THE
MITROPA CUP
1927-1992

A Statistical Record

Dirk Karsdorp

The Author

Dirk Karsdorp was born on 5th October 1946 in Molenaarsgraaf, the Netherlands.

After high school, he spent several years working as a clerk at a large steel company before switching to IT and he then worked in that business for many years.

Working with computers became a hobby as well as a profession and, after taking early retirement, Dirk continued to use computers along with his iPad. Of course, the internet has now become an almost inexhaustible source of information when it comes to gathering statistical information about soccer.

Dirk's interest in football statistics began in the 1960s when he first collated seasonal summaries of results and began to document team line-ups. As there were no personal computers available in the sixties, all this data was recorded on paper, using a typewriter.

The first information Dirk collated was for the European Champions Clubs' Cup (now the UEFA Champions League) and the European Cup Winners' Cup, soon followed by the Inter-Cities Fairs Cup (which later became the UEFA Cup and is now the UEFA Europa League), as well as the International Football Cup (later called the UEFA Intertoto Cup). After this, other Cups followed including the Mitropa Cup, Latin Cup, Alpen Cup and the Balkan Cup. Dirk also took an interest in the club tournaments of South America and similar club tournaments from Africa, Asia, North and Central America, Arabia and Oceania.

In the era before the internet, most of the data was collected through correspondence with the various football associations and participating clubs. With the arrival of the internet, a new world of information opened up. Furthermore, the contacts Dirk has made with fellow statisticians at home and abroad have made an important contribution both to this book and also to the wide range of other football statistics which he has collated.

The extensive database Dirk has built over the years has been used in several publications by other statisticians. Soccer Books Limited have now produced a number of titles in collaboration with Dirk including a number which are listed on the back page of this book.

British Library Cataloguing in Publication Data
A catalogue record for this book is available from the British Library

ISBN: 978-1-86223-320-1

Copyright © 2015, SOCCER BOOKS LIMITED (01472 696226)
72 St. Peter's Avenue, Cleethorpes, N.E. Lincolnshire, DN35 8HU, England
Web site   www.soccer-books.co.uk   e-mail   info@soccer-books.co.uk

Printed in the UK by 4Edge Ltd.

FOREWORD

The Mitropa Cup was the first major European club competition which was played between teams from Central European countries and operated in various guises between 1927 and 1992.

In the years following the end of World War I, football flourished in the countries which had been part of the defunct Austro-Hungarian Empire and this led to the introduction of professional leagues in Austria in 1924, Hungary in 1925 and Czechoslovakia in 1926. It soon became clear that a competition between the top clubs from each of these countries (by now among the strongest in Europe) would provide financial support and also further their standing in the game. With this concept in mind, Hugo Meisl, head of the Austrian Football Association (ÖFB), arranged a meeting in Venice on 17th July 1927 where the Mitropa Cup was born.

Officially known as *La Coupe de l'Europe Centrale*, the first matches in the Mitropa Cup were played on 14th August 1927 with two teams each from Austria, Czechoslovakia, Hungary and Yugoslavia entering a straight knock-out competition with each tie played over two legs. These teams were the league Champions plus either the runners-up or the Cup winners of each country. In the first Mitropa Cup final, the Czech team AC Sparta Prague defeated SK Rapid Wien 7-4 on aggregate. From 1929 onwards, two Italian teams replaced the Yugoslavian entrants but otherwise the format remained the same until 1934 when the number of entrants was doubled and four teams entered from each participating country. An additional knock-out round was added at the first stage of the competition to accommodate these new teams. In 1936, four Swiss clubs entered, playing other teams in a preliminary round before the competition proper and in 1937 the total number of entrants was reduced to 16 teams. One team each from Romania and Yugoslavia joined the competition and the number of clubs from the other countries were reduced to either 2 or 3. Austria withdrew from the competition in 1938 following the Anschluss by Nazi Germany but the total number of entrants remained at 16 for this year. However, the following year there were just 8 entrants, two each from Hungary, Czechoslovakia and Italy and one each from Romania and Yugoslavia. The strength of the Mitropa Cup during this golden era of the 1930s can be clearly seen in the achievements of the national teams of the countries involved. Italy won the World Cup in both 1934 and 1938, Czechoslovakia and Hungary were the other finalists in 1934 and 1938 respectively. Of the eleven countries competing in the first three World Cup tournaments, five entered teams in the Mitropa Cup. Despite the onset of war in September 1939, a tournament was played in 1940 and was only abandoned following the semi-finals in June and early July.

After the end of World War II in Europe in 1944, conditions were extremely difficult throughout much of the continent and it was not until 1951 when a replacement for the Mitropa Cup was held under the name of the Zentropa Cup. Just four teams entered the tournament (two from Austria and one each from Italy and Yugoslavia), and SK Rapid Wien lifted the trophy. After this small competition, it was to be another 4 years before the Mitropa Cup was revived and the 1955 competition was much more substantial with 10 entrants from 5 countries vying for the trophy.

The Mitropa Cup then continued to run for most years in a variety of different formats (and under the name of the Danube Cup in 1958) until the final match was held in 1992. The introduction of more prestigious competitions including the European Cup, Cup-Winners' Cup, Fairs Cup and later the UEFA Cup led to an ongoing decline in the importance of the Mitropa Cup and, by the 1980s, it was competed for by the Second Division Champions of each of the participating countries. The last ever match in the competition was played on 29th May 1992 and the Yugoslav team FK Borac Banja Luka were the final winners of the Mitropa Cup.

This book provides as full a statistical record as is currently available for the whole 65-year span of the Mitropa Cup and statistics for most games are complete. However, it has not been possible to discover the complete data for all of the games and the author, Dirk Karsdorp, would be very grateful to receive any additional information which readers may have available. Please contact Dirk via Soccer Books Limited using the following e-mail address:

info@soccer-books.co.uk

In compiling this book, Dirk has enjoyed help from a number of fellow statisticians and would like to extend particular thanks to Imrich Varga for his assistance.

1927

QUARTER-FINALS

14-08-1927   Stadion BSK, Beograd: B.S.K. Beograd – Hungária FC Budapest   2-4 (0-2)
B.S.K. Beograd: Milorad GLIGORIJEVIC, Svetolzar POPOVIC, Milorad MITROVIC,
Milorad ARSENIJEVIC, Sava MARINKOVIC, Ljubisa DJORDJEVIC, Blagoje
MARJANOVIC, Ivan BEK, Kuzman SOTIROVIC, Nikola MARJANOVIC, Dragutin
NAJDANOVIC. (Coach: Adolf ENGEL).
Hungária FC Budapest: János BIRI, Gyula MÁNDI-MANDL, György OLÁH, Gábor
KOMPÓTI-KLÉBER, János KVASZ, Béla REBRÓ, Gyula SENKEY (II), György MOLNÁR,
Zoltán OPATA, György SKVAREK, Rudolf JENY. (Coach: Gyula FELDMANN).
Goals: B.S.K. Beograd: 1-2 Kuzman SOTIROVIC (50' penalty), 2-4 Nikola MARJANOVIC
(86').
Hungária FC Budapest: 0-1 János KVASZ (15'), 0-2 György SKVAREK (35'), 1-3 Rudolf
JENY (58'), 1-4 Zoltán OPATA (72').
Referee: Emil GÖBEL (AUT)   Attendance: 5.000

14-08-1927   Rapid-Platz, Wien: SK Rapid Wien – NK Hajduk Split   8-1 (1-1)
SK Rapid Wien: Walter FEIGL, Franz KRAL, Leopold NITSCH, Johann RICHTER, Josef
SMISTIK (I), Josef MADLMAYER, Karl WONDRAK, Johann HORVATH, Johann
HOFFMANN, Johann LUEF, Ferdinand WESSELY. (Coach: Eduard BAUER).
NK Hajduk Split: Otmar GAZZARI (ITA), Lorenzo GAZZARI (ITA), Janko RODIN
(expulsion 68'), Miroslav DESKOVIC, Mihovil BOROVCIC-KURIR, Veljko PODUJE, Sime
PODUJE, Leo LEMESIC, Mirko BONACIC, Anton BONACIC, Vinko RADIC. (Coach: Luka
KALITERNA).
Goals: SK Rapid Wien: 1-1 Johann HOFFMANN (34'), 2-1 Johann HOFFMANN (46'), 3-1
Karl WONDRAK (50'), 4-1 Johann HOFFMANN (54'), 5-1 Ferdinand WESSELY (61'), 6-1
Ferdinand WESSELY (66'), 7-1 Johann HORVATH (70'), 8-1 Johann LUEF (80').
NK Hajduk Split: 0-1 Mirko BONACIC (1').
Referee: Ladislav STEPANOVSKY (TCH)   Attendance: 18.000

14-08-1927   Stadión Sparta/Letná, Praha: AC Sparta Praha – WSC Admira Wien   5-1 (3-1)
AC Sparta Praha: Frantisek HOCHMAN, Antonín PERNER, Karel STEINER, Frantisek
KOLENATY, Karel "Káda" PESEK, Ferdinand HAJNY, Jan MALOUN, Adolf PATEK
(AUT), Josef SILNY, Evzen VESELY, Josef HOREJS (AUT). (Coach: John DICK (ENG)).
WSC Admira Wien: Friedrich FRANZL, Georg VOCI, Anton JANDA, Rudolf WOSTRAK,
Anton KOCH, Karl SCHOTT, Ignaz SIGL, Johann KLIMA, Karl STOIBER, Anton SCHALL,
Franz RUNGE. (Coach: Hans SKOLAUT).
Goals: AC Sparta Praha: 1-0 Evzen VESELY (2'), 2-0 Evzen VESELY (8'), 3-1 Jan
MALOUN (41'), 4-1 Josef HOREJS (46'), 5-1 Josef HOREJS (53').
WSC Admira Wien: 2-1 Franz RUNGE (10').
Referee: Erno GÖRÖ (HUN)   Attendance: 8.000

21-08-1927   Stadion Graanski, Zagreb: NK Hajduk Split – SK Rapid Wien   0-1 (0-0)
NK Hajduk Split: Otmar GAZZARI (ITA), Lorenzo GAZZARI (ITA), Janko RODIN,
Miroslav DESKOVIC, Mihovil BOROVCIC-KURIR, Veljko PODUJE, Sime PODUJE, Leo
LEMESIC, Mirko BONACIC, Anton BONACIC, Vinko RADIC. (Coach: Luka
KALITERNA).
SK Rapid Wien: Walter FEIGL, Franz KRAL, Leopold NITSCH, Johann RICHTER, Josef
SMISTIK (I), Josef MADLMAYER, Karl WONDRAK, Johann HORVATH, Johann
HOFFMANN, Johann LUEF, Ferdinand WESSELY. (Coach: Eduard BAUER).
Goal: SK Rapid Wien: 0-1 Johann HOFFMANN (81').
Referee: Bohumil ZENÍSEK (TCH)   Attendance: 6.000

21-08-1927   Stadión Slavia/Letná, Praha: SK Slavia Praha – Újpesti TE   4-0 (2-0)
SK Slavia Praha: Frantisek PLÁNICKA, Zdenek KUMMERMANN, Emil SEIFERT,
Frantisek CERNICKY, Josef PLETICHA, Karel CIPERA, Kalmán BOBOR, Jindich
SOLTYS, Karel BEJBL, Frantisek SVOBODA, Josef KRATOCHVIL. (Coach: John
MADDEN (SCO)).
Újpesti TE: József BENEDA, Károly FOGL (II), József FOGL (III), József VÍG-WILHELM
(I), Lajos LUTZ (II), LUTZ (III), Adalbert STRÖCK/Albert TÖRÖK, János VÍG-WILHELM
(II), Pál JÁVOR-JAKUBE, József SCHALLER, Gábor P.SZABÓ. (Coach: Imre POZSONYI).
Goals: SK Slavia Praha: 1-0 Jindich SOLTYS (18'), 2-0 Josef KRATOCHVIL (32'), 3-0
Frantisek SVOBODA (65' penalty), 4-0 Karel BEJBL (84').
Referee: Ernest FÁBRIS (YUG)   Attendance: 12.000
*(Adalbert STRÖCK/Albert TÖRÖK was of Romanian descent and played for the national
teams of both Romania and Hungary. The spelling of his name used in both countries is shown)*

27-08-1927   WAC-Platz, Wien: WSC Admira Wien – AC Sparta Praha   5-3 (2-0)
WSC Admira Wien: Friedrich FRANZL, Anton JANDA, Georg VOCI, Rudolf WOSTRAK,
Anton KOCH, Karl SCHOTT, Ignaz SIGL, Johann KLIMA, Karl STOIBER, Anton SCHALL,
Franz RUNGE. (Coach: Hans SKOLAUT).
AC Sparta Praha: Frantisek HOCHMAN, Antonín PERNER, Karel STEINER, Frantisek
KOLENATY, Karel "Káda" PESEK, Ferdinand HAJNY, Jan MALOUN, Adolf PATEK
(AUT), Josef SILNY, Evzen VESELY, Josef HOREJS (AUT). (Coach: John DICK (ENG)).
Goals: WSC Admira Wien: 1-0 Anton SCHALL (13'), 2-0 Ignaz SIGL (43' penalty), 3-1
Anton SCHALL (50'), 4-1 Franz RUNGE (52'),
5-1 Karl STOIBER (60').
AC Sparta Praha: 2-1 Josef SILNY (48'), 5-2 Evzen VESELY (73'), 5-3 Evzen VESELY
(79').
Referee: József SCHLISSER (HUN)   Attendance: 17.000

28-08-1927   Hungária körút, Budapest: Hungária FC Budapest – B.S.K. Beograd   4-0 (2-0)
Hungária FC Budapest: János BIRI, Gyula MÁNDI-MANDL, Géza BALASITS, Gábor
KOMPÓTI-KLÉBER, János KVASZ, Bélo REBRÓ, Zoltán OPATA, György MOLNÁR,
György ORTH, György SKVAREK, Rudolf JENY. (Coach: Gyula FELDMANN).
B.S.K. Beograd: Milorad GLIGORIJEVIC, Svetolzar POPOVIC, Milorad MITROVIC,
Milorad ARSENIJEVIC, Sava MARINKOVIC, Ljubisa DJORDJEVIC, Blagoje
MARJANOVIC, Ivan BEK, Kuzman SOTIROVIC (expulsion 83'), Milorad DRAGICEVIC,
Dragutin NAJDANOVIC. (Coach: Adolf ENGEL).
Goals: Hungária FC Budapest: 1-0 György ORTH (37'), 2-0 György MOLNÁR (44'), 3-0
György ORTH (81'), 4-0 Géza BALASITS (90' penalty).
Referee: József SCHLISSER (HUN)   Attendance: 18.000

6

28-08-1927   Megyeri ut, Budapest: Újpestı TE – SK Slavia Praha   2-2 (0-0)
Újpesti TE: BÁCSAY, Károly FOGL (II), József FOGL (III), Ferenc BORSÁNYI, Lajos
LUTZ (II), LUTZ (III), Adalbert STRÖCK/Albert TÖRÖK, János VÍG-WILHELM (II),
MORAVCSIK, Pál JÁVOR-JAKUBE, Gábor P.SZABÓ. (Coach: Imre POZSONYI).
SK Slavia Praha: Frantisek PLÁNICKA, Zdenek KUMMERMANN, Emil SEIFERT,
Frantisek CERNICKY, Josef PLETICHA, Karel CIPERA, Kalmán BOBOR, Jindich
SOLTYS, Karel BEJBL, Josef KRATOCHVIL, Antonín PUC. (Coach: John MADDEN
(SCO)).
Goals: Újpesti TE: 1-0 József FOGL (57' penalty), 2-1 József FOGL (80' penalty).
SK Slavia Praha: 1-1 Antonín PUC (68'), 2-2 Antonín PUC (82').
Referee: Eugen BRAUN (AUT)   Attendance: 9.000

SEMI-FINALS

04-09-1927   Hungária körút, Budapest: Hungária FC Budapest – AC Sparta Praha   2-2 (1-1)
Hungária FC Budapest: János BIRI, Gyula MÁNDI-MANDL, Ferenc KOCSIS, Gábor
KOMPÓTI-KLÉBER, János KVASZ, Bélo REBRÓ, Zoltán OPATA, György MOLNÁR,
György ORTH, Ferenc HÍRES-HIZER, Rudolf JENY. (Coach: Gyula FELDMANN).
AC Sparta Praha: Frantisek HOCHMAN, Antonín PERNER, Karel STEINER, Frantisek
KOLENATY, Karel "Káda" PESEK, Ferdinand HAJNY, Jan MALOUN, Adolf PATEK
(AUT), Josef SILNY, Evzen VESELY, Josef HOREJS (AUT). (Coach: John DICK (ENG)).
Goals: Hungária FC Budapest: 1-0 Zoltán OPATA (30'), 2-2 Rudolf JENY (69').
AC Sparta Praha: 1-1 Adolf PATEK (34'), 1-2 Josef SILNY (64').
Referee: Eugen BRAUN (AUT)   Attendance: 15.500

28-09-1927   Stadión Slavia/Letná, Praha: SK Slavia Praha – SK Rapid Wien   2-2 (2-0)
SK Slavia Praha: Frantisek PLÁNICKA, Zdenek KUMMERMANN, Emil SEIFERT, Antonín
VODICKA, Josef PLETICHA, Frantisek CERNICKY, Kalmán BOBOR, Frantisek
SVOBODA, Karel BEJBL, Antonín PUC, Josef KRATOCHVIL. (Coach: John MADDEN
(SCO)).
SK Rapid Wien: Walter FEIGL, Otto JELLINEK, Leopold NITSCH, Johann RICHTER, Josef
SMISTIK (I), Josef MADLMAYER, Franz WESELIK, Johann HOFFMANN, Johann
HORVATH, Johann LUEF, Ferdinand WESSELY. (Coach: Eduard BAUER).
Goals: SK Slavia Praha: 1-0 Josef KRATOCHVIL (9'), 2-0 Antonín PUC (12').
SK Rapid Wien: 2-1 Johann HORVATH (58'), 2-2 Johann LUEF (59').
Referee: Sándor BÍRÓ (HUN)   Attendance: 12.000

02-10-1927   Stadión Sparta/Letná, Praha: AC Sparta Praha – Hungária FC Budapest   0-0
AC Sparta Praha: Frantisek HOCHMAN, Antonín PERNER, Karel STEINER, Frantisek
KOLENATY, Karel "Káda" PESEK, Ferdinand HAJNY, Jan MALOUN, Adolf PATEK
(AUT), Josef SILNY, Evzen VESELY, Josef HOREJS (AUT). (Coach: John DICK (ENG)).
Hungária FC Budapest: János BIRI, Gyula MÁNDI-MANDL, Ferenc KOCSIS, Bélo REBRÓ,
Gábor KOMPÓTI-KLÉBER, Josef SCHNEIDER (AUT), József BRAUN, Kálmán KONRÁD,
Zoltán OPATA, György SKVAREK, Ferenc HÍRES-HIZER. (Coach: Gyula FELDMANN).
Referee: Eugen BRAUN (AUT)   Attendance: 22.000

*(Hungária FC Budapest played with Kálmán KONRÁD who was not eligible to play according
to the Mitropa Cup rules. However, there was no subsequent rematch and AC Spartak Praha
progressed to the final).*

7

02-10-1927   Hohe Warte, Wien: SK Rapid Wien – SK Slavia Praha   2-1 (0-1)
SK Rapid Wien: Walter FEIGL, Otto JELLINEK, Leopold NITSCH, Johann RICHTER, Josef
SMISTIK (I), Josef MADLMAYER, Karl WONDRAK, Johann HORVATH, Richard (Rigo)
KUTHAN, Johann LUEF, Ferdinand WESSELY. (Coach: Eduard BAUER).
SK Slavia Praha: Frantisek PLÁNICKA, Zdenek KUMMERMANN, Emil SEIFERT,
Frantisek CERNICKY, Josef PLETICHA, Antonín VODICKA, Kalmán BOBOR, Frantisek
SVOBODA, Karel BEJBL, Antonín PUC, Josef KRATOCHVIL. (Coach: John MADDEN
(SCO)).
Goals: SK Rapid Wien: 1-1 Karl WONDRAK (80'), 2-1 Ferdinand WESSELY (83').
SK Slavia Praha: 0-1 Antonín PUC (41').
Referee: Sándor BÍRÓ (HUN)   Attendance: 32.000

FINAL

30-10-1927   Stadión Sparta/Letná, Praha: AC Sparta Praha – SK Rapid Wien   6-2 (3-2)
AC Sparta Praha: Frantisek HOCHMAN, Jaroslav BURGR, Antonín PERNER, Frantisek
KOLENATY, Karel "Káda" PESEK, Ferdinand HAJNY, Adolf PATEK (AUT), Josef SÍMA,
Alois MYCLÍK, Josef SILNY, Josef HOREJS (AUT). (Coach: John DICK (ENG)).
SK Rapid Wien: Walter FEIGL, Otto JELLINEK, Leopold CZEJKA, Josef MADLMAYER,
Josef SMISTIK (I), Leopold NITSCH, Karl WONDRAK, Franz WESELIK, Richard (Rigo)
KUTHAN, Johann HORVATH, Ferdinand WESSELY. (Coach: Eduard BAUER).
Goals: AC Sparta Praha: 1-0 Karel "Káda" PESEK (1'), 2-0 Josef SÍMA (14'), 3-1 Josef
SILNY (33'), 4-2 Adolf PATEK (62'), 5-2 Josef SILNY (76'), 6-2 Adolf PATEK (78').
SK Rapid Wien: 2-1 Franz WESELIK (15'), 3-2 Ferdinand WESSELY (34' penalty).
Referee: Raphaël VAN PRAAG (BEL)   Attendance: 25.000

13-11-1927   Hohe Warte, Wien: SK Rapid Wien – AC Sparta Praha   2-1 (1-0)
SK Rapid Wien: Walter FEIGL, Roman SCHRAMSEIS, Leopold NITSCH, Johann
RICHTER, Josef SMISTIK (I), Josef MADLMAYER, Eduard BAUER, Johann HORVATH,
Franz WESELIK, Johann LUEF, Ferdinand WESSELY. (Coach: Eduard BAUER).
AC Sparta Praha: Frantisek HOCHMAN, Jaroslav BURGR, Antonín PERNER (expulsion
62'), Frantisek KOLENATY, Karel "Káda" PESEK, Ferdinand HAJNY, Adolf PATEK
(AUT), Josef SILNY, Alois MYCLÍK, Josef SÍMA, Josef HOREJS (AUT). (Coach: John
DICK (ENG)).
Goals: SK Rapid Wien: 1-0 Franz WESELIK (5'), 2-0 Johann LUEF (55').
AC Sparta Praha: 2-1 Josef SILNY (82').
Referee: Willem EYMERS (HOL)   Attendance: 38.000

(The Coach of SK Rapid Wien, Eduard BAUER, had nominated himself as outside right).

*** AC Sparta Praha won the Cup ***

8

1928

QUARTER-FINALS

15-08-1928   WAC-Platz, Wien: WSC Admira Wien – SK Slavia Praha   3-1 (1-0)
WSC Admira Wien: Friedrich FRANZL, Georg VOCI, Anton JANDA, Ludwig STROH, Anton KOCH, Karl SCHOTT, Ignaz SIGL, Johann KLIMA, Karl STOIBER, Anton SCHALL, Franz RUNGE. (Coach: Hans SKOLAUT).
SK Slavia Praha: Frantisek PLÁNICKA, Antonín VODICKA, Frantisek CERNICKY, Emil SEIFERT, Josef PLETICHA, Karel CIPERA, Frantisek JUNEK, Jindrich SOLTYS, Frantisek SVOBODA, Antonín PUC, Josef KRATOCHVIL. (Coach: John MADDEN (SCO)).
Goals: WSC Admira Wien: 1-0 Ignaz SIGL (45'), 2-0 Franz RUNGE (56'), 3-1 Anton SCHALL (75').
SK Slavia Praha: 2-1 Frantisek JUNEK (72' penalty).
Referee: Achille Gama MALCHER (ITA)   Attendance: 16.000

19-08-1928   Stadion B.S.K., Beograd:
            B.S.K. Beograd – Ferencvárosi TC Budapest   0-7 (0-4)
B.S.K. Beograd: Milorad GLIGORIJEVIC, Svetolzar POPOVIC, Milorad MITROVIC, Milorad ARSENIJEVIC, Sava MARINKOVIC, Ljubisa DJORDJEVIC, Blagoje MARJANOVIC, Djordje VUJADINOVIC, Kuzman SOTIROVIC, Milorad DRAGICEVIC, Dragutin NAJDANOVIC. (Coach: Adolf ENGEL).
Ferencvárosi TC Budapest: Ignác AMSEL, Géza TAKÁCS (I), János HUNGLER, Károly FURMANN, Antal LYKA, Elemér BERKESSY, Imre KOSZTA, József TAKÁCS (II), József TURAY, Ferenc SZEDLACSIK, Vilmos KOHUT. (Coach: István TÓTH-POTYA).
Goals: Ferencvárosi TC Budapest: 0-1 József TAKÁCS (II) (1'), 0-2 József TURAY (3'), 0-3 József TURAY (9'), 0-4 József TAKÁCS (II) (34'), 0-5 József TAKÁCS (II) (76'), 0-6 József TURAY (80'), 0-7 József TAKÁCS (II) (87').
Referee: Emil GÖBEL (AUT)   Attendance: 4.000

19-08-1928   Stadión Slavia/Letná, Praha: SK Slavia Praha – WSC Admira Wien   3-3 (1-2)
SK Slavia Praha: Frantisek PLÁNICKA, Antonín VODICKA, Frantisek CERNICKY, Josef SUCHY, Josef PLETICHA, Karel CIPERA, Kalmán BOBOR, Jindrich SOLTYS, Frantisek SVOBODA, Antonín PUC, Josef KRATOCHVIL. (Coach: John MADDEN (SCO)).
WSC Admira Wien: Friedrich FRANZL, Georg VOCI, Anton JANDA, Johann KLIWITSCH, Anton KOCH, Karl SCHOTT, Ignaz SIGL, Johann KLIMA, Karl STOIBER, Anton SCHALL, Franz RUNGE. (Coach: Hans SKOLAUT).
Goals: SK Slavia Praha: 1-1 Josef KRATOCHVIL (29'), 2-2 Josef KRATOCHVIL (50'), 3-2 Frantisek SVOBODA (69').
WSC Admira Wien: 0-1 Karl STOIBER (23'), 1-2 Anton SCHALL (32'), 3-3 Franz RUNGE (83').
Referee: Achille Gama MALCHER (ITA)   Attendance: 17.000

9

20-08-1928   Rapid-Platz, Wien: SK Rapid Wien – Hungária FC Budapest 6-4 (2-1)
SK Rapid Wien: Franz GRIFTNER, Anton WITSCHEL, Roman SCHRAMSEIS, Josef
FRÜHWIRTH, Josef SMISTIK (I), Josef MADLMAYER, Willibald KIRBES, Franz
WESELIK, Richard (Rigo) KUTHAN, Johann HORVATH, Ferdinand WESSELY. (Coach:
Eduard BAUER).
Hungária FC Budapest: Ferenc FEHÉR, Gyula MÁNDI-MANDL, Ferenc KOCSIS, Gábor
KOMPÓTI-KLÉBER, Lajos WÉBER, Josef SCHNEIDER (AUT), Mór HAÁR, György
MOLNÁR, Jenő KALMÁR, György SKVAREK, Ferenc HÍRES-HIRZER. (Coach: Béla
RÉVÉSZ).
Goals: SK Rapid Wien: 1-1 Richard (Rigo) KUTHAN (18'), 2-1 Franz WESELIK (32'), 3-2
Johann HORVATH (57'), 4-3 Ferdinand WESSELY (68'), 5-3 Johann HORVATH (73'), 6-3
Ferdinand WESSELY (78').
Hungária FC Budapest: 0-1 György MOLNÁR (16'), 2-2 Jenő KALMÁR (50'), 3-3 Ferenc
HÍRES-HIRZER (63'), 6-4 Jenő KALMÁR (83').
Referee: Gustav KRIST (TCH)   Attendance: 20.000

25-08-1928   Hungária körút, Budapest: Hungária FC Budapest – SK Rapid Wien 3-1 (3-0)
Hungária FC Budapest: József ÚJVÁRI, Gyula MÁNDI-MANDL, Ferenc KOCSIS, Gábor
KOMPÓTI-KLÉBER, Lajos WÉBER, Josef SCHNEIDER (AUT), Mór HAÁR, György
MOLNÁR, Jenő KALMÁR, György SKVAREK, Ferenc HÍRES-HIRZER. (Coach: Béla
RÉVÉSZ).
SK Rapid Wien: Franz GRIFTNER, Anton WITSCHEL, Roman SCHRAMSEIS, Josef
FRÜHWIRTH, Josef SMISTIK (I), Josef MADLMAYER, Willibald KIRBES, Franz
WESELIK, Wilhelm CERNIC, Johann HORVATH, Ferdinand WESSELY. (Coach: Eduard
BAUER).
Goals: Hungária FC Budapest: 1-0 Jenő KALMÁR (13'), 2-0 György MOLNÁR (32'), 3-0
György MOLNÁR (40').
SK Rapid Wien: 3-1 Jenő KALMÁR (72' *own goal*).
Referee: Gustav KRIST (TCH)   Attendance: 20.000

26-08-1928   Hungária körút, Budapest:
                      Ferencvárosi TC Budapest – B.S.K. Boegrad 6-1 (4-1)
Ferencvárosi TC Budapest: Ignác AMSEL, Géza TAKÁCS (I), János HUNGLER, Károly
FURMANN, Antal LYKA, Elemér BERKESSY, Imre KOSZTA, József TAKÁCS (II), József
TURAY, Ferenc SZEDLACSIK, Vilmos KOHUT. (Coach: István TÓTH-POTYA).
B.S.K. Beograd: Milorad GLIGORIJEVIC, Svetolzar POPOVIC, Milorad MITROVIC,
Milorad ARSENIJEVIC, Sava MARINKOVIC, Ljubisa DJORDJEVIC, Blagoje
MARJANOVIC, Djordje VUJADINOVIC, Kuzman SOTIROVIC, Milorad DRAGICEVIC,
Dragutin NAJDANOVIC. (Coach: Adolf ENGEL).
Goals: Ferencvárosi TC Budapest: 1-0 Ferenc SZEDLACSIK (5'), 2-1 József TAKÁCS (II)
(30'), 3-1 József TAKÁCS (II) (32'), 4-1 József TURAY (37'), 5-1 József TURAY (70'), 6-1
József TURAY (85').
B.S.K. Beograd: 1-1 Blagoje MARJANOVIC (15' penalty).
Referee: József SCHLISSER (HUN)   Attendance: 20.000

10

26-08-1928   Stadion Gradjandski, Zagreb:
                HSK Gradjanski Zagreb – SK Viktoria Zizkov   3-2 (1-1)
HSK Gradjanski Zagreb: Maksimilijan MIHELCIC, Zvonimir GMAJNICKI, Franjo
MANTLER, Rudolf HITREC, Viktor PIKIC, Dragutin BABIC, Nikola BABIC, Antun
GUMHALTER, Emil PERSKA, Slavin CINDRIC, Franja GILER. (Coach: Imre POZSONYI
(HUN)).
SK Viktoria Zizkov: Václav BENDA, Karel STEINER, Frantisek STEHLÍK, Vilém KÖNIG,
Antonín KLICPERA, Matej STEPÁN, Karel PODRAZIL, Jaroslav SRBA, Karel MEDUNA,
Karel HROMÁDKA, Václav BAYER. (Coach: none).
Goals: HSK Gradjanski Zagreb: 1-0 Emil PERSKA (24'), 2-1 Slavin CINDRIC (54'), 3-1
Slavin CINDRIC (57').
SK Viktoria Zizkov: 1-1 Karel PODRAZIL (40'), 3-2 Václav BAYER (84').
Referee: Eugen BRAUN (AUT)   Attendance: 6.000

01-09-1928   Hohe Warte, Wien: SK Rapid Wien – Hungária FC Budapest   1-0 (0-0)
SK Rapid Wien: Franz GRIFTNER, Anton WITSCHEL, Roman SCHRAMSEIS, Josef
FRÜHWIRTH, Josef SMISTIK (I), Josef MADLMAYER, Willibald KIRBES, Franz
WESELIK, Richard (Rigo) KUTHAN, Johann HORVATH, Ferdinand WESSELY. (Coach:
Eduard BAUER).
Hungária FC Budapest: József ÚJVÁRI, Gyula MÁNDI-MANDL, Ferenc KOCSIS, Gábor
KOMPÓTI-KLÉBER, Lajos WÉBER, Josef SCHNEIDER (AUT), Mór HAÁR, György
MOLNÁR, Jenõ KALMÁR, György SKVAREK, Ferenc HÍRES-HIRZER. (Coach: Béla
RÉVÉSZ).
Goal: SK Rapid Wien: 1-0 Anton WITSCHEL (99').
Referee: Albino CARRARO (ITA)   Attendance: 35.000

(Play-off game which was decided following extra-time)

02-09-1928   Stadión Na ohrade, Praha:
                SK Viktoria Zizkov – HSK Gradjanski Zagreb   6-1 (2-0)
SK Viktoria Zizkov: Václav BENDA, Karel STEINER, Frantisek STEHLÍK, Vilém KÖNIG,
Antonín KLICPERA, Matej STEPÁN, Karel PODRAZIL, Jaroslav SRBA, Karel MEDUNA,
Jan DVORÁCEK, Václav BAYER. (Coach: none).
HSK Gradjanski Zagreb: Maksimilijan MIHELCIC, Zvonimir GMAJNICKI, Franjo
MANTLER, Rudolf HITREC, Viktor PIKIC, Dragutin BABIC, Nikola BABIC, Antun
GUMHALTER, Emil PERSKA, Slavin CINDRIC, Franja GILER. (Coach: Imre POZSONYI
(HUN)).
Goals: SK Viktoria Zizkov: 1-0 Karel PODRAZIL (26'), 2-0 Jan DVORÁCEK (29'), 3-0
Karel STEINER (55'), 4-0 Karel MEDUNA (57'), 5-0 Karel PODRAZIL (59'), 6-1 Jaroslav
SRBA (83').
HSK Gradjanski Zagreb: 5-1 Slavin CINDRIC (80').
Referee: Emil GÖBEL (AUT)   Attendance: 11.000

11

SEMI-FINALS

08-09-1928   Stadión Sparta/Letná, Praha: SK Viktoria Zizkov – SK Rapid Wien 4-3 (2-3)
SK Viktoria Zizkov: Václav BENDA, Karel STEINER, Frantisek STEHLÍK, Vilém KÖNIG,
Antonín KLICPERA, Matej STEPÁN, Karel PODRAZIL, Jaroslav SRBA, Karel MEDUNA,
Jan DVORÁCEK, Václav BAYER. (Coach: none).
SK Rapid Wien: Franz GRIFTNER, Anton WITSCHEL, Roman SCHRAMSEIS (expulsion
43'), Josef FRÜHWIRTH, Josef SMISTIK (I), Josef MADLMAYER, Willibald KIRBES,
Johann LUEF, Franz WESELIK, Johann HORVATH, Ferdinand WESSELY. (Coach: Eduard
BAUER).
Goals: SK Viktoria Zizkov: 1-0 Karel STEINER (9' penalty), 2-3 Jan DVORÁCEK (44'), 3-3
Jan DVORÁCEK (63'), 4-3 Jan DVORÁCEK (64').
SK Rapid Wien: 1-1 Franz WESELIK (12'), 1-2 Franz WESELIK (27'), 1-3 Franz WESELIK
(37').
Referee: Otto ZANDER (GER)   Attendance: 16.000

09-09-1928   Hohe Warte, Wien: WSC Admira Wien – Ferencvárosi TC Budapest 1-2 (1-1)
WSC Admira Wien: Friedrich FRANZL, Georg VOCI, Anton JANDA, Johann KLIWITSCH,
Anton KOCH, Karl SCHOTT, Ignaz SIGL, Johann KLIMA, Karl STOIBER, Anton SCHALL,
Franz RUNGE. (Coach: Hans SKOLAUT).
Ferencvárosi TC Budapest: Ignác AMSEL, Géza TAKÁCS (I), János HUNGLER, Antal
LYKA, Márton BUKOVI, Elemér BERKESSY, Imre KOSZTA, József TAKÁCS (II), József
TURAY, Ferenc SZEDLACSIK, Vilmos KOHUT. (Coach: István TÓTH-POTYA).
Goals: WSC Admira Wien: 1-1 Ignaz SIGL (21').
Ferencvárosi TC Budapest: 0-1 József TURAY (3'), 1-2 József TAKÁCS (II) (54').
Referee: József SCHLISSER (HUN)   Attendance: 20.000

16-09-1928   Rapid-Platz, Wien: SK Rapid Wien – SK Viktoria Zizkov 3-2 (2-1)
SK Rapid Wien: Franz GRIFTNER, Anton WITSCHEL, Roman SCHRAMSEIS, Josef
FRÜHWIRTH, Josef SMISTIK (I), Josef MADLMAYER, Willibald KIRBES, Johann LUEF,
Franz WESELIK, Johann HORVATH, Ferdinand WESSELY. (Coach: Eduard BAUER).
SK Viktoria Zizkov: Václav BENDA, Karel STEINER, Frantisek STEHLÍK, Vilém KÖNIG,
Antonín KLICPERA, Matej STEPÁN, Karel PODRAZIL, Otto NOVÁK, Karel MEDUNA,
Jan DVORÁCEK, Václav BAYER. (Coach: none).
Goals: SK Rapid Wien: 1-0 Ferdinand WESSELY (1'), 2-0 Franz WESELIK (15'), 3-1 Johann
HORVATH (47').
SK Viktoria Zizkov: 2-1 Jan DVORÁCEK (25'), 3-2 Karel PODRAZIL (64').
Referee: Alfred BIRLEM (GER)   Attendance: 26.000

16-09-1928   Üllöi ut, Budapest: Ferencvárosi TC Budapest – WSC Admira Wien 1-0 (1-0)
Ferencvárosi TC Budapest: Ignác AMSEL, Géza TAKÁCS (I), János HUNGLER, Antal
LYKA, Márton BUKOVI, Elemér BERKESSY, Mór RÁZSÓ, József TAKÁCS (II), József
TURAY, Ferenc SZEDLACSIK, Vilmos KOHUT. (Coach: István TÓTH-POTYA).
WSC Admira Wien: Friedrich FRANZL, Georg VOCI, Anton JANDA, Johann KLIWITSCH,
Anton KOCH, Karl SCHOTT, Ignaz SIGL, Johann KLIMA, Karl STOIBER, Anton SCHALL,
Franz RUNGE. (Coach: Hans SKOLAUT).
Goal: Ferencvárosi TC Budapest: 1-0 Mór RÄZSÓ (33').
Referee: Rinaldo BARLASSINA (ITA)   Attendance: 20.000

12

23-09-1928   Rapid-Platz, Wien: SK Rapid Wien - SK Viktoria Zizkov 3-1 (3-1)
SK Rapid Wien: Franz GRIFTNER, Anton WITSCHEL, Roman SCHRAMSEIS, Iosef
FRÜHWIRTH, Josef SMISTIK (I), Josef MADLMAYER, Willibald KIRBES, Johann LUEF,
Ferdinand WESSELY, Johann HORVATH, Franz WESELIK. (Coach: Eduard BAUER).
SK Viktoria Zizkov: Václav BENDA, Karel STEINER, Frantisek STEHLÍK, Vilém KÖNIG,
Antonín KLICPERA, Matej STEPÁN, Karel PODRAZIL, Otto NOVÁK, Karel MEDUNA,
Jan DVORÁCEK, Václav BAYER. (Coach: none).
Goals: SK Rapid Wien: 1-0 Johann HORVATH (8'), 2-0 Johann HORVATH (14' penalty),
3-0 Franz WESELIK (32').
SK Viktoria Zizkov: 3-1 Otto NOVÁK (38').
Referee: Carlo DANI (ITA)   Attendance: 15.000

(Play-off game)

FINAL

28-10-1928   Üllöi ut, Budapest: Ferencvárosi TC Budapest – SK Rapid Wien 7-1 (3-0)
Ferencvárosi TC Budapest: Ignác AMSEL, Géza TAKÁCS (I), János HUNGLER, Károly
FURMANN, Márton BUKOVI, Elemér BERKESSY, Imre KOSZTA, József TAKÁCS (II),
József TURAY, Ferenc SZEDLACSIK, Vilmos KOHUT. (Coach: István TÓTH-POTYA).
SK Rapid Wien: Franz HRIBAR, Roman SCHRAMSEIS, Franz KRAL, Josef FRÜHWIRTH,
Josef SMISTIK (I), Josef MADLMAYER, Willibald KIRBES, Franz WESELIK, Johann
HOFMANN, Johann HORVATH, Ferdinand WESSELY. (Coach: Eduard BAUER).
Goals: Ferencvárosi TC Budapest: 1-0 Ferenc SZEDLACSIK (15'), 2-0 József TAKÁCS (II)
(18'), 3-0 Ferenc SZEDLACSIK (20'), 4-0 Vilmos KOHUT (56'), 5-0 Vilmos KOHUT (58'),
6-0 József TAKÁCS (II) (64'), 7-0 József TAKÁCS (II) (76').
SK Rapid Wien: 7-1 Johann HORVATH (85').
Referee: Albino CARRARO (ITA)   Attendance: 20.000

11-11-1928   Hohe Warte, Wien: SK Rapid Wien – Ferencvárosi TC Budapest 5-3 (3-2)
SK Rapid Wien: Franz HRIBAR, Roman SCHRAMSEIS, Anton WITSCHEL, Johann
HOFMANN, Josef MADLMAYER, Josef FRÜHWIRTH, Willibald KIRBES, Franz
WESELIK, Richard (Rigo) KUTHAN, Johann HORVATH, Ferdinand WESSELY. (Coach:
Eduard BAUER).
Ferencvárosi TC Budapest: Ignác AMSEL, Géza TAKÁCS (I), János HUNGLER, Károly
FURMANN, Márton BUKOVI, Elemér BERKESSY, Imre KOSZTA, József TAKÁCS (II),
József TURAY, Ferenc SZEDLACSIK, Vilmos KOHUT. (Coach: István TÓTH-POTYA).
Goals: SK Rapid Wien: 1-0 Willibald KIRBES (5'), 2-0 Willibald KIRBES (22'), 3-2
Ferdinand WESSELY (37'), 4-2 Franz WESELIK (50'), 5-2 Ferdinand WESSELY (53').
Ferencvárosi TC Budapest: 2-1 Vilmos KOHUT (33'), 2-2 József TURAY (36'), 5-3 Ferenc
SZEDLACSIK (79').
Referee: Albino CARRARO (ITA)   Attendance: 20.000

*** Ferencvarosi TC Budapest won the Cup ***

13

1929

QUARTER-FINALS

22-06-1929   Hungária körút, Budapest: Újpesti TE – AC Sparta Praha 6-1 (2-0)
Újpesti TE: János (Acht) AKNAI, Károly KŐVÁGÓ, József FOGL (III), Ferenc BORSÁNYI, János (Kvasz) KÖVES, János (Wilhelm) VÍG (I), Imre KOSZTA, Stefan AUER/István AVAR, Rudolf VEDER, Imre HARMAT, Gábor P.SZABÓ. (Coach: Lajos BÁNYAI).
AC Sparta Praha: Frantisek HOCHMAN, Jaroslav BURGR, Antonín PERNER, Ferdinard HAJNY, Karel "Káda" PESEK, Antonín CARVAN, Antonín JIRAN, Adolf PATEK (AUT), Otto HAFTL (GER), Josef SILNY, Jan "Madelon" KNOBLOCH. (Coach: John DICK (ENG)).
Goals: Újpesti TE: 1-0 Gábor P.SZABÓ (4' penalty), 2-0 Gábor P.SZABÓ (8' penalty), 3-0 Stefan AUER/István AVAR (47'), 4-0 Stefan AUER/István AVAR (49'), 5-0 Rudolf VEDER (67'), 6-0 Stefan AUER/István AVAR (75').
AC Sparta Praha: 6-1 Josef SILNY (85').
Referee: Moritz FUCHS (GER)   Attendance: 5.000

(Stefan AUER/István AVAR was of German descent and played for the national teams of both Romania and Hungary. The spelling of his name as used in both countries is shown).

23-06-1929   Stadio Comunale "Benito Mussolini", Torino:
                Juventus FC Torino – SK Slavia Praha 1-0 (0-0)
Juventus FC Torino: Giampiero COMBI, Virginio ROSETTA, Umberto CALIGARIS, Oreste BARALE, Mario VARGLIEN (I), Lino MOSCA, Federico MUNERATI, Luigi CEVENINI (III), Antonio VOJAK (I), Carlo CROTTI, Alfredo BARISONE. (Coach: George AITKEN (ENG)).
SK Slavia Praha: Frantisek PLÁNICKA, Frantisek CERNICKY, Antonín NOVÁK, Antonín VODICKA, Josef PLETICHA, Karel CIPERA, Frantisek JUNEK, Jindich SOLTYS, Frantisek SVOBODA, Antonín PUC, Bohumil JOSKA. (Coach: John MADDEN (SCO)).
Goal: Juventus FC Torino: 1-0 Federico MUNERATI (62').
Referee: Ferenc MAJORSZKY (HUN)   Attendance: 20.000

23-06-1929   Rapid-Platz, Wien: SK Rapid Wien – Genova 1893 CC 5-1 (3-1)
SK Rapid Wien: Franz HRIBAR, Roman SCHRAMSEIS, Leopold CZEJKA, Josef MADLMAYER, Joset SMISTIK (I), Johann LUEF, Willibald KIRBES, Franz WESELIK, Matthias KABUREK, Johann HORVATH, Ferdinand WESSELY. (Coach: Eduard BAUER).
Genova 1893 CC: Giovanni DE PRÀ, Umberto LOMBARDO, Giuseppe SPIGNO, Ottavio BARBIERI, Luigi BURLANDO, Amilcare GILARDONI, Gino PUERARI, Giovanni CHIECCHI (III), Luigi LEONE, Ottorino CASANOVA, Birgilio Felice LEVRATTO.. (Coach: Renzo DE VECCHI).
Goals: SK Rapid Wien: 1-0 Franz WESELIK (8'), 2-1 Ferdinand WESSELY (30' PENALTY), 3-1 Willibald KIRBES (39'), 4-1 Ferdinand WESSELY (72'), 5-1 Franz WESELIK (82').
Genova 1893 CC: 1-1 Giovanni CHIECCHI (III) (12').
Referee: Ladislav STEPANOVSKY (TCH)   Attendance: 22.000

14

23-06-1929   Hungária körút, Budapest: Hungária FC Budapest – First Vienna FC   1-4 (1-3)
Hungária FC Budapest: József ÚJVÁRI, Gyula MÁNDI-MANDL, Ferenc KOCSIS, Béla
REBRÓ, Gábor KOMPÓTI-KLÉBER, Josef SCHNEIDER (AUT), István JECKL, György
MOLNÁR, Jenő KALMÁR, György SKVAREK, Ferenc HÍRES-HIRZER. (Coach: Béla
RÉVÉSZ).
First Vienna FC: Karl HORESCHOVSKY, Karl RAINER, Josef BLUM, Otto KALLER,
Leopold HOFMANN, Leonhard MACHU, Leopold MARAT, Karl GERHOLD, Friedrich
(Fritz) GSCHWEIDL, Franz ZILLBAUER, Leopold GIEBISCH. (Coach: Ferdinand
FRITHUM).
Goals: Hungária FC Budapest: 1-1 György SKVAREK (14').
First Vienna FC: 0-1 Leopold GIEBISCH (6'), 1-2 Karl GERHOLD (20'), 1-3 Karl
GERHOLD (35'), 1-4 Friedrich (Fritz) GSCHWEIDL (68').
Referee: Frantisek CEJNAR (TCH)   Attendance: 7.000

03-07-1929   Stadión Sparta/Letná, Praha: AC Sparta Praha – Újpesti TE   2-0 (1-0)
AC Sparta Praha: Frantisek HOCHMAN, Jaroslav BURGR, Antonín HOJER, Ferdinard
HAJNY, Karel "Káda" PESEK, Antonín CARVAN, Antonín JIRAN, Adolf PATEK (AUT),
Otto HAFTL (GER), Josef SILNY, Jan "Madelon" KNOBLOCH. (Coach: John DICK (ENG)).
Újpesti TE: János (Acht) AKNAI, Károly KŐVÁGÓ, József FOGL (III) (expulsion 61'),
Ferenc BORSÁNYI, János (Kvasz) KÖVES, János (Wilhelm) VÍG (I), Imre KOSZTA, Stefan
AUER/István AVAR, Rudolf VEDER, Imre HARMAT, Gábor P.SZABÓ. (Coach: Lajos
BÁNYAI).
Goals: AC Sparta Praha: 1-0 Jan "Madelon" KNOBLOCH (42'), 2-0 Jan "Madelon"
KNOBLOCH (72').
Referee: Rinaldo BARLASSINA (ITA)   Attendance: 22.000

06-07-1929   Stadión Slavia/Letná, Praha: SK Slavia Praha – Juventus FC Torino   3-0 (0-0)
SK Slavia Praha: Frantisek PLÁNICKA, Antonín NOVÁK, Ladislav ZENÍSEK, Karel
CIPERA, Josef PLETICHA, Antonín VODICKA, Frantisek JUNEK, Bohumil JOSKA,
Frantisek SVOBODA, Antonín PUC, Josef KRATOCHVIL. (Coach: John MADDEN (SCO)).
Juventus FC Torino: Giampiero COMBI, Virginio ROSETTA, Umberto CALIGARIS, Oreste
BARALE, Mario VARGLIEN (I) (expulsion 84'), Lino MOSCA, Federico MUNERATI,
Luigi CEVENINI (III), Antonio VOJAK (I), Carlo CROTTI, Alfredo BARISONE. (Coach:
George AITKEN (ENG)).
Goals: SK Slavia Praha: 1-0 Frantisek JUNEK (49'), 2-0 Frantisek JUNEK (69'), 3-0 Bohumil
JOSKA (75').
Referee: Ferenc MAJORSZKY (HUN)   Attendance: 20.000

07-07-1929   Stadio "Luigi Ferraris", Marassi, Genova:
                    Genova 1893 CC – SK Rapid Wien   0-0
Genova 1893 CC: Giovanni DE PRÀ, Umberto LOMBARDO, Giuseppe SPIGNO, Ottavio
BARBIERI, Luigi BURLANDO, Amilcare GILARDONI, Gino PUERARI, Ercole BODINI
(I), Giovanni CHIECCHI (III), Ottorino CASANOVA, Birgilio Felice LEVRATTO.. (Coach:
Renzo DE VECCHI).
SK Rapid Wien: Franz HRIBAR, Roman SCHRAMSEIS, Leopold CZEJKA, Josef
MADLMAYER, Josef SMISTIK (I), Johann LUEF, Willibald KIRBES, Franz WESELIK,
Matthias KABUREK, Johann HORVATH, Ferdinand WESSELY. (Coach: Eduard BAUER).
Referee: Ladislav STEPANOVSKY (TCH)   Attendance: 15.000

15

07-07-1929   Hohe Warte. Wien: First Vienna FC – Hungária FC Budapest 1-0 (0-0)
First Vienna FC: Karl HORESCHOVSKY, Karl RAINER, Josef BLUM, Otto KALLER,
Leopold HOFMANN, Leonhard MACHU, Leopold MARAT, Karl GERHOLD, Friedrich
(Fritz) GSCHWEIDL, Franz ZILLBAUER, Leopold GIEBISCH. (Coach: Ferdinand
FRITHUM).
Hungária FC Budapest: Ern NÉMETH, Gyula MÁNDI-MANDL, Ferenc KOCSIS, Henrik
NÁDLER, Gábor KOMPÓTI-KLÉBER, Josef SCHNEIDER (AUT), István JECKL, Jenö
KALMÁR, Gusztáv SEBES, Ferenc HÍRES-HIRZER, József ORMOS. (Coach: Béla
RÉVÉSZ).
Goal: First Vienna FC: 1-0 Friedrich (Fritz) GSCHWEIDL (75').
Referee: Cesare LENTI (ITA)   Attendance: 18.000

SEMI-FINALS

18-08-1929   Hohe Warte, Wien: First Vienna FC – SK Slavia Praha 3-2 (2-1)
First Vienna FC: Robert FRIEDL, Karl RAINER, Josef BLUM, Otto KALLER, Leopold
HOFMANN, Leonhard MACHU, Anton BROSENBAUER, Karl GERHOLD, Friedrich (Fritz)
GSCHWEIDL, Franz ZILLBAUER, Leopold GIEBISCH. (Coach: Ferdinand FRITHUM).
SK Slavia Praha: Frantisek PLÁNICKA, Antonín NOVÁK, Ladislav ZENÍSEK, Antonín
VODICKA, Josef PLETICHA, Karel CIPERA, Frantisek JUNEK, Bohumil JOSKA, Frantisek
SVOBODA, Antonín PUC, Josef KRATOCHVIL. (Coach: John MADDEN (SCO)).
Goals: First Vienna FC: 1-1 Karl GERHOLD (25'), 2-1 Leopold GIEBISCH (40'), 3-1
Friedrich (Fritz) GSCHWEIDL (50').
SK Slavia Praha: 0-1 Antonín PUC (10'), 3-2 Antonín PUC (89').
Referee: Ferenc KLUG (HUN)   Attendance: 12.000

21-08-1929   Újpesti pálya, Budapest: Újpesti TE – SK Rapid Wien 2-1 (1-0)
Újpesti TE: János (Acht) AKNAI, Károly KÕVÁGÓ, József FOGL (III), Ferenc BORSÁNYI,
János (Kvasz) KÖVES, János (Wilhelm) VÍG (I), Adalbert STRÖCK/Albert TÖRÖK, Stefan
AUER/István AVAR, Rudolf VEDER, Imre HARMAT, Gábor P.SZABÓ. (Coach: Lajos
BÁNYAI).
SK Rapid Wien: Franz HRIBAR, Roman SCHRAMSEIS, Leopold CZEJKA, Josef
MADLMAYER, Josef SMISTIK (I), Johann LUEF, Willibald KIRBES, Franz WESELIK,
Matthias KABUREK, Johann HORVATH, Ferdinand WESSELY. (Coach: Eduard BAUER).
Goals: Újpesti TE: 1-0 János (Kvasz) KÖVES (16'), 2-1 Adalbert STRÖCK/Albert TÖRÖK
(80').
SK Rapid Wien: 1-1 Franz WESELIK (46').
Referee: Ferenc MAJORSZKY (HUN)   Attendance: 6.000

25-08-1929   Rapid-Platz, Wien: SK Rapid Wicn – Újpesti TE 3-2 (2-0)
SK Rapid Wien: Franz HRIBAR, Roman SCHRAMSEIS, Leopold CZEJKA, Josef
MADLMAYER, Josef SMISTIK (I), Johann LUEF, Willibald KIRBES, Franz WESELIK,
Matthias KABUREK, Johann HORVATH, Ferdinand WESSELY. (Coach: Eduard BAUER).
Újpesti TE: János (Acht) AKNAI, Károly KÕVÁGÓ, József FOGL (III), Ferenc BORSÁNYI,
János (Kvasz) KÖVES, János (Wilhelm) VÍG (I), Adalbert STRÖCK/Albert TÖRÖK, Stefan
AUER/István AVAR, Rudolf VEDER, Imre HARMAT, Gábor P.SZABÓ. (Coach: Lajos
BÁNYAI).
Goals: SK Rapid Wien: 1-0 Franz WESELIK (1'), 2-0 Willibald KIRBES (27'), 3-1 Johann
HORVATH (52').
Újpesti TE: 2-1 Stefan AUER/István AVAR (48'), 3-2 Stefan AUER/István AVAR (61').
Referee: Ladislav STEPANOVSKY (TCH)   Attendance: 22.000

16

28-08-1929   Stadión Slavia/Letná, Praha: SK Slavia Praha – First Vienna FC   4-2 (0-0)
SK Slavia Praha: Frantisek PLÁNICKA, Antonín NOVÁK, Ladislav ZENÍSEK, Antonín
VODICKA, Josef PLETICHA, Karel CIPERA, Frantisek JUNEK, Bohumil JOSKA, Frantisek
SVOBODA, Antonín PUC, Josef KRATOCHVIL. (Coach: John MADDEN (SCO)).
First Vienna FC: Robert FRIEDL, Karl RAINER, Josef BLUM, Otto KALLER, Leopold
HOFMANN, Leonhard MACHU, Anton BROSENBAUER, Karl GERHOLD, Friedrich (Fritz)
GSCHWEIDL, Franz ZILLBAUER, Leopold GIEBISCH. (Coach: Ferdinand FRITHUM).
Goals: SK Slavia Praha: 1-1 Antonín PUC (54'), 2-1 Antonín PUC (65'), 3-1 Bohumil JOSKA
(82'), 4-1 Frantisek JUNEK (84').
First Vienna FC: 0-1 Leopold GIEBISCH (51'), 4-2 Karl GERHOLD (89').
Referee: Ferenc KLUG (HUN)   Attendance: 22.000

25-09-1929   Stadión Slavia/Letná, Praha: Újpesti TE – SK Rapid Wien   3-1 (0-1)
Újpesti TE: János (Acht) AKNAI, Károly KÕVÁGÓ, József FOGL (III), Ferenc BORSÁNYI,
János (Kvasz) KÖVES, János (Wilhelm) VÍG (I), Adalbert STRÖCK/Albert TÖRÖK, Stefan
AUER/István AVAR, István MÉSZÁROS, Illés SPITZ, Gábor P.SZABÓ. (Coach: Lajos
BÁNYAI).
SK Rapid Wien: Franz HRIBAR, Roman SCHRAMSEIS, Leopold CZEJKA (expulsion 116'),
Josef MADLMAYER, Josef SMISTIK (I), Johann LUEF, Willibald KIRBES (expulsion 116'),
Franz WESELIK, Richard (Rigo) KUTHAN, Johann HORVATH, Ferdinand WESSELY.
(Coach: Eduard BAUER).
Goals: Újpesti TE: 1-1 Stefan AUER/István AVAR (53'), 2-1 Stefan AUER/István AVAR
(101'), 3-1 Stefan AUER/István AVAR (116').
SK Rapid Wien: 0-1 János (Wilhelm) VÍG (I) (26' own goal).
Referee: Albino CARRARO (ITA)   Attendance: 14.000

(Play-off game. Extra-time required)

FINAL

03-11-1929   Hungária körút, Budapest: Újpesti TE – SK Slavia Praha   5-1 (1-1)
Újpesti TE: János AKNAI-ACHT, Károly KÕVÁGÓ, József FOGL (III), Ferenc BORSÁNYI,
János KÖVES, János VÍG-WILHELM (I), Adalbert STRÖCK/Albert TÖRÖK, Stefan
AUER/István AVAR, István MÉSZÁROS, Illés SPITZ, Gábor P.SZABÓ. (Coach: Lajos
BÁNYAI).
SK Slavia Praha: Frantisek PLÁNICKA, Ladislav ZENÍSEK, Antonín NOVÁK, Antonín
VODICKA, Josef PLETICHA, Karel CIPERA, Frantisek JUNEK, Bohumil JOSKA, Frantisek
SVOBODA, Antonín PUC, Josef KRATOCHVIL. (Coach: John MADDEN (SCO)).
Goals: Újpesti TE: 1-0 Illés SPITZ (42'), 2-1 Stefan AUER/István AVAR (60'), 3-1 Adalbert
STRÖCK/Albert TÖRÖK (67'), 4-1 Illés SPITZ (69'),
5-1 Gábor P.SZABÓ (80').
SK Slavia Praha: 1-1 Antonín PUC (44').
Referee: Eugen BRAUN (AUT)   Attendance: 18.000

17

17-11-1929   Stadión Slavia/Letná, Praha: SK Slavia Praha – Újpesti TE   2-2 (1-0)
SK Slavia Praha: Frantisek PLÁNICKA, Ladislav ZENÍSEK, Antonín NOVÁK, Antonín
VODICKA, Josef PLETICHA, Karel CIPERA, Frantisek JUNEK, Bohumil JOSKA, Frantisek
SVOBODA, Antonín PUC, Josef KRATOCHVIL. (Coach: John MADDEN (SCO)).
Újpesti TE: János AKNAI-ACHT, Károly KÕVÁGÓ, József FOGL (III), Ferenc BORSÁNYI,
János KÖVES, János VÍG-WILHELM (I), Adalbert STRÖCK/Albert TÖRÖK, Stefan
AUER/István AVAR, István MÉSZÁROS, Illés SPITZ, Gábor P.SZABÓ. (Coach: Lajos
BÁNYAI).
Goals: SK Slavia Praha: 1-0 Frantisek JUNEK (28'), 2-0 Josef KRATOCHVIL (57' penalty).
Újpesti TE: 2-1 Gábor P.SZABÓ (84'), 2-2 Stefan AUER/István AVAR (86').
Referee: Eugen BRAUN (AUT)   Attendance: 22.000
(Frantisek JUNEK missed a penalty)

*** Újpesti TE won the Cup ***

18

1930

FIRST ROUND

19-06-1930   Stadión Slavia/Letná, Praha:
SK Slavia Praha – Ferencvárosi TC Budapest   2-2 (1-1)
SK Slavia Praha: Frantisek PLÁNICKA, Ladislav ZENÍSEK, Antonín NOVÁK, Antonín VODICKA, Adolf SIMPERSKÝ, Václav SUBRT, Franktisek JUNEK, Jindrich SOLTYS, Frantisek SVOBODA, Antonín PUC, Bohumil JOSKA. (Coach: John MADDEN (SCO)).
Ferencvárosi TC Budapest: Ignác ARNSEL, Géza TAKÁCS (I), Lajos KORÁNYI, Antal LYKA, Márton BUKOVI, Elernér BERKESSY, Mihály TÁNCOS, József TAKÁCS (II), József TURAY, Géza TOLDI, Vilmos KOHUT. (Coach: Zoltán BLUM).
Goals: SK Slavia Praha: 1-0 Frantisek SVOBODA (23'), 2-2 Jindrich SOLTYS (85').
Ferencvárosi TC Budapest: 1-1 Géza TOLDI (30'), 1-2 József TAKÁCS (II) (47').
Referee: Hans Walter FRANKENSTEIN (AUT)   Attendance: 14.000

12-07-1930   Stadión Sparta/Letná, Praha: AC Sparta Praha – First Vienna FC   2-1 (0-0)
AC Sparta Praha: Karel HÁTLE, Jaroslav BURGR, Antonín HOJER, Jan "Madelon" KNOBLOCH, Karel "Káda" PESEK, Antonín CARVAN, Václav "Baron" BRABEC, Josef KOSTÁLEK, Raymond BRAINE (BEL), Josef SILNÝ, Karel HEJMA. (Coach: John DICK (ENG)).
First Vienna FC: Karl HORESCHOVSKY, Otto KALLER, Josef BLUM, Willy SCHADEN, Leopold HOFMANN, Leonhard MACHU, Anton BROSENBAUER, Johann PENZINGER, Friedrich (Fritz) GSCHWEIDL, Gustav TÖGEL, Leopold GIEBISCH. (Coach: Ferdinand FRITHUM).
Goals: AC Sparta Praha: 1-0 Josef SILNÝ (61'), 2-1 Raymond BRAINE (86').
First Vienna FC: 1-1 Friedrich (Fritz) GSCHWEIDL (64').
Referee: Albino CARRARO (ITA)   Attendance: 15.000

12-07-1930   Üllöi ut, Budapest: Ferencvárosi TC Budapest – SK Slavia Praha   1-0 (0-0)
Ferencvárosi TC Budapest: Ignác ARNSEL, Géza TAKÁCS (I), Lajos KORÁNYI, Antal LYKA, Gábor OBITZ, Elernér BERKESSY, Mihály TÁNCOS, József TAKÁCS (II), József TURAY, Géza TOLDI, Vilmos KOHUT. (Coach: Zoltán BLUM).
SK Slavia Praha: Frantisek PLÁNICKA, Frantisek CERNICKÝ, Antonín NOVÁK, Antonín VODICKA, Adolf SIMPERSKÝ, Vilém KÖNIG, Franktisek JUNEK, Jindrich SOLTYS, Frantisek SVOBODA, Antonín PUC, Josef KRATOCHVÍL. (Coach: John MADDEN (SCO)).
Goal: Ferencvárosi TC Budapest: 1-0 Mihály TÁNCOS (80' penalty).
Referee: Cesare LENTI (ITA)   Attendance: 10.000

13-07-1930   Stadio Comunale Luigi Ferraris, Genova:
Genoa 1893 CC – SK Rapid Wien   1-1 (0-0)
Genoa 1893 CC: Manlio BACIGALUPO, Umberto LOMBARDO, Giuseppe SPIGNO, Ottavio BARBIERI, Angelo ALBERTONI, Mario PARODI, Gino PUERARI, Ercole BODINI (I), Elvio BANCHERO (I), Ottorino CASANOVA, Virgilio Felice LEVRATTO. (Coach: Géza SZEKANY (HUN)).
SK Rapid Wien: Josef BUGALA, Roman SCHRAMSEIS, Leopold CZEJKA, Karl RAPPAN, Josef SMISTIK (I), Johann WANA, Willibald KIRBES, Franz WESELIK, Matthias KABUREK, Johann LUEF, Ferdinand WESSELY. (Coach: Eduard BAUER).
Goals: Genoa 1893 CC: 1-0 Elvio BANCHERO (49').
SK Rapid Wien: 1-1 Johann LUEF (62').
Referee: Ladislav STEPANOVSKY (TCH)   Attendance: 12.000

19

15-07-1930   Hungária körút, Budapest: Újpesti TE – AS Ambrosiana Milano 2-4 (1-2)
Újpesti TE: János (Acht) AKNAI, Gyula DUDÁS, József FOGL (III), Ferenc BORSÁNYI,
Béla VOLENTIK, János (Wilhelm) VÍG (I), Adalbert STRÖCK/Albert TÖRÖK, Stefan
AUER/István AVAR, János (Kvasz) KÖVES, Illés SPITZ, Gábor P.SZABÓ. (Coach: Lajos
BÁNYAI).
AS Ambrosiana Milano: Valentino DEGANI, Guido GIANFARDONI, Luigi ALLEMANDI,
Enrico RIVOLTA, Giuseppe VIANI, Armando CASTELLAZZI, Umberto VISENTIN (III),
Pietro SERANTONI, Giuseppe MEAZZA, Antonio BLASEVICH, Leopoldo CONTI. (Coach:
Árpád WEISZ (HUN)).
Goals: Újpesti TE: 1-0 Stefan AUER/István AVAR (12'), 2-2 Gábor P.SZABÓ (56' penalty).
AS Ambrosiana Milano: 1-1 Antonio BLASEVICH (29'), 1-2 Giuseppe MEAZZA (37'), 2-3
Giuseppe MEAZZA (60'), 2-3 Umberto VISENTIN (76').
Referee: Hans Walter FRANKENSTEIN (AUT)   Attendance: 25.000

*(Adalbert STRÖCK/Albert TÖRÖK was of Romanian descent and played for both the national
teams of Romania and Hungary. Stefan AUER/István AVAR was of German descent and also
played for both the national teams of Romania and Hungary. The spelling of the names of
these players as used in both countries is shown).*

19-07-1930   Hohe Warte, Wien: First Vienna FC – AC Sparta Praha 2-3 (1-3)
First Vienna FC: Karl HORESCHOVSKY, Karl RAINER, Josef BLUM, Otto KALLER,
Leopold HOFMANN, Leonhard MACHU, Anton BROSENBAUER, Josef ADELBRECHT,
Friedrich (Fritz) GSCHWEIDL, Gustav TÖGEL, Leopold GIEBISCH. (Coach: Ferdinand
FRITHUM).
AC Sparta Praha: Karel HÁTLE, Jaroslav BURGR, Antonín HOJER, Jan "Madelon"
KNOBLOCH, Karel "Káda" PESEK, Antonín CARVAN, Karel PODRAZIL, Josef
KOSTÁLEK, Raymond BRAINE (BEL), Josef SILNÝ, Karel HEJMA. (Coach: John DICK
(ENG)).
Goals: First Vienna FC: 1-1 Otto KALLER (9'), 2-3 Josef ADELBRECHT (70').
AC Sparta Praha: 0-1 Josef KOSTÁLEK, (4'), 1-2 Karel HEJMA (19'), 1-3 Raymond
BRAINE (22').
Referee: Albino CARRARO (ITA)   Attendance: 20.000

20-07-1930   Stadio Calistico di San Siro, Milano:
              AS Ambrosiana Milano – Újpesti TE 2-4 (1-2)
AS Ambrosiana Milano: Valentino DEGANI, Guido GIANFARDONI, Luigi ALLEMANDI,
Enrico RIVOLTA, Giuseppe VIANI, Armando CASTELLAZZI, Umberto VISENTIN (III),
Pietro SERANTONI, Giuseppe MEAZZA, Antonio BLASEVICH, Leopoldo CONTI. (Coach:
Árpád WEISZ (HUN)).
Újpesti TE: János (Acht) AKNAI, Gyula DUDÁS, József FOGL (III), Ferenc BORSÁNYI,
Béla VOLENTIK, János (Wilhelm) VÍG (I), Adalbert STRÖCK/Albert TÖRÖK, Stefan
AUER/István AVAR, János SÓLYOM, Illés SPITZ, Gábor P.SZABÓ. (Coach: Lajos
BÁNYAI).
Goals: AS Ambrosiana Milano: 1-0 Giuseppe MEAZZA (4'), 2-2 Giuseppe MEAZZA (47').
Újpesti TE: 1-1 Illés SPITZ (13'), 1-2 János SÓLYOM (34'), 2-3 János SÓLYOM (69'), 2-4
Gábor P.SZABÓ (83' penalty).
Referee: Hans Walter FRANKENSTEIN (AUT)   Attendance: 20.000

31-08-1930   Stadion Neufeld, Bern· Újpesti TE – AS Ambrosiana Milano   1-1 (0-0)
Újpesti TE: János (Acht) AKNAI, Gyula DUDÁS, Károly KÖVÁGÓ, Ferenc BORSÁNYI,
Béla VOLENTIK, János (Wilhelm) VÍG (I), Adalbert STRÖCK/Albert TÖRÖK, Stefan
AUER/István AVAR, János SÓLYOM, Illés SPITZ, Gábor P.SZABÓ. (Coach: Lajos
BÁNYAI).
AS Ambrosiana Milano: Valentino DEGANI (expulsion 95'), Giovanni BOLZONI, Luigi
ALLEMANDI, Enrico RIVOLTA, Giuseppe VIANI, Armando CASTELLAZZI, Umberto
VISENTIN (III), Pietro SERANTONI, Giuseppe MEAZZA, Antonio BLASEVICH, Leopoldo
CONTI. (Coach: Árpád WEISZ (HUN)).
Goals: Újpesti TE: 1-1 Stefan AUER/István AVAR (71').
AS Ambrosiana Milano: 0-1 Giuseppe MEAZZA (64').
Referee: Paul RUOFF (SUI)   Attendance: 7.000

*(Play-off game with extra-time played. The match was abandoned after 113 minutes due to
poor light and a replay was required).*

03-09-1930   Rapid-Platz, Wien: SK Rapid Wien – Genoa 1893 CC   6-1 (2-1)
SK Rapid Wien: Josef BUGALA, Roman SCHRAMSEIS, Leopold CZEJKA, Karl RAPPAN,
Josef SMISTIK (I), Johann WANA, Willibald KIRBES, Franz WESELIK, Matthias
KABUREK, Johann LUEF, Ferdinand WESSELY. (Coach: Eduard BAUER).
Genoa 1893 CC: Manlio BACIGALUPO, Giuseppe SPIGNO, Angelo STRATA, Ottavio
BARBIERI, Luigi BURLANDO, Amilcare GILARDINO, Gino PUERARI, Elvio
BANCHERO (I), Virgilio Felice LEVRATTO, Ottorino CASANOVA, Quinto ROSSO.
(Coach: Géza SZEKANY (HUN)).
Goals: SK Rapid Wien: 1-1 Willibald KIRBES (9'), 2-1 Johann LUEF (16'), 3-1 Ferdinand
WESSELY (57'), 4-1 Franz WESELIK (76'), 5-1 Franz WESELIK (81'), 6-1 Ferdinand
WESSELY (83').
Genoa 1893 CC: 0-1 Virgilio Felice LEVRATTO (3').
Referee: Paul RUOFF (SUI)   Attendance: 16.500

14-09-1930   Arena Civica, Milano: AS Ambrosiana Milano – Újpesti TE   5-3 (3-1)
AS Ambrosiana Milano: Valentino DEGANI, Giovanni BOLZONI, Luigi ALLEMANDI,
Enrico RIVOLTA, Giuseppe VIANI, Armando CASTELLAZZI, Umberto VISENTIN (III),
Pietro SERANTONI, Giuseppe MEAZZA, Antonio BLASEVICH, Leopoldo CONTI. (Coach:
Árpád WEISZ (HUN)).
Újpesti TE: János (Acht) AKNAI, Gyula DUDÁS, Károly KÖVÁGÓ, Ferenc BORSÁNYI,
Béla VOLENTIK, János (Wilhelm) VÍG (I), Adalbert STRÖCK/Albert TÖRÖK, Stefan
AUER/István AVAR, János SÓLYOM, Illés SPITZ, Gábor P.SZABÓ. (Coach: Lajos
BÁNYAI).
Goals: AS Ambrosiana Milano: 1-0 Leopoldo CONTI (25'), 2-0 Giuseppe MEAZZA (35'), 3-0
Giuseppe MEAZZA (38'), 4-2 Pietro SERANTONI (76'), 5-2 Umberto VISENTIN (80').
Újpesti TE: 3-1 Stefan AUER/István AVAR (44'), 3-2 Stefan AUER/István AVAR (50'), 5-3
János SÓLYOM (90').
Referee: Dr.Peco BAUWENS (GER)   Attendance: 20.000

(Play-off game replay).

21

SEMI-FINALS

08-09-1930   Rapid-Platz, Wien: SK Rapid Wien – Ferencvárosi TC Budapest 5-1 (3-0)
SK Rapid Wien: Josef BUGALA, Roman SCHRAMSEIS, Leopold CZEJKA, Karl RAPPAN,
Josef SMISTIK (I), Johann WANA, Willibald KIRBES, Franz WESELIK, Matthias
KABUREK, Stefan SKOUMAL, Ferdinand WESSELY. (Coach: Eduard BAUER).
Ferencvárosi TC Budapest: József HÁDA, Géza TAKÁCS (I), Lajos KORÁNYI, Károly
FURMANN, Antal LYKA, Elernér BERKESSY, Gyula LÁZÁR, Mihály TÁNCOS, József
TURAY, Géza TOLDI, Vilmos KOHUT. (Coach: Zoltán BLUM).
Goals: SK Rapid Wien: 1-0 Matthias KABUREK (1'), 2-0 Matthias KABUREK (14'), 3-0
Ferdinand WESSELY (30' penalty), 4-0 Matthias KABUREK (66'), 5-1 Ferdinand
WESSELY (80').
Ferencvárosi TC Budapest: 4-1 Vilmos KOHUT (70').
Referee: Sophus HANSEN (DEN)   Attendance: 18.000

28-09-1930   Arena Civica, Milano: AS Ambrosiana Milano – AC Sparta Praha 2-2 (1-2)
AS Ambrosiana Milano: Valentino DEGANI, Giovanni BOLZONI, Luigi ALLEMANDI,
Enrico RIVOLTA, Giuseppe VIANI, Armando CASTELLAZZI, Umberto VISENTIN (III),
Pietro SERANTONI, Giuseppe MEAZZA, Antonio BLASEVICH, Leopoldo CONTI. (Coach:
Árpád WEISZ (HUN)).
AC Sparta Praha: Ladislav BELÍK, Jaroslav BURGR, Josef CTYROKÝ, Jan "Madelon"
KNOBLOCH, Karel "Káda" PESEK, Erich SRBEK, Karel PODRAZIL, Josef KOSTÁLEK,
Raymond BRAINE (BEL), Josef SILNÝ, Karel HEJMA. (Coach: John DICK (ENG)).
Goals: AS Ambrosiana Milano: 1-2 Pietro SERANTONI (27'), 2-2 Pietro SERANTONI (67').
AC Sparta Praha: 0-1 Josef KOSTÁLEK (1'), 0-2 Josef KOSTÁLEK (15').
Referee: John LANGENUS (BEL)   Attendance: 15.000

12-10-1930   Stadión Sparta/Letná, Praha:
               AC Sparta Praha – AS Ambrosiana Milano 6-1 (1-0)
AC Sparta Praha: Ladislav BELÍK, Jaroslav BURGR, Josef CTYROKÝ, Jan "Madelon"
KNOBLOCH, Karel "Káda" PESEK, Erich SRBEK, Karel PODRAZIL, Josef KOSTÁLEK,
Raymond BRAINE (BEL), Josef SILNÝ, Karel HEJMA. (Coach: John DICK (ENG)).
AS Ambrosiana Milano: Pietro MIGLIO, Giovanni BOLZONI, Luigi ALLEMANDI, Enrico
RIVOLTA, Giuseppe VIANI, Armando CASTELLAZZI, Umberto VISENTIN (III), Pietro
SERANTONI, Giuseppe MEAZZA, Luigi FERRERO, Antonio BLASEVICH. (Coach: Árpád
WEISZ (HUN)).
Goals: AC Sparta Praha: 1-0 Raymond BRAINE (33'), 2-0 Armando CASTELLAZZI (49' *own
goal*), 3-0 Josef SILNÝ (53'), 4-0 Raymond BRAINE (70'), 5-0 Karel PODRAZIL (72'), 6-0
Karel HEJMA (85').
AS Ambrosiana Milano: 6-1 Luigi FERRERO (88').
Referee: Sophus HANSEN (DEN)   Attendance: 32.000

15-10-1930   Üllöi ut, Budapest: Ferencvárosi TC Budapest – SK Rapid Wien 1-0 (1-0)
Ferencvárosi TC Budapest: József HÁDA, Lajos KORÁNYI, László PAPP, Károly
FURMANN, Antal LYKA, Elernér BERKESSY, Gyula LÁZÁR, Jozsef TAKÁCS (II), József
TURAY, Géza TOLDI, Vilmos KOHUT. (Coach: Zoltán BLUM).
SK Rapid Wien: Josef BUGALA, Roman SCHRAMSEIS, Leopold CZEJKA, Karl RAPPAN,
Josef SMISTIK (I), Johann WANA, Willibald KIRBES, Franz WESELIK, Matthias
KABUREK, Johann LUEF, Ferdinand WESSELY. (Coach: Eduard BAUER).
Goal: Ferencvárosi TC Budapest: 1-0 Jozsef TAKÁCS (24').
Referee: Otto OLSSON (SWE)   Attendance: 8.000

22

FINAL

02-11-1930   Stadión Sparta/Letná, Praha: AC Sparta Praha – SK Rapid Wien   0-2 (0-1)
AC Sparta Praha: Ladislav BELÍK, Jaroslav BURGR, Antonín HOJER, Jan "Madelon"
KNOBLOCH, Karel "Káda" PESEK, Erich SRBEK, Adolf PATEK (AUT), Josef
KOSTÁLEK, Raymond BRAINE (BEL), Josef SILNÝ, Karel HEJMA. (Coach: John DICK
(ENG)).
SK Rapid Wien: Josef BUGALA, Roman SCHRAMSEIS, Leopold CZEJKA, Karl RAPPAN,
Josef SMISTIK (I), Johann WANA, Willibald KIRBES, Franz WESELIK, Matthias
KABUREK, Johann LUEF, Ferdinand WESSELY. (Coach: Eduard BAUER).
Goals: SK Rapid Wien: 0-1 Johann LUEF (9'), 0-2 Franz WESELIK (57').
Referee: Sophus HANSEN (DEN)   Attendance: 25.000
(Antonín HOJER missed a penalty in the 8th minute).

12-11-1930   Hohe Warte, Wien: SK Rapid Wien – AC Sparta Praha   2-3 (1-2)
SK Rapid Wien: Josef BUGALA, Roman SCHRAMSEIS, Leopold CZEJKA, Josef
FRÜHWIRTH, Josef SMISTIK (I), Josef MADLMAYER, Willibald KIRBES, Franz
WESELIK, Matthias KABUREK, Johann LUEF, Ferdinand WESSELY. (Coach: Eduard
BAUER).
AC Sparta Praha: Ladislav BELÍK, Jaroslav BURGR, Josef CTYROKÝ, Jan "Madelon"
KNOBLOCH, Karel "Káda" PESEK, Erich SRBEK, Karel PODRAZIL, Josef KOSTÁLEK,
Raymond BRAINE (BEL), Josef SILNÝ, Karel HEJMA. (Coach: John DICK (ENG)).
Goals: SK Rapid Wien: 1-0 Matthias KABUREK (17'), 2-2 Josef SMISTIK (68').
AC Sparta Praha: 1-1 Josef KOSTÁLEK (25'), 1-2 Josef KOSTÁLEK (27'), 2-3 Josef
KOSTÁLEK (87').
Referee: Sophus HANSEN (DEN)   Attendance: 40.000

*** SK Rapid Wien won the Cup ***

1931

QUARTER-FINALS

27-06-1931   Hohe Warte, Wien: First Vienna FC – Debreceni Bocskai FC   3-0 (2-0)
First Vienna FC: Karl HORESCHOVSKY, Karl RAINER, Josef BLUM, Otto KALLER,
Leopold HOFMANN, Leonhard MACHU, Leopold MARAT, Josef ADELBRECHT, Friedrich
(Fritz) GSCHWEIDL, Gustav TÖGEL, Franz ERDL. (Coach: Ferdinand FRITHUM).
Debreceni Bocskai FC: András BUDAI, Lajos MOHAROS, Imre MOLNÁR, István
VILLÁNYI, János MÓRÉ, Rezsö KEVICZKY, Imre MARKOS, János GYURCSÓ, Pál
TELEKI, Attila MÁTÉFFY, József ORMOS. (Coach: Zsigmond KÁLDY).
Goals: First Vienna FC: 1-0 Friedrich (Fritz) GSCHWEIDL (8'), 2-0 Friedrich (Fritz)
GSCHWEIDL (40'), 3-0 Leopold HOFMANN (64').
Referee: Gustav KRIST (TCH)   Attendance: 8.000

05-07-1931   Diószegi úti, Debrecen: Debreceni Bocskai FC – First Vienna FC   0-4 (0-1)
Debreceni Bocskai FC: András BUDAI, Lajos MOHAROS, Imre MOLNÁR, István
VILLÁNYI, János MÓRÉ, Rezsö KEVICZKY, Imre MARKOS, Jen VINCE, Pál TELEKI,
Attila MÁTÉFFY, József ORMOS. (Coach: Zsigmond KÁLDY).
First Vienna FC: Karl HORESCHOVSKY, Karl RAINER, Josef BLUM, Otto KALLER,
Leopold HOFMANN, Leonhard MACHU, Leopold MARAT, Josef ADELBRECHT, Friedrich
(Fritz) GSCHWEIDL, Gustav TÖGEL, Franz ERDL. (Coach: Ferdinand FRITHUM).
Goals: First Vienna FC: 0-1 Gustav TÖGEL (20'), 0-2 Josef ADELBRECHT (49'), 0-3 Franz
ERDL (63'), 0-4 Franz ERDL (88').
Referee: Gustav KRIST (TCH)   Attendance: 5.000

07-07-1931   Stadión Slavia/Letná, Praha: SK Slavia Praha – AS Roma   1-1 (1-1)
SK Slavia Praha: Frantisek PLÁNICKA, Ladislav ZENÍSEK, Antonín NOVÁK, Antonín
VODICKA, Adolf SIMPERSKÝ, Frantisek CERNICKÝ, Franktisek JUNEK, Stefan
CAMBAL, Frantisek SVOBODA, Antonín PUC, Bohumil JOSKA. (Coach: Josef "Staplík"
SLOUP).
AS Roma: Guido MASETTI, Mario DE MICHELI, Renato BODINI (II), Attilio FERRARIS
(IV), Dr.Fulvio BERNARDINI, Raffaele D'AQUINO, Raffaele COSTANTINO, Cesare
Augusto FASANELLI, Rodolfo VOLK, Nicolás Italo LOMBARDO (ARG), Antonio CHINI
Ludueña (ARG). (Coach: Herbert BURGESS (ENG)).
Goals: SK Slavia Praha: 1-1 Antonín NOVÁK (30' penalty).
AS Roma: 0-1 Rodolfo VOLK (13').
Referee: René MERCET (SUI)   Attendance: 30.000

12-07-1931   Campo Sportivo Testaccio, Roma: AS Roma – SK Slavia Praha   2-1 (1-1)
AS Roma: Guido MASETTI, Mario DE MICHELI, Renato BODINI (II), Attilio FERRARIS
(IV), Dr. Fulvio BERNARDINI, Raffaele D'AQUINO, Raffaele COSTANTINO, Cesare
Augusto FASANELLI, Rodolfo VOLK, Nicolás Italo LOMBARDO (ARG), Antonio CHINI
Ludueña (ARG). (Coach: Herbert BURGESS (ENG)).
SK Slavia Praha: Frantisek PLÁNICKA, Ladislav ZENÍSEK, Antonín NOVÁK, Antonín
VODICKA, Stefan CAMBAL, Frantisek CERNICKÝ, Franktisek JUNEK, Frantisek
SVOBODA, Václáv BÁRA, Antonín PUC, Frantisek FAIT. (Coach: Josef "Staplík" SLOUP).
Goals: AS Roma: 1-1 Raffaele COSTANTINO (41'), 2-1 Rodolfo VOLK (47').
SK Slavia Praha: 0-1 Antonín PUC (15').
Referee: René MERCET (SUI)   Attendance: 14.000

12-07-1931   Stade Comunale "Benito Mussolini", Torino:
                Juventus FC Torino – AC Sparta Praha 2-1 (1-0)
Juventus FC Torino: Ezio SCLAVI, Virginio ROSETTA, Umberto CALIGARIS, Giovanni
VARGLIEN (II), Mario VARGLIEN (I), Luigi BERTOLINI, Federico MUNERATI, Renato
CESARINI (ARG), Giovanni VECCHINA, Giovanni FERRARI, Raimundo Bibiani ORSI
(ARG). (Coach: Carlo CARCANO).
AC Sparta Praha: Josef NEMEC, Jaroslav BURGR, Josef CTYROKÝ, Jan "Madelon"
KNOBLOCH, Karel "Káda" PESEK, Erich SRBEK, Karel PODRAZIL, Otto HAFTL (GER),
Raymond BRAINE (BEL), Oldrich NEJEDLÝ, Josef SILNÝ. (Coach: John DICK (ENG)).
Goals: Juventus FC Torino: 1-0 Renato CESARINI (39'), 2-1 Federico MUNERATI (88').
AC Sparta Praha: 1-1 Raymond BRAINE (60').
Referee: Dr.Adolf MIESZ (AUT)   Attendance: 15.000
(Ezio SCLAVI saved an 80th minute penalty taken by Raymond BRAINE).

22-07-1931   Stadión Sparta/Letná, Praha: AC Sparta Praha – Juventus FC Torino 1-0 (0-0)
AC Sparta Praha: Josef NEMEC, Jaroslav BURGR, Josef CTYROKÝ, Jan "Madelon"
KNOBLOCH, Karel "Káda" PESEK, Erich SRBEK, Karel PODRAZIL, Otto HAFTL (GER),
Raymond BRAINE (BEL), Josef SILNÝ, Karel SOKOLÁ. (Coach: John DICK (ENG)).
Juventus FC Torino: Ezio SCLAVI, Virginio ROSETTA, Umberto CALIGARIS, Giovanni
VARGLIEN (II), Mario VARGLIEN (I), Luigi BERTOLINI, Federico MUNERATI, Renato
CESARINI (ARG), Giovanni VECCHINA, Giovanni FERRARI, Raimundo Bibiani ORSI
(ARG). (Coach: Carlo CARCANO).
Goal: AC Sparta Praha: 1-0 Otto HAFTL (61').
Referee: Dr.Adolf MIESZ (AUT)   Attendance: 35.000

12-08-1931   Hungária körút, Budapest:
                Hungária FC Budapest – Wiener Athletiksport-Club 1-5 (0-0)
Hungária FC Budapest: József ÚJVÁRI, János NAGY, Gyula MÁNDI-MANDL, Gábor
KOMPÓTI-KLÉBER, Jenö KALMÁR, Gusztáv SEBES, Pál TITKOS, László CSEH, József
HÉJAS-HAUER, Gyula BARÁTKY, Ferenc HÍRES-HIRZER. (Coach: Imre SENKEY).
Wiener Athletiksport-Club: Rudolf HIDEN, Johann BECHER, Karl SESTA, Georg BRAUN,
Vlastimil BORECZKY (TCH), Otto JANY, Franz CISAR, Heinrich MÜLLER, Heinrich
HILTL, Josef HANKE (GER), Karl HUBER. (Coach: Karl GEYER).
Goals: Hungária FC Budapest: 1-5 Gyula BARÁTKY (90').
Wiener Athletiksport-Club: 0-1 Heinrich HILTL (51'), 0-2 Josef HANKE (61'), 0-3 Karl
HUBER (66'), 0-4 Josef HANKE (69'), 0-5 Heinrich HILTL (87').
Referee: Gustav KRIST (TCH)   Attendance: 10.000

19-08-1931   WAC-Platz, Wien:
                Wiener Athletiksport-Club – Hungária FC Budapest 1-3 (0-2)
Wiener Athletiksport-Club: Rudolf HIDEN, Johann BECHER, Karl SESTA, Georg BRAUN,
Vlastimil BORECZKY (TCH), Rudolf KUBESCH, Franz CISAR, Heinrich MÜLLER,
Heinrich HILTL, Josef HANKE (GER), Karl HUBER. (Coach: Karl GEYER).
Hungária FC Budapest: József ÚJVÁRI, János NAGY, Gyula MÁNDI-MANDL, Gábor
KOMPÓTI-KLÉBER, Jenö KALMÁR, Gusztáv SEBES, Pál TITKOS, László CSEH, József
HÉJAS-HAUER, Gyula BARÁTKY, Ferenc HÍRES-HIRZER. (Coach: Imre SENKEY).
Goals: Wiener Athletiksport-Club: 1-3 Josef HANKE (82').
Hungária FC Budapest: 0-1 László CSEH (2'), 0-2 Jenö KALMÁR (3'), 0-3 Pál TITKOS
(47').
Referee: Gustav KRIST (TCH)   Attendance: 15.000

25

02-09-1931   WAC-Platz, Wien: AC Sparta Praha – Juventus FC Torino 3-2 (1-1)
AC Sparta Praha: Josef NEMEC, Jaroslav BURGR, Josef CTYROKÝ, Jan "Madelon"
KNOBLOCH (expulsion 87'), Karel "Káda" PESEK, Erich SRBEK, Karel PODRAZIL, Otto
HAFTL (GER), Raymond BRAINE (BEL), Oldrich NEJEDLÝ, Josef SILNÝ. (Coach: John
DICK (ENG)).
Juventus FC Torino: Ezio SCLAVI, Virginio ROSETTA, Umberto CALIGARIS (expulsion
83'), Mario VARGLIEN (I), Luis Felipe MONTI (ARG), Luigi BERTOLINI, Giovanni
VECCHINA, Renato CESARINI (ARG) (expulsion 87'), José MAGLIO (ARG) (expulsion
37'), Giovanni FERRARI, Raimundo Bibiani ORSI (ARG). (Coach: Carlo CARCANO).
Goals: AC Sparta Praha: 1-1 Karel PODRAZIL (26'), 2-1 Oldrich NEJEDLÝ (59'), 3-1 Josef
SILNÝ (70').
Juventus FC Torino: 0-1 Raimundo Bibiani ORSI (24'), 3-2 Giovanni FERRARI (90').
Referee: Paul RUOFF (SUI)   Attendance: 8.000

SEMI-FINALS

10-09-1931   WAC-Platz, Wien: Wiener Athletiksport-Club – AC Sparta Praha 2-3 (1-1)
Wiener Athletiksport-Club: Rudolf HIDEN, Johann BECHER, Karl SESTA, Georg BRAUN,
Ernst LÖWINGER, Rudolf KUBESCH, Franz CISAR, Heinrich MÜLLER, Heinrich HILTL,
Josef HANKE (GER), Karl HUBER. (Coach: Karl GEYER).
AC Sparta Praha: Josef NEMEC, Jaroslav BURGR, Josef CTYROKÝ, Jan "Madelon"
KNOBLOCH, Karel "Káda" PESEK, Erich SRBEK, Karel PODRAZIL, Otto HAFTL (GER),
Raymond BRAINE (BEL), Oldrich NEJEDLÝ, Josef SILNÝ. (Coach: John DICK (ENG)).
Goals: Wiener Athletiksport-Club: 1-1 Heinrich HILTL (45'), 2-2 Rudolf KUBESCH (74'
penalty).
AC Sparta Praha: 0-1 Otto HAFTL (20'), 1-2 Oldrich NEJEDLÝ (70'), 2-3 Oldrich NEJEDLÝ
(86').
Referee: John LANGENUS (BEL)   Attendance: 12.000

17-09-1931   Stadión Sparta/Letná, Praha:
               AC Sparta Praha – Wiener Athletiksport-Club 3-4 (0-1)
AC Sparta Praha: Josef NEMEC, Jaroslav BURGR, Josef CTYROKÝ, Jan "Madelon"
KNOBLOCH, Karel "Káda" PESEK, Erich SRBEK, Karel PODRAZIL, Otto HAFTL (GER),
Raymond BRAINE (BEL), Oldrich NEJEDLÝ, Josef SILNÝ. (Coach: John DICK (ENG)).
Wiener Athletiksport-Club: Rudolf HIDEN, Johann BECHER, Karl SESTA, Georg BRAUN,
Ernst LÖWINGER, Rudolf KUBESCH, Franz CISAR, Heinrich MÜLLER, Heinrich HILTL,
Josef HANKE (GER), Karl HUBER. (Coach: Karl GEYER).
Goals: AC Sparta Praha: 1-3 Oldrich NEJEDLÝ (57'), 2-3 Otto HAFTL (62'), 3-3 Josef
SILNÝ (64').
Wiener Athletiksport-Club: 0-1 Karl SESTA (29'), 0-2 Heinrich HILTL (50'), 0-3 Heinrich
HILTL (55'), 3-4 Heinrich HILTL (88').
Referee: John LANGENUS (BEL)   Attendance: 26.000

20-09-1931   Campo Sportivo Testaccio, Roma: AS Roma – First Vienna FC   2-3 (1-2)
AS Roma: Guido MASETTI, Mario DE MICHELI, Renato BODINI (II), Attilio FERRARIS
(IV), Dr. Fulvio BERNARDINI, Raffaele D'AQUINO, Raffaele COSTANTINO, Cesare
Augusto FASANELLI, Rodolfo VOLK, Nicolás Italo LOMBARDO (ARG), Antonio CHINI
Ludueña (ARG). (Coach: Herbert BURGESS (ENG)).
First Vienna FC: Karl HORESCHOVSKY, Karl RAINER, Josef BLUM, Otto KALLER,
Leopold HOFMANN, Willibald SCHMAUS, Anton BROSENBAUER, Josef ADELBRECHT,
Friedrich (Fritz) GSCHWEIDL, Gustav TÖGEL, Leopold MARAT. (Coach: Ferdinand
FRITHUM).
Goals: AS Roma: 1-0 Antonio CHINI Ludueña (3'), 2-3 Cesare Augusto FASANELLI (55').
First Vienna FC: 1-1 Leopold MARAT (33'), 1-2 Josef BLUM (34'), 1-3 Friedrich (Fritz)
GSCHWEIDL (51').
Referee: René MERCET (SUI)   Attendance: 13.000

24-09-1931   Hohe Warte, Wien: First Vienna FC – AS Roma   3-1 (3-0)
First Vienna FC: Karl HORESCHOVSKY, Karl RAINER, Josef BLUM, Otto KALLER,
Leopold HOFMANN, Willibald SCHMAUS, Anton BROSENBAUER, Josef ADELBRECHT,
Friedrich (Fritz) GSCHWEIDL, Gustav TÖGEL, Leopold MARAT. (Coach: Ferdinand
FRITHUM).
AS Roma: Guido MASETTI, Mario DE MICHELI, Renato BODINI (II), Attilio FERRARIS
(IV), Dr. Fulvio BERNARDINI, Raffaele D'AQUINO (expulsion 10'), Raffaele
COSTANTINO, Cesare Augusto FASANELLI, Rodolfo VOLK, Nicolás Italo LOMBARDO
(ARG), Antonio CHINI Ludueña (ARG). (Coach: Herbert BURGESS (ENG)).
Goals: First Vienna FC: 1-0 Leopold MARAT (9'), 2-0 Josef BLUM (27' penalty), 3-0
Leopold MARAT (30').
AS Roma: 3-1 Rodolfo VOLK (65').
Referee: René MERCET (SUI)   Attendance: 20.000
(Guido MASETTI saved a 10th minute penalty taken by Josef BLUM).

07-10-1931   Stadión Sparta/Letná, Praha:
                AC Sparta Praha – Wiener Athletiksport-Club   0-2 (0-1)
AC Sparta Praha: Josef NEMEC, Jaroslav BURGR, Josef CTYROKÝ, Jan "Madelon"
KNOBLOCH, Karel "Káda" PESEK, Erich SRBEK, Karel PODRAZIL, Otto HAFTL (GER),
Raymond BRAINE (BEL), Oldrich NEJEDLÝ, Josef SILNÝ. (Coach: John DICK (ENG)).
Wiener Athletiksport-Club: Rudolf HIDEN, Johann BECHER, Karl SESTA, Georg BRAUN,
Ernst LÖWINGER, Rudolf KUBESCH, Franz CISAR, Heinrich MÜLLER, Heinrich HILTL,
Josef HANKE (GER), Karl HUBER. (Coach: Karl GEYER).
Goals: Wiener Athletiksport-Club: 0-1 Franz CISAR (37'), 0-2 Heinrich HILTL (50').
Referee: Albino CARRARO (ITA)   Attendance: 25.000

(Play-off game).

27

08-11-1931   Stadion Hardturm, Zürich:
                        First Vienna FC – Wiener Athletiksport-Club   3-2 (1-2)
First Vienna FC: Karl HORESCHOVSKY, Karl RAINER, Josef BLUM, Willibald
SCHMAUS, Leopold HOFMANN, Leonhard MACHU, Anton BROSENBAUER, Josef
ADELBRECHT, Friedrich (Fritz) GSCHWEIDL, Gustav TÖGEL, Franz ERDL. (Coach:
Ferdinand FRITHUM).
Wiener Athletiksport-Club: Rudolf HIDEN, Johann BECHER, Karl SESTA, Georg BRAUN,
Ernst LÖWINGER, Rudolf KUBESCH, Franz CISAR, Heinrich MÜLLER, Heinrich HILTL,
Josef HANKE (GER), Karl HUBER. (Coach: Karl GEYER).
Goals: First Vienna FC: 1-2 Gustav TÖGEL (30'), 2-2 Josef ADELBRECHT (63'), 3-2 Johann
BECHER (87' *own goal*).
Wiener Athletiksport-Club: 0-1 Josef HANKE (2'), 0-2 Heinrich MÜLLER (22').
Referee: Francesco MATTEA (ITA)   Attendance: 20.000

12-11-1931   Hohe Warte, Wien: Wiener Athletiksport-Club – First Vienna FC   1-2 (0-2)
Wiener Athletiksport-Club: Rudolf HIDEN, Johann BECHER, Karl SESTA, Georg BRAUN,
Ernst LÖWINGER, Rudolf KUBESCH, Wilhelm CUTTI, Heinrich MÜLLER, Heinrich
HILTL, Josef HANKE (GER), Karl HUBER. (Coach: Karl GEYER).
First Vienna FC: Karl HORESCHOVSKY, Karl RAINER, Josef BLUM, Willibald
SCHMAUS, Leopold HOFMANN, Leonhard MACHU, Anton BROSENBAUER, Josef
ADELBRECHT, Friedrich (Fritz) GSCHWEIDL, Gustav TÖGEL, Franz ERDL. (Coach:
Ferdinand FRITHUM).
Goals: Wiener Athletiksport-Club: 1-2 Josef HANKE (65').
First Vienna FC: 0-1 Franz ERDL (6'), 0-2 Franz ERDL (41').
Referee: Rinaldo BARLASSINA (ITA)   Attendance: 25.000

*** First Vienna FC won the Cup ***

28

1932

QUARTER-FINALS

10-06-1932   Stadio del Littoriale, Bologna: Bologna Sportiva – AC Sparta Praha   5-0 (4-0)
Bologna Sportiva: Mario GIANNI, Eraldo MONZEGLIO, Felice GASPERI, Mario
MONTESANTO, Gastone BALDI, Gastone MARTELLI, Bruno MAINI, Raffaele SANSONE
(URU), Angelo SCHIAVIO, Francisco FEDULLO (URU), Carlo REGUZZONI. (Coach:
József NAGY (HUN)).
AC Sparta Praha: Antonín LEDVINA, Jaroslav BURGR, Antonín PERNER,Josef
KOSTÁLEK, Jan "Madelon" KNOBLOCH, Erich SRBEK, Karel PODRAZIL, Josef SILNÝ,
Raymond BRAINE (BEL) (expulsion 60'), Oldrich NEJEDLÝ, Karel SOKOLÁR. (Coach:
Antonín HOJER).
Goals: Bologna Sportiva: 1-0 Carlo REGUZZONI (2'), 2-0 Bruno MAINI (16'), 3-0 Bruno
MAINI (20'), 4-0 Angelo SCHIAVIO (43'), 5-0 Gastone BALDI (68').
Referee: Dr.Adolf MIESZ (AUT)   Attendance: 22.000

18-06-1932   Stadión Slavia/Letná, Praha: SK Slavia Praha – WSC Admira Wien   3-0 (1-0)
SK Slavia Praha: Frantisek PLÁNICKA, Ladislav ZENÍSEK, Adolf FIALA, Antonín
VODICKA, Stefan CAMBAL, Frantisek CERNICKÝ, Franktisek JUNEK, Frantisek
SVOBODA, Jirí SOBOTKA, Vlastimil KOPECKÝ, Antonín PUC. (Coach: Josef "Staplík"
SLOUP).
WSC Admira Wien: Rudolf ZÖHRER, Robert PAVLICEK, Anton JANDA, Karl
SZOLDATICS, Johann URBANEK, Johann KLIMA, Leopold FACCO, Leopold VOGL,
Wilhelm HAHNEMANN, Anton SCHALL, Adolf VOGL. (Coach: Hans SKOLAUT).
Goals: SK Slavia Praha: 1-0 Frantisek SVOBODA (32'), 2-0 Vlastimil KOPECKÝ (72'), 3-0
Frantisek SVOBODA (77').
Referee: Ferenc KLUG (HUN)   Attendance: 22.000

25-06-1932   Hohe Warte, Wien: First Vienna FC – Újpesti TE   5-3 (2-3)
First Vienna FC: Karl HORESCHOVSKY, Karl RAINER, Josef BLUM, Otto KALLER,
Leopold HOFMANN, Willibald SCHMAUS, Anton BROSENBAUER, Josef ADELBRECHT,
Friedrich (Fritz) GSCHWEIDL, Gustav TÖGEL, Franz SCHÖNWETTER. (Coach: Ferdinand
FRITHUM).
Újpesti TE: Rezsö HUBA, Károly KÖVÁGÓ, József FOGL (III), Ferenc BORSÁNYI, Miklos
SÁROS, Antal SZALAY, Adalbert STRÖCK/Albert TÖRÖK, Stefan AUER/István AVAR,
Pál JÁVOR-JAKUBE, Károly KIS, Gábor P.SZABÓ. (Coach: Lajos BÁNYAI).
Goals: First Vienna FC: 1-0 Franz SCHÖNWETTER (11'), 2-2 Franz SCHÖNWETTER (30'),
3-3 Josef ADELBRECHT (60'), 4-3 Gustav TÖGEL (83'), 5-3 Franz SCHÖNWETTER (90').
Újpesti TE: 1-1 Pál JÁVOR-JAKUBE (14'), 1-2 Pál JÁVOR-JAKUBE (18'), 2-3 Gábor
P.SZABÓ (35').
Referee: Camillo CAIRONI (ITA)   Attendance: 12.000

26-06-1932   Praterstadion, Wien: WSC Admira Wien – SK Slavia Praha   1-0 (0-0)
WSC Admira Wien: Rudolf ZÖHRER, Robert PAVLICEK, Anton JANDA, Karl
SZOLDATICS, Johann URBANEK, Johann KLIMA, Leopold FACCO, Leopold VOGL,
Wilhelm HAHNEMANN, Anton SCHALL, Adolf VOGL. (Coach: Hans SKOLAUT).
SK Slavia Praha: Frantisek PLÁNICKA, Ladislav ZENÍSEK, Adolf FIALA, Antonín
VODICKA, Stefan CAMBAL, Frantisek CERNICKÝ, Franktisek JUNEK, Frantisek
SVOBODA, Jirí SOBOTKA, Vlastimil KOPECKÝ, Antonín PUC. (Coach: Josef "Staplík"
SLOUP).
Goal: WSC Admira Wien: 1-0 Leopold VOGL (64').
Referee: Rinaldo BARLASSINA (ITA)   Attendance: 30.000

28-06-1932   Stadión Sparta/Letná, Praha: AC Sparta Praha – Bologna Sportiva   3-0 (2-0)
AC Sparta Praha: Josef NEMEC, Jaroslav BURGR, Josef CTYROKÝ, Josef KOSTÁLEK,
Karel "Káda" PESEK, Erich SRBEK, Karel PODRAZIL, Frantisek PELCNER, Raymond
BRAINE (BEL), Oldrich NEJEDLÝ, Frantisek FÁBERA. (Coach: Antonín HOJER).
Bologna Sportiva: Mario GIANNI, Eraldo MONZEGLIO, Felice GASPERI, Aldo DONATI,
Mario MONTESANTO, Gastone MARTELLI, Bruno MAINI, Raffaele SANSONE (URU),
Geraldo OTTANI, Francisco FEDULLO (URU), Carlo REGUZZONI. (Coach: József NAGY
(HUN)).
Goals: AC Sparta Praha: 1-0 Oldrich NEJEDLÝ (33' penalty), 2-0 Aldo DONATI (34' *own
goal*), 3-0 Karel PODRAZIL (62').
Referee: Eugen BRAUN (AUT)   Attendance: 16.000

29-06-1932   Hungária körút, Budapest: Újpesti TE – First Vienne FC   1-1 (1-1)
Újpesti TE: Rezsö HUBA, Károly KÖVÁGÓ, Jenö LIGETI, Ferenc BORSÁNYI, Miklos
SÁROS, Antal SZALAY, Adalbert STRÖCK/Albert TÖRÖK, Stefan AUER/István AVAR,
Pál JÁVOR-JAKUBE, Illés VÖRÖS, Gábor P.SZABÓ. (Coach: Lajos BÁNYAI).
First Vienna FC: Karl HORESCHOVSKY, Karl RAINER, Josef BLUM, Leonhard MACHU,
Leopold HOFMANN, Willibald SCHMAUS, Anton BROSENBAUER, Josef ADELBRECHT,
Friedrich (Fritz) GSCHWEIDL, Gustav TÖGEL, Franz SCHÖNWETTER. (Coach: Ferdinand
FRITHUM).
Goals: Újpesti TE: 1-0 Stefan AUER/István AVAR (38').
First Vienna FC: 1-1 Anton BROSENBAUER (40').
Referee: Bohumil ZENÍSEK (TCH)   Attendance: 8.000

29-06-1932   Stadio Comunale "Benito Mussolini", Torino:
                  Juventus FC Torino – Ferencvárosi TC Budapest   4-0 (2-0)
Juventus FC Torino: Giampiero COMBI, Virginio ROSETTA, Umberto CALIGARIS, Mario
VARGLIEN (I), Luis Felipe MONTI (ARG), Luigi BERTOLINI, Pedro Sernagiotto
"MINISTRINHO" (BRA), Renato CESARINI (ARG), Giovanni VECCHINA, Giovanni
FERRARI, Raimundo Bibiani ORSI (ARG). (Coach: Carlo CARCANO).
Ferencvárosi TC Budapest: József HÁDA, Géza TAKÁCS (I), Lajos KORÁNYI, Antal
LYKA, Dr.György SÁROSI, Gyula LÁZÁR, Mihály TÁNCOS, József TAKÁCS (II), József
TURAY, Géza TOLDI, Vilmos KOHUT. (Coach: Zoltán BLUM).
Goals: Juventus FC Torino: 1-0 Raimundo Bibiani ORSI (14'), 2-0 Renato CESARINI (44'),
3-0 Renato CESARINI (56'), 4-0 Pedro Sernagiotto "MINISTRINHO" (59').
Referee: Frantisek CEJNAR (TCH)   Attendance: 12.000

03-07-1932   Üllöi ut, Budapest: Ferencvárosi TC Budapest – Juventus FC Torino 3-3 (2-2)
Ferencvárosi TC Budapest: József HÁDA, Géza TAKÁCS (I), Lajos KORÁNYI, Antal
LYKA, Dr.György SÁROSI, Gyula LÁZÁR, Mihály TÁNCOS, József TAKÁCS (II), József
TURAY, Géza TOLDI, Vilmos KOHUT. (Coach: Zoltán BLUM).
Juventus FC Torino: Giampiero COMBI, Virginio ROSETTA, Umberto CALIGARIS, Mario
VARGLIEN (I), Luis Felipe MONTI (ARG), Luigi BERTOLINI, Pedro Sernagiotto
"MINISTRINHO" (BRA), Renato CESARINI (ARG), Giovanni VECCHINA, Giovanni
FERRARI, Raimundo Bibiani ORSI (ARG). (Coach: Carlo CARCANO).
Goals: Ferencvárosi TC Budapest: 1-0 György SÁROSI (15' penalty), 2-0 György SÁROSI
(18' penalty), 3-3 György SÁROSI (80' penalty).
Juventus FC Torino: 2-1 Raimundo Bibiani ORSI (25'), 2-2 Renato CESARINI (30'), 2-3
Renato CESARINI (65').
Referee: Eugen BRAUN (AUT)   Attendance: 9.000

SEMI-FINALS

06-07-1932   Stadión Slavia/Letná, Praha: SK Slavia Praha – Juventus FC Torino 4-0 (3-0)
SK Slavia Praha: Frantisek PLÁNICKA, Ladislav ZENÍSEK, Adolf FIALA, Antonín
VODICKA, Stefan CAMBAL, Frantisek CERNICKÝ, Franktisek JUNEK, Jirí SOBOTKA,
Frantisek SVOBODA, Vlastimil KOPECKÝ, Antonín PUC. (Coach: Josef "Staplík" SLOUP).
Juventus FC Torino: Giampiero COMBI, Virginio ROSETTA, Umberto CALIGARIS, Mario
VARGLIEN (I), Luis Felipe MONTI (ARG), Luigi BERTOLINI, Pedro Sernagiotto
"MINISTRINHO" (BRA), Renato CESARINI (ARG) (expulsion 81'), Giovanni VECCHINA,
Giovanni FERRARI, Raimundo Bibiani ORSI (ARG). (Coach: Carlo CARCANO).
Goals: SK Slavia Praha: 1-0 Vlastimil KOPECKÝ (25'), 2-0 Frantisek SVOBODA (29'), 3-0
Vlastimil KOPECKÝ (37'), 4-0 Adolf FIALA (81' penalty).
Referee: Eugen BRAUN (AUT)   Attendance: 30.000

10-07-1932   Stadio Comunale "Benito Mussolini", Torino:
                    Juventus FC Torino – SK Slavia Praha 2-0 (2-0)
Juventus FC Torino: Giampiero COMBI, Virginio ROSETTA, Umberto CALIGARIS, Mario
VARGLIEN (I), Luis Felipe MONTI (ARG), Luigi BERTOLINI, Pedro Sernagiotto
"MINISTRINHO" (BRA), Renato CESARINI (ARG), Giovanni VECCHINA, Giovanni
FERRARI, Raimundo Bibiani ORSI (ARG). (Coach: Carlo CARCANO).
SK Slavia Praha: Frantisek PLÁNICKA, Ladislav ZENÍSEK, Adolf FIALA, Antonín
VODICKA, Stefan CAMBAL, Frantisek CERNICKÝ, Franktisek JUNEK, Frantisek
SVOBODA, Jirí SOBOTKA, Vlastimil KOPECKÝ, Antonín PUC. (Coach: Josef "Staplík"
SLOUP).
Goals: Juventus FC Torino: 1-0 Renato CESARINI (15'), 2-0 Raimundo Bibiani ORSI (41'
penalty).
Referee: Dr.Adolf MIESZ (AUT)   Attendance: 18.000

(The match was abandoned in the 46th minute).

10-07-1932   Stadio del Littoriale, Bologna: Bologna Sportiva – First Vienna FC   2-0 (0-0)
Bologna Sportiva: Mario GIANNI, Eraldo MONZEGLIO, Felice GASPERI, Mario
MONTESANTO, Gastone BALDI, Gastone MARTELLI, Bruno MAINI, Raffaele SANSONE
(URU), Angelo SCHIAVIO, Francisco FEDULLO (URU), Carlo REGUZZONI. (Coach:
József NAGY (HUN)).
First Vienna FC: Karl HORESCHOVSKY, Karl RAINER, Josef BLUM, Otto KALLER,
Leopold HOFMANN, Willibald SCHMAUS, Anton BROSENBAUER, Josef ADELBRECHT,
Friedrich (Fritz) GSCHWEIDL, Gustav TÖGEL, Franz SCHÖNWETTER. (Coach: Ferdinand
FRITHUM).
Goals: Bologna Sportiva: 1-0 Bruno MAINI (60'), 2-0 Raffaele SANSONE (89').
Referee: Frantisek CEJNAR (TCH)   Attendance: 18.000

17-07-1932   Hohe Warte, Wien: First Vienna FC – Bologna Sportiva   1-0 (1-0)
First Vienna FC: Karl HORESCHOVSKY, Karl RAINER, Josef BLUM, Otto KALLER,
Leopold HOFMANN, Leonhard MACHU, Anton BROSENBAUER, Josef ADELBRECHT,
Friedrich (Fritz) GSCHWEIDL, Gustav TÖGEL, Franz SCHÖNWETTER. (Coach: Ferdinand
FRITHUM).
Bologna Sportiva: Mario GIANNI, Eraldo MONZEGLIO, Felice GASPERI, Mario
MONTESANTO, Gastone BALDI, Gastone MARTELLI, Bruno MAINI, Raffaele SANSONE
(URU), Angelo SCHIAVIO, Francisco FEDULLO (URU), Carlo REGUZZONI. (Coach:
József NAGY (HUN)).
Goal: First Vienna FC: 1-0 Franz SCHÖNWETTER (13' penalty).
Referee: René MERCET (SUI)   Attendance: 15.000
(Josef BLUM missed a 7th minute penalty)

FINAL

*Due to problems in the abandoned match between Juventus FC Torino and SK Slavia Praha on
on 10th July 1932, both teams were ejected from the tournament.*

*Bologna Sportiva were therefore named winners of the trophy without playing any further
matches.*

*** **Bologna Sportiva won the Cup** ***

1933

QUARTER-FINALS

21-06-1933   Stadión Slavia/Letná, Praha: SK Slavia Praha – FK Austria Wien 3-1 (2-1)
SK Slavia Praha: Frantisek PLÁNICKA, Ladislav ZENÍSEK, Adolf FIALA, Antonín
VODICKA, Stefan CAMBAL, Adolf SIMPERSKÝ, Franktisek JUNEK, Frantisek
SVOBODA, Jirí SOBOTKA, Vlastimil KOPECKÝ, Bohumil JOSKA. (Coach: Josef "Staplík"
SLOUP).
FK Austria Wien: Johann BILLICH, Karl GRAF, Walter NAUSCH, Matthias NAJEMNIK,
Johann MOCK, Karl GALL, Josef MOLZER, Josef STROH, Matthias SINDELAR, Viktor
SPECHTL, Rudolf VIERTL. (Coach: Josef BLUM).
Goals: SK Slavia Praha: 1-1 Vlastimil KOPECKÝ (27'), 2-1 Frantisek SVOBODA (30'), 3-1
Vlastimil KOPECKÝ (49').
FK Austria Wien: 0-1 Ladislav ZENÍSEK (11' own goal).
Referee: Ferenc KLUG (HUN)   Attendance: 25.000

22-06-1933   Hungária körút, Budapest: Újpesti TE – Juventus FC Torino 2-4 (0-2)
Újpesti TE: György HÓRI, László STERNBERG-SÁTORI, Gyula FUTÓ, Antal SZALAY,
György SZÜCS, Miklos SÁROS, Ferenc PUSZTAI, Stefan AUER/István AVAR, Pál JÁVOR-
JAKUBE, Károly DËRI, Gábor P.SZABÓ. (Coach: Zoltán BLUM).
Juventus FC Torino: Giampiero COMBI, Virginio ROSETTA, Umberto CALIGARIS, Mario
VARGLIEN (I), Luis Felipe MONTI (ARG), Luigi BERTOLINI, Pedro Sernagiotto
"MINISTRINHO" (BRA), Giovanni VARGLIEN (II), Felice Placido BOREL (II), Giovanni
FERRARI, Raimundo Bibiani ORSI (ARG). (Coach: Carlo CARCANO).
Goals: Újpesti TE: 1-4 Ferenc PUSZTAI (78'), 2-4 Pál JÁVOR-JAKUBE (87').
Juventus FC Torino: 0-1 Giovanni VARGLIEN (II) (7'), 0-2 Felice Placido BOREL (II) (14'),
0-3 Pedro Sernagiotto "MINISTRINHO" (65'), 0-4 Raimundo Bibiani ORSI (77').
Referee: Alois BERANEK (AUT)   Attendance: 12.000

25-06-1933   Hungária körút, Budapest: Hungária FC Budapest – AC Sparta Praha 2-3 (1-2)
Hungária FC Budapest: Antal SZABÓ, Gyula MÁNDI-MANDL, Károly KIS, Gyula
BARÁTKY, Gusztáv SEBES, Imre EGRI, Ferenc SZEGÖ, László CSEH, Jenö KALMÁR,
János DUDÁS, Pál TITKOS. (Coach: Imre SENKEY).
AC Sparta Praha: Antonín LEDVINA, Jaroslav BURGR, Josef CTYROKÝ, Josef
KOSTÁLEK, Jaroslav BOUCEK, Jan "Madelon" KNOBLOCH, Josef SEDLÁCEK, Frantisek
KLOZ, Raymond BRAINE (BEL), Oldrich NEJEDLÝ, Josef SILNÝ. (Coach: Antonín
HOJER).
Goals: Hungária FC Budapest: 1-0 Jenö KALMÁR (29'), 2-3 János DUDÁS (82').
AC Sparta Praha: 1-1 Frantisek KLOZ (37'), 1-2 Jaroslav BOUCEK (45'), 1-3 Josef SILNÝ
(57').
Referee: Hans Walter FRANKENSTEIN (AUT)   Attendance: 8.000

25-06-1933   Hohe Warte, Wien: First Vienna FC – AS Ambrosiana-Inter Milano 1-0 (1-0)
First Vienna FC: Karl HORESCHOVSKY, Karl RAINER, Willibald SCHMAUS, Otto
KALLER, Leopold HOFMANN, Leonhard MACHU, Anton BROSENBAUER, Josef
ADELBRECHT, Siegfried WORTMANN, Gustav TÖGEL, Franz ERDL. (Coach: Ferdinand
FRITHUM).
AS Ambrosiana-Inter Milano: Carlo CERESOLI, Paolo AGOSTEO, Luigi ALLEMANDI,
Alfredo PITTO, Giuseppe VIANI, Armando CASTELLAZZI, Francisco FRIONE (II) (URU),
Pietro SERANTONI, Giuseppe MEAZZA, Attilio José DEMARÍA (I) (ARG), Virgilio Felice
LEVRATTO. (Coach: Árpád WEISZ (HUN)).
Goal: First Vienna FC: 1-0 Gustav TÖGEL (18').
Referee: Mihály Iványi IVÁNCSICS (HUN)   Attendance: 30.000

29-06-1933   Stadio Comunale "Benito Mussolini", Torino:
                    Juventus FC Torino – Újpesti TE 6-2 (3-1)
Juventus FC Torino: Giampiero COMBI, Virginio ROSETTA, Umberto CALIGARIS, Mario
VARGLIEN (I), Luis Felipe MONTI (ARG) (expulsion 55'), Luigi BERTOLINI, Pedro
Sernagiotto "MINISTRINHO" (BRA), Giovanni VARGLIEN (II), Felice Placido BOREL (II),
Giovanni FERRARI, Raimundo Bibiani ORSI (ARG). (Coach: Carlo CARCANO).
Újpesti TE: György HÓRI, László STERNBERG-SÁTORI, Antal SZALAY, Antal SZALAY,
György SZÜCS, Miklos SÁROS, Ferenc PUSZTAI, Stefan AUER/István AVAR, Pál JÁVOR-
JAKUBE, Károly DÉRI, Gábor P.SZABÓ. (Coach: Zoltán BLUM).
Goals: Juventus FC Torino: 1-1 Raimundo Bibiani ORSI (29'), 2-1 Giovanni VARGLIEN (II)
(36'), 3-1 Giovanni VARGLIEN (II) (40'), 4-2 Raimundo Bibiani ORSI (72'), 5-2 Raimundo
Bibiani ORSI (73' penalty), 6-2 Raimundo Bibiani ORSI (88').
Újpesti TE: 0-1 Pál JÁVOR-JAKUBE (17'), 3-2 Stefan AUER/István AVAR (69').
Referee: Bohumil ZENÍSEK (TCH)   Attendance: 22.000

29-06-1933   Stadión Sparta/Letná, Praha:
                    AC Sparta Praha – Hungária FC Budapest 2-1 (1-0)
AC Sparta Praha: Antonín LEDVINA, Jaroslav BURGR, Josef CTYROKÝ, Josef
KOSTÁLEK, Jaroslav BOUCEK, Jan "Madelon" KNOBLOCH, Josef SEDLÁCEK, Frantisek
KLOZ, Raymond BRAINE (BEL), Oldrich NEJEDLÝ, Josef SILNÝ. (Coach: Antonín
HOJER).
Hungária FC Budapest: Antal SZABÓ, József GERGELY, Károly KIS, Gyula BARÁTKY,
Gusztáv SEBES, Imre EGRI, Ferenc SZEGÖ, László CSEH, Jenö KALMÁR, János DUDÁS,
Pál TITKOS. (Coach: Imre SENKEY).
Goals: AC Sparta Praha: 1-0 Frantisek KLOZ (28' penalty), 2-1 Frantisek KLOZ (70').
Hungária FC Budapest: 1-1 László CSEH (70').
Referee: Francesco MATTEA (ITA)   Attendance: 15.000

02-07-1933   Praterstadion, Wien: FK Austria Wien – SK Slavia Prha 3-0 (1-0)
FK Austria Wien: Johann BILLICH, Karl GRAF, Walter NAUSCH, Matthias NAJEMNIK,
Johann MOCK, Karl GALL, Josef MOLZER, Josef STROH, Matthias SINDELAR, Viktor
SPECHTL, Rudolf VIERTL. (Coach: Josef BLUM).
SK Slavia Praha: Frantisek PLÁNICKA, Ladislav ZENÍSEK, Adolf FIALA, Antonín
VODICKA, Stefan CAMBAL, Adolf SIMPERSKÝ, Franktisek JUNEK, Frantisek
SVOBODA, Jirí SOBOTKA, Vlastimil KOPECKÝ, Bohumil JOSKA. (Coach: Josef "Staplík"
SLOUP).
Goals: FK Austria Wien: 1-0 Rudolf VIERTL (29'), 2-0 Rudolf VIERTL (55'), 3-0 Matthias
SINDELAR (77').
Referee: Rinaldo BARLASSINA (ITA)   Attendance: 30.000

02-07-1933   Arena Civica, Parco Sempione, Milano:
                    AS Ambrosiana-Inter Milano – First Vienna FC   4-0 (1-0)
AS Ambrosiana-Inter Milano: Carlo CERESOLI, Paolo AGOSTEO, Luigi ALLEMANDI,
Alfredo PITTO, Giuseppe VIANI, Armando CASTELLAZZI, Francisco FRIONE (II) (URU),
Pietro SERANTONI, Giuseppe MEAZZA, Attilio José DEMARÍA (I) (ARG), Virgilio Felice
LEVRATTO. (Coach: Árpád WEISZ (HUN)).
First Vienna FC: Karl HORESCHOVSKY, Karl RAINER, Willibald SCHMAUS, Otto
KALLER, Leopold HOFMANN, Leonhard MACHU, Anton BROSENBAUER, Josef
ADELBRECHT, Siegfried WORTMANN, Gustav TÖGEL, Franz ERDL. (Coach: Ferdinand
FRITHUM).
Goals: AS Ambrosiana-Inter Milano: 1-0 Giuseppe MEAZZA (38'), 2-0 Giuseppe MEAZZA
(51'), 3-0 Francisco FRIONE (II) (66'), 4-0 Giuseppe MEAZZA (86').
Referee: Frantisek CEJNAR (TCH)   Attendance: 30.000

SEMI-FINALS

09-07-1933   Praterstadion, Wien: FK Austria Wien – Juventus FC Torino   3-0 (1-0)
FK Austria Wien: Johann BILLICH, Karl GRAF, Walter NAUSCH, Matthias NAJEMNIK,
Johann MOCK, Karl GALL, Josef MOLZER, Josef STROH, Matthias SINDELAR, Viktor
SPECHTL, Rudolf VIERTL. (Coach: Josef BLUM).
Juventus FC Torino: Giampiero COMBI, Virginio ROSETTA, Umberto CALIGARIS, Mario
VARGLIEN (I), Luis Felipe MONTI (ARG) (expulsion 85'), Luigi BERTOLINI, Pedro
Sernagiotto "MINISTRINHO" (BRA), Giovanni VARGLIEN (II), Felice Placido BOREL (II),
Giovanni FERRARI, Raimundo Bibiani ORSI (ARG). (Coach: Carlo CARCANO).
Goals: FK Austria Wien: 1-0 Matthias SINDELAR (3'), 2-0 Rudolf VIERTL (52'), 3-0 Viktor
SPECHTL (88').
Referee: Abraham KLEIN (HUN)   Attendance: 50.000

09-07-1933   Arena Civica, Parco Sempione, Milano:
                    AS Ambrosiana-Inter Milano – AC Sparta Praha   4-1 (4-0)
AS Ambrosiana-Inter Milano: Carlo CERESOLI, Paolo AGOSTEO, Luigi ALLEMANDI,
Alfredo PITTO, Giuseppe VIANI, Armando CASTELLAZZI, Francisco FRIONE (II) (URU),
Pietro SERANTONI, Giuseppe MEAZZA, Attilio José DEMARÍA (I) (ARG), Virgilio Felice
LEVRATTO. (Coach: Árpád WEISZ (HUN)).
AC Sparta Praha: Antonín LEDVINA, Jaroslav BURGR, Josef CTYROKÝ, Josef
KOSTÁLEK, Jaroslav BOUCEK, Josef SEDLÁCEK, Frantisek PELCNER, Frantisek KLOZ,
Raymond BRAINE (BEL), Oldrich NEJEDLÝ, Ludvík KOUBEK. (Coach: Antonín HOJER).
Goals: AS Ambrosiana-Inter Milano: 1-0 Virgilio Felice LEVRATTO (8'), 2-0 Attilio José
DEMARÍA (35'), 3-0 Attilio José DEMARÍA (40'), 4-0 Attilio José DEMARÍA (44').
AC Sparta Praha: 4-1 Oldrich NEJEDLÝ (64').
Referee: Dr. Adolf MIESZ (AUT)   Attendance: 28.000

16-07-1933   Stadio Comunale "Benito Mussolini", Torino:
Juventus FC Torino – FK Austria Wien   1-1 (1-0)
Juventus FC Torino: Giampiero COMBI, Virginio ROSETTA, Umberto CALIGARIS, Mario VARGLIEN (I), Giovanni VARGLIEN (II), Luigi BERTOLINI, Pedro Sernagiotto "MINISTRINHO" (BRA), Renato CESARINI (ARG), Felice Placido BOREL (II), Giovanni FERRARI, Raimundo Bibiani ORSI (ARG). (Coach: Carlo CARCANO).
FK Austria Wien: Johann BILLICH, Karl GRAF, Walter NAUSCH, Matthias NAJEMNIK, Johann MOCK, Karl GALL, Josef MOLZER, Josef STROH, Matthias SINDELAR, Viktor SPECHTL, Rudolf VIERTL. (Coach: Josef BLUM).
Goals: Juventus FC Torino: 1-0 Giovanni FERRARI (21').
FK Austria Wien: 1-1 Josef MOLZER (85').
Referee: Frantisek CEJNAR (TCH)   Attendance: 15.000

16-07-1933   Stadión Sparta/Letná, Praha:
AC Sparta Praha – AS Ambrosiana-Inter Milano   2-2 (1-2)
AC Sparta Praha: Antonín LEDVINA, Jaroslav BURGR, Josef CTYROKÝ, Josef KOSTÁLEK, Jaroslav BOUCEK, Jan "Madelon" KNOBLOCH, Josef SEDLÁCEK, Frantisek KLOZ, Raymond BRAINE (BEL), Oldrich NEJEDLÝ, Ludvík KOUBEK. (Coach: Antonín HOJER).
AS Ambrosiana-Inter Milano: Carlo CERESOLI, Paolo AGOSTEO, Luigi ALLEMANDI, Alfredo PITTO, Giuseppe VIANI, Armando CASTELLAZZI, Francisco FRIONE (II) (URU), Pietro SERANTONI, Giuseppe MEAZZA, Attilio José DEMARÍA (I) (ARG), Renato DE MANZANO. (Coach: Árpád WEISZ (HUN)).
Goals: AC Sparta Praha: 1-0 Frantisek KLOZ (25'), 2-2 Frantisek KLOZ (60').
AS Ambrosiana-Inter Milano: 1-1 Pietro SERANTONI (30'), 1-2 Attilio José DEMARÍA (40').
Referee: Alois BERANEK (AUT)   Attendance: 35.000

FINAL

03-09-1933   Arena Civica, Parco Sempione, Milano:
AS Ambrosiana-Inter Milano – FK Austria Wien   2-1 (2-0)
AS Ambrosiana-Inter Milano: Carlo CERESOLI, Paolo AGOSTEO, Luigi ALLEMANDI, Alfredo PITTO, Ricardo Gregorio FACCIO Porta (URU), Armando CASTELLAZZI, Francisco FRIONE (II) (URU), Renato DE MANZANO, Giuseppe MEAZZA, Attilio José DEMARÍA (I) (ARG), Virgilio Felice LEVRATTO. (Coach: Árpád WEISZ (HUN)).
FK Austria Wien: Johann BILLICH, Karl GRAF, Walter NAUSCH, Matthias NAJEMNIK, Johann MOCK, Karl GALL, Josef MOLZER, Josef STROH, Matthias SINDELAR, Camillo JERUSALEM, Rudolf VIERTL. (Coach: Josef BLUM).
Goals: AS Ambrosiana-Inter Milano: 1-0 Giuseppe MEAZZA (40'), 2-0 Virgilio Felice LEVRATTO (41').
FK Austria Wien: 2-1 Rudolf VIERTL (77').
Referee: Ferenc KLUG (HUN)   Attendance: 35.000
(Carlo CERESOLI saved a 23rd minute a penalty taken by Josef STROH).

08-09-1933   Praterstadion, Wien.

FK Austria Wien – AS Ambrosiana-Inter Milano   3-1 (1 0)

FK Austria Wien: Johann BILLICH, Karl GRAF, Walter NAUSCH, Matthias NAJEMNIK, Johann MOCK, Karl ADAMEK, Josef MOLZER, Josef STROH, Matthias SINDELAR, Camillo JERUSALEM, Rudolf VIERTL. (Coach: Josef BLUM).

AS Ambrosiana-Inter Milano: Carlo CERESOLI, Paolo AGOSTEO, Luigi ALLEMANDI (expulsion 77'), Alfredo PITTO, Giuseppe VIANI, Ricardo Gregorio FACCIO Porta (URU), Francisco FRIONE (II) (URU), Pietro SERANTONI, Giuseppe MEAZZA, Attilio José DEMARÍA (I) (ARG) (expulsion 75'), Armando CASTELLAZZI. (Coach: Árpád WEISZ (HUN)).

Goals: FK Austria Wien: 1-0 Matthias SINDELAR (45' penalty), 2-0 Matthias SINDELAR (80'), 3-1 Matthias SINDELAR (88').

AS Ambrosiana-Inter Milano: 2-1 Giuseppe MEAZZA (85').

Referee: Frantisek CEJNAR (TCH)   Attendance: 58.000

*** FK Austria Wien won the Cup ***

1934

FIRST ROUND

12-06-1934   Stadión Sparta/Letná, Praha:
AC Sparta Praha – Hungária FC Budapest   1-2 (0-1)
AC Sparta Praha: Rudolf FRANC, Jaroslav BURGR, Josef CTYROKÝ, Josef KOSTÁLEK, Jaroslav BOUCEK, Erich SRBEK, Václav HRUSKA, Bohuslav KOMBEREC, Ferdinand FACSINEK, Oldrich NEJEDLÝ, Géza KALOCSAY. (Coach: Ferenc SZEDLACSEK (HUN)).
Hungária FC Budapest: Antal SZABÓ, Gyula MÁNDI-MANDL, Károly KIS, Imre EGRI, Gusztáv SEBES, János DUDÁS, László FENYVESI, István KARDOS, László CSEH, József TURAY, Pál TITKOS. (Coach: Imre SENKEY).
Goals: AC Sparta Praha: 1-1 Oldrich NEJEDLÝ (70').
Hungária FC Budapest: 0-1 János DUDÁS (39'), 1-2 László CSEH (88').
Referee: Camillo CAIRONI (ITA)   Attendance: 22.000

16-06-1934   Hungária körút, Budapest: Hungária FC Budapest – AC Sparta Praha   4-5 (3-4)
Hungária FC Budapest: Antal SZABÓ, Gyula MÁNDI-MANDL, Károly KIS, Imre EGRI, Gusztáv SEBES, János DUDÁS, László FENYVESI, István KARDOS, László CSEH, József TURAY, Pál TITKOS. (Coach: Imre SENKEY).
AC Sparta Praha: Rudolf FRANC, Jaroslav BURGR, Josef CTYROKÝ, Josef KOSTÁLEK, Jaroslav BOUCEK, Erich SRBEK, Václav HRUSKA, Ferdinand FACSINEK, Raymond BRAINE (BEL), Oldrich NEJEDLÝ, Géza KALOCSAY. (Coach: Ferenc SZEDLACSEK (HUN)).
Goals: Hungária FC Budapest: 1-1 Pál TITKOS (10'), 2-2 József TURAY (22'), 3-2 Pál TITKOS (24'), 4-5 János DUDÁS (73').
AC Sparta Praha: 0-1 Raymond BRAINE (1'), 1-2 Ferdinand FACSINEK (13'), 3-3 Ferdinand FACSINEK (29'), 3-4 Oldrich NEJEDLÝ (34'), 3-5 Václav HRUSKA (49').
Referee: Hans Walter FRANKENSTEIN (AUT)   Attendance: 6.000

16-06-1934   Praterstadion, Wien: FK Austria Wien – Újpesti TE   1-2 (1-2)
FK Austria Wien: Willibald MÜLLNER, Karl GRAF, Ernst KAIT, Matthias NAJEMNIK, Johann MOCK, Karl GALL, Josef MOLZER, Josef STROH, Matthias SINDELAR, Viktor SPECHTL, Rudolf VIERTL. (Coach: Josef BLUM).
Újpesti TE: György HÓRI, Gyula FUTÓ, László STERNBERG-SÁTORI, Gyula SERES, György SZÜCS, Antal SZALAY, István TAMÁSSY, Ferenc PUSZTAI, Pál JÁVOR-JAKUBE, Géza KOCSIS, Gábor P.SZABÓ. (Coach: István TÓTH-POTYA).
Goals: FK Austria Wien: 1-1 Matthias SINDELAR (16' penalty).
Újpesti TE: 0-1 Géza KOCSIS (3'), 1-2 Gábor P.SZABÓ (31' penalty).
Referee: Raffaele SCORZONI (ITA)   Attendance: 12.000

17-06-1934   Üllüi ut, Budapest:
Ferencvárosi TC Budapest – Floridsdorfer AC Wien   8-0 (5-0)
Ferencvárosi TC Budapest: József HÁDA, Nándor BÁN, Lajos KORÁNYI, Antal LYKA,
János MÓRÉ, Gyula LÁZÁR, Károly RÁTKAI, Gyula POLGÁR, Dr.György SÁROSI, Géza
TOLDI, Tibor KEMÉNY. (Coach: Zoltán BLUM).
Floridsdorfer AC Wien: Karl SCHARL, Josef BERNARD, Rudolf SCHLAUF, Johann
MÜLLER, Johann HOFMANN, Franz RADAKOVICH, Johann WEISS, Josef CHLOUPEK,
Johann DOSTAL, Karl GRABER, Karl LANGER. (Coach: Karl JISZDA).
Goals: Ferencvárosi TC Budapest: 1-0 Tibor KEMÉNY (4'), 2-0 Károly RÁTKAI (15'), 3-0
Géza TOLDI (23'), 4-0 Gyula POLGÁR (27'), 5-0 Gyula POLGÁR (35'), 6-0 Dr.György
SÁROSI (59'), 7-0 Dr.György SÁROSI (62'), 8-0 Josef BERNARD (76' *own goal*).
Referee: Ján BIZÍK (TCH)   Attendance: 10.000

17-06-1934   Stadión SK Kladno, Kladno:
SK Kladno – AS Ambrosiana-Inter Milano   1-1 (0-1)
SK Kladno: Karel TICHÝ, Frantisek NEJEDLÝ, Emil HABR, Václav BOUSKA, Karel
KRAUS, Antonín CERNÝ, Václav VRAGA, Frantisek KLOZ, Miroslav PROCHÁZKA,
Frantisek BUBENÍCEK, Josef JUNEK. (Coach: Josef PLETICHA).
AS Ambrosiana-Inter Milano: Carlo CERESOLI, Paolo AGOSTEO, Luigi ALLEMANDI,
Alfredo PITTO, Giovanni BATTISTONI, Armando CASTELLAZZI, Francisco FRIONE (II)
(URU), Attilio José DEMARÍA (I) (ARG), Giuseppe MEAZZA, Alfredo MAZZONI, Eligio
VECCHI. (Coach: Gyula FELDMANN (HUN)).
Goals: SK Kladno: 1-1 Frantisek BUBENÍCEK (88' penalty).
AS Ambrosiana-Inter Milano: 0-1 Giuseppe MEAZZA (25').
Referee: Alois BERANEK (AUT)   Attendance: 15.000

17-06-1934   Stadio Comunale "Benito Mussolini", Torino:
Juventus FC Torino – Teplitzer FK   4-2 (3-1)
Juventus FC Torino: Giampiero COMBI, Virginio ROSETTA, Umberto CALIGARIS,
Giovanni VARGLIEN (II), Mario VARGLIEN (I), Luigi BERTOLINI, Pedro Sernagiotto
"MINISTRINHO" (BRA), Renato CESARINI (ARG), Felice Placido BOREL (II), Giovanni
FERRARI, Raimundo Bibiani ORSI (ARG). (Coach: Carlo CARCANO).
Teplitzer FK: Ehrenfried PATZELT (GER), Géza CSAPO (HUN), Heinrich SCHÖBKE
(GER), Franz KOWANZ (GER), Martin WATZATA (GER), Willy MIZERA (GER), Karl
HABERSTROH (GER), Jenö ROTH (HUN), Tomás PORUBSKÝ, Josef MILLNER (GER),
Rudolf ZOSEL (GER).
Goals: Juventus FC Torino: 1-1 Felice Placido BOREL (20'), 2-1 Renato CESARINI (25'), 3-1
Renato CESARINI (43'), 4-2 Giovanni FERRARI (58').
Teplitzer FK: 0-1 Karl HABERSTROH (6'), 3-2 Rudolf ZOSEL (52').
Referee: Mihály Iványi IVÁNCSICS (HUN)   Attendance: 11.000

17-06-1934   Stadio del Littoriale, Bologna:
Bologna Sportiva – Debreceni Bocskai FC   2-0 (2-0)
Bologna Sportiva: Mario GIANNI, Eraldo MONZEGLIO, Felice GASPERI, Aldo DONATI,
Francesco OCHIUZZI, Gastone MARTELLI, Bruno MAINI, Giordano CORSI, Angelo
SCHIAVIO, Francisco FEDULLO (URU), Carlo REGUZZONI. (Coach: Lajos Nemes
KOVÁCS (HUN)).
Debreceni Bocskai FC: József ALBERTI, József VÁGÓ, József JANZSÓ, István PALOTÁS,
Lajos ÓDRY, Zoltán SZANISZLÓ, Imre MARKOS, Jenö VINCZE, Pál TELEKI, István
DÓCZÉ, Sándor HEVESI. (Coach: Edwin HERZOG).
Goals: Bologna Sportiva: 1-0 Carlo REGUZZONI (3'), 2-0 Angelo SCHIAVIO (31').
Referee: Gustav KRIST (TCH)   Attendance: 12.000

17-06-1934   Praterstadion, Wien: WSC Admira Wien – AC Napoli   0-0
WSC Admira Wien: Peter PLATZER, Robert PAVLICEK, Anton JANDA, Johann
URBANEK, Karl HUMMENBERGER, Josef MIRSCHITZKA, Ignaz SIGL, Wilhelm
HAHNEMANN, Karl STOIBER, Karl DURSPEKT, Adolf VOGL. (Coach: Hans
SKOLAUT).
AC Napoli: Giuseppe CAVANNA, Giovanni VINCENZI, Luigi CASTELLO, Maggiorino
MONGERO, Enrico COLOMBARI, Alberto RIVOLTA, Umberto VISENTIN (III), Antonio
VOJAK (I), Attila SALLUSTRO (I) (PAR), Gino ROSETTI, Pietro FERRARIS (II). (Coach:
William GARBUTT (ENG)).
Referee: Bohumil ZENÍSEK (TCH)   Attendance: 10.000

19-06-1934   Stadión Slavia/Letná, Praha: SK Slavia Praha – SK Rapid Wien   1-3 (0-1)
SK Slavia Praha: Frantisek PLÁNICKA, Ladislav ZENÍSEK, Adolf FIALA, Antonín
VODICKA, Adolf SIMPERSKÝ, Jaromír SKÁLA (AUT), Franktisek JUNEK, Frantisek
SVOBODA, Jirí SOBOTKA, Vlastimil KOPECKÝ, Antonín PUC. (Coach: Kálmán
KONRÁD (HUN)).
SK Rapid Wien: Rudolf RAFTL, Karl JESTRAB, Leopold CZEJKA, Franz WAGNER, Josef
SMISTIK (I), Johann PESSER, Johann OSTERMANN, Karl HOCHREITER, Josef BICAN,
Franz BINDER, Alois OHRENBERGER. (Coach: Eduard BAUER).
Goals: SK Slavia Praha: 1-3 Frantisek SVOBODA (76').
SK Rapid Wien: 0-1 Karl HOCHREITER (40'), 0-2 Karl HOCHREITER (48'), 0-3 Josef
BICAN (75').
Referee: Rinaldo BARLASSINA (ITA)   Attendance: 30.000

23-06-1934   Hohe Warte, Wien:
              Floridsdorfer AC Wien – Ferencvárosi TC Budapest   1-2 (0-0)
Floridsdorfer AC Wien: Karl SCHARL, Josef BERNARD, Rudolf SCHLAUF, Johann
MÜLLER, Johann HOFMANN, Franz RADAKOVICH, Johann WEISS, Josef CHLOUPEK,
Josef HANKE (GER), Johann DOSTAL, Karl LANGER. (Coach: Karl JISZDA).
Ferencvárosi TC Budapest: József HÁDA, Nándor BÁN, Lajos KORÁNYI, Antal LYKA,
János MÓRÉ, Gyula LÁZÁR, Károly RÁTKAI, Gyula POLGÁR, Dr.György SÁROSI, Géza
TOLDI, Tibor KEMÉNY. (Coach: Zoltán BLUM).
Goals: Floridsdorfer AC Wien: 1-0 Josef HANKE (50').
Ferencvárosi TC Budapest: 1-1 Gyula LÁZÁR (70'), 1-2 Dr.György SÁROSI (85').
Referee: Albert MULTER (GER)   Attendance: 800

24-06-1934   Megyeri ut, Budapest: Újpesti TE – FK Austria Wien   2-1 (1-1)
Újpesti TE: György HÓRI, Gyula FUTÓ, László STERNBERG-SÁTORI, Ferenc
BORSÁNYI, György SZÜCS, Antal SZALAY, István TAMÁSSY, Ferenc PUSZTAI, Pál
JÁVOR-JAKUBE, Géza KOCSIS, Gábor P.SZABÓ. (Coach: István TÓTH-POTYA).
FK Austria Wien: Willibald MÜLLNER, Wilhelm LUDWIG, Ernst KAIT, Matthias
NAJEMNIK, Johann MOCK, Walter NAUSCH, Viktor SPECHTL, Josef STROH, Matthias
SINDELAR, Camillo JERUSALEM, Karl GALL. (Coach: Josef BLUM).
Goals: Újpesti TE: 1-0 Gábor P.SZABÓ (17' penalty), 2-1 Ferenc PUSZTAI (85').
FK Austria Wien: 1-1 Viktor SPECHTL (43').
Referee: Gustav KRIST (TCH)   Attendance: 15.000

40

24-06-1934   Stadión Teplitzer FK, Teplice: Teplitzer FK – Juventus FC Torino   0-1 (0-1)
Teplitzer FK: Ehrenfried PATZELT (GER), Heinrich SCHÖBKE (GER), Wilhelm
NÁHLOVSKÝ, Erwin KOVACS (HUN), Martin WATZATA (GER), Willy MIZERA (GER),
Karl HABERSTROH (GER), Jenö ROTH (HUN), Tomás PORUBSKÝ, Josef MILLNER
(GER), Rudolf ZOSEL (GER).
Juventus FC Torino: Giampiero COMBI, Virginio ROSETTA, Umberto CALIGARIS, Mario
VARGLIEN (I), Luis Felipe MONTI (ARG), Luigi BERTOLINI, Giovanni VARGLIEN (II),
Renato CESARINI (ARG), Felice Placido BOREL (II), Giovanni FERRARI, Raimundo
Bibiani ORSI (ARG). (Coach: Carlo CARCANO).
Goal: Juventus FC Torino: 0-1 Giovanni VARGLIEN (18').
Referee: Alois BERANEK (AUT)   Attendance: 12.000

24-06-1934   Arena Civica, Parco Sempione, Milano:
             AS Ambrosiana-Inter Milano – SK Kladno   2-3 (1-1)
AS Ambrosiana-Inter Milano: Carlo CERESOLI, Paolo AGOSTEO, Luigi ALLEMANDI,
Alfredo PITTO, Giovanni BATTISTONI, Felíx DEMARÍA (II) (ARG), Francisco FRIONE
(II) (URU), Attilio José DEMARÍA (I) (ARG), Giuseppe MEAZZA, Alfredo MAZZONI,
Eligio VECCHI. (Coach: Gyula FELDMANN (HUN)).
SK Kladno: Jirí TICHÝ, Frantisek NEJEDLÝ, Emil HABR, Václav BOUSKA, Karel KRAUS,
Antonín CERNÝ, Miroslav PROCHÁZKA, Frantisek KLOZ, Frantisek BUBENÍCEK, Josef
JUNEK, Karel HROMÁDKA. (Coach: Josef PLETICHA).
Goals: AS Ambrosiana-Inter Milano: 1-0 Giuseppe MEAZZA (4'), 2-1 G. MEAZZA (47').
SK Kladno: 1-1 Frantisek BUBENÍCEK (42' penalty), 2-2 Frantisek KLOZ (54'), 2-3
Frantisek KLOZ (80').
Referee: Dr.Adolf MIESZ (AUT)   Attendance: 20.000

24-06-1934   Diószegi úti, Debrecen: Debreceni Bocskai FC – Bologna Sportiva   2-1 (1-0)
Debreceni Bocskai FC: József ALBERTI, József VÁGÓ, József JANZSÓ, István PALOTÁS,
Lajos ÓDRY, Zoltán SZANISZLÓ, Imre MARKOS, Jenö VINCZE, Pál TELEKI, István
DÓCZÉ, Sándor HEVESI. (Coach: Edwin HERZOG).
Bologna Sportiva: Mario GIANNI, Eraldo MONZEGLIO, Felice GASPERI, Mario
MONTESANTO, Francesco OCHIUZZI, Gastone MARTELLI, Bruno MAINI, Giordano
CORSI, Angelo SCHIAVIO, Francisco FEDULLO (URU), Carlo REGUZZONI. (Coach:
Lajos Nemes KOVÁCS (HUN)).
Goals: Debreceni Bocskai FC: 1-0 Sándor HEVESI (20'), 2-1 Jenö VINCZE (67').
Bologna Sportiva: 1-1 Carlo REGUZZONI (49').
Referee: Eugen BRAUN (AUT)   Attendance: 12.000

24-06-1934   Stadio "Ascarelli", Napoli: AC Napoli – WSC Admira Wien   2-2 (1-0)
AC Napoli: Giuseppe CAVANNA, Giovanni VINCENZI, Luigi CASTELLO, Maggiorino
MONGERO, Enrico COLOMBARI, Alberto RIVOLTA, Umberto VISENTIN (III), Antonio
VOJAK (I), Attila SALLUSTRO (I) (PAR), Gino ROSETTI, Pietro FERRARIS (II). (Coach:
William GARBUTT (ENG)).
WSC Admira Wien: Peter PLATZER, Robert PAVLICEK, Anton JANDA, Johann
URBANEK, Karl HUMMENBERGER, Josef MIRSCHITZKA, Ignaz SIGL, Karl
DURSPEKT, Karl STOIBER, Wilhelm HAHNEMANN, Adolf VOGL. (Coach: Hans
SKOLAUT).
Goals: AC Napoli: 1-0 Attila SALLUSTRO (17'), 2-0 Antonio VOJAK (56' penalty).
WSC Admira Wien: 2-1 Wilhelm HAHNEMANN (69'), 2-2 Adolf VOGL (75').
Referee: Ferenc KLUG (HUN)   Attendance: 12.000

41

24-06-1934   Rapid-Platz, Wien: SK Rapid Wien – SK Slavia Praha 1-1 (1-0)
SK Rapid Wien: Rudolf RAFTL, Karl JESTRAB, Leopold CZEJKA, Franz WAGNER, Josef
SMISTIK (I), Johann PESSER, Johann OSTERMANN, Karl HOCHREITER, Josef BICAN,
Franz BINDER, Alois OHRENBERGER. (Coach: Eduard BAUER).
SK Slavia Praha: Frantisek PLÁNICKA, Antonín PECH, Adolf FIALA, Jaromír SKÁLA
(AUT), Adolf SIMPERSKÝ, Rudolf KRCIL, Franktisek JUNEK, Vojtech BRADÁC, Jirí
SOBOTKA, Frantisek SVOBODA, Antonín PUC. (Coach: Kálmán KONRÁD (HUN)).
Goals: SK Rapid Wien: 1-0 Franz BINDER (10').
SK Slavia Praha: 1-1 Vojtech BRADÁC (67').
Referee: Ferenc MAJORSZKY (HUN)   Attendance: 16.000

26-06-1934   Stadión Sparta/Letná, Praha:
                      AC Sparta Praha- Hungária FC Budapest 5-2 (3-2)
AC Sparta Praha: Bohumil KLENOVEC, Jaroslav BURGR, Josef CTYROKÝ, Josef
KOSTÁLEK, Jaroslav BOUCEK, Erich SRBEK, Václav HRUSKA, Ferdinand FACSINEK,
Raymond BRAINE (BEL), Oldrich NEJEDLÝ, Géza KALOCSAY. (Coach: Ferenc
SZEDLACSEK (HUN)).
Hungária FC Budapest: Antal SZABÓ, Gyula MÁNDI-MANDL, Sándor BÍRÓ, János SZABÓ
(IV), Gusztáv SEBES, Károly KIS, László FENYVESI, László CSEH, József TURAY, János
DUDÁS, Pál TITKOS. (Coach: Imre SENKEY).
Goals: AC Sparta Praha: 1-1 Václav HRUSKA (8'), 2-2 Ferdinand FACSINEK (22'), 3-2
Raymond BRAINE (33' penalty), 4-2 Raymond BRAINE (75'), 5-2 Ferdinand FACSINEK
(86').
Hungária FC Budapest: 0-1 János DUDÁS (2'), 1-2 László FENYVESI (15').
Referee: Hans Walter FRANKENSTEIN (AUT)   Attendance: 13.000

(Play-off game)

*The results of all three matches played between AC Sparta Praha and Hungária FC Budapest
(on 12th June 1934, 16th June 1934 and 26th June 1934) were annulled after it was found that
Ferdinand FACSINEK was not eligible to play for AC Sparta Praha at that point as his full
transfer fee had not been paid. Both teams were ordered to play each other once again.*

01-07-1934   Stadion Letzigrund, Zürich: WSC Admira Wien – AC Napoli 5-0 (1-0)
WSC Admira Wien: Peter PLATZER, Robert PAVLICEK, Anton JANDA, Johann
URBANEK, Karl HUMMENBERGER, Josef MIRSCHITZKA, Ignaz SIGL, Karl
DURSPEKT, Karl STOIBER, Wilhelm HAHNEMANN, Adolf VOGL. (Coach: Hans
SKOLAUT).
AC Napoli: Giuseppe CAVANNA, Giovanni VINCENZI, Luigi CASTELLO, Maggiorino
MONGERO, Enrico COLOMBARI, Alberto RIVOLTA, Umberto VISENTIN (III), Antonio
VOJAK (I), Attila SALLUSTRO (I) (PAR), Gino ROSETTI, Pietro FERRARIS (II). (Coach:
William GARBUTT (ENG)).
Goals: WSC Admira Wien: 1-0 Adolf VOGL (2'), 2-0 Wilhelm HAHNEMANN (48'), 3-0
Robert PAVLICEK (53' penalty), 4-0 Karl DURSPEKT (62'), 5-0 Karl HUMMENBERGER
(78').
Referee: Hans WÜTHRICH (SUI)   Attendance: 9.000

(Play-off game).

08-07-1934   Hungária körút, Budapest: Hungária FC Budapest – AC Sparta Praha   2-1 (1-0)
Hungária FC Budapest: Antal SZABÓ, Gyula MÁNDI-MANDL, Sándor BÍRÓ, János SZABÓ
(IV), Gusztáv SEBES, Károly KIS, László FENYVESI, László CSEH, József TURAY, János
DUDÁS, Pál TITKOS. (Coach: Imre SENKEY).
AC Sparta Praha: Bohumil KLENOVEC, Jaroslav BURGR, Josef CTYROKÝ, Josef
KOSTÁLEK, Jaroslav BOUCEK, Erich SRBEK, Václav HRUSKA, Ferdinand FACSINEK,
Raymond BRAINE (BEL), Oldrich NEJEDLÝ, Géza KALOCSAY. (Coach: Ferenc
SZEDLACSEK (HUN)).
Goals: Hungária FC Budapest: 1-0 József TURAY (16'), 2-1 László CSEH (56').
AC Sparta Praha: 1-1 Ferdinand FACSINEK (49').
Referee: Hans Walter FRANKENSTEIN (AUT)   Attendance: 10.000

11-07-1934   Stadión Sparta/Letná, Praha:
             AC Sparta Praha – Hungária FC Budapest   2-1 (0-0)
AC Sparta Praha: Bohumil KLENOVEC, Josef KOSTÁLEK, Jaroslav BURGR, Josef
SEDLÁCEK, Jaroslav BOUCEK, Erich SRBEK, Václav HRUSKA, Ferdinand FACSINEK,
Raymond BRAINE (BEL), Oldrich NEJEDLÝ, Géza KALOCSAY. (Coach: Ferenc
SZEDLACSEK (HUN)).
Hungária FC Budapest: Antal SZABÓ, Gyula MÁNDI-MANDL, Sándor BÍRÓ, János SZABÓ
(IV), Gusztáv SEBES, Károly KIS, László FENYVESI, László CSEH, József TURAY, János
DUDÁS, Pál TITKOS. (Coach: Imre SENKEY).
Goals: AC Sparta Praha: 1-0 Géza KALOCSAY (68'), 2-1 Erich SRBEK (85').
Hungária FC Budapest: 1-1 János DUDÁS (80').
Referee: Alois BERANEK (AUT)   Attendance: 15.000

15-07-1934   Praterstadion, Wien: AC Sparta Praha – Hungária FC Budapest   1-1 (1-1)
AC Sparta Praha: Bohumil KLENOVEC, Jaroslav BURGR, Josef CTYROKÝ, Josef
SEDLÁCEK, Jaroslav BOUCEK, Erich SRBEK, Václav HRUSKA, Josef KOSTÁLEK,
Raymond BRAINE (BEL), Ferdinand FACSINEK, Géza KALOCSAY. (Coach: Ferenc
SZEDLACSEK (HUN)).
Hungária FC Budapest: Antal SZABÓ, Károly KIS, Sándor BÍRÓ, János SZABÓ (IV),
Gusztáv SEBES, János DUDÁS, László FENYVESI, István KARDOS, László CSEH, József
TURAY, Pál TITKOS. (Coach: Imre SENKEY).
Goals: AC Sparta Praha: 1-0 Josef KOSTÁLEK (27').
Hungária FC Budapest: 1-1 László CSEH (52').
Referee: Hans Walter FRANKENSTEIN (AUT)   Attendance: 12.000
(Play-off game. AC Sparta Praha won by the drawing of lots after extra time had been played).

QUARTER-FINALS

30-06-1934   Üllöi út, Budapest: Ferencvárosi TC Budapest – SK Kladno   6-0 (3-0)
Ferencvárosi TC Budapest: József HÁDA, Nándor BÁN, Lajos KORÁNYI, Antal LYKA,
János MÓRÉ, Gyula LÁZÁR, Károly RÁTKAI, Gyula POLGÁR, Dr.György SÁROSI, Géza
TOLDI, Tibor KEMÉNY. (Coach: Zoltán BLUM).
SK Kladno: Karel TICHÝ, Frantisek NEJEDLÝ, Emil HABR, Václav BOUSKA, Karel
KRAUS, Antonín CERNÝ, Frantisek KLOZ, Frantisek BUBENÍCEK, Miroslav
PROCHÁZKA, Josef JUNEK, Karel HROMÁDKA. (Coach: Josef PLETICHA).
Goals: Ferencvárosi TC Budapest: 1-0 Dr.György SÁROSI (5'), 2-0 Géza TOLDI (9'), 3-0
Dr.György SÁROSI (29' penalty), 4-0 Dr.György SÁROSI (58' penalty), 5-0 Gyula POLGÁR
(71'), 6-0 Tibor KEMÉNY (81').
Referee: Camillo CAIRONI (ITA)   Attendance: 15.000

43

01-07-1934   Megyeri út, Budapest: Újpesti TE – Juventus FC Torino 1-3 (1-1)
Újpesti TE: György HÓRI, Gyula FUTÓ, László STERNBERG-SÁTORI, Gyula SERES,
György SZÜCS, Antal SZALAY, István TAMÁSSY, Ferenc PUSZTAI, Gábor KISS, Géza
KOCSIS, Gábor P.SZABÓ. (Coach: István TÓTH-POTYA).
Juventus FC Torino: Giampiero COMBI, Virginio ROSETTA, Umberto CALIGARIS, Mario
VARGLIEN (I), Luis Felipe MONTI (ARG), Renato CESARINI (ARG), Giovanni
VARGLIEN (II), Pietro SERANTONI, Felice Placido BOREL (II), Giovanni FERRARI,
Raimundo Bibiani ORSI (ARG). (Coach: Carlo CARCANO).
Goals: Újpesti TE: 1-1 Gábor P.SZABÓ (43').
Juventus FC Torino: 0-1 Giovanni FERRARI (15'), 1-2 Felice Placido BOREL (74'), 1-3
Felice Placido BOREL (78').
Referee: Bohumil ZENÍSEK (TCH)   Attendance: 18.000

01-07-1934   Stadio del Littoriale, Bologna: Bologna Sportiva – SK Rapid Wien 6-1 (2-1)
Bologna Sportiva: Mario GIANNI, Dino FIORINI, Felice GASPERI, Mario MONTESANTO,
Aldo DONATI, Giordano CORSI, Bruno MAINI, Mario PERAZZOLO, Angelo SCHIAVIO,
Francisco FEDULLO (URU), Carlo REGUZZONI. (Coach: Lajos Nemes KOVÁCS (HUN)).
SK Rapid Wien: Rudolf RAFTL, Karl JESTRAB, Leopold CZEJKA, Franz WAGNER, Josef
SMISTIK (I), Johann PESSER, Johann OSTERMANN, Karl HOCHREITER, Josef BICAN,
Franz BINDER, Alois OHRENBERGER. (Coach: Eduard BAUER).
Goals: Bologna Sportiva: 1-0 Mario PERAZZOLO (20'), 2-0 Angelo SCHIAVIO (39'), 3-1
Angelo SCHIAVIO (49'), 4-1 Carlo REGUZZONI (53'), 5-1 Dino FIORINI (59'), 6-1 Carlo
REGUZZONI (87').
SK Rapid Wien: 2-1 Franz BINDER (40' penalty).
Referee: Ferenc KLUG (HUN)   Attendance: 18.000

08-07-1934   Stadión SK Kladno, Kladno:
               SK Kladno – Ferencvárosi TC Budapest 4-1 (0-0)
SK Kladno: Karel TICHÝ, Frantisek NEJEDLÝ, Emil HABR, Alois SVEC, Karel KRAUS,
Václav BOUSKA, Karel HROMÁDKA, Frantisek KLOZ, Miroslav PROCHÁZKA, Frantisek
BUBENÍCEK, Josef JUNEK. (Coach: Josef PLETICHA).
Ferencvárosi TC Budapest: József HÁDA, Nándor BÁN, Lajos KORÁNYI, Antal LYKA,
János MÓRÉ, Gyula LÁZÁR, Károly RÁTKAI, Gyula POLGÁR, Béla SZÉKELY, Géza
TOLDI, Tibor KEMÉNY. (Coach: Zoltán BLUM).
Goals: SK Kladno: 1-0 Miroslav PROCHÁZKA (46'), 2-0 Frantisek BUBENÍCEK (53'), 3-0
Karel HROMÁDKA (62'), 4-1 Miroslav PROCHÁZKA (88').
Ferencvárosi TC Budapest: 3-1 Géza TOLDI (82').
Referee: Raffaele SCORZONI (ITA)   Attendance: 4.000

08-07-1934   Stadio Comunale "Benito Mussolini", Torino:
               Juventus FC Torino – Újpesti TE 1-1 (0-1)
Juventus FC Torino: Giampiero COMBI, Virginio ROSETTA, Umberto CALIGARIS, Mario
VARGLIEN (I), Luis Felipe MONTI (ARG), Luigi BERTOLINI, Pedro Sernagiotto
"MINISTRINHO" (BRA), Pietro SERANTONI, Felice Placido BOREL (II), Giovanni
FERRARI, Raimundo Bibiani ORSI (ARG). (Coach: Carlo CARCANO).
Újpesti TE: György HÓRI, Gyula FUTÓ, László STERNBERG-SÁTORI, Gyula SERES,
György SZÜCS, Antal SZALAY, István TAMÁSSY, Ferenc PUSZTAI, Gábor KISS, Géza
KOCSIS, Gábor P.SZABÓ. (Coach: István TÓTH-POTYA).
Goals: Juventus FC Torino: 1-1 Felice Placido BOREL (52').
Újpesti TE: 0-1 Géza KOCSIS (3').
Referee: Dr.Adolf MIESZ (AUT)   Attendance: 12.000

44

08-07-1934   Praterstadion, Wien: SK Rapid Wien – Bologna Sportiva 4-1 (1-1)
SK Rapid Wien: Rudolf RAFTL, Karl JESTRAB, Leopold CZEJKA, Franz WAGNER, Josef
SMISTIK (I), Johann PESSER, Johann OSTERMANN, Matthias KABUREK, Josef BICAN,
Franz BINDER, Alois OHRENBERGER. (Coach: Eduard BAUER).
Bologna Sportiva: Mario GIANNI, Eraldo MONZEGLIO (expulsion 65'), Felice GASPERI,
Mario MONTESANTO, Aldo DONATI, Giordano CORSI, Dino FIORINI, Mario
PERAZZOLO, Bruno MAINI, Francisco FEDULLO (URU), Carlo REGUZZONI. (Coach:
Lajos Nemes KOVÁCS (HUN)).
Goals: SK Rapid Wien: 1-0 Franz BINDER (2'), 2-1 Franz BINDER (70' penalty), 3-1 Franz
BINDER (79' penalty), 4-1 Franz BINDER (85').
Bologna Sportiva: 1-1 Carlo REGUZZONI (41').
Referee: Bohumil ZENÍSEK (TCH)   Attendance: 20.000
(Mario GIANNI saved a penalty taken by Franz BINDER).

18-07-1934   Praterstadio, Wien: WSC Admira Wien – AC Sparta Praha 4-0 (3-0)
WSC Admira Wien: Peter PLATZER, Robert PAVLICEK, Anton JANDA, Johann
URBANEK, Karl HUMMENBERGER, Josef MIRSCHITZKA, Ignaz SIGL, Karl
DURSPEKT, Karl STOIBER, Wilhelm HAHNEMANN, Adolf VOGL. (Coach: Hans
SKOLAUT).
AC Sparta Praha: Bohumil KLENOVEC, Jaroslav BURGR, Josef CTYROKÝ, Josef
KOSTÁLEK, Jaroslav BOUCEK, Erich SRBEK, Frantisek PELCNER, Václav HRUSKA,
Oldrich NEJEDLÝ, Oldrich ZAJÍCEK, Géza KALOCSAY. (Coach: Ferenc SZEDLACSEK
(HUN)).
Goals: WSC Admira Wien: 1-0 Karl STOIBER (33'), 2-0 Wilhelm HAHNEMANN (40'), 3-0
Karl STOIBER (42'), 4-0 Adolf VOGL (67').
Referee: Mihály Iványi IVÁNCSISC (HUN)   Attendance: 20.000

22-07-1934   Stadión Sparta/Letná, Praha: AC Sparta Praha – WSC Admira Wien 3-2 (0-2)
AC Sparta Praha: Bohumil KLENOVEC, Jaroslav BURGR, Josef CTYROKÝ, Josef
SEDLÁCEK, Jaroslav BOUCEK, Erich SRBEK, Václav HRUSKA, Josef KOSTÁLEK,
Raymond BRAINE (BEL), Oldrich NEJEDLÝ, Oldrich ZAJÍCEK. (Coach: Ferenc
SZEDLACSEK (HUN)).
WSC Admira Wien: Peter PLATZER, Robert PAVLICEK, Anton JANDA, Johann
URBANEK, Karl HUMMENBERGER, Josef MIRSCHITZKA, Ignaz SIGL, Karl
DURSPEKT, Karl STOIBER, Wilhelm HAHNEMANN, Adolf VOGL. (Coach: Hans
SKOLAUT).
Goals: AC Sparta Praha: 1-2 Josef SEDLÁCEK (58'), 2-2 Josef SEDLÁCEK (62'), 3-2
Oldrich ZAJÍCEK (86').
WSC Admira Wien: 0-1 Karl DURSPEKT (13'), 0-2 Karl DURSPEKT (40').
Referee: Rinaldo BARLASSINA (ITA)   Attendance: 14.000
(Peter PLATZER stopped a penalty)

15-07-1934   Üllöi ut, Budapest: Ferencvárosi TC Budapest – Bologna Sportiva 1-1 (1-1)
Ferencvárosi TC Budapest: József HÁDA, Nándor BÁN, Lajos KORÁNYI, Antal LYKA,
János MÓRÉ, Gyula LÁZÁR, Mihály TÁNCOS, Gyula POLGÁR, Dr.György SÁROSI, Géza
TOLDI, Sándor BARNA. (Coach: Zoltán BLUM).
Bologna Sportiva: Mario GIANNI, Dino FIORINI, Felice GASPERI, Mario MONTESANTO,
Aldo DONATI, Giordano CORSI, Bruno MAINI, Mario PERAZZOLO, Angelo SCHIAVIO,
Francisco FEDULLO (URU), Carlo REGUZZONI. (Coach: Lajos Nemes KOVÁCS (HUN)).
Goals: Ferencvárosi TC Budapest: 1-0 Géza TOLDI (9').
Bologna Sportiva: 1-1 Bruno MAINI (13').
Referee: Eugen BRAUN (AUT)   Attendance: 19.000
(József HÁDA saved a 33rd minute penalty taken by Angelo SCHIAVIO).

22-07-1934   Stadio del Littoriale, Bologna:
              Bologna Sportiva – Ferencvárosi TC Budapest 5-1 (2-1)
Bologna Sportiva: Mario GIANNI, Eraldo MONZEGLIO, Felice GASPERI, Mario
MONTESANTO, Aldo DONATI, Giordano CORSI, Bruno MAINI, Mario PERAZZOLO,
Angelo SCHIAVIO, Francisco FEDULLO (URU), Carlo REGUZZONI. (Coach: Lajos Nemes
KOVÁCS (HUN)).
Ferencvárosi TC Budapest: József HÁDA, Nándor BÁN, Lajos KORÁNYI, Antal LYKA,
János MÓRÉ, Gyula LÁZÁR, Mihály TÁNCOS, Gyula POLGÁR, Dr.György SÁROSI, Géza
TOLDI, Tibor KEMÉNY. (Coach: Zoltán BLUM).
Goals: Bologna Sportiva: 1-0 Mario PERAZZOLO (5'), 2-1 Bruno MAINI (30'), 3-1 Angelo
SCHIAVIO (48'), 4-1 Angelo SCHIAVIO (51'), 5-1 Carlo REGUZZONI (77').
Ferencvárosi TC Budapest: 1-1 Dr.György SÁROSI (7').
Referee: Gustav KRIST (TCH)   Attendance: 23.000

25-07-1934   Praterstadion, Wien: WSC Admira Wien – Juventus FC Torino 3-1 (1-0)
WSC Admira Wien: Peter PLATZER, Robert PAVLICEK, Anton JANDA, Johann
URBANEK, Karl HUMMENBERGER, Josef MIRSCHITZKA, Ignaz SIGL, Karl
DURSPEKT, Karl STOIBER, Wilhelm HAHNEMANN, Adolf VOGL. (Coach: Hans
SKOLAUT).
Juventus FC Torino: Giampiero COMBI, Duilio SANTAGOSTINO, Umberto CALIGARIS,
Giovanni VARGLIEN (II), Mario VARGLIEN (I), Luigi BERTOLINI, Pietro SERANTONI,
Renato CESARINI (ARG), Felice Placido BOREL (II), Giovanni FERRARI, Raimundo
Bibiani ORSI (ARG). (Coach: Carlo CARCANO).
Goals: WSC Admira Wien: 1-0 Adolf VOGL (13'), 2-0 Wilhelm HAHNEMANN (46'), 3-0
Ignaz SIGL (48').
Juventus FC Torino: 3-1 Raimundo Bibiani ORSI (87').
Referee: Ferenc KLUG (HUN)   Attendance: 16.000

29-07-1934   Stadio Comunale del Littorio, Genova:
              Juventus FC Torino – WSC Admira Wien   2-1 (2-1)
Juventus FC Torino: Giampiero COMBI, Duilio SANTAGOSTINO, Umberto CALIGARIS,
Mario VARGLIEN (I), Luis Felipe MONTI (ARG), Luigi BERTOLINI, Giovanni
VARGLIEN (II), Pietro SERANTONI, Felice Placido BOREL (II), Giovanni FERRARI,
Raimundo Bibiani ORSI (ARG). (Coach: Carlo CARCANO).
WSC Admira Wien: Peter PLATZER, Robert PAVLICEK, Anton JANDA, Johann
URBANEK, Karl HUMMENBERGER, Josef MIRSCHITZKA, Ignaz SIGL, Karl
DURSPEKT, Karl STOIBER, Wilhelm HAHNEMANN, Adolf VOGL. (Coach: Hans
SKOLAUT).
Goals: Juventus FC Torino: 1-0 Felice Placido BOREL (13'), 2-0 Raimundo Bibiani ORSI
(30').
WSC Admira Wien: 2-1 Adolf VOGL (43').
Referee: Mihály Iványi IVÁNCSISC (HUN)   Attendance: 16.000

FINALS

05-09-1934   Praterstadion, Wien: WSC Admira Wien – Bologna Sportiva   3-2 (0-2)
WSC Admira Wien: Peter PLATZER, Robert PAVLICEK, Anton JANDA, Johann
URBANEK, Karl HUMMENBERGER, Josef MIRSCHITZKA, Ignaz SIGL, Wilhelm
HAHNEMANN, Karl STOIBER, Anton SCHALL, Adolf VOGL. (Coach: Hans SKOLAUT).
Bologna Sportiva: Mario GIANNI, Eraldo MONZEGLIO, Felice GASPERI, Mario
MONTESANTO, Aldo DONATI, Giordano CORSI, Bruno MAINI, Raffaele SANSONE
(URU), Aldo SPIVACH, Francisco FEDULLO (URU), Carlo REGUZZONI. (Coach: Lajos
Nemes KOVÁCS (HUN)).
Goals: WSC Admira Wien: 1-2 Karl STOIBER (56'), 2-2 Adolf VOGL (58'), 3-2 Anton
SCHALL (60').
Bologna Sportiva: 0-1 Aldo SPIVACH (7'), 0-2 Carlo REGUZZONI (25').
Referee: William Walter WALDEN (ENG)   Attendance: 50.000

09-09-1934   Stadio del Littoriale, Bologna:
              Bologna Sportiva – WSC Admira Wien   5-1 (4-1)
Bologna Sportiva: Mario GIANNI, Eraldo MONZEGLIO, Felice GASPERI, Mario
MONTESANTO, Aldo DONATI, Giordano CORSI, Bruno MAINI, Raffaele SANSONE
(URU), Angelo SCHIAVIO, Francisco FEDULLO (URU), Carlo REGUZZONI. (Coach:
Lajos Nemes KOVÁCS (HUN)).
WSC Admira Wien: Peter PLATZER, Robert PAVLICEK, Anton JANDA, Johann
URBANEK, Karl HUMMENBERGER, Josef MIRSCHITZKA, Leopold VOGL, Karl
DURSPEKT, Karl STOIBER, Wilhelm HAHNEMANN, Adolf VOGL. (Coach: Hans
SKOLAUT).
Goals: Bologna Sportiva: 1-0 Bruno MAINI (21'), 2-1 Carlo REGUZZONI (33'), 3-1 Carlo
REGUZZONI (40'), 4-1 Francisco FEDULLO (44'), 5-1 Carlo REGUZZONI (88').
WSC Admira Wien: 1-1 Adolf VOGL (32' penalty).
Referee: Arthur James JEWELL (ENG)   Attendance: 25.000

*** **Bologna Sportiva won the Cup** ***

47

1935

15-06-1935   Praterstadion, Wien: WSC Admira Wien – Hungária FC Budapest   3-2 (2-0)
WSC Admira Wien: Peter PLATZER, Robert PAVLICEK, Anton JANDA, Johann
URBANEK, Karl HUMMENBERGER, Josef MIRSCHITZKA, Leopold VOGL, Wilhelm
HAHNEMANN, Karl STOIBER, Karl DURSPEKT, Adolf VOGL. (Coach: Hans
SKOLAUT).
Hungária FC Budapest: József ÚJVÁRI, Gyula MÁNDI-MANDL, Károly KIS, Imre EGRI,
Gusztáv SEBES, János DUDÁS, Ferenc SAS, Heinrich MÜLLER (AUT), József HADRÉVI,
László CSEH, Pál TITKOS. (Coach: Imre SENKEY).
Goals: WSC Admira Wien: 1-0 Karl DURSPEKT (36'), 2-0 Wilhelm HAHNEMANN (40'),
3-2 Leopold VOGL (74').
Hungária FC Budapest: 2-1 Heinrich MÜLLER (59'), 2-2 Heinrich MÜLLER (61').
Referee: Camillo CAIRONI (ITA)   Attendance: 10.000

16-06-1935   Campo Sportivo Testaccio, Roma:
               AS Roma – Ferencvárosi TC Budapest   3-1 (2-1)
AS Roma: Guido MASETTI, Eraldo MONZEGLIO, Andrea GADALDI, Evaristo FRISONI
(II), Dr.Fulvio BERNARDINI, Antonio FUSCO, Angelo CATTANEO, Alejandro SCOPELLI
Casanova (ARG), Enrique GUAITA (ARG), Franco SCARAMELLI, Ernesto TOMASI.
(Coach: Luigi BARBESINO).
Ferencvárosi TC Budapest: József HÁDA, Gyula POLGÁR, Lajos KORÁNYI, Antal LYKA,
Dr.György SÁROSI, Gyula LÁZÁR, Mihály TÁNCOS, Gyula KISS, Géza TOLDI, János
MÓRÉ, Tibor KEMÉNY. (Coach: Zoltán BLUM).
Goals: AS Roma: 1-0 Alejandro SCOPELLI Casanova (23'), 2-0 Angelo CATTANEO (29'),
3-1 Alejandro SCOPELLI Casanova (72').
Ferencvárosi TC Budapest: 2-1 János MÓRÉ (40').
Referee: Hans Walter FRANKENSTEIN (AUT)   Attendance: 12.000

16-06-1935   Üllöi ut, Budapest: Újpesti TE – AC Fiorentina Firenze   0-2 (0-2)
Újpesti TE: György HÓRI, Gyula FUTÓ, László STERNBERG-SÁTORI, Gyula SERES,
György SZÜCS, Ferenc BORSÁNYI, Ferenc PUSZTAI, Pál JÁVOR-JAKUBE, Jenö
VINCZE, Stefan AUER/István AVAR, István BALOGH. (Coach: Béla JÁNOSY).
AC Fiorentina Firenze: Ugo AMORETTI, Lorenzo GAZZARI, Renzo MAGLI, Mario
PIZZIOLO (I), Giuseppe BIGOGNO, Bruno NERI, Cherubino COMINI, Cesare Augusto
FASANELLI, Vinicio VIANI (II), Mario PERAZZOLO, Carlos GRINGA (URU). (Coach:
Guido ARA).
Goals: AC Fiorentina Firenze: 0-1 Cherubino COMINI (21'), 0-2 Carlos GRINGA (37').
Referee: Gustav KRIST (TCH)   Attendance: 8.000

16-06-1935   Arena Civica, Parco Sempione, Milano:
AS Ambrosiana-Inter Milano – FK Austria Wien   2-5 (0-2)
AS Ambrosiana-Inter Milano: Carlo CERESOLI, Giuseppe BALLERIO, Ernesto
MASCHERONI (URU), Ferruccio GHIDINI, Ricardo Gregorio FACCIO Porta (URU),
Armando CASTELLAZZI, Roberto PORTA, Natale MASERA, Giuseppe MEAZZA, Attilio
José DEMARÍA (I) (ARG), Alfredo Ciríaco DEVINCENZI (ARG). (Coach: Gyula
FELDMANN (HUN)).
FK Austria Wien: Rudolf ZÖHRER, Karl ANDRITZ, Karl SESTA, Karl ADAMEK, Johann
MOCK, Walter NAUSCH, Josef MOLZER, Josef STROH, Matthias SINDELAR, Camillo
JERUSALEM, Rudolf VIERTL. (Coach: Josef BLUM).
Goals: AS Ambrosiana-Inter Milano: 1-4 Giuseppe MEAZZA (69'), 2-4 Giuseppe MEAZZA
(73').
FK Austria Wien: 0-1 Rudolf VIERTL (15'), 0-2 Matthias SINDELAR (25'), 0-3 Josef
STROH (58'), 0-4 Camillo JERUSALEM (63'), 2-5 Josef STROH (75').
Referee: Bruno PFÜTZNER (TCH)   Attendance: 18.000

16-06-1935   Na rybnícku, Brno: SK Zidenice – SK Rapid Wien   3-2 (1-0)
SK Zidenice: Karel BURKERT, Frantisek NEJEDLÝ, Karel CERNÝ, Josef SMOLKA,
Stephan POSPICHAL (AUT), Frantisek NOVÁK, Frantisek STERC, Jaroslav MOTÁK,
Václav PRUSA, Karel KLÍMA, Oldrich RULC. (Coach: Jenö KONRAD (HUN)).
SK Rapid Wien: Rudolf RAFTL, Karl JESTRAB, Ludwig TAUSCHEK, Franz WAGNER,
Josef SMISTIK (I), Stefan SKOUMAL, Johann OSTERMANN, Karl HOCHREITER,
Matthias KABUREK, Franz BINDER, Johann PESSER. (Coach: Eduard BAUER).
Goals: SK Zidenice: 1-0 Václav PRUSA (25'), 2-0 Václav PRUSA (51'), 3-0 Václav PRUSA
(55').
SK Rapid Wien: 3-1 Karl HOCHREITER (79'), 3-2 Matthias KABUREK (85').
Referee: Pál VON HERTZKA (HUN)   Attendance: 12.000

16-06-1935   Stadión Viktoria, Plzen: SK Viktoria Plzen – Juventus FC Torino   3-3 (2-2)
SK Viktoria Plzen: Václav DEDIC, Bohumil MUDRA, Johann WANA (AUT), Jaroslav
VLCEK, Antonín BIRÓ, Jaroslav BESTÁK, Václav HORÁK, Ladislav CULÍK, Karel HESS,
Vilém CERVENÝ, Vladimír BÍNA. (Coach: Jindrich PROVITA).
Juventus FC Torino: Cesare VALINASSO, Virginio ROSETTA, Alfredo FONI, Mario
VARGLIEN (I), Luis Felipe MONTI (ARG), Luigi BERTOLINI, Armando DIENA, Felice
Placido BOREL (II), Guglielmo GABETTO, Giovanni FERRARI, Renato CESARINI (ARG).
(Player-coach: Virginio ROSETTA).
Goals: SK Viktoria Plzen: 1-0 Vladimír BÍNA (19'), 2-2 Antonín BIRÓ (36'), 3-2 Karel HESS
(61').
Juventus FC Torino: 1-1 Felice Placido BOREL (25'), 1-2 Giovanni FERRARI (33'), 3-3
Felice Placido BOREL (62').
Referee: Mihály Iványi IVÁNCSISC (HUN)   Attendance: 16.000

49

16-06-1935   Temesvári körút, Szeged: Szeged FC – SK Slavia Praha 1-4 (1-2)
Szeged FC: József PÁLINKÁS, József MIKLÓSI, Lajos RAFFAI, János GYURCSÓ, Kálmán
SOMOGYI, Pál BERTÓK, Mátyás KORÁNYI, Kálmán BOGNÁR, Gyula VASTAG, István
MESTER, Béla BERECZ. (Coach: Béla RETI-REBRO).
SK Slavia Praha: Jaroslav VOJTA, Václav KLUS, Ferdinand DAUCÍK, Antonín VODICKA,
Stefan CAMBAL, Rudolf KRCIL, Jan HERMÁNEK, Vlastimil KOPECKÝ, Vojtech
BRADÁC, Antonín PUC, Rudolf VYTLACIL (AUT). (Coach: Kálmán KONRÁD (HUN)).
Goals: Szeged FC: 1-2 Kálmán BOGNÁR (30').
SK Slavia Praha: 0-1 Vlastimil KOPECKÝ (13'), 0-2 Vlastimil KOPECKÝ (17'), 1-3
Vlastimil KOPECKÝ (54'), 1-4 Vojtech BRADÁC (84').
Referee: Dr.Adolf MIESZ (AUT)   Attendance: 8.000

18-06-1935   Praterstadion, Wien: First Vienna FC – AC Sparta Praha 1-1 (1-0)
First Vienna FC: Viktor HAVLICEK, Karl RAINER, Willibald SCHMAUS, Otto KALLER,
Leopold HOFMANN, Leonhard MACHU (expulsion 74'), Franz ERDL, Friedrich (Fritz)
GSCHWEIDL, Richard FISCHER, Josef MAYBÖCK, Wilhelm HOLEC. (Player-coach:
Friedrich (Fritz) GSCHWEIDL).
AC Sparta Praha: Bohumil KLENOVEC, Jaroslav BURGR, Josef CTYROKÝ, Josef
KOSTÁLEK, Jaroslav BOUCEK (expulsion 76'), Erich SRBEK, Václav HRUSKA, Ferdinand
FACSINEK, Raymond BRAINE (BEL), Oldrich NEJEDLÝ, Géza KALOCSAY. (Coach:
Ferenc SZEDLACSEK (HUN)).
Goals: First Vienna FC: 1-0 Wilhelm HOLEC (35').
AC Sparta Praha: 1-1 Oldrich NEJEDLÝ (70').
Referee: Otello SASSI (ITA)   Attendance: 6.500

22-06-1935   Üllöi út, Budapest: Ferencvárosi TC Budapest – AS Roma 8-0 (3-0)
Ferencvárosi TC Budapest: József HÁDA, Gyula POLGÁR, Lajos KORÁNYI, Antal LYKA,
János MÓRÉ, Gyula LÁZÁR, Mihály TÁNCOS, Gyula KISS, Dr.György SÁROSI, Géza
TOLDI, Tibor KEMÉNY. (Coach: Zoltán BLUM).
AS Roma: Guido MASETTI, Eraldo MONZEGLIO, Andrea GADALDI, Evaristo FRISONI
(II), Dr.Fulvio BERNARDINI, Antonio FUSCO, Angelo CATTANEO, Alejandro SCOPELLI
Casanova (ARG), Enrique GUAITA (ARG), Franco SCARAMELLI, Ernesto TOMASI.
(Coach: Luigi BARBESINO).
Goals: Ferencvárosi TC Budapest: 1-0 Dr.György SÁROSI (23' penalty), 2-0 Dr.György
SÁROSI (30'), 3-0 Dr.György SÁROSI (38' penalty), 4-0 Géza TOLDI (57'), 5-0 Dr.György
SÁROSI (62' penalty), 6-0 Tibor KEMÉNY (76'), 7-0 Tibor KEMÉNY (79'), 8-0 Gyula KISS
(89').
Referee: Bruno PFÜTZNER (TCH)   Attendance: 12.000

50

22-06-1935   Stadión Sparta/Letná, Praha: AC Sparta Praha – First Vienna FC   5-3 (2-1)
AC Sparta Praha: Bohumil KLENOVEC, Jaroslav BURGR, Josef CTYROKÝ, Josef
KOSTÁLEK, Raymond BRAINE (BEL), Erich SRBEK, Václav HRUSKA, Josef
SEDLÁCEK, Oldrich ZAJÍCEK, Oldrich NEJEDLÝ, Géza KALOCSAY. (Coach: Ferenc
SZEDLACSEK (HUN)).
First Vienna FC: Viktor HAVLICEK, Karl RAINER, Willibald SCHMAUS, Otto KALLER,
Leopold HOFMANN, Franz ERDL, Franz HIERLEITHNER, Josef MAYBÖCK, Richard
FISCHER, Gustav POLLAK, Wilhelm HOLEC. (Player-coach: Friedrich (Fritz)
GSCHWEIDL).
Goals: AC Sparta Praha: 1-1 Oldrich ZAJÍCEK (14'), 2-1 Raymond BRAINE (45'), 3-1
Oldrich NEJEDLÝ (47'), 4-2 Oldrich ZAJÍCEK (50' penalty), 5-3 Oldrich ZAJÍCEK (85').
First Vienna FC: 0-1 Richard FISCHER (8'), 3-2 Gustav POLLAK (47'), 4-3 Gustav
POLLAK (71' penalty).
Referee: Ferenc MAJORSZKY (HUN)   Attendance: 12.000

23-06-1935   Hungária körút, Budapest:
               Hungária FC Budapest – WSC Admira Wien   7-1 (1-0)
Hungária FC Budapest: József ÚJVÁRI, Gyula MÁNDI-MANDL, Károly KIS, Imre EGRI,
Gusztáv SEBES, János DUDÁS, Ferenc SAS, Heinrich MÜLLER (AUT), László CSEH,
József TURAY, Pál TITKOS. (Coach: Imre SENKEY).
WSC Admira Wien: Peter PLATZER, Robert PAVLICEK, Anton JANDA (expulsion 90'),
Johann URBANEK, Karl HUMMENBERGER, Josef MIRSCHITZKA, Leopold VOGL,
Wilhelm HAHNEMANN (expulsion 77'), Karl STOIBER, Karl DURSPEKT, Adolf VOGL.
(Coach: Hans SKOLAUT).
Goals: Hungária FC Budapest: 1-0 Pál TITKOS (32'), 2-0 László CSEH (60'), 3-0 László
CSEH (73'), 4-1 László CSEH (82'), 5-1 Pál TITKOS (84'), 6-1 Pál TITKOS (87'), 7-1
Heinrich MÜLLER (88' penalty).
WSC Admira Wien: 3-1 Karl HUMMENBERGER (77').
Referee: Frantisek CEJNAR (TCH)   Attendance: 6.000

23-06-1935   Stadio Comunale "Giovanni Berta", Firenze:
               AC Fiorentina Firenze – Újpesti TE   4-3 (2-1)
AC Fiorentina Firenze: Ugo AMORETTI, Lorenzo GAZZARI, Renzo MAGLI, Mario
PIZZIOLO (I), Giuseppe BIGOGNO, Bruno NERI, Cherubino COMINI, Mario
PERAZZOLO, Cesare Augusto FASANELLI, Cinzio SCAGLIOTTI, Carlos GRINGA (URU).
(Coach: Guido ARA).
Újpesti TE: Ferenc SZIKLAI, Gyula FUTÓ, László STERNBERG-SÁTORI, Gyula SERES,
György SZÜCS, Ferenc BORSÁNYI, Lipót KÁLLAI, Pál JÁVOR-JAKUBE, Jenö VINCZE,
Stefan AUER/István AVAR, István TAMÁSSY. (Coach: Béla JÁNOSY).
Goals: AC Fiorentina Firenze: 1-0 Cesare Augusto FASANELLI (27'), 2-1 Cesare Augusto
FASANELLI (43'), 3-1 Cherubino COMINI (47'), 4-3 Cesare Augusto FASANELLI (83').
Újpesti TE: 1-1 Stefan AUER/István AVAR (29'), 3-2 Stefan AUER/István AVAR (49'), 3-3
Gyula SERES (70').
Referee: Adolf ROSENBERGER (AUT)   Attendance: 15.000

51

23-06-1935   Praterstadion, Wien:
                FK Austria Wien – AS Ambrosiana-Inter Milano   3-1 (2-1)
FK Austria Wien: Rudolf ZÖHRER, Karl ANDRITZ, Karl SESTA, Karl ADAMEK, Johann
MOCK, Walter NAUSCH, Josef MOLZER, Josef STROH, Matthias SINDELAR, Camillo
JERUSALEM, Rudolf VIERTL. (Coach: Josef BLUM).
AS Ambrosiana-Inter Milano: Valentino DEGANI, Giuseppe BALLERIO, Ernesto
MASCHERONI (URU), Alfredo PITTO, Ricardo Gregorio FACCIO Porta (URU), Armando
CASTELLAZZI, Roberto PORTA, Natale MASERA, Giuseppe MEAZZA, Attilio José
DEMARÍA (I) (ARG), Alfredo Ciríaco DEVINCENZI (ARG). (Coach: Gyula FELDMANN
(HUN)).
Goals: FK Austria Wien: 1-0 Matthias SINDELAR (13'), 2-1 Matthias SINDELAR (30'), 3-1
Matthias SINDELAR (70').
AS Ambrosiana-Inter Milano: 1-1 Attilio José DEMARÍA (25').
Referee: Ferenc KLUG (HUN)   Attendance: 55.000

23-06-1935   Praterstadion, Wien: SK Rapid Wien – SK Zidenice 2-2 (1-2)
SK Rapid Wien: Rudolf RAFTL, Karl JESTRAB, Ludwig TAUSCHEK, Franz WAGNER,
Josef SMISTIK (I), Stefan SKOUMAL, Johann OSTERMANN, Karl HOCHREITER,
Matthias KABUREK, Franz BINDER, Johann PESSER. (Coach: Eduard BAUER).
SK Zidenice: Karel BURKERT, Frantisek NEJEDLÝ, Karel CERNÝ, Josef SMOLKA,
Stephan POSPICHAL (AUT), Frantisek NOVÁK, Frantisek STERC, Oldrich NÝVLT, Václav
PRUSA, Jaroslav MOTÁK, Oldrich RULC. (Coach: Jenö KONRAD (HUN)).
Goals: SK Rapid Wien: 1-0 Franz BINDER (6'), 2-2 Matthias KABUREK (56').
SK Zidenice: 1-1 Oldrich NÝVLT (43'), 1-2 Oldrich RULC (44').
Referee: Francesco MATTEA (ITA)   Attendance: 55.000

23-06-1935   Stadio Comunale "Benito Mussolini", Torino:
                Juventus FC Torino – SK Viktoria Plzen 5-1 (3-0)
Juventus FC Torino: Cesare VALINASSO, Virginio ROSETTA, Alfredo FONI, Mario
VARGLIEN (I), Luis Felipe MONTI (ARG), Luigi BERTOLINI, Armando DIENA, Felice
Placido BOREL (II), Guglielmo GABETTO, Giovanni FERRARI, Renato CESARINI (ARG).
(Player-coach: Virginio ROSETTA).
SK Viktoria Plzen: Václav DEDIC, Bohumil MUDRA, Johann WANA (AUT), Jaroslav
VLCEK, Antonín BIRÓ, Jaroslav BESTÁK, Václav HORÁK, Ladislav CULÍK, Karel HESS,
Vilém CERVENÝ, Vladimír BÍNA. (Coach: Jindrich PROVITA).
Goals: Juventus FC Torino: 1-0 Giovanni FERRARI (6'), 2-0 Felice Placido BOREL (25'), 3-0
Armando DIENA (39'), 4-0 Felice Placido BOREL (69'), 5-1 Giovanni FERRARI (87').
SK Viktoria Plzen: 4-1 Václav HORÁK (80').
Referee: Alois BERANEK (AUT)   Attendance: 14.000

23-06-1935   Stadión Slavia/Letná, Praha: SK Slavia Praha – Szeged FC   0-1 (0-0)
SK Slavia Praha: Jaroslav VOJTA, Václav KLUS, Ferdinand DAUCÍK, Antonín VODICKA,
Stefan CAMBAL, Rudolf KRCIL, Jan HERMÁNEK, Vlastimil KOPECKÝ, Jirí SOBOTKA,
Antonín PUC, Rudolf VYTLACIL (AUT). (Coach: Kálmán KONRÁD (HUN)).
Szeged FC: József PÁLINKÁS, József MIKLÓSI, Lajos RAFFAI, János GYURCSÓ, Kálmán
SOMOGYI, Pál BERTÓK, Mátyás KORÁNYI, Kálmán BOGNÁR, Gyula VASTAG, István
MESTER, Béla BERECZ. (Coach: Béla RETI-REBRO).
Goal: Szeged FC: 0-1 István MESTER (50').
Referee: Raffaele SCORZONI (ITA)   Attendance: 7.000

52

QUARTER-FINALS

29-06-1935   Stadión Slavia/Letná, Praha: SK Slavia Praha – FK Austria Wien   1-0 (1-0)
SK Slavia Praha: Frantisek PLÁNICKA, Václav KLUS, Ferdinand DAUCÍK, Antonín
VODICKA, Stefan CAMBAL, Rudolf KRCIL, Rudolf VYTLACIL (AUT), Jirí SOBOTKA,
Vojtech BRADÁC, Vlastimil KOPECKÝ, Antonín PUC. (Coach: Kálmán KONRÁD (HUN)).
FK Austria Wien: Rudolf ZÖHRER, Karl ANDRITZ, Karl SESTA, Karl ADAMEK, Johann
MOCK, Walter NAUSCH, Josef MOLZER, Josef STROH, Matthias SINDELAR, Camillo
JERUSALEM, Rudolf VIERTL. (Coach: Josef BLUM).
Goal: SK Slavia Praha: 1-0 Vojtech BRADÁC (23').
Referee: Rinaldo BARLASSINA (ITA)   Attendance: 15.000

30-06-1935   Stadión Sparta/Letná, Praha:
                     AC Sparta Praha – AC Fiorentina Firenze   7-1 (2-0)
AC Sparta Praha: Bohumil KLENOVEC, Jaroslav BURGR, Josef CTYROKÝ, Josef
KOSTÁLEK, Jaroslav BOUCEK, Erich SRBEK, Ferdinand FACSINEK, Oldrich ZAJÍCEK,
Raymond BRAINE (BEL), Oldrich NEJEDLÝ, Géza KALOCSAY. (Coach: Ferenc
SZEDLACSEK (HUN)).
AC Fiorentina Firenze: Ugo AMORETTI, Lorenzo GAZZARI, Renzo MAGLI, Mario
PIZZIOLO (I), Giuseppe BIGOGNO, Bruno NERI, Cherubino COMINI, Mario
PERAZZOLO, Vinicio VIANI (II), Cesare Augusto FASANELLI, Carlos GRINGA (URU).
(Coach: Guido ARA).
Goals: AC Sparta Praha: 1-0 Oldrich ZAJÍCEK (23'), 2-0 Oldrich NEJEDLÝ (40'), 3-1
Oldrich NEJEDLÝ (52'), 4-1 Géza KALOCSAY (58'), 5-1 Ferdinand FACSINEK (60'), 6-1
Raymond BRAINE (79'), 7-1 Ferdinand FACSINEK (79').
AC Fiorentina Firenze: 2-1 Carlos GRINGA (48').
Referee: Mihály Iványi IVÁNCSISC (HUN)   Attendance: 18.000

30-06-1935   Na rybnícku, Brno: SK Zidenice – Ferencvárosi TC Budapest   4-2 (2-0)
SK Zidenice: Karel BURKERT, Jozef NEDER, Karel CERNÝ, Josef SMOLKA, Stephan
POSPICHAL (AUT), Ladislau RAFFINSKY (ROM), Frantisek STERC, Oldrich NÝVLT,
Václav PRUSA, Jaroslav MOTÁK, Oldrich RULC. (Coach: Jenö KONRAD (HUN)).
Ferencvárosi TC Budapest: József HÁDA, Gyula POLGÁR, Lajos KORÁNYI, Antal LYKA,
János MÓRÉ, Gyula LÁZÁR, Mihály TÁNCOS, Gyula KISS, Dr.György SÁROSI, Géza
TOLDI, Tibor KEMÉNY. (Coach: Zoltán BLUM).
Goals: SK Zidenice: 1-0 Oldrich RULC (12'), 2-0 Oldrich NÝVLT (30'), 3-2 Frantisek
STERC (54'), 4-2 Václav PRUSA (88').
Ferencvárosi TC Budapest: 2-1 Gyula KISS (49'), 2-2 Dr.György SÁROSI (51').
Referee: Raffaele SCORZONI (ITA)   Attendance: 17.000

30-06-1935   Hungária körút, Budapest:
               Hungária FC Budapest – Juventus FC Torino   1-3 (0-0)
Hungária FC Budapest: József ÚJVÁRI, Gyula MÁNDI-MANDL, Károly KIS, Imre EGRI,
Gusztáv SEBES, János DUDÁS, Ferenc SAS, Heinrich MÜLLER (AUT), László CSEH,
József TURAY, Pál TITKOS. (Coach: Imre SENKEY).
Juventus FC Torino: Cesare VALINASSO, Virginio ROSETTA, Alfredo FONI, Mario
VARGLIEN (I), Luis Felipe MONTI (ARG), Luigi BERTOLINI, Armando DIENA, Felice
Placido BOREL (II), Guglielmo GABETTO, Giovanni FERRARI, Renato CESARINI (ARG).
(Player-coach: Virginio ROSETTA).
Goals: Hungária FC Budapest: 1-3 Heinrich MÜLLER (75' penalty).
Juventus FC Torino: 0-1 Giovanni FERRARI (51'), 0-2 Guglielmo GABETTO (65'), 0-3
Armando DIENA (67').
Referee: Alois BERANEK (AUT)   Attendance: 17.000

06-07-1935   Stadio Comunale "Giovanni Berta", Firenze:
               AC Fiorentina Firenze – AC Sparta Praha   3-1 (2-0)
AC Fiorentina Firenze: Ugo AMORETTI, Renzo MAGLI, Aldo QUERCI, Mario PIZZIOLO
(I), Achille PICCINI, Bruno NERI, János NEHODOMA (HUN), Cesare Augusto
FASANELLI, Vinicio VIANI (II), Alfonso NEGRO (USA), Carlos GRINGA (URU). (Coach:
Guido ARA).
AC Sparta Praha: Bohumil KLENOVEC, Jaroslav BURGR, Josef CTYROKÝ, Josef
KOSTÁLEK, Jaroslav BOUCEK, Erich SRBEK, Ferdinand FACSINEK, Oldrich ZAJÍCEK,
Raymond BRAINE (BEL), Oldrich NEJEDLÝ, Géza KALOCSAY. (Coach: Ferenc
SZEDLACSEK (HUN)).
Goals: AC Fiorentina Firenze: 1-0 Vinicio VIANI (30' penalty), 2-0 Alfonso NEGRO (35'),
3-0 Vinicio VIANI (51').
AC Sparta Praha: 3-1 Ferdinand FACSINEK (58').
Referee: Hans Walter FRANKENSTEIN (AUT)   Attendance: 10.000

06-07-1935   Üllöi ut, Budapest: Ferencvárosi TC Budapest – SK Zidenice   6-1 (2-1)
Ferencvárosi TC Budapest: József HÁDA, Gyula POLGÁR, Lajos KORÁNYI, Antal LYKA,
János MÓRÉ, Gyula LÁZÁR, Mihály TÁNCOS, Gyula KISS, Dr.György SÁROSI, Géza
TOLDI, Tibor KEMÉNY. (Coach: Zoltán BLUM).
SK Zidenice: Karel BURKERT, Jozef NEDER, Karel CERNÝ, Josef SMOLKA, Stephan
POSPICHAL (AUT), Ladislau RAFFINSKY (ROM), Frantisek STERC, Oldrich NÝVLT,
Josef TICHÝ, Jaroslav MOTÁK, Oldrich RULC. (Coach: Jenö KONRAD (HUN)).
Goals: Ferencvárosi TC Budapest: 1-0 Dr.György SÁROSI (9'), 2-1 Gyula KISS (43'), 3-1
Dr.György SÁROSI (47'), 4-1 Géza TOLDI (54'), 5-1 Mihály TÁNCOS (66'), 6-1 Géza
TOLDI (85').
SK Zidenice: 1-1 Frantisek STERC (16').
Referee: Dr.Adolf MIESZ (AUT)   Attendance: 15.000

54

06-07-1935   Stadio Comunale "Benito Mussolini", Torino:
Juventus FC Torino – Hungária FC Budapest   1-1 (1-0)
Juventus FC Torino: Cesare VALINASSO, Virginio ROSETTA, Alfredo FONI, Mario
VARGLIEN (I), Luis Felipe MONTI (ARG), Luigi BERTOLINI, Armando DIENA, Felice
Placido BOREL (II), Guglielmo GABETTO, Giovanni FERRARI, Renato CESARINI (ARG).
(Player-coach: Virginio ROSETTA).
Hungária FC Budapest: József ÚJVÁRI, Károly KIS, Sándor BÍRÓ, Imre EGRI, Gusztáv
SEBES, János DUDÁS, Ferenc SAS, Heinrich MÜLLER (AUT), László CSEH, József
TURAY, Pál TITKOS. (Coach: Imre SENKEY).
Goals: Juventus FC Torino: 1-0 Giovanni FERRARI (15').
Hungária FC Budapest: 1-1 Pál TITKOS (48').
Referee: Ján BIZÍK (TCH)   Attendance: 9.000

07-07-1935   Praterstadion, Wien: FK Austria Wien – SK Slavia Praha   2-1 (1-1)
FK Austria Wien: Rudolf ZÖHRER, Karl ANDRITZ, Karl SESTA, Karl ADAMEK, Johann
MOCK, Walter NAUSCH, Josef MOLZER, Josef STROH, Matthias SINDELAR, Camillo
JERUSALEM, Rudolf VIERTL. (Coach: Josef BLUM).
SK Slavia Praha: Frantisek PLÁNICKA, Václav KLUS, Ferdinand DAUCÍK, Antonín
VODICKA, Stefan CAMBAL, Rudolf KRCIL, Jan HERMÁNEK, Vojtech BRADÁC,
Frantisek SVOBODA, Vlastimil KOPECKÝ, Rudolf VYTLACIL (AUT). (Coach: Kálmán
KONRÁD (HUN)).
Goals: FK Austria Wien: 1-1 Camillo JERUSALEM (23'), 2-1 Josef STROH (53').
SK Slavia Praha: 0-1 Vojtech BRADÁC (17').
Referee: Pál VON HERTZKA (HUN)   Attendance: 45.000

14-07-1935   Praterstadion, Wien: FK Austria Wien – SK Slavia Praha   5-2 (3-0)
FK Austria Wien: Rudolf ZÖHRER, Matthias NAJEMNIK, Karl SESTA, Karl ADAMEK,
Johann MOCK, Karl GALL, Josef MOLZER, Josef STROH, Matthias SINDELAR, Walter
NAUSCH, Rudolf VIERTL. (Coach: Josef BLUM).
SK Slavia Praha: Frantisek PLÁNICKA, Václav KLUS, Ferdinand DAUCÍK, Antonín
VODICKA, Stefan CAMBAL, Rudolf KRCIL, Rudolf VYTLACIL (AUT), Vojtech
BRADÁC, Jirí SOBOTKA, Vlastimil KOPECKÝ, Antonín PUC. (Coach: Kálmán KONRÁD
(HUN)).
Goals: FK Austria Wien: 1-0 Rudolf VIERTL (16'), 2-0 Matthias SINDELAR (34'), 3-0 Josef
MOLZER (37'), 4-0 Walter NAUSCH (58'), 5-1 Josef STROH (71').
SK Slavia Praha: 4-1 Antonín PUC (60'), 5-2 Rudolf VYTLACIL (88').
Referee: Francesco MATTEA (ITA)   Attendance: 50.000
(Play-off)

55

16-07-1935   Stadión Sparta/Letná, Praha: AC Sparta Praha – Juventus FC Torino 2-0 (1-0)
AC Sparta Praha: Bohumil KLENOVEC, Jaroslav BURGR, Josef CTYROKÝ, Josef
KOSTÁLEK, Jaroslav BOUCEK, Erich SRBEK, Ferdinand FACSINEK, Oldrich ZAJÍCEK,
Raymond BRAINE (BEL), Oldrich NEJEDLÝ, Géza KALOCSAY. (Coach: Ferenc
SZEDLACSEK (HUN)).
Juventus FC Torino: Cesare VALINASSO, Virginio ROSETTA, Alfredo FONI, Mario
VARGLIEN (I), Luis Felipe MONTI (ARG) (expulsion 67'), Luigi BERTOLINI, Gastone
PRENDATO, Felice Placido BOREL (II), Guglielmo GABETTO, Giovanni FERRARI,
Renato CESARINI (ARG). (Player-coach: Virginio ROSETTA).
Goals: AC Sparta Praha: 1-0 Ferdinand FACSINEK (43'), 2-0 Oldrich ZAJÍCEK (67'
penalty).
Referee: Alois BERANEK (AUT)   Attendance: 36.000

21-07-1935   Stadio Comunale "Benito Mussolini", Torino:
                   Juventus FC Torino – AC Sparta Praha 3-1 (1-0)
Juventus FC Torino: Cesare VALINASSO, Virginio ROSETTA, Alfredo FONI, Mario
VARGLIEN (I), Luis Felipe MONTI (ARG), Luigi BERTOLINI, Gastone PRENDATO,
Felice Placido BOREL (II), Guglielmo GABETTO, Giovanni FERRARI, Renato CESARINI
(ARG). (Player-coach: Virginio ROSETTA).
AC Sparta Praha: Bohumil KLENOVEC, Jaroslav BURGR, Josef CTYROKÝ, Josef
KOSTÁLEK, Jaroslav BOUCEK, Erich SRBEK, Ferdinand FACSINEK, Oldrich ZAJÍCEK,
Raymond BRAINE (BEL), Oldrich NEJEDLÝ, Géza KALOCSAY. (Coach: Ferenc
SZEDLACSEK (HUN)).
Goals: Juventus FC Torino: 1-0 Gastone PRENDATO (1'), 2-0 Felice Placido BOREL (52'),
3-1 Felice Placido BOREL (90').
AC Sparta Praha: 2-1 Oldrich NEJEDLÝ (65').
Referee: Mihály Iványi IVÁNCSISC (HUN)   Attendance: 17.000
(Bohumil KLENOVEC saved an 85th minute penalty).

21-07-1935   Üllöi út, Budapest: Ferencvárosi TC Budapest – FK Austria Wien 4-2 (1-1)
Ferencvárosi TC Budapest: József HÁDA, Gyula POLGÁR, Lajos KORÁNYI, Antal LYKA,
János MÓRÉ, Gyula LÁZÁR, Mihály TÁNCOS, Gyula KISS, Dr.György SÁROSI, Géza
TOLDI, Tibor KEMÉNY. (Coach: Zoltán BLUM).
FK Austria Wien: Rudolf ZÖHRER, Matthias NAJEMNIK, Karl SESTA, Karl ADAMEK,
Walter NAUSCH, Karl GALL, Josef MOLZER, Josef STROH, Matthias SINDELAR, Franz
SCHILLING, Rudolf VIERTL. (Coach: Josef BLUM).
Goals: Ferencvárosi TC Budapest: 1-1 Dr.György SÁROSI (38'), 2-1 Gyula KISS (47'), 3-1
Dr.György SÁROSI (61'), 4-2 Gyula KISS (85').
FK Austria Wien: 0-1 Matthias SINDELAR (35'), 3-2 Matthias SINDELAR (80').
Referee: Bruno PFÜTZNER (TCH)   Attendance: 28.000

28-07-1935   Rankhof, Basel: AC Sparta Praha – Juventus FC Torino   5-1 (3-0)
AC Sparta Praha: Bohumil KLENOVEC, Jaroslav BURGR, Josef CTYROKÝ, Josef
KOSTÁLEK, Jaroslav BOUCEK, Erich SRBEK, Ferdinand FACSINEK, Oldrich ZAJÍCEK,
Raymond BRAINE (BEL), Oldrich NEJEDLÝ, Géza KALOCSAY. (Coach: Ferenc
SZEDLACSEK (HUN)).
Juventus FC Torino: Cesare VALINASSO, Virginio ROSETTA, Alfredo FONI, Mario
VARGLIEN (I), Luis Felipe MONTI (ARG), Luigi BERTOLINI, Gastone PRENDATO,
Felice Placido BOREL (II), Guglielmo GABETTO, Giovanni FERRARI, Renato CESARINI
(ARG). (Player-coach: Virginio ROSETTA).
Goals: AC Sparta Praha: 1-0 Oldrich ZAJÍCEK (21'), 2-0 Raymond BRAINE (37'), 3-0
Ferdinand FACSINEK (40'), 4-1 Raymond BRAINE (85'), 5-1 Oldrich ZAJÍCEK (87').
Juventus FC Torino: 3-1 Alfredo FONI (70' penalty).
Referee: Albert Edward FOGG (ENG)   Attendance: 8.000

(Play-off game).

28-07-1935   Praterstadion, Wien: FK Austria Wien – Ferencvárosi TC Budapest 3-2 (1-1)
FK Austria Wien: Rudolf ZÖHRER, Matthias NAJEMNIK, Karl SESTA, Karl ADAMEK,
Walter NAUSCH, Karl ANDRITZ, Josef MOLZER, Josef STROH, Matthias SINDELAR,
Camillo JERUSALEM, Rudolf VIERTL. (Coach: Josef BLUM).
Ferencvárosi TC Budapest: József HÁDA, Gyula POLGÁR, Lajos KORÁNYI, Antal LYKA,
János MÓRÉ, Gyula LÁZÁR, Mihály TÁNCOS, Gyula KISS, Dr.György SÁROSI, Géza
TOLDI, Tibor KEMÉNY. (Coach: Zoltán BLUM).
Goals: FK Austria Wien: 1-0 Matthias SINDELAR (29'), 2-1 Camillo JERUSALEM (46'), 3-1
Karl ADAMEK (58' penalty).
Ferencvárosi TC Budapest: 1-1 Géza TOLDI (43'), 3-2 Géza TOLDI (68').
Referee: Bruno PFÜTZNER (TCH)   Attendance: 55.000

FINAL

08-09-1935   Üllöi ut, Budapest: Ferencvárosi TC Budapest – AC Sparta Praha 2-1 (2-0)
Ferencvárosi TC Budapest: József HÁDA, Gyula POLGÁR, Lajos KORÁNYI, Károly
MIKES, János MÓRÉ, Nándor BÁN, Mihály TÁNCOS, Gyula KISS, Dr.György SÁROSI,
Géza TOLDI, Tibor KEMÉNY. (Coach: Zoltán BLUM).
AC Sparta Praha: Bohumil KLENOVEC, Jaroslav BURGR, Josef CTYROKÝ, Josef
KOSTÁLEK, Jaroslav BOUCEK, Erich SRBEK, Ferdinand FACSINEK, Oldrich ZAJÍCEK,
Raymond BRAINE (BEL), Oldrich NEJEDLÝ, Géza KALOCSAY. (Coach: Ferenc
SZEDLACSEK (HUN)).
Goals: Ferencvárosi TC Budapest: 1-0 Géza TOLDI (16'), 2-0 Gyula KISS (27').
AC Sparta Praha: 2-1 Raymond BRAINE (71').
Referee: William Walter WALDEN (ENG)   Attendance: 34.000

15-09-1935   Stadión Strahov (Masaryk), Praha:
AC Sparta Praha – Ferencvárosi TC Budapest 3-0 (2-0)
AC Sparta Praha: Bohumil KLENOVEC, Jaroslav BURGR, Josef CTYROKÝ, Josef
KOSTÁLEK, Jaroslav BOUCEK, Erich SRBEK, Ferdinand FACSINEK, Oldrich ZAJÍCEK,
Raymond BRAINE (BEL), Oldrich NEJEDLÝ, Géza KALOCSAY. (Coach: Ferenc
SZEDLACSEK (HUN)).
Ferencvárosi TC Budapest: József HÁDA, Gyula POLGÁR, Lajos KORÁNYI, Károly
MIKES, János MÓRÉ, Nándor BÁN, Mihály TÁNCOS, Gyula KISS, Dr.György SÁROSI,
Géza TOLDI, Tibor KEMÉNY. (Coach: Zoltán BLUM).
Goals: AC Sparta Praha: 1-0 Ferdinand FACSINEK (26'), 2-0 Raymond BRAINE (34'), 3-0
Raymond BRAINE (69').
Referee: Albert Edward FOGG (ENG)   Attendance: 56.000

*** AC Sparta Praha won the Cup ***

58

1936

07-06-1936   Praterstadion, Wien: FK Austria Wien – Grasshopper-Club Zürich 3-1 (2-0)
FK Austria Wien: Johann KOVAR, Wilhelm KOPETKO, Walter NAUSCH, Karl ADAMEK,
Johann MOCK, Karl GALL, Franz RIEGLER, Josef STROH, Matthias SINDELAR, Camillo
JERUSALEM, Rudolf VIERTL. (Coaches: Kálmán KONRÁD (HUN) & Walter NAUSCH).
Grasshopper-Club Zürich: Willy MAIRE, Severino (Sevi) MINELLI, Walter WEILER (II),
Dr.Sigmund GUTTORMSEN (NOR), Sirio VERNATI (ITA), Oskar RAUCH, Alfred (Fredy)
BICKEL, Aurelio VACCANI, Friedrich (Fritz) WAGNER, Max (Xam) ABEGGLEN (II),
Heinrich VITA (AUT). (Coach: Karl RAPPAN (AUT)).
Goals: FK Austria Wien: 1-0 Matthias SINDELAR (7'), 2-0 Camillo JERUSALEM (37'), 3-0
Franz RIEGLER (61').
Grasshopper-Club Zürich: 3-1 Alfred BICKEL (90').
Referee: Bruno PFÜTZNER (TCH)   Attendance: 7.500

07-06-1936   Na rybnícku, Brno: SK Zidenice – Lausanne-Sports 5-0 (2-0)
SK Zidenice: Karel BURKERT, Jozef NEDER, Karel CERNÝ, Josef SMOLKA, Stephan
POSPICHAL (AUT), Frantisek NOVÁK, Frantisek STERC, Karel NEPALA, Václav PRUSA,
Karel HESS, Oldrich RULC. (Coach: Antonín CARVAN).
Lausanne-Sports: Frank SÉCHEHAYE, August LEHMANN, Hans STALDER, Adolfo
SPILLER, Robert WEILLER (GER), Jean BICHSEL, Adolf STELZER, Lozan KOTSEV
(BUL), Willy JAEGGI (IV), Jacques SPAGNOLI, Jean-Pierre ROCHAT. (Coach: Alwin
RIEMKE (GER)).
Goals: SK Zidenice: 1-0 Václav PRUSA (10'), 2-0 Karel NEPALA (17'), 3-0 Frantisek
STERC (47'), 4-0 Karel HESS (70'), 5-0 Václav PRUSA (80').
Referee: Hans Walter FRANKENSTEIN (AUT)   Attendance: 15.000

07-06-1936   Stadion Neufeld, Bern: FC Bern – AC Torino 1-4 (0-2)
FC Bern: Ernst TREUBERG, Otto HÄNNI, William (Willy) BAUMGARTNER, Hans
LUDER, James Chadwick (Jimmy) TOWNLEY (ENG), Otto KOHLER, Alfons WEBER,
Engelbert BÖSCH, Leopold (Poldi) KIELHOLZ, Carlo PINTÉR (HUN), Leo-Paul (Leo)
BILLETER. (Coach: Robert PACHE).
AC Torino: Giuseppe MAINA, Luigi BRUNELLA, Osvaldo FERRINI, Cesare GALLEA,
Frederico ALLASIO, Filippo PRATO, Mario BO, Fioravante BALDI (III), Remo GALLI,
Pietro BUSCAGLIA, Onesto SILANO. (Coach: Clemens CARGNELLI (AUT)).
Goals: FC Bern: 1-2 Leo BILLETER (67').
AC Torino: 0-1 Fioravante BALDI (5'), 0-2 Remo GALLI (35'), 1-3 Remo GALLI (73'), 1-4
Pietro BUSCAGLIA (89').
Referee: Mihály Iványi IVÁNCSISC (HUN)   Attendance: 5.000

59

07-06-1936   Stadion Förrlibuck, Zürich:
                Young Fellows Zürich – Phöbus FC Budapest   0-3 (0-1)
Young Fellows Zürich: Gustav (Gusti) SCHLEGEL, Emil KUPFER, Hans NYFFELER, Max
NOLDIN, Anton CISERI (I), Robert KAES, Eugen DIEBOLD, Eduard MÜLLER, Alessandro
(Mucho) FRIGERIO, Gustav TÖGEL (AUT), Giuseppe BOSSI. (Coach: József (Csibi)
WINKLER (HUN)).
Phöbus FC Budapest: Gyula CSIKÓS, Lajos WÉBER, Jenö FEKETE, Ferenc BORSÁNYI,
Sándor MEGYERI, József PÉTER, Bertalan BÉKY, Sándor SZIKÁR, Dr.József SOLTI,
András TURAY (II), Gábor P.SZABÓ. (Coach: Lajos BÁNYAI).
Goals: Phöbus FC Budapest: 0-1 Bertalan BÉKY (21'), 0-2 Gábor P.SZABÓ (46'), 0-3
Dr.József SOLTI (78').
Referee: Raffaele SCORZONI (ITA)   Attendance: 5.500

14-06-1936   Stadion Hardturm, Zürich:
                Grasshopper-Club Zürich – FK Austria Wien   1-1 (1-0)
Grasshopper-Club Zürich: Willy MAIRE, Severino (Sevi) MINELLI, Walter WEILER (II),
Dr.Sigmund GUTTORMSEN (NOR), Sirio VERNATI (ITA), Oskar RAUCH, Alfred (Fredy)
BICKEL, Heinrich VITA (AUT), Friedrich (Fritz) WAGNER, Max (Xam) ABEGGLEN (II),
Max FAUGUEL. (Coach: Karl RAPPAN (AUT)).
FK Austria Wien: Rudolf ZÖHRER, Wilhelm KOPETKO, Karl SESTA, Karl ADAMEK,
Johann MOCK, Karl GALL, Franz RIEGLER, Josef STROH, Matthias SINDELAR, Camillo
JERUSALEM, Rudolf VIERTL. (Coach: Kálmán KONRÁD (HUN)).
Goals: Grasshopper-Club Zürich: 1-0 Max FAUGUEL (14').
FK Austria Wien: 1-1 Josef STROH (76').
Referee: Pál VON HERTZKA (HUN)   Attendance: 7.000

14-06-1936   Stade Olympique de la Pontaise, Lausanne:
                Lausanne-Sports – SK Zidenice   2-1 (1-0)
Lausanne-Sports: Frank SÉCHEHAYE, August LEHMANN, Hans STALDER, Adolfo
SPILLER, Robert WEILLER (GER), Jean BICHSEL, Adolf STELZER, Lozan KOTSEV
(BUL), Willy JAEGGI (IV), Jacques SPAGNOLI, Jean-Pierre ROCHAT. (Coach: Alwin
RIEMKE (GER)).
SK Zidenice: Karel BURKERT, Jozef NEDER, Karel CERNÝ, Josef SMOLKA, Stephan
POSPICHAL (AUT), Frantisek NOVÁK, Frantisek STERC, Karel NEPALA, Václav PRUSA,
Karel HESS, Oldrich RULC. (Coach: Antonín CARVAN).
Goals: Lausanne-Sports: 1-0 Lozan KOTSEV (15') 2-1 Willy JAEGGI (70').
SK Zidenice: 1-1 Karel NEPALA (65').
Referee: Giuseppe SCARPI (ITA)   Attendance: 6.000

14-06-1936   Campo "Torino" di Corso Filadelfia, Torino: AC Torino – FC Bern   7-1 (2-0)
AC Torino: Giuseppe MAINA, Luigi BRUNELLA, Osvaldo FERRINI, Cesare GALLEA,
Antonio JANNI, Filippo PRATO, Mario BO, Fioravante BALDI (III), Remo GALLI, Pietro
BUSCAGLIA, Onesto SILANO. (Coach: Clemens CARGNELLI (AUT)).
FC Bern: Ernst TREUBERG, Otto HÄNNI, William (Willy) BAUMGARTNER, Hans
LUDER, James Chadwick (Jimmy) TOWNLEY (ENG), Otto KOHLER, Alfons WEBER,
Leo-Paul (Leo) BILLETER, Carlo PINTÉR (HUN), Engelbert BÖSCH, Arturo CAVALLI.
(Coach: Robert PACHE).
Goals: AC Torino: 1-0 Mario BO (14'), 2-0 Pietro BUSCAGLIA (26'), 3-1 Remo GALLI
(62'), 4-1 Fioravante BALDI (70'), 5-1 Fioravante BALDI (78'), 6-1 Pietro BUSCAGLIA
(83'), 7-1 Onesto SILANO (88').
FC Bern: 2-1 Alfons WEBER (49').
Referee: Adolf ROSENBERGER (AUT)   Attendance: 10.000

14-06-1936   Phöbus pálya, Budapest:
            Phöbus FC Budapest – Young Fellows Zürich   6-2 (1-0)
Phöbus FC Budapest: Gyula CSIKÓS, Lajos WÉBER, Jenö FEKETE, Ferenc BORSÁNYI,
Sándor MEGYERI, József PÉTER, Bertalan BÉKY, Sándor SZIKÁR, Dr.József SOLTI,
András TURAY (II), Gábor P.SZABÓ. (Coach: Lajos BÁNYAI).
Young Fellows Zürich: Gustav (Gusti) SCHLEGEL, Georg WIDMER, Hans NYFFELER,
Eduard MÜLLER, Anton CISERI (I), Robert KAES, Eugen DIEBOLD, SACCANI,
Alessandro (Mucho) FRIGERIO, Gustav TÖGEL (AUT), Giuseppe BOSSI. (Coach: József
(Csibi) WINKLER (HUN)).
Goals: Phöbus FC Budapest: 1-0 András TURAY (22'), 2-0 Dr.József SOLTI (69' penalty),
3-1 Gábor P.SZABÓ (79'), 4-1 Dr.József SOLTI (81'), 5-1 Bertalan BÉKY (84'), 6-1 András
TURAY (86').
Young Fellows Zürich: 2-1 Gustav TÖGEL (76'), 6-2 Alessandro (Mucho) FRIGERIO (88').
Referee: Ján BIZÍK (TCH)   Attendance: 4.000

FIRST ROUND

20-06-1936   Stadión Sparta/Letná, Praha:
            AC Sparta Praha – Phöbus FC Budapest   5-2 (2-2)
AC Sparta Praha: Bohumil KLENOVEC, Jaroslav BURGR, Josef CTYROKÝ, Josef
KOSTÁLEK, Jaroslav BOUCEK, Erich SRBEK, Ferdinand FACSINEK, Josef SEDLÁCEK,
Oldrich ZAJÍCEK, Oldrich NEJEDLÝ, Géza KALOCSAY. (Coach: Ferenc SZEDLACSEK
(HUN)).
Phöbus FC Budapest: Gyula CSIKÓS, Lajos WÉBER, Jenö FEKETE, Ferenc BORSÁNYI,
Sándor MEGYERI, József PÉTER, Bertalan BÉKY, Sándor SZIKÁR, Dr.József SOLTI,
András TURAY (II), Gábor P.SZABÓ. (Coach: Lajos BÁNYAI).
Goals: AC Sparta Praha: 1-0 Oldrich NEJEDLÝ (3'), 2-1 Oldrich ZAJÍCEK (34' penalty), 3-2
Ferdinand FACSINEK (49'), 4-1 Oldrich NEJEDLÝ (52'), 5-2 Jaroslav BOUCEK (83').
Phöbus FC Budapest: 1-1 Gábor P.SZABÓ (17'), 2-2 András TURAY (44').
Referee: Hans Walter FRANKENSTEIN (AUT)   Attendance: 18.000

20-06-1936   Hungária körút, Budapest: Hungária FC Budapest – First Vienna FC   0-2 (0-0)
Hungária FC Budapest: Antal SZABÓ, Károly KIS, Sándor BÍRÓ, Gusztáv SEBES, József
TURAY, János DUDÁS, Ferenc SAS, Heinrich MÜLLER (AUT), István KARDOS, László
CSEH, Pál TITKOS. (Coach: Imre SENKEY).
First Vienna FC: Viktor HAVLICEK, Karl RAINER, Willibald SCHMAUS, Otto KALLER,
Leopold HOFMANN, Leonhard MACHU, Josef MOLZER, Friedrich (Fritz) GSCHWEIDL,
Richard FISCHER, Gustav POLLAK, Franz ERDL. (Player-coach: Friedrich (Fritz)
GSCHWEIDL).
Goals: First Vienna FC: 0-1 Franz ERDL (55'), 0-2 Franz ERDL (83').
Referee: Gustav KRIST (TCH)   Attendance: 7.500

21-06-1936   Üllöi ut, Budapest: Ferencvárosi TC Budapest – SK Slavia Praha 5-2 (4-1)
Ferencvárosi TC Budapest: József HÁDA, Lajos KORÁNYI, László PAPP, Béla PÓSA,
Gyula POLGÁR, Gyula LÁZÁR, Mihály TÁNCOS, Gyula KISS, Dr.György SÁROSI, Géza
TOLDI, Tibor KEMÉNY. (Coach: Zoltán BLUM).
SK Slavia Praha: Frantisek PLÁNICKA, Adolf FIALA, Ferdinand DAUCÍK, Karel PRUCHA,
Josef TRUHLÁR, Bedrich JEZBERA, Václav HORÁK, Bedrich VACEK, Vojtech BRADÁC,
Vlastimil KOPECKÝ, Rudolf VYTLACIL (AUT). (Coach: Jan REICHARDT).
Goals: Ferencvárosi TC Budapest: 1-0 Mihály TÁNCOS (5'), 2-0 Dr.György SÁROSI (6'),
3-1 Dr.György SÁROSI (32'), 4-1 Dr.György SÁROSI (35'), 5-2 Dr.György SÁROSI (83'
penalty).
SK Slavia Praha: 2-1 Vojtech BRADÁC (10'), 4-2 Václav HORÁK (54').
Referee: Rinaldo BARLASSINA (ITA)   Attendance: 12.000

21-06-1936   Campo "Torino" di Corso Filadelfia, Torino:
                AC Torino – Újpesti TE   2-0 (1-0)
AC Torino: Giuseppe MAINA, Luigi BRUNELLA, Osvaldo FERRINI, Cesare GALLEA,
Antonio JANNI, Filippo PRATO, Mario BO, Fioravante BALDI (III), Remo GALLI, Pietro
BUSCAGLIA, Onesto SILANO. (Coach: Clemens CARGNELLI (AUT)).
Újpesti TE: György HÓRI, Gyula FUTÓ, László STERNBERG-SÁTORI, Gyula SERES,
György SZÜCS, Antal SZALAY, Ferenc PUSZTAI, Jenö VINCZE, Lipót KÁLLAI, István
BALOGH, Géza KOCSIS. (Coach: Béla JÁNOSY).
Goals: AC Torino: 1-0 Pietro BUSCAGLIA (30'), 2-0 Onesto SILANO (51').
Referee: Ján BIZÍK (TCH)   Attendance: 12.000

21-06-1936   Praterstadion, Wien: WSC Admira Wien – SK Prostejov 0-4 (0-1)
WSC Admira Wien: Peter PLATZER, Robert PAVLICEK, Wilhelm LUDWIG, Johann
URBANEK, Karl HUMMENBERGER, Siegfried JOKSCH, Leopold VOGL, Wilhelm
HAHNEMANN, Karl STOIBER, Josef BICAN, Adolf VOGL. (Coach: Hans SKOLAUT).
SK Prostejov: Frantisek SRÁM, Josef SUCHÝ, Vilém LUGR, Václav BOUSKA, Josef
STROBL (AUT), Oldrich KVAPIL, Leopold HENCL, Ladislav CULÍK, Jan MELKA, Rudolf
DROZD, Antonín DUFEK. (Coach: Rudolf KRENEK).
Goals: SK Prostejov: 0-1 Rudolf DROZD (9'), 0-2 Antonín DUFEK (48'), 0-3 Rudolf DROZD
(78'), 0-4 Rudolf DROZD (84').
Referee: Rinaldo BARLASSINA (ITA)   Attendance: 23.000

21-06-1936   Praterstadion, Wien: SK Rapid Wien – AS Roma 3-1 (2-0)
SK Rapid Wien: Rudolf RAFTL, Karl JESTRAB, Ludwig TAUSCHEK, Franz SMISTIK (II),
Josef (Pepi) SMISTIK (I), Stefan SKOUMAL, Johann OSTERMANN, Johann MEISTER,
Franz BINDER, Walter PROBST, Wilhelm Lukas (Harry) AUREDNIK. (Coach: Eduard
BAUER).
AS Roma: Giovanni ZUCCA, Eraldo MONZEGLIO, Luigi ALLEMANDI, Ernesto TOMASI,
Dr.Fulvio BERNARDINI, Andrea GADALDI, Angelo CATTANEO, Pietro SERANTONI,
Dante DI BENEDETTI, Otello SUBINAGHI, Domenico D'ALBERTO. (Coach: Luigi
BARBESINO).
Goals: SK Rapid Wien: 1-0 Walter PROBST (21'), 2-0 Franz BINDER (30'), 3-1 Franz
BINDER (62').
AS Roma: 2-1 Dante DI BENEDETTI (59').
Referee: Ferenc MAJORSZKY (HUN)   Attendance: 23.000

21-06-1936   Stadio del Littoriale, Bologna: Bologna Sportiva – FK Austria Wien   2-1 (2-0)
Bologna Sportiva: Mario GIANNI, Dino FIORINI, Felice GASPERI, Mario MONTESANTO,
Michele ANDREOLO Frodella (URU), Giordano CORSI, Bruno MAINI, Raffaele SANSONE
(URU), Angelo SCHIAVIO, Francisco FEDULLO (URU), Carlo REGUZZONI. (Coach:
Árpád WEISZ (HUN)).
FK Austria Wien: Rudolf ZÖHRER, Karl ANDRITZ, Karl SESTA, Karl ADAMEK, Johann
MOCK, Walter NAUSCH, Franz RIEGLER, Josef STROH, Matthias SINDELAR, Camillo
JERUSALEM, Rudolf VIERTL. (Coaches: Walter NAUSCH & Kálmán KONRÁD (HUN)).
Goals: Bologna Sportiva: 1-0 Bruno MAINI (6'), 2-0 Angelo SCHIAVIO (21').
FK Austria Wien: 2-1 Rudolf VIERTL (77' penalty).
Referee: Julius BRÜLL (TCH)   Attendance: 13.000

21-06-1936   Na rybnícka, Brno: SK Zidenice – AS Ambrosiana-Inter Milano   2-3 (0-2)
SK Zidenice: Karel BURKERT, Jozef NEDER, Karel CERNÝ, Josef SMOLKA, Stephan
POSPICHAL (AUT), Frantisek NOVÁK, Frantisek STERC, Karel NEPALA, Václav PRUSA,
Karel HESS, Oldrich RULC. (Coach: Antonín CARVAN).
AS Ambrosiana-Inter Milano: Giuseppe PERUCHETTI, Giuseppe BALLERIO, Ernesto
MASCHERONI (URU), Valentino SALA, Egidio TURCHI, Ugo LOCATELLI, Annibale
FROSSI, Attilio José DEMARÍA (I) (ARG), Giuseppe MEAZZA, Giovanni FERRARI, Pietro
FERRARIS (II). (Coach: Gyula FELDMANN (HUN)).
Goals: SK Zidenice: 1-2 Karel NEPALA (51'), 2-2 Karel HESS (73').
AS Ambrosiana-Inter Milano: 0-1 Giuseppe MEAZZA (7'), 0-2 Annibale FROSSI (39'), 2-3
Giuseppe MEAZZA (85').
Referee: Ferenc KLUG (HUN)   Attendance: 19.000
(Giuseppe PERUCHETTI saved a 36th minute penalty).

26-06-1936   Stadión Sparta/Letná, Praha:
                    SK Slavia Praha – Ferencvárosi TC Budapest   4-0 (2-0)
SK Slavia Praha: Frantisek PLÁNICKA, Adolf FIALA, Ferdinand DAUCÍK, Bedrich
JEZBERA, Karel PRUCHA, Josef TRUHLÁR, Václav HORÁK, Bedrich VACEK, Vojtech
BRADÁC, Vlastimil KOPECKÝ, Rudolf VYTLACIL (AUT). (Coach: Jan REICHARDT).
Ferencvárosi TC Budapest: József HÁDA, Lajos KORÁNYI, László PAPP, Béla PÓSA,
Gyula POLGÁR, Gyula LÁZÁR, Mihály TÁNCOS, Gyula KISS, Dr.György SÁROSI, Géza
TOLDI, Tibor KEMÉNY. (Coach: Zoltán BLUM).
Goals: SK Slavia Praha: 1-0 Bedrich VACEK (11'), 2-0 Vlastimil KOPECKÝ (13'), 3-0
Rudolf VYTLACIL (83'), 4-0 Václav HORÁK (87').
Referee: Dr.Adolf MIESZ (AUT)   Attendance: 15.000

27-06-1936   Berlini útca, Budapest: Phöbus FC Budapest – AC Sparta Praha   4-2 (2-0)
Phöbus FC Budapest: Gyula CSIKÓS, Lajos WÉBER, Jenö FEKETE, Ferenc BORSÁNYI,
Sándor MEGYERI, József PÉTER, Bertalan BÉKY, Sándor SZIKÁR, Dr.József SOLTI,
András TURAY (II), Gábor P.SZABÓ. (Coach: Lajos BÁNYAI).
AC Sparta Praha: Bohumil KLENOVEC, Jaroslav BURGR, Josef CTYROKÝ, Josef
KOSTÁLEK, Jaroslav BOUCEK, Erich SRBEK, Ferdinand FACSINEK, Oldrich ZAJÍCEK,
Raymond BRAINE (BEL), Oldrich NEJEDLÝ, Géza KALOCSAY. (Coach: Ferenc
SZEDLACSEK (HUN)).
Goals: Phöbus FC Budapest: 1-0 Sándor SZIKÁR (28'), 2-0 Bertalan BÉKY (37'), 3-1 Gábor
P.SZABÓ (76'), 4-1 Sándor SZIKÁR (87').
AC Sparta Praha: 2-1 Oldrich ZAJÍCEK (49'), 4-2 Oldrich NEJEDLÝ (89').
Referee: Francesco MATTEA (ITA)   Attendance: 15.000

28-06-1936   Praterstadion, Wien: First Vienna FC – Hungária FC Budapest 5-1 (1-0)
First Vienna FC: Viktor HAVLICEK, Karl RAINER, Willibald SCHMAUS, Otto KALLER, Leopold HOFMANN, Leonhard MACHU, Josef MOLZER, Friedrich (Fritz) GSCHWEIDL, Richard FISCHER, Gustav POLLAK, Franz ERDL. (Player-coach: Friedrich (Fritz) GSCHWEIDL).
Hungária FC Budapest: Antal SZABÓ, Károly KIS, Sándor BÍRÓ, Gusztáv SEBES, József TURAY, János DUDÁS, Ferenc SAS, Heinrich MÜLLER (AUT), István KARDOS, László CSEH, Pál TITKOS. (Coach: Imre SENKEY).
Goals: First Vienna FC: 1-0 Friedrich (Fritz) GSCHWEIDL (3'), 2-0 Gustav POLLAK (50'), 3-1 Gustav POLLAK (77'), 4-1 Gustav POLLAK (87'), 5-1 Gustav POLLAK (90').
Hungária FC Budapest: 2-1 Heinrich MÜLLER (60').
Referee: Karl WUNDERLIN (SUI)   Attendance: 32.000

28-06-1936   Megyeri út, Budapest: Újpesti TE – AC Torino 5-0 (1-0)
Újpesti TE: György HÓRI, Gyula FUTÓ, László STERNBERG-SÁTORI, Gyula SERES, György SZÜCS, Antal SZALAY, Ferenc PUSZTAI, Jenő VINCZE, Lipót KÁLLAI, Gyula ZSENGELLÉR, Géza KOCSIS. (Coach: Béla JÁNOSY).
AC Torino: Giuseppe MAINA, Luigi BRUNELLA, Osvaldo FERRINI (expulsion 84'), Cesare GALLEA (expulsion 85'), Antonio JANNI, Filippo PRATO, Mario BO, Fioravante BALDI (III), Remo GALLI, Pietro BUSCAGLIA, Onesto SILANO. (Coach: Clemens CARGNELLI (AUT)).
Goals: Újpesti TE: 1-0 Géza KOCSIS (14'), 2-0 Jenő VINCZE (55'), 3-0 Ferenc PUSZTAI (67'), 4-0 Gyula ZSENGELLÉR (83' penalty), 5-0 Jenő VINCZE (85').
Referee: Bruno PFÜTZNER (TCH)   Attendance: 10.000

28-06-1936   Stadión SK Prostejov, Prostejov: SK Prostejov – WSC Admira Wien 2-3 (0-2)
SK Prostejov: Frantisek SRÁM, Josef SUCHÝ, Vilém LUGR, Václav BOUSKA, Josef STROBL (AUT), Oldrich KVAPIL, Leopold HENCL, Ladislav CULÍK (expulsion 13'), Jan MELKA, Rudolf DROZD, Antonín DUFEK. (Coach: Rudolf KRENEK).
WSC Admira Wien: Peter PLATZER, Wilhelm LUDWIG, Otto MARISCHKA, Siegfried JOKSCH, Johann URBANEK (expulsion 51'), Karl STOIBER (expulsion 70'), Leopold VOGL (expulsion 41'), Wilhelm HAHNEMANN, Karl HUMMENBERGER (expulsion 70'), Josef BICAN (expulsion 85'), Adolf VOGL. (Coach: Hans SKOLAUT).
Goals: SK Prostejov: 1-2 Josef STROBL (67'), 2-3 Rudolf DROZD (89').
WSC Admira Wien: 0-1 Wilhelm HAHNEMANN (2'), 0-2 Josef BICAN (9'), 1-3 Josef BICAN (70').
Referee: Pál VON HERTZKA (HUN)   Attendance: 10.000

28-06-1936   Campo Sportivo Testaccio, Roma: AS Roma – SK Rapid Wien 5-1 (4-0)
AS Roma: Archimede NARDI, Eraldo MONZEGLIO, Andrea GADALDI, Evaristo FRISONI (II), Dr.Fulvio BERNARDINI, Ernesto TOMASI, Angelo CATTANEO, Pietro SERANTONI, Dante DI BENEDETTI, Otello SUBINAGHI, Domenico D'ALBERTO. (Coach: Luigi BARBESINO).
SK Rapid Wien: Rudolf RAFTL, Karl JESTRAB, Ludwig TAUSCHEK, Franz SMISTIK (II), Josef (Pepi) SMISTIK (I), Stefan SKOUMAL, Johann OSTERMANN, Johann MEISTER, Franz BINDER, Walter PROBST, Wilhelm Lukas (Harry) AUREDNIK. (Coach: Eduard BAUER).
Goals: AS Roma: 1-0 Pietro SERANTONI (6'), 2-0 Ludwig TAUSCHEK (21' own goal), 3-0 Pietro SERANTONI (35'), 4-0 Domenico D'ALBERTO (44'), 5-0 Otello SUBINAGHI (50').
SK Rapid Wien: 5-1 Franz BINDER (89').
Referee: William BANGERTER (SUI)   Attendance: 10.000

64

28-06-1936   Praterstadion, Wien. FK Austria Wien – Bologna Sportiva   4-0 (2-0)
FK Austria Wien: Rudolf ZÖHRER, Karl ANDRITZ, Karl SESTA, Karl ADAMEK, Johann
MOCK, Walter NAUSCH, Franz RIEGLER, Josef STROH, Matthias SINDELAR, Camillo
JERUSALEM, Rudolf VIERTL. (Coaches: Kálmán KONRÁD (HUN) & Walter NAUSCH).
Bologna Sportiva: Mario GIANNI, Dino FIORINI, Felice GASPERI, Mario MONTESANTO,
Michele ANDREOLO Frodella (URU), Aldo DONATI, Bruno MAINI, Amedeo BIAVATI,
Raffaele SANSONE (URU), Francisco FEDULLO (URU), Carlo REGUZZONI. (Coach:
Árpád WEISZ (HUN)).
Goals: FK Austria Wien: 1-0 Camillo JERUSALEM (12'), 2-0 Josef STROH (31'), 3-0
Matthias SINDELAR (88'), 4-0 Camillo JERUSALEM (90').
Referee: Mihály Iványi IVÁNCSISC (HUN)   Attendance: 32.000

29-06-1936   Arena Civica, Parco Sempione, Milano:
                AS Ambrosiana-Inter Milano – SK Zidenice   8-1 (4-0)
AS Ambrosiana-Inter Milano: Giuseppe PERUCHETTI, Giuseppe BALLERIO, Ernesto
MASCHERONI (URU), Valentino SALA, Egidio TURCHI, Ugo LOCATELLI, Annibale
FROSSI, Attilio José DEMARÍA (I) (ARG), Giuseppe MEAZZA, Giovanni FERRARI, Pietro
FERRARIS (II). (Coach: Gyula FELDMANN (HUN)).
SK Zidenice: Karel BURKERT, Jozef NEDER, Karel CERNÝ, Josef SMOLKA, Stephan
POSPICHAL (AUT), Antonín SUCHÁNEK, Frantisek STERC, Karel NEPALA, Václav
PRUSA, Karel HESS, Oldrich RULC. (Coach: Antonín CARVAN).
Goals: AS Ambrosiana-Inter Milano: 1-0 Giuseppe MEAZZA (3'), 2-0 Attilio José
DEMARÍA (4'), 3-0 Giuseppe MEAZZA (17'), 4-0 Annibale FROSSI (18'), 5-0 Giuseppe
MEAZZA (57'), 6-0 Giovanni FERRARI (60'), 7-0 Giuseppe MEAZZA (81'), 8-0 Giuseppe
MEAZZA (85').
SK Zidenice: 8-1 Karel HESS (89').
Referee: Alois BERANEK (AUT)   Attendance: 15.000

QUARTER-FINALS

04-07-1936   Stadión Sparta/Letná, Praha: AC Sparta Praha – AS Roma   3-0 (2-0)
AC Sparta Praha: Bohumil KLENOVEC, Josef KOSTÁLEK, Josef CTYROKÝ, Ludovít
RADÓ, Jaroslav BOUCEK, Erich SRBEK, Ferdinand FACSINEK, Oldrich ZAJÍCEK,
Raymond BRAINE (BEL), Oldrich NEJEDLÝ, Géza KALOCSAY. (Coach: Ferenc
SZEDLACSEK (HUN)).
AS Roma: Archimede NARDI, Eraldo MONZEGLIO, Andrea GADALDI, Evaristo FRISONI
(II), Dr.Fulvio BERNARDINI, Ernesto TOMASI, Angelo CATTANEO, Pietro SERANTONI,
Dante DI BENEDETTI, Otello SUBINAGHI, Domenico D'ALBERTO. (Coach: Luigi
BARBESINO).
Goals: AC Sparta Praha: 1-0 Oldrich ZAJÍCEK (19'), 2-0 Ferdinand FACSINEK (45'), 3-0
Oldrich NEJEDLÝ (69').
Referee: Mihály Iványi IVÁNCSISC (HUN)   Attendance: 19.000

05-07-1936   Stadión SK Prostejov, Prostejov: SK Prostejov – Újpesti TE   0-1 (0-0)
SK Prostejov: Frantisek SRÁM, Josef SUCHÝ, Vilém LUGR, Václav BOUSKA, Josef
STROBL (AUT), Oldrich KVAPIL, Leopold HENCL, Alois SEPER, Jan MELKA, Rudolf
DROZD, Antonín DUFEK. (Coach: Rudolf KRENEK).
Újpesti TE: György HÓRI, Gyula FUTÓ, László STERNBERG-SÁTORI, Gyula SERES,
György SZÜCS, Antal SZALAY, Ferenc PUSZTAI, Jenö VINCZE, Lipót KÁLLAI, Gyula
ZSENGELLÉR, Géza KOCSIS. (Coach: Béla JÁNOSY).
Goal: Újpesti TE: 0-1 Gyula ZSENGELLÉR (56').
Referee: Rinaldo BARLASSINA (ITA)   Attendance: 7.000

05-07-1936   Praterstadion, Wien: First Vienna FC – AS Ambrosiana-Inter Milano   2-0 (2-0)
First Vienna FC: Viktor HAVLICEK, Karl RAINER, Willibald SCHMAUS, Otto KALLER, Leopold HOFMANN, Leonhard MACHU, Josef MOLZER, Friedrich (Fritz) GSCHWEIDL, Richard FISCHER, Gustav POLLAK, Franz ERDL. (Player-coach: Friedrich (Fritz) GSCHWEIDL).
AS Ambrosiana-Inter Milano: Giuseppe PERUCHETTI, Giuseppe BALLERIO, Ernesto MASCHERONI (URU), Valentino SALA, Egidio TURCHI, Ugo LOCATELLI, Annibale FROSSI, Attilio José DEMARÍA (I) (ARG), Giuseppe MEAZZA, Giovanni FERRARI, Pietro FERRARIS (II). (Coach: Gyula FELDMANN (HUN)).
Goals: First Vienna FC: 1-0 Leonhard MACHU (33' penalty), 2-0 Gustav POLLAK (37').
Referee: Gustav KRIST (TCH)   Attendance: 37.000

05-07-1936   Praterstadion, Wien: FK Austria Wien – SK Slavia Praha   3-0 (0-0)
FK Austria Wien: Rudolf ZÖHRER, Karl ANDRITZ, Karl SESTA, Karl ADAMEK, Johann MOCK, Walter NAUSCH, Franz RIEGLER, Josef STROH, Matthias SINDELAR, Camillo JERUSALEM, Rudolf VIERTL. (Coaches: Kálmán KONRÁD (HUN) & Walter NAUSCH).
SK Slavia Praha: Frantisek PLÁNICKA, Adolf FIALA, Ferdinand DAUCÍK, Antonín VODICKA, Karel PRUCHA, Josef TRUHLÁR, Václav HORÁK, Bedrich VACEK, Vojtech BRADÁC, Vlastimil KOPECKÝ, Rudolf VYTLACIL (AUT). (Coach: Jan REICHARDT).
Goals: FK Austria Wien: 1-0 Franz RIEGLER (61'), 2-0 Josef STROH (68'), 3-0 Camillo JERUSALEM (84').
Referee: Ferenc MAJORSZKY (HUN)   Attendance: 23.000

12-07-1936   Campo Sportivo Testaccio, Roma: AS Roma – AC Sparta Praha   1-1 (1-1)
AS Roma: Guido MASETTI, Eraldo MONZEGLIO, Luigi ALLEMANDI, Evaristo FRISONI (II), Dr.Fulvio BERNARDINI, Ernesto TOMASI, Angelo CATTANEO, Pietro SERANTONI, Dante DI BENEDETTI, Otello SUBINAGHI, Domenico D'ALBERTO. (Coach: Luigi BARBESINO).
AC Sparta Praha: Bohumil KLENOVEC, Josef KOSTÁLEK, Josef CTYROKÝ, Ludovít RADÓ, Jaroslav BOUCEK, Erich SRBEK, Ferdinand FACSINEK, Oldrich ZAJÍCEK, Raymond BRAINE (BEL), Oldrich NEJEDLÝ, Géza KALOCSAY. (Coach: Ferenc SZEDLACSEK (HUN)).
Goals: AS Roma: 1-0 Dante DI BENEDETTI (1').
AC Sparta Praha: 1-1 Ferdinand FACSINEK (2').
Referee: Dr.Adolf MIESZ (AUT)   Attendance: 12.000

12-07-1936   Megyeri ut, Budapest: Újpesti TE – SK Prostejov   2-0 (2-0)
Újpesti TE: György HÓRI, Gyula FUTÓ, László STERNBERG-SÁTORI, Gyula SERES, György SZÜCS, Antal SZALAY, Ferenc PUSZTAI, Jenö VINCZE, Lipót KÁLLAI, Gyula ZSENGELLÉR, Géza KOCSIS. (Coach: Béla JÁNOSY).
SK Prostejov: Frantisek SRÁM, Josef SUCHÝ, Vilém LUGR, Václav BOUSKA, Josef STROBL (AUT), Oldrich KVAPIL, Leopold HENCL, Ladislav CULIK, Jan MELKA, Rudolf DROZD, Antonín DUFEK. (Coach: Rudolf KRENEK).
Goals: Újpesti TE: 1-0 Géza KOCSIS (25'), 2-0 Lipót KÁLLAI (27').
Referee: Hans Walter FRANKENSTEIN (AUT)   Attendance: 12.000

12-07-1936   Arena Civica, Parco Sempione, Milano:
AS Ambrosiana-Inter Milano – First Vienna FC   4-1 (1-1)
AS Ambrosiana-Inter Milano: Giuseppe PERUCHETTI, Giuseppe BALLERIO, Ernesto
MASCHERONI (URU), Valentino SALA, Egidio TURCHI, Ugo LOCATELLI, Annibale
FROSSI, Attilio José DEMARÍA (I) (ARG), Giuseppe MEAZZA, Giovanni FERRARI, Pietro
FERRARIS (II). (Coach: Gyula FELDMANN (HUN)).
First Vienna FC: Viktor HAVLICEK, Karl RAINER, Willibald SCHMAUS, Otto KALLER,
Leopold HOFMANN, Leonhard MACHU, Josef MOLZER, Friedrich (Fritz) GSCHWEIDL,
Franz ERDL, Gustav POLLAK, Wilhelm HOLEC. (Player-coach: Friedrich (Fritz)
GSCHWEIDL).
Goals: AS Ambrosiana-Inter Milano: 1-0 Giuseppe MEAZZA (9'), 2-1 Pietro FERRARIS
(46'), 3-1 Pietro FERRARIS (65'), 4-1 Attilio José DEMARÍA (82').
First Vienna FC: 1-1 Wilhelm HOLEC (38').
Referee: Ferenc KLUG (HUN)   Attendance: 15.000
(Egidio TURCHI missed a 62nd minute penalty).

13-07-1936   Stadión Slavia/Letná, Praha: SK Slavia Praha – FK Austria Wien   1-0 (0-0)
SK Slavia Praha: Frantisek PLÁNICKA, Adolf FIALA, Ferdinand DAUCÍK, Josef
TRUHLÁR, Karel PRUCHA, Rudolf KRCIL, Václav HORÁK, Bedrich VACEK, Vojtech
BRADÁC, Vlastimil KOPECKÝ, Rudolf VYTLACIL (AUT). (Coach: Jan REICHARDT).
FK Austria Wien: Rudolf ZÖHRER, Karl ANDRITZ, Karl SESTA, Karl ADAMEK
(expulsion 80'), Johann MOCK, Walter NAUSCH, Franz RIEGLER, Josef STROH, Matthias
SINDELAR, Camillo JERUSALEM, Rudolf VIERTL. (Coaches: Kálmán KONRÁD (HUN)
& Walter NAUSCH).
Goal: SK Slavia Praha: 1-0 Vojtech BRADÁC (66').
Referee: Raffaele SCORZONI (ITA)   Attendance: 26.000

SEMI-FINALS

19-07-1936   Megyeri út, Budapest: Újpesti TE – FK Austria Wien 1-2 (1-0)
Újpesti TE: György HÓRI, Gyula FUTÓ, László STERNBERG-SÁTORI, Gyula SERES,
György SZÜCS, Antal SZALAY, Jenö VINCZE, Lipót KÁLLAI, Gyula ZSENGELLÉR,
Géza KOCSIS, Ferenc PUSZTAI. (Coach: Béla JÁNOSY).
FK Austria Wien: Rudolf ZÖHRER, Karl ANDRITZ, Karl SESTA, Karl ADAMEK, Johann
MOCK, Walter NAUSCH, Franz RIEGLER, Josef STROH, Matthias SINDELAR, Camillo
JERUSALEM, Rudolf VIERTL. (Coaches: Kálmán KONRÁD (HUN) & Walter NAUSCH).
Goals: Újpesti TE: 1-0 Lipót KÁLLAI (4').
FK Austria Wien: 1-1 Josef STROH (64'), 1-2 Rudolf VIERTL (80').
Referee: Rinaldo BARLASSINA (ITA)   Attendance: 12.000

19-07-1936   Arena Civica, Parco Sempione, Milano:
            AS Ambrosiana-Inter Milano – AC Sparta Praha   3-5 (3-3)
AS Ambrosiana-Inter Milano: Giuseppe PERUCHETTI, Giuseppe BALLERIO, Ernesto
MASCHERONI (URU), Valentino SALA, Egidio TURCHI, Ugo LOCATELLI, Annibale
FROSSI, Attilio José DEMARÍA (I) (ARG), Giuseppe MEAZZA, Giovanni FERRARI, Pietro
FERRARIS (II). (Coach: Gyula FELDMANN (HUN)).
AC Sparta Praha: Bohumil KLENOVEC, Josef KOSTÁLEK, Josef CTYROKÝ, Ludovít
RADÓ, Jaroslav BOUCEK, Erich SRBEK, Ferdinand FACSINEK, Oldrich ZAJÍCEK,
Raymond BRAINE (BEL), Oldrich NEJEDLÝ, Géza KALOCSAY. (Coach: Ferenc
SZEDLACSEK (HUN)).
Goals: AS Ambrosiana-Inter Milano: 1-2 Giovanni FERRARI (15'), 2-2 Giuseppe MEAZZA
(31'), 3-2 Pietro FERRARIS (36').
AC Sparta Praha: 0-1 Oldrich NEJEDLÝ (9'), 0-2 Raymond BRAINE (12'), 3-3 Oldrich
NEJEDLÝ (39'), 3-4 Raymond BRAINE (72'), 3-5 Oldrich ZAJÍCEK (80').
Referee: Dr.Adolf MIESZ (AUT)   Attendance: 19.000

26-07-1936   Praterstadion, Wien: FK Austria Wien – Újpesti TE 5-2 (1-1)
FK Austria Wien: Rudolf ZÖHRER, Karl ANDRITZ, Karl SESTA, Karl ADAMEK, Johann
MOCK, Walter NAUSCH, Franz RIEGLER, Josef STROH, Matthias SINDELAR, Camillo
JERUSALEM, Rudolf VIERTL. (Coaches: Kálmán KONRÁD (HUN) & Walter NAUSCH).
Újpesti TE: György HÓRI, Gyula FUTÓ, László STERNBERG-SÁTORI, Gyula SERES,
György SZÜCS, Antal SZALAY, Jenö VINCZE, Lipót KÁLLAI, Gyula ZSENGELLÉR,
Géza KOCSIS, Ferenc PUSZTAI. (Coach: Béla JÁNOSY).
Goals: FK Austria Wien: 1-1 Camillo JERUSALEM (37'), 2-2 Matthias SINDELAR (53'), 3-2
Camillo JERUSALEM (56'), 4-2 Matthias SINDELAR (65'), 5-2 Josef STROH (68').
Újpesti TE: 0-1 Gyula ZSENGELLÉR (10'), 1-2 Gyula ZSENGELLÉR (49').
Referee: Gustav KRIST (TCH)   Attendance: 37.000

26-07-1936   Stadión Sparta/Letná, Praha:
            AC Sparta Praha – AS Ambrosiana-Inter Milano 3-2 (1-1)
AC Sparta Praha: Bohumil KLENOVEC, Josef KOSTÁLEK, Josef CTYROKÝ, Ludovít
RADÓ, Jaroslav BOUCEK, Erich SRBEK, Ferdinand FACSINEK, Oldrich ZAJÍCEK,
Raymond BRAINE (BEL), Oldrich NEJEDLÝ, Géza KALOCSAY. (Coach: Ferenc
SZEDLACSEK (HUN)).
AS Ambrosiana-Inter Milano: Giuseppe PERUCHETTI, Giuseppe BALLERIO, Ernesto
MASCHERONI (URU), Piero ANTONA, Egidio TURCHI, Ugo LOCATELLI, Annibale
FROSSI, Giuseppe MEAZZA, Giovanni FERRARI, Pietro FERRARIS (II), Eligio VECCHI.
(Coach: Gyula FELDMANN (HUN)).
Goals: AC Sparta Praha: 1-0 Raymond BRAINE (10'), 2-1 Oldrich ZAJÍCEK (59' penalty),
3-2 Raymond BRAINE (83').
AS Ambrosiana-Inter Milano: 1-1 Giuseppe MEAZZA (15'), 2-2 Annibale FROSSI (71').
Referee: Alois BERANEK (AUT)   Attendance: 36.000

06-09-1936   Praterstadion, Wien: FK Austria Wien – AC Sparta Praha   0-0
FK Austria Wien: Rudolf ZÖHRER, Karl ANDRITZ, Karl SESTA, Karl ADAMEK, Johann
MOCK, Walter NAUSCH, Franz RIEGLER, Josef STROH, Matthias SINDELAR, Camillo
JERUSALEM, Rudolf VIERTL. (Coaches: Kálmán KONRÁD (HUN) & Walter NAUSCH).
AC Sparta Praha: Bohumil KLENOVEC, Jaroslav BURGR, Josef CTYROKÝ, Josef
KOSTÁLEK, Jaroslav BOUCEK, Ludovít RADÓ, Ferdinand FACSINEK, Oldrich ZAJÍCEK,
Raymond BRAINE (BEL), Oldrich NEJEDLÝ, Géza KALOCSAY. (Coach: Ferenc
SZEDLACSEK (HUN)).
Referee: Giuseppe SCARPI (ITA)   Attendance: 41.600

13-09-1936   Stadión Strahov (Masaryk), Praha:
                     AC Sparta Praha – FK Austria Wien   0-1 (0-0)
AC Sparta Praha: Bohumil KLENOVEC, Jaroslav BURGR, Josef CTYROKÝ, Josef
KOSTÁLEK, Jaroslav BOUCEK, Ludovít RADÓ, Ferdinand FACSINEK, Oldrich ZAJÍCEK,
Raymond BRAINE (BEL), Oldrich NEJEDLÝ, Géza KALOCSAY. (Coach: Ferenc
SZEDLACSEK (HUN)).
FK Austria Wien: Rudolf ZÖHRER, Karl ANDRITZ, Karl SESTA, Karl ADAMEK, Johann
MOCK, Walter NAUSCH, Franz RIEGLER, Josef STROH, Matthias SINDELAR, Camillo
JERUSALEM, Rudolf VIERTL. (Coaches: Kálmán KONRÁD (HUN) & Walter NAUSCH).
Goal: FK Austria Wien: 0-1 Camillo JERUSALEM (67').
Referee: Rinaldo BARLASSINA (ITA)   Attendance: 58.000

*** FK Austria Wien won the Cup ***

69

1937

12-06-1937   Arena Venus, Bucursti: ASC Venus Bucuresti – Újpesti TE   4-6 (1-2)
ASC Venus Bucuresti: Carol BURDAN, Lazar SFERA, Gheorghe ALBU, Andrei
BARBULESCU, Vasile GAIN, Nicolae GORGORIN, Silviu PLOESTEANU, Iuliu BODOLA,
Constantin (Kostas) HUMIS (GRE), Petr VÂLCOV, Lucian GRUIN. (Coach: Ferenc
PLATTKÓ (HUN)).
Újpesti TE: László HAVAS, Gyula FUTÓ, Péter JOÓS, Gyula SERES, György SZÜCS, Antal
SZALAY, Ferenc PUSZTAI, Géza KOCSIS, Lipót KÁLLAI, Gyula ZSENGELLÉR, Mátyás
TÓTH. (Coach: Béla JÁNOSY).
Goals: ASC Venus Bucuresti: 1-1 Constantin (Kostas) HUMIS (25'), 2-2 Silviu
PLOESTEANU (47'), 3-2 Lucian GRUIN (55'), 4-3 Constantin (Kostas) HUMIS (71').
Újpesti TE: 0-1 Mátyás TÓTH (15'), 1-2 Lipót KÁLLAI (35'), 3-3 Gyula ZSENGELLÉR
(60'), 4-4 Géza KOCSIS (72'), 4-5 Gyula ZSENGELLÉR (81'), 4-6 Gyula ZSENGELLÉR
(90').
Referee: Bruno PFÜTZNER (TCH)   Attendance: 18.000
(Iuliu BODOLA was also known as Gyula BODOLA)
(Constantin (Kostas) HUMIS name in Greek was Kostas CHOUMIS)

13-06-1937   Stadion Hardturm, Zürich: Grasshopper-Club Zürich – SK Prostejov   4-3 (2-0)
Grasshopper-Club Zürich: Willy HUBER, Severino (Sevi) MINELLI, Walter WEILER (II),
Hermann SPRINGER, Sirio VERNATI, Dr.Sigmund GUTTORMSEN (NOR), Alfred (Fredy)
BICKEL, Friedrich (Fritz) WAGNER, Eugen RUPF, Max (Xam) ABEGGLEN (II), Max
FAUGUEL. (Coach: Karl RAPPAN (AUT)).
SK Prostejov: Frantisek RITICKA, Karel BERNÁSEK, Rudolf KOS, Václav BOUSKA, Josef
STROBL (AUT), Oldrich KVAPIL, Rudolf DROZD, Vojtech KASTL (expulsion 90'), Jan
MELKA, Frantisek KUCHTA, Antonín DUFEK. (Coach: Rudolf KRENEK).
Goals: Grasshopper-Club Zürich: 1-0 Eugen RUPF (20'), 2-0 Eugen RUPF (33'), 3-1 Severino
(Sevi) MINELLI (51' penalty), 4-3 Alfred (Fredy) BICKEL (78').
SK Prostejov: 2-1 Frantisek KUCHTA (47'), 3-2 Jan MELKA (55'), 3-3 Jan MELKA (59').
Referee: Hans Walter FRANKENSTEIN (AUT)   Attendance: 3.500
(Frantisek RITICKA saved an 88th minute penalty taken by Eugen RUPF)
(Sirio VERNATI had become a naturalised Swiss)

13-06-1937   Stadio del Littoriale, Bologna: Bologna AGC – FK Austria Wien   1-2 (1-0)
Bologna AGC: Carlo CERESOLI, Dino FIORINI, Felice GASPERI, Mario MONTESANTO,
Michele ANDREOLO Frodella (URU), Giordano CORSI, Giovanni BUSONI, Raffaele
SANSONE (URU), Angelo SCHIAVIO, Francisco FEDULLO (URU), Carlo REGUZZONI.
(Coach: Árpád WEISZ (HUN)).
FK Austria Wien: Rudolf ZÖHRER, Wilhelm KOPETKO, Karl SESTA, Karl ADAMEK,
Johann MOCK, Karl ANDRITZ, Franz RIEGLER, Walter NAUSCH, Matthias SINDELAR,
Camillo JERUSALEM, Leopold NEUMER. (Coaches: Matthias SINDELAR & Walter
NAUSCH).
Goals: Bologna AGC: 1-0 Carlo REGUZZONI (35').
FK Austria Wien: 1-1 Leopold NEUMER (66'), 1-2 Matthias SINDELAR (75').
Referee: Pál VON HERTZKA (HUN)   Attendance: 17.000

13-06-1937   Stadión Slavia/Letnán, Praha:
            SK Slavia Praha – Ferencvárosi TC Budapest   2-2 (1-1)
SK Slavia Praha: Frantisek PLÁNICKA, Adolf FIALA, Ferdinand DAUCÍK, Antonín
VODICKA, Karel PRUCHA, Josef TRUHLÁR, Rudolf TOMAN, Bedrich VACEK, Jirí
SOBOTKA, Vlastimil KOPECKÝ, Rudolf VYTLACIL (AUT). (Coach: Jan REICHARDT).
Ferencvárosi TC Budapest: József HÁDA, Sándor TÁTRAI, Lajos KORÁNYI, László
HÁMORI, Gyula POLGÁR, Gyula LÁZÁR, Mihály TÁNCOS, Gyula KISS, Dr.György
SÁROSI, Géza TOLDI, Tibor KEMÉNY. (Coach: József SÁNDOR).
Goals: SK Slavia Praha: 1-0 Jirí SOBOTKA (20'), 2-2 Rudolf VYTLACIL (89').
Ferencvárosi TC Budapest: 1-1 Dr.György SÁROSI (31'), 1-2 Géza TOLDI (65').
Referee: Giuseppe SCARPI (ITA)   Attendance: 23.000

13-06-1937   Hungária körút, Budapest: Hungária FC Budapest – SS Lazio Roma 1-1 (0-0)
Hungária FC Budapest: Antal SZABÓ, Károly KIS, Sándor BÍRÓ, Gusztáv SEBES, József
TURAY, János DUDÁS, Ferenc SAS, Heinrich MÜLLER (AUT), László CSEH, István
KARDOS, Pál TITKOS. (Coach: Alfréd SCHAFFER).
SS Lazio Roma: Giacomo BLASON, Benedetto ZACCONI, Alfredo MONZA, Giuseppe
BALDO, Giuseppe VIANI, Luigi MILANO, Umberto BUSANI, Libero Turiddo MARCHINI,
Silvio PIOLA, Giovanni RICCARDI, Giovanni COSTA. (Coach: József VIOLA (HUN)).
Goals: Hungária FC Budapest: 1-1 László CSEH (69').
SS Lazio Roma: 0-1 Silvio PIOLA (57').
Referee: Gustav KRIST (TCH)   Attendance: 8.000

13-06-1937   Praterstadion, Wien: WSC Admira Wien – AC Sparta Praha 1-1 (0-0)
WSC Admira Wien: Peter PLATZER, Anton SCHALL, Otto MARISCHKA, Johann
URBANEK, Willibald HAHN, Siegfried JOKSCH, Leopold VOGL, Wilhelm
HAHNEMANN, Karl STOIBER, Franz SCHILLING, Adolf VOGL. (Coach: Hans
SKOLAUT).
AC Sparta Praha: Bohumil KLENOVEC, Jaroslav BURGR, Josef CTYROKÝ, Josef
KOSTÁLEK, Jaroslav BOUCEK, Karel KOLSKÝ, Ferdinand FACSINEK, Karel SENECKÝ,
Oldrich ZAJÍCEK, Oldrich NEJEDLÝ, Géza KALOCSAY. (Coach: Ferenc SZEDLACSEK
(HUN)).
Goals: WSC Admira Wien: 1-0 Karl STOIBER (55').
AC Sparta Praha: 1-1 Karel SENECKÝ (73').
Referee: Rinaldo BARLASSINA (ITA)   Attendance: 22.000

13-06-1937   Praterstadion, Wien: First Vienna FC – Young Fellows Zürich 2-1 (1-1)
First Vienna FC: Viktor HAVLICEK, Karl RAINER, Willibald SCHMAUS, Otto KALLER,
Leopold HOFMANN, Leonhard MACHU, Josef MOLZER, Friedrich (Fritz) GSCHWEIDL,
Richard FISCHER, Ferdinand BARILLY, Franz ERDL. (Player-coach: Friedrich (Fritz)
GSCHWEIDL).
Young Fellows Zürich: Gustav (Gusti) SCHLEGEL, Karl KUHN, Hans NYFFELER, Robert
KAES, VONTHRON, Eduard MÜLLER, Eugen DIEBOLD, René SAUVAIN, PALI,
Alessandro (Mucho) FRIGERIO, LIENHARD. (Coach: Otto HAFTL (GER)).
Goals: First Vienna FC: 1-1 Friedrich (Fritz) GSCHWEIDL (36'), 2-1 Josef MOLZER (76').
Young Fellows Zürich: 0-1 LIENHARD (18').
Referee: Jaroslac VLCEK (TCH)   Attendance: 23.000

71

13-06-1937   Stadio "Luigi Ferraris", Marassi, Genova:
          AC Genova 1893 – HSK Gradanski Zagreb 3-1 (2-0)
AC Genova 1893: Manlio BACIGALUPO, Paolo AGOSTEO, Mario GENTA, Pietro
PASTORINO, Giuseppe BIGOGNO, Emanuele FRIGLIOLA, Pietro ARCARI (III), Mario
PERAZZOLO, Carlo SERVETTI, Luigi SCARABELLO, Alfredo MARCHIONNESCHI.
(Coach: Hermann FELSNER (AUT)).
HSK Gradanski Zagreb: Franja GLAZER, Bernard HÜGL, August BIVEC, Dimitruje
KOVACEVIC, Ivan JAZBINSEK, Mirko KOKOTOVIC, Ivan MEDARIC, Milan
ANTOLKOVIC, August LESNIK, Svetozar DJANIC, Branko PLESE. (Coach: Márton
BUKOVI (HUN)).
Goals: AC Genova 1893: 1-0 Pietro ARCARI (4'), 2-0 Paolo AGOSTEO (30' penalty), 3-0
Carlo SERVETTI (47').
HSK Gradanski Zagreb: 3-1 Mirko KOKOTOVIC (68' penalty).
Referee: Mihály Iványi IVÁNCSISC (HUN)   Attendance: 12.000

20-06-1937   Megyeri út, Budapest: Újpesti TE – ASC Venus Bucuresti 4-1 (2-0)
Újpesti TE: László HAVAS, Gyula FUTÓ, Péter JOÓS, Gyula SERES, György SZÜCS, Antal
SZALAY, Géza KOCSIS, Jenö VINCZE, Lipót KÁLLAI, Gyula ZSENGELLÉR, Mátyás
TÓTH. (Coach: Béla JÁNOSY).
ASC Venus Bucuresti: Nicolae IORADCHESCU, Lazar SFERA, Gheorghe ALBU, Alfred
EISENBEISSER, Vasile GAIN, Theodor BEFFA (GRE), Silviu PLOESTEANU, Iuliu
BODOLA, Constantin (Kostas) HUMIS (GRE), Petr VÂLCOV, Lucian GRUIN. (Coach:
Ferenc PLATTKÓ (HUN)).
Goals: Újpesti TE: 1-0 Gyula ZSENGELLÉR (29'), 2-0 Jenö VINCZE (43'), 3-0 Lipót
KÁLLAI (63'), 4-1 Gyula ZSENGELLÉR (84').
ASC Venus Bucuresti: 3-1 Constantin (Kostas) HUMIS (63').
Referee: Francesco MATTEA (ITA)   Attendance: 7.500
(Alfred EISENBEISSER was also known as Alfred (Fredi) FIERARU – this was the Romanian
verson of his name).

20-06-1937   Stadión SK Prostejov, Prostejov:
          SK Prostejov – Grasshopper-Club Zürich 2-2 (1-1)
SK Prostejov: Frantisek RITICKA, Karel BERNÁSEK, Rudolf KOS, Václav BOUSKA, Josef
STROBL (AUT), Oldrich KVAPIL, Bohumil PROSEK, Rudolf DROZD, Jan MELKA,
Frantisek KUCHTA, Antonín DUFEK. (Coach: Rudolf KRENEK).
Grasshopper-Club Zürich: Willy HUBER, Severino (Sevi) MINELLI, Walter WEILER (II),
Oskar RAUCH, Sirio VERNATI, Hermann SPRINGER, Alfred (Fredy) BICKEL, Josef
ARTIMOVIC (AUT), Eugen RUPF, Max (Xam) ABEGGLEN (II), Max FAUGUEL. (Coach:
Karl RAPPAN (AUT)).
Goals: SK Prostejov: 1-0 Frantisek KUCHTA (8'), 2-2 Rudolf DROZD (70').
Grasshopper-Club Zürich: 1-1 Eugen RUPF (24'), 1-2 ARTMOVIC (55').
Referee: Mihajlo POPOVIC (YUG)   Attendance: 8.000

72

20-06-1937   Stadion Gradanski, Zagreb:
HSK Gradanski Zagreb – AC Genova 1893   0 3 (0-3)
HSK Gradanski Zagreb: Franja GLAZER, Bernard HÜGL, August BIVEC, Dimitruje
KOVACEVIC, Ivan JAZBINSEK, Mirko KOKOTOVIC, Ivan MEDARIC, Milan
ANTOLKOVIC, August LESNIK, Svetozar DJANIC, Branko PLESE. (Coach: Márton
BUKOVI (HUN)).
AC Genova 1893: Manlio BACIGALUPO, Paolo AGOSTEO, Mario GENTA, Pietro
PASTORINO, Giuseppe BIGOGNO, Mario PERAZZOLO, Pietro ARCARI (III), Cesare
Augsuto FASANELLI, Carlo SERVETTI, Luigi SCARABELLO, Alfredo
MARCHIONNESCHI. (Coach: Hermann FELSNER (AUT)).
Goals: AC Genova 1893: 0-1 Alfredo MARCHIONNESCHI (6'), 0-2 Carlo SERVETTI (12'),
0-3 Cesare Augsuto FASANELLI (43').
Referee: Alois BERANEK (AUT)   Attendance: 7.000

25-06-1937   Praterstadion, Wien: FK Austria Wien – Bologna AGC   5-1 (2-0)
FK Austria Wien: Rudolf ZÖHRER, Wilhelm KOPETKO, Karl SESTA, Karl ADAMEK,
Johann MOCK, Karl ANDRITZ, Franz RIEGLER, Walter NAUSCH, Matthias SINDELAR,
Camillo JERUSALEM, Leopold NEUMER. (Coaches: Matthias SINDELAR & Walter
NAUSCH).
Bologna AGC: Carlo CERESOLI, Dino FIORINI, Felice GASPERI, Mario MONTESANTO,
Michele ANDREOLO Frodella (URU), Giordano CORSI, Bruno MAINI, Raffaele SANSONE
(URU), Angelo SCHIAVIO, Francisco FEDULLO (URU), Carlo REGUZZONI. (Coach:
Árpád WEISZ (HUN)).
Goals: FK Austria Wien: 1-0 Matthias SINDELAR (3'), 2-0 Walter NAUSCH (18'), 3-0
Walter NAUSCH (59'), 4-0 Walter NAUSCH (62'), 5-0 Camillo JERUSALEM (82').
Bologna AGC: 5-1 Angelo SCHIAVIO (90').
Referee: Bohumil ZENÍSEK (TCH)   Attendance: 38.000

25-06-1937   Stadión Sparta/Letná, Praha: AC Sparta Praha – WSC Admira Wien   2-2 (2-2)
AC Sparta Praha: Bohumil KLENOVEC, Jaroslav BURGR, Josef CTYROKÝ, Josef
KOSTÁLEK, Jaroslav BOUCEK, Karel KOLSKÝ, Ferdinand FACSINEK, Karel SENECKÝ,
Josef ZEMAN, Oldrich NEJEDLÝ, Géza KALOCSAY. (Coach: Ferenc SZEDLACSEK
(HUN)).
WSC Admira Wien: Peter PLATZER, Anton SCHALL, Otto MARISCHKA, Johann
URBANEK, Willibald HAHN, Siegfried JOKSCH, Leopold VOGL, Wilhelm
HAHNEMANN, Karl STOIBER, Franz SCHILLING, Adolf VOGL. (Coach: Hans
SKOLAUT).
Goals: AC Sparta Praha: 1-0 Karel SENECKÝ (8'), 2-2 Josef ZEMAN (19').
WSC Admira Wien: 1-1 Wilhelm HAHNEMANN (11'), 1-2 Leopold VOGL (14').
Referee: Gábor BORONKAY (HUN)   Attendance: 30.000

27-06-1937   Üllöi út, Budapest: Ferencvárosi FC Budapest – SK Slavia Praha   3-1 (1-0)
Ferencvárosi TC Budapest: József HÁDA, Sándor TÁTRAI, Lajos KORÁNYI, László
HÁMORI, Gyula POLGÁR, Gyula LÁZÁR, Mihály TÁNCOS, Gyula KISS, Dr.György
SÁROSI, Géza TOLDI, Tibor KEMÉNY. (Coach: József SÁNDOR).
SK Slavia Praha: Frantisek PLÁNICKA, Adolf FIALA, Ferdinand DAUCÍK, Antonín
VODICKA, Karel PRUCHA, Josef TRUHLÁR, Václav HORÁK, Frantisek SVOBODA, Jirí
SOBOTKA, Vlastimil KOPECKÝ, Antonín PUC. (Coach: Jan REICHARDT).
Goals: Ferencvárosi TC Budapest: 1-0 Géza TOLDI (32'), 2-0 Dr.György SÁROSI (55'), 3-0
Géza TOLDI (65').
SK Slavia Praha: 4-1 Antonín PUC (89').
Referee: Dr.Adolf MIESZ (AUT)   Attendance: 20.000

73

27-06-1937   Stadio Nazionale del Partito Nazionale Fascista, Roma:
                SS Lazio Roma – Hungária FC Budapest   3-2 (2-0)
SS Lazio Roma: Giacomo BLASON, Benedetto ZACCONI, Alfredo MONZA, Giuseppe
BALDO, Giuseppe VIANI, Luigi MILANO, Umberto BUSANI, Libero Turiddo MARCHINI,
Silvio PIOLA, Bruno CAMOLESE, Giovanni COSTA. (Coach: József VIOLA (HUN)).
Hungária FC Budapest: Antal SZABÓ, Károly KIS, Sándor BÍRÓ, Gusztáv SEBES, József
TURAY, János DUDÁS, Ferenc SAS, Heinrich MÜLLER (AUT), László CSEH, István
KARDOS, Pál TITKOS. (Coach: Alfréd SCHAFFER).
Goals: SS Lazio Roma: 1-0 Silvio PIOLA (2'), 2-0 Silvio PIOLA (39'), 3-0 Giovanni COSTA
(49').
Hungária FC Budapest: 3-1 László CSEH (59'), 3-2 László CSEH (70').
Referee: Hans WÚTHRICH (SUI)   Attendance: 18.000

27-06-1937   Stadion Letzigrund, Zürich:
                Young Fellows Zürich – First Vienna FC   1-0 (1-0)
Young Fellows Zürich: FÄH, Karl KUHN, Hans NYFFELER, Robert KAES, VONTHRON,
Eduard MÜLLER, Eugen DIEBOLD, Alessandro (Mucho) FRIGERIO, PALI, Gustav TÖGEL
(AUT), LIENHARD. (Coach: Otto HAFTL (GER)).
First Vienna FC: Viktor HAVLICEK, Karl RAINER, Otto KALLER, Rudolf PATZKA,
Leopold HOFMANN, Leonhard MACHU, Josef MOLZER, Adolf LAUDON, Friedrich (Fritz)
GSCHWEIDL, Ferdinand BARILLY, Franz ERDL. (Player-coach: Friedrich (Fritz)
GSCHWEIDL).
Goal: Young Fellows Zürich: 1-0 PALI (24').
Referee: Raffaele SCORZONI (ITA)   Attendance: 6.000

29-06-1937   Hungária körút, Budapest: AC Sparta Praha – WSC Admira Wien   0-2 (0-0)
AC Sparta Praha: Bohumil KLENOVEC, Jaroslav BURGR, Josef CTYROKÝ, Josef
KOSTÁLEK, Jaroslav BOUCEK, Karel KOLSKÝ, Josef ZEMAN, Karel SENECKÝ, Oldrich
ZAJÍCEK, Oldrich NEJEDLÝ, Géza KALOCSAY. (Coach: Ferenc SZEDLACSEK (HUN)).
WSC Admira Wien: Peter PLATZER, Anton SCHALL, Otto MARISCHKA, Johann
URBANEK, Willibald HAHN, Siegfried JOKSCH, Leopold VOGL, Wilhelm
HAHNEMANN, Karl STOIBER, Franz SCHILLING, Adolf VOGL. (Coach: Hans
SKOLAUT).
Goals: WSC Admira Wien: 0-1 Leopold VOGL (50'), 0-2 Franz SCHILLING (80').
Referee: Rinaldo BARLASSINA (ITA)   Attendance: 8.000

(Play-off game).

29-06-1937   Stadion Hardturm, Zürich: Young Fellows Zürich – First Vienna FC   0-2 (0-0)
Young Fellows Zürich: FÄH, Karl KUHN, Hans NYFFELER, Robert KAES, VONTHRON,
Eduard MÜLLER, Eugen DIEBOLD, PALI, Alessandro (Mucho) FRIGERIO, Anton CISERI
(I), LIENHARD. (Coach: Otto HAFTL (GER)).
First Vienna FC: Viktor HAVLICEK, Karl RAINER, Otto KALLER, Rudolf PATZKA,
Leopold HOFMANN, Leonhard MACHU, Josef MOLZER, Friedrich (Fritz) GSCHWEIDL,
Richard FISCHER, Gustav POLLAK, Franz ERDL. (Player-coach: Friedrich (Fritz)
GSCHWEIDL).
Goals: First Vienna FC: 0-1 Richard FISCHER (50'), 0-2 Friedrich (Fritz) GSCHWEIDL
(85').
Referee: Raffaele SCORZONI (ITA)   Attendance: 4.000
(Play-off game).

04-07-1937   Praterstadion, Wien: WSC Admira Wien – AC Genova 1893   2-2 (0-0)
WSC Admira Wien: Peter PLATZER, Anton SCHALL, Otto MARISCHKA, Johann
URBANEK, Willibald HAHN, Franz RADAKOVICH, Leopold VOGL, Wilhelm
HAHNEMANN, Karl STOIBER, Franz SCHILLING, Adolf VOGL. (Coach: Hans
SKOLAUT).
AC Genova 1893: Manlio BACIGALUPO, Paolo AGOSTEO (expulsion 83'), Renato
VIGNOLINI, Arrigo MORSELLI, Giuseppe BIGOGNO, Emanuele FIGLIOLA (URU), Pietro
ARCARI (III), Mario PERAZZOLO, Carlo SERVETTI, Luigi SCARABELLO, Alfredo
MARCHIONNESCHI. (Coach: Hermann FELSNER (AUT)).
Goals: WSC Admira Wien: 1-0 Franz SCHILLING (56'), 2-2 Anton SCHALL (85' penalty).
AC Genova 1893: 1-1 Alfredo MARCHIONNESCHI (72'), 1-2 Carlo SERVETTI (80').
Referee: Mihály Iványi IVÁNCSISC (HUN)   Attendance: 44.000

04-07-1937   Praterstadion, Wien: FK Austria Wien – Újpesti TE   5-4 (1-2)
FK Austria Wien: Rudolf ZÖHRER, Wilhelm KOPETKO, Karl SESTA, Karl ADAMEK,
Johann MOCK, Karl ANDRITZ, Franz RIEGLER, Walter NAUSCH, Matthias SINDELAR,
Camillo JERUSALEM, Leopold NEUMER. (Coaches: Matthias SINDELAR & Walter
NAUSCH).
Újpesti TE: László HAVAS, Gyula FUTÓ, Péter JOÓS, Gyula SERES, György SZÜCS, Antal
SZALAY, Géza KOCSIS, Jenö VINCZE, Gyula ZSENGELLÉR, Lipót KÁLLAI, Mátyás
TÓTH. (Coach: Béla JÁNOSY).
Goals: FK Austria Wien: 1-1 Leopold NEUMER (19'), 2-2 Matthias SINDELAR (57'), 3-2
Walter NAUSCH (63'), 4-2 Karl SESTA (68'), 5-4 Walter NAUSCH (79').
Újpesti TE: 0-1 Géza KOCSIS (16'), 1-2 Gyula ZSENGELLÉR (41'), 4-3 Gyula
ZSENGELLÉR (72'), 4-4 Gyula ZSENGELLÉR (75').
Referee: Bruno PFÜTZNER (TCH)   Attendance: 47.000

04-07-1937   Stadio Nazionale del Partito Nazionale Fascista, Roma:
            SS Lazio Roma – Grasshopper-Club Zürich   6-1 (3-1)
SS Lazio Roma: Giacomo BLASON, Benedetto ZACCONI, Alfredo MONZA, Giuseppe
BALDO, Giuseppe VIANI, Luigi MILANO, Umberto BUSANI, Libero Turiddo MARCHINI,
Silvio PIOLA, Bruno CAMOLESE, Giovanni COSTA. (Coach: József VIOLA (HUN)).
Grasshopper-Club Zürich: Willy HUBER, Severino (Sevi) MINELLI, Walter WEILER (II),
Hermann SPRINGER, Sirio VERNATI, Dr.Sigmund GUTTORMSEN (NOR), Alfred (Fredy)
BICKEL, Josef ARTIMOVIC (AUT), Eugen RUPF, Max (Xam) ABEGGLEN (II), Max
FAUGUEL. (Coach: Karl RAPPAN (AUT)).
Goals: SS Lazio Roma: 1-1 Umberto BUSANI (14'), 2-1 Libero Turiddo MARCHINI (30'),
3-1 Silvio PIOLA (35'), 4-1 Umberto BUSANI (74'), 5-1 Silvio PIOLA (77'), 6-1 Silvio
PIOLA (83').
Grasshopper-Club Zürich: 0-1 Max FAUGUEL (5').
Referee: Dr.Adolf MIESZ (AUT)   Attendance: 11.000

04-07-1937   Üllöi út, Budapest: Ferencvárosi TC Budapest – First Vienna FC   2-1 (2-1)
Ferencvárosi TC Budapest: József HÁDA, Sándor TÁTRAI, Lajos KORÁNYI, László
HÁMORI, Gyula POLGÁR, Gyula LÁZÁR, Mihály TÁNCOS, Gyula KISS, Dr.György
SÁROSI, Géza TOLDI, László GYETVAI. (Coach: József SÁNDOR).
First Vienna FC: Viktor HAVLICEK, Karl RAINER, Otto KALLER, Rudolf PATZKA,
Leopold HOFMANN, Leonhard MACHU, Josef MOLZER, Friedrich (Fritz) GSCHWEIDL,
Richard FISCHER, Gustav POLLAK, Franz ERDL. (Player-coach: Friedrich (Fritz)
GSCHWEIDL).
Goals: Ferencvárosi TC Budapest: 1-1 Dr.György SÁROSI (14'), 2-1 Géza TOLDI (24').
First Vienna FC: 0-1 Gustav POLLAK (9').
Referee: Giuseppe SCARPI (ITA)   Attendance: 15.000
(Sándor TÁTRAI missed a penalty).

11-07-1937   AC Genova 1893 – WSC Admira Wien

*The return match was cancelled due to the misbehaviour of both sets of players during and
after the first match. Furthermore, the referee Mihály Iványi IVÁNCSICS was banned from
officiating at Mitropa Cup matches and both teams were expelled from the competition.*

11-07-1937   Üllöi út, Budapest: Újpesti TE – FK Austria Wien   1-2 (0-1)
Újpesti TE: László HAVAS, Gyula FUTÓ, Péter JOÓS, Gyula SERES, György SZÜCS,
István BALOGH, Géza VINCZE, Gyula ZSENGELLÉR, Lipót KÁLLAI,
Mátyás TÓTH. (Coach: Béla JÁNOSY).
FK Austria Wien: Rudolf ZÖHRER, Karl ANDRITZ, Karl SESTA, Karl ADAMEK, Johann
MOCK, Walter NAUSCH, Franz RIEGLER, Josef STROH, Matthias SINDELAR, Camillo
JERUSALEM, Leopold NEUMER. (Coaches: Matthias SINDELAR & Walter NAUSCH).
Goals: Újpesti TE: 1-2 Géza KOCSIS (84' penalty).
FK Austria Wien: 0-1 Matthias SINDELAR (43'), 0-2 Camillo JERUSALEM (59').
Referee: Rinaldo BARLASSINA (ITA)   Attendance: 28.000

11-07-1937   Stadion Hardturm, Zürich:
                    Grasshopper-Club Zürich – SS Lazio Roma   3-2 (2-1)
Grasshopper-Club Zürich: Willy HUBER, Severino (Sevi) MINELLI, Walter WEILER (II),
Hermann SPRINGER, Sirio VERNATI, Dr.Sigmund GUTTORMSEN (NOR), Alfred (Fredy)
BICKEL, Friedrich (Fritz) WAGNER, Josef ARTIMOVIC (AUT), Max (Xam) ABEGGLEN
(II), Heinrich KRISMER. (Coach: Karl RAPPAN (AUT)).
SS Lazio Roma: Giacomo BLASON, Benedetto ZACCONI, Alfredo MONZA, Giuseppe
BALDO, Giuseppe VIANI, Luigi MILANO, Umberto BUSANI, Libero Turiddo MARCHINI,
Silvio PIOLA, Bruno CAMOLESE, Giovanni COSTA. (Coach: József VIOLA (HUN)).
Goals: Grasshopper-Club Zürich: 1-1 KRISMER (35'), 2-1 Alfred (Fredy) BICKEL (39'), 3-2
Alfred (Fredy) BICKEL (79').
SS Lazio Roma: 0-1 Libero Turiddo MARCHINI (23'), 2-2 Silvio PIOLA (52').
Referee: Pál VON HERTZKA (HUN)   Attendance: 7.000

11-07-1937   Praterstadion, Wien: First Vienna FC – Ferencvárosi TC Budapest   1-0 (0-0)
First Vienna FC: Viktor HAVLICEK, Karl RAINER, Otto KALLER, Rudolf PATZKA,
Leopold HOFMANN, Leonhard MACHU, Josef MOLZER, Friedrich (Fritz) GSCHWEIDL,
Richard FISCHER, Gustav POLLAK, Franz ERDL. (Player-coach: Friedrich (Fritz)
GSCHWEIDL).
Ferencvárosi TC Budapest: József HÁDA, Sándor TÁTRAI, Lajos KORÁNYI, László
HÁMORI, Dr.György SÁROSI, Gyula LÁZÁR, Mihály BÍRÓ, Gyula KISS, László JAKOB,
Géza TOLDI, László GYETVAI. (Coach: József SÁNDOR).
Goal: First Vienna FC: 1-0 Gustav POLLAK (20' penalty).
Referee: Ján BIZÍK (TCH)   Attendance: 12.000

14-07-1937   Üllöi út, Budapest: Ferencvárosi TC Budapest – First Vienna FC   2-1 (2-0)
Ferencvárosi TC Budapest: József HÁDA, Sándor TÁTRAI, Lajos KORÁNYI, László
HÁMORI, Gyula POLGÁR, Gyula LÁZÁR, Mihály TÁNCOS, Gyula KISS, Dr.György
SÁROSI, Géza TOLDI, László GYETVAI. (Coach: József SÁNDOR).
First Vienna FC: Viktor HAVLICEK, Karl RAINER, Willibald SCHMAUS, Rudolf
PATZKA, Leopold HOFMANN, Leonhard MACHU, Josef MOLZER, Otto KALLER,
Friedrich (Fritz) GSCHWEIDL, Gustav POLLAK, Franz ERDL. (Player-coach: Friedrich
(Fritz) GSCHWEIDL).
Goals: Ferencvárosi TC Budapest: 1-0 Géza TOLDI (24'), 2-0 Géza TOLDI (38').
First Vienna FC: 2-1 Otto KALLER (57').
Referee: Rinaldo BARLASSINA (ITA)   Attendance: 16.000

(Play-off game).

SEMI-FINALS

18-07-1937   Praterstadion, Wien: FK Austria Wien – Ferencvárosi TC Budapest   4-1 (2-0)
FK Austria Wien: Rudolf ZÖHRER, Karl ANDRITZ, Karl SESTA, Karl ADAMEK, Johann
MOCK, Walter NAUSCH, Franz RIEGLER, Josef STROH, Matthias SINDELAR, Camillo
JERUSALEM, Leopold NEUMER. (Coaches: Matthias SINDELAR & Walter NAUSCH).
Ferencvárosi TC Budapest: József HÁDA, Sándor TÁTRAI, Lajos KORÁNYI, László
HÁMORI, Dr.György SÁROSI, Gyula LÁZÁR, Mihály BÍRÓ, Gyula KISS, Gyula POLGÁR,
Géza TOLDI, László GYETVAI. (Coach: József SÁNDOR).
Goals: FK Austria Wien: 1-0 Camillo JERUSALEM (15'), 2-0 Josef STROH (39'), 3-1
Camillo JERUSALEM (57'), 4-1 Matthias SINDELAR (62').
Ferencvárosi TC Budapest: 2-1 Dr.György SÁROSI (49' penalty).
Referee: Hans WÜTHRICH (SUI)   Attendance: 32.000

25-07-1937   Üllöi út, Budapest: Ferencvárosi TC Budapest – FK Austria Wien   6-1 (2-1)
Ferencvárosi TC Budapest: József HÁDA, Sándor TÁTRAI, Lajos KORÁNYI, László
HÁMORI, Gyula POLGÁR, Gyula LÁZÁR, Mihály TÁNCOS, Gyula KISS, Dr.György
SÁROSI, Géza TOLDI, Tibor KEMÉNY. (Coach: József SÁNDOR).
FK Austria Wien: Rudolf ZÖHRER, Karl ANDRITZ, Karl SESTA, Karl ADAMEK, Johann
MOCK, Walter NAUSCH, Franz RIEGLER, Josef STROH, Matthias SINDELAR, Camillo
JERUSALEM, Leopold NEUMER. (Coaches: Matthias SINDELAR & Walter NAUSCH).
Goals: Ferencvárosi TC Budapest: 1-0 Tibor KEMÉNY (7'), 2-0 Dr.György SÁROSI (25'), 3-
1 Gyula KISS (57'), 4-1 Tibor KEMÉNY (63'), 5-1 Dr.György SÁROSI (77'), 6-1 Géza
TOLDI (83').
FK Austria Wien: 2-1 Matthias SINDELAR (43').
Referee: Generoso DATTILO (ITA)   Attendance: 22.000

SS Lazio Roma received a bye to the Final following the expulsion of AC Genova 1893 and WSC Admira Wien in the previous round.

FINAL

12-09-1937   Üllöi út, Budapest: Ferencvárosi TC Budapest – SS Lazio Roma   4-2 (1-1)
Ferencvárosi TC Budapest: József HÁDA, Sándor TÁTRAI, Lajos KORÁNYI, Béla
MAGDA, Gyula POLGÁR, Béla SZÉKELY, Mihály TÁNCOS, Gyula KISS, Dr.György
SÁROSI, Géza TOLDI, Tibor KEMÉNY. (Coach: Emil RAUCHMAUL).
SS Lazio Roma: Giacomo BLASON, Benedetto ZACCONI, Alfredo MONZA, Giuseppe
BALDO, Giuseppe VIANI, Luigi MILANO, Umberto BUSANI, Libero Turiddo MARCHINI,
Silvio PIOLA, Bruno CAMOLESE, Giovanni COSTA. (Coach: József VIOLA (HUN)).
Goals: Ferencvárosi TC Budapest: 1-0 Géza TOLDI (22'), 2-1 Dr.György SÁROSI (53'), 3-1
Dr.György SÁROSI (59' penalty), 4-2 Dr.György SÁROSI (73' penalty).
SS Lazio Roma: 1-1 Umberto BUSANI (26'), 3-2 Silvio PIOLA (64').
Referee: Gustav KRIST (TCH)   Attendance: 32.000

24-10-1937   Stadio Nazionale del Partito Nazionale Fascista, Roma:
                   SS Lazio Roma – Ferencvárosi TC Budapest   4-5 (4-3)
SS Lazio Roma: Vincenzo PROVERA, Benedetto ZACCONI, Alfredo MONZA, Giuseppe
BALDO, Giuseppe VIANI, Luigi MILANO, Umberto BUSANI, Libero Turiddo MARCHINI,
Silvio PIOLA, Bruno CAMOLESE, Giovanni COSTA. (Coach: József VIOLA (HUN)).
Ferencvárosi TC Budapest: József HÁDA, Sándor TÁTRAI, Lajos KORÁNYI, Béla
MAGDA, Gyula POLGÁR, Gyula LÁZÁR, Mihály TÁNCOS, Gyula KISS, Dr.György
SÁROSI, Géza TOLDI, Tibor KEMÉNY. (Coach: Emil RAUCHMAUL).
Goals: SS Lazio Roma: 1-0 Giovanni COSTA (4'), 2-2 Silvio PIOLA (19'), 3-2 Silvio PIOLA
(24'), 4-2 Silvio PIOLA (36').
Ferencvárosi TC Budapest: 1-1 Dr.György SÁROSI (6' penalty), 1-2 Dr.György SÁROSI (8'),
4-3 Géza TOLDI (37'), 4-4 Gyula KISS (71'), 4-5 Dr.György SÁROSI (80').
Referee: Hans WÜTHRICH (SUI)   Attendance: 35.000

*** Ferencvárosi TC Budapest won the Cup ***

78

1938

FIRST ROUND

26-06-1938   Stadio "Luigi Ferraris", Marassi, Genova:
                AC Genova 1893 – AC Sparta Praha   4-2 (4-1)
AC Genova 1893: Rodolfo AGOSTINI, Mario GENTA, Michele BORELLI, Carlo VILLA,
Giuseppe BIGOGNO, Emanuele FIGLIOLA (URU), Pietro ARCARI (III), Mario
PERAZZOLO, Sergio BERTONI, Luigi SCARABELLO, Angelo CATTANEO. (Coach:
William GARBUTT (ENG)).
AC Sparta Praha: Bohumil KLENOVEC, Jaroslav BURGR, Josef CTYROKÝ, Josef
KOSTÁLEK, Jaroslav BOUCEK, Karel KOLSKÝ, Jan RÍHA, Karel SENECKÝ, Josef
ZEMAN, Oldrich NEJEDLÝ, Ludovít RADÓ. (Coach: Ferenc SZEDLACSEK (HUN)).
Goals"AC Genova 1893: 1-0 Sergio BERTONI (3'), 2-0 Angelo CATTANEO (4'), 3-0 Luigi
SCARABELLO (16'), 4-1 Mario PERAZZOLO (21').
AC Sparta Praha: 3-1 Oldrich NEJEDLÝ (17'), 4-2 Ludovít RADÓ (47').
Referee: Pál VON HERTZKA (HUN)   Attendance: 12.000

26-06-1938   Arena Civica, Parco Sempione, Milano:
                AS Ambrosiana-Inter Milano – Kispesti AC   4-2 (0-2)
AS Ambrosiana-Inter Milano: Giuseppe PERUCHETTI, Carmelo BUONOCORE, Duilio
SETTI, Ugo LOCATELLI, Renato OLMI, Piero ANTONA, Antonio FERRARA (II),
Giuseppe MEAZZA, Giorgio BARSANTI, Giovanni FERRARI, Pietro FERRARIS (II).
(Coach: Armando CASTELLAZZI).
Kispesti AC: János GERGÖ, Károly OLAJKÁR (I), Andor ÓNODI, Károly RÁTKAI,
Dr.László VARGA, József VÍG, Mihály KINCSES, Sándor OLAJKÁR (II), József NEMES,
Károly DÉRI, Imre SERÉNYI. (Coach: Ferenc PUSKÁS Sr.).
Goals: AS Ambrosiana-Inter Milano: 1-2 Pietro FERRARIS (67'), 2-2 Giuseppe MEAZZA
(75'), 3-2 Pietro FERRARIS (76'), 4-2 Giovanni FERRARI (81').
Kispesti AC: 0-1 Károly DÉRI (19'), 0-2 Sándor OLAJKÁR (21').
Referee: Dionisi-Nicolae XIFANDO (ROM)   Attendance: 18.000

26-06-1938   Megyeri út, Budapest: Újpesti TE – FC Rapid Bucuresti   4-1 (1-0)
Újpesti TE: Ferenc SZIKLAI, Gyula FUTÓ, Jenö FEKETE, Antal SZALAY, György SZÜCS,
István BALOGH, Géza KOCSIS, Jenö VINCZE, Lipót KÁLLAI, Gyula ZSENGELLÉR,
György SZEDER. (Coach: László STERNBERG-SÁTORI).
FC Rapid Bucuresti: Petre RADULESCU, Stefan WETZER, Nicolae ROSCULE, Vintila
COSSINI, Gheorghe RASINARU, Ladislau RAFFINSKY, Ion BOGDAN, Ioachim
MOLDOVEANU, Stefan AUER/István AVAR (HUN), Gyula BARÁTKY (HUN), Alexandru
CUEDAN. (Coach: Eduard BAUER (AUT)).
Goals: Újpesti TE: 1-0 Gyula ZSENGELLÉR (11'), 2-0 Gyula ZSENGELLÉR (46'), 3-0
Gyula ZSENGELLÉR (66'), 4-1 Jenö VINCZE (90').
FC Rapid Bucuresti: 3-1 Ladislau RAFFINSKY (83' penalty).
Referee: Ján BIZÍK (TCH)   Attendance: 13.000
(Gyula BARÁTKY was also known by his Romanian name: Iuliu BARÁTKY)
(Ladislau RAFFINSKY was also known by his Hungarian name: László RAFFINSKY)

79

26-06-1938   Na rybnícku, Brno: SK Zidenice – Ferencvárosi TC Budapest 3-1 (0-0)
SK Zidenice: Vojtech ANDRASÍK, Eduard VANEK, Jozef NEDER, Josef CURDA, Stephan
POSPICHAL (AUT), Bohumil CHOCHOLOUS, Vladimír CABANA, Géza CSAPO (HUN),
Karel NEPALA, Jan STLOUKAL, Oldrich RULC. (Coach: Jenö KONRÁD (HUN)).
Ferencvárosi TC Budapest: József HÁDA, Sándor TÁTRAI, Lajos KORÁNYI, Béla
MAGDA, Gyula POLGÁR, Gyula LÁZÁR, Mihály BÍRÓ, Gyula KISS, Dr.György SÁROSI,
Géza TOLDI, Tibor KEMÉNY. (Coach: György HLAVAY).
Goals: SK Zidenice: 1-0 Oldrich RULC (55'), 2-0 Karel NEPALA (60'), 3-0 Karel NEPALA
(68').
Ferencvárosi TC Budapest: 3-1 Gyula KISS (74').
Referee: Raffaele SCORZONI (ITA)   Attendance: 15.000

26-06-1938   Hungária körút, Budapest: Hungária FC Budapest – Juventus Torino 3-3 (0-3)
Hungária FC Budapest: Antal SZABÓ, Károly KIS, Sándor BÍRÓ, Gusztáv SEBES, József
TURAY, János DUDÁS, Ferenc SAS, László CSEH, István KARDOS, Heinrich MÜLLER
(AUT), Géza SZABÓ (III). (Coach: Alfréd SCHAFFER).
Juventus Torino: Alfredo BODOIRA, Alfredo FONI, Pietro RAVA, Teobaldo DEPETRINI,
Luis Felipe MONTI (ARG), Mario VARGLIEN (I), Savino BELLINI, Lodovico DE
FILIPPIS, Guglielmo GABETTO, Carlo BUSCAGLIA, Luigi BUSDON. (Coach: Virginio
ROSETTA).
Goals: Hungária FC Budapest: 1-3 István KARDOS (48'), 2-3 István KARDOS (57'), 3-3
István KARDOS (88').
Juventus Torino: 0-1 Guglielmo GABETTO (26'), 0-2 Luigi BUSDON (35'), 0-3 Savino
BELLINI (41').
Referee: Leon VOGL (TCH)   Attendance: 14.000

26-06-1938   Arena Venus, Bucuresti: FC Ripensia Timisoara- Milan AS 3-0 (3-0)
FC Ripensia Timisoara: Dumitru PAVLOVICI, Rudolf BÜRGER, Vasile CHIROIU, Tibor
NAGY, Rudolf KOTORMÁNY, Vasile DEHELEANU, Silviu BINDEA, Zoltán BEKE,
Adalbert MARKSTEINER, Gheorghe CIOLAC, Stefan DOBAY. (Coach: József POZSÁR
(HUN)).
Milan AS: Luigi DIAMANTE, Luigi PERVERSI, Giuseppe BONIZZONI, Sereno
GIANESELLO, Antonio BORTOLETTI, Mario LOETTI, Egidio CAPRA, Giuseppe
ANTONINI, Aldo BOFFI, Elisio GABARDO, Remo COSSIO. (Coach: Jozef BANAS
(TCH)).
Goals: FC Ripensia Timisoara: 1-0 Adalbert MARKSTEINER (33'), 2-0 Adalbert
MARKSTEINER (35'), 3-0 Stefan DOBAY (38').
Referee: Abraham KLEIN (HUN)   Attendance: 25.000
*(Adalbert MARKSTEINER was also known by both his Hungarian name (Béla MAROSVÁRI)
and his Romanian name (Adalbert MARCU))*
(Stefan DOBAY was also known by his native name: István DOBAY)

80

26-06-1938   Stadión SK Kladno, Kladno: SK Kladno – HASK Zagreb   3-1 (2-1)
SK Kladno: Karel TICHÝ, Emanuel SMEJKAL, Frantisek KUSALA, Frantisek BENES,
Václav SVATON, Václav NOVÝ, Frantisek KLOZ, Jan SEIDL, Miroslav PROCHÁZKA,
Josef JUNEK, Adolf SKÁLA. (Coach: Karel KRAUS).
HASK Zagreb: Vladimir ZMARA, Zlatko GOLAC, Boro KONSTANTINOVIC, Nikola
PAJEVIC, Ivan GAJER, Nikola DUKOVIC, Ivan MEDARIC, Ratko KACIJAN, Ivan
HITREC, Stjepan HORVAT, Milevoj FINK. (Coach: Zoltán OPATA (HUN)).
Goals: SK Kladno: 1-0 Frantisek KLOZ (14'), 2-0 Frantisek KLOZ (40'), 3-1 Adolf SKÁLA
(47').
HASK Zagreb: 2-1 Ratko KACIJAN (41').
Referee: Mihály Iványi IVÁNCSISC (HUN)   Attendance: 8.000

26-06-1938   Stadion BSK, Beograd: BSK Beograd – SK Slavia Praha   2-3 (1-3)
BSK Beograd: Srdan MRKUSIC, Djordje STOJILJKOVIC, Ernest DUBAC, Petar MANOLA,
Prvoslav DRAGICEVIC, Gustav LEHNER, Svetislav GLISOVIC, Svetislav VALJAREVIC,
Vojin (Skoba) BOZOVIC, Djordje (Djokica) VUJADINOVIC, Ján PODHRADSKÝ. (Coach:
Alex NEMESCH).
SK Slavia Praha: Alexej BOKSAY, Antonín CERNÝ, Ferdinand DAUCÍK, Václav BOUSKA,
Otakar NOZÍR, Vlastimil KOPECKÝ, Václav HORÁK, Ladislav SIMUNEK, Vojtech
BRADÁC, Josef BICAN, Rudolf VYTLACIL (AUT). (Coach: Jan REICHARDT).
Goals: BSK Beograd: 1-3 Ján PODHRADSKÝ (41'), 2-3 Vojin (Skoba) BOZOVIC (89').
SK Slavia Praha: 0-1 Rudolf VYTLACIL (8'), 0-2 Vojtech BRADÁC (14'), 0-3 Václav
HORÁK (23').
Referee: Raffaele SCORZONI (ITA)   Attendance: 8.000

02-07-1938   Stadión Sparta/Letná, Praha: AC Sparta Praha – AC Genova 1893   1-1 (0-1)
AC Sparta Praha: Bohumil KLENOVEC, Jaroslav BURGR, Josef CTYROKÝ, Josef
KOSTÁLEK, Jaroslav BOUCEK, Karel KOLSKÝ, Jan RÍHA, Karel SENECKÝ, Josef
ZEMAN, Oldrich NEJEDLÝ, Ludovít RADÓ. (Coach: Ferenc SZEDLACSEK (HUN)).
AC Genova 1893: Rodolfo AGOSTINI, Mario GENTA, Michele BORELLI, Mario
PERAZZOLO, Giuseppe BIGOGNO, Emanuele FIGLIOLA (URU), Pietro ARCARI (III),
Arrigo MORSELLI, Sergio BERTONI, Luigi SCARABELLO, Angelo CATTANEO. (Coach:
William GARBUTT (ENG)).
Goals: AC Sparta Praha: 1-1 Josef ZEMAN (74').
AC Genova 1893: 0-1 Sergio BERTONI (33').
Referee: Mihajlo POPOVIC (YUG)   Attendance: 30.000

02-07-1938   Üllöi út, Budapest: Kispesti AC – AS Ambrosiana-Inter Milano   1-1 (0-1)
Kispesti AC: János GERGÖ, Károly OLAJKÁR (I), Andor ÓNODI, Károly RÁTKAI,
Dr.László VARGA, József VÍG, Mihály KINCSES, Károly MONOSTORI, József NEMES,
Károly DÉRI, Imre SERÉNYI. (Coach: Ferenc PUSKÁS Sr.).
AS Ambrosiana-Inter Milano: Giuseppe PERUCHETTI, Carmelo BUONOCORE, Duilio
SETTI, Ugo LOCATELLI, Ezio MENEGHELLO, Piero ANTONA, Antonio FERRARA (II),
Giuseppe MEAZZA, Pietro FERRARIS (II), Giovanni FERRARI, Enrico CANDIANI.
(Coach: Armando CASTELLAZZI).
Goals: Kispesti AC: 1-1 Dr.László VARGA (66').
AS Ambrosiana-Inter Milano: 0-1 Giuseppe MEAZZA (40' penalty).
Referee: Gustav KRIST (TCH)   Attendance: 7.000

81

03-07-1938   Stadion Giuleti, Bucuresti: FC Rapid Bucuresti – Újpesti TE   4-0 (0-0)
FC Rapid Bucuresti: Petre RADULESCU, Stefan WETZER, Nicolae ROSCULE, Vintila
COSSINI, Gheorghe RASINARU, Ladislau RAFFINSKY, Ion BOGDAN, Ioachim
MOLDOVEANU, Stefan AUER/István AVAR (HUN), Iosif LENGHERIU, Alexandru
CUEDAN. (Coach: Eduard BAUER (AUT)).
Újpesti TE: Ferenc SZIKLAI, Gyula FUTÓ, Jenö FEKETE, Sándor ÁDÁM, György SZÜCS,
Péter JOÓS, Ferenc PUSZTAI, Jenö VINCZE, Gyula ZSENGELLÉR, Lipót KÁLLAI, György
SZEDER. (Coach: László STERNBERG-SÁTORI).
Goals: FC Rapid Bucuresti: 1-0 Alexandru CUEDAN (63'), 2-0 Ioachim MOLDOVEANU
(69'), 3-0 Stefan AUER/István AVAR (81'), 4-0 Ion BOGDAN (90').
Referee: Bruno PFÜTZNER (TCH)   Attendance: 15.000

03-07-1938   Üllöi út, Budapest: Ferencvárosi TC Budapest – SK Zidenice   3-0 (1-0)
Ferencvárosi TC Budapest: József HÁDA, Sándor TÁTRAI, Lajos KORÁNYI, Béla
MAGDA, Gyula POLGÁR, Gyula LÁZÁR, Mihály BÍRÓ, Gyula KISS, Dr.György SÁROSI,
Géza TOLDI, Tibor KEMÉNY. (Coach: György HLAVAY).
SK Zidenice: Vojtech ANDRASÍK, Eduard VANEK, Jozef NEDER, Josef CURDA, Stephan
POSPICHAL (AUT), Bohumil CHOCHOLOUS, Vladimír CABANA, Géza CSAPO (HUN),
Karel NEPALA, Jan STLOUKAL, Oldrich RULC. (Coach: Jenö KONRÁD (HUN)).
Goals: Ferencvárosi TC Budapest: 1-0 Gyula POLGÁR (21'), 2-0 Géza TOLDI (51'), 3-0
Gyula POLGÁR (65').
Referee: Giuseppe SCARPI (ITA)   Attendance: 15.000

03-07-1938   Stadio Comunale "Benito Mussolini", Torino:
                      Juventus Torino – Hungária FC Budapest   6-1 (4-0)
Juventus Torino: Ugo AMORETTI, Alfredo FONI, Pietro RAVA, Teobaldo DEPETRINI,
Luis Felipe MONTI (ARG), Mario VARGLIEN (I), Savino BELLINI, Lodovico DE
FILIPPIS, Guglielmo GABETTO, Carlo BUSCAGLIA, Luigi BUSDON. (Coach: Virginio
ROSETTA).
Hungária FC Budapest: Antal SZABÓ, Károly KIS, Sándor BÍRÓ, Gusztáv SEBES, József
TURAY, János DUDÁS, Ferenc SAS, László CSEH, István KARDOS, Heinrich MÜLLER
(AUT), Géza SZABÓ (III). (Coach: Alfréd SCHAFFER).
Goals: Juventus Torino: 1-0 Carlo BUSCAGLIA (2' penalty), 2-0 Carlo BUSCAGLIA (26'),
3-0 Luigi BUSDON (38'), 4-0 Lodovico DE FILIPPIS (41'), 5-1 Savino BELLINI (73'), 6-1
Guglielmo GABETTO (86').
Hungária FC Budapest: 4-1 István KARDOS (63').
Referee: Ján BIZÍK (TCH)   Attendance: 8.000

03-07-1938   Stadio Calistico di San Siro, Milano:
                      Milan AS – FC Rpensia Timisoara   3-1 (2-1)
Milan AS: Luigi DIAMANTE, Luigi PERVERSI, Giuseppe BONIZZONI, Mario
PROVAGLIO, Antonio BORTOLETTI, Mario LOETTI, Egidio CAPRA, Ezio LOIK,
Giuseppe ANTONINI, Pietro BUSCAGLIA, Remo COSSIO. (Coach: Jozef BANAS (TCH)).
FC Ripensia Timisoara: Dumitru PAVLOVICI, Rudolf BÜRGER, Vasile CHIROIU, Tibor
NAGY, Rudolf KOTORMÁNY, Cornel LAZAR, Silviu BINDEA, Zoltán BEKE, Adalbert
MARKSTEINER, Gheorghe CIOLAC, Stefan DOBAY. (Coach: József POZSÁR (HUN)).
Goals: Milan AS: 1-1 Remo COSSIO (27'), 2-1 Ezio LOIK (37'), 3-1 Remo COSSIO (58'
penalty).
FC Ripensia Timisoara: 0-1 Silviu BINDEA (12').
Referee: Milenko PODUBSKI (YUG)   Attendance: 12.000

03-07-1938   Stadion HASK, Zagreb: HASK Zagreb – SK Kladno 2-1 (1-0)
HASK Zagreb: Vladimir ZMARA, Zlatko GOLAC, Boro KONSTANTINOVIC, Nikola
PAJEVIC, Ivan GAJER, Nikola DUKOVIC, Ivan MEDARIC, Ratko KACIJAN, Ivan
HITREC, Stjepan HORVAT, Milevoj FINK. (Coach: Zoltán OPATA (HUN)).
SK Kladno: Karel TICHÝ, Emanuel SMEJKAL, Frantisek KUSALA, Frantisek BENES,
Václav SVATON, Václav NOVÝ, Vojtech RASPLICKA, Frantisek KLOZ, Jan SEIDL, Josef
JUNEK, Adolf SKÁLA. (Coach: Karel KRAUS).
Goals: HASK Zagreb: 1-0 Ivan HITREC (13'), 2-1 Ratko KACIJAN (88').
SK Kladno: 1-1 Frantisek KLOZ (47').
Referee: Mario CIAMBERLINI (ITA)   Attendance: 8.000

04-07-1938   Stadión Slavia/Letná, Praha: SK Slavia Praha – BSK Beograd 2-1 (1-0)
SK Slavia Praha: Alexej BOKSAY, Antonín CERNÝ, Ferdinand DAUCÍK, Václav BOUSKA,
Otakar NOZÍR, Vlastimil KOPECKÝ, Václav HORÁK, Ladislav SIMUNEK, Vojtech
BRADÁC, Josef BICAN, Rudolf VYTLACIL (AUT). (Coach: Jan REICHARDT).
BSK Beograd: Anton PUHAR, Djordje STOJILJKOVIC, Ernest DUBAC, Petar MANOLA,
Gustav LEHNER, Bruno KNEZEVIC, Svetislav GLISOVIC, Djordje (Djokica)
VUJADINOVIC, Blagoje (Mosa) MARJANOVIC, Vojin (Skoba) BOZOVIC, Ján
PODHRADSKÝ. (Coach: Alex NEMESCH).
Goals: SK Slavia Praha: 1-0 Ladislav SIMUNEK (12'), 2-1 Josef BICAN (82' penalty).
BSK Beograd: 1-1 Ján PODHRADSKÝ (55').
Referee: Gábor BORONKAY (HUN)   Attendance: 25.000

QUARTER-FINALS

10-07-1938   Arena Venus, Bucuresti:
              FC Ripensia Timisoara – Ferencvárosi TC Budapest 4-5 (3-3)
FC Ripensia Timisoara: Dumitru PAVLOVICI, Rudolf BÜRGER, Vasile CHIROIU, Tibor
NAGY, Rudolf KOTORMÁNY, Cornel LAZAR, Silviu BINDEA, Zoltán BEKE, Adalbert
MARKSTEINER, Alexandru SCHWARTZ, Stefan DOBAY. (Coach: József POZSÁR
(HUN)).
Ferencvárosi TC Budapest: József HÁDA, Sándor TÁTRAI, Lajos KORÁNYI, Béla
MAGDA, Gyula POLGÁR, Gyula LÁZÁR, Mihály TÁNCOS, Gyula KISS, Dr.György
SÁROSI, Géza TOLDI, Tibor KEMÉNY. (Coach: György HLAVAY).
Goals: FC Ripensia Timisoara: 1-0 Silviu BINDEA (9'), 2-3 Silviu BINDEA (43'), 3-3 Silviu
BINDEA (45'), 4-4 Silviu BINDEA (81').
Ferencvárosi TC Budapest: 1-1 Géza TOLDI (14'), 1-2 Géza TOLDI (15'), 1-3 Dr.György
SÁROSI (33'), 3-4 Géza TOLDI (55'), 4-5 Mihály TÁNCOS (86').
Referee: Rinaldo BARLASSINA (ITA)   Attendance: 22.000

10-07-1938   Stadio Comunale "Benito Mussolini", Torino:
Juventus Torino – SK Kladno   4-2 (2-2)
Juventus Torino: Ugo AMORETTI, Alfredo FONI, Pietro RAVA, Teobaldo DEPETRINI,
Luis Felipe MONTI (ARG), Mario VARGLIEN (I), Savino BELLINI, Lodovico DE
FILIPPIS, Guglielmo GABETTO, Ernesto TOMASI, Luigi BUSDON. (Coach: Virginio
ROSETTA).
SK Kladno: Karel TICHÝ, Emanuel SMEJKAL, Frantisek KUSALA, Frantisek BENES,
Václav SVATON, Václav NOVÝ, Vojtech RASPLICKA, Frantisek KLOZ, Jan SEIDL, Josef
JUNEK, Karel SEDLICKÝ. (Coach: Karel KRAUS).
Goals: Juventus Torino: 1-0 Luigi BUSDON (5'), 2-2 Ernesto TOMASI (40'), 3-2 Luis Felipe
MONTI (85'), 4-2 Lodovico DE FILIPPIS (86').
SK Kladno: 1-1 Frantisek KLOZ (24'), 1-2 Jan SEIDL (30').
Referee: Abraham KLEIN (HUN)   Attendance: 8.000

10-07-1938   Stadio "Luigi Ferraris", Marassi, Genova:
AC Genova 1893 – FC Rapid Bucuresti   3-0 (1-0)
AC Genova 1893: Rodolfo AGOSTINI, Mario GENTA, Michele BORELLI, Mario
PERAZZOLO, Giuseppe BIGOGNO, Emanuele FIGLIOLA (URU), Pietro ARCARI (III),
Arrigo MORSELLI, Sergio BERTONI, Luigi SCARABELLO, Angelo CATTANEO. (Coach:
William GARBUTT (ENG)).
FC Rapid Bucuresti: Petre RADULESCU, Stefan WETZER, Nicolae ROSCULE, Vintila
COSSINI, Gheorghe RASINARU, Ladislau RAFFINSKY, Ion BOGDAN, Ioachim
MOLDOVEANU, Stefan AUER/István AVAR (HUN), Iosif LENGHERIU, Alexandru
CUEDAN. (Coach: Eduard BAUER (AUT)).
Goals: AC Genova 1893: 1-0 Luigi SCARABELLO (41'), 2-0 Luigi SCARABELLO (66'),
3-0 Arrigo MORSELLI (85').
Referee: Jaroslav VLCEK (TCH)   Attendance: 10.000

11-07-1938   Stadión Slavia/Letná, Praha:
SK Slavia Praha – AS Ambrosiana-Inter Milano   9-0 (2-0)
SK Slavia Praha: Alexej BOKSAY, Antonín CERNÝ, Ferdinand DAUCÍK, Karel PRUCHA,
Otakar NOZÍR, Vlastimil KOPECKÝ, Václav HORÁK, Ladislav SIMUNEK, Vojtech
BRADÁC, Josef BICAN, Rudolf VYTLACIL (AUT). (Coach: Jan REICHARDT).
AS Ambrosiana-Inter Milano: Giuseppe PERUCHETTI, Carmelo BUONOCORE, Duilio
SETTI, Ugo LOCATELLI, Renato OLMI, Piero ANTONA, Antonio FERRARA (II),
Giuseppe MEAZZA, Aldo CAMPATELLI, Giovanni FERRARI, Pietro FERRARIS (II).
(Coach: Armando CASTELLAZZI).
Goals: SK Slavia Praha: 1-0 Josef BICAN (32'), 2-0 Václav HORÁK (34'), 3-0 Rudolf
VYTLACIL (48'), 4-0 Josef BICAN (54'), 5-0 Vojtech BRADÁC (59'), 6-0 Josef BICAN
(60'), 7-0 Václav HORÁK (61'), 8-0 Josef BICAN (69'), 9-0 Rudolf VYTLACIL (74').
Referee: Pál VON HERTZKA (HUN)   Attendance: 20.000

17-07-1938   Üllöi út, Budapest:
Ferencvárosi TC Budapest – FC Ripensia Timisoara   4-1 (2-0)
Ferencvárosi TC Budapest: József HÁDA, Sándor TÁTRAI, Lajos KORÁNYI, Béla
MAGDA, Gyula POLGÁR, Gyula LÁZÁR, Mihály TÁNCOS, Gyula KISS, Dr.György
SÁROSI, Géza TOLDI, Tibor KEMÉNY. (Coach: György HLAVAY).
FC Ripensia Timisoara: Dumitru PAVLOVICI, Rudolf BÜRGER, Vasile CHIROIU, Tibor
NAGY, Rudolf KOTORMÁNY, Cornel LAZAR, Silviu BINDEA, Zoltán BEKE, Adalbert
MARKSTEINER, Gheorghe CIOLAC, Stefan DOBAY. (Coach: József POZSÁR (HUN)).
Goals: Ferencvárosi TC Budapest: 1-0 Dr.György SÁROSI (25'), 2-0 Dr.György SÁROSI
(37'), 3-0 Dr.György SÁROSI (61'), 4-0 Géza TOLDI (75').
FC Ripensia Timisoara: 4-1 Stefan DOBAY (89').
Referee: Generoso DATTILO (ITA)   Attendance: 24.000

17-07-1938   Stadión SK Kladno, Kladno: SK Kladno – Juventus Torino   1-2 (1-1)
SK Kladno: Karel TICHÝ, Emanuel SMEJKAL, Frantisek KUSALA, Frantisek BENES,
Václav SVATON, Václav NOVÝ, Vojtech RASPLICKA, Frantisek KLOZ, Jan SEIDL, Josef
JUNEK, Karel SEDLICKÝ. (Coach: Karel KRAUS).
Juventus Torino: Ugo AMORETTI, Alfredo FONI, Pietro RAVA, Teobaldo DEPETRINI,
Luis Felipe MONTI (ARG), Mario VARGLIEN (I), Savino BELLINI, Lodovico DE
FILIPPIS, Guglielmo GABETTO, Ernesto TOMASI, Luigi BUSDON. (Coach: Virginio
ROSETTA).
Goals: SK Kladno: 1-0 Frantisek KLOZ (7').
Juventus Torino: 1-1 Guglielmo GABETTO (39'), 1-2 Guglielmo GABETTO (89').
Referee: Dionisi-Nicolae XIFANDO (ROM)   Attendance: 15.000

17-07-1938   Stadion Giulesti, Bucuresti: FC Rapid Bucuresti – AC Genova 1893   2-1 (1-1)
FC Rapid Bucuresti: Petre RADULESCU, Stefan WETZER, Nicolae ROSCULE, Vintila
COSSINI, Gheorghe RASINARU, Ladislau RAFFINSKY, Ion BOGDAN, Ioachim
MOLDOVEANU, Stefan AUER/István AVAR (HUN), Gyula BARÁTKY (HUN), Alexandru
CUEDAN. (Coach: Eduard BAUER (AUT)).
AC Genova 1893: Rodolfo AGOSTINI, Mario GENTA, Michele BORELLI, Mario
PERAZZOLO, Giuseppe BIGOGNO, Emanuele FIGLIOLA (URU), Pietro ARCARI (III),
Arrigo MORSELLI, Sergio BERTONI, Luigi SCARABELLO, Angelo CATTANEO. (Coach:
William GARBUTT (ENG)).
Goals: FC Rapid Bucuresti: 1-0 Gyula BARÁTKY (3'), 2-1 Alexandru CUEDAN (65').
AC Genova 1893: 1-1 Angelo CATTANEO (15').
Referee: Leon VOGL (TCH)   Attendance: 15.000

17-07-1938   Arena Civica, Parco Sempione, Milano:
AS Ambrosiana-Inter Milano – SK Slavia Praha   3-1 (1-1)
AS Ambrosiana-Inter Milano: Giuseppe PERUCHETTI, Giuseppe BALLERIO, Duilio SETTI,
Ugo LOCATELLI, Renato OLMI, Bruno VALE, Annibale FROSSI, Lorenzo SUBER,
Giuseppe MEAZZA, Giovanni FERRARI, Enrico CANDIANI. (Coach: Armando
CASTELLAZZI).
SK Slavia Praha: Alexej BOKSAY, Antonín CERNÝ, Ferdinand DAUCÍK, Karel PRUCHA,
Otakar NOZÍR, Vlastimil KOPECKÝ, Václav HORÁK, Ladislav SIMUNEK, Josef BICAN,
Vojtech BRADÁC, Rudolf VYTLACIL (AUT). (Coach: Jan REICHARDT).
Goals: AS Ambrosiana-Inter Milano: 1-1 Giovanni FERRARI (27'), 2-1 Annibale FROSSI
(56'), 3-1 Giovanni FERRARI (90').
SK Slavia Praha: 0-1 Rudolf VYTLACIL (25').
Referee: Mihály Iványi IVÁNCSISC (HUN)   Attendance: 6.000

85

24-07-1938   Stadio Comunale "Benito Mussolini", Torino:
Juventus Torino – Ferencvárosi TC Budapest   3-2 (2-1)
Juventus Torino: Ugo AMORETTI, Alfredo FONI, Pietro RAVA, Teobaldo DEPETRINI,
Luis Felipe MONTI (ARG), Mario VARGLIEN (I), Carlo BUSCAGLIA, Lodovico DE
FILIPPIS, Guglielmo GABETTO, Ernesto TOMASI, Luigi BUSDON. (Coach: Virginio
ROSETTA).
Ferencvárosi TC Budapest: József HÁDA, Sándor TÁTRAI, Lajos KORÁNYI, Béla
MAGDA, Gyula POLGÁR, Gyula LÁZÁR, Mihály TÁNCOS, Gyula KISS, Dr.György
SÁROSI, Géza TOLDI, Tibor KEMÉNY. (Coach: György HLAVAY).
Goals: Juventus Torino: 1-0 Lodovico DE FILIPPIS (30'), 2-0 Carlo BUSCAGLIA (35'), 3-1
Ernesto TOMASI (60').
Ferencvárosi TC Budapest: 2-1 Dr.György SÁROSI (44'), 3-2 Dr.György SÁROSI (63').
Referee: Ján BIZÍK (TCH)   Attendance: 11.000

24-07-1938   Stadio "Luigi Ferraris", Marassi, Genova:
AC Genova 1893 – SK Slavia Praha   4-2 (2-1)
AC Genova 1893: Rodolfo AGOSTINI, Mario GENTA, Michele BORELLI, Carlo VILLA,
Giuseppe BIGOGNO, Emanuele FIGLIOLA (URU), Pietro ARCARI (III), Mario
PERAZZOLO, Arrigo MORSELLI, Luigi SCARABELLO, Angelo CATTANEO. (Coach:
William GARBUTT (ENG)).
SK Slavia Praha: Alexej BOKSAY, Antonín CERNÝ, Ferdinand DAUCÍK, Karel PRUCHA,
Otakar NOZÍR, Vlastimil KOPECKÝ, Václav HORÁK, Ladislav SIMUNEK, Josef BICAN,
Vojtech BRADÁC, Rudolf VYTLACIL (AUT). (Coach: Jan REICHARDT).
Goals: AC Genova 1893: 1-0 Emanuele FIGLIOLA (29'), 2-0 Arrigo MORSELLI (35'), 3-2
Arrigo MORSELLI (68'), 4-2 Angelo CATTANEO (83').
SK Slavia Praha: 2-1 Václav HORÁK (38'), 2-2 Rudolf VYTLACIL (58').
Referee: Mihajlo POPOVIC (YUG)   Attendance: 8.000

31-07-1938   Üllöi út, Budapest: Ferencvárosi TC Budapest – Juventus Torino   2-0 (0-0)
Ferencvárosi TC Budapest: József HÁDA, Sándor TÁTRAI, Gyula POLGÁR, Béla MAGDA,
Béla SÁROSI (III), Gyula LÁZÁR, Mihály TÁNCOS, Gyula KISS, Dr.György SÁROSI,
Géza TOLDI, Tibor KEMÉNY. (Coach: György HLAVAY).
Juventus Torino: Ugo AMORETTI, Alfredo FONI, Pietro RAVA, Giovanni VARGLIEN (II),
Luis Felipe MONTI (ARG), Mario VARGLIEN (I), Lodovico DE FILIPPIS, Teobaldo
DEPETRINI, Luigi BUSDON, Ernesto TOMASI, Carlo BUSCAGLIA. (Coach: Virginio
ROSETTA).
Goals: Ferencvárosi TC Budapest: 1-0 Dr.György SÁROSI (78'), 2-0 Tibor KEMÉNY (85').
Referee: Leon VOGL (TCH)   Attendance: 33.000

01-08-1938   Stadión Slavia/Letná, Praha: SK Slavia Praha – AC Genova 1893   4-0 (2-0)
SK Slavia Praha: Alexej BOKSAY, Antonín CERNÝ, Ferdinand DAUCÍK, Karel PRUCHA,
Otakar NOZÍR, Vlastimil KOPECKÝ, Václav HORÁK, Ladislav SIMUNEK, Josef BICAN,
Vojtech BRADÁC, Rudolf VYTLACIL (AUT). (Coach: Jan REICHARDT).
AC Genova 1893: Rodolfo AGOSTINI, Mario GENTA, Michele BORELLI, Mario
PERAZZOLO, Giuseppe BIGOGNO, Emanuele FIGLIOLA (URU), Pietro ARCARI (III),
Arrigo MORSELLI, Sergio BERTONI, Luigi SCARABELLO, Angelo CATTANEO. (Coach:
William GARBUTT (ENG)).
Goals: SK Slavia Praha: 1-0 Josef BICAN (10'), 2-0 Josef BICAN (14'), 3-0 J. BICAN (67'),
4-0 Josef BICAN (78').
Referee: Pál VON HERTZKA (HUN)   Attendance: 30.000

FINAL

04-09-1938   Stadión Strahov (Masaryk), Praha:
SK Slavia Praha – Ferencvárosi TC Budapest   2-2 (2-1)
SK Slavia Praha: Alexej BOKSAY, Antonín CERNÝ, Ferdinand DAUCÍK, Karel PRUCHA,
Karel DAUCÍK, Vlastimil KOPECKÝ, Václav HORÁK, Ladislav SIMUNEK, Josef BICAN,
Vojtech BRADÁC, Rudolf VYTLACIL (AUT). (Coach: Jan REICHARDT).
Ferencvárosi TC Budapest: József HÁDA, Sándor TÁTRAI, Gyula POLGÁR, Béla MAGDA,
Béla SÁROSI (III), Gyula LÁZÁR, Mihály TÁNCOS, Gyula KISS, Dr.György SÁROSI,
Géza TOLDI, Tibor KEMÉNY. (Coach: György HLAVAY).
Goals: SK Slavia Praha: 1-1 Josef BICAN (36'), 2-1 Ladislav SIMUNEK (44').
Ferencvárosi TC Budapest: 0-1 Tibor KEMÉNY (30'), 2-2 Gyula KISS (63').
Referee: Henry Norman MEE (ENG)   Attendance: 45.000

11-09-1938   Üllöi út, Budapest: Ferencvárosi TC Budapest – SK Slavia Praha   0-2 (0-0)
Ferencvárosi TC Budapest: József HÁDA, Sándor TÁTRAI, Gyula POLGÁR, Béla MAGDA,
Béla SÁROSI (III), Gyula LÁZÁR, Mihály TÁNCOS, Gyula KISS, Dr.György SÁROSI,
Géza TOLDI, Tibor KEMÉNY. (Coach: György HLAVAY).
SK Slavia Praha: Alexej BOKSAY, Antonín CERNÝ, Ferdinand DAUCÍK, Karel PRUCHA,
Otakar NOZÍR, Vlastimil KOPECKÝ, Ladislav SIMUNEK, Bedrich VACEK, Josef BICAN,
Vojtech BRADÁC, Rudolf VYTLACIL (AUT). (Coach: Jan REICHARDT).
Goals: SK Slavia Praha: 0-1 Rudolf VYTLACIL (57'), 0-2 Ladislav SIMUNEK (71').
Referee: Arthur James JEWELL (ENG)   Attendance: 40.000

*** SK Slavia Praha won the Cup ***

1939

QUARTER-FINALS

17-06-1939   Üllöi út, Budapest: Ferencvárosi TC Budapest – AC Sparta Praha   2-3 (2-1)
Ferencvárosi TC Budapest: József HÁDA, Sándor TÁTRAI, Kornél SZOYKA, Béla
MAGDA, Béla SÁROSI (III), Béla PÓSA, Gyula LÁZÁR, Dr.György SÁROSI, Gyula
POLGÁR, István KISZELY, László GYETVAI. (Coach: György HLAVAY).
AC Sparta Praha: Alois VECHET, Jaroslav BURGR, Josef CTYROKÝ, Josef KOSTÁLEK,
Jaroslav BOUCEK, Karel KOLSKÝ, Jan RÍHA, Karel SENECKÝ, Josef ZEMAN, Josef
LUDL, Oldrich NEJEDLÝ. (Coach: Ferenc SZEDLACSEK (HUN)).
Goals: Ferencvárosi TC Budapest: 1-0 Gyula LÁZÁR (25'), 2-0 István KISZELY (29').
AC Sparta Praha: 2-1 Josef LUDL (42'), 2-2 Jan RÍHA (57'), 2-3 Oldrich NEJEDLÝ (64').
Referee: Giuseppe SCARPI (ITA)   Attendance: 8.000

18-06-1939   Arena Civica, Parco Sempione, Milano:
                    AS Ambrosiana-Inter Milano – Újpesti TE   2-1 (2-1)
AS Ambrosiana-Inter Milano: Orlando SAIN, Carmelo BUONOCORE, Duilio SETTI,
Alessandro PUPPO, Renato OLMI, Aldo CAMPATELLI, Annibale FROSSI, Attilio José
DEMARÍA (I) (ARG), Umberto GUARNIERI, Enrico CANDIANI, Pietro FERRARIS (II).
(Coach: Clemens CARGNELLI (AUT)).
Újpesti TE: Ferenc SZIKLAI, Gyula FUTÓ, Jenö FEKETE, Antal SZALAY, György SZÜCS,
István BALOGH, Sándor ÁDÁM, Jenö VINCZE, Gyula ZSENGELLÉR, Lipót KÁLLAI,
Géza KOCSIS. (Coach: Béla GUTTMANN).
Goals: AS Ambrosiana-Inter Milano: 1-0 Attilio José DEMARÍA (17'), 2-0 Umberto
GUARNIERI (23').
Újpesti TE: 2-1 Jenö VINCZE (34').
Referee: Frederick W.WORTH (ENG)   Attendance: 10.000

18-06-1939   Arena Venus, Bucuresti: ASC Venus Bucuresti – Bologna AGC   1-0 (1-0)
ASC Venus Bucuresti: Nicolae IORDACHESCU, Lazar SFERA, Gheorghe ALBU, Rudolf
DEMETROVICI, Alfred EISENBEISSER, Ion LUPAS, Cornel ORZA, Silviu
PLOESTEANU, Iuliu BODOLA, Petr VÂLCOV, Nicolae ENE. (Coach: Béla JÁNOSY
(HUN)).
Bologna AGC: Pietro FERRARI, Mario PAGOTTO, Secondo RICCI, Bruno MAINI, Michele
ANDREOLO Frodella (URU), Giordano CORSI, Amedeo BIAVATI, Raffaele SANSONE
(URU), Héctor (Ettore) PURICELLI (URU) (expulsion 60'), Francisco FEDULLO (URU),
Carlo REGUZZONI. (Coach: Árpád WEISZ (HUN)).
Goal: ASC Venus Bucuresti: 1-0 Nicolae ENE (9').
Referee: Ferenc MAJORSZKY (HUN)   Attendance: 12.000

25-06-1939   Megyeri út, Budapest: Újpesti TE – AS Ambrosiana-Inter Milano 3-1 (1-0)
Újpesti TE: Ferenc SZIKLAI, Gyula FUTÓ, Jenö FEKETE, Antal SZALAY, György SZÜCS,
István BALOGH, Sándor ÁDÁM, Jenö VINCZE, Gyula ZSENGELLÉR, Lipót KÁLLAI,
Géza KOCSIS. (Coach: Béla GUTTMANN).
AS Ambrosiana-Inter Milano: Orlando SAIN, Carmelo BUONOCORE, Duilio SETTI, Ugo
LOCATELLI, Renato OLMI, Aldo CAMPATELLI, Annibale FROSSI, Attilio José
DEMARÍA (I) (ARG), Umberto GUARNIERI, Giuseppe MEAZZA, Pietro FERRARIS (II).
(Coach: Clemens CARGNELLI (AUT)).
Goals: Újpesti TE: 1-0 Lipót KÁLLAI (5'), 2-1 Gyula ZSENGELLÉR (85'), 3-1 Géza
KOCSIS (89').
AS Ambrosiana-Inter Milano: 1-1 Pietro FERRARIS (78').
Referee: Leslie E.DALE (ENG)   Attendance: 10.000

25-06-1939   Stadio del Littoriale, Bologna:
                        Bologna AGC – ASC Venus Bucuresti 5-0 (1-0)
Bologna AGC: Pietro FERRARI, Dino FIORINI, Secondo RICCI, Mario PAGOTTO, Michele
ANDREOLO Frodella (URU), Giordano CORSI, Amedeo BIAVATI, Raffaele SANSONE
(URU), Bruno MAINI, Pietro ANDREOLI, Carlo REGUZZONI. (Coach: Árpád WEISZ
(HUN)).
ASC Venus Bucuresti: Nicolae IORDACHESCU, Lazar SFERA, Gheorghe ALBU, Alfred
EISENBEISSER, Vasile GAIN, Ion LUPAS, Nicolae ENE, Cornel ORZA, Silviu
PLOESTEANU, Iuliu BODOLA, Traian IORDACHE. (Coach: Béla JÁNOSY (HUN)).
Goals: Bologna AGC: 1-0 Raffaele SANSONE (20'), 2-0 Bruno MAINI (46'), 3-0 Bruno
MAINI (68'), 4-0 Carlo REGUZZONI (75'), 5-0 Carlo REGUZZONI (88').
Referee: Gustav KRIST (TCH)   Attendance: 7.000

25-06-1939   Stadion BSK, Beograd: BSK Beograd – SK Slavia Praha 3-0 (1-0)
BSK Beograd: Anton PUHAR, Djordje STOJILJKOVIC, Ernest DUBAC, Petar MANOLA,
Gustav LEHNER, Bruno KNEZEVIC, Svetislav GLISOVIC, Djordje (Djokica)
VUJADINOVIC, Blagoje (Mosa) MARJANOVIC, Vojin (Skoba) BOZOVIC, Ján
PODHRADSKÝ. (Coach: Alex NEMESCH).
SK Slavia Praha: Alexej BOKSAY, Josef TRUHLÁR, Ferdinand DAUCÍK, Karel PRUCHA,
Otakar NOZÍR, Vlastimil KOPECKÝ, Václav HORÁK, Bedrich VACEK, Josef BICAN,
Vojtech BRADÁC, Rudolf VYTLACIL (AUT). (Coach: Jan REICHARDT).
Goals: BSK Beograd: 1-0 Vojin (Skoba) BOZOVIC (29'), 2-0 Djordje (Djokica)
VUJADINOVIC (71'), 3-0 Svetislav GLISOVIC (75').
Referee: Raffaele SCORZONI (ITA)   Attendance: 6.000

01-07-1939   Stadión Sparta/Letná, Praha:
                        AC Sparta Praha – Ferencvárosi TC Budapest 0-2 (0-0)
AC Sparta Praha: Alois VECHET, Jaroslav BURGR, Josef CTYROKÝ, Josef KOSTÁLEK,
Jaroslav BOUCEK, Karel KOLSKÝ, Jan RÍHA, Karel SENECKÝ, Josef ZEMAN, Josef
LUDL, Oldrich NEJEDLÝ. (Coach: Ferenc SZEDLACSEK (HUN)).
Ferencvárosi TC Budapest: József HÁDA, Sándor TÁTRAI, Kornél SZOYKA, Béla
MAGDA, Béla SÁROSI (III), Gyula LÁZÁR, Mihály TÁNCOS, Dr.György SÁROSI, Gyula
POLGÁR, István KISZELY, László GYETVAI. (Coach: György HLAVAY).
Goals: Ferencvárosi TC Budapest: 0-1 Dr.György SÁROSI (70'), 0-2 István KISZELY (74').
Referee: Generoso DATTILO (ITA)   Attendance: 29.000

89

03-07-1939   Stadión Slaviá/Letná, Praha: SK Slavia Praha – BSK Beograd   2-1 (2-1)
SK Slavia Praha: Alexej BOKSAY, Josef TRUHLÁR, Ferdinand DAUCÍK, Karel PRUCHA, Otakar NOZÍR, Oldrich ZAJÍCEK, Václav HORÁK, Bedrich VACEK, Josef BICAN, Vlastimil KOPECKÝ, Rudolf VYTLACIL (AUT) (expulsion 45'). (Coach: Jan REICHARDT).
BSK Beograd: Srdan MRKUSIC, Djordje STOJILJKOVIC, Ernest DUBAC, Petar MANOLA, Prvoslav DRAGICEVIC, Gustav LEHNER, Svetislav GLISOVIC, Djordje (Djokica) VUJADINOVIC (expulsion 45'), Vojin (Skoba) BOZOVIC, Svetislav VALJAREVIC, Ján PODHRADSKÝ. (Coach: Alex NEMESCH).
Goals: SK Slavia Praha: 1-0 Josef BICAN (5'), 2-1 Josef BICAN (45').
BSK Beograd: 1-1 Ján PODHRADSKÝ (15').
Referee: Dionisi-Nicolae XIFANDO (ROM)   Attendance: 15.000
(Srdan MRKUSIC saved a 57th minute penalty taken by Josef BICAN).

SEMI-FINALS

09-07-1939   Stadion BSK, Beograd: BSK Beograd – Újpesti TE   4-2 (2-1)
BSK Beograd: Srdan MRKUSIC, Djordje STOJILJKOVIC, Ernest DUBAC, Petar MANOLA, Prvoslav DRAGICEVIC, Gustav LEHNER, Svetislav GLISOVIC, Djordje (Djokica) VUJADINOVIC, Vojin (Skoba) BOZOVIC, Frane MATOSIC, Dobrivoje ZECEVIC. (Coach: István MÉSZÁROS (HUN)).
Újpesti TE: Ferenc SZIKLAI, Gyula FUTÓ, Jenö FEKETE, Antal SZALAY, György SZÜCS, István BALOGH, Sándor ÁDÁM, Jenö VINCZE, Gyula ZSENGELLÉR, Lipót KÁLLAI, Géza KOCSIS. (Coach: Béla GUTTMANN).
Goals: BSK Beograd: 1-0 Vojin (Skoba) BOZOVIC (18'), 2-0 Vojin (Skoba) BOZOVIC (23'), 3-1 Djordje (Djokica) VUJADINOVIC (48'), 4-2 Antal SZALAY (82' own goal).
Újpesti TE: 2-1 Géza KOCSIS (41'), 3-2 Gyula ZSENGELLÉR (53' penalty).
Referee: Albert Edward EIBA (ENG)   Attendance: 16.000

09-07-1939   Stadio del Littoriale, Bologna:
                   Bologna AGC – Ferencvárosi TC Budapest   3-1 (0-1)
Bologna AGC: Pietro FERRARI, Mario PAGOTTO, Secondo RICCI, Bruno MAINI, Michele ANDREOLO Frodella (URU), Giordano CORSI, Amedeo BIAVATI, Raffaele SANSONE (URU), Héctor (Ettore) PURICELLI (URU), Pietro ANDREOLI, Carlo REGUZZONI. (Coach: Árpád WEISZ (HUN)).
Ferencvárosi TC Budapest: József HÁDA, Sándor TÁTRAI, Kornél SZOYKA, Béla MAGDA, Béla SÁROSI (III), Gyula LÁZÁR, Mihály TÁNCOS, Gyula POLGÁR, Dr.György SÁROSI, István KISZELY, László GYETVAI. (Coach: György HLAVAY).
Goals: Bologna AGC: 1-1 Héctor (Ettore) PURICELLI (64'), 2-1 Héctor (Ettore) PURICELLI (70'), 3-1 Héctor (Ettore) PURICELLI (71').
Ferencvárosi TC Budapest: 0-1 István KISZELY (37').
Referee: Robert C.GREENWOOD (ENG)   Attendance: 20.000

15-07-1939   Megyeri út, Budapest: Újpesti TE – BSK Beograd   7-1 (1-1)
Újpesti TE: Ferenc SZIKLAI, Gyula FUTÓ, Jenö FEKETE, Antal SZALAY, György SZÜCS,
István BALOGH, Sándor ÁDÁM, Jenö VINCZE, Gyula ZSENGELLÉR, Lipót KÁLLAI,
Géza KOCSIS. (Coach: Béla GUTTMANN).
BSK Beograd: Srdan MRKUSIC, Djordje STOJILJKOVIC, Ernest DUBAC, Petar MANOLA,
Prvoslav DRAGICEVIC, Gustav LEHNER, Svetislav GLISOVIC, Djordje (Djokica)
VUJADINOVIC, Vojin (Skoba) BOZOVIC, Frane MATOSIC, Dobrivoje ZECEVIC. (Coach:
István MÉSZÁROS (HUN)).
Goals: Újpesti TE: 1-1 Jenö VINCZE (43'), 2-1 Gyula ZSENGELLÉR (50'), 3-1 Gyula
ZSENGELLÉR (62'), 4-1 Gyula ZSENGELLÉR (72'), 5-1 Jenö VINCZE (80'), 6-1 Gyula
ZSENGELLÉR (84'), 7-1 Gyula ZSENGELLÉR (88').
BSK Beograd: 0-1 Frane MATOSIC (30').
Referee: Rinaldo BARLASSINA (ITA)   Attendance: 15.000

16-07-1939   Üllöi út, Budapest: Ferencvárosi TC Budapest – Bologna AGC   4-1 (1-1)
Ferencvárosi TC Budapest: József HÁDA, Sándor TÁTRAI, Kornél SZOYKA, Béla
MAGDA, Béla SÁROSI (III), Gyula LÁZÁR, Mihály TÁNCOS, Gyula KISS, Dr.György
SÁROSI, Géza TOLDI, László GYETVAI. (Coach: György HLAVAY).
Bologna AGC: Pietro FERRARI, Mario PAGOTTO, Secondo RICCI, Bruno MAINI, Michele
ANDREOLO Frodella (URU), Giordano CORSI, Amedeo BIAVATI, Raffaele SANSONE
(URU), Héctor (Ettore) PURICELLI (URU), Pietro ANDREOLI, Carlo REGUZZONI.
(Coach: Árpád WEISZ (HUN)).
Goals: Ferencvárosi TC Budapest: 1-0 Géza TOLDI (2'), 2-1 Géza TOLDI (64'), 3-1 Géza
TOLDI (84'), 4-1 Géza TOLDI (86').
Bologna AGC: 1-1 Héctor (Ettore) PURICELLI (42').
Referee: James M.WILSHIRE (ENG)   Attendance: 18.000

FINAL

23-07-1939   Üllöi út, Budapest: Ferencvárosi TC Budapest – Újpesti TE   1-4 (0-2)
Ferencvárosi TC Budapest: József HÁDA, Sándor TÁTRAI, Kornél SZOYKA, Béla
MAGDA, Béla SÁROSI (III), Gyula LÁZÁR, Mihály TÁNCOS, Gyula KISS, Dr.György
SÁROSI, Géza TOLDI, László GYETVAI. (Coach: György HLAVAY).
Újpesti TE: Ferenc SZIKLAI, Gyula FUTÓ, Jenö FEKETE, Antal SZALAY, György SZÜCS,
István BALOGH, Sándor ÁDÁM, Jenö VINCZE, Gyula ZSENGELLÉR, Lipót KÁLLAI,
Géza KOCSIS. (Coach: Béla GUTTMANN).
Goals: Ferencvárosi TC Budapest: 1-3 Dr.György SÁROSI (73').
Újpesti TE: 0-1 Gyula ZSENGELLÉR (9'), 0-2 Géza KOCSIS (10'), 0-3 Géza KOCSIS (53'),
1-4 Gyula ZSENGELLÉR (74').
Referee: Gustav KRIST (TCH)   Attendance:12.000

91

30-07-1939   Megyeri út, Budapest: Újpesti TE – Ferencvárosi TC Budapest 2-2 (0-2)
Újpesti TE: Ferenc SZIKLAI, Gyula FUTÓ, Jenö FEKETE, Antal SZALAY, György SZÜCS,
István BALOGH, Sándor ÁDÁM, Jenö VINCZE, Gyula ZSENGELLÉR, Lipót KÁLLAI,
Géza KOCSIS. (Coach: Béla GUTTMANN).
Ferencvárosi TC Budapest: József PÁLINKÁS, Sándor TÁTRAI, Kornél SZOYKA, Gyula
POLGÁR, Béla SÁROSI (III), Gyula LÁZÁR, Mihály BÍRÓ, Dr.György SÁROSI, Géza
TOLDI, István KISZELY, László GYETVAI. (Coach: György HLAVAY).
Goals: Újpesti TE: 1-2 Sándor ÁDÁM (54'), 2-2 István BALOGH (82').
Ferencvárosi TC Budapest: 0-1 István KISZELY (15' penalty), 0-2 István KISZELY (29').
Referee: Generoso DATTILO (ITA)   Attendance: 15.000

*** Újpesti TE won the Cup ***

1940

QUARTER-FINALS

16-06-1940   Hungária körút, Budapest:
Hungária FC Budapest – CS Rapid Bucuresti   1-2 (1-1)
Hungária FC Budapest: Antal SZABÓ (I), Károly KIS, Sándor BÍRÓ, NÉGYESI, József
TURAY, János DUDÁS, Bertalan BÉKY, József VIDOR, István KARDOS, Heinrich
MÜLLER (AUT), Pál TITKOS. (Coach: Imre SENKEY)
CS Rapid Bucuresti: Petre RADULESCU, Iosif SLIVATZ, Iosif LENGHERIU, Vintila
COSSINI, Gheorghe RASINARU, Ioachim MOLDOVEANU, Willy Vilmos (Vilim) SIPOS
(HUN), Johann WETZER (III), Iuliu BARÁTKY, Dan GAVRILESCU, Ion BOGDAN.
(Coach: Stefan AUER/István AVAR (HUN)).
Goals: Hungária FC Budapest: 1-0 József VIDOR (24').
CS Rapid Bucuresti: 1-1 Károly KIS (29' own goal), 1-2 Willy Vilmos (Vilim) SIPOS (56').
Referee: Milenko PODUBSKI (YUG)   Attendance: 4.000
(Iuliu BARÁTKY was also known by his Hungarian name: Gyula BARÁTKY).

17-06-1940   Stadion BSK, Beograd: BSK Beograd – ASC Venus Bucuresti   3-0 (1-0)
BSK Beograd: Srdan MRKUSIC, Djordje STOJILJKOVIC, Ernest DUBAC, Petar MANOLA,
Prvoslav DRAGICEVIC, Gustav LEHNER, Svetislav GLISOVIC, Vojin BOZOVIC, Djordje
VUJADINOVIC, Svetislav VALJAREVIC, Milorad NIKOLIC. (Coach: Aleksandar
POPOVIC).
ASC Venus Bucuresti: Mircea DAVID, Lazar SFERA, Alexandru NEGRESCU, Rudolf
DEMETROVICI, Augustin IUHÁSZ, Ion LUPAS, Nicolae ENE, Silviu PLOESTEANU, Iuliu
BODOLA, Constantin (Kostas) HUMIS (GRE), Traian IORDACHE. (Coach: Béla JÁNOSY
(HUN)).
Goals: BSK Beograd: 1-0 Svetislav VALJAREVIC (6'), 2-0 Svetislav GLISOVIC (63'), 3-0
Milorad NIKOLIC (84').
Referee: József UJVARI (HUN)   Attendance: 10.000
(Augustin IUHÁSZ was also known by his Hungarian name: Gusztáv JUHÁSZ).

19-06-1940   Stadion Koturaska (Gradjanski Stadion), Zagreb:
1.HSK Gradjanski Zagreb – Újpesti TE   4-0 (1-0)
1.HSK Gradjanski Zagreb: Emil URCH, Miroslav (Meho) BROZOVIC, Ivan BELOSEVIC,
Svetozar (Milan) DJANIC, Ivan Oskar JAZBINSEK, Mirko KOKOTOVIC, Zvonimir
CIMERMANCIC, Franjo WÖLFL, August LESNIK, Milan ANTOLKOVIC, Drago
ZALANT. (Coach: Márton BUKOVI (HUN)).
Újpesti TE: Ferenc SZIKLAI, Gyula FUTÓ, Péter JOÓS, Antal SZALAY (I), János TEMES,
István BALOGH (I), Géza KOCSIS, Jenö VINCZE, György SZÜCS, Gyula ZSENGELLÉR,
Mátyás TÓTH (III). (Coach: István MÉSZÁROS).
Goals: 1.HSK Gradjanski Zagreb: 1-0 Ferenc SZIKLAI (2' own goal), 2-0 Zvonimir
CIMERMANCIC (69'), 3-0 Drago ZALANT (74'), 4-0 Drago ZALANT (90').
Attendance: 6.000

19-06-1940   Stadion Slavija, Sarajevo:
SK Slavija Sarajevo – Ferencvárosi TC Budapest 3-0 (2-0)
SK Slavija Sarajevo: KRSTALOVIC, Slavko ZAGORAC, PAVLIC, MARJANOVIC,
GLAVOSEVIC, PETKOVIC, VIDOVIC, SALIPUR, Milan RAJLIC, Predrag DJAJIC,
LAZAROVIC. (Coach: Vilmos WILHELM (HUN)).
Ferencvárosi TC Budapest: Gyula CSIKÓS, Dr.Kornél SZOYKA, Gyula POLGÁR, Gyula
LÁZÁR, Béla SÁROSI (III), Béla PÓSA, Mihály BÍRÓ (II), Gyula KISS, István KISZELY,
Károly BERÉNYI, László GYETVAI. (Coach: Lajos DIMÉNY).
Goals: SK Slavija Sarajevo: 1-0 SALIPUR (9'), 2-0 Milan RAJLIC (36'), 3-0 Milan RAJLIC
(65').
Attendance: 8.000

22-06-1940   Megyeri út, Budapest: Újpesti TE – 1.HSK Gradjanski Zagreb 0-1 (0-0)
Újpesti TE: Ferenc SZIKLAI, Gyula FUTÓ, Jenö FEKETE, Antal SZALAY (I), János
TEMES, István BALOGH (I), Sándor ÁDÁM, Jenö VINCZE, Gyula ZSENGELLÉR, Lipót
KÁLLAI, Géza KOCSIS. (Coach: István MÉSZÁROS).
1.HSK Gradjanski Zagreb: Emil URCH, Miroslav (Meho) BROZOVIC, Ivan BELOSEVIC,
Svetozar (Milan) DJANIC, Ivan Oskar JAZBINSEK, Mirko KOKOTOVIC, Zvonimir
CIMERMANCIC, Franjo WÖLFL, August LESNIK, Milan ANTOLKOVIC, Drago
ZALANT. (Coach: Bernard (Benda) HÜGL).
Goal: 1.HSK Gradjanski Zagreb: 0-1 János TEMES (61' *own goal*).
Attendance: 5.000

23-06-1940   Arena Venus, Bucuresti: ASC Venus Bucuresti – BSK Beograd 0-1 (0-1)
ASC Venus Bucuresti: Mircea DAVID, Lazar SFERA, Alexandru NEGRESCU, Rudolf
DEMETROVICI, Augustin IUHÁSZ, Ion LUPAS, Cornel ORZA, Silviu PLOESTEANU,
Constantin (Kostas) HUMIS (GRE), Petre VILCOV, Traian IORDACHE. (Coach: Béla
JÁNOSY (HUN)).
BSK Beograd: Srdan MRKUSIC, Djordje STOJILJKOVIC, Ernest DUBAC, Petar MANOLA,
Prvoslav DRAGICEVIC, Gustav LEHNER, Svetislav GLISOVIC, Djordje VUJADINOVIC,
Vojin BOZOVIC, Svetislav VALJAREVIC, Milorad NIKOLIC. (Coach: Aleksandar
POPOVIC).
Goal: BSK Beograd: 0-1 Vojin BOZOVIC (16').
Referee: Theodor KISS (HUN)

23-06-1940   Stadionul "ANEF", Bucuresti:
CS Rapid Bucuresti – Hungária FC Budapest 3-0 (2-0)
CS Rapid Bucuresti: Petre RADULESCU, Iosif SLIVATZ, Iosif LENGHERIU, Vintila
COSSINI, Gheorghe RASINARU, Ioachim MOLDOVEANU, Willy Vilmos (Vilim) SIPOS
(HUN), Johann WETZER (III), Stefan AUER/István AVAR (HUN), Iuliu BARÁTKY, Ion
BOGDAN. (Player-coach: Stefan AUER/István AVAR (HUN)).
Hungária FC Budapest: Antal SZABÓ (I), Károly KIS, Sándor BÍRÓ, NÉGYESI, Gusztáv
SEBES, János DUDÁS, Bertalan BÉKY, József VIDOR, Jenö KALMÁR, Heinrich MÜLLER
(AUT), Géza SZABÓ (III). (Coach: Imre SENKEY).
Goals: CS Rapid Bucuresti: 1-0 Willy Vilmos (Vilim) SIPOS (39'), 2-0 Ion BOGDAN (42'),
3-0 Iuliu BARÁTKY (72').
Referee: BAZART (YUG)   Attendance: 25.000

94

23-06-1940   Üllői út, Budapest:
Ferencvárosi TC Budapest – SK Slavija Sarajevo   11-0 (5-0)
Ferencvárosi TC Budapest: Gyula CSIKÓS, Dr.Kornél SZOYKA, Gyula POLGÁR, Gyula
LÁZÁR, Béla SÁROSI (III), Béla PÓSA, Mihály BÍRÓ (II), Gyula KISS, Károly FINTA,
Dr.György SÁROSI, László GYETVAI. (Coach: Lajos DIMÉNY).
SK Slavija Sarajevo: KRSTALOVIC, Slavko ZAGORAC, PAVLIC, MARJANOVIC,
GLAVOSEVIC, PETKOVIC, VIDOVIC, SALIPUR, Milan RAJLIC, Predrag DJAJIC,
BEBETIC (expulsion 72'). (Coach: Vilmos WILHELM (HUN)).
Goals: Ferencvárosi TC Budapest: 1-0 Dr.György SÁROSI (5'), 2-0 Gyula KISS (21'), 3-0
Károly FINTA (24'), 4-0 Károly FINTA (30'), 5-0 László GYETVAI (36'), 6-0 Dr.György
SÁROSI (54'), 7-0 Dr.György SÁROSI (57'), 8-0 Mihály BÍRÓ (63'), 9-0 Dr.György
SÁROSI (77'), 10-0 Dr.György SÁROSI (80'), 11-0 Mihály BÍRÓ (83').
Attendance: 11.000

SEMI-FINALS

29-06-1940   Stadion BSK, Beograd: BSK Beograd – Ferencvárosi TC Budapest   1-0 (1-0)
BSK Beograd: Srdan MRKUSIC, Djordje STOJILJKOVIC, Ernest DUBAC, Petar MANOLA,
Prvoslav DRAGICEVIC, Gustav LEHNER, Svetislav GLISOVIC, Svetislav VALJAREVIC,
Vojin BOZOVIC, Djordje VUJADINOVIC, Milorad NIKOLIC. (Coach: Aleksandar
POPOVIC).
Ferencvárosi TC Budapest: Gyula CSIKÓS, Dr.Kornél SZOYKA, Béla PÓSA, Gyula LÁZÁR,
Gyula POLGÁR, Béla SÁROSI (III), Mihály BÍRÓ (II), Gyula KISS, Károly FINTA, István
KISZELY, László GYETVAI. (Coach: Lajos DIMÉNY).
Goal: BSK Beograd: 1-0 Svetislav GLISOVIC (32').
Attendance: 10.000

30-06-1940   Stadion Koturaska (Gradjanski Stadion), Zagreb:
1.HSK Gradjanski Zagreb – CS Rapid Bucuresti   0-0
1.HSK Gradjanski Zagreb: Emil URCH, Miroslav (Meho) BROZOVIC, Ivan BELOSEVIC,
Svetozar (Milan) DJANIC, Ivan Oskar JAZBINSEK, Mirko KOKOTOVIC, Zvonimir
CIMERMANCIC, Franjo WÖLFL, August LESNIK, Milan ANTOLKOVIC, Florijan
MATEKALO. (Coach: Márton BUKOVI (HUN)).
CS Rapid Bucuresti: Petre RADULESCU, Iosif SLIVATZ, Iosif LENGHERIU, Vintila
COSSINI, Gheorghe RASINARU, Ioachim MOLDOVEANU, Ion BOGDAN, Francisc
SIMKO, Iuliu BARÁTKY, Dan GAVRILESCU, Stefan AUER/István AVAR (HUN). (Player-
coach: Stefan AUER/István AVAR (HUN)).

07-07-1940   Stadionul "ANEF", Bucuresti:
CS Rapid Bucuresti – 1.HSK Gradjanski Zagreb   0-0
CS Rapid Bucuresti: Petre RADULESCU, Iosif SLIVATZ, Iosif LENGHERIU, Vintila
COSSINI, Gheorghe RASINARU, Ioachim MOLDOVEANU, Willy Vilmos (Vilim) SIPOS
(HUN), Francisc SIMKO, Iuliu BARÁTKY, Stefan AUER/István AVAR (HUN), Ion
BOGDAN. (Player-coach: Stefan AUER/István AVAR (HUN)).
1.HSK Gradjanski Zagreb: Emil URCH, Miroslav (Meho) BROZOVIC, Ivan BELOSEVIC,
Svetozar (Milan) DJANIC, Ivan Oskar JAZBINSEK, Mirko KOKOTOVIC, Zvonimir
CIMERMANCIC, Franjo WÖLFL, August LESNIK, Milan ANTOLKOVIC, Florijan
MATEKALO. (Coach: Márton BUKOVI (HUN)).
Referee: Todor ATANASOV (BUL)

07-07-1940   Üllöi út, Budapest: Ferencvárosi TC Budapest – BSK Beograd   2-0 (0-0)
Ferencvárosi TC Budapest: Gyula CSIKÓS, Dr.Kornél SZOYKA, Béla PÓSA, Béla SÁROSI
(III), Gyula POLGÁR, Gyula LÁZÁR, Mihály BÍRÓ (II), Gyula KISS, Károly FINTA,
Dr.György SÁROSI, László GYETVAI. (Coach: Lajos DIMÉNY).
BSK Beograd: Srdan MRKUSIC, Djordje STOJILJKOVIC, Ernest DUBAC, Petar MANOLA,
Prvoslav DRAGICEVIC, Gustav LEHNER, Svetislav GLISOVIC, Svetislav VALJAREVIC,
Vojin BOZOVIC, Djordje VUJADINOVIC, Milorad NIKOLIC. (Coach: Aleksandar
POPOVIC).
Goals: Ferencvárosi TC Budapest: 1-0 Dr.György SÁROSI (65'), 2-0 Gyula LÁZÁR (72').
Attendance: 12.000

10-07-1940   Gradski Stadion, Subotica:
                    1.HSK Gradjanski Zagreb – CS Rapid Bucuresti   1-1 (1-1)
1.HSK Gradjanski Zagreb: Emil URCH, Miroslav (Meho) BROZOVIC, Ivan BELOSEVIC,
Svetozar (Milan) DJANIC, Ivan Oskar JAZBINSEK, Mirko KOKOTOVIC, Branko (Isusek)
PLESE, Zvonimir CIMERMANCIC, Franjo WÖLFL, Milan ANTOLKOVIC, Florijan
MATEKALO. (Coach: Márton BUKOVI (HUN)).
CS Rapid Bucuresti: Petre RADULESCU, Iosif SLIVATZ, Iosif LENGHERIU, Ion COSTEA,
Johann WETZER (III), Ioachim MOLDOVEANU, Florian RADU, Francisc SIMKO, Iuliu
BARÁTKY, Dan GAVRILESCU, Ion BOGDAN. (Player-coach: Stefan AUER/István AVAR
(HUN)).
Goals: 1.HSK Gradjanski Zagreb: 1-0 Zvonimir CIMERMANCIC (1').
CS Rapid Bucuresti: 1-1 Ion BOGDAN (14').
Referee: Alois BERANEK (AUT)   Attendance: 6.000

(Play-off match. CS Rapid Bucuresti won the game on the toss of a coin).

FINAL

The tournament was abandoned due to problems caused by the onset of World War II.

Zentropa Cup

1951

03-07-1951   Praterstadion, Wien: SC Wacker Wien – NK Dinamo Zagreb   4-1 (2-0)
SC Wacker Wien: Franz PELIKAN, Franz PAVUZA, Wilhelm MACHO, Franz PRAK, Josef
CIZEK, Theodor BRINEK Jr., Ernst BOKON, Theodor (Turl) WAGNER, Richard
BROUSEK, Wilhelmd (Willi) HAHNEMANN, Walter HAUMMER. (Coach: Eduard (Edi)
FRÜHWIRTH).
NK Dinamo Zagreb: Branko STINCIC, Svemir DELIC, Tomislav CRNKOVIC, Vladimir-
Drago HORVAT (I), Ivica HORVAT (II), Kresimir PUKSEC, Branko REZEK, Zvonimir
CIMERMANCIC, Franjo WÖLFL, Zeljko CAJKOVSKI (II), Dionizije DVORNIC. (Coach:
Bernard HÜGL).
Goals: SC Wacker Wien: 1-0 Ernst BOKON (20'), 2-0 Walter HAUMMER (30'), 3-1 Theodor
BRINEK Jr. (59'), 4-1 Richard BROUSEK (89').
NK Dinamo Zagreb: 2-1 Ivica HORVAT (II) (54').
Referee: Giacomo BERTOLIO (ITA)   Attendance: 26.000

03-07-1951   Praterstadion, Wien: SK Rapid Wien – SS Lazio Roma   5-0 (2-0)
SK Rapid Wien: Walter ZEMAN, Maximilian (Max) MERKEL, Ernst Franz Hermann
HAPPEL, Alfred TEINITZER, Gerhard HANAPPI, Erich MÜLLER, Robert KÖRNER (I),
Johann (Hans) RIEGLER, Leopold GERNHARDT, Erich PROBST, Alfred KÖRNER (II).
(Coach: Johann (Hans) PESSER).
SS Lazio Roma: Lucidio SENTIMENTI (IV), Francesco ANTONAZZI, Zeffiro FURIASSI,
Romolo ALZANI, Stefano MALACARNE, Mario MAGRINI, Aldo PUCCINELLI, Enrique
FLAMINI (ARG), Gulesin SUKRU (TUR), Flavio CECCONI, Vittorio SENTIMENTI (V).
(Coach: Mario SPERONE).
Goals: SK Rapid Wien: 1-0 Erich PROBST (15'), 2-0 Alfred KÖRNER (43'), 3-0 Erich
PROBST (51'), 4-0 Erich PROBST (62'), 5-0 Gerhard HANAPPI (71').
Referee: Marian MATANCIC (YUG)   Attendance: 23.000

3rd & 4th PLACE MATCH

05-07-1951   Praterstadion, Wien: NK Dinamo Zagreb – SS Lazio Roma   2-0 (1-0)
NK Dinamo Zagreb: Branko STINCIC, Svemir DELIC, Tomislav CRNKOVIC, Vladimir-Drago HORVAT (I), Ivica HORVAT (II), Branko REZEK, Bozidar SENCAR, Zvonimir CIMERMANCIC, Dionizije DVORNIC, Zeljko CAJKOVSKI (II), Aleksandar BENKO (I). (Coach: Bernard HÜGL).
SS Lazio Roma: Lucidio SENTIMENTI (IV), Francesco ANTONAZZI, Zeffiro FURIASSI, Romolo ALZANI, Stefano MALACARNE, Mario MAGRINI, Aldo PUCCINELLI, Enrique FLAMINI (ARG), Gulesin SUKRU (TUR), Mido BIMBI, Vittorio SENTIMENTI (V). (Coach: Mario SPERONE).
Goals: NK Dinamo Zagreb: 1-0 Zeljko CAJKOVSKI (19'), 2-0 Dionizije DVORNIC (86').
Referee: BENEK (AUT)   Attendance: 3.000

FINAL

05-07-1951   Praterstadion, Wien: SK Rapid Wien – SC Wacker Wien   3-2 (1-1)
SK Rapid Wien: Josef MUSIL, Maximilian (Max) MERKEL, Ernst Franz Hermann HAPPEL, Erich MÜLLER, Gerhard HANAPPI, Alfred TEINITZER, Robert KÖRNER (I), Johann (Hans) RIEGLER, Leopold GERNHARDT, Erich PROBST, Alfred KÖRNER (II). (Coach: Johann (Hans) PESSER).
SC Wacker Wien: Franz PELIKAN, Franz PAVUZA, Wilhelm MACHO, Ernst KOZLICEK, Josef CIZEK, Franz PRAK, Ernst BOKON, Theodor (Turl) WAGNER, Richard BROUSEK, Wilhelmd (Willi) HAHNEMANN, Ernst Josef FORETH. (Coach: Eduard (Edi) FRÜHWIRTH).
Goals: SK Rapid Wien: 1-1 Leopold GERNHARDT (40'), 2-2 Erich PROBST (58'), 3-2 Ernst Franz Hermann HAPPEL (90' penalty).
SC Wacker Wien: 0-1 Theodor (Turl) WAGNER (32'), 1-2 Ernst Josef FORETH (50').
Referee: CAMPANI (ITA)   Attendance: 9.000

*** SK Rapid Wien won the Cup ***

1955

PRELIMINARY ROUND

29-06-1955   Népstadion, Budapest:
Budapesti Vörös Lobogó SE – SC Wacker Wien   3-3 (1-2)
Budapesti Vörös Lobogó SE: Árpád FAZEKAS, József KOVÁCS (II), János BÖRZSEI, Mihály LANTOS, Imre KOVÁCS (I), József ZAKARIÁS, Károly SÁNDOR, Endre KÁRÁSZ, Nándor HIDEGKUTI, Gábor ARATÓ, István SZIMCSÁK (I). (Coach: Tibor KEMÉNY).
SC Wacker Wien: Franz PELIKAN, Franz CHALUPETZKY, Walter KOLLMANN, Ernst Josef FORETH, Paul KOZLICEK (I), Anton WOLF, Adalbert KAUBEK, Theodor (Turl) WAGNER, Richard BROUSEK, Ernst KOZLICEK (II), Walter HAUMMER.
Goals: Budapesti Vörös Lobogó SE: 1-0 Gábor ARATÓ (8'), 2-2 Endre KÁRÁSZ (53'), 3-2 Endre KÁRÁSZ (58').
SC Wacker Wien: 1-1 Adalbert KAUBEK (10'), 1-2 Walter HAUMMER (17'), 3-3 Adalbert KAUBEK (66').
Referee: Francesco LIVERANI (ITA)   Attendance: 45.000

29-06-1955   Novi Sad: FK Vojvodina Novi Sad – AS Roma   4-1 (2-1)
FK Vojvodina Novi Sad: RISTIC, SELENA, Zarko NIKOLIC, MALENCIC, Sima MILOVANOV, Dobroslav KRSTIC (II), Novak ROGANOVIC, Zdravko RAJKOV, Vujadin BOSKOV, Alexander IVOS (expulsion 75'), Radomir KRSTIC (I). (Coach: Gustav LECHNER).
AS Roma: Giuseppe MORO, Giosuè STUCCHI, Alberto ELIANI (expulsion 82'), Raoul BORTOLETTO, Luigi GIULIANO (expulsion 75'), Arcadio VENTURI, Alcides Edgardo GHIGGIA (URU), Celestino CELIO, Giancarlo (Carlo) GALLI, Armando CAVAZZUTI, Stefano (István) Etienne NYERS (FRA). (Coach: György SÁROSI (HUN)).
Goals: FK Vojvodina Novi Sad: 1-0 Radomir KRSTIC (I) (9'), 2-0 Alexander IVOS (20'), 3-1 Alexander IVOS (46'), 4-1 Zdravko RAJKOV (78').
AS Roma: 2-1 Stefano NYERS (34').
Referee: Andor DOROGI (HUN)   Attendance: 18.000

02-07-1955   Praterstadion, Wien:
SC Wacker Wien – Budapesti Vörös Lobogó SE   2-2 (2-2)
SC Wacker Wien: Franz PELIKAN, Franz CHALUPETZKY, Walter KOLLMANN, Ernst Josef FORETH, Paul KOZLICEK (I), Anton WOLF, Adalbert KAUBEK, Theodor (Turl) WAGNER, Richard BROUSEK, Ernst KOZLICEK (II), Walter HAUMMER.
Budapesti Vörös Lobogó SE: Árpád FAZEKAS, József KOVÁCS (II), János BÖRZSEI, Mihály LANTOS, Imre KOVÁCS (I), József ZAKARIÁS, Károly SÁNDOR, Nándor HIDEGKUTI, Péter PALOTÁS, Endre KÁRÁSZ, István SZIMCSÁK (I). (Coach: Tibor KEMÉNY).
Goals: SC Wacker Wien: 1-1 József KOVÁCS (20' *own goal*), 2-1 Adalbert KAUBEK (40').
Budapesti Vörös Lobogó SE: 0-1 Franz CHALUPETZKY (1' *own goal*), 2-2 Nándor HIDEGKUTI (42').
Referee: Leo LEMESIC (YUG)   Attendance: 22.000

99

03-07-1955   Stadio Olimpico, Roma: AS Roma – FK Vojvodina Novi Sad 4-5 (3-1)
AS Roma: Giuseppe MORO, Luigi GIULIANO, Alberto ELIANI, Raoul BORTOLETTO,
Amos CARDARELLI, Arcadio VENTURI, Alcides Edgardo GHIGGIA (URU), Celestino
CELIO, Giancarlo (Carlo) GALLI, Egidio GUARNACCI, Stefano (István) Etienne NYERS
(FRA). (Coach: György SÁROSI (HUN)).
FK Vojvodina Novi Sad: RISTIC, SELENA, Zarko NIKOLIC, BLANARIK, Sima
MILOVANOV, Dobroslav KRSTIC (II), Novak ROGANOVIC, Zdravko RAJKOV, Vujadin
BOSKOV, Alexander IVOS, Radomir KRSTIC (I). (Coach: Gustav LECHNER).
Goals: AS Roma: 1-0 GALLI (10'), 2-0 Carlo GALLI (12'), 3-0 Carlo GALLI (28'), 4-1 Luigi
GIULIANO (56').
FK Vojvodina Novi Sad: 3-1 Radomir KRSTIC (I) (34'), 4-2 Zdravko RAJKOV (63'), 4-3
Zdravko RAJKOV (66'), 4-4 Zdravko RAJKOV (87'), 4-5 Zdravko RAJKOV (89').
Referee: Friedrich (Fritz) SEIPELT (AUT)   Attendance: 40.000

05-07-1955   Praterstadion, Wien:
              SC Wacker Wien – Budapesti Vörös Lobogó SE 1-5 (1-3)
SC Wacker Wien: Franz PELIKAN, Franz CHALUPETZKY, Walter KOLLMANN, Ernst
Josef FORETH, Paul KOZLICEK (I), Anton WOLF, Adalbert KAUBEK, Theodor (Turl)
WAGNER, Richard BROUSEK, Ernst KOZLICEK (II), Walter HAUMMER.
Budapesti Vörös Lobogó SE: Árpád FAZEKAS, József KOVÁCS (II), Imre KOVÁCS (I),
Mihály LANTOS, Ferenc KOVÁCS (III), József ZAKARIÁS, Károly SÁNDOR, Endre
KÁRÁSZ, Nándor HIDEGKUTI, János MOLNÁR, István SZIMCSÁK (I). (Coach: Tibor
KEMÉNY).
Goals: SC Wacker Wien: 1-2 Richard BROUSEK (20' penalty).
Budapesti Vörös Lobogó SE: 0-1 Nándor HIDEGKUTI (13'), 0-2 János MOLNÁR (14'), 1-3
János MOLNÁR (39'), 1-4 János MOLNÁR (50'), 1-5 Nándor HIDEGKUTI (70').
Referee: Jaroslav VLCEK (TCH)   Attendance: 16.000

(Play-off match).

QUARTER-FINALS

06-07-1955   Népstadion, Budapest: Budapesti Honvéd SE – Wiener Sportklub 5-2 (3-2)
Budapesti Honvéd SE: Lajos FARAGÓ, László RÁKÓCZI, Gyula LÓRÁNT, Antal KOTÁSZ,
József BOZSIK, Nándor BÁNYAI, László BUDAI (II), Sándor KOCSIS, Lajos TICHÝ,
Ferenc PUSKÁS, Zoltán CZIBOR. (Coach: Jenö KALMÁR).
Wiener Sportklub: Rudolf SZANWALD, Erich HASENKOPF, Johann MACH, Heinrich
BÜLLWATSCH, Erwin STADLMAYR, Leopold BARSCHANDT, Stefan SZOKOL, Johann
HOWANIETZ, Karl MIESSLER, Erich HOF, Walter HORAK. (Coach: Johann (Hans)
PESSER).
Goals: Budapesti Honvéd SE: 1-1 Lajos TICHÝ (11'), 2-1 Sándor KOCSIS (13'), 3-2 Ferenc
PUSKÁS (23' penalty), 4-2 Sándor KOCSIS (72'), 5-2 Sándor KOCSIS (81').
Wiener Sportklub: 0-1 Karl MIESSLER (3'), 2-2 Karl MIESSLER (18').
Referee: Ecio DAMJANI (YUG)   Attendance: 40.000

06-07-1955   Novi Sad: FK Vojvodina Novi Sad – Slovan UNV Bratislava   0-0
FK Vojvodina Novi Sad: RISTIC, SELENA, Sima MILOVANOV, Zarko NIKOLIC,
BLANARIC, Dobroslav KRSTIC (II), Novak ROGANOVIC, Zdravko RAJKOV, Vujadin
BOSKOV, Alexander IVOS, Radomir KRSTIC (I). (Coach: Gustav LECHNER).
Slovan UNV Bratislava: Karol TIBENSKÝ, Vojtech JANKOVIC, Michal VICAN, Mikulás
CIRKA, Jozef JAJCAJ, Michal BENEDIKOVIC, Jozef VENGLOS, Anton BÍLÝ, Viktor
TEGELHOFF, Emil PAZICKÝ, Pavol MOLNÁR. (Coach: Leopold STASTNÝ).
Referee: Johann PRIBYL (AUT)   Attendance: 18.000

06-07-1955   Bologna: FC Bologna – U.D.A. Praha   2-4 (1-2)
FC Bologna: Anselmo GIORCELLI, Guglielmo GIOVANNINI, Bruno FAVALLI, Tage Ivan
Linde JENSEN (DEN), Fedele GRECO, Dino BALLACI, Giorgio VALENTINUZZI, Gino
PIVATTELI, Gino CAPPELLO, Ugo POZZAN, Cesarino CERVELATTI. (Coach: Giuseppe
Ferruccio (Gipo) VIANI).
U.D.A. Praha: Václav PAVLIS, Jirí JECNÝ, Ladislav NOVÁK, Jirí TRNKA, Svatopluk
PLUSKAL, Milan DVORÁK, Arnost PAZDERA, Josef MASOPUST, Jaroslav
BOROVICKA, Ladislav PRÁDA, Tadeás KRAUS. (Coach: Karel KOLSKÝ).
Goals: FC Bologna: 1-2 Gino PIVATELLI (44'), 2-3 Gino PIVATELLI (68' penalty).
U.D.A. Praha: 0-1 Josef MASOPUST (9'), 0-2 Ladislav PRÁDA (24'), 1-3 Ladislav PRÁDA
(65'), 2-4 Josef MASOPUST (71').
Referee: Vasa STEFANOVIC (YUG)   Attendance: 12.000

09-07-1955   Wiener Sportklub-Platz, Wien:
                   Wiener Sportklub – Budapesti Honvéd SE   4-5 (1-2)
Wiener Sportklub: Rudolf SZANWALD, Erich HASENKOPF, Johann MACH, Heinrich
BÜLLWATSCH, Erwin STADLMAYR, Leopold BARSCHANDT, Stefan SZOKOL, Johann
HOWANIETZ, Karl MIESSLER, Erich HOF, Walter HORAK. (Coach: Johann (Hans)
PESSER).
Budapesti Honvéd SE: Lajos FARAGÓ, László RÁKÓCZI, Tibor PALICSKÓ, Antal
KOTÁSZ, József BOZSIK, Nándor BÁNYAI, László BUDAI (II), Sándor KOCSIS, Ferenc
MACHOS, Ferenc PUSKÁS, Zoltán CZIBOR. (Coach: Jenö KALMÁR).
Goals: Wiener Sportklub: 1-0 Walter HORAK (22'), 2-3 Stefan SZOKOL (60'), 3-4 Karl
MIESSLER (63' penalty), 4-5 Erich HOF (90').
Budapesti Honvéd SE: 1-1 Zoltán CZIBOR (24'), 1-2 Sándor KOCSIS (26'), 1-3 Ferenc
PUSKÁS (54'), 2-4 József BOZSIK (61'), 3-5 Zoltán CZIBOR (78').
Referee: Cesare JONNI (ITA)   Attendance: 13.000

09-07-1955   Népstadion, Budapest:
                   Budapesti Vörös Lobogó SE – NK Hajduk Split   6-0 (4-0)
Budapesti Vörös Lobogó SE: Árpád FAZEKAS, József KOVÁCS (II), János BÖRZSEI,
Ferenc KOVÁCS (III), Imre KOVÁCS (I), József ZAKARIÁS, Károly SÁNDOR, Endre
KÁRÁSZ, Nándor HIDEGKUTI, János MOLNÁR, István SZIMCSÁK (I). (Coach: Tibor
KEMÉNY).
NK Hajduk Split: Ante VULIC, Ljubomir KOKEZA, Davor GRCIC (II), Bozo BROKETA,
Lenko GRCIC (I), Slavko LUSTICA, Sulejman REBAC, Bernard VUKAS, Frane MATOSIC,
Josko VIDOSEVIC, Nikola RADOVIC.
Goals: Budapesti Vörös Lobogó SE: 1-0 János MOLNÁR (4'), 2-0 István SZIMCSÁK (12'),
3-0 Károly SÁNDOR (32'), 4-0 Endre KÁRÁSZ (37'), 5-0 Károly SÁNDOR (51'), 6-0
Nándor HIDEGKUTI (70').
Referee: ZOLKO (Nationality not known)   Attendance: 15.000

101

10-07-1955   Bratislava: Slovan UNV Bratislava – FK Vojvodina Novi Sad   3-0 (1-0)
Slovan UNV Bratislava: Karol TIBENSKÝ, Vojtech JANKOVIC, Michal VICAN, Mikulás
CIRKA, Michal BENEDIKOVIC, Jozef JAJCAJ, Jozef VENGLOS, Anton BÍLÝ, Viktor
TEGELHOFF, Emil PAZICKÝ, CURGALI. (Coach: Leopold STASTNÝ).
FK Vojvodina Novi Sad: RISTIC, SELENA, Sima MILOVANOV, Zarko NIKOLIC, Vujadin
BOSKOV, Dobroslav KRSTIC (II), Novak ROGANOVIC, Zdravko RAJKOV, Todor
VESELINOVIC, Alexander IVOS, Radomir KRSTIC (I). (Coach: Gustav LECHNER).
Goals: Slovan UNV Bratislava: 1-0 Emil PAZICKY (17'), 2-0 Anton BILY (51'), 3-0 Anton
BILY (78').
Referee: János PÓSA-POLARECZKY (HUN)   Attendance: 45.000

10-07-1955   Praha: U.D.A. Praha – FC Bologna   3-0 (2-0)
U.D.A. Praha: Václav PAVLIS, Jirí JECNÝ, Ladislav NOVÁK, Ivo URBAN, Jirí HLEDIK,
Milan DVORÁK, Arnost PAZDERA, Josef MASOPUST, Jaroslav BOROVICKA, Ladislav
PRÁDA, Tadeás KRAUS. (Coach: Karel KOLSKÝ).
FC Bologna: Anselmo GIORCELLI, Guglielmo GIOVANNINI, Dino BALLACI, Tage Ivan
Linde JENSEN (DEN), Fedele GRECO, Giorgio VALENTINUZZI, Francesco
PANTALEONI, Ugo POZZAN, Gino PIVATTELI, José GARCIA (URU), Cesarino
CERVELATTI. (Coach: Giuseppe Ferruccio (Gipo) VIANI).
Goals: U.D.A. Praha: 1-0 Ladislav PRÁDA (12'), 2-0 Tadeás KRAUS (29'), 3-0 Tadeás
KRAUS (89').
Referee: Sándor HARANGOZÓ (HUN)   Attendance: 50.000

13-07-1955   Stadion Stari plac, Split:
              NK Hajduk Split – Budapesti Vörös Lobogó SE   3-2 (0-0)
NK Hajduk Split: Ante VULIC, Ljubomir KOKEZA, Davor GRCIC (II), Bozo BROKETA,
Lenko GRCIC (I), Slavko LUSTICA, Sulejman REBAC, Bernard VUKAS, Frane MATOSIC,
Josko VIDOSEVIC, Nikola RADOVIC.
Budapesti Vörös Lobogó SE: Árpád FAZEKAS, József KOVÁCS (II), János BÖRZSEI,
Ferenc KOVÁCS (III), Imre KOVÁCS (I), József ZAKARIÁS, Károly SÁNDOR, Endre
KÁRÁSZ, Nándor HIDEGKUTI, János MOLNÁR, István SZIMCSÁK (I). (Coach: Tibor
KEMÉNY).
Goals: NK Hajduk Split: 1-0 Frane MATOSIC (49'), 2-2 Bernard VUKAS (70'), 3-2 Josko
VIDOSEVIC (79').
Budapesti Vörös Lobogó SE: 1-1 Nándor HIDEGKUTI (64'), 1-2 Károly SÁNDOR (66').
Referee: Riccardo PIERI (ITA)   Attendance: 11.000

SEMI-FINALS

17-07-1955   Praha: U.D.A. Praha – Slovan UNV Bratislava   0-0
U.D.A. Praha: Václav PAVLIS, Jirí JECNÝ, Jirí HLEDIK, Ladislav NOVÁK, Ivo URBAN,
Milan DVORÁK, Arnost PAZDERA, Josef MASOPUST, Jirí TRNKA, Ladislav PRÁDA,
Tadeás KRAUS. (Coach: Karel KOLSKÝ).
Slovan UNV Bratislava: Karol TIBENSKÝ, Vojtech JANKOVIC, Michal VICAN, Mikulás
CIRKA, Jozef JAJCAJ, Michal BENEDIKOVIC, Jozef VENGLOS, Emil ÁRPÁS, Viktor
TEGELHOFF, Emil PAZICKÝ, Pavol MOLNÁR. (Coach: Leopold STASTNÝ).
Referee: János PÓSA-POLARECZKY (HUN)   Attendance: 25.000

18-07-1955   Népstadion, Budapest:
        Budapesti Honvéd SE – Budapesti Vörös Lobogó SE   5-2 (3-2)
Budapesti Honvéd SE: László HEINRICH, László RÁKÓCZI, Tibor PALICSKÓ, Antal
KOTÁSZ, József BOZSIK, Nándor BÁNYAI, László BUDAI (II), Sándor KOCSIS, Ferenc
MACHOS, Ferenc PUSKÁS, Zoltán CZIBOR. (Coach: Jenö KALMÁR).
Budapesti Vörös Lobogó SE: Árpád FAZEKAS, József KOVÁCS (II), János BÖRZSEI,
Ferenc KOVÁCS (III), Imre KOVÁCS (I), József ZAKARIÁS, Károly SÁNDOR, Endre
KÁRÁSZ, Nándor HIDEGKUTI, János MOLNÁR, István SZIMCSÁK (I). (Coach: Tibor
KEMÉNY).
Goals: Budapesti Honvéd SE: 1-0 Ferenc MACHOS (10'), 2-0 Zoltán CZIBOR (12'), 3-0
Sándor KOCSIS (14'), 4-2 Sándor KOCSIS (53'), 5-2 Ferenc MACHOS (79').
Budapesti Vörös Lobogó SE: 3-1 János MOLNÁR (16'), 3-2 Endre KÁRÁSZ (40').
Referee: Friedrich (Fritz) SEIPELT (AUT)   Attendance: 75.000

22-07-1955   Bratislava: Slovan UNV Bratislava – U.D.A. Praha   2-2 (0-2)
Slovan UNV Bratislava: Karol TIBENSKÝ, Vojtech JANKOVIC, Michal VICAN, Mikulás
CIRKA, Jozef JAJCAJ, Michal BENEDIKOVIC, Jozef VENGLOS, Anton BÍLÝ, Viktor
TEGELHOFF, Emil PAZICKÝ, Pavol MOLNÁR. (Coach: Leopold STASTNÝ).
U.D.A. Praha: Václav PAVLIS, Jirí JECNÝ, Jirí HLEDIK, Ladislav NOVÁK, Ivo URBAN,
Milan DVORÁK, Arnost PAZDERA, Josef MASOPUST, Jaroslav BOROVICKA, Ladislav
PRÁDA, Tadeás KRAUS. (Coach: Karel KOLSKÝ).
Goals: Slovan UNV Bratislava: 1-2 Michal VICAN (70' penalty), 2-2 Jozef JAJCAJ (88').
U.D.A. Praha: 0-1 Tadeás KRAUS (21'), 0-2 Arnost PAZDERA (25').
Referee: Johann PRIBYL (AUT)   Attendance: 20.000

23-07-1955   Népstadion, Budapest:
        Budapesti Vörös Lobogó SE – Budapesti Honvéd SE   5-1 (4-1)
Budapesti Vörös Lobogó SE: Árpád FAZEKAS, József KOVÁCS (II), János BÖRZSEI,
Ferenc KOVÁCS (III), Imre KOVÁCS (I), József ZAKARIÁS, Endre KÁRÁSZ, Gábor
ARATÓ, Nándor HIDEGKUTI, János MOLNÁR, István SZIMCSÁK (I). (Coach: Tibor
KEMÉNY).
Budapesti Honvéd SE: Lajos FARAGÓ, László RÁKÓCZI, Tibor PALICSKÓ, Antal
KOTÁSZ, József BOZSIK, Nándor BÁNYAI, László BUDAI (II), Sándor KOCSIS, Ferenc
MACHOS, Ferenc PUSKÁS, Zoltán CZIBOR. (Coach: Jenö KALMÁR).
Goals: Budapesti Vörös Lobogó SE: 1-0 János MOLNÁR (4'), 2-0 Imre KOVÁCS (22'
penalty), 3-0 János MOLNÁR (37'), 4-0 János MOLNÁR (42'), 5-1 Imre KOVÁCS (66').
Budapesti Honvéd SE: 4-1 Ferenc PUSKÁS (44').
Referee: Friedrich MAYER (AUT)   Attendance: 50.000

25-07-1955   Brno: U.D.A. Praha – Slovan UNV Bratislava   2-1 (0-0)
U.D.A. Praha: Václav PAVLIS, Jirí JECNÝ, Jirí HLEDIK, Ladislav NOVÁK, Svatopluk
PLUSKAL, Milan DVORÁK, Ladislav HLAVÁCEK, Ladislav PRÁDA, Josef MASOPUST,
Jan HERTL, Tadeás KRAUS. (Coach: Karel KOLSKÝ).
Slovan UNV Bratislava: Viliam SCHROJF, Vojtech JANKOVIC, Michal VICAN, Mikulás
CIRKA, Jozef JAJCAJ, Michal BENEDIKOVIC, Emil ÁRPÁS, Anton BÍLÝ, Viktor
TEGELHOFF, Emil PAZICKÝ, Pavol MOLNÁR. (Coach: Leopold STASTNÝ).
Goals: U.D.A. Praha: 1-0 Svatopluk PLUSKAL (52'), 2-0 Ladislav HLAVÁCEK (59').
Slovan UNV Bratislava: 2-1 Viktor TEGELHOFF (66').
Referee: Friedrich MAYER (AUT)   Attendance: 40.000
(Play-off match).

FINAL

30-07-1955   Népstadion, Budapest: Budapesti Vörös Lobogó SE – U.D.A. Praha 6-0 (4-0)
Budapesti Vörös Lobogó SE: Árpád FAZEKAS, József KOVÁCS (II), János BÖRZSEI,
Ferenc KOVÁCS (III), Imre KOVÁCS (I), József ZAKARIÁS, Károly SÁNDOR, Endre
KÁRÁSZ, Nándor HIDEGKUTI, János MOLNÁR, István SZIMCSÁK (I). (Coach: Tibor
KEMÉNY).
U.D.A. Praha: Václav PAVLIS, Jirí JECNÝ, Jirí HLEDIK, Ladislav NOVÁK, Josef
MASOPUST, Milan DVORÁK, Ladislav HLAVÁCEK, Arnost PAZDERA, Jaroslav
BOROVICKA, Ladislav PRÁDA, Tadeás KRAUS. (Coach: Karel KOLSKÝ).
Goals: Budapesti Vörös Lobogó SE: 1-0 Nándor HIDEGKUTI (4'), 2-0 Endre KÁRÁSZ (12'),
3-0 Nándor HIDEGKUTI (14'), 4-0 Nándor HIDEGKUTI (43'), 5-0 Ladislav NOVÁK (71'
own goal), 6-0 János MOLNÁR (76').
Referee: Friedrich MAYER (AUT)   Attendance: 70.000

04-08-1955   Stadión Strahov (Masaryk), Praha:
                  U.D.A. Praha – Budapesti Vörös Lobogó SE   1-2 (1-0)
U.D.A. Praha: Václav PAVLIS, Jirí JECNÝ, Jirí HLEDIK, Ladislav NOVÁK, Svatopluk
PLUSKAL, Jan HERTL, Ladislav HLAVÁCEK, Josef MASOPUST, Milan DVORÁK,
Ladislav PRÁDA, Arnost PAZDERA. (Coach: Karel KOLSKÝ).
Budapesti Vörös Lobogó SE: Árpád FAZEKAS, József KOVÁCS (II), János BÖRZSEI,
Ferenc KOVÁCS (III), Imre KOVÁCS (I), József ZAKARIÁS, Károly SÁNDOR, Nándor
HIDEGKUTI, Péter PALOTÁS, Endre KÁRÁSZ, István SZIMCSÁK (I). (Coach: Tibor
KEMÉNY).
Goals: U.D.A. Praha: 1-0 Ladislav PRÁDA (31').
Budapesti Vörös Lobogó SE: 1-1 Nándor HIDEGKUTI (55'), 1-2 Péter PALOTÁS (88').
Referee: Friedrich MAYER (AUT)   Attendance: 50.000

*** Budapesti Vörös Lobogó SE won the Cup ***

1956

QUARTER-FINALS

23-06-1956   Praterstadion, Wien: SC Wacker Wien – FK Partizan Beograd   1-1 (0-0)
SC Wacker Wien: Franz PELIKAN, Franz CHALUPETZKY, Walter KOLLMANN, Ernst
Josef FORETH, Paul KOZLICEK (I), Anton WOLF, Adalbert KAUBEK, Richard
BROUSEK, Ferdinand SMETANA, Ernst KOZLICEK (II), Walter HAUMMER. (Coach: Jenö
KALMÁR (HUN)).
FK Partizan Beograd: Slavko STOJANOVIC, Bruno BELIN, Branko ZEBEC, Cedomir
LAZAREVIC, Ranko BOROZAN, Bozidar PAJEVIC, Prvoslav MIHAJLOVIC (I), Stanoje
JOCIC, Marko VALOK, Tomislav KALOPEROVIC, Antun HERCEG. (Coach: Aleksandar
TOMASEVIC).
Goals: SC Wacker Wien: 1-1 Richard BROUSEK (49').
FK Partizan Beograd: 0-1 Marko VALOK (46').
Referee: Jaroslav VLCEK (TCH)   Attendance: 15.000

*(Double game played on the same day and at the same venue as the game between SK Rapid
Wien and Slovan UNV Bratislava)*

23-06-1956   Praterstadion, Wien: SK Rapid Wien – Slovan UNV Bratislava   3-0 (0-0)
SK Rapid Wien: Herbert GARTNER, Paul HALLA, Robert DIENST, Franz GOLOBIC, Josef
HÖLTL, Karl GIESSER, Robert KÖRNER (I), Johann RIEGLER, Gerhard HANAPPI, Alfred
KÖRNER (II), Josef BERTALAN. (Coach: Franz WAGNER).
Slovan UNV Bratislava: Viliam SCHROJF, Pavol BENA, Michal VICAN, Vojtech
JANKOVIC, Jozef JAJCAJ, Jozef VENGLOS, Anton MORAVCÍK, Július KOVÁC, Anton
BÍLÝ, Jozef OBERT, Pavol MOLNÁR. (Coach: Leopold STASTNÝ).
Goals: SK Rapid Wien: 1-0 Robert KÖRNER (65'), 2-0 Robert KÖRNER (67'), 3-0 Gerhard
HANAPPI (72').
Referee: Sándor HARANGOZÓ (HUN)   Attendance: 15.000

*(Double game played on the same day and at the same venue as the game between SC Wacker
Wien and FK Partizan Beograd)*

24-06-1956   Stadion J.N.A., Beograd:
                    FK Crvena Zvezda Beograd – Budapesti Vörös Lobogó SE   1-1 (1-1)
FK Crvena Zvezda Beograd: Vladimir BEARA, Branko STANKOVIC, Ljubomir SPAJIC,
Miljan ZEKOVIC, Rajko MITIC, Lazar TASIC, Anton RUDINSKI, Dragoslav
SEKULARAC, Ivan TOPLAK, Borivoje (Bora) KOSTIC, Stevan VESELINOVIC. (Coach:
Milovan CIRIC).
Budapesti Vörös Lobogó SE: Sándor GELLÉR, János BÖRZSEI, Ferenc KOVÁCS (III), Imre
KOVÁCS (I), József ZAKARIÁS, Károly SÁNDOR, Mihály LANTOS, Péter PALOTÁS,
Ferenc SIPOS, István SZOLNOK, István SZIMCSÁK (I). (Coach: Béla VOLENTIK).
Goals: FK Crvena Zvezda Beograd: 1-1 Borivoje (Bora) KOSTIC (40').
Budapesti Vörös Lobogó SE: 0-1 Károly SÁNDOR (35').
Referee: Alfred GRILL (AUT)   Attendance: 50.000

24-06-1956   Népstadion, Budapest: Budapesti Vasas SC – U.D.A. Praha   2-0 (0-0)
Budapesti Vasas SC: Mihály KAMARÁS, László SÁROSI, Károly KONTHA, Gyula
TELEKI, Dezsö BUNDZSÁK, Pál BERENDI, József RADULY, Lajos CSORDÁS, Gyula
SZILÁGYI (I), László KASZÁS, Sándor LENKEI. (Coach: Lajos BARÓTI).
U.D.A. Praha: Bretislav DOLEJSÍ, Jan HERTL, Jirí CADEK, Ladislav NOVÁK, Svatopluk
PLUSKAL, Josef MASOPUST, Ladislav HLAVÁCEK, Milan DVORÁK, Ladislav PRÁDA,
Jaroslav BOROVICKA, Karol DOBAY. (Coach: Karel KOLSKÝ).
Goals: Budapesti Vasas SC: 1-0 Lajos CSORDÁS (82'), 2-0 Sándor LENKEI (84').
Referee: Vasa STEFANOVIC (YUG)   Attendance: 50.000

30-06-1956   Bratislava: Slovan UNV Bratislava – SK Rapid Wien   3-1 (0-0)
Slovan UNV Bratislava: Viliam SCHROJF, Pavol BENA, Michal VICAN, Vojtech
JANKOVIC, Jozef JAJCAJ, Jozef VENGLOS, Vlastimil HLAVÁTY, Anton MORAVCÍK,
Július KOVÁC, Anton BÍLÝ, Pavol MOLNÁR. (Coach: Leopold STASTNÝ).
SK Rapid Wien: Herbert GARTNER, Paul HALLA, Robert DIENST, Franz GOLOBIC, Josef
HÖLTL, Karl GIESSER, Robert KÖRNER (I), Johann RIEGLER, Gerhard HANAPPI, Alfred
KÖRNER (II), Josef BERTALAN. (Coach: Franz WAGNER).
Goals: Slovan UNV Bratislava: 1-0 Anton MORAVCIK (47'), 2-0 Július KOVÁC (60'
penalty), 3-1 Vlastimil HLAVÁTY (84').
SK Rapid Wien: 2-1 Gerhard HANAPPI (81').
Referee: István ZSOLT (HUN)   Attendance: 45.000

30-06-1956   Stadión Strahov (Masaryk), Praha:
                    U.D.A. Praha –Budapesti Vasas SC   2-2 (1-1)
U.D.A. Praha: Bretislav DOLEJSÍ, Jan HERTL, Jirí JECNÝ, Ladislav NOVÁK, Svatopluk
PLUSKAL, Josef MASOPUST, Ladislav HLAVÁCEK, Milan DVORÁK, Ladislav PRÁDA,
Ivo URBAN, Jaroslav BOROVICKA. (Coach: Karel KOLSKÝ).
Budapesti Vasas SC: Mihály KAMARÁS, László SÁROSI, Károly KONTHA, Gyula
TELEKI, Dezsö BUNDZSÁK, Pál BERENDI, József RADULY, Lajos CSORDÁS, Gyula
SZILÁGYI (I), János SZILÁGYI (II), Sándor LENKEI. (Coach: Lajos BARÓTI).
Goals: U.D.A. Praha: 1-1 Josef MASOPUST (33'), 2-2 Ladislav PRÁDA (65').
Budapesti Vasas SC: 0-1 Lajos CSORDÁS (13'), 1-2 Sándor LENKEI (51').
Referee: LAMESIC (YUG)   Attendance: 45.000

01-07-1956   Stadion J.N.A., Beograd: FK Partizan Beograd – SC Wacker Wien   1-1 (0-0)
FK Partizan Beograd: Slavko STOJANOVIC, Bruno BELIN, Cedomir LAZAREVIC, Bozidar
PAJEVIC, Branko ZEBEC, Miodrag JOVANOVIC, Branislav (Boba) MIHAILOVIC, Stanoje
JOCIC, Marko VALOK, Tomislav KALOPEROVIC, Miroslav MARKOVIC. (Coach:
Aleksandar TOMASEVIC).
SC Wacker Wien: Franz PELIKAN, Franz CHALUPETZKY, Walter KOLLMANN, Ernst
Josef FORETH, Paul KOZLICEK (I), Anton WOLF, Theodor (Turl) WAGNER (II), Johann
WINDISCH, Ernst KOZLICEK (II), Ferdinand SMETANA, Walter HAUMMER. (Coach:
Jenö KALMÁR (HUN)).
Goals: FK Partizan Beograd: 1-1 Stanoje JOCIC (88').
SC Wacker Wien: 0-1 Theodor (Turl) WAGNER (72').
Referee: Martin MACKO (TCH)   Attendance: 25.000

106

01-07-1956   Népstadion, Budapest:
             Budapesti Vörös Lobogó SE – FK Crvena Zvezda Beograd   5-3 (2-2)
Budapesti Vörös Lobogó SE: Sándor GELLÉR, János BÖRZSEI, Ferenc KOVÁCS (III), Imre
KOVÁCS (I), József ZAKARIÁS, Károly SÁNDOR, Mihály LANTOS, Péter PALOTÁS,
Nándor HIDEGKUTI, István SZOLNOK, István SZIMCSÁK (I). (Coach: Béla VOLENTIK).
FK Crvena Zvezda Beograd: Vladimir BEARA, Branko STANKOVIC, Ljubomir SPAJIC,
Miljan ZEKOVIC, Vladimir POPOVIC, Rajko MITIC, Lazar TASIC, Anton RUDINSKI,
Dragoslav SEKULARAC, Ivan TOPLAK, Borivoje (Bora) KOSTIC. (Coach: Milovan
CIRIC).
Goals: Budapesti Vörös Lobogó SE: 1-0 Lazar TASIC (2' own goal), 2-1 Ljubomir SPAJIC
(38' own goal), 3-3 Nándor HIDEGKUTI (48'), 4-3 István SZOLNOK (64'), 5-3 Péter
PALOTÁS (66').
FK Crvena Zvezda Beograd: 1-1 Ivan TOPLAK (26'), 2-2 Borivoje (Bora) KOSTIC (44'), 2-3
Borivoje (Bora) KOSTIC (..').
Referee: Friedrich MAYER (AUT)   Attendance: 45.000

03-07-1956   Stadion J.N.A., Beograd: FK Partizan Beograd – SC Wacker Wien   4-0 (4-0)
FK Partizan Beograd: Slavko STOJANOVIC, Bruno BELIN, Cedomir LAZAREVIC, Bozidar
PAJEVIC, Branko ZEBEC, Miodrag JOVANOVIC, Prvoslav MIHAJLOVIC (I), Stanoje
JOCIC, Marko VALOK, Tomislav KALOPEROVIC, Miroslav MARKOVIC. (Coach:
Aleksandar TOMASEVIC).
SC Wacker Wien: Franz PELIKAN, Johann STEUP, Walter KOLLMANN, Ernst Josef
FORETH, Paul KOZLICEK (I), Anton WOLF, Franz CHALUPETZKY, Ferdinand
SMETANA, Johann WINDISCH, Ernst KOZLICEK (II), Walter HAUMMER. (Coach: Jenö
KALMÁR (HUN)).
Goals: FK Partizan Beograd: 1-0 Tomislav KALOPEROVIC (25'), 2-0 Tomislav
KALOPEROVIC (40'), 3-0 Miroslav MARKOVIC (43'), 4-0 Tomislav KALOPEROVIC
(45').
Referee: Antonin RUZICKA (TCH)   Attendance: 8.000

(Play-off match).

SEMI-FINALS

07-07-1956   Praterstadion, Wien: SK Rapid Wien – Budapesti Vörös Lobogó SE   3-3 (1-0)
SK Rapid Wien: Herbert GARTNER, Paul HALLA, Robert DIENST, Franz GOLOBIC, Josef
HÖLTL, Karl GIESSER, Robert KÖRNER (I), Johann RIEGLER, Gerhard HANAPPI, Alfred
KÖRNER (II), Josef BERTALAN. (Coach: Franz WAGNER).
Budapesti Vörös Lobogó SE: Sándor GELLÉR, József KOVÁCS (II), János BÖRZSEI, Imre
KOVÁCS (I), József ZAKARIÁS, Károly SÁNDOR, Mihály LANTOS, Péter PALOTÁS,
Nándor HIDEGKUTI, István SZOLNOK, István SZIMCSÁK (I). (Coach: Béla VOLENTIK).
Goals: SK Rapid Wien: 1-0 Alfred KÖRNER (12'), 2-0 Robert KÖRNER (47' penalty), 3-0
Alfred KÖRNER (60').
Budapesti Vörös Lobogó SE: 3-1 Nándor HIDEGKUTI (61'), 3-2 Nándor HIDEGKUTI (73'),
3-3 Péter PALOTÁS (75').
Referee: Veljko ROMCEVIC (YUG)   Attendance: 45.000

08-07-1956   Stadion J.N.A., Beograd:
            FK Partizan Beograd – Budapesti Vasas SC   1-0 (1-0)
FK Partizan Beograd: Slavko STOJANOVIC, Bruno BELIN, Cedomir LAZAREVIC, Miodrag
JOVANOVIC, Branko ZEBEC, Bozidar PAJEVIC, Mihalj MESAROS, Prvoslav
MIHAJLOVIC (I), Marko VALOK, Tomislav KALOPEROVIC, Miroslav MARKOVIC.
(Coach: Kiril SIMONOVSKI).
Budapesti Vasas SC: Mihály KAMARÁS, László SÁROSI, Károly KONTHA, Gyula
TELEKI, Dezsö BUNDZSÁK, Pál BERENDI, József RADULY, Lajos CSORDÁS, Gyula
SZILÁGYI (I), János SZILÁGYI (II), Sándor LENKEI. (Coach: Lajos BARÓTI).
Goal: FK Partizan Beograd: 1-0 Marko VALOK (20').
Referee: Friedrich MAYER (AUT)   Attendance: 40.000

14-07-1956   Népstadion, Budapest: Budapesti Vasas SC – FK Partizan Beograd   6-1 (3-1)
Budapesti Vasas SC: Mihály KAMARÁS, Béla KÁRPÁTI, Károly KONTHA, Gyula
TELEKI, Dezsö BUNDZSÁK, Pál BERENDI, József RADULY, Lajos CSORDÁS, Gyula
SZILÁGYI (I), János SZILÁGYI (II), Sándor LENKEI. (Coach: Lajos BARÓTI).
FK Partizan Beograd: Slavko STOJANOVIC, Bruno BELIN, Cedomir LAZAREVIC, Miodrag
JOVANOVIC, Branko ZEBEC (expulsion 84'), Bozidar PAJEVIC, Prvoslav MIHAJLOVIC
(I), Marko VALOK (expulsion 79'), Tomislav KALOPEROVIC, Stjepan BOBEK, Miroslav
MARKOVIC. (Coach: Kiril SIMONOVSKI).
Goals: Budapesti Vasas SC: 1-0 Gyula SZILÁGYI (3'), 2-0 Lajos CSORDÁS (9'), 3-1 Dezsö
BUNDZSÁK (38'), 4-1 Lajos CSORDÁS (78'), 5-1 Sándor LENKEI (83'), 6-1 Lajos
CSORDÁS (88').
FK Partizan Beograd: 2-1 Miroslav MARKOVIC (31').
Referee: Martin MACKO (TCH)   Attendance: 80.000

*(Double game played on the same day and at the same venue as the game between Budapesti
Vörös Lobogó SE and SK Rapid Wien).*

14-07-1956   Népstadion, Budapest:
            Budapesti Vörös Lobogó SE – SK Rapid Wien   3-4 (1-3)
Budapesti Vörös Lobogó SE: Sándor GELLÉR, József KOVÁCS (II), János BÖRZSEI, Imre
KOVÁCS (I), József ZAKARIÁS, Károly SÁNDOR, Mihály LANTOS, Péter PALOTÁS,
Nándor HIDEGKUTI, István SZOLNOK, István SZIMCSÁK (I). (Coach: Béla VOLENTIK).
SK Rapid Wien: Herbert GARTNER, Paul HALLA, Robert DIENST, Franz GOLOBIC, Josef
HÖLTL, Lambert LENZINGER, Robert KÖRNER (I), Bruno MEHSAROSCH, Gerhard
HANAPPI, Alfred KÖRNER (II), Josef BERTALAN. (Coach: Franz WAGNER).
Goals: Budapesti Vörös Lobogó SE: 1-3 István SZOLNOK (29'), 2-3 Péter PALOTÁS (48'),
3-3 Péter PALOTÁS (50').
SK Rapid Wien: 0-1 Gerhard HANAPPI (10'), 0-2 Gerhard HANAPPI (17'), 0-3 Alfred
KÖRNER (20'), 3-4 Bruno MEHSAROSCH (83').
Referee: Jaroslav VLCEK (TCH)   Attendance: 80.000

*(Double game played on the same day and at the same venue as the game between Budapesti
Vasas SC and FK Partizan Beograd).*

FINAL

21-07-1956   Praterstadion, Wien: SK Rapid Wien – Budapesti Vasas SC 3-3 (3-1)
SK Rapid Wien: Herbert GARTNER, Paul HALLA, Robert DIENST, Franz GOLOBIC, Josef
HÖLTL, Karl GIESSER, Robert KÖRNER (I), Bruno MEHSAROSCH, Gerhard HANAPPI,
Alfred KÖRNER (II), Josef BERTALAN. (Coach: Franz WAGNER).
Budapesti Vasas SC: Mihály KAMARÁS, Béla KÁRPÁTI, Károly KONTHA, Gyula
TELEKI, Dezsö BUNDZSÁK, Pál BERENDI, József RADULY, Lajos CSORDÁS, Gyula
SZILÁGYI (I), László SÁROSI, Sándor LENKEI. (Coach: Lajos BARÓTI).
Goals: SK Rapid Wien: 1-1 Alfred KÖRNER (3'), 2-1 Alfred KÖRNER (14'), 3-1 Bruno
MEHSAROSCH (19').
Budapesti Vasas SC: 0-1 Gyula SZILÁGYI (2'), 3-2 Dezsö BUNDZSÁK (47'), 3-3 Lajos
CSORDÁS (58').
Referee: Vincenzo ORLANDINI (ITA)   Attendance: 52.000

28-07-1956   Népstadion, Budapest: Budapesti Vasas SC – SK Rapid Wien 1-1 (1-0)
Budapesti Vasas SC: Mihály KAMARÁS, Béla KÁRPÁTI, Károly KONTHA, Gyula
TELEKI, Dezsö BUNDZSÁK, Pál BERENDI, József RADULY, Lajos CSORDÁS, Gyula
SZILÁGYI (I), László SÁROSI, Sandor LENKEI. (Coach: Lajos BARÓTI).
SK Rapid Wien: Herbert GARTNER, Paul HALLA, Franz GOLOBIC, Josef HÖLTL, Karl
GIESSER, Johann RIEGLER, Robert KÖRNER (I), Bruno MEHSAROSCH, Gerhard
HANAPPI, Alfred KÖRNER (II), Josef BERTALAN. (Coach: Franz WAGNER).
Goals: Budapesti Vasas SC: 1-0 Gyula SZILÁGYI (3').
SK Rapid Wien: 1-1 Josef BERTALAN (60').
Referee: Giorgio BERNARDI (ITA)   Attendance: 104.000

04-08-1956   Népstadion, Budapest: Budapesti Vasas SC – SK Rapid Wien 9-2 (3-1)
Budapesti Vasas SC: Mihály KAMARÁS, Béla KÁRPÁTI, Károly KONTHA, Gyula
TELEKI, Dezsö BUNDZSÁK, Pál BERENDI, József RADULY, Lajos CSORDÁS, Gyula
SZILÁGYI (I), László SÁROSI, Sándor LENKEI. (Coach: Lajos BARÓTI).
SK Rapid Wien: Herbert GARTNER, Paul HALLA, Franz GOLOBIC, Josef HÖLTL, Karl
GIESSER, Johann RIEGLER, Robert KÖRNER (I), Bruno MEHSAROSCH, Gerhard
HANAPPI, Lambert LENZINGER, Josef BERTALAN. (Coach: Franz WAGNER).
Goals: Budapesti Vasas SC: 1-0 Lajos CSORDÁS (21'), 2-0 Lajos CSORDÁS (28'), 3-1
József RADULY (43'), 4-1 Gyula SZILÁGYI (47'), 5-1 Gyula SZILÁGYI (52'), 6-1 Gyula
SZILÁGYI (56'), 7-1 Gyula SZILÁGYI (70'), 8-1 József RADULY (80'), 9-2 Gyula TELEKI
(88').
SK Rapid Wien: 2-1 Johann RIEGLER (32'), 8-2 Johann RIEGLER (85').
Referee: Jaroslav VLCEK (TCH)   Attendance: 104.000

(Final Play-off match).

*** **Budapesti Vasas SC won the Cup** ***

1957

QUARTER-FINALS

29-06-1957   Praterstadion, Wien: SK Rapid Wien – M.T.K. Budapest 1-1 (0-1)
SK Rapid Wien: Herbert GARTNER, Josef HÖLTL, Ernst Franz Hermann HAPPEL, Franz
GOLOBIC, Gerhard HANAPPI, Lothar BILEK, Paul HALLA, Johann RIEGLER, Robert
DIENST, Alfred KÖRNER (II), Josef BERTALAN. (Coach: Maximilian (Max) MERKEL).
M.T.K. Budapest: Sándor GELLÉR, Tibor PALICSKÓ, Ferenc SIPOS, Mihály LANTOS,
Imre KOVÁCS (I), Ferenc GÁL, Károly SÁNDOR, Nándor HIDEGKUTI, László BÖDÖR,
János MOLNÁR, Endre KÁRÁSZ. (Coach: Márton BUKOVI).
Goals: SK Rapid Wien: 1-1 Paul HALLA (62').
M.T.K. Budapest: 0-1 László BÖDÖR (15').
Referee: Jaroslav VLCEK (TCH)   Attendance: 35.000

30-06-1957   Népstadion, Budapest: Vasas SC – First Vienna FC 3-0 (1-0)
Vasas SC: Ferenc KOVALIK, Béla KÁRPÁTI, Károly KONTHA, László SÁROSI, János
SZILÁGYI (II), Pál BERENDI, József RADULY, Antal BÁRFI, Gyula SZILÁGYI (I), Dezsö
BUNDZSÁK, Sándor LENKEI. (Coach: Lajos BARÓTI).
First Vienna FC: Bruno ENGELMEIER, Alfred UMGEHER, Rudolf RÖCKL, Karl
NICKERL, Karl KOLLER, Johann OBST, Herbert GROHS, Johann (Hans) BUZEK, Karl
JERICHA, Otto WALZHOFER, Alfred PICHLER. (Coach: Leopold HOFMANN).
Goals: Vasas SC: 1-0 Gyula SZILÁGYI (31'), 2-0 Sándor LENKEI (59'), 3-0 Dezsö
BUNDZSÁK (79').
Referee: Borce NEDELKOVSKI (YUG)   Attendance: 35.000

30-06-1957   Bratislava: Slovan UNV Bratislava – FK Vojvodina Novi Sad 1-0 (0-0)
Slovan UNV Bratislava: Viliam SCHROJF, Mikulás CIRKA, Michal VICAN, Vojtech
JANKOVIC, Anton URBAN, Jozef VENGLOS, Jozef OBERT, Július KOVÁC, Anton
MORAVCÍK, Emil PAZICKÝ, Július KÁNÁSSY. (Coach: Leopold STASTNÝ).
FK Vojvodina Novi Sad: András VERES, Novak ROGANOVIC, Dobroslav KRSTIC (II),
Zarko NIKOLIC, Vujadin BOSKOV, Luka MALESEV, Zdravko RAJKOV, Todor
VESELINOVIC, Alexander IVOS, Dragoljub BLAZIC, Radomir KRSTIC (I). (Coach: Antal
LYKA).
Goal: Slovan UNV Bratislava: 1-0 Vojtech JANKOVIV (85').
Referee: Károly BALLA (HUN)   Attendance: 45.000

30-06-1957   JNA Stadion, Beograd: FK Crvena Zvezda Beograd – Dukla Praha 1-1 (1-1)
FK Crvena Zvezda Beograd: Srboljub KRIVOKUCA, Branko STANKOVIC, Ljubomir
SPAJIC, Miljan ZEKOVIC, Vladimir POPOVIC (I), Lazar TASIC, Jovan COKIC, Ivan
TOPLAK, Rajko MITIC, Borivoje (Bora) KOSTIC, Anton RUDINSKI. (Coach: Milovan
CIRIC).
Dukla Praha: Václav PAVLIS, Jirí JECNÝ, Jirí CADEK, Ladislav NOVÁK, Svatopluk (Svata)
PLUSKAL, Josef MASOPUST, Ivo URBAN, Milan DVORÁK, Jaroslav BOROVICKA,
Frantisek SAFRÁNEK, Josef VACENOVSKÝ. (Coach: Karel KOLSKÝ).
Goals: FK Crvena Zvezda Beograd: 1-0 Ivan TOPLAK (25').
Dukla Praha: 1-1 Frantisek SAFRÁNEK (43').
Referee: Alfred GRILL (AUT)   Attendance: 20.000

110

06-07-1957   Népstadion, Budapest: M.T.K. Budapest – SK Rapid Wien   3-3 (1-2)
M.T.K. Budapest: Sándor GELLÉR, Tibor PALICSKÓ, Ferenc SIPOS, Mihály LANTOS,
Imre KOVÁCS (I), Ferenc GÁL, Károly SÁNDOR, Nándor HIDEGKUTI, László BÖDÖR,
János MOLNÁR, Endre KÁRÁSZ. (Coach: Márton BUKOVI).
SK Rapid Wien: Herbert GARTNER, Paul HALLA, Ernst Franz Hermann HAPPEL, Franz
GOLOBIC, Gerhard HANAPPI, Lothar BILEK, Robert KÖRNER (I), Josef HÖLTL, Robert
DIENST, Alfred KÖRNER (II), Josef BERTALAN. (Coach: Maximilian (Max) MERKEL).
Goals: M.T.K. Budapest: 1-0 Nándor HIDEGKUTI (14'), 2-3 Endre KÁRÁSZ(63'), 3-3
László BÖDÖR (77').
SK Rapid Wien: 1-1 Ferenc SIPOS (21' *own goal*), 1-2 Robert DIENST (43'), 1-3 Mihály
LANTOS (48' *own goal*).
Referee: Alojz OBTULOVIC (YUG)   Attendance: 40.000

06-07-1957   Hohe Warte, Wien: First Vienna FC – Vasas SC   2-1 (0-0)
First Vienna FC: Bruno ENGELMEIER, Alfred UMGEHER, Rudolf RÖCKL, Karl
NICKERL, Karl KOLLER, Julius SCHWEIGER, Herbert GROHS, Otto WALZHOFER,
Johann (Hans) BUZEK, Johann (Hans) MENASSE, Alfred PICHLER. (Coach: Leopold
HOFMANN).
Vasas SC: Ferenc KOVALIK, Béla KÁRPÁTI, Károly KONTHA, László SÁROSI, János
SZILÁGYI (II), Pál BERENDI, József RADULY, Antal BÁRFI, Gyula SZILÁGYI (I), Dezsö
BUNDZSÁK, Sándor LENKEI. (Coach: Lajos BARÓTI).
Goals: First Vienna FC: 1-0 Alfred PICHLER (49'), 2-0 Alfred PICHLER (59').
Vasas SC: 2-1 Sándor LENKEI (65').
Referee: Vasa STEFANOVIC (YUG)   Attendance: 15.000

06-07-1957   Praha: Dukla Praha – FK Crvena Zvezda Beograd   1-1 (0-0)
Dukla Praha: Václav PAVLIS, Jirí JECNÝ, Jirí CADEK, Ladislav NOVÁK, Svatopluk (Svata)
PLUSKAL, Ivo URBAN, Josef VACENOVSKÝ, Milan DVORÁK, Jaroslav BOROVICKA,
Josef MASOPUST, Karol DOBAY. (Coach: Karel KOLSKÝ).
FK Crvena Zvezda Beograd: Srboljub KRIVOKUCA, Branko STANKOVIC, Ljubomir
SPAJIC, Miljan ZEKOVIC, Rajko MITIC, Lazar TASIC, Vladimir DURKOVIC, Ivan
TOPLAK, Vladimir POPOVIC (I), Borivoje (Bora) KOSTIC, Anton RUDINSKI. (Coach:
Milovan CIRIC).
Goals: Dukla Praha: 1-1 Svatopluk (Svata) PLUSKAL (86').
FK Crvena Zvezda Beograd: 0-1 Borivoje (Bora) KOSTIC (50').
Referee: Friedrich MAYER (AUT)   Attendance: 15.000

07-07-1957   Novi Sad: FK Vojvodina Novi Sad – Slovan UNV Bratislava   6-0 (4-0)
FK Vojvodina Novi Sad: András VERES, Novak ROGANOVIC, Dobroslav KRSTIC (II),
Zarko NIKOLIC, Vujadin BOSKOV, Luka MALESEV, Zdravko RAJKOV, Todor (Toza)
VESELINOVIC, Alexander IVOS, Dragoljub BLAZIC, Radomir KRSTIC (I). (Coach: Antal
LYKA).
Slovan UNV Bratislava: Viliam SCHROJF, Mikulás CIRKA, Michal VICAN, Vojtech
JANKOVIC, Jozef OBERT, Anton URBAN, Milan BALÁZÍK, Anton MORAVCÍK, Anton
BÍLÝ, Emil PAZICKÝ, Július KÁNÁSSY. (Coach: Leopold STASTNÝ).
Goals: FK Vojvodina Novi Sad: 1-0 Dragoljub BLAZIC (3'), 2-0 Aleksandar IVOS (13'), 3-0
Todor (Toza) VESELINOVIC (31'), 4-0 Aleksandar IVOS (34'), 5-0 Todor (Toza)
VESELINOVIC (46' penalty), 6-0 Zdravko RAJKOV (90').
Referee: György DANKO (HUN)   Attendance: 12.000

111

10-07-1957   Bratislava: Dukla Praha – FK Crvena Zvzeda Beograd   0-1 (0-0)
Dukla Praha: Václav PAVLIS, Ivo URBAN, Jirí CADEK, Ladislav NOVÁK, Svatopluk
(Svata) PLUSKAL, Josef MASOPUST, PONES, Milan DVORÁK, Jaroslav BOROVICKA,
Josef VACENOVSKÝ, Karol DOBAY. (Coach: Karel KOLSKÝ).
FK Crvena Zvezda Beograd: Srboljub KRIVOKUCA, Branko STANKOVIC, Ljubomir
SPAJIC, Miljan ZEKOVIC, Vladimir POPOVIC (I), Lazar TASIC, Ivan POPOVIC (II), Ivan
TOPLAK, Rajko MITIC, Borivoje (Bora) KOSTIC, Anton RUDINSKI. (Coach: Milovan
CIRIC).
Goal: FK Crvena Zvezda Beograd: 0-1 Ivan POPOVIC (82').
Referee: Friedrich (Fritz) SEIPELT (AUT)   Attendance: 20.000
(Play-off match).

11-07-1957   Praterstadion, Wien: SK Rapid Wien – M.T.K. Budapest   4-1 (0-1)
SK Rapid Wien: Herbert GARTNER, Paul HALLA, Ernst Franz Hermann HAPPEL, Franz
GOLOBIC, Gerhard HANAPPI, Lothar BILEK, Robert KÖRNER (I), Johann RIEGLER,
Robert DIENST, Alfred KÖRNER (II), Josef HÖLTL. (Coach: Maximilian (Max) MERKEL).
M.T.K. Budapest: Sándor GELLÉR, Tibor PALICSKÓ, Ferenc SIPOS, Mihály LANTOS,
Imre KOVÁCS (I), Ferenc GÁL, Károly SÁNDOR, Nándor HIDEGKUTI, László BÖDÖR,
János MOLNÁR, Endre KÁRÁSZ. (Coach: Márton BUKOVI).
Goals: SK Rapid Wien: 1-1 Alfred KÖRNER (51'), 2-1 Robert KÖRNER (54'), 3-1 Johann
RIEGLER (60'), 4-1 Johann RIEGLER (66').
M.T.K. Budapest: 0-1 Károly SÁNDOR (36').
Referee: Vasa STEFANOVIC (YUG)   Attendance: 25.000
(Play-off match).

SEMI-FINALS

14-07-1957   JNA Stadion, Beograd: FK Crvena Zvezda Beograd – Vasas SC   1-3 (1-0)
FK Crvena Zvezda Beograd: Srboljub KRIVOKUCA, Branko STANKOVIC, Ljubomir
SPAJIC, Miljan ZEKOVIC, Vladimir POPOVIC (I), Lazar TASIC, Anton RUDINSKI, Rajko
MITIC, Ivan POPOVIC (II), Ivan TOPLAK, Borivoje (Bora) KOSTIC. (Coach: Milovan
CIRIC).
Vasas SC: Ferenc KOVALIK, Béla KÁRPÁTI, Pál PALÁSTI, László SÁROSI, János
SZILÁGYI (II), Pál BERENDI, József RADULY, Antal BÁRFI, Gyula SZILÁGYI (I), Dezsö
BUNDZSÁK, Sándor LENKEI. (Coach: Lajos BARÓTI).
Goals: FK Crvena Zvezda Beograd: 1-0 Vladimir POPOVIC (18').
Vasas SC: 1-1 Antal BÁRFI (60'), 1-2 Dezsö BUNDZSÁK (71' penalty), 1-3 Gyula
SZILÁGYI (83').
Referee: Carl Erich STEINER (AUT)   Attendance: 38.000

16-07-1957   Praterstadion, Wien: SK Rapid Wien – FK Vojvodina Novi Sad   3-0 (2-0)
SK Rapid Wien: Herbert GARTNER, Paul HALLA, Ernst Franz Hermann HAPPEL, Franz
GOLOBIC, Gerhard HANAPPI, Lothar BILEK, Robert KÖRNER (I), Johann RIEGLER,
Robert DIENST, Alfred KÖRNER (II), Josef HÖLTL. (Coach: Maximilian (Max) MERKEL).
FK Vojvodina Novi Sad: András VERES, Novak ROGANOVIC, Dobroslav KRSTIC (II),
Zarko NIKOLIC, Vujadin BOSKOV, Luka MALESEV, Zdravko RAJKOV, Todor
VESELINOVIC, Alexander IVOS, Dragoljub BLAZIC, Radomir KRSTIC (I). (Coach: Antal
LYKA).
Goals: SK Rapid Wien: 1-0 Johann RIEGLER (23'), 2-0 Johann RIEGLER (33'), 3-0 Ernst
Franz Hermann HAPPEL (75').
Referee: Sándor HARANGOZÓ (HUN)   Attendance: 25.000

20-07-1957   Népstadion, Budapest: Vasas SC – Crvena Zvezda Beograd 3-2 (1-1)
Vasas SC: Ferenc KOVALIK, Béla KÁRPÁTI, Pál PALÁSTI, László SÁROSI, János
SZILÁGYI (II), Pál BERENDI, József RADULY, Dezsö BUNDZSÁK, Gyula SZILÁGYI (I),
Gyula TELEKI, Sándor LENKEI. (Coach: Lajos BARÓTI).
FK Crvena Zvezda Beograd: Srboljub KRIVOKUCA, Novak TOMIC, Ljubomir SPAJIC,
Miljan ZEKOVIC, Rajko MITIC, Vladimir POPOVIC (I), Vladimir DURKOVIC, Lazar
TASIC, Ivan POPOVIC (II), Borivoje (Bora) KOSTIC, Anton RUDINSKI. (Coach: Milovan
CIRIC).
Goals: Vasas SC: 1-1 Gyula SZILÁGYI, 2-1 Gyula TELEKI, 3-2 Gyula TELEKI,.
FK Crvena Zvezda Beograd: 0-1 Borivoje (Bora) KOSTIC, 2-2 Lazar TASIC.
Referee: Martin MACKO (TCH)   Attendance: 45.000

21-07-1957   Novi Sad: FK Vojvodina Novi Sad – SK Rapid Wien 4-1 (2-1)
FK Vojvodina Novi Sad: András VERES, Novak ROGANOVIC, Dobroslav KRSTIC (II),
Zarko NIKOLIC, Vujadin BOSKOV, Luka MALESEV, Zdravko RAJKOV, Todor
VESELINOVIC, Milan VUKELIC, Alexander IVOS, Radomir KRSTIC (I). (Coach: Antal
LYKA).
SK Rapid Wien: Herbert GARTNER, Paul HALLA, Ernst Franz Hermann HAPPEL, Franz
GOLOBIC, Gerhard HANAPPI, Lothar BILEK, Lambert LENZINGER, Johann RIEGLER,
Robert DIENST, Karl GIESSER, Alfred KÖRNER (II). (Coach: Maximilian (Max)
MERKEL).
Goals: FK Vojvodina Novi Sad: 1-0 Alexander IVOS (4'), 2-0 Milan VUKELIC (16'), 3-1
Todor VESELINOVIC (72'), 4-1 Milan VUKELIC (85').
SK Rapid Wien: 2-1 Johann RIEGLER (29').
Referee: Jaroslav VLCEK (TCH)   Attendance: 35.000

SK Rapid Wien withdrew from the play-off so FK Vojvodina progressed to the Final.

FINAL

28-07-1957   Népstadion, Budapest: Vasas SC– FK Vojvodina Novi Sad 4-0 (1-0)
Vasas SC: Ferenc KOVALIK, Béla KÁRPÁTI, Gyula TELEKI, László SÁROSI, János
SZILÁGYI (II), Pál BERENDI, József RADULY, Lajos CSORDÁS, Gyula SZILÁGYI (I),
Dezsö BUNDZSÁK, Sándor LENKEI. (Coach: Lajos BARÓTI).
FK Vojvodina Novi Sad: András VERES, Novak ROGANOVIC, Dobroslav KRSTIC (II),
Zarko NIKOLIC, Vujadin BOSKOV, Luka MALESEV, Zdravko RAJKOV, Todor
VESELINOVIC, Stevan BENA, Alexander IVOS, Radomir KRSTIC (I). (Coach: Antal
LYKA).
Goals: VASAS SC: 1-0 Dezsö BUNDZSÁK (42'), 2-0 Gyula SZILÁGYI (48'), 3-0 Lajos
CSORDÁS (55'), 4-0 Dezsö BUNDZSÁK (70').
Attendance: 92.000

04-08-1957   Gradski Stadion, Novi Sad: FK Vojvodina Novi Sad – Vasas SC 2-1 (0-1)
FK Vojvodina Novi Sad: András VERES, Novak ROGANOVIC, Dobroslav KRSTIC (II),
Zarko NIKOLIC, Vujadin BOSKOV, Luka MALESEV, Zdravko RAJKOV, Todor
VESELINOVIC, Milan VUKELIC, Alexander IVOS, Radomir KRSTIC (I). (Coach: Antal
LYKA).
Vasas SC: Ferenc KOVALIK, Béla KÁRPÁTI, Károly KONTHA, László SÁROSI, János
SZILÁGYI (II), Pál BERENDI, József RADULY, Dezsö BUNDZSÁK, Gyula SZILÁGYI (I),
Gyula TELEKI, Sándor LENKEI. (Coach: Lajos BARÓTI).
Goals: FK Vojvodina Novi Sad: 1-1 Milan VUKELIC (20'), 2-1 Milan VUKELIC (..').
Vasas SC: 0-1 Dezsö BUNDZSÁK (2').
Attendance: 20.000

*** Vasas SC won the Cup ***

Danube Cup (Donaupokel)

1958

FIRST ROUND

24-05-1958   Beograd: FK Crvena Zvezda Beograd – Dukla Pardubice   2-0 (0-0)
FK Crvena Zvezda Beograd: Jovan GAJIC, Dimitrije STOJANOVIC, Miljan ZEKOVIC, Ranko BOROZAN, Ljubomir SPAJIC, Lazar TASIC, Nikola STIPIC, Vojislav SRDIC, Selimir MILOSEVIC (..' Ivan POPOVIC), Vladimir DURKOVIC, Borivoje (Bora) KOSTIC. (Coach: Milorad PAVIC).
Dukla Pardubide: Karol BOBOK, Telesfor HALMO, Miroslav OSTÁDAL, Kvetoslav NOVÁK, Prokop DANEK, VOVORSKÝ, Karel LICHTNÉGL, Kael NEPOMUCKÝ, Bedrich SONKA, ANTALA, Fáfa MORÁVEK. (Coach: Stefan CAMBAL).
Goals: FK Crvena Zvezda Beograd: 1-0 Borivoje (Bora) KOSTIC (54'), 2-0 Ranko BOROZAN (89').
Referee: Vilmos HERNÁDI (HUN)   Attendance: 8.000

25-05-1958   Bányász Stadion, Tatabánya:
              Tatabányai Bányász SC – FK Lokomotiv Sofia   1-4 (0-2)
Tatabányai Bányász SC: István FEKETE, Ferenc FARSANG, Sándor KOVÁCS, János LUGOSI (46' Sándor HETÉNYI), László HÁRI, Sándor MOLNÁR, István SZOVJÁK, Gyula BÍRÓ, András DOMBAI, Béla PELLER, Ferenc BECK. (Coach: Károly LAKAT).
FK Lokomotiv Sofia: Yosif Yordanov YOSIFOV, Vasil METODIEV, Ivan DIMITROV, Todor VELEV, Metodi NESTOROV, Dimitar DRAGOMIROV, STAKOV (37' STAMOV), STANIMIROV, Nikola KOTKOV Todorov, Spiro DEBARSKI, MALINOV. (Coach: Aleksandar POPOV).
Goals: Tatabányai Bányász SC: 1-3 István SZOVJÁK (69').
FK Lokomotiv Sofia: 0-1 STAKOV (29'), 0-2 Spiro DEBARSKI (35'), 0-3 Spiro DEBARSKI (59'), 1-4 Nikola KOTKOV (89').
Attendance: 5.000

25-05-1958   Stadion Závodu Jana Svermy, Brno:
              TJ Rudá Hvezda Brno – Salgótarjáni BTC   3-0 (1-0)
TJ Rudá Hvezda Brno: Zdenek PLACHETA, Karel KOHLIK, Bohuslav SLÁMA, Stanislav NAVRÁTIL, Arnost MACHOVSKÝ, Jirí SÓN (78' Bronislav DANDA), Zdenek KOLÁCEK, Miroslav MIKESKA, Ladislav PRÁDA, Zdenek HAJSKÝ, Josef PÍSA. (Coach: Josef EREMIÁS).
Salgótarjáni BTC: Géza OLÁH (I), Dezsö OLÁH (II) (46' László BABLENA), Mihály JANCSIK, Sándor JEDLICSKA, Gyula SÁNDOR, Róbert DÁVID, László JAGODICS, Béla CSÁKI, Tibor BODON, Géza KORUHELY, Ferenc TALIGA. (Coach: György SZÜCS).
Goals: TJ Rudá Hvezda Brno: 1-0 Ladislav PRÁDA (14'), 2-0 Zdenek HAJSKÝ (67'), 3-0 Karel KOLÁCEK (73').
Referee: MARKOVIC (YUG)   Attendance: 8.000

25-05-1958   Kragujevac: FK Partizan Beograd – DSO Tatran Presov   4-2 (3-0)
FK Partizan Beograd: Slavko STOJANOVIC, Bruno BELÍN, Aleksandar JONCIC, Fahrudin
JUSUFI, Tomislav KALOPEROVIC, Bozidar PAJEVIC, Josip (Mico) DUVANCIC, Miroslav
REDE, Milan VUKELIC, Draguljub BLAZIC, Anton HERCEG.
DSO Tatran Presov: Alois VECERKA, Anton VARGA, Alexander FELSZEGHY, Frantisek
SEMESI, Andrej CEPCEK, Jozef BOMBA, Ladislav PAVLOVIC, Rudolf PAVLOVIC, Karol
PETROS, Jozef GAVRON, Ján FERIANCÍK.
Goals: FK Partizan Beograd: 1-0 Frantisek SEMESI (16' *own goal*), 2-0 Josip (Mico)
DUVANZIC (18'), 3-0 Miroslav REDE (42'), 4-1 Anton HERCEG (53').
DSO Tatran Presov: 3-1 Ladislav PAVLOVIC (52'), 4-2 Rudolf PAVLOVIC (88').
Referee: Károly BALLA (HUN)   Attendance: 15.000

25-05-1958   Népstadion, Budapest:
                    Ferencvárosi TC Budapest – FK Radnicki Beograd   3-3 (1-3)
Ferencvárosi TC Budapest: Géza GULYÁS, Antal THOMANN, Ernö FORGÁCS, Károly
LÁNG (46' József DÁLNOKI (II)), Imre OMBÓDI, Dr.Ferenc DÉKÁNY, Tamás KERTÉSZ,
Pál OROSZ, Miklós BORSOS, Oszkár VILEZSÁL, Gyula RÁKOSI. (Coach: Sándor
TÁTRAI).
FK Radnicki Beograd: Blagoje VIDINIC, Djura COKIC, Milorad DISKIC, BACKOVIC,
Milan LJUBENOVIC, Radmilo RISTIC, ROSTIC, BUGJA, Zoran PRLJINCEVIC, Ljubomir
OGNJANOVIC (II), SAVIC.
Goals: Ferencvárosi TC Budapest: 1-3 Gyula RÁKOSI (43'), 2-3 Gyula RÁKOSI (77'), 3-3
Miklós BORSOS (82').
FK Radnicki Beograd: 0-1 Zoran PRLJINCEVIC (21'), 0-2 Zoran PRLJINCEVIC (27'), 0-3
Zoran PRLJINCEVIC (32').
Attendance: 30.000

25-05-1958   Stadion EDEN, Praha: Dynamo Praha – CS Stiinta Timisoara 5-3 (1-3)
Dynamo Praha: ..., ..., ..., Jirí TRNKA, Jírí VLASÁK, Jirí NEDVÍDEK, Milos URBAN, Alois
HERCÍK, Otto HEMELE, Ladislav SVOBODA (..' Jan ANDREJKOVIC), Jirí PESEK.
(Coach: Josef FOREJT).
CS Stiinta Timisoara: ..., PESKOV, Petre CADARIU, Iuliu BOROS, GIRLEANU, ... (Coach:
Dinca SCHILERU).
Goals: Dynamo Praha: 1-3 Jirí PESEK (34'), 2-3 Jirí PESEK (79'), 3-3 Jirí PESEK (82'), 4-3
Milos URBAN (85'), 5-3 Milos URBAN (89' penalty).
CS Stiinta Timisoara: 0-1 Petre CADARIU (..'), 0-2 Iuliu BOROS (..'), 0-3 GIRLEANU (..').
Attendance: 10.000

25-05-1958   Stadionul "23 August", Bucuresti:
                    C.C.A. Bucuresti – M.T.K. Budapest   2-3 (1-1)
C.C.A. Bucuresti: Ion VOINESCU, Vasile ZAVODA (II), Alexandru APOLZAN, Victor
DUMITRESCU, Emerich Alexandru (Imre) JENEI (HUN), Tiberiu BONE, Gheorghe
CACOVEANU, Gheorghe CONSTANTIN, Ion ALEXANDRESCU (65'
CONTANTINESNU), Francisc ZAVODA (I), Nicolae TATARU. (Coach: Gheorghe
POPESCU).
M.T.K. Budapest: Róbert BÁRTFAI, Ferenc GÁL, Péter PALOTÁS, László SZIMCSÁK (II),
Imre KOVÁCS (I), Ferenc KOVÁCS (III), Endre KÁRÁSZ, Gábor BUKOVI, László BÖDÖR
(73' Gábor ARATÓ), János MOLNÁR, István SZIMCSÁK (I). (Coach: Márton BUKOVI).
Goals: C.C.A. Bucuresti: 1-0 Gheorghe CACOVEANU (35'), 2-1 Nicolae TATARU (59').
M.T.K. Budapest: 1-1 Gábor BUKOVI (43'), 2-2 László BÖDÖR (70'), 2-3 Gábor BUKOVI
(88').
Attendance: 50.000

116

27-05-1958   Stadion Vasil Levski, Sofia: Levski Sofia – FK Vojvodina Novi Sad 1-0 (1-0)
Levski Sofia: Ivan DERVENTSKI, Pavel VASILEV, Blagoi FILIPOV, Boris APOSTOLOV,
Ioncho ARSOV, Ivan GEORGIEV, Liuben GAIDEROV, Peyo PEEV (..' Stefan ABADJIEV),
Dimitar YORDANOV, Hristo ILIEV, Aleksandar Dimitrov KOSTOV. (Coach: Georgi
PACHEDJIEV).
FK Vojvodina Novi Sad: Lazar VASIC, Novak ROGANOVIC (..' Luka MALESEV), Zarko
NIKOLIC, Mladen VUCINIC, Imre BLANARIK, Nedeljko BULATOVIC, Stevan
VODALOV, Cedomir SENTIN, Stevan BENA, Aleksandar IVOS, Radomir KRSTIC. (Coach:
Antal LUKA).
Goal: Levski Sofia: 1-0 Dimitar YORDANOV (30').
Referee: SCHULLER (ROM)   Attendance: 40.000

31-05-1958   Kohász Stadion, Salgótarján:
              Salgótarjáni BTC – TJ Rudá Hvezda Brno 3-1 (1-1)
Salgótarjáni BTC: Géza OLÁH (I), Gyula SÁNDOR, Mihály JANCSIK, Lajos AGÓCS, Tibor
BODON, Róbert DÁVID, László BABLENA (46' Sándor JEDLICSKA), Béla CSÁKI, László
JAGODICS, Ferenc TALIGA, Nándor CHLADNI. (Coach: György SZÜCS).
TJ Rudá Hvezda Brno: Zdenek PLACHETA, Karel KOHLIK, Bohuslav SLÁMA, Stanislav
NAVRÁTIL, Jirí SÓN, Arnost MACHOVSKÝ (70' Borívoj VOBORNÝ), Zdenek
KOLÁCEK, Miroslav MIKESKA, Jirí ZAMASTIL, Zdenek HAJSKÝ, Bronislav DANDA.
(Coach: Josef EREMIÁS).
Goals: Salgótarjáni BTC: 1-0 László JAGODICS (2'), 2-1 László JAGODICS (61'), 3-1 Tibor
BODON (80').
TJ Rudá Hvezda Brno: 1-1 Bronislav DANDA (37').
Attendance: 6.000

31-05-1958   Népstadion, Budapest: M.T.K. Budapest – C.C.A. Bucuresti 6-2 (4-1)
M.T.K. Budapest: Róbert BÁRTFAI, László SZIMCSÁK (II) (46' Tibor PALICSKÓ), Péter
PALOTÁS, Mihály LANTOS, Imre KOVÁCS (I), Ferenc KOVÁCS (III), Endre KÁRÁSZ,
Gábor BUKOVI, László BÖDÖR, János MOLNÁR, István SZIMCSÁK (I). (Coach: Márton
BUKOVI).
C.C.A. Bucuresti: Constantin (Costica) TOMA (46' Ion VOINESCU), Vasile ZAVODA (II),
Alexandru APOLZAN, Victor DUMITRESCU, Emerich Alexandru (Imre) JENEI (HUN) (46'
ONISTE), Tiberiu BONE, Gheorghe CACOVEANU, Gheorghe CONSTANTIN, Ion
ALEXANDRESCU, Francisc ZAVODA (I), Nicolae TATARU. (Coach: Gheorghe
POPESCU).
Goals: M.T.K. Budapest: 1-0 Mihály LANTOS (2'), 2-1 János MOLNÁR (21'), 3-1 László
BÖDÖR (..'), 4-1 János MOLNÁR (..'), 5-2 János MOLNÁR (68'), 6-2 Vasile ZAVODA (78'
own goal).
C.C.A. Bucuresti: 1-1 Gheorghe CONSTANTIN (10'), 4-2 Péter PALOTÁS (57' *own goal*).
Attendance: 9.000

117

01-06-1958   Stadion Karadjordje, Novi Sad:
             FK Vojvodina Novi Sad – Levski Sofia 5-0 (2-0)
FK Vojvodina Novi Sad: Lazar VASIC, Stevan BENA, Mladen VUCINIC, Imre BLANARIK
(..' Stevan VODALOV), Zarko NIKOLIC, Luka MALESEV, Silvester TAKAC, Aleksandar
IVOS, Cedomir SENTIN, Nedeljko BULATOVIC, Radomir KRSTIC. (Coach: Antal LUKA).
Levski Sofia: Ivan DERVENTSKI, Petar DONCHEV, Boris APOSTOLOV, Ioncho ARSOV,
Blagoi FILIPOV, Ivan GEORGIEV, Stefan ABADJIEV, Peyo PEEV, Dimitar YORDANOV,
Hristo ILIEV, Aleksandar Dimitrov KOSTOV. (Coach: Georgi PACHEDJIEV).
Goals: FK Vojvodina Novi Sad: 1-0 Nedeljko BULATOVIC (29'), 2-0 Silvester TAKAC
(40'), 3-0 Silvester TAKAC (72'), 4-0 Radomir KRSTIC (73'), 5-0 Aleksandar IVOS (78').
Referee: Milan FENCL (TCH)   Attendance: 7.000

01-06-1958   Stadion Tatran, Presov: DSO Tatran Presov – FK Partizan Beograd 4-1 (0-1)
DSO Tatran Presov: Alois VECERKA, Anton VARGA, Jozef BOMBA, Alexander
FELSZÉGHY, Frantisek SEMESI, Ján FERIANCÍK, Ladislav PAVLOVIC, Rudolf
PAVLOVIC, Karol PETROS (68' Jozef FERENC), Jozef GAVRON, Gejza SIMANSKÝ.
FK Partizan Beograd: Slavko STOJANOVIC, Bruno BELÍN, Aleksandar JONCIC, Fahrudin
JUSUFI, Tomislav KALOPEROVIC, Bozidar PAJEVIC, Anton HERCEG, Josip (Mico)
DUVANCIC (..' Miroslav REDE), Milan VUKELIC, Draguljub BLAZIC, Branislav
MIHAJLOVIC.
Goals: DSO Tatran Presov: 1-1 Jozef GAVRON (54'), 2-1 Ladislav PAVLOVIC (57'), 3-1
Gejza SIMANSKÝ (82'), 4-1 Jozef GAVRON (86').
FK Partizan Beograd: 0-1 Tomislav KALOPEROVIC (38').
Referee: Károly BALLA (HUN)   Attendance: 14.000

01-06-1958   StadionZemun, Zemun:
             FK Radnicki Beograd – Ferencvárosi TC Budapest 2-1 (2-0)
FK Radnicki Beograd: Blagoje VIDINIC, Djura COKIC, Milorad DISKIC, BACKOVIC,
Milan LJUBENOVIC, Radmilo RISTIC, ROSTIC, BUGJA, Zoran PRLJINCEVIC, Ljubomir
OGNJANOVIC (II), SAVIC.
Ferencvárosi TC Budapest: Géza GULYÁS, Antal THOMANN, Ernö FORGÁCS, Imre
OMBÓDI, András GERENDÁS, Dr.Ferenc DÉKÁNY, Tamás KERTÉSZ, Pál OROSZ,
Miklós BORSOS (46' József DÁLNOKI (II)), Oszkár VILEZSÁL, Gyula RÁKOSI. (Coach:
Sándor TÁTRAI).
Goals: FK Radnicki Beograd: 1-0 Zoran PRLJINCEVIC (8' penalty), 2-0 Zoran
PRLJINCEVIC (34').
Ferencvárosi TC Budapest: 2-1 József DÁLNOKI (60').
Referee: Piki KRONER (ROM)   Attendance: 15.000

01-06-1958   National Stadion Vasil Levski, Sofia:
             FK Lokomotiv Sofia – Tatabányai Bányász SC 0-1 (0-0)
FK Lokomotiv Sofia: Yosif Yordanov YOSIFOV, Vasil METODIEV, Ivan DIMITROV,
Todor VELEV, Metodi NESTOROV, Dimitar DRAGOMIROV, SANOV, STANIMIROV,
Nikola KOTKOV Todorov (73' MIHAYLOV), Spiro DEBARSKI, MALINOV. (Coach:
Aleksandar POPOV).
Tatabányai Bányász SC: István FEKETE, Ferenc FARSANG, Viktor KÖRNYEI, János
LUGOSI, Sándor KOVÁCS, Sándor MOLNÁR (73' András DOMBAI), Ferenc BECK, Gyula
BÍRÓ, István SZOVJÁK,), László HÁRI, Gyula MACSALI. (Coach: Károly LAKAT).
Goal: Tatabányai Bányász SC: 0-1 István SZOVJÁK (88').
Referee: Borce NEDELKOVSKI (YUG)   Attendance: 12.000

118

01-06-1958   Stadion Klementa Gottwalda, Pardubice:
              Dukla Pardubice – FK Crvena Zvezda Beograd   0-0
Dukla Pardubice: Karol BOBOK, Telesfor HALMO, Prokop DANEK, Miroslav OSTÁDAL,
Kvetoslav NOVÁK, Karel VOVORSKÝ, Karel LICHTNÉGL, Jirí GRUNT, Bedrich SONKA
(..' Josef SUMMERAUER), Karel NEPOMUCKÝ, Frantisek MORÁVEK. (Coach: Stefan
CAMBAL).
FK Crvena Zvezda Beograd: Jovan GAJIC, Dimitrije STOJANOVIC, Miljan ZEKOVIC,
Ranko BOROZAN, Ljubomir SPAJIC, Lazar TASIC, Nikola STIPIC, Branko MILANOVIC,
Ivan POPOVIC, Borivoje (Bora) KOSTIC, Vojislav SRDIC. (Coach: Milorad PAVIC).
Referee: Gyula EMSBERGER (HUN)   Attendance: 12.000

01-06-1958   Timisoara: CS Stiinta Timisoara – TJ Dynamo Praha   3-0 (2-0)
CS Stiinta Timisoara: Petre CURCAN, STURECA, Octavian BRINZEI, Lucretiu FLORESCU,
Petre COJEREANU, Cornel TANASE, GIRLEANU, Iosif LERETER, COJAREANU, Petre
CADARIU, Ioan CIOSESCU. (Coach: Dinca SCHILERU).
TJ Dynamo Praha: Alois JONÁK, Jirí HILDEBRAND, Jirí TRNKA, Jan ANDREJKOVIC,
Jirí VLASÁK, Jirí NEDVÍDEK, Milos URBA, Alois HERCÍK, Ota HEMELE, Ladislav
SVOBODA, Miroslav LINHART.
Goals: CS Stiinta Timisoara: 1-0 Ioan CIOSESCU (20'), 2-0 Ioan CIOSESCU (35'), 3-0 Petre
CADARIU (74').

QUARTER-FINALS

08-06-1958   Stadion Karadjordje, Novi Sad:
              FK Vojvodina Novi Sad – TJ Rudá Hvezda Brno   0-0
FK Vojvodina Novi Sad: Lazar VASIC, Ilija BELIC, Mladen VUCINIC, Cedomir SENTIN,
Zarko NIKOLIC, Luka MALESEV, Stevan VODALOV, Silvester TAKAC (..' Nedeljko
BULATOVIC), Stevan BENA, Aleksandar IVOS, Radomir KRSTIC. (Coach: Antal LUKA).
TJ Rudá Hvezda Brno: Zdenek PLACHETA, Karel KOHLÍK, Bohuslav SLÁMA, Stanislav
NAVRÁTIL, Arnost MACHOVSKÝ, Vlastimil BUBNÍK, Zdenek KOLÁCEK, Jaromír
SALAJ, Jirí ZAMASTIL, Zdenek HAJSKÝ, Bronislav DANDA. (Coach: Josef EREMIÁS).
Referee: Gyula BALLA (HUN)   Attendance: 6.000

08-06-1958   Stadión Tatra, Presov: DSO Tatran Presov – M.T.K. Budapest   1-0 (0-0)
DSO Tatran Presov: Alois VECERKA, Andrej CEPCEK, Jozef BOMBA, Alexander
FELSZÉGHY, Frantisek SEMESI, Ján FERIANCÍK, Ladislav PAVLOVIC, Rudolf
PAVLOVIC, Karol PETROS, Jozef GAVRON, Gejza SIMANSKÝ.
M.T.K. Budapest: Róbert BÁRTFAI, László SZIMCSÁK (II), Péter PALOTÁS, Mihály
LANTOS, Imre KOVÁCS (I), Ferenc KOVÁCS (III), Endre KÁRÁSZ, Gábor BUKOVI,
László BÖDÖR, János MOLNÁR, István SZIMCSÁK (I). (Coach: Márton BUKOVI).
Goal: DSO Tatran Presov: 1-0 Rudolf PAVLOVIC (72').
Referee: Zivko BAJIC (YUG)   Attendance: 13.000

08-06-1958   City Stadion Zemun, Beograd:
FK Radnicki Beograd – CS Stiinta Timisoara 4-2 (1-0)
FK Radnicki Beograd: Blagoje VIDINIC, Djura COKIC, Jovan BACKOVIC, Milan
LJUBENOVIC, Milorad DISKIC, Radmilo RISTIC, Nemanja ROSIC, Aleksandar BUDA,
Zoran PRLJINCEVIC, Ljubomir OGNJANOVIC, Jovan SAVIC. (Coach: Illés SPITZ (HUN)).
CS Stiinta Timisoara: Alfred (Fredi) FUCHS, Ion ZBARCEA, Lucretiu FLORESCU, Petre
COJEREANU, Octavian BRINZEI, Cornel TANASE, FIRLEANU, Petre CADARIU, Ioan
CIOSESCU, Iosif LERETER, Iuliu BOROS (..' FOLIN). (Coach: Dinca SCHILERU).
Goals: FK Radnicki Beograd: 1-0 Zoran PRLJINCEVIC (26' penalty), 2-2 Zoran
PRLJINCEVIC (60'), 3-2 Nemanja ROSIC (71'), 4-2 Aleksandar BUDA (75').
CS Stiinta Timisoara: 1-1 Petre CADARIU (46'), 1-2 Ioan CIOSESCU (55').
Referee: Vilmos HERNÁDI (HUN)   Attendance: 5.500

08-06-1958   Stadion Vasil Levski, Sofia:
FK Lokomotiv Sofia – FK Crvena Zvezda Beograd 4-4 (2-2)
FK Lokomotiv Sofia: Yosif Yordanov YOSIFOV, Vasil METODIEV, Todor VELEV, Metodi
NESTOROV, Ivan DIMITROV, STANIMIROV, DEJEV, Nikola KOTKOV Todorov,
TAKOV, Spiro DEBARSKI, MALINOV. (Coach: Aleksandar POPOV).
FK Crvena Zvezda Beograd: Jovan GAJIC (..' Tatomir RADUNOVIC), Dimitrije
STOJANOVIC, Miljan ZEKOVIC, Ranko BOROZAN, Ljubomir SPAJIC, Lazar TASIC,
Nikola STIPIC, Branko MILANOVIC, Ivan POPOVIC, Borivoje (Bora) KOSTIC, Vojislav
SRDIC (..' Selimir MILOSEVIC). (Coach: Milorad PAVIC).
Goals: FK Lokomotiv Sofia: 1-1 TAKO V (5'), 2-2 MALINOV (41'), 3-2 Metodi
NESTOROV (49'), 4-3 DEJEV (67').
FK Crvena Zvezda Beograd: 0-1 Borivoje (Bora) KOSTIC (4'), 1-2 Borivoje (Bora) KOSTIC
(29'), 3-3 Borivoje (Bora) KOSTIC (51'), 4-4 Borivoje (Bora) KOSTIC (68').
Referee: Mihai POPA (ROM)   Attendance: 30.000

14-06-1958   Staion TJ Spartak, Brno: TJ Rudá Hvezda Brno – FK Vojvodina Novi Sad 0-0
TJ Rudá Hvezda Brno: Zdenek PLACHETA, Karel KOHLÍK, Bohuslav SLÁMA, Stanislav
NAVRÁTIL, Arnost MACHOVSKÝ, Vlastimil BUBNÍK, Zdenek KOLÁCEK, Jaromír
SALAJ, Jirí ZAMASTIL, Zdenek HAJSKÝ, Bronislav DANDA. (Coach: Josef EREMIÁS).
FK Vojvodina Novi Sad: Lazar VASIC, Stevan BENA, Mladen VUCINIC, Luka MALESEV,
Zarko NIKOLIC, Nedeljko BULATOVIC, Stevan VODALOV (..' Silvester TAKAC),
Cedomir SENTIN, Ilija BELIC, Aleksandar IVOS, Radomir KRSTIC. (Coach: Antal LUKA).
Referee: Gyula BALLA (HUN)   Attendance: 15.000
(TJ Rudá Hvezda Brno won on the toss of a coin).

14-06-1958   Hungária körút, Budapest: M.T.K. Budapest – DSO Tatran Presov 4-3 (4-1)
M.T.K. Budapest: József GELEI, Tibor PALICSKÓ, Péter PALOTÁS, László SZIMCSÁK
(II), Imre KOVÁCS (I), Ferenc KOVÁCS (III), Endre KÁRÁSZ (5' Gábor ARATÓ), Gábor
BUKOVI, László BÖDÖR, János MOLNÁR, István SZIMCSÁK (I). (Coach: Márton
BUKOVI).
DSO Tatran Presov: Alois VECERKA, Anton VARGA, Jozef BOMBA, Alexander
FELSZÉGHY, Frantisek SEMESI, Ján FERIANCÍK, Ladislav PAVLOVIC, Rudolf
PAVLOVIC, József FERENCZ (46' Karol PETROS), Jozef GAVRON, Gejza SIMANSKÝ.
Goals: M.T.K. Budapest: 1-0 László BÖDÖR (11'), 2-0 János MOLNÁR (16'), 3-1 Imre
KOVÁVS (21'), 4-1 János MOLNÁR (30').
DSO Tatran Presov: 2-1 Ladislav PAVLOVIC (20'), 4-2 Karol PETROS (50'), 4-3 Ladislav
PAVLOVIC (75' penalty).
Referee: Konstantin DINOV Sotirov (BUL)   Attendance: 18.000
(DSO Tatran Presov won on the toss of a coin).

120

15-06-1958   JNA Stadion, Beograd:
          FK Crvena Zvezda Beograd – FK Lokomotiv Sofia 1-0 (0-0)
FK Crvena Zvezda Beograd: Tatomir RADUNOVIC, Dimitrije STOJANOVIC, Miljan
ZEKOVIC, Ranko BOROZAN, Ljubomir SPAJIC, Lazar TASIC, Nikola STIPIC, Branko
MILANOVIC, Selimir MILOSEVIC (..' Ivan POPOVIC), Borivoje (Bora) KOSTIC, Vojislav
SRDIC. (Coach: Milorad PAVIC).
FK Lokomotiv Sofia: Yosif Yordanov YOSIFOV, STANIMIROV, Ivan DIMITROV, Todor
VELEV, Metodi NESTOROV, DRAGOMIROV, TAKOV, Petar MIHAYLOV, Nikola
KOTKOV Todorov, Spiro DEBARSKI, MALINOV. (Coach: Aleksandar POPOV).
Goal: FK Crvena Zvezda Beograd: 1-0 Borivoje (Bora) KOSTIC (86').
Referee: Gyula GERE (HUN)   Attendance: 10.000

15-06-1958   Stadion 23 august, Timisoara:
          CS Stiinta Timisoara – FK Radnicki Beograd 1-3 (0-0)
CS Stiinta Timisoara: Mircea ENACHESCU, Ion ZBARCEA, Octavian BRINZEI,
SURESKU, Petre COJEREANU, Cornel TANASE, GRIJANU, Petre CADARIU, Ioan
CIOSESCU, Iosif LERETER, MINCHARU. (Coach: Dinca SCHILERU).
FK Radnicki Beograd: Blagoje VIDINIC, Djura COKIC, Jovan BACKOVIC, Milan
LJUBENOVIC, Milorad DISKIC, Radmilo RISTIC, Nemanja ROSIC, Aleksandar BUDA,
Zoran PRLJINCEVIC, Ljubomir OGNJANOVIC, Jovan SAVIC. (Coach: Illés SPITZ (HUN)).
Goals: CS Stiinta Timisoara: 1-1 Octavian BRINZEI (67').
FK Radnicki Beograd: 0-1 Jovan SAVIC (55'), 1-2 Jovan SAVIC (73'), 1-3 Jovan SAVIC
(78').
Referee: Karel JÜNGER (TCH)   Attendance: 25.000

SEMI-FINALS

22-06-1958   Presov: DSO Tatran Presov – TJ Rudá Hvezda Brno 0-0
DSO Tatran Presov: Alois VECERKA, Anton VARGA, Andrej CEPCEK, Jozef BOMBA,
Frantisek SEMESI, Ján FERIANCÍK, Ladislav PAVLOVIC, Rudolf PAVLOVIC, Karol
PETROS, Jozef GAVRON, Gejza SIMANSKÝ.
TJ Rudá Hvezda Brno: Zdenek PLACHETA, Karel KOHLÍK, Bohumil SLÁMA (expulsion
60'), Jirí NAVRÁTIL, Zdenek MACHOVSKÝ, Jirí SÓN, Zdenek KOLÁCEK, Borívoj
VOBORNÝ, Vlastimil BUBNIK, Zdenek HAJSKÝ, Bronislav DANDA. (Coach: Josef
EREMIÁS).
Referee: Vilmos HERNÁDI (HUN)   Attendance: 7.000

22-06-1958   City stadion Zemun, Beograd:
          FK Radnicki Beograd – FK Crvena Zvezda Beograd 1-2 (1-1)
FK Radnicki Beograd: Blagoje VIDINIC, Djura COKIC, Jovan BACKOVIC, Milan
LJUBENOVIC, Milorad DISKIC, Radmilo RISTIC, Nemanja ROSIC, Aleksandar BUDA,
Zoran PRLJINCEVIC, Ljubomir OGNJANOVIC, Jovan SAVIC. (Coach: Illés SPITZ (HUN)).
FK Crvena Zvezda Beograd: Tatomir RADUNOVIC, Dimitrije STOJANOVIC, Miljan
ZEKOVIC (..' Radojko POPADIC), Ranko BOROZAN, Ljubomir SPAJIC, Lazar TASIC,
Nikola STIPIC, Branko MILANOVIC, Ivan POPOVIC, Borivoje (Bora) KOSTIC, Selimir
MILOSEVIC. (Coach: Milorad PAVIC).
Goals: FK Radnicki Beograd: 1-1 Zoran PRLJINCEVIC (27').
FK Crvena Zvezda Beograd: 0-1 Nikola STIPIC (17'), 1-2 Nikola STIPIC (52').
Referee: Konstantin DINOV Sotirov (BUL)   Attendance: 4.000

28-06-1958   Brno: TJ Rudá Hvezda Brno – DSO Tatran Presov   3-0 (2-0)
TJ Rudá Hvezda Brno: Zdenek PLACHETA, Zdenek MACHOVSKÝ, Karel KOHLIK, Jirí
NAVRÁTIL, Borívoj VOBORNÝ, Jirí SÓN, Zdenek KOLÁCEK, Bronislav DANDA,
Vlastimil BUBNIK, Zdenek HAJSKÝ, KOLOUCH. (Coach: Josef EREMIÁS).
DSO Tatran Presov: Alois VECERKA, Anton VARGA, Jozef BOMBA, Alexander
FELSZÉGHY, Frantisek SEMESI, Ján FERIANCÍK, Ladislav PAVLOVIC, Rudolf
PAVLOVIC, Karol PETROS, Jozef GAVRON (46' Jozef FERENC), Gejza SIMANSKÝ.
Goals: TJ Rudá Hvezda Brno: 1-0 Bronislav DANDA (8'), 2-0 Vlastimil BUBNIK (15'), 3-0
Zdenék HAJSKY (80').
Referee: Vilmos HERNÁDI (HUN)   Attendance: 4.000

29-06-1958   JNA Stadion, Beograd:
                    FK Crvena Zvezda Beograd – FK Radnicki Beograd   0-0
FK Crvena Zvezda Beograd: Tatomir RADUNOVIC, Novak TOMIC, Dimitrije
STOJANOVIC, Ranko BOROZAN, Ljubomir SPAJIC, Vladimir POPOVIC, Nikola STIPIC,
Branko MILANOVIC, Selimir MILOSEVIC (..' Ivan POPOVIC), Borivoje (Bora) KOSTIC,
Dragoslav SEKULARAC. (Coach: Milorad PAVIC).
FK Radnicki Beograd: Blagoje VIDINIC, Djura COKIC, MRDALJ, Milan LJUBENOVIC,
Milorad DISKIC, Radmilo RISTIC, Nemanja ROSIC, Aleksandar BUDA, Zoran
PRLJINCEVIC, Ljubomir OGNJANOVIC, Jovan SAVIC. (Coach: Illés SPITZ (HUN)).
Referee: Piki KRONER (ROM)   Attendance: 16.000

FINAL

06-07-1958   JNA Stadion, Beograd:
                    FK Crvena Zvezda Beograd – TJ Rudá Hvezda Brno   4-1 (2-1)
FK Crvena Zvezda Beograd: Tatomir RADUNOVIC, Novak TOMIC, Ljubisa SPAJIC,
Dimitrije STOJANOVIC, Ranko BOROZAN, Vladimir POPOVIC, Nikola STIPIC, Branko
MILANOVIC, Selimir MILOSEVIC, Dragoslav SEKULARAC, Borivoje (Bora) KOSTIC.
(Coach: Milorad PAVIC).
TJ Rudá Hvezda Brno: Zdenek PLACHETA, Karel KOHLÍK, Bohumil SLÁMA, Jirí
NAVRÁTIL, Zdenek MACHOVSKÝ, Jirí SÓN, Zdenek KOLÁCEK, Bronislav DANDA,
Vlastimil BUBNIK, Zdenek HAJSKÝ, Miroslav MIKESKA. (Coach: Josef EREMIÁS).
Goals: FK Crvena Zvezda Beograd: 1-0 Selimir MILOSEVIC (5'), 2-0 Borivoje (Bora)
KOSTIC (6'), 3-1 Borivoje (Bora) KOSTIC (59'), 4-1 Branko MILANOVIC (86').
TJ Rudá Hvezda Brno: 2-1 Zdenek KOLÁCEK (39').
Referee: Piki KRONER (ROM)   Attendance: 22.000

12-07-1958   Brno: TJ Rudá Hvezda Brno – FK Crvena Zvezda Beograd   2-3 (0-2)
TJ Rudá Hvezda Brno: Zdenek PLACHETA, Karel KOHLÍK, Bohumil SLÁMA, Jirí
NAVRÁTIL, Zdenek MACHOVSKÝ, Jirí SÓN, Zdenek KOLÁCEK, Bronislav DANDA (51'
Borívoj VOBORNÝ), Vlastimil BUBNIK, Zdenek HAJSKÝ, Miroslav MIKESKA. (Coach:
Josef EREMIÁS).
FK Crvena Zvezda Beograd: Tatomir RADUNOVIC, Novak TOMIC, Ljubisa SPAJIC,
Dimitrije STOJANOVIC, Vladimir POPOVIC, Ranko BOROZAN, Nikola STIPIC, Branko
MILANOVIC, Selimir MILOSEVIC, Dragoslav SEKULARAC, Borivoje (Bora) KOSTIC.
(Coach: Milorad PAVIC).
Goals: TJ Rudá Hvezda Brno: 1-3 Zdenek HAJSKÝ (50'), 2-3 Zdenek HAJSKÝ (76').
FK Crvena Zvezda Beograd: 0-1 Borivoje (Bora) KOSTIC (5'), 0-2 Dragoslav SEKULARAC
(14'), 0-3 Selimir MILOSEVIC (46').
Referee: Petar Khristov DJONEV (BUL)   Attendance: 13.000

*** FK Crvena Zvezda Beograd won the Cup ***

1959

04-07-1959   WAC-Platz, Wien: Wiener AC – Budapesti Honvéd SE   2-1 (0-1)
Wiener AC: Franz PELIKAN, Helmut JANECEK, Karl KOWANZ, Herbert MACH, Lambert
LENZINGER, Bohumil HRSUKA, Karl SCHRÖTTER, Stefan SZOKOLL, Ernst
KALTENBRUNNER (II), Franz SCHILLING, Kurt REITER.
Budapesti Honvéd SE: Lajos FARAGÓ, János SZÖCS, István SOLTI, Zoltán DUDÁS, István
TÖRÖCSIK (I), Antal KOTÁSZ, István GILICZ, László KAZINCZY, Ferenc MACHOS,
Lajos TICHÝ, János SZILASI. (Coach: Károly SÓS).
Goals: Wiener AC: 1-1 Stefan SZOKOLL (89'), 2-1 Ernst KALTENBRUNNER (90').
Budapesti Honvéd SE: 0-1 János SZILASI (39').
Referee: Giulio CAMPANATI (ITA)   Attendance: 7.000

05-07-1959   Budapest: M.T.K. Budapest – TJ Dynamo Praha   5-0 (3-0)
M.T.K. Budapest: Sándro GELLÉR, Tibor PALICSKÓ, Ferenc SIPOS, Mihály LANTOS,
István NAGY, Ferenc KOVÁCS (III), Károly SÁNDOR (35' BOTHA), István KUTI, László
BÖDÖR, János MOLNÁR, István SZIMCSÁK (I). (Coach: Nándor HIDEGKUTI).
TJ Dynamo Praha: Bretislav DOLEJSÍ, Jirí HILDEBRANDT, Václav ZAMAZAL, Josef
KETTNER, Jirí VLASÁK, Jirí NEDVÍDEK, Milos URBAN, Otto HEMELE, Robert
HOCHMAN, Milos STÁDLER, Frantisek MORÁVEK. (Coach: Vlastimil KOPECKÝ).
Goals: M.T.K. Budapest: 1-0 István SZIMCSÁK (1'), 2-0 Mihály LANTOS (20' penalty), 3-0
János MOLNÁR (38'), 4-0 László BÖDÖR (48'), 5-0 János MOLNÁR (79').
Referee: Francesco LIVERANI (ITA)   Attendance: 15.000

05-07-1959   Stadion Karadjordje, Novi Sad:
               FK Vojvodina Novi Sad – First Vienna FC   1-0 (1-0)
FK Vojvodina Novi Sad: Andras VERES, Novak ROGAN?VIC, Mladen VUCINIC, Stevan
BENA, Zarko NIKOLIC, Cedomir SENTIN, Stevan SEKERES, Silvester TAKAC, Todor
VESELINOVIC, Aleksandar IVOS, Zdravko RAJKOV. (Coach: Antal LUKA).
First Vienna FC: Kurt SCHMIED, Hermann KOZICH (I), Josef WEBORA, Karl NICKERL,
Karl KOLLER, Julius SCHWEIGER, Erich MEDVETH, Helmut SENEKOWITSCH, Herbert
GROHS, Karl JERICHA, Alfred PICHLER. (Coach: Richard FISCHER).
Goal: FK Vojvodina Novi Sad: 1-0 Aleksandar IVOS (19').
Referee: Vilmos HERNÁDI (HUN)   Attendance: 12.000

05-07-1959   Bazaly Stadion, Ostrava: DSO Baník Ostrava – FK Partizan Beograd   1-1 (1-0)
DSO Baník Ostrava: Frantisek DVORÁK (I), Bedrich KÖHLER, Karel DVORÁK (III),
Prokop DANEK, Josef ONDRACKA, Zdenek STANCO, Zdenek KOSNOVSKÝ, Tomás
POSPÍCHAL, Jirí KRIZÁK, Miroslav WIECEK, Vilém ZÁVALSKÝ. (Coach: Jaroslav
VEJVODA).
FK Partizan Beograd: Milutin SOSKIC, Milan KRANJCIC, Bruno BELÍN, Aleksandar
JONCIC, Fahrudin JUSUFI, Jovan MILADINOVIC, Zvezdan CEBINAC, Lazar RADOVIC
(30' Milan VUKELIC), Tomislav KALOPEROVIC, Milan GALIC, Branislav MIHAJLOVIC.
(Coach: Illés SPLITZ (HUN)).
Goals: DSO Baník Ostrava: 1-0 Miroslav WIECEK (35').
FK Partizan Beograd: 1-1 Milan VUKELIC (61').
Referee: Friedrich (Fritz) SEIPELT (AUT)   Attendance: 18.000

124

10-07-1959   Stadion Eden, Praha: TJ Dynamo Praha – M.T.K. Budapest 4-2 (1-1)
TJ Dynamo Praha: Alois JONÁK, Jirí HILDEBRANDT (..' Josef MORAVEC), Václav
ZAMAZAL, Milos STÁDLER, Jirí VLASÁK, Jirí NEDVIDEK, Milos URBAN, Alois
HERCÍK, Robert HOCHMAN, Ladislav SVOBODA, Frantisek MORÁVEK. (Coach:
Vlastimil KOPECKÝ).
M.T.K. Budapest: Sándor GELLÉR, Tibor PALICSKÓ, Ferenc SIPOS, József DANSZKY,
István NAGY, Ferenc KOVÁCS (III), BOTHA, István KUTI, László BÖDÖR, János
MOLNÁR, István SZIMCSÁK (I). (Coach: Nándor HIDEGKUTI).
Goals: TJ Dynamo Praha: 1-0 Frantisek MORÁVEK (9'), 2-1 Frantisek MORÁVEK (50'
penalty), 3-1 Frantisek MORÁVEK (51' penalty), 4-1 Milos STÁDLER (60').
M.T.K. Budapest: 1-1 István NAGY (28'), 4-2 János MOLNÁR (75').
Referee: Carl Erich STEINER (AUT)   Attendance: 15.000

11-07-1959   JNA Stadion, Beograd: FK Partizan Beograd – DSO Baník Ostrava 3-2 (0-1)
FK Partizan Beograd: Milutin SOSKIC, Milan KRANJCIC, Aleksandar JONCIC, Fahrudin
JUSUFI, Bruno BELÍN, Jovan MILADINOVIC, Zvezdan CEBINAC, Lazar RADOVIC,
Tomislav KALOPEROVIC, Milan GALIC, Branislav MIHAJLOVIC. (Coach: Illés SPLITZ
(HUN)).
DSO Baník Ostrava: Frantisek DVORÁK (I), Bedrich KÖHLER, Prokop DANEK, Josef
VLADYKA, Josef ONDRACKA, Zdenek STANCO, Zdenek KOSNOVSKÝ, Tomás
POSPÍCHAL, Jirí KRIZÁK, Miroslav WIECEK, Vilém ZÁVALSKÝ. (Coach: Jaroslav
VEJVODA).
Goals: FK Partizan Beograd: 1-2 Tomislav KALOPEROVIC (80' penalty), 2-2 Zoran
MILADINOVIC (90'+), 3-2 Tomislav KALOPEROVIC (102').
DSO Baník Ostrava: 0-1 Tomás POSPÍCHAL (16'), 0-2 Jirí KRIZÁK (56').
Referee: István ZSOLT (HUN)   Attendance: 15.000
(After extra time)

11-07-1959   Hohe Warte, Wien: First Vienna FC – FK Vojvodina Novi Sad 3-3 (0-2)
First Vienna FC: Kurt SCHMIED, Hermann KOZICH (II), Josef WEBORA, Karl NICKERL,
Karl KOLLER, Julius SCHWEIGE Rudolf GRASSERBAUER, Helmut SENEKOWITSCH,
Josef GELEGS (II) (44' Johann LA ER), Karl JERICHA, Alfred PICHLER. (Coach:
Richard FISCHER).
FK Vojvodina Novi Sad: András VERÉS, Slavko SVINJAREVIC, Novak ROGANOVIC,
Mladen VUCINIC, Stevan BENA, Cedomir SENTIN, Zdravko RAJKOV, Aleksandar IVOS,
Stevan SEKERES, Todor VESELINOVIC, Radomir KRSTIC (I). (Coach: Ratomir CABRIC).
Goals: First Vienna FC: 1-2 Helmut SENEKOWITSCH (50'), 2-3 Helmut SENEKOWITSCH
(63'), 3-3 Karl JERICHA (75').
FK Vojvodina Novi Sad: 0-1 Todor VESELINOVIC (25'), 0-2 Aleksandar IVOS (26'), 1-3
Radomir KRSTIC (60').
Referee: Karol GALBA (TCH)   Attendance: 5.000

12.07-1959   Bozsik József Stadion, Budapest:
               Budapesti Honvéd SE – Wiener AC 7-0 (3-0)
Budapesti Honvéd SE: Lajos FARAGÓ, János SZÖCS (..' Ferenc TÖRÖCSIK (II)), Nándor
BÁNYAI, Zoltán DUDÁS, József BOZSIK, Antal KOTÁSZ, László MAROSI, István
TÖRÖCSIK (I), Lajos TICHÝ, István GILICZ, János SZILASI. (Coach: Károly SÓS).
Wiener AC:
Goals: Budapesti Honvéd SE: 1-0 István GILICZ (18'), 2-0 István TÖRÖCSIK (23'), 3-0
János SZÖCS (27' penalty), 4-0 Lajos TICHÝ (58'), 5-0 Lajos TICHÝ (78'), 6-0 János
SZILASI (80'), 7-0 István GILICZ (85').
Attendance: 10.000

125

SEMI-FINALS

18-07-1959   JNA Stadion, Beograd:
             FK Partizan Beograd – Budapesti Honvéd SE   3-3 (1-1)
FK Partizan Beograd: Milutin SOSKIC, Milan KRANJCIC, Fahrudin JUSUFI, Bruno BELÍN,
Aleksandar JONCIC, Velibor VASOVIC, Zvezdan CEBINAC, Lazar RADOVIC (..' Vladimir
KOVACEVIC), Jovan MILADINOVIC, Tomislav KALOPEROVIC, Branislav
MIHAJLOVIC. (Coach: Illés SPLITZ (HUN)).
Budapesti Honvéd SE: Lajos FARAGÓ, János SZÖCS (..' Ferenc TÖRÖCSIK (II)), Nándor
BÁNYAI, Zoltán DUDÁS, József BOZSIK, Antal KOTÁSZ, László MAROSI, István
TÖRÖCSIK (I), Lajos TICHÝ, István GILICZ, János SZILASI. (Coach: Károly SÓS).
Goals: FK Partizan Beograd: 1-1 Branislav MIHAJLOVIC (44'), 2-1 József BOZSIK (49' own
goal), 3-3 Tomislav KALOPEROVIC (80' penalty).
Budapesti Honvéd SE: 0-1 Lajos TICHÝ (1'), 2-2 József BOZSIK (56'), 2-3 László MAROSI
(58').
Referee: Jindrich KARAS (TCH)   Attendance: 35.000

18-07-1959   Népstadion, Budapest: M.T.K. Budapest – FK Vojvodina Novi Sad   2-1 (0-0)
M.T.K. Budapest: Sándor GELLÉR, Tibor PALICSKÓ, Mihály LANTOS, István NAGY,
Ferenc SIPOS, Ferenc KOVÁCS (III), Gábor ARATÓ, István KUTI, László BÖDÖR, János
MOLNÁR, István SZIMCSÁK (I). (Coach: Márton BUKOVI).
FK Vojvodina Novi Sad: Lazar VASIC, Slavko SVINJAREVIC, Mladen VUCINIC, Stevan
BENA, Novak ROGANOVIC, Cedomir SENTIN, Stevan SEKERES, Aleksandar IVOS,
Todor VESELINOVIC, Josip DUVANDZIC, Radomir KRSTIC (I). (Coach: Antal LUKA).
Goals: M.T.K. Budapest: 1-1 János MOLNÁR (57'), 2-1 Ferenc SIPOS (63').
FK Vojvodina Novi Sad: 0-1 Aleksandar IVOS (50').
Referee: Alfred GRILL (AUT)   Attendance: 15.000

26-07-1959   Bozsik József Stadion, Budapest:
             Budapesti Honvéd SE – FK Partizan Beograd   2-2 (2-0)
Budapesti Honvéd SE: Lajos FARAGÓ, János SZÖCS, Nádor BÁNYAI, Zoltán DUDÁS,
József BOZSIK, Antal KOTÁSZ, László MAROSI, LászKAZINCZY, Lajos TICHÝ, István
GILICZ, János SZILASI. (Coach: Károly SÓS).
FK Partizan Beograd: Milutin SOSKIC, Fahrudin JUSUFI, Bruno BELÍN, Milan KRANJCIC,
Aleksandar JONCIC, Jovan MILADINOVIC, Zvezdan CEBINAC, Lazar RADOVIC (..'
Milan VUKELIC), Tomislav KALOPEROVIC, Milan GALIC, Branislav MIHAJLOVIC.
(Coach: Illés SPLITZ (HUN)).
Goals: Budapesti Honvéd SE: 1-0 Lajos TICHÝ (19'), 2-0 Lajos TICHÝ (35').
FK Partizan Beograd: 2-1 Antal KOTÁSZ (62' own goal), 2-2 Milan GALIC (84').
Referee: Friedrich (Fritz) SEIPELT (AUT)   Attendance: 25.000

(Budapesti Honvéd SE won on the toss of a coin).

27-07-1959   Stadion Karadjordje, Novi Sad:
             FK Vojvodina Novi Sad – M.T.K. Budapest   0-0
FK Vojvodina Novi Sad: Andras VERES, Slavko SVINJAREVIC, Mladen VUCINIC, Stevan
BENA, Zarko NIKOLIC, Cedomir SENTIN, Novak ROGANOVIC, Josip DUVANDZIC (..'
Silvester TAKAC), Stevan SEKERES, Aleksandar IVOS, Miladin RADICEVIC. (Coach:
Antal LUKA).
M.T.K. Budapest: Sándor GELLÉR, Tibor PALICSKÓ, Mihály LANTOS, Ferenc GÁL,
Ferenc SIPOS, Ferenc KOVÁCS (III), Sándor BÓTA, István NAGY, László BÖDÖR (..'
Gábor ARATÓ), János MOLNÁR, István SZIMCSÁK (I). (Coach: Márton BUKOVI).
Referee: ROLEK (TCH)   Attendance: 15.000

126

FINAL

19-08-1959   Népstadion, Budapest: Budapesti Honvéd SE – M.T.K. Budapest 4-3
Budapesti Honvéd SE: Lajos FARAGÓ, Ferenc TÖRÖCSIK (II), János SZÖCS (..' Antal
GALAMBOS), Zoltán DUDÁS, József BOZSIK, Antal KOTÁSZ, László MAROSI, István
TÖRÖCSIK (I), Lajos TICHÝ, István GILICZ, Zoltán REGÖS. (Coach: Károly SÓS).
M.T.K. Budapest: Sándor GELLÉR (..' József GELEI), Tibor PALICSKÓ, Ferenc SIPOS,
Mihály LANTOS, István NAGY, Ferenc KOVÁCS (III), Károly SÁNDOR, István KUTI (..'
József HALMAI), László BÖDÖR, János MOLNÁR, István SZIMCSÁK (I). (Coach: Márton
BUKOVI).
Goals: Budapesti Honvéd SE: Lajos TICHÝ, Lajos TICHÝ, Lajos TICHÝ, István GILICZ.
M.T.K. Budapest: János MOLNÁR, Károly SÁNDOR, István SZIMCSÁK (I).
Attendance: 20.000

09-09-1959   Népstadion, Budapest: M.T.K. Budapest – Budapesti Honvéd SE 2-2
M.T.K. Budapest: József GELEI, Tibor PALICSKÓ, Ferenc SIPOS, Mihály LANTOS, István
NAGY, Ferenc KOVÁCS (III), Károly SÁNDOR, László BÖDÖR, Gyula SAS, János
MOLNÁR, István SZIMCSÁK (I). (Coach: Márton BUKOVI).
Budapesti Honvéd SE: Lajos FARAGÓ, Ferenc TÖRÖCSIK (II), István TÖRÖCSIK (I),
Zoltán DUDÁS, József BOZSIK, Antal KOTÁSZ, László BUDAI (II), László KAZINCZY,
Lajos TICHÝ, István GILICZ, János SZILASI (..' András CSINOS). (Coach: Károly SÓS).
Goals: M.T.K. Budapest: János MOLNÁR, Gyula SAS.
Budapesti Honvéd SE: Lajos TICHÝ, András CSINOS.
Attendance: 60.000

*** Budapesti Honvéd SE won the Cup ***

127

1960

03-07-1960   Hohe Warte, Wien: Wiener Sportklub – Dukla Praha 2-1 (1-0)
Wiener Sportklub: Rudolf SZANWALD, Johann WINDISCH, Heinrich BÜLLWATSCH,
Wilhelm KAINRATH, Rudolf OSLANDSKÝ, Leipold BARSCHANDT, Karl SKERLAN,
Josef HAMERL, Adolf KNOLL, Erich HOF (I), Egon STAMPFER. (Coach: Josef STROH).
Dukla Praha: Pavol KOUBA, Karel CHRUDIMSKÝ, Jiří CADEK, Ivo URBAN, Stanislav
JARÁBEK, Milan DVORÁK, Rudolf TAUCHEN, Rudolf KUCERA (70' Jan
BRUMOVSKÝ), Jiří SURA, Jaroslav BOROVICKA, Josef JELÍNEK.
Goals: Wiener Sportklub: 1-0 Josef HAMERL (25'), 2-1 Adolf KNOLL (89').
Dukla Praha: 1-1 Jiří SURA (31').
Referee: István ZSOLT (HUN)   Attendance: 25.000

*(Double game played on the same day and at the same venue as the game between First
Vienna FC and Vasas SC).*

03-07-1960   Rudolfsheim-Fünfhaus: Wiener AC – FK Vojvodina Novi Sad 2-2 (1-2)
Wiener AC: Franz PELIKAN, Helmut JANECEK, Herbert MACH, Josef NEMANSKY, Karl
KOWANZ, Bohumil HRSUKA, HAJCAR, Friedrich (Fritz) CEJKA, Ernst/Günter (Name not
certain) KALTENBRUNNER, Norbert SCHILLING, Stefan SZOKOLL.
FK Vojvodina Novi Sad: Zdravko BRKLJACIC, Slavko SVINJAREVIC, Stevan SEKERES,
Stevan BENA, Novak ROGANOVIC, Josip DUVANCIC, Laslo BORBELJ, Zdravko
RAJKOV, Sylvester TAKAC, Alexander IVOS, Radoslav ZLOPASA.
Goals: Wiener AC: 1-1 Ernst/Günter (Name not certain) KALTENBRUNNER (20'), 2-2
Norbert SCHILLING (62').
FK Vojvodina Novi Sad: 0-1 Sylvester TAKAC (16'), 1-2 Zdravko RAJKOV (32').
Referee: Milan FENCL (TCH)   Attendance: 6.000

03-07-1960   City Stadium, Mostar: FK Velez Mostar – US Alessandria 4-1 (1-0)
FK Velez Mostar: Ivan CURKOVIC, Zdravko RODIN, Meho HANDZIC, Vlado
SLISKOVIC, Dane PRAJO, Franjo DZIDIC (46' Mensud DILBEROVIC), LIPOSINOVIC,
BLAZIC, Sulejman REBAC, Milorad LAZOVIC, Kruno RADILJEVIC. (Coach: Ratomir
CABRIC).
US Alessandria: Luciano ARBIZZANI, Aldo NARDI, Giovanni GIACOMAZZI, Cirano
SNIDERO, Antonio SCHIAVONI, Umberto BONIARDI, Mario MORRIGI, Romano FORIN,
MORANTI, Remo MARMO, Vittorio REGENI.
Goals: FK Velez Mostar: 1-0 Milorad LAZOVIC (40'), 2-0 LIPOSINOVIC (54'), 3-1
Sulejman REBAC (79'), 4-1 Sulejman REBAC (87').
US Alessandria: 2-1 Romano FORIN (71').
Referee: Antonin RUZICKA (TCH)   Attendance: 6.000

03-07-1960   Udine: AC Udinese – FK Austria Wien 2-0 (1-0)
AC Udinese: Luigi BERTOSSI, Luigi GIGANTE, Renato VALENTI, Renzo SASSI, Giorgio
ODLING, Massimo GIACOMINI, Luis PENTRELLI (ARG), Enzo MENEGOTTI, Lorenzo
BETTINI, Roberto MANGANOTTO, Alberto FONTANESI.
FK Austria Wien: Paul SCHWEDA, Oskar FISCHER, Nobert KRASA, Johann LÖSER, Adolf
BLUTSCH, Erich MEDVETH, Franz PFEIFFER (46' Horst HIRNSCHRODT), Johann
RIEGLER, Horst NEMEC, Ernst FIALA, Walter SCHLEGER.
Goals: AC Udinese: 1-0 Oskar FISCHER (23' *own goal*), 2-0 Lorenzo BETTINI (84').
Referee: Acio DAMJANI (YUG)   Attendance: 11.000

03-07-1960   Bányász Stadion, Tatabánya:
Tatabányai Bányász SC – TJ Cervená Hviezda Bratislava 2-1 (1-1)
Tatabányai Bányász SC: Gyula GROSICS, Ferenc FARSANG, Imre MÉSZÁROS, Gyula
MACSALI, József SCHÉDL, József POLGÁR, István SVOZJÁK, Gyula BÍRÓ, László
RAPAI, László TÖRÖK, Mihály DEMETER. (Coach: Károly LAKAT).
TJ Cervená Hviezda Bratislava: Frantisek HLAVATÝ, Gustáv MRÁZ, Vladimír WEISS (I),
Ján FERIANCÍK, Stefan MATLÁK, Dezider CIMRA (44' Eduard GÁBORÍK), Kazimír
GAJDOS, Adolf SCHERER, Ladislav KACÁNI, Jozef OBERT, Valerián BARTALSKÝ.
Goals: Tatabányai Banyasz SC: 1-1 Gyula BÍRÓ (34'), 2-1 László RAPAI (81').
TJ Cervená Hviezda Bratislava: 0-1 József POLGAR (5' own goal).
Referee: Friedrich (Fritz) SEIPELT (AUT)   Attendance: 12.000

03-07-1960   Stadión Tehelné pole, Bratislava:
DSO Spartak Kovosmalt Trnava – AS Roma 2-0 (1-0)
DSO Spartak Kovosmalt Trnava: Jozef ONDRUSKA, Juraj KADLEC, Stefan PSENKO,
Stefan SLANINA, Karol TIBENSKÝ, Milan GALBICKA, Jozef STIBRÁNYI, Valérian
SVEC (84' Jaroslav BENEDIK), Ján STURDÍK, Jozef ADAMEC, Milan BARTÁK.
AS Roma: Fabio CUDICINI, Giosuè STUCCHI, Giovanni GRIFFITH, Alfio FONTANA,
Giacomo LOSI, Luigi GIULIANO, Lamberto LEONARDI, Manlio COMPAGNO, Alberto
ORLANDO, Franco ZAGLIO, Arne Bengt SELMOSSON (SWE). (Coach: Alfredo FONI).
Goals: DSO Spartak Kovosmalt Trnava: 1-0 Jozef ADAMEC (13' penalty), 2-0 Valérian
SVEC (72').
Referee: Zivko BAJIC (YUG)   Attendance: 27.000

03-07-1960   Stadion Kosevo, Sarajevo: FK Sarajevo – M.T.K. Budapest 1-2 (0-1)
FK Sarajevo: Ranko PLANINIC, Petar BANJAC (..' Kemal DZEMIDZIC), Ibrahim (Ibro)
BIOGRADLIC, Vladimir CONC, Momcilo STANIC, Srboljub MARKUSEVIC, Ivica MIOC,
Asim FERHATOVIC, Salih SEHOVIC, Ivica PETKOVIC, Zijad ARSLANAGIC. (Coach:
Semso KAPETANOVIC).
M.T.K. Budapest: Sándor GELLÉR, Tibor PALICSKÓ, Mihály LANTOS, Ferenc GÁL,
Ferenc SIPOS, Ferenc KOVÁCS (III), Sándor BÓTA, Mihály LACZKÓ, István NAGY, János
MOLNÁR, István SZIMCSÁK. (Coach: Gyula SZÜCS).
Goals: FK Sarajevo: 1-1 Ivica PETKOVIC (54').
M.T.K. Budapest: 0-1 Sándor BÓTA (2'), 1-2 János MOLNÁR (76').
Referee: Igino RIGATO (ITA)   Attendance: 14.000

03-07-1960   Stadion JNA., Beograd:
FK Partizan Beograd – Slovan UNV Bratislava 2-1 (1-1)
FK Partizan Beograd: Slavko STOJANOVIC, Aleksandar JONCIC, Bozidar PAJEVIC, Bruno
BELÍN, Ilija MITIC, Velibor VASOVIC, Zvezdan CEBINAC, Milan VUKELIC, Lazar
RADOVIC, Vladimir KOVACEVIC (46' KIS), Branislav MIHAJLOVIC. (Coach: Stjepan
BOBEK).
Slovan UNV Bratislava: Ferdinand HASON, Mikulás CIRKA, Vojtech JANKOVIC, Frantisek
KISS, Anton URBAN, Anton TROCHTA, Ludovít CVETLER, Ivan MRÁZ, Jozef
VENGLOS, Anton BÍLÝ, Stefdan DEMOVIC.
Goals: FK Partizan Beograd: 1-0 Milan VUKELIC (13'), 2-1 Velibor VASOVIC (72').
Slovan UNV Bratislava: 1-1 Bozidar PAJEVIC (39' own goal).
Referee: Carl Erich STEINER (AUT)   Attendance: 17.000

03-07-1960   Stadio La Favorita, Palermo: UD Palermo – Diósgyöri VTK Miskolc 1-2 (0-2)
UD Palermo: Riccardo TOROS (46' Vincenzo BIONDO), Antonio DE BELLIS, Enzo
BENEDETTI, FRANCAVILLA, Mario COCCO, Alberto MALAVASI, Ulderico
SACCHELLA, Ricciotti GREATTI, Gianni SANDRI, Stefano BERNINI, Bruno BALDI.
(Coach: Fioravante BALDI).
Diósgyöri VTK Miskolc: Zoltán HÓDI, Gyula WERNER, Oszkár SZIGETI, Tibor PAULÁS,
Sándor TÖRÖK, Ernö SOLYMOSI, József IVÁN, József CSÁNYI, László KISS (I), József
FEKETE (40' László PAPP), János PÁL (I). (Coach: Gábor KISS).
Goals: UD Palermo: 1-2 Gianni SANDRI (48').
Diósgyöri VTK Miskolc: 0-1 József IVÁN (28'), 0-2 József FEKETE (32').
Referee: Václav KORELUS (TCH)   Attendance: 8.000

03-07-1960   Linz: Linzer ASK – Spartak Praha Stalingrad 1-3 (1-2)
Linzer ASK: Helmut KITZMÜLLER, Heribert TRÜBRIG, Gerhard STURMBERGER (..'
Clemens LUSENBERGER), ECKER, Alfred TEINITZER, Günter PRASCHAK,
SPIELMANN, Ferdinand ZECHMEISTER, Hermann FÜRST, Rudolf SABETZER, Karl
HÖFER.
Spartak Praha Stalingrad: André HOUSKA, Ladislav MISKOVIC, Pavel TRCKA, Miroslav
POHUNEK, Václav JANOVSKÝ, Frantisek FIKTUS, Frantisek MOTTL, Zdenek KOPSA,
Vladimír KOS, Ladislav HUBÁLEK, Karel KAURA.
Goals: Linzer ASK: 1-0 SPIELMANN (7').
Spartak Praha Stalingrad: 1-1 Zdenek KOPSA (18'),1-2 Zdenek KOPSA (44'), 1-3 Zdenek
KOPSA (79').
Referee: Vilmos HERNÁDI (HUN)   Attendance: 3.000

(SPIELMANN appeared as a guest player).

03-07-1960   Hohe Warte, Wien: First Vienna FC – Vasas SC 2-3 (1-3)
First Vienna FC: Kurt SCHMIED, Alfred PICHLER, Josef WEBORA, KOLARIK, Helmut
SENEKOWITSCH, Alfons DIRNBERGER, Johann LAHNER, Walter MEDVETH, Hans
BUZEK, Herbert GROHS, POLSTER.
Vasas SC: Antal SZENTMIHÁLYI, Béla KÁRPÁTI, Kálmán MÉSZÖLY, Kálmán IHÁSZ,
Dezsö BUNDZSÁK, Pál BERENDI, Sándor LENKEI, Ferenc MACHOS, Gyula SZILÁGYI
(I), Miklós BORSOS, Imre MATHESZ. (Coach: Rudolf ILLOVSZKY).
Goals: First Vienna FC: 1-3 Herbert GROHS (43'), 2-3 Hans BUZEK (80').
Vasas SC: 0-1 Gyula SZILÁGYI (27'), 0-2 Miklós BORSOS (31'), 0-3 Ferenc MACHOS
(35').
Attendance: 20.000

*(Double game played on the same day and at the same venue as the game between Wiener
Sportklub and Dukla Praha).*

03-07-1960   Népstadion, Budapest:
                        Ferencvárosi TC Budapest – 1.Simmeringer SC 1-2 (0-1)
Ferencvárosi TC Budapest: Ferenc LANDI, Ferenc BERTA, Sándor MÁTRAI, Jenö
DALNOKI, György KOCSIS, Ferenc DÉKÁNY, Gábor NAGY, Pál OROSZ, Oszkár
VILEZSÁL, Gyula RÁKOSI, Dr.Máté FENYVESI (..' Flórián ALBERT). (Coach: Sándor
TÁTRAI).
1.Simmeringer SC:
Goals: Ferencvárosi TC Budapest: 1-1 Flórián ALBERT (57').
1.Simmeringer SC: 0-1 Erwin NINAUS (23'), 1-2 Franz NEUBAUER (70').
Attendance: 60.000

03-07-1960   Stadio Renato Dall'Aia, Bologna: FC Bologna – NK Hajdik Split   1-3 (1-1)
FC Bologna: Anselmo GIORCELLI, Battista ROTA, Mirko PAVINATO, Carlo FURLANIS,
Fedele GRECO, Eugenio FASCETTI, Antonio Mimmo RENNA, Cesarino CERVELLATI,
Claudio VERONESI (46' Luciano BONFADA), Sergio CAMPANA, NARDI. (Coach:
Federico ALLASIO).
NK Hajduk Split: Ante VULIC, KRAGIC, Stjepan ILIC, Pavle GAROV, Davor GRCIC,
RADAKOVIC, Vladimir (Geza) SENAUER, Radivoje OGNJANOVIC, Zlatko PAPEC,
Bernard VUKAS, Zvonko BEGO (II). (Coach: Milovan CIRIC).
Goals: FC Bologna: 1-1 Cesarino CERVELLATI (43').
NK Hajduk Split: 0-1 Zlatko PAPEC (32'), 1-2 Zlatko PAPEC (54'), 1-3 Vladimir (Geza)
SENAUER (76').
Referee: Josef STOLL (AUT)   Attendance: 6.000

03-07-1960   Stadion Na Bazalech, Ostrava:
             Baník Ostrava OKD – O.F.K. Beograd   2-1 (1-1)
Baník Ostrava OKD: Vladimir MOKROHAJSKÝ, Bedrich KÖHLER, Karel DVORÁK (III),
Josef ONDRACKA, Prokop DANEK, Zdenek STANCO, Zdenek KOSNOVSKÝ, Jirí
VECEREK, MIKECKA (..' Frantisek SINDELAR), Tomás POSPÍCHAL, Frantisek
VALOSEK. (Coach: Frantisek BUFKA).
O.F.K. Beograd: Srboljub KRIVOKUCA, Milos GRUJIC, Radovan GOJKOV, Momcilo
GAVRIC, Dragoljub MARIC, Sava ANTIC, Ranko BOROZAN, Zivko JOSIC, Josip
SKOBLAR, Vladan MLADENOVIC, Sreten BANOVIC.
Goals: Baník Ostrava OKD: 1-0 Frantisek VALOSEK (30'), 2-1 Momcilo GAVRIC (88' own
goal).
O.F.K. Beograd: 1-1 Vladan MLADENOVIC (31').
Referee: Andor DOROGI (HUN)   Attendance: 15.000

03-07-1960   Népstadion, Budapest: Újpesti Dózsa SC – AC Fiorentina   0-1 (0-0)
Újpesti Dózsa SC: Gábor TÖRÖK, Károly RAJNA, József GYÖRVÁRI, József SZINI, Pál
VÁRHIDI, György BORSÁNYI, Béla KUHARSZKI, János GÖRÖCS, István HALÁPI,
László PATAKI, Mihály TÓTH.
AC Fiorentina: Giuliano SARTI, Saul MALATRASI, Enzo ROBOTTI, Giuseppe
CHIAPELLA, Alberto ORZAN, Claudio RIMBALDO, Kurt Roland HAMRIN (SWE),
Francisco Ramón LOJACONO (ARG), Miguel Ángel MONTUORI (ARG), Renato
BENAGLIA, Fianfranco PETRIS.
Goal: AC Fiorentina: 0-1 Kurt Roland HAMRIN (60').
Referee: Leo LEMESIC (YUG)   Attendance: 60.000

10-07-1960   Vojvodina Stadium, Novi Sad:
             FK Vojvodina Novi Sad – Wiener AC   5-0 (2-0)
FK Vojvodina Novi Sad: Andras VERES, Slavko SVINJAREVIC, Mladen VUCINIC, Laslo
BORBELJ, Novak ROGANOVIC, Stevan BENA (..' Radoslav ZLOPASA), Zdravko
RAJKOV, Sylvester TAKAC, Alexander IVOS, Djordje PAVLIC, Cedomir SENTIN.
Wiener AC: Franz PELIKAN, Herbert LENZINGER, Herbert MACH, Josef NEMANSKY,
Karl KOWANZ, Bohumil HRSUKA, HAJCAR, PEJIN, Ernst/Günter (Name not certain)
KALTENBRUNNER, Norbert SCHILLING, Stefan SZOKOLL (..' RAJTER).
Goals: FK Vojvodina Novi Sad: 1-0 Zdravko RAJKOV (4'), 2-0 Djordje PAVLIC (27'), 3-0
Zdravko RAJKOV (50'). 4-0 Djordje PAVLIC (65'), 5-0 Alexander IVOS (87').
Referee: Giulio CAMPANATI (ITA)   Attendance: 12.000

131

10-07-1960   Népstadion, Budapest: Vasas SC – First Vienna FC   3-1 (0-1)
Vasas SC: Antal SZENTMIHÁLYI, Béla KÁRPÁTI, Kálmán MÉSZÖLY, Kálmán IHÁSZ,
Dezsö BUNDZSÁK, Pál BERENDI, Sándor LENKEI, Lajos CSORDÁS (..' János FARKAS),
Ferenc MACHOS, Miklós BORSOS, Imre MATHESZ. (Coach: Rudolf ILLOVSZKY).
First Vienna FC: Kurt SCHMIED, Hermann KOZICH (II), Josef WEBORA, Alfred
PICHLER, Karl KOLLER, Alfons DIRNBERGER, Johann LAHNER, Helmut
SENEKOWITSCH, Hans BUZEK, Herbert GROHS, FISCHL.
Goals: Vasas SC: 1-1 Imre MATHESZ (60'), 2-1 Ferenc MACHOS (61'), 3-1 János FARKAS
(74').
First Vienna FC: 0-1 Herbert GROHS (19').
Attendance: 30.000

10-07-1960   Stadión Vrsovice, Praha: Spartak Praha Stalingad – Linzer ASK   3-1 (1-0)
Spartak Praha Stalingrad: André HOUSKA, Ladislav MISKOVIC, Pavel TRCKA, Miroslav
POHUNEK, Václav JANOVSKÝ, Frantisek FIKTUS, Frantisek MOTTL, Zdenek KOPSA,
Josef KRAL (46' Ladislav HUBÁLEK), Vladimír KOS, Karel KAURA.
Linzer ASK: Helmut KITZMÜLLER, Heribert TRÜBRIG, Clemens LUSENBERGER, Alfred
TEINITZER, Gerhard STURMBERGER, Günter PRASCHAK, Ernst KOZLICEK (I), Paul
KOZLICEK (II) (75' ECKER), Ferdinand ZECHMEISTER, Rudolf SABETZER, Karl
HÖFER.
Goals: Spartak Praha Stalingrad: 1-0 Josef KRAL (31'), 2-0 Frantisek MOTTL (79'), 3-0 Karel
KAURA (82').
Linzer ASK: 3-1 Ernst KOZLICEK (I) (89').
Referee: István ZSOLT (HUN)   Attendance: 15.000

10-07-1960   Stadión Tehelné pole, Bratislava:
                    Slovan UNV Bratislava – FK Partizan Beograd   4-1 (3-0)
Slovan UNV Bratislava: Ferdinand HASON, Mikulás CIRKA, Frantisek KISS, Vojtech
JANKOVIC (40' Zdeno VELECKÝ), Anton URBAN, Anton TROCHTA, Ludovít
CVETLER, Ivan MRÁZ, Jozef VENGLOS, Anton BÍLÝ, Stefdan DEMOVIC.
FK Partizan Beograd: Slavko STOJANOVIC, Bruno BELÍN, Bozidar PAJEVIC, Velimir
SOMBOLAC, Ilija MITIC, Velibor VASOVIC, Zvezdan CEBINAC, Vladimir (Vladica)
KOVACEVIC, Milan VUKELIC, Lazar RADOVIC, Branislav MIHAJLOVIC.
Goals: Slovan UNV Bratislava: 1-0 Ludovit CVETLER (1'), 2-0 Iván MRÁZ (9'), 3-0 Anton
BILÝ (32'), 4-1 Anton BILÝ (76').
FK Partizan Beograd: 3-1 Vladimir (Vladica) KOVACEVIC (73').
Referee: Vilmos HERNÁDI (HUN)   Attendance: 25.000

10-07-1960   Simmering-Platz, Simmering:
                    1.Simmeringer SC – Ferencvárosi TC Budapest   1-5 (1-1)
1.Simmeringer SC:
Ferencvárosi TC Budapest: György HORVÁTH, Ferenc BERTA, Sándor MÁTRAI, Jenö
DALNOKI, Oszkár VILEZSÁL, György KOCSIS, Zoltán FRIEDMANSZKY, Pál OROSZ,
Flórián ALBERT, Gyula RÁKOSI, Dr.Máté FENYVESI. (Coach: Sándor TÁTRAI).
Goals: 1.Simmeringer SC: 1-1 Franz LÖFFELMANN (26' penalty).
Ferencvárosi TC Budapest: 0-1 Dr.Máté FENYVESI (3'), 1-2 Flórián ALBERT (62'), 1-3
Franz LÖFFELMANN (64' *own goal*), 1-4 Zoltán FRIEDMANSZKY (74'), 1-5 Jenö
DALNOKI (90').
Attendance: 11.000

10-07-1960   Stadion Tehelné pole, Bratislava:
                TJ Cervená Hviezda Bratislava – Tatabányai Banyasz SC   3 3 (2-0)
TJ Cervená Hviezda Bratislava: Frantisek HLAVATÝ, Stefan MATLÁK, Vladimír WEISS (I),
Ján FERIANCÍK, Eduard GÁBORÍK, Jirí SON, Kazimír GAJDOS, Adolf SCHERER, Jozef
OBERT (46' Bohdan UJVÁRY), Ladislav KACÁNI, Valerián BARTALSKÝ.
Tatabányai Bányász SC: Gyula GROSICS, Imre MÉSZÁROS (..' József SCHÉDL), József
POLGÁR, Ferenc FARSANG, Gyula BÍRÓ, Gyula MACSALI, István SVOZJÁK, László
LAHOS, László RAPAI, László TÖRÖK, Mihály DEMETER. (Coach: Károly LAKAT).
Goals: TJ Cervená Hviezda Bratislava: 1-0 Ladislava KACANI (26'), 2-0 Kazimir GAJDOS
(34'), 3-3 Jirí SON (87').
Tatabányai Banyasz SC: 1-2 László TOROK (51'), 2-2 László LAHOS (72' penalty), 2-3
István SZOVJAK (78').
Referee: Leo LEMESIC (YUG)   Attendance: 25.000

10-07-1960   Stadio Flaminio, Roma:
                AS Roma – DSO Spartak Kovosmalt Trnava   1-0 (1-0)
AS Roma: Fabio CUDICINI, Giosuè STUCCHI, Giovanni GRIFFITH, Alfio FONTANA,
Giacomo LOSI, Maurizio THERMES, Manlio COMPAGNO, Paolo PRESTIN (46' Sergio
TENENTE), Gualtiero BRUNELLI, Luigi GIULIANO, Arne Bengt SELMOSSON (SWE).
(Coach: Alfredo FONI).
DSO Spartak Kovosmalt Trnava: Imrich STACHO (76' Jozef ONDRUSKA), Juraj KADLEC,
Stefan PSENKO, Stefan SLANINA, Karol TIBENSKY, Milan GALBICKA, Jozef
STIBRÁNYI, Valérian SVEC, Ján STURDÍK (46' Ján HORVÁTH), Jozef ADAMEC, Milan
BARTÁK.
Goal: AS Roma: 1-0 Arne Bengt SELMOSSON (32').
Referee: Viktor Ernst CHEBAT (AUT)   Attendance: 15.000

10-07-1960   Omladinski Stadion, Beograd:
                O.F.K. Beograd – Baník Ostrava OKD   3-2 (1-1)
O.F.K. Beograd: Srboljub KRIVOKUCA, Milos GRUJIC, Momcilo GAVRIC, Dragoljub
MARIC, Radovan GOJKOV, Sava ANTIC, Ranko BOROZAN, Zivko JOSIC (..' Veroslav
MLADENOVIC), Josip SKOBLAR, Vladan MLADENOVIC, Spasoje SAMARDZIC.
Baník Ostrava OKD: Vladimir MOKROHAJSKÝ, Bedrich KÖHLER, Karel DVORÁK (III),
Josef ONDRACKA, Prokop DANEK, Zdenek STANCO, Zdenek KOSNOVSKÝ, Jirí
VECEREK, Frantisek SINDELAR, Tomás POSPÍCHAL, Frantisek VALOSEK. (Coach:
Frantisek BUFKA).
Goals: O.F.K. Beograd: 1-0 Josip SKOBLAR (3'), 2-1 Ranko BOROZAN (47'), 3-1 Sava
ANTIC (80').
Baník Ostrava OKD: 1-1 Frantisek SINDELAR (38'), 3-2 Frantisek VALOSEK (89').
Referee: Francesco LIVERANI (ITA)   Attendance: 3.475

10-07-1960   Népstadion, Budapest: M.T.K. Budapest – FK Sarajevo   2-1 (1-1)
M.T.K. Budapest: Sándor GELLÉR, Tibor PALICSKÓ, Mihály LANTOS, Ferenc GÁL (..'
Mihály LACZKÓ), Ferenc SIPOS, Ferenc KOVÁCS (III), László BÖDÖR, István NAGY,
István KUTI, János MOLNÁR, István SZIMCSÁK (I). (Coach: Imre KOVÁCS).
FK Sarajevo: Ranko PLANINIC, Kemal DZEMIDZIC, Ibrahim (Ibro) BIOGRADLIC,
Vladimir CONC, Mladen STIPIC, Srboljub MARKUSEVIC, Ivica PETKOVIC, Asim
FERHATOVIC, Salih SEHOVIC, Zijad ARSLANAGIC, Dobrivoje ZIVKOV. (Coach: Semso
KAPETANOVIC).
Goals: M.T.K. Budapest: 1-0 István KUTI (4'), 2-1 Mihály LACZKÓ (85').
FK Sarajevo: 1-1 Zijad ARSLANAGIC (35').
Referee: Milan FENCL (TCH)   Attendance: 50.000

10-07-1960   Stadion Stari plac, Split: NK Hajduk Split – FC Bologna 1-0 (1-0)
NK Hajduk Split: Ante VULIC, KRAGIC, Stjepan ILIC, RADAKOVIC, Davor GRCIC, Pavle
GAROV, Vladimir (Geza) SENAUER, Radivoje OGNJANOVIC, Zlatko PAPEC, Bernard
VUKAS, Zvonko BEGO (II). (Coach: Milovan CIRIC).
FC Bologna: Anselmo GIORCELLI, Battista ROTA, Mirko PAVINATO, Carlo FURLANIS,
Fedele GRECO, Ezio PASCUTTI, Antonio Mimmo RENNA, Mario ROSSINI, Claudio
VERONESI, Luciano BONFADA, NARDI. (Coach: Federico ALLASIO).
Goal: NK Hajduk Split: 1-0 Radivoje OGNJANOVICH (44').
Referee: Carl Erich STEINER (AUT)   Attendance: 12.000

10-07-1960   Stadio Comunale, Firenze: AC Fiorentina – Újpesti Dózsa SC 0-2 (0-1)
AC Fiorentina: Enrico ALBERTOSI, Saul MALATRASI, Enzo ROBOTTI, Giuseppe
CHIAPELLA, Alberto ORZAN, Claudio RIMBALDO, Kurt Roland HAMRIN (SWE), Miguel
Ángel MONTUORI (ARG), Eugenio FANTINI, Renato BENAGLIA, Fianfranco PETRIS.
Újpesti Dózsa SC: Gábor TÖRÖK, Károly RAJNA, József GYÖRVÁRI, József SZINI, Pál
VÁRHIDI, György BORSÁNYI, Béla KUHARSZKI, János GÖRÖCS, Ferenc SZUSZA,
István HALÁPI (46' László PATAKI), Mihály TÓTH.
Goals: Újpesti Dózsa SC: 0-1 Ferenc SZUSZA (23'), 0-2 János GÖRÖCS (87').
Referee: Friedrich (Fritz) SEIPELT (AUT)   Attendance: 15.000

10-07-1960   Stadion Juliska, Praha: Dukla Praha – Wiener Sportklub 2-1 (1-0)
Dukla Praha: Pavol KOUBA, Karel CHRUDIMSKÝ, Jirí CADEK, Ivo URBAN, Stanislav
JARÁBEK, Milan DVORÁK, Jan BRUMOVSKÝ, Rudolf KUCERA, Jirí SURA, Jaroslav
BOROVICKA, Rudolf TAUCHEN (65' Josef JELÍNEK).
Wiener Sportklub: Rudolf SZANWALD, Johann WINDISCH, Heinrich BÜLLWATSCH,
Erich HASENKOPF, Rudolf OSLANDSKY, Leipold BARSCHANDT, Johann SCHICKER,
Adolf KNOLL, Erich HOF (I), Wilhelm KAINRATH, Egon STAMPFER. (Coach: Josef
STROH).
Goals: Dukla Praha: 1-0 Rudolf KUCERA (25'), 2-0 Jirí SURA (65').
Wiener Sportklub: 2-1 Erich HOF (I) (80').
Referee: Andor DOROGI (HUN)   Attendance: 10.000

10-07-1960   DVTK Stadion, Miskolc: Diósgyöri VTK Miskolc – UD Palermo 0-2 (0-0)
Diósgyöri VTK Miskolc: Zoltán HÓDI, Gyula WERNER, Tibor PAULÁS, Sándor TÖRÖK,
Oszkár SZIGETI, Ernö SOLYMOSI, József IVÁN, József CSÁNYI, László KISS (I) (46'
István KOVÁCS), János PÁL (I), József FEKETE. (Coach: Gábor KISS).
UD Palermo: Vincenzo BIONDO (46' Riccardo TOROS), Antonio DE BELLIS,
FRANCAVILLA, Mario COCCO, Enzo BENEDETTI, Alberto MALAVASI, Ulderico
SACCHELLA, Ricciotti GREATTI, Eliseo LODI, Stefano BERNINI, Bruno BALDI. (Coach:
Fioravante BALDI).
Goals: UD Palermo: 0-1 BALDI (62'), 0-2 Ulderico SACCHELLA (78').
Referee: Zivko BAJIC (YUG)   Attendance: 22.000

134

10-07-1960   Red Star-Platz, Fünfhaus: FK Austria Wien – AC Udinese 4-2 (2-0)
FK Austria Wien: Paul SCHWEDA, Oskar FISCHER, Giose KOSCHIER, Johann LÖSER,
Adolf BLUTSCH, Erich MEDVETH, Horst HIRNSCHRODT, Johann RIEGLER, Horst
NEMEC, Ernst FIALA, Walter SCHLEGER.
AC Udinese: Luigi BERTOSSI, Luigi GIGANTE, Renato VALENTI, Renzo SASSI
(expulsion), Giorgio ODLING, Massimo GIACOMINI, Luis PENTRELLI (ARG), Enzo
MENEGOTTI, Lorenzo BETTINI, Roberto MANGANOTTO (46' MAZZOLENI), DI
BENEDETTI.
Goals: FK Austria Wien: 1-0 Johann RIEGLER (20'), 2-0 Renzo SASSI (22' *own goal*), 3-0
Johann RIEGLER (48'), 4-2 Horst NEMEC (88')..
AC Udinese: 3-1 Massimo GIACOMINI (51'), 3-2 Lorenzo BETTINI (87').
Referee: Václav KORELUS (TCH)   Attendance: 11.000

(Giose KOSCHIER was a guest player from Admira Wien)

10-07-1960   Alessandria: US Alessandria – FK Velez Mostar 1-2 (1-0)
US Alessandria: Luciano ARBIZZANI (46' PESCI), Aldo NARDI, Rocco MELIDEO, Cirano
SNIDERO, Antonio SCHIAVONI, GIOLITTI, Mario MORRIGI, Romano FORIN,
Alessandro VITALI, MARANGI, Remo MARMO.
FK Velez Mostar: Ivan CURKOVIC, Zdravko RODIN, Meho HANDZIC, Vlado
SLISKOVIC, Dane PRAJO, Kruno RADILJEVIC, LIPOSINOVIC, Franjo DZIDIC, Sulejman
REBAC, BLAZIC, Milorad LAZOVIC. (Coach: Ratomir CABRIC).
Goals: US Alessandria: 1-0 Romano FORIN (16').
FK Velez Mostar: 1-1 Sulejman REBAC (60'), 1-2 Sulejman REBAC (87').
Referee: Karol GALBA (TCH)

Pos	Country	Pld	W	D	L	GF	GA	GD	Pts
1	*Hungary*	*12*	*8*	*1*	*3*	*25*	*16*	*+9*	*17*
2	Yugoslavia	12	7	1	4	26	18	+8	15
3	Czechoslovakia	12	6	1	5	24	18	+6	13
4	Italy	12	4	0	8	12	20	-8	8
5	Austria	12	3	1	8	17	32	-15	7

*** Hungary won the Cup as their teams had the best record ***

135

1961-1962

GROUP 1

18-06-1961   Stadion na Dolicku Praha:
Spartak Praha Stalingrad – FK Austria Wien   1-2 (1-2)
Spartak Praha Stalingrad: André HOUSKA, Václav JANOVSKÝ, Pavel TRCKA, Miroslav
POHUNEK, Frantisek FIKTUS, Frantisek KOKTA, Frantisek MOTTL, Zdenek KOPSA,
Milan KRATOCHVÍL, PISA, Karel KAURA.
FK Austria Wien: Paul SCHWEDA, Heinz KRAL, Karl STOTZ, Nobert KRASA, Johann
LÖSER, Horst PAPROTH (FRG), Theodor BAUMGÄRTNER, Johann RIEGLER, Horst
NEMEC, Ernst FIALA, Walter SCHLEGER.
Goals: Spartak Praha Stalingrad: 1-0 Milan KRATOCHVÍL (3').
FK Austria Wien: 1-1 Horst NEMEC (14'), 1-2 Johann RIEGLER (20').
Referee: Igino RIGATO (ITA)   Attendance: 8.000

18-06-1961   Genova: UC Sampdoria – FC Bologna   1-1 (1-0)
UC Sampdoria: Franco SATTOLO, Guido VINCENZI, Paolo MAROCCHI, Mario
BERGAMASCHI, Gaudenzio BERNASCONI, Azeglio VICINI, Giuseppe RECAGNO, Ernst
OCWIRK (AUT), Luigi TOSCHI, Karl Lennart SKOGLUND (SWE), Ernesto Bernardo Tito
CUCCHIARONI (ARG).
FC Bologna: Rino RADO, Bruno CAPRA, Edmondo LORENZINI, Paride TUMBURUS,
Guglielmo BURELLI, Carlo FURLANIS, Marino PERANI, Cesarino CERVELLATI, Giulio
BONAFIN, Héctor (Ettore) DE MARCO (URU), Ezio PASCUTTI. (Coach: Fulvio
BERNARDINI).
Goals: UC Sampdoria: 1-0 Karl Lennart SKOGLUND (36').
FC Bologna: 1-1 Ezio PASCUTTI (73').
Referee: Francesco FRANCESCON (ITA)

25-06-1961   Praha: Spartak Praha Stalingrad – FC Bologna   1-3 (0-1)
Spartak Praha Stalingrad: André HOUSKA, Václav JANOVSKÝ, Pavel TRCKA, Miroslav
POHUNEK, Frantisek FIKTUS, Frantisek KOKTA, Frantisek MOTTL, Zdenek KOPSA,
Milan KRATOCHVÍL, Josef PISA, Karel KAURA.
FC Bologna: Rino RADO, Bruno CAPRA, Edmondo LORENZINI, Carlo FURLANIS, Bruno
TAVERNA, Paride TUMBURUS, Antonio RENNA, Cesarino CERVELLATI, Giulio
BONAFIN, Héctor (Ettore) DE MARCO (URU), Claudio VERONESI. (Coach: Fulvio
BERNARDINI).
Goals: Spartak Praha Stalingrad: 1-3 Karel KAURA (76').
FC Bologna: 0-1 Héctor (Ettore) DE MARCO (4'), 0-2 Claudio VERONESI (62'), 0-3 Claudio
VERONESI (63').
Referee: Carl Erich STEINER (AUT)   Attendance: 6.000

136

25-06-1961   Praterstadion, Wien: FK Austria Wien – UC Sampdoria 5-2 (2-0)
FK Austria Wien: Gernot FRAYDL, Erich STROBL, Karl STOTZ, Heinz KRAL, Johann
LÖSER, Horst PAPROTH (FRG), Anton HERZOG, Johann RIEGLER, Horst NEMEC, Ernst
FIALA, Dr.Walter SCHLEGER.
UC Sampdoria: Ugo ROSIN, Glauco TOMASIN, Paolo MAROCCHI, Mario
BERGAMASCHI, Gaudenzio BERNASCONI, Azeglio VICINI, Severino LOJODICE, Ernst
OCWIRK (AUT), Luigi TOSCHI, Karl Lennart SKOGLUND (SWE), Ernesto Bernardo Tito
CUCCHIARONI (ARG).
Goals: FK Austria Wien: 1-0 Horst NEMEC (26'), 2-0 Horst NEMEC (36'), 3-0 Johann
RIEGLER (51'), 4-2 Dr.Walter SCHLEGER (81'), 5-2 Ernst FIALA (82').
UC Sampdoria: 3-1 Karl Lennart SKOGLUND (57'), 3-2 Severino LOJODICE (59').
Referee: Adolf MACH (TCH)   Attendance: 6.000

02-07-1961   Genova: UC Sampdoria – Spartak Praha Stalingrad 1-1 (0-1)
UC Sampdoria: Ugo ROSIN, Glauco TOMASIN, Gaetano VERGAZZOLA, Mario
BERGAMASCHI, Gaudenzio BERNASCONI, Azeglio VICINI, Severino LOJODICE,
Vujadin BOSKOV (YUG), Luigi TOSCHI, Todor (Toza) VESELINOVIC (YUG), Ernesto
Bernardo Tito CUCCHIARONI (ARG).
Spartak Praha Stalingrad: André HOUSKA, Ladislav MISKOVIC, Miroslav POHUNEK,
Václav JANOVSKÝ, Pavel TRCKA, Frantisek KOKTA, Frantisek MOTTL, Zdenek KOPSA,
Milan KRATOCHVÍL, Josef PISA, Karel KAURA.
Goals: UC Sampdoria: 1-1 Severino LOJODICE (59').
Spartak Praha Stalingrad: 0-1 Zdenek KOPSA (36').
Referee: Friedrich (Fritz) SEIPELT (AUT)   Attendance: 12.000

02-07-1961   Bologna: FC Bologna – FK Austria Wien 2-1 (1-0)
FC Bologna: Rino RADO, Bruno CAPRA, Franco MARINI, Carlo FURLANIS, Bruno
TAVERNA, Paride TUMBURUS, Antonio RENNA, Cesarino CERVELLATI, SLAWOSKI,
Héctor (Ettore) DE MARCO (URU), Claudio VERONESI. (Coach: Fulvio BERNARDINI).
FK Austria Wien: Gernot FRAYDL, Erich STROBL, Karl STOTZ, Heinz KRAL, Johann
LÖSER, Horst PAPROTH (FRG), Rudolf STARK, Anton HERZOG, Horst NEMEC, Ernst
FIALA, Dr.Walter SCHLEGER.
Goals: FC Bologna: 1-0 Héctor (Ettore) DE MARCO (13'), 2-0 Héctor (Ettore) DE MARCO
(61').
FK Austria Wien: 2-1 Horst NEMEC 74').
Referee: Alojz OBTULOVIC (TCH)   Attendance: 8.000

Pos	Team	Pld	W	D	L	GF	GA	GD	Pts
1	FC Bologna (ITA)	3	2	1	0	6	3	+3	5
2	FK Austria Wien (AUT)	3	2	0	1	8	5	+3	4
3	UC Sampdoria (ITA)	3	0	2	1	4	7	-3	2
4	Spartak Praha Stalingrad (TCH)	3	0	1	2	3	6	-3	1

*** FC Bologna qualified for the semi-finals ***

GROUP 2

18-06-1961   Linzer Stadion "Gugl", Linz: SV Stickstoff Linz – AC Torino   3-5 (0-4)
SV Stickstoff Linz: WEIKERTSCHLAGER, Franz SCHIERHUBER, Alfred PRIBIL, Karl
CIZL, KAISERSEDER, Leopold BARSCHANDT, Oskar KOHLHAUSER, Theodor (Turl)
WAGNER (I), WINDISCH, Alfred WAGNER (II), Anton POLSTER.
AC Torino: Lido VIERI (29' Antonio ODASSO), Piero SCESA, Antonio GERBAUDO,
Vincenzo (Enzo) BEARZOT, Remo LANCIONI, Giancarlo VERSOLATTO, Giancarlo
DANOVA, Italo MAZZERO, Marcos Alberto LOCATELLI (ARG), Giancarlo CELLA (42'
Vincenzo TRASPEDINI), Ulisse GUALTIERI. (Coach: Benjamin César SANTOS Fernández
(ARG)).
Goals: SV Stickstoff Linz: 1-5 Theodor (Turl) WAGNER (I) (76' penalty), 2-5 Oskar
KOHLHAUSER (78'), 3-5 Oskar KOHLHAUSER (89').
AC Torino: 0-1 Giancarlo DANOVA (9'), 0-2 Giancarlo DANOVA (14'), 0-3 Ulisse
GUALTIERI (29'), 0-4 Giancarlo DANOVA (41'), 0-5 Giancarlo DANOVA (68').
Referee: Václav KORELUS (TCH)   Attendance: 2.000

18-06-1961   Bratislava: UD Cervena Hviezda Bratislava – TJ Slovan Nitra   2-4 (1-2)
UD Cervena Hviezda Bratislava: Frantisek HLAVATÝ, Vladimír WEISS (I), Ottmar
DEUTSCH, Ján FERIANCÍK, Stefan MATLÁK, Titus BUBERNÍK, Kazimír GAJDOS,
Valerián SVEC (43' Bohdan UJVÁRY), Dezider CIMRA, Ladislav KACÁNI, Milan
DOLINSKÝ. (Coach: Karol BORHY).
TJ Slovan Nitra: Viliam PADÚCH, Andrej ISTÓK, Marián STANÍK, Eduard DOBAI, Jozef
FOJTÍK, Ladislav PUTYERA, Milan NAVRÁTIL, Stefan GYUREK, Michal PUCHER,
Viliam HRNCÁR, Vladimír BACHRATÝ. (Coach: Karol BUCKO).
Goals: UD Cervena Hviezda Bratislava: 1-0 Milan DOLINSKÝ (1'), 2-3 Kazimír GAJDOS
(63').
TJ Slovan Nitra: 1-1 Jozef FOJTÍK (20'), 1-2 Vladimír BACHRATÝ (33'), 1-3 Michal
PUCHER (56'), 2-4 Viliam HRNCÁR (75').
Referee: Alojz OBTULOVIC (TCH)   Attendance: 5.000

25-06-1961   Nitra: TJ Slovan Nitra – AC Torino   5-1 (2-0)
TJ Slovan Nitra: Viliam PADÚCH, Andrej ISTÓK, Marián STANÍK, Eduard DOBAI, Jozef
FOJTÍK, Milan BARTÁK, Milan NAVRÁTIL, Michal PUCHER, Ladislav PUTYERA,
Viliam HRNCÁR, Vladimír BACHRATÝ. (Coach: Karol BUCKO).
AC Torino: Lido VIERI, Luciano BUZZACCHERA, Mauro LESSI, Giorgio FERRINI,
Antonio GERBAUDO, Giancarlo VERSOLATTO, Giancarlo DANOVA, Marcos Alberto
LOCATELLI (ARG), Vincenzo TRASPEDINI (27' Enrico ALBRIGI), Italo MAZZERO,
Ulisse GUALTIERI. (Coach: Benjamin César SANTOS Fernández (ARG)).
Goals: TJ Slovan Nitra: 1-0 Milan BARTÁK (9'), 2-0 Viliam HRNCÁR (19'), 3-0 Michal
PUCHER (46'), 4-0 Milan NAVRÁTIL (61'), 5-1 Vladimír BACHRATÝ (71').
AC Torino: 4-1 Ulisse GUALTIERI (64').
Referee: Viktor Ernst CHEBAT (AUT)   Attendance: 12.000

25-06-1961   Bratislava: UD Cervena Hviezda Bratislava – SV Stickstoff Linz   8-2 (4-0)
UD Cervena Hviezda Bratislava: Frantisek HLAVATÝ, Stefan MATLÁK, Jirí TICHÝ,
Vladimír WEISS (I), Titus BUBERNÍK, Ján FERIANCÍK, Kazimír GAJDOS, Adolf
SCHERER, Eduard GÁBORÍK, Ladislav KACÁNI (43' Bohdan UJVÁRY), Milan
DOLINSKÝ. (Coach: Karol BORHY).
SV Stickstoff Linz: FILZ (77' Helmut KRÖGER), Franz SCHIERHUBER, Alfred PRIBIL,
Othmar BUCHBERGER, KAISERSEDER, Leopold BARSCHANDT, Oskar
KOHLHAUSER, Theodor (Turl) WAGNER (I), WINDISCH, Alfred WAGNER (II) (44'
BACHL), Anton POLSTER.
Goals: UD Cervena Hviezda Bratislava: 1-0 Milan DOLINSKÝ (6'), 2-0 Kazimír GAJDOS
(9'), 3-0 Titus BUBERNÍK (12'), 4-0 Milan DOLINSKÝ (24'), 5-1 Adolf SCHERER (58'),
6-2 Titus BUBERNÍK (77'), 7-2 Milan DOLINSKÝ (79'), 8-2 Milan DOLINSKÝ (82').
SV Stickstoff Linz: 4-1 Alfred WAGNER (II) (54' penalty), 5-2 Anton POLSTER (63').
Referee: Raoul RIGHI (ITA)   Attendance: 10.000

02-07-1961   Torino: AC Torino – UD Cervena Hviezda Bratislava   2-4 (1-2)
AC Torino: Lido VIERI, Piero SCESA, Antonio GERBAUDO, Vincenzo (Enzo) BEARZOT,
Remo LANCIONI, Giancarlo VERSOLATTO, Enrico ALBRIGI, Marcos Alberto
LOCATELLI (ARG), Ulisse GUALTIERI, Italo MAZZERO, Giancarlo DANOVA. (Coach:
Benjamin César SANTOS Fernández (ARG)).
UD Cervena Hviezda Bratislava: Frantisek HLAVATÝ, Stefan MATLÁK, Jirí TICHÝ,
Vladimír WEISS (I), Titus BUBERNÍK, Ján FERIANCÍK, Kazimír GAJDOS, Adolf
SCHERER, Eduard GÁBORÍK, Ladislav KACÁNI, Milan DOLINSKÝ. (Coach: Karol
BORHY).
Goals: AC Torino: 1-0 Marcos Alberto LOCATELLI (18'), 2-4 Italo MAZZERO (64'
penalty).
UD Cervena Hviezda Bratislava: 1-1 Milan DOLINSKÝ (28'), 1-2 Adolf SCHERER (29'),
1-3 Milan DOLINSKÝ (48'), 1-4 Remo LANCIONI (58' *own goal*).
Referee: Alfred HABERFELLNER (AUT)   Attendance: 5.800

02-07-1961   Linzer Stadion "Gugl", Linz: SV Stickstoff Linz – TJ Slovan Nitra   4-4 (2-2)
Goals: SV Stickstoff Linz: 1-0 Oskar KOHLHAUSER (6'), 2-1 Anton POLSTER (12'), 3-1
Oskar KOHLHAUSER (66'), 4-3 Anton POLSTER (76').
TJ Slovan Nitra: 1-1 Viliam HRNCÁR (9'), 2-2 Michal PUCHER (20'), 3-3 Viliam HRNCÁR
(75' penalty), 4-4 Michal PUCHER (79').
Referee: Giuseppe ADAMI (ITA)   Attendance: 500

Pos	Team	Pld	W	D	L	GF	GA	GD	Pts
1	*TJ Slovan Nitra (TCH)*	*3*	*2*	*1*	*0*	*13*	*7*	*+6*	*5*
2	UD Cervena Hviezda Bratislava (TCH)	3	2	0	1	14	8	+6	4
3	AC Torino (ITA)	3	1	0	2	8	12	-4	2
4	SV Stickstoff Linz (AUT)	3	0	1	2	9	17	-8	1

*** TJ Slovan Nitra qualified for the semi-finals ***

139

18-06-1961   Wien: 1.Wiener Neustädter SC – Linzer ASK   4-1 (2-0)
1.Wiener Neustädter SC: …, Janos KEREKI (HUN), Martin LEFOR (I), …
Linzer ASK: …, Paul KOZLICEK (II), …
Goals: 1.Wiener Neustädter SC: 1-0 Martin LEFOR (23'), 2-0 Janos KEREKI (25'), 3-0
Manfred PICHLER (48'), 4-1 Martin LEFOR (79').
Linzer ASK: 3-1 Paul KOZLICEK (II) (55').
Attendance: 1.500

21-06-1961   Stadio Moretti, Udine: AC Udinese – TJ SONP Kladno   2-1
AC Udinese: Luigi BERTOSSI, Gianfranco GARBUGLIA, Armando SEGATO, Renzo
SASSI, Vasco TAGLIAVINI, Massimo GIACOMINI, Osvaldo BAGNOLI, Roberto
MANGANOTTO, Luis PENTRELLI (ARG), Mario MEREGHETTI, Francesco CANELLA.
(Coach: Giuseppe BIGOGNO).
TJ SONP Kladno: Zdenek DLOUHY, Zdenek HOLOUBEK, Josef LINHART, Jan FÁBERA,
Jan CHVOJKA (..' Josef MAJER), Zdenek KOFENT, Antonín SOLC, Josef HÁJEK, Josef
KADRABA, Miroslav RYS, Karel NEMECEK.
Goals: AC Udinese: 1-0 Luis PENTRELLI (3'), 2-0 Luis PENTRELLI (31').
TJ SONP Kladno: 2-1 Karel NEMECEK (34').
Referee: Ferdinand MARSCHALL (AUT)

(The match was abandoned in the 41st minute and then replayed on 23rd August 1961).

25-06-1961   Wien: 1.Wiener Neustädter SC – TJ SONP Kladno   0-5 (0-2)
Goals: TJ SONP Kladno: 0-1 Josef KADRABA (41'), 0-2 Antonín SOLC (45'), 0-3 Josef
MAJER (47'), 0-4 Josef MAJER (70'), 0-5 Josef KADRABA (89').
Referee: Bruno DE MARCHI (ITA)   Attendance: 1.600

25-06-1961   Linzer Stadion, Linz: Linzer ASK – AC Udinese   2-2 (1-1)
Linzer ASK: Helmut KITZMÜLLER, Heribert TRÜBRIG, Tomislav CRNKOVIC (YUG),
Heinz OBERPARLEITER, Anton RIHS, Ernst KOZLICEK (I), Hermann FÜRST, Paul
KOZLICEK (II), László NEMETH (HUN), Rudolf SABETZER, Ferdinand ZECHMEISTER.
AC Udinese: Luigi BERTOSSI, Pier Luigi DEL BENE, Renato VALENTI, Renzo SASSI,
Vasco TAGLIAVINI, LEGATTI, Osvaldo BAGNOLI, Luis PENTRELLI (ARG), Massimo
GIACOMINI, Franco DE CECCO, MANTANUZZI. (Coach: Giuseppe BIGOGNO).
Goals: Linzer ASK: 1-1 Ernst KOZLICEK (I) (19'), 2-2 Ernst KOZLICEK (I) (89').
AC Udinese: 0-1 Luis PENTRELLI (1'), 1-2 Osvaldo BAGNOLI (73').
Referee: Alojz OBTULOVIC (TCH)   Attendance: 2.500

02-07-1961   Stadio Moretti, Udine: AC Udinese – 1.Wiener Neustädter SC   4-1 (3-1)
AC Udinese: Dino ZOFF, Pier Luigi DEL BENE, Renato VALENTI, Renzo SASSI, Vasco
TAGLIAVINI, Massimo GIACOMINI, Osvaldo BAGNOLI, Luis PENTRELLI (ARG),
Franco DE CECCO, Mario MEREGHETTI, Roberto MANGAROTTO. (Coach: Giuseppe
BIGOGNO).
1.Wiener Neustädter SC: TRENDL, Franz NUSSBAUMER, Manfred REITER, Rudolf
NEUDAUER, STEIGERN, Hubert HUTFLESS, Martin LEFOR (I), WINDERL, Alfred
HOFFMANN, Janos KEREKI (HUN), FRANCOLIN. (Coach: Adolf HUBER).
Goals: AC Udinese: 1-0 Osvaldo BAGNOLI (6'), 2-0 Mario MEREGHETTI (10'), 3-1 Franco
DE CECCO (37'), 4-1 Franco DE CECCO (65').
1.Wiener Neustädter SC: 2-1 Janos KEREKI (22').
Referee: Václav KORELUS (TCH)   Attendance: 1.000

02-07-1961   Kladno: TJ SONP Kladno – Linzer ASK   1-1 (0-0)
TJ SONP Kladno: Jaroslav MATUCHA, KOSAR, Josef LINHART, Jan FÁBERA, Miroslav
RYS, Zdenek KOFENT, Antonín SOLC, Josef MAJER, Josef KADRABA, Josef HÁJEK,
Karel NEMECEK. (Coach: Jirí KUCHLER).
Linzer ASK: Helmut KITZMÜLLER, Heribert TRÜBRIG, Tomislav CRNKOVIC (YUG),
Heinz OBERPARLEITER, Gerhard STURMBERGER (..' Siegfried HINTRINGER), Ernst
KOZLICEK (I), Anton RIHS, Paul KOZLICEK (II), Hermann FÜRST, Rudolf SABETZER,
Ferdinand ZECHMEISTER.
Goals: TJ SONP Kladno: 1-0 Josef HÁJEK (50').
Linzer ASK: 1-1 Paul KOZLICEK (II) (57').
Referee: Carlo GAMBROTTA (ITA)   Attendance: 4.000

23-08-1961   Stadio Moretti, Udine: AC Udinese – TJ SONP Kladno   3-2 (2-2)
AC Udinese: Dino ZOFF (46' Franco DINELLI), Guglielmo BURELLI, Remo BARBIANI,
Renzo SASSI, Vasco TAGLIAVINI, Armando SEGATO, Luis PENTRELLI (ARG),
Giancarlo (Carlo) GALLI (46' Candido BERETTA), Giulio BONAFIN, Kurt Irving
ANDERSSON (SWE), Leif MORTENSEN (DEN). (Coach: Giuseppe BIGOGNO).
TJ SONP Kladno: Jaroslav MATUCHA, Zdenek HOLOUBEK, Jan FÁBERA, KOSART,
Josef LINHART, Miroslav RYS, Antonín SOLC, Josef MAJER, Josef KADRABA, Josef
HÁJEK, Karel NEMECEK (46' Petr KALINA).
Goals: AC Udinese: 1-0 Kurt Irving ANDERSSON (10'), 2-1 Luis PENTRELLI (20'), 3-2
Kurt Irving ANDERSSON (117').
TJ SONP Kladno: 1-1 Karel NEMECEK (19') , 2-2 Josef HÁJEK (35').
Referee: Friedrich MAYER (AUT)

(This was the replay of the abandoned match from 21st June 1961)
(The referee played two 15 minutes halves of extra time in error)

Pos	Team	Pld	W	D	L	GF	GA	GD	Pts
1	AC Udinese (ITA)	3	2	1	0	9	5	+4	5
2	TJ SONP Kladno (TCH)	3	1	1	1	8	4	+4	3
3	Linzer ASK (AUT)	3	0	2	1	4	7	-3	2
4	1.Wiener Neustädter SC (AUT)	3	1	0	2	5	10	-5	2

*** AC Udinese and TJ SONP Kladno qualified for the semi-finals ***

SEMI-FINALS

01-11-1961   Kladno: TJ SONP Kladno – FC Bologna   1-2 (1-0)
TJ SONP Kladno: Jaroslav MATUCHA, Zdenek HOLOUBEK, Josef LINHART, Zdenek
KOFENT, Miroslav RYS, Petr KALINA, Antonín SOLC, Bohumil RICHTRMOC, Josef
KADRABA, Josef HÁJEK, Karel NEMECEK (46' Václav FERTEK).
FC Bologna: Rino RADO, Franco MARINI, Edmondo LORENZINI, Paride TUMBURUS,
Lorenzo NONINO, Romano FOGLI, Marino PERANI (46' Luciano BONFADA), Bruno
FRANZINI, Harald Ingemann NIELSEN (DEN), Héctor (Ettore) DE MARCO (URU),
Antonio RENNA. (Coach: Fulvio BERNARDINI).
Goals: TJ SONP Kladno: 1-0 Josef KADRABA (12').
FC Bologna: 1-1 Héctor (Ettore) DE MARCO (76'), 1-2 Antonio RENNA (80').
Referee: Lajos HORVÁTH (HUN)   Attendance: 3.500

01-11-1961   Nitra: TJ Slovan Nitra – AC Udinese   4-3 (3-0)
TJ Slovan Nitra: Michal KUBACKA, Ladislav PUTYERA, Marián STANÍK, Andrej ISTÓK,
Jozef FOJTÍK, Emil KISÝ, Milan NAVRÁTIL, Dusan KONÍK, Michal PUCHER, Viliam
HRNCÁR, Vladimír BACHRATÝ. (Coach: Karol BUCKO).
AC Udinese: Franco DINELLI, Flavio COLAOTTO, Guglielmo BURELLI, Remo
BARBIANI, Candido BERETTA, Roberto MANGANOTTO, Francesco CANELLA, Kurt
Irving ANDERSSON (SWE), Orlando ROZZONI, Armando SEGATO, Leif MORTENSEN
(DEN).
Goals: TJ Slovan Nitra: 1-0 Viliam HRNCÁR (4'), 2-0 Michal PUCHER (22'), 3-0 Emil KISÝ
(43'), 4-3 Viliam HRNCÁR (88').
AC Udinese: 3-1 Leif MORTENSEN (49'), 3-2 Armando SEGATO (53' penalty), 3-3
Francesco CANELLA (61').
Referee: Eduard BABAUCZEK (AUT)   Attendance: 6.000

15-11-1961   Bologna: FC Bologna – TJ SONP Kladno   1-0 (0-0)
FC Bologna: Attilio SANTARELLI (46' Rino RADO), Bruno CAPRA, Edmondo
LORENZINI, Lorenzo NONINO, Francesco JANICH, Bruno FRANZINI, Marino PERANI,
Mario ROSSINI, Luís "VINÍCIO" Vinícius de Menenzes (BRA), Cesarino CERVELLATI,
Antonio RENNA. (Coach: Fulvio BERNARDINI).
TJ SONP Kladno: Jaroslav MATUCHA, Zdenek HOLOUBEK, Jan FÁBERA, KOSART,
Josef LINHART, Zdenek KOFENT, Antonín SOLC, RICHTERMOC, Josef KADRABA,
Miroslav RYS, Josef HÁJEK.
Goal: FC Bologna: 1-0 Mario ROSSINI (65').
Referee: Carl Erich STEINER (AUT)   Attendance: 8.000

29-11-1961   Stadio Moretti, Udine: AC Udinese – TJ Slovan Nitra   1-1 (0-0)
AC Udinese: Gianni ROMANO, Guglielmo BURELLI, Armando SEGATO, Candido
BERETTA, Vasco TAGLIAVINI, Roberto MANGANOTTO, Francesco CANELLA,
Giuseppe DEL ZOTTO (46' Giulio BONAFIN), Orlando ROZZONI, Kurt Irving
ANDERSSON (SWE), Arne Bengt SELMOSSON (SWE).
TJ Slovan Nitra: Viliam PADÚCH, Ladislav PUTYERA, Marián STANÍK, Andrej ISTÓK,
Jozef FOJTÍK, Dusan KONÍK, Emil KISÝ, Milan NAVRÁTIL, Michal PUCHER, Vladimír
BACHRATÝ, Viliam HRNCÁR. (Coach: Karol BUCKO).
Goals: AC Udinese: 1-1 Francesco CANELLA (58').
TJ Slovan Nitra: 0-1 Michal PUCHER/Milan NAVRÁTIL (49').
Referee: Jenö SRAMKÓ (HUN)

FINAL

14-03-1962   Nitra: TJ Slovan Nitra – FC Bologna   2-2 (1-1)
TJ Slovan Nitra: Michal KUBACKA, Andrej ISTÓK, Jozef FOJTÍK, Ladislav PUTYERA,
Dusan KONÍK, Emil KISÝ, Milan NAVRÁTIL, Ján DINGA, Michal PUCHER, Vladimír
BACHRATÝ, Viliam HRNCÁR. (Coach: Karol BUCKO).
FC Bologna: Rino RADO, Edmondo LORENZINI, Bruno TAVERNA, Mirko PAVINATO,
Carlo FURLANIS, Mario ROSSINI, Marino PERANI, Bruno FRANZINI, Harald Ingemann
NIELSEN (DEN), Héctor (Ettore) DE MARCO (URU), Antonio RENNA. (Coach: Fulvio
BERNARDINI).
Goals: TJ Slovan Nitra: 1-0 Vladimir BACHRATÝ (8'), 2-2 Viliam HRNCÁR (76' penalty).
FC Bologna: 1-1 Haral Ingemann NIELSEN (42'), 1-2 Marino PERANI (54' penalty).
Referee: János PÓSA-POLARECZKY (HUN)   Attendance: 10.000

04-04-1962   Bologna: FC Bologna – TJ Slovan Nitra   3-0 (1-0)
FC Bologna: Paolo CIMPIEL, Edmondo LORENZINI, Mirko PAVINATO, Paride
TUMBURUS, Bruno TAVERNA, Romano FOGLI, Marino PERANI, Mario ROSSINI,
Harald Ingemann NIELSEN (DEN), Héctor (Ettore) DE MARCO (URU), Ezio PASCUTTI.
(Coach: Fulvio BERNARDINI).
TJ Slovan Nitra: Viliam PADÚCH, Andrej ISTÓK, Marián STANÍK, Ladislav PUTYERA,
Emil KISÝ, Dusan KONÍK, Ján DINGA, Michal PUCHER, Vladimír BACHRATÝ, Stefan
GYUREK, Viliam HRNCÁR. (Coach: Karol BUCKO).
Goals: FC Bologna: 1-0 Héctor (Ettore) DE MARCO (21'), 2-0 Ezio PASCUTTI (46'), 3-0
Harald Ingemann NIELSEN (54').
Referee: Konstantin ZECEVIC (YUG)   Attendance: 2.500

*** FC Bologna won the Cup ***

1962

GROUP 1

12-05-1962   Stadio Torino "Filadelfia", Torino:
            FC Juventus – NK Dinamo Zagreb   4-1 (1-1)
FC Juventus: Roberto ANZOLIN, Ernesto CASTANO (expulsion 88'), Benito SARTI, Flavio
EMOLI, Giancarlo BERCELLINO (I), Gianfranco LEONCINI, Gino STACCHINI, Humberto
Jorge ROSA (ARG), Salvatore CALVANESE, Bruno NICOLÉ, Giorgio STIVANELLO.
(Coach: Carlo PAROLA).
NK Dinamo Zagreb: Zlatko SKORIC, Mirko BRAUN, Josip SIKIC, Ivan SANTEK, Ivan
SANGULIN, Pavle GAROV, Tomislav KNEZ (expulsion 88'), OSIM, Rudolf BELIN, Zlatko
PAPEC, Ivica CVITKOVIC. (Coach: Milan ANTOLKOVIC).
Goals: FC Juventus: 1-1 Bruno NICOLÉ (20'), 2-1 Humberto Jorge ROSA (54'), 3-1 Gino
STACCHINI (67'), 4-1 Humberto Jorge ROSA (85').
NK DInamo Zagreb: 0-1Pavle GAROV (10').
Referee: János PÓSA-POLARECZKY (HUN)   Attendance: 1.500

(OSIM appeared as a guest player).

13-05-1962   Népstadion, Budapest:
            Ferencvárosi TC Budapest – DSO Spartak Hradec Králové   1-2 (1-0)
Ferencvárosi TC Budapest: György HORVÁTH, Dezsö NOVÁK, László KISS (III), Jenö
DALNOKI, Oszkár VILEZSÁL, György KOCSIS, Zoltán BORBÁS (II), Tibor CSERNAI
(II), Zoltán VARGA, Pál OROSZ, József KÖKÉNY. (Coach: József MÉSZÁROS).
DSO Spartak Hradec Králové: Jindrich JINDRA, Jirí CERNY, Zdenek PICMAN, Rudolf
RUNSTUK, Zdenek KREJCI, Jiró KOMÁNEK, Edmund SCHMIDT, Ladislav POKORNÝ,
Milous KVACEK, Bedrich SONKA, Zdenek ZIKÁN. (Coach: Oldrich SUBRT).
Goals: Ferencvárosi TC Budapest: 1-0 József KÖKÉNY (..').
DSO Spartak Hradec Králové: 1-1 Edmund SCHMIDT (..'), 1-2 Jirí KOMÁNEK (..').
Referee: Zivko BAJIC (YUG)   Attendance: 30.000

20-05-1962   Hradec Králové:
            DSO Spartak Hradec Králové – Ferencvárosi TC Budapest   1-0 (1-0)
DSO Spartak Hradec Králové: Jindrich JINDRA, Jirí CERNY, Zdenek PICMAN, Rudolf
RUNSTUK, Jiró KOMÁNEK, DEUTSCH, Edmund SCHMIDT, Ladislav POKORNÝ,
Bedrich SONKA, Milous KVACEK, Zdenek ZIKÁN. (Coach: Oldrich SUBRT).
Ferencvárosi TC Budapest: György SZÁGER, Dezsö NOVÁK, András GERENDÁS, Jenö
DALNOKI, Oszkár VILEZSÁL, György KOCSIS, Zoltán BORBÁS (II), Tibor CSERNAI
(II), Zoltán VARGA, Lajos NÉMETH, József KÖKÉNY. (Coach: József MÉSZÁROS).
Goal: DSO Spartak Hradec Králové: 1-0 Bedrich SONKA (20').
Referee: Trajan IVANOVSKI (YUG)   Attendance: 8.000

20-05-1962   Stadion Maksimir, Zagreb: NK Dinamo Zagreb – FC Juventus 2-1 (2-1)
NK Dinamo Zagreb: Gordan IROVIC, Josip SIKIC, Mirko BRAUN, Rudolf BELIN, Marijan
BRNCIC, Ivan SANTEK, Ivica CVITKOVIC, RUDIC, Zeljko PERUSIC, Berislav RIBIC,
Luka LIPOSINOVIC. (Coach: Milan ANTOLKOVIC).
FC Juventus: Roberto ANZOLIN, Bruno GARZENA, Gianfranco BOZZAO, Benito SARTI,
Giancarlo BERCELLINO (I), Gianfranco LEONCINI, Gino STACCHINI, Humberto Jorge
ROSA (ARG), Salvatore CALVANESE, Bruno MAZZIA, Giorgio STIVANELLO. (Coach:
Carlo PAROLA).
Goals: NK Dinamo Zagreb: 1-0 RUDIC (1'), 2-1 Ivica CVITKOVIC (19').
FC Juventus: 1-1 Gino STACCHINI (6').
Referee: Gyula BALLA (HUN)   Attendance: 8.000

(Bruno GARZENA received an official warning)
(RUDIC appeared as a guest from his usual club NK Novi Sad)

27-05-1962   Stadio Torino "Filadelfia", Torino:
                FC Juventus – DSO Spartak Hradec Králové 3-2 (3-2)
FC Juventus: Giuseppe GASPARI, Ernesto CASTANO, Benito SARTI, Flavio EMOLI,
Giancarlo BERCELLINO (I), Gianfranco LEONCINI, Gino STACCHINI, John William
CHARLES (WAL), Salvatore CALVANESE, Bruno NICOLÉ, Giorgio STIVANELLO.
(Coach: Carlo PAROLA).
DSO Spartak Hradec Králové: Jindrich JINDRA, Jirí CERNY, Rudolf RUNSTUK, Jiró
KOMÁNEK, Zdenek PICMAN, Zdenek KREJCI, Edmund SCHMIDT, Milous KVACEK,
Bedrich SONKA, Ladislav POKORNÝ, Zdenek ZIKÁN. (Coach: Oldrich SUBRT).
Goals: FC Juventus: 1-0 Gino STACCHINI (1'), 2-1 Ernesto CASTANO (25'), 3-1 Gino
STACCHINI (43').
DSO Spartak Hradec Králové: 1-1 Ladislav POKORNÝ (23'), 3-2 Milous KVACEK (34').
Referee: Aleksandar SKORIC (YUG)   Attendance: 6.000

27-05-1962   Stadion Maksimir, Zagreb:
                NK Dinamo Zagreb – Ferencvárosi TC Budapest 2-0 (2-0)
NK Dinamo Zagreb: Gordan IROVIC, Josip SIKIC, Mirko BRAUN, Zeljko PERUSIC, Rudolf
BELIN, Ivan SANTEK, Ivica CVITKOVIC, Slaven ZAMBATA, Damir PETRUNIC, Luka
LIPOSINOVIC, Ilijas PASIC. (Coach: Milan ANTOLKOVIC).
Ferencvárosi TC Budapest: György SZÁGER, Dezsö NOVÁK, András GERENDÁS, Jenö
DALNOKI, Oszkár VILEZSÁL, György KOCSIS, Zoltán BORBÁS (II), Lajos NÉMETH,
Zoltán VARGA, Pál OROSZ, József KÖKÉNY. (Coach: József MÉSZÁROS).
Goals: NK Dinamo Zagreb: 1-0 Slaven ZAMBATA (11'), 2-0 Damir PETRUNIC (20').
Referee: Milan FENCL (TCH)   Attendance: 20.000

03-06-1962   Hradec Králové: DSO Spartak Hradec Králové – FC Juventus 2-0 (1-0)
DSO Spartak Hradec Králové: Jindrich JINDRA, Jirí CERNY, Rudolf RUNSTUK, Jirí
KOMÁNEK, Zdenek PICMAN, Zdenek KREJCI, Edmund SCHMIDT, Milous KVACEK,
Bedrich SONKA, Ladislav POKORNÝ, Zdenek ZIKÁN. (Coach: Oldrich SUBRT).
FC Juventus: Roberto ANZOLIN, Ernesto CASTANO, Benito SARTI (expulsion 65'), Flavio
EMOLI, Giancarlo BERCELLINO (I), Bruno MAZZIA, Gino STACCHINI, Humberto Jorge
ROSA (ARG), Salvatore CALVANESE, Bruno NICOLÉ, Giorgio ROSSANO. (Coach: Carlo
PAROLA).
Goals: DSO Spartak Hradec Králové: 1-0 Ladislav POKORNÝ (6'), 2-0 Rudolf TAUCHEN
(74').
Referee: Zivko BAJIC (YUG)

03-06-1962   Népstadion, Budapest:
Ferencvárosi TC Budapest – NK Dinamo Zagreb 1-5 (0-3)
Ferencvárosi TC Budapest: György SZÁGER, András GERENDÁS, Dezsö NOVÁK, Jenö
DALNOKI, Oszkár VILEZSÁL, György KOCSIS, József KÖKÉNY, Zoltán VARGA, Tibor
CSERNAI (II), Pál OROSZ, Zoltán FRIEDMANSZKY. (Coach: József MÉSZÁROS).
NK Dinamo Zagreb: Gordan IROVIC, Josip SIKIC, Mirko BRAUN, Zeljko PERUSIC, Rudolf
BELIN, Ivan SANTEK, Ivica CVITKOVIC, Slaven ZAMBATA, Damir PETRUNIC, RUDIC,
Ilijas PASIC. (Coach: Milan ANTOLKOVIC).
Goals: Ferencvárosi TC Budapest: 1-4 Dezsö NOVÁK (67').
NK Dinamo Zagreb: 0-1 Slaven ZAMBATA (3'), 0-2 RUDIC (5'), 0-3 Ivan SANTEK (31'),
0-4 Ilijas PASIC (61'), 1-5 RUDIC (70').
Referee: Adolf MACH (TCH)   Attendance: 35.000

10-06-1962   Spartak Stadion, Hradec Králové:
DSO Spartak Hradec Králové – NK Dinamo Zagreb 3-2 (2-1)
DSO Spartak Hradec Králové: Jindrich JINDRA, Jirí CERNY, Rudolf RUNSTUK, Zdenek
KREJCI, Zdenek PICMAN, Jirí KOMÁNEK, Milous KVACEK, Ladislav POKORNÝ,
Bedrich SONKA, Rudolf TAUCHEN, Zdenek ZIKÁN. (Coach: Oldrich SUBRT).
NK Dinamo Zagreb: Gordan IROVIC, Josip SIKIC, Mirko BRAUN, Zeljko PERUSIC, Rudolf
BELIN, Ivan SANTEK, Ivica CVITKOVIC, Slaven ZAMBATA, Damir PETRUNIC, RUDIC,
Luka LIPOSINOVIC. (Coach: Milan ANTOLKOVIC).
Goals: DSO Spartak Hradec Králové: 1-1 Milous KVACEK (15'), 2-1 Rudolf TAUCHEN
(30'), 3-2 Zdenek ZIKÁN (73').
NK Dinamo Zagreb: 0-1 Slaven ZAMBATA (16'), 2-2 Slaven ZAMBATA (65').
Referee: Jozsef KATONA (HUN)   Attendance: 9.000

10-06-1962   Népstadion, Budapest: Ferencvárosi TC Budapest – FC Juventus 0-1 (0-1)
Ferencvárosi TC Budapest: György HORVÁTH, Antal THOMANN, András GERENDÁS,
Dezsö NOVÁK, Oszkár VILEZSÁL, György KOCSIS, József KÖKÉNY, Zoltán VARGA,
Lajos NÉMETH, Pál OROSZ, Zoltán FRIEDMANSZKY. (Coach: József MÉSZÁROS).
FC Juventus: Roberto ANZOLIN, Ernesto CASTANO, Gianfranco LEONCINI, Flavio
EMOLI, Giancarlo BERCELLINO (I), Bruno MAZZIA, Gino STACCHINI, Humberto
Giorgio ROSA (ARG), Bruno NICOLÉ, John William CHARLES (WAL), Giorgio
STIVANELLO (..' Giorgio ROSSANO). (Coach: Carlo PAROLA).
Goal: FC Juventus: 0-1 Humberto Giorgio ROSA (41').
Referee: V.TYL (TCH)

17-06-1962   Stadio Torino "Filadelfia", Torino:
FC Juventus – Ferencvárosi TC Budapest 1-1 (0-0)
FC Juventus: Roberto ANZOLIN, Ernesto CASTANO, Benito SARTI, Flavio EMOLI,
Giancarlo BERCELLINO (I), Gianfranco LEONCINI, Gino STACCHINI, Humberto Giorgio
ROSA (ARG), Bruno NICOLÉ, John William CHARLES (WAL), Giorgio STIVANELLO.
(Coach: Carlo PAROLA).
Ferencvárosi TC Budapest: György HORVÁTH, Antal THOMANN, András GERENDÁS,
Dezsö NOVÁK, Oszkár VILEZSÁL, György KOCSIS, József KÖKÉNY, Zoltán VARGA,
Lajos NÉMETH, Pál OROSZ, Zoltán FRIEDMANSZKY. (Coach: József MÉSZÁROS).
Goals: FC Juventus: 1-1 Humberto Giorgio ROSA (71').
Ferencvárosi TC Budapest: 0-1 Lajos NÉMETH (49').
Referee: Pavel SPOTÁK (TCH)

146

17-06-1962   Maksimir Stadion, Zagreb:
                     NK Dinamo Zagreb – DSO Spartak Hradec Králové   2-1 (1-0)
NK Dinamo Zagreb: Gordan IROVIC, Josip SIKIC, Mirko BRAUN, Ivan SANTEK, Zeljko
PERUSIC, Rudolf BELIN, Ivica CVITKOVIC, Slaven ZAMBATA, Damir PETRUNIC,
RUDIC, Ilijas PASIC. (Coach: Milan ANTOLKOVIC).
DSO Spartak Hradec Králové: Jindrich JINDRA, Jirí CERNY, Rudolf RUNSTUK, Zdenen
KREJCI, Zdenek PICMAN, Jirí KOMÁNEK, Milous KVACEK, Ladislav POKORNÝ,
Bedrich SONKA, Rudolf TAUCHEN, Zdenek ZIKÁN. (Coach: Oldrich SUBRT).
Goals: NK Dinamo Zagreb: 1-0 Slaven ZAMBATA (10'), 2-1 Rudolf BELIN (84').
DSO Spartak Hradec Králové: 1-1 Rudolf TAUCHEN (60').
Referee: Lajos ARANYOSI (HUN)   Attendance: 10.000

Pos	Team	Pld	W	D	L	GF	GA	GD	Pts
1	NK Dinamo Zagreb (YUG)	6	4	0	2	14	10	+4	8
2	DSO Spartak Hradec Králové (TCH)	6	4	0	2	11	8	+3	8
3	FC Juventus (ITA)	6	3	1	2	10	8	+2	7
4	Ferencvárosi TC Budapest (HUN)	6	0	1	5	3	12	-9	1

*** NK Dinamo Zagreb qualified for the semi-finals ***

GROUP 2

13-05-1962   Stadion J.N.A., Beograd: FK Partizan Beograd –TJ Baník Ostrava   2-2 (1-0)
FK Partizan Beograd: Jovan CURCIC, Velimir SOMBOLAC, Ljubomir MIHAJLOVIC, Milan
VUKELIC, Dragoslav JOVANOVIC, Velibor VASOVIC, Joakim VISLAVSKI, Radivoje
OGNJANOVIC, Branislav MIHAJLOVIC, Lazar RADOVIC, Vladimir PETROVIC. (Coach:
Stjepan BOBEK).
Baník Ostrava OKD: Frantisek DVORÁK (I), Bedrich KÖHLER, Karel DVORÁK (III), Josef
ONDRACKA, Prokop DANEK, Jan KNIEZEK, Karel PALIVEC, Miroslav WIECEK,
Frantisek SINDELÁR, Miroslav MIKESKA, Frantisek VALOSEK. (Coach: Frantisek
BUFKA).
Goals: FK Partizan Beograd: 1-0 Velibor VASOVIC (24'), 2-0 Branislav MIHAJLOVIC (56').
TJ Baník Ostrava: 2-1 Miroslav WIECEK (71'), 2-2 Frantisek SINDELÁR (86').
Referee: Raoul RIGHI (ITA)   Attendance: 7.000

13-05-1962   Stadio Comunale, Bergamo: Atalanta Bergamo – M.T.K. Budapest   0-0
Atalanta Bergamo: Zaccaria COMETTI, Giovanni Battista ROTA, Livio RONCOLI,
Flemming Gert NIELSEN (DEN), Piero GARDONI, Umberto COLOMBO, Angelo
DOMENGHINI, Dino DA COSTA (BRA), Enrico NOVA, Fermo FAVINI, Ejnar Kurt
CHRISTENSEN (DEN). (Coach: Ferruccio VALCAREGGI).
M.T.K. Budapest: Ferenc KOVALIK, István JENEI, József DANSZKY, Ernö SOLYMOSI,
LOSAS, Ferenc KOVÁCS (III), Sándor FALISZEK, Mihály LACZKO, István KUTI, László
BÖDÖR, István SZIMCSÁK (I).
Attendance: 3.000

147

20-05-1962   Budapest: M.T.K. Budapest – Atalanta Bergamo 1-1 (1-1)
M.T.K. Budapest: Ferenc KOVALIK, István JENEI, Ernö SOLYMOSI, Mihály VASAS,
József DANSZKY, Ferenc KOVÁCS (III), Sándor FALISZEK, László BÖDÖR, István KUTI,
Mihály LACZKÓ, István SZIMCSÁK (I).
Atalanta Bergamo: Zaccaria COMETTI, Giovanni Battista ROTA, Livio RONCOLI, Umberto
COLOMBO, Piero GARDONI, Flemming Gert NIELSEN (DEN), Rinaldo OLIVIERI, Dino
DA COSTA (BRA), Enrico NOVA, Ejnar Kurt CHRISTENSEN (DEN), Angelo
DOMEGHINI. (Coach: Ferruccio VALCAREGGI).
Goals: M.T.K. Budapest: 1-0 Umberto COLOMBO (40' *own goal*).
Atalanta Bergamo: 1-1 Ejnar Kurt CHRISTENSEN (44').

20-05-1962   Ostrava: TJ Baník Ostrava – FK Partizan Beograd 1-1 (1-1)
TJ Baník Ostrava: Vladimir MOKROHAJSKÝ, Bedrich KÖHLER, Karel DVORÁK (III),
Josef ONDRACKA, Prokop DANEK, Jan KNIEZEK, Karel PALIVEC, Jirí VECEREK,
Frantisek SINDELÁR, Miroslav MIKESKA, Frantisek VALOSEK. (Coach: Frantisek
BUFKA).
FK Partizan Beograd: Jovan CURCIC, Velimir SOMBOLAC, Ljubomir MIHAJLOVIC, Milan
VUKELIC, Dragoslav JOVANOVIC, Velibor VASOVIC, Joakim VISLAVSKI, Radivoje
OGNJANOVIC, Branislav MIHAJLOVIC, Lazar RADOVIC, Mustafa HASANAGIC.
(Coach: Stjepan BOBEK).
Goals: TJ Baník Ostrava: 1-0 Karel PALIVEC (1').
FK Partizan Beograd: 1-1 Branislav MIHAJLOVIC (27').
Referee: Alfio GRIGNANI (ITA)   Attendance: 5.000

27-05-1962   Népstadion, Budapest: M.T.K. Budapest – TJ Baník Ostrava 4-2 (2-1)
M.T.K. Budapest:
TJ Baník Ostrava: Vladimir MOKROHAJSKÝ, Bedrich KÖHLER, Prokop DANEK, Karel
DVORÁK (III), Jan CHLOPEK, Jan KNIEZEK, Karel PALIVEC, Miroslav WIECEK,
Miroslav MIKESKA, Milan SIRÝ, Frantisek VALOSEK. (Coach: Frantisek BUFKA).
Goals: M.T.K. Budapest: 1-0 István KUTI (14'), 2-0 Mihály LACZKÓ (27'), 3-1 István
SZIMCSÁK (56'), 4-2 László POVÁZSAI (63').
TJ Baník Ostrava: 2-1 Frantisek VALOSEK (40'), 3-2 Miroslav WIECEK (61').
Referee: Carlo GAMBAROTTA (ITA)   Attendance: 15.000

28-05-1962   Stadio Comunale, Bergamo:
                   Atalanta Bergamo – FK Partizan Beograd 3-3 (1-2)
Atalanta Bergamo: Zaccaria COMETTI, Giovanni Battista ROTA, Livio RONCOLI,
Flemming Gert NIELSEN (DEN), Piero GARDONI, Umberto COLOMBO, Rinaldo
OLIVIERI, Dino DA COSTA (BRA), Enrico NOVA, Ejnar Kurt CHRISTENSEN (DEN),
Angelo DOMENGHINI. (Coach: Paolo TABANELLI).
FK Partizan Beograd: Jovan CURCIC, Velimir SOMBOLAC, Ljubomir MIHAJLOVIC,
Dragoslav JOVANOVIC, Velibor (Bora) MILUTINOVIC, Velibor VASOVIC, Zvezdan
CEBINAC, Milan VUKELIC, Branislav MIHAJLOVIC, Lazar RADOVIC, Joakim
VISLAVSKI. (Coach: Stjepan BOBEK).
Goals: Atalanta Bergamo: Dino DA COSTA (2x), Ejnar Kurt CHRISTENSEN.
FK Partizan Beograd: Branislav MIHAJLOVIC, Velibor VASOVIC, Joakim VISLAVSKI.
Referee: Gyula GERE (HUN)   Attendance: 15.000

03-06-1962   Stadion J.N.A., Beograd: FK Partizan Beograd – Atalanta Bergamo   2-2 (1-0)
FK Partizan Beograd: Jovan CURCIC, Velimir SOMBOLAC, Ljubomir MIHAJLOVIC, Dragoslav JOVANOVIC, Velibor (Bora) MILUTINOVIC, Velibor VASOVIC, Zvezdan CEBINAC, Milan VUKELIC, Branislav MIHAJLOVIC, Lazar RADOVIC, Joakim VISLAVSKI. (Coach: Stjepan BOBEK).
Atalanta Bergamo: Zaccaria COMETTI, Giovanni Battista ROTA, Livio RONCOLI, Flemming Gert NIELSEN (DEN), Piero GARDONI, Umberto COLOMBO, Rinaldo OLIVIERI, Dino DA COSTA (BRA), Enrico NOVA, Ejnar Kurt CHRISTENSEN (DEN), Angelo DOMENGHINI. (Coach: Paolo TABANELLI).
Goals: FK Partizan Beograd: 1-0 Velibor VASOVIC (1'), 2-0 Milan VUKELIC (70').
Atalanta Bergamo: 2-1 Angelo DOMENGHINI (72'), 2-2 Enrico NOVA (83').
Referee: Gábor SOÓS (HUN)   Attendance: 15.500

03-06-1962   Bazaly Stadion, Ostrava: TJ Baník Ostrava – M.T.K. Budapest   3-1 (3-0)
TJ Baník Ostrava: Frantisek DVORÁK (I), Bedrich KÖHLER, Prokop DANEK, Jan KNIEZEK, Josef ONDRACKA, Jan CHLOPEK, Miroslav MIKESKA, Miroslav WIECEK, Frantisek SINDELÁR, Milan SIRÝ, Frantisek VALOSEK. (Coach: Frantisek BUFKA).
M.T.K. Budapest: Ferenc KOVALIK, István JENEI, József DANSZKY, Ernö SOLYMOSI, Mihály VASAS, Ferenc KOVÁCS (III), László BÖDÖR, Mihály LACZKÓ, István KUTI, László POVÁZSAI, István SZIMCSÁK (I). (Coach: Imre KOVÁCS).
Goals: TJ Baník Ostrava: 1-0 Frantisek VALOSEK (23'), 2-0 Ferenc KOVÁCS (33' *own goal*), 3-0 Miroslav WIECEK (35').
M.T.K. Budapest: 3-1 Ferenc KOVÁCS (58' penalty).
Referee: Gennaro MARCHESE (ITA)   Attendance: 9.400

10-06-1962   Stadion J.N.A., Beograd: FK Partizan Beograd – M.T.K. Budapest   2-1 (2-1)
FK Partizan Beograd: Jovan CURCIC, Velimir SOMBOLAC, Ljubomir MIHAJLOVIC, Lazar RADOVIC, Velibor (Bora) MILUTINOVIC, Dragoslav JOVANOVIC, Zvezdan CEBINAC, Mustafa HASANAGIC, Milan VUKELIC, Branislav MIHAJLOVIC, Joakim VISLAVSKI. (Coach: Stjepan BOBEK).
M.T.K. Budapest: Ferenc KOVALIK, György KESZEI, Ernö SOLYMOSI, Mihály VASAS, József DANSZKY, Ferenc KOVÁCS (III), Sándor FALISZEK, László BÖDÖR, Mihály LACZKÓ, László POVÁZSAI, István SZIMCSÁK (I).
Goals: FK Partizan Beograd: 1-0 Velibor (Bora) MILUTINOVIC (13'), 2-1 Lazar RADOVIC (38').
M.T.K. Budapest: 1-1 László BÖDÖR (22').
Referee: Gastone ROVERSI (ITA)   Attendance: 15.000

10-06-1962   Ostrava: TJ Baník Ostrava – Atalanta Bergamo   0-0
TJ Baník Ostrava: Vladimir MOKROHAJSKÝ, Bedrich KÖHLER, Prokop DANEK, Jan KNIEZEK, Josef ONDRACKA, Jan CHLOPEK, Miroslav MIKESKA, Miroslav WIECEK, Frantisek SINDELÁR, Milan SIRY, Stanislav KUROVSKÝ. (Coach: Jaroslav SIMONEK).
Atalanta Bergamo: Zaccaria COMETTI, Alfredo PESENTI, Livio RONCOLI, Flemming Gert NIELSEN (DEN), Piero GARDONI, Umberto COLOMBO, Angelo DOMENGHINI, Dino DA COSTA (BRA), Enrico NOVA, Ejnar Kurt CHRISTENSEN (DEN), Luciano MAGISTRELLI. (Coach: Paolo TABANELLI).
Referee: Aleksandar SKORIC (YUG)   Attendance: 10.000

149

17-06-1962   Népstadion, Budapest: M.T.K. Budapest – FK Partizan Beograd 4-1 (3-0)
M.T.K. Budapest: László TAKÁCS, György KESZEI, Ernö SOLYMOSI, Mihály VASAS,
József DANSZKY, Ferenc KOVÁCS (III), István KUTI, László BÖDÖR, Mihály LACZKÓ,
László POVÁZSAI, István SZIMCSÁK (I).
FK Partizan Beograd: Stanoje MILORADOVIC, Velimir SOMBOLAC, Ljubomir
MIHAJLOVIC, Lazar RADOVIC, Velibor (Bora) MILUTINOVIC, Dragoslav JOVANOVIC,
Zvezdan CEBINAC, Mustafa HASANAGIC, Milan VUKELIC, Branislav MIHAJLOVIC,
Joakim VISLAVSKI. (Coach: Stjepan BOBEK).
Goals: M.T.K. Budapest: 1-0 László BÖDÖR (5'), 2-0 László BÖDÖR (17'), 3-0 László
POVÁZSAI (18'), 4-1 László POVÁZSAI (75').
FK Partizan Beograd: 3-1 Branislav MIHAJLOVIC (60').
Referee: Concetto LO BELLO (ITA)   Attendance: 10.000

17-06-1962   Stadio Comunale, Bergamo: Atalanta Bergamo – TJ Baník Ostrava 8-2 (5-1)
Atalanta Bergamo: Zaccaria COMETTI, Giovanni Batista ROTA, Livio RONCOLI, Flemming
Gert NIELSEN (DEN), Piero GARDONI, Umberto COLOMBO, Angelo DOMENGHINI,
Dino DA COSTA (BRA), Enrico NOVA, Ejnar Kurt CHRISTENSEN (DEN), Luciano
MAGISTRELLI. (Coach: Paolo TABANELLI).
TJ Baník Ostrava: Frantisek DVORÁK (I), Karel DVORÁK (III), Prokop DANEK, Jan
KNIEZEK, Josef ONDRACKA, Bedrich KÖHLER, Milan SIRY, Miroslav WIECEK,
Miroslav MIKESKA, Frantisek SINDELÁR, CHLOPEK. (Coach: Jaroslav SIMONEK).
Goals: Atalanta Bergamo: 1-0 Enrico NOVA (1'), 2-0 Dino DA COSTA (4'), 3-0 Angelo
DOMENGHINI (26'), 4-1 Dino DA COSTA (36'), 5-1 Luciano MAGISTRELLI (44'), 6-1
Dino DA COSTA (46'), 7-1 Luciano MAGISTRELLI (64'), 8-1 Ejnar Kurt CHRISTENSEN
(65').
TJ Baník Ostrava: 3-1 Miroslav WIECEK (32'), 8-2 Miroslav WIECEK (87').
Referee: Konstantin ZECEVIC (YUG)

Pos	Team	Pld	W	D	L	GF	GA	GD	Pts
1	*Atalanta Bergamo (ITA)*	*6*	*1*	*5*	*0*	*14*	*8*	*+6*	*7*
2	M.T.K. Budapest (HUN)	6	2	2	2	11	9	+2	6
3	FK Partizan Beograd (YUG)	6	1	4	1	11	13	-2	6
4	TJ Baník Ostrava (TCH)	6	1	3	2	10	16	-6	5

*** Atalanta Bergamo qualified for the semi-finals ***

GROUP 3

13-05-1962   Népstadion, Budapest:
              Budapesti Honvéd SE – Slovan UNV Bratislava 2-1 (2-0)
Budapesti Honvéd SE: Béla TAKÁCS (I), László MAROSI, Sándor JÓZSA, Zoltán DUDÁS,
Mihály ROZMIS, Antal KOTÁSZ, György NAGY, Károly BALOGH, Ferenc NÓGRÁDI,
Imre KOMORA, Sándor KATONA. (Coach: László RÁKÓCZI).
Slovan UNV Bratislava: Alexander VENCEL (I), Frantisek KISS, Anton URBAN, Vojtech
JANKOVIC, Jozef VENGLOS, Stefan KRÁL, Ludovít CVETLER, Anton MORAVCÍK, Ivan
MRÁZ, Jozef OBERT, Milan BALÁZIK. (Coach: Karol BORHY).
Goals: Budapesti Honvéd SE: 1-0 Sándor KATONA (13'), 2-0 Ferenc NÓGRÁDI (38').
Slovan UNV Bratislava: 2-1 Jozef OBERT (50').
Referee: Borce NEDELKOVSKI (YUG)   Attendance: 20.000

13-05-1962   Stadio Comunale, Bologna:
FC Bologna – FK Crvena Zvezda Beograd 2-1 (1-1)
FC Bologna: Attilio SANTARELLI, Bruno CAPRA, Edmondo LORENZINI, Carlo
FURLANIS, Mirko PAVINATO, Romano FOGLI, Antonio RENNA, Bruno FRANZINI,
Harald Ingemann NIELSEN (DEN), Héctor (Ettore) DE MARCO (URU), Luís "VINÍCIO"
Vinícius de Menenzes (BRA) (expulsion). (Coach: Fulvio BERNARDINI).
FK Crvena Zvezda Beograd: Mirko STOJANOVIC, Milanko CUK, Tomislav MILICEVIC,
Luka MALESEV, Novak TOMIC, Slobodan SKRBIC, Nikola STIPIC, Dusan MARAVIC,
Antun RUDINSKI, BECEJAC, Selimir MILOSEVIC.
Goals: FC Bologna: 1-1 Héctor (Ettore) DE MARCO (19'), 2-1 Harald Ingemann NIELSEN
(75').
FK Cvrena Zvezda Beograd: 0-1 Dusan MARAVIC (9').
Referee: István ZSOLT (HUN)   Attendance: 10.000
(BECEJAC appeared as a guest player).

20-05-1962   Bratislava: Slovan UNV Bratislava – Budapesti Honvéd SE 2-1 (0-0)
Slovan UNV Bratislava: Alexander VENCEL (I), Anton URBAN, Alexander HORVÁTH,
Vojtech JANKOVIC, Stefan KRÁL, Jozef VENGLOS, Ivan MRÁZ, Anton MORAVCÍK,
Ludovít CVETLER, Jozef OBERT, Stefan DEMOVIC. (Coach: Karol BORHY).
Budapesti Honvéd SE: Béla TAKÁCS (I), László MAROSI, Sándor JÓZSA, Zoltán DUDÁS,
Antal GALAMBOS, Antal KOTÁSZ, György NAGY, Károly BALOGH, Ferenc NÓGRÁDI,
Imre KOMORA, Sándor KATONA. (Coach: László RÁKÓCZI).
Goals: Slovan UNV Batislava: 1-0 Alexander HORVÁTH (53'), 2-0 Stefan DEMOVIC (87').
Budapesti Honvéd SE: 2-1 Antal KOTÁSZ (90').
Referee: Konstantin ZECEVIC (YUG)   Attendance: 7.000

20-05-1962   Stadion J.N.A., Beograd: FK Crvena Zvezda Beograd – FC Bologna 4-2 (4-0)
FK Crvena Zvezda Beograd: Mirko STOJANOVIC, Milanko CUK, Novak TOMIC, Luka
MALESEV, Milan COP, Slobodan SKRBIC, Nikola STIPIC, Dusan MARAVIC, Antun
RUDINSKI, Zoran PRLJINCEVIC, Spasoje SAMARDZIC.
FC Bologna: Paolo CIMPIEL, Bruno CAPRA, Edmondo LORENZINI, Carlo FURLANIS,
Mirko PAVINATO, Romano FOGLI, Antonio RENNA, Bruno FRANZINI, Harald Ingemann
NIELSEN (DEN), Héctor (Ettore) DE MARCO (URU), Cesarino CERVELLATI. (Coach:
Fulvio BERNARDINI).
Goals: FK Crvena Zvezda Beograd: 1-0 Nikola STIPIC (9'), 2-0 Spasoje SAMARDZIC (23'),
3-0 Spasoje SAMARDZIC (35'), 4-0 Zoran PRLJINCEVIC (37').
FC Bologna: 4-1 Harald Ingemann NIELSEN (46'), 4-2 Harald Ingemann NIELSEN (74').
Referee: Gyula BALLA (HUN)   Attendance: 10.000
(Milan COP and Zoran PRLJINCEVIC (from Radnicki Beograd) and Spasoje SAMARDZIC
(OFK Beograd) were all playing as guests).

27-05-1962   Stadion J.N.A., Beograd:
FK Crvena Zvezda Beograd – Budapesti Honvéd SE 1-0 (0-0)
FK Crvena Zvezda Beograd: Mirko STOJANOVIC, Novak TOMIC, Milanko CUK, Blagoje
MITIC, Milan COP, Slobodan SKRBIC, Nikola STIPIC, Dusan MARAVIC, Zoran
PRLJINCEVIC, OBRADOVIC, Selimir MILOSEVIC.
Budapesti Honvéd SE: Béla TAKÁCS (I), László MAROSI, János SZÖCS, Zoltán DUDÁS,
Antal GALAMBOS, Antal KOTÁSZ, György NAGY, Károly BALOGH, Ferenc NÓGRÁDI,
Imre KOMORA, Sándor KATONA. (Coach: László RÁKÓCZI).
Goal: FK Crvena Zvezda Beograd: 1-0 Selimir MILOSEVIC (78').
Referee: Miroslav KUKÁS (TCH)   Attendance: 12.000
(OBRADOVIC was a guestplayer)

27-05-1962   Stadio Comunale, Bologna: FC Bologna – Slovan UNV Bratislava 3-0 (1-0)
FC Bologna: Paolo CIMPIEL, Bruno CAPRA, Franco MARINI, Carlo FURLANIS, Mirko
PAVINATO, Romano FOGLI, Luciano BONFADA, Cesarino CERVELLATI, Harald
Ingemann NIELSEN (DEN), Héctor (Ettore) DE MARCO (URU), Luís "VINÍCIO" Vinícius
de Menenzes (BRA). (Coach: Fulvio BERNARDINI).
Slovan UNV Bratislava: Alexander VENCEL (I), Anton URBAN, Vojtech JANKOVIC, Jozef
VENGLOS, Frantisek KISS, Stefan KRÁL, Ivan MRÁZ, Ludovít CVETLER, Anton
MORAVCÍK, Jozef OBERT, Milan BALÁZIK. (Coach: Karol BORHY).
Goals: FC Bologna: 1-0 Héctor (Ettore) DE MARCO (1'), 2-0 Luís "VINÍCIO" Vinícius de
Menenzes (56'), 3-0 Héctor (Ettore) DE MARCO (82').
Referee: Rikard PETROSIC (YUG)

03-06-1962   Bratislava: Slovan UNV Bratislava – FC Bologna 2-1 (0-0)
Slovan UNV Bratislava: Alexander VENCEL (I), Anton URBAN, Alexander HORVÁTH,
Frantisek KISS, Stefan KRÁL, Jozef VENGLOS, Zdeno VELECKÝ, Ludovít CVETLER,
Anton MORAVCÍK, Jozef OBERT, Anton BÍLÝ. (Coach: Karol BORHY).
FC Bologna: Paolo CIMPIEL, Bruno CAPRA, Mirko PAVINATO, Franco MARINI, Carlo
FURLANIS, Romano FOGLI, Luís "VINÍCIO" Vinícius de Menenzes (BRA), Cesarino
CERVELLATI, Harald Ingemann NIELSEN (DEN), Héctor (Ettore) DE MARCO (URU),
Renzo RAGONESI. (Coach: Fulvio BERNARDINI).
Goals: Slovan UNV Bratislava: 1-0 Anton BÍLÝ (49'), 2-1 Zdeno VELECKÝ (74').
FC Bologna: 1-1 Harald Ingemann NIELSEN (62').
Referee: Konstantin ZECEVIC (YUG)   Attendance: 18.000

03-06-1962   Népstadion, Budapest:
              Budapesti Honvéd SE – FK Crvena Zvezda Beograd 2-3 (2-1)
Budapesti Honvéd SE: Béla TAKÁCS (I), László MAROSI, János SZÖCS, Zoltán DUDÁS,
Antal GALAMBOS, Antal KOTÁSZ, György NAGY, Ferenc NÓGRÁDI, Károly BALOGH,
Imre KOMORA, Sándor KATONA. (Coach: László RÁKÓCZI).
FK Crvena Zvezda Beograd: Mirko STOJANOVIC, Novak TOMIC, Milanko CUK, Slobodan
SKRBIC, Milan COP, Luka MALESEV, Nikola STIPIC, Dusan MARAVIC, Selimir
MILOSEVIC, Zoran PRLJINCEVIC, Anton RUDINSKI.
Goals: Budapesti Honvéd SE: 1-0 Ferenc NÓGRÁDI (12'), Sándor KATONA (44').
FK Crvena Zvezda Beograd: Anton RUDINSKI (36'), 2-2 Zoran PRLJINCEVIC (63'), 2-3
Zoran PRLJINCEVIC (80').
Referee: Milan FENCL (TCH)   Attendance: 20.000

10-06-1962   Bratislava: Slovan UNV Bratislava – FK Crvena Zvezda Beograd 1-0 (1-0)
Slovan UNV Bratislava: Ferdinand HASON, Frantisek KISS, Anton URBAN, Vojtech
JANKOVIC, Stefan KRÁL, Jozef VENGLOS, Zdeno VELECKÝ, Ludovít CVETLER, Anton
MORAVCIK, Jozef OBERT, Anton BÍLÝ. (Coach: Anton BULLA).
FK Crvena Zvezda Beograd: Mirko STOJANOVIC, Novak TOMIC, Milanko CUK, Slobodan
SKRBIC, Milan COP, Luka MALESEV, Nikola STIPIC, Dusan MARAVIC, Selimir
MILOSEVIC, Zoran PRLJINCEVIC, Anton RUDINSKI.
Goal: Slovan UNV Bratislava: 1-0 Ludovít CVETLER (7').
Referee: Karoly SCHOPP (HUN)   Attendance: 9.000

152

10-06-1962   Népstadion, Budapest: Budapesti Honvéd SE – FC Bologna 1-2 (1-1)
Budapesti Honvéd SE: Béla TAKÁCS (I), István LÉVAI, Sándor JÓZSA, Zoltán DUDÁS, Mihály ROZMIS, Antal KOTÁSZ, István TAKÁCS (II), Imre KOMORA, Antal TUSSINGER, Ferenc NÓGRÁDI, Sándor KATONA. (Coach: László RÁKÓCZI).
FC Bologna: Paolo CIMPIEL, Bruno CAPRA, Franco MARINI, Carlo FURLANIS, Mirko PAVINATO, Lorenzo NONINO, Antonio RENNA, Héctor (Ettore) DE MARCO (URU), Harald Ingemann NIELSEN (DEN), Romano FOGLI, Renzo RAGONESI. (Coach: Fulvio BERNARDINI).
Goals: Budapesti Honvéd SE: 1-1 Antal TUSSINGER (44').
FC Bologna: 0-1 Harald Ingemann NIELSEN (4'), 1-2 Harald Ingemann NIELSEN (74').
Attendance: 5.000

17-06-1962   Stadion J.N.A., Beograd:
                      FK Crvena Zvezda Beograd – Slovan UNV Bratislava   2-2 (2-1)
FK Crvena Zvezda Beograd: Mirko STOJANOVIC, Novak TOMIC, Tomislav MILICEVIC, Luka MALESEV, Milan COP, Blagoje MITIC, Nikola STIPIC, Dusan MARAVIC, Selimir MILOSEVIC, Zoran PRLJINCEVIC, Slobodan MILOSAVLJEVIC.
Slovan UNV Bratislava: Ferdinand HASON, Frantisek KISS, Anton URBAN, Vojtech JANKOVIC, Stefan KRÁL, Jozef VENGLOS, Zdeno VELECKÝ, Ludovít CVETLER, Anton MORAVCIK, Jozef OBERT, Anton BÍLÝ. (Coach: Anton BULLA).
Goals: FK Crvena Zvezda Beograd: 1-0 Slobodan MILOSAVLJEVIC (15'), 2-0 Dusan MARAVIC (19').
Slovan UNV Bratislava: 2-1 Jozef OBERT (24'), 2-2 Anton BÍLÝ (78').
Referee: Lajos HORVÁTH (HUN)   Attendance: 3.000

17-06-1962   Stadio Littoriale, Bologna: FC Bologna – Budapesti Honvéd SE 5-1 (2-1)
FC Bologna: Paolo CIMPIEL, Bruno CAPRA, Mirko PAVINATO, Paride TUMBURUS, Francesco JANICH, Romano FOGLI, Antonio RENNA, Héctor (Ettore) DE MARCO (URU), Harald Ingemann NIELSEN (DEN), Giacomo BULGARELLI, Ezio PASCUTTI. (Coach: Fulvio BERNARDINI).
Budapesti Honvéd SE: Béla TAKÁCS (I), István LÉVAI, László MAROSI, Zoltán DUDÁS, Ferenc NÓGRÁDI, Mihály ROZMIS, István TAKÁCS (II), Károly BALOGH, Antal TUSSINGER, Imre KOMORA, Sándor KATONA. (Coach: László RÁKÓCZI).
Goals: FC Bologna: 1-1 Ezio PASCUTTI (36'), 2-1 Harald Ingemann NIELSEN (41'), 3-1 Harald Ingemann NIELSEN (67'), 4-1 Héctor (Ettore) DE MARCO (73'), 5-1 Harald Ingemann NIELSEN (85').
Budapesti Honvéd SE: 0-1 Károly BALOGH (23').

Pos	Team	Pld	W	D	L	GF	GA	GD	Pts
1	*FC Bologna (ITA)*	*6*	*4*	*0*	*2*	*15*	*9*	*+6*	*8*
2	FK Crvena Zvezda Beograd (YUG)	6	3	1	2	11	9	+2	7
3	Slovan UNV Bratislava (TCH)	6	3	1	2	8	9	-1	7
4	Budapesti Honvéd SE (HUN)	6	1	0	5	7	14	-7	2

*** FC Bologna qualified for the semi-finals ***

153

13-05-1962   Gradski Stadion, Novi Sad:
FK Vojvodina Novi Sad – TJ Spartak Kovosmalt Trnava   0-1 (0-1)
FK Vojvodina Novi Sad: András VERES, Mladen VUCINIC, Dimitrije RADOVIC, Stevan
SEKERES, Zarko NIKOLIC, Stevan BENA, Silvester TAKAC, Djordje MILIC, Ljubisa
STEFANOVIC, Petar MIJATOVIC, EKMEDZIC. (Coach: Franja HIRMAN).
TJ Spartak Kovosmalt Trnava: Jozef ONDRUSKA, Stefan SLEZÁK, Milan PÚCHLY, Ivan
STEFKO, Stanislav JARÁBEK, Marián KOZINKA, Emil ADAMEC, Ján HORVATH,
Valerián SVEC, Vojtech BEDNÁRIK, Jozef STIBRÁNYI.
Goal: TJ Spartak Kovosmalt Trnava: 0-1 Valerián SVEC (8').
Referee: Giulio CAMPANATI (ITA)   Attendance: 9.000

15-05-1962   Stadio Comunale, Firenze: AC Fiorentina – Vasas SC   0-0
AC Fiorentina: Giuliano SARTI, Alberto ORZAN, Sergio CASTELLETTI, Amilcare
FERRETTI, Piero GONFIANTINI, Claudio RIMBALDO, Kurt Roland HAMRIN (SWE), Can
BARTÚ (TUR), Luigi MILAN, Lucio DELL'ANGELO, Gianfranco PETRIS. (Coach:
Ferruccio VALCAREGGI).
Vasas SC: József GELEI, Béla KÁRPÁTI, Dezsö BUNDZSÁK, Sándor BAKOS, Antal
BÁRFI, Pál BERENDI, Imre MATHESZ, Mihály KÉKESI, Ferenc MACHOS, László PÁL
(I), Tibor PÁL (II). (Coach: Rudolf ILLOVSZKY).

20-05-1962   Népstadion, Budapest: Vasas SC – AC Fiorentina   3-1 (2-0)
Vasas SC: József GELEI, Béla KÁRPÁTI, Sándor BAKOS, Antal BÁRFI, Dezsö
BUNDZSÁK, Pál BERENDI, Imre MATHESZ, Mihály KÉKESI, Ferenc MACHOS, László
PÁL (I), Tibor PÁL (II). (Coach: Rudolf ILLOVSZKY).
AC Fiorentina: Giuliano SARTI, Saul MALATRASI, Sergio CASTELLETTI, Amilcare
FERRETTI, Alberto ORZAN, Claudio RIMBALDO, Kurt Roland HAMRIN (SWE), Can
BARTÚ (TUR), Luigi MILAN, Lucio DELL'ANGELO, Gianfranco PETRIS. (Coach:
Ferruccio VALCAREGGI).
Goals: Vasas SC: 1-0 Ferenc MACHOS (8'), 2-0 Ferenc MACHOS (25'), 3-1 Ferenc
MACHOS (63').
AC Fiorentina: 2-1 Kurt Ronald HAMRIN (59').

20-05-1962   Trnava: TJ Spartak Kovosmalt Trnava – FK Vojvodina Novi Sad   0-0
TJ Spartak Kovosmalt Trnava: Jozef ONDRUSKA, Stefan SLEZÁK, Milan PÚCHLY, Ivan
STEFKO, Stanislav JARÁBEK, Marián KOZINKA, Emil ADAMEC, Ján HORVÁTH,
Valerián SVEC, Vojtech BEDNÁRIK, Jozef STIBRÁNYI.
FK Vojvodina Novi Sad: Ilija PANTELIC, Mladen VUCINIC, Stevan SEKERES, Dimitrije
RADOVIC, Zarko NIKOLIC, Stevan BENA, Silvester TAKAC, Cedomir SENTIN, Djordje
PAVLIC, Petar MIJATOVIC, Nedeljko DUGANDZIJA. (Coach: Franja HIRMAN).
Referee: Bruno DE MARCHI (ITA)   Attendance: 4.000

27-05-1962   Népstadion, Budapest: Vasas SC – TJ Spartak Kovosmalt Trnava 5-0 (2-0)
Vasas SC: József GELEI, Béla KÁRPÁTI, Dezsö BUNDZSÁK, Sándor BAKOS, Antal
BÁRFI, Pál BERENDI, Imre MATHESZ, Mihály KÉKESI, Ferenc MACHOS, László PÁL
(I), Tibor PÁL (II). (Coach: Rudolf ILLOVSZKY).
TJ Spartak Kovosmalt Trnava: Jozef ONDRUSKA, Milan PÚCHLY, Stanislav JARÁBEK,
Stefan SLEZÁK, Ivan STEFKO, Marián KOZINKA, emil ADAMEC, Kamil MAJERNIK,
Valerián SVEC, Vojtech BEDNÁRIK, Stefan KUCHÁR.
Goals: Vasas SC: 1-0 László PAL (I) (7'), 2-0 László PAL (14'), 3-0 Dezsö BUNDZSÁK
(64'), 4-0 Tibor PAL (II) (68'), 5-0 László PAL (I) (89').
Referee: Antonio SBARDELLA (ITA)

27-05-1962   Stadio Comunale, Firenze: AC Fiorentina – FK Vojvodina Novi Sad 0-1 (0-1)
AC Fiorentina: Giuliano SARTI, Saul MALATRASI, Sergio CASTELLETTI, SERENO,
Sergio ORLANDI, Claudio RIMBALDO, Kurt Roland HAMRIN (SWE), Can BARTÚ
(TUR), Fernando VENERANDA, Luigi MILAN, Gianfranco PETRIS. (Coach: Ferruccio
VALCAREGGI).
FK Vojvodina Novi Sad: András VERES, Mladen VUCINIC, Dimitrije RADOVIC, Zarko
NIKOLIC, Cedomir SENTIN, Stevan SEKERES, Silvester TAKAC, Stevan BENA, Djordje
PAVLIC, Petar MIJATOVIC, Nedeljko DUGANDZIJA. (Coach: Franja HIRMAN).
Goal: FK Vojvodina Novi Sad: 0-1 Djordje PAVLIC (23').
Referee: Jozsef KATONA (HUN)   Attendance: 9.000

03-06-1962   Gradski Stadion, Novi Sad:
              FK Vojvodina Novi Sad – AC Fiorentina 2-2 (0-2)
FK Vojvodina Novi Sad: András VERES, Mladen VUCINIC, Dimitrije RADOVIC, Stevan
SEKERES, Zarko NIKOLIC, Cedomir SENTIN, Silvester TAKAC, Djordje MILIC, Djordje
PAVLIC, Petar MIJATOVIC, Nedeljko DUGANDZIJA. (Coach: Franja HIRMAN).
AC Fiorentina: Giuliano SARTI, Saul MALATRASI, Giampaolo BAGAGLI, Amilcare
FERRETTI, Alberto ORZAN, Claudio RIMBALDO, Kurt Roland HAMRIN (SWE), Can
BARTÚ (TUR), Luigi MILAN, Gianfranco PETRIS, Sergio ORLANDI. (Coach: Ferruccio
VALCAREGGI).
Goals: FK Vojvodina Novi Sad: 1-2 Giampaolo BAGAGLI (48' *own goal*), 2-2 Djordje
PAVLIC (67').
AC Fiorentina: 0-1 Kurt Roland HAMRIN (6'), 0-2 Can BARTÚ (24').
Referee: Lajos ARANYOSI (HUN)   Attendance: 14.000

03-06-1962   Stadión Spartak, Trnava:
              TJ Spartak Kovosmalt Trnava – Vasas SC 2-2 (1-1)
TJ Spartak Kovosmalt Trnava: Jozef ONDRUSKA, Milan PÚCHLY, Stanislav JARÁBEK,
Stefan SLEZÁK, Vojtech BEDNÁRIK, Marián KOZINKA, Emil ADAMEC, Kamil
MAJERNIK, Ján STURDÍK, Valerián SVEC, Stefan KUCHÁR.
Vasas SC: József GELEI, György ROZSNYÓI, Dezsö BUNDZSÁK, Sándor BAKOS, Antal
BÁRFI, Pál BERENDI, Imre MATHESZ, Mihály KÉKESI, Ferenc MACHOS, László PÁL
(I), Tibor PÁL (II). (Coach: Rudolf ILLOVSZKY).
Goals: TJ Spartak Kovosmalt Trnava: 1-1 Marián KOZINKA (42'), 2-1 Valerián SVEC (52').
Vasas SC: 0-1 Mihály KEKESI (11'), 2-2 László PAL (I) (72').
Referee: Francesco FRANCESCON (ITA)   Attendance: 6.000

10-06-1962   Gradski Stadion, Novi Sad: FK Vojvodina Novi Sad – Vasas SC 0-3 (0-1)
FK Vojvodina Novi Sad: Ilija PANTELIC, Mladen VUCINIC, Zarko NIKOLIC, Dimitrije
RADOVIC, Stevan BENA, Cedomir SENTIN, Silvester TAKAC, Stevan SEKERES, Djordje
PAVLIC, Petar MIJATOVIC, Nedeljko DUGANDZIJA. (Coach: Franja HIRMAN).
Vasas SC: József GELEI, Károly NAGY, Dezsö BUNDZSÁK, Sándor BAKOS, Antal
BÁRFI, Pál BERENDI, Imre MATHESZ, Mihály KÉKESI, Ferenc MACHOS, László PÁL
(I), Tibor PÁL (II). (Coach: Rudolf ILLOVSZKY).
Goals: Vasas SC: 0-1 László PÁL (I) (5'), 0-2 Ferenc MACHOS (54'), 0-3 Dezsö
BUNDZSÁK (63' penalty).
Referee: Piero ANGELINI (ITA)   Attendance: 20.000

10-06-1962   Trnava: TJ Spartak Kovosmalt Trnava – AC Fiorentina 3-4 (1-0)
TJ Spartak Kovosmalt Trnava: Jozef ONDRUSKA, Stefan SLEZÁK, Stanislav JARÁBEK,
Milan PÚCHLY, Ján HORVÁTH, Marián KOZINKA, Vojtech BEDNÁRIK, Valerián SVEC,
Ján STURDÍK, Ivan STEFKO, Stefan KUCHÁR.
AC Fiorentina: Giuliano SARTI, Saul MALATRASI, Sergio CASTELLETTI, Amilcare
FERRETTI, Alberto ORZAN, Claudio RIMBALDO, Kurt Roland HAMRIN (SWE), Rino
MARCHESI, Luigi MILAN, Lucio DELL'ANGELO, Can BARTÚ (TUR). (Coach: Ferruccio
VALCAREGGI).
Goals: TJ Spartak Kovosmalt Trnava: 1-0 Valerián SVEC (3' penalty), 2-2 Ján STURDIK
(73'), 3-4 Vojtech BEDNÁRIK (89').
AC Fiorentina: 1-1 Lucio DELL'ANGELO (49'), 1-2 Kurt Roland HAMRIN (57'), 2-3 Kurt
Roland HAMRIN (75'), 2-4 Kurt Roland HAMRIN (87').
Referee: Borce NEDELKOVSKI (YUG)   Attendance: 5.000

17-06-1962   Népstadion, Budapest: Vasas SC – FK Vojvodina Novi Sad 3-1 (0-1)
Vasas SC: József GELEI, Károly NAGY, Dezsö BUNDZSÁK, Sándor BAKOS, Antal
BÁRFI, Pál BERENDI, Imre MATHESZ, Mihály KÉKESI, Ferenc MACHOS, László PÁL
(I), Tibor PÁL (II). (Coach: Rudolf ILLOVSZKY).
FK Vojvodina Novi Sad: András VERES, Dimitrije RADOVIC, Zarko NIKOLIC, Mladen
VUCINIC, Stevan SEKERES, Stevan BENA, Silvester TAKAC, Cedomir SENTIN, Djordje
MILIC, Radivoj RADOSAV, Nedeljko DUGANDZIJA. (Coach: Franja HIRMAN).
Goals: Vasas SC: 1-1 László PÁL (I) (56'), 2-1 Imre MATHESZ (65'), 3-1 Dezsö
BUNDZSÁK (87' penalty).
FK Vojvodina Novi Sad: 0-1 Djordje MILIC (34').
Referee: Giulio CAMPANATI (ITA)   Attendance: 20.000

17-06-1962   Stadio Comunale, Firenze:
              AC Fiorentina – TJ Spartak Kovosmalt Trnava 6-1 (4-1)
AC Fiorentina: Giuliano SARTI, Enzo ROBOTTI, Sergio CASTELLETTI, Amilcare
FERRETTI, Alberto ORZAN, Rino MARCHESI, Kurt Roland HAMRIN (SWE), Luigi
MILAN, Can BARTÚ (TUR), Lucio DELL'ANGELO, Gianfranco PETRIS. (Coach: Nandor
HIDEGKUTI (HUN)).
TJ Spartak Kovosmalt Trnava: Imrich STACHO, Stefan SLEZÁK, Stanislav JARÁBEK,
Milan PÚCHLY, Marián KOZINKA, Frantisek CAMBAL, Vojtech BEDNÁRIK, Ján
HORVÁTH, Kamil MAJERNÍK, Valerián SVEC, Ivan STEFKO.
Goals: AC Fiorentina: 1-1 Kurt Roland HAMRIN (13'), 2-1 Kurt Roland HAMRIN (24'), 3-1
Lucio DELL'ANGELO (42'), 4-1 Can BARTU (43'), 5-1 Kurt Roland HAMRIN (74'), 6-1
Kurt Roland HAMRIN (85').
TJ Spartak Kovosmalt Trnava: 0-1 Ján HORVÁTH (7').
Referee: Zivko BAJIC (YUG)

156

Pos	Team	Pld	W	D	L	GF	GA	GD	Pts
1	*Vasas SC (HUN)*	*6*	*4*	*2*	*0*	*16*	*4*	*+12*	*10*
2	AC Fiorentina (ITA)	6	2	2	2	13	10	+3	6
3	FK Vojvodina Novi Sad (YUG)	6	1	2	3	4	9	-5	4
4	TJ Spartak Kovosmalt Trnava (TCH)	6	1	2	3	7	17	-10	4

*** Vasas SC qualified for the semi-finals ***

SEMI-FINALS

23-06-1962   Maksimir Stadion, Zagreb: NK Dinamo Zagreb – FC Bologna 1-1 (1-0)
NK Dinamo Zagreb: Gordan IROVIC, Josip SIKIC, Mirko BRAUN, Ivan SANTEK, Vlatko MARKOVIC, Rudolf BELIN, Ivica CVITKOVIC, Slaven ZAMBATA, Zeljko PERUSIC, Drazan JERKOVIC, Tomislav KNEZ. (Coach: Milan ANTOLKOVIC).
FC Bologna: Paolo CIMPIEL, Bruno CAPRA, Mirko PAVINATO, Paride TUMBURUS, Francesco JANICH, Romano FOGLI, Antonio RENNA, Héctor (Ettore) DE MARCO (URU), Giacomo BULGARELLI, Harald Ingemann NIELSEN (DEN), Ezio PASCUTTI. (Coach: Fulvio BERNARDINI).
Goals: NK Dinamo Zagreb: 1-0 Slaven ZAMBATA (43').
FC Bologna: 1-1 Antonio RENNA (52').
Referee: Václav KORELUS (TCH)   Attendance: 20.000

23-06-1962   Stadio Comunale, Bergamo: Atalanta Bergamo – Vasas SC   1-0 (0-0)
Atalanta Bergamo: Zaccaria COMETTI, Battista ROTA, Piero GARDONI, Livio RONCOLI, Flemming NIELSEN, Umberto COLOMBO, Angelo DOMEGHINI, Dino DA COSTA, Enrico NOVA, Kurt CHRISTENSEN, Luciano MAGISTRELLI. (Coach: Ferruccio VALCAREGGI).
Vasas SC: Antal SZENTMIHÁLYI, Mihály FÓRIZS, Dezsö BUNDZSÁK, Sándor BAKOS, Imre MATHESZ, Pál BERENDI, Mihály KÉKESI, János FARKAS, Ferenc MACHOS, László PÁL (I), Tibor PÁL (II). (Coach: Rudolf ILLOVSZKY).
Goal: Atalanta Bergamo: 1-0 Luciano MAGISTRELLI (63').
Attendance: 25.000

30-06-1962   Népstadion, Budapest: Vasas SC – Atalanta Bergamo   3-1
Vasas SC: Antal SZENTMIHÁLYI, Kálmán IHÁSZ, Kálmán MÉSZÖLY, László SÁROSI, Dezsö BUNDZSÁK, Pál BERENDI, Imre MATHESZ, János FARKAS, Ferenc MACHOS, László PÁL (I), Tibor PÁL (II). (Coach: Rudolf ILLOVSZKY).
Atalanta Bergamo: Zaccaria COMETTI, Battista ROTA, Livio RONCOLI, Flemming NIELSEN, Piero GARDONI, Umberto COLOMBO, Rinaldo OLIVIERI, Dino DA COSTA, Enrico NOVA, Kurt CHRISTENSEN, Angelo DOMEGHINI. (Coach: Ferruccio VALCAREGGI).
Goals: Vasas SC: 1-1 János FARKAS (16'), 2-1 László PÁL (I) (..'), 3-1 János FARKAS (..').
Atalanta Bergamo: 0-1 Dino DA COSTA (7').

30-06-1962   Bologna: FC Bologna – NK Dinamo Zagreb   2-1 (2-0)
FC Bologna: Paolo CIMPIEL, Bruno CAPRA, Mirko PAVINATO, Paride TUMBURUS, Francesco JANICH, Romano FOGLI, Antonio RENNA, Héctor (Ettore) DE MARCO (URU), Giacomo BULGARELLI, Renzo RAGONESI, Ezio PASCUTTI. (Coach: Fulvio BERNARDINI).
NK Dinamo Zagreb: Gordan IROVIC, Josip SIKIC, Mirko BRAUN, Ivan SANTEK, Vlatko MARKOVIC, Zeljko PERUSIC, Ivica CVITKOVIC, Slaven ZAMBATA, Zeljko MATUS, Drazan JERKOVIC, Ilijas PASIC. (Coach: Milan ANTOLKOVIC).
Goals: FC Bologna: 1-0 Antonio RENNA (24'), 2-0 Ezio PASCUTTI (41').
NK Dinamo Zagreb: 2-1 Drazan JERKOVIC (46').
Referee: SICZ (HUN)   Attendance: 10.000

FINAL

26-09-1962   Népstadion, Budapest: Vasas SC – FC Bologna   5-1
Vasas SC: Antal SZENTMIHÁLYI, Kálmán IHÁSZ, Kálmán MÉSZÖLY, László SÁROSI, Dezsö BUNDZSÁK, Pál BERENDI, Mihály KÉKESI, János FARKAS, Ferenc MACHOS, László PÁL (I), Tibor PÁL (II). (Coach: Rudolf ILLOVSZKY).
FC Bologna: Attilio SANTARELLI, Franco MARINI, Francesco JANICH, Edmondo LORENZINI, Paride TUMBURUS, Bruno FRANZINI, Marino PERANI, Héctor (Ettore) DE MARCO (URU), Harald Ingemann NIELSEN (DEN), Helmut HALLER (FRG), Ezio PASCUTTI. (Coach: Fulvio BERNARDINI).
Goals: Vasas SC: Dezsö BUNDZSÁK, Dezsö BUNDZSÁK, Dezsö BUNDZSÁK, Dezsö BUNDZSÁK, Ferenc MACHOS.
FC Bologna: Harald NIELSEN.

17-10-1962   Stadio Littoriale, Bologna: FC Bologna – Vasas SC   2-1 (0-0)
FC Bologna: Paolo CIMPIEL, Bruno CAPRA, Mirko PAVINATO, Carlo FURLANIS, Francesco JANICH, Romano FOGLI, Marino PERANI, Bruno FRANZINI, Giacomo BULGARELLI, Helmut HALLER (FRG), Antonio RENNA (expulsion 83'). (Coach: Fulvio BERNARDINI).
Vasas SC: Antal SZENTMIHÁLYI, Kálmán IHÁSZ, Sándor BAKOS, Dezsö BUNDZSÁK, Kálmán MÉSZÖLY (expulsion 83'), Pál BERENDI, Mihály KÉKESI, János FARKAS, Ferenc MACHOS, László PÁL (I), Tibor PÁL (II). (Coach: Rudolf ILLOVSZKY).
Goals: FC Bologna: 1-0 Giacomo BULGARELLI (48'), 2-0 Helmut HALLER (65').
Vasas SC: 2-1 László PÁL (I) (67').

*** Vasas SC won the Cup ***

158

1963

QUARTER-FINALS

29-05-1963   Népstadion, Budapest: Vasas SC – TJ Baník Ostrava   5-0 (3-0)
Vasas SC: László VARGA, Kálmán IHÁSZ, Kálmán MÉSZÖLY, László SÁROSI, Gyula
SAS, Pál BERENDI, István BOZÓ, Tibor PÁL (II), Ferenc MACHOS, László PÁL (I), Imre
MATHESZ. (Coach: Rudolf ILLOVSZKY).
TJ Baník Ostrava: Frantisek DVORÁK, Bedrich KÖHLER, Prokop DANEK, Karel DVORÁK
(II), Zdenek STANCO, Frantisek SINDELÁR, Jan KNIEZEK, Miroslav WIECEK, Miroslav
MIKESKA, Milan SIRÝ, Frantisek VALOSEK. (Coach: Frantisek BUFKA).
Goals: Vasas SC: 1-0 László PÁL (..'), 2-0 Ferenc MACHOS (..' penalty), 3-0 Ferenc
MACHOS (..'), 4-0 Tibor PÁL (..'), 5-0 Ferenc MACHOS (..').
Referee: Giuseppe ADAMI (ITA)   Attendance: 25.000

29-05-1963   Budapest: M.T.K. Budapest – FC Bologna   1-1 (1-0)
M.T.K. Budapest: Sándor LANCZKOR, György KESZEI, István JENEI, István NAGY, József
DANSZKY, Ferenc SIPOS, Gyula MAJOR, László BÖDÖR, István KUTI, Mihály LACZKÓ,
István SZIMCSÁK (I). (Coach: Imre KOVÁCS).
FC Bologna: Rino RADO, Bruno CAPRA, Carlo FURLANIS, Paride TUMBURUS,
Francesco JANICH, Romano FOGLI, Sidio CORRADI, Bruno FRANZINI, Domenico PACE,
Héctor (Ettore) DE MARCO (URU), Antonio RENNA. (Coach: Fulvio BERNARDINI).
Goals: M.T.K. Budapest: 1-0 István KUTI (14').
FC Bologna: 1-1 Sándor LANCZKOR (79' *own goal*).
Referee: Alfred HABERFELLNER (AUT)

(Note: other sources indicate the Bologna scorer was: 1-1 Héctor (Ettore) DE MARCO (79'))

29-05-1963   Hohe Warte, Wien: Admira-Energie Wien – AC Torino   1-0 (1-0)
Admira-Energie Wien: Johann DRAXELMAYER, Ferdinand KOLARIK, Emmerich
SOMMER, Werner BEDERNIK, Giuseppe Francesco Carlo KOSCHIER, Michael
BREIBERT, Günter KALTENBRUNNER (II), Peter REITER, Alfred KÖRNER, José Roque
Paes "TRAÇAIA" (BRA), Josef HAMERL. (Coach: Johann (Hans) PESSER).
AC Torino: Lido VIERI, Luciano TENEGGI, Luciano BUZZACCHERA, Giovanni
MIALICH, Antonio GERBAUDO, Giampaolo PIACERI, Antonio CARDILLO, Giorgio
FERRINI, Gerald Archibald (Gerry) HITCHENS (ENG), Marcos Alberto LOCATELLI
(ARG), Carlo CRIPPA. (Coach: Giacinto Delfino ELLENA).
Goal: Admira-Energie Wien: 1-0 Günter KALTENBRUNNER (7').
Referee: Adolf MACH (TCH)   Attendance: 5.000

29-05-1963   Sarajavo: FK Zeljeznicar Sarajevo – FK Austria Wien   4-1 (2-1)
FK Zeljeznicar Sarajevo: Vasilije RADOVIC, Miljan STAKA, Sulejman KULOVIC,
Vjekoslav KRAJNC, Enver KAPIDZIC, Rastislav MATIC, Djuro SMAJLOVIC (II), Ivica
OSIM, Ahmet DIZDAREVIC, Drago SMAJLOVIC (I), Zvonko DUSPARA. (Coach: Vlatko
KONJEVOD).
FK Austria Wien: Fernot FRAYDL, Peter VARGO, Karl STOTZ, Johann LÖSER, Adolf
(Dolfi) BLUTSCH, Horst PAPROTH (FRG), Johann GEYER, Waldemar Graziano
"JACARÉ" (BRA), Alfred GAGER, Horst NEMEC, Dr.Walter SCHLEGER. (Coach: Eduard
(Edi) FRÜHWIRTH).
Goals: FK Zeljeznicar Sarajevo: 1-1 Drago SMAJLOVIC (29'), 2-1 Drago SMAJLOVIC
(44'), 3-1 Ivica OSIM (54'), 4-1 Drago SMAJLOVIC (68').
FK Austria Wien: 0-1 Waldemar Graziano "JACARÉ" (13').
Referee: Milan FENCL (TCH)   Attendance: 18.000

05-06-1963   Stadio Comunale, Torino: AC Torino – Admira-Energie Wien   5-1 (1-0)
AC Torino: Silvano VINCENZI, Fabrizio POLETTI, Luciano BUZZACCHERA, Vincenzo
(Enzo) BEARZOT, Remo LANCIONI, Amilcare FERRETTI, Giampaolo PIACERI, Marcos
Alberto LOCATELLI (ARG), Gerald Archibald (Gerry) HITCHENS (ENG), Joaquim PEIRÓ
Lucas (ESP), Antonio CARDILLO. (Coach: Giacinto Delfino ELLENA).
Admira-Energie Wien: Johann DRAXELMAYER, Ferdinand KOLARIK, Emmerich
SOMMER, Bohumil HRUSKA, Giuseppe Francesco Carlo KOSCHIER, Walter STAMM,
José Roque Paes "TRAÇAIA" (BRA), Günter KALTENBRUNNER, Alfred KÖRNER, Josef
HAMERL, Karl SKERLAN. (Coach: Johann (Hans) PESSER).
Goals: AC Torino: 1-0 Joaquim PEIRÓ Lucas (1'), 2-1 Joaquim PEIRÓ Lucas (48'), 3-1
Gerald Archibald (Gerry) HITCHENS (96' penalty), 4-1 Joaquim PEIRÓ Lucas (100'), 5-1
Amilcare FERRETTI (112').
Admira-Energie Wien: 1-1 Alfred KÖRNER (47').
Referee: Branko CAHUN (YUG)   Attendance: 3.000
(After extra time)

05-06-1963   Stadio Comunale, Bologna: FC Bologna – M.T.K. Budapest   0-1 (0-0)
FC Bologna: Rino RADO, Bruno CAPRA, Mirko PAVINATO, Carlo FURLANIS, Lorenzo
NONINO, Romano FOGLI, Sidio CORRADI, Bruno FRANZINI, Domenico PACE, Héctor
(Ettore) DE MARCO (URU), Antonio RENNA. (Coach: Fulvio BERNARDINI).
M.T.K. Budapest: Sándor LANCZKOR, György KESZEI, István JENEI, István NAGY, József
DANSZKY, Tibor PALICSKÓ, Gyula MAJOR, Mihály LACZKÓ, László BÖDÖR, István
KUTI, István SZIMCSÁK (I). (Coach: Imre KOVÁCS).
Goal: M.T.K. Budapest: 0-1 István KUTI (59').
Referee: Aleksandar SKORIC (YUG)

05-06-1963   Bazaly Stadion, Ostrava: TJ Baník Ostrava – Vasas SC   1-1 (1-0)
TJ Baník Ostrava: Vladimir MOKROHAJSKÝ, Bedrich KÖHLER, Prokop DANEK, Jan
KNIEZEK, Jirí LACIGA, Zdenek STANCO, Eduard SMÍD, Miroslav WIECEK, Frantisek
SINDELÁR, Milan SIRÝ, Frantisek VALOSEK. (Coach: Frantisek BUFKA).
Vasas SC: László VARGA, Kálmán IHÁSZ, Kálmán MÉSZÖLY, Sándor BAKOS, Gyula
SAS, Pál BERENDI, István BOZÓ, Mihály KÉKESI, Dezsö BUNDZSÁK, László PÁL (I),
Tibor PÁL (II). (Coach: Rudolf ILLOVSZKY).
Goals: TJ Baník Ostrava: Jirí LACIGA.
Vasas SC: László PÁL.

05-06-1963   Wacker-Platz, Wien: FK Austria Wien – FK Zeljeznicar Sarajevo   2-0 (0-0)
FK Austria Wien: Fernot FRAYDL, Peter VARGO, Adolf (Dolfi) BLUTSCH, Franz
SWOBODA, Alfred GAGER, Horst PAPROTH (FRG), Johann GEYER, Waldemar Graziano
"JACARÉ" (BRA), Ernst FIALA, Horst NEMEC, Dr.Walter SCHLEGER. (Coach: Eduard
(Edi) FRÜHWIRTH).
FK Zeljeznicar Sarajevo: Vasilije RADOVIC, Miljan STAKA, Sulejman KULOVIC,
Vjekoslav KRAJNC, Enver KAPIDZIC, Rastislav MATIC, Sefik AZABAGIC, Kasim
KOKOT, Drago SMAJLOVIC (I), Ivica OSIM, Zvonko DUSPARA. (Coach: Vlatko
KONJEVOD).
Goals: FK Austra Wien: 1-0 Horst NEMEC (60'), 2-0 Waldemar Graziano "JACARÉ" (73').
Referee: Lajos ARANYOSI (HUN)   Attendance: 10.000

SEMI-FINALS

12-06-1963   Népstadion, Budapest: Vasas SC – AC Torino   5-1 (3-0)
Vasas SC: László VARGA, Kálmán IHÁSZ, László SÁROSI, Gyula SAS, Kálmán
MÉSZÖLY, Pál BERENDI, István BOZÓ, Mihály KÉKESI, Ferenc MACHOS, László PÁL
(I), Tibor PÁL (II). (Coach: Rudolf ILLOVSZKY).
AC Torino: Lido VIERI, Fabrizio POLETTI, Luciano BUZZACCHERA, Giovanni MIALICH,
Luciano TENEGGI, Amilcare FERRETTI, Giampaolo PIACERI, Giorgio FERRINI, Gerald
Archibald (Gerry) HITCHENS (ENG), Marcos Alberto LOCATELLI (ARG), Carlo CRIPPA.
(Coach: Giacinto Delfino ELLENA).
Goals: Vasas SC: 1-0 Ferenc MACHOS (13'), 2-0 Mihály KÉKESI (34'), 3-0 Ferenc
MACHOS (45' penalty), 4-1 László PÁL (73'), 5-1 László PÁL (84').
AC Torino: 3-1 Gianpaolo PIACERI (48').
Referee: Konstantin ZECEVIC (YUG)   Attendance: 30.000

12-06-1963   Stadion Kosevo, Sarajevo:
                FK Zeljeznicar Sarajevo – M.T.K. Budapest   1-1 (0-1)
FK Zeljeznicar Sarajevo: Vasilije RADOVIC, Miljan STAKA, Sulejman KULOVIC,
Vjekoslav KRAJNC, Mahmut KAPIDZIC, Rastislav MATIC, Sefik AZABAGIC, Kasim
KOKOT, Drago SMAJLOVIC (I), Ivica OSIM, Zvonko DUSPARA. (Coach: Vlatko
KONJEVOD).
M.T.K. Budapest: Sándor LANCZKOR, György KESZEI, István JENEI, István NAGY, József
DANSZKY, Tibor PALICSKÓ, Gyula MAJOR, Mihály LACZKÓ, László BÖDÖR, István
KUTI, István SZIMCSÁK (I). (Coach: Imre KOVÁCS).
Goals: FK Zeljeznicar Sarajevo: 1-1 Drago SMAJLOVIC (62').
M.T.K. Budapest: 0-1 József DANSZKY (2').
Referee: Dimitris WLACHOJANIS (AUT)   Attendance: 10.000

19-06-1963   Stadio Comunale, Torino: AC Torino – Vasas SC   2-1 (1-0)
AC Torino: Lido VIERI, Fabrizio POLETTI, Luciano TENEGGI, Roberto ROSATO, Antonio
GERBAUDO, Amilcare FERRETTI, Giancarlo DANOVA, Marcos Alberto LOCATELLI
(ARG), Gerald Archibald (Gerry) HITCHENS (ENG), Joaquim PEIRÓ Lucas (ESP),
Giampaolo PIACERI. (Coach: Giacinto Delfino ELLENA).
Vasas SC: László VARGA, Kálmán IHÁSZ, László SÁROSI, Gyula SAS, Kálmán
MÉSZÖLY, Pál BERENDI, István BOZÓ, Mihály KÉKESI, Ferenc MACHOS, Dezsö
BUNDZSÁK, László PÁL (I). (Coach: Rudolf ILLOVSZKY).
Goals: AC Torino: 1-0 Gerald Archibald (Gerry) HITCHENS (20'), 2-1 Marcos Alberto
LOCATELLI (75').
Vasas SC: 1-1 Antonio GERBAUDO (69' own goal).
Referee: Alojz OBTULOVIC (TCH)

19-06-1963   Népstadion, Budapest: M.T.K. Budapest – FK Zeljeznicar Sarajevo 1-0 (1-0)
M.T.K. Budapest: Sándor LANCZKOR, István JENEI, György KESZEI, Ferenc KOVÁCS
(III), József DANSZKY, Mihály VASAS, Gyula MAJOR, Mihály LACZKÓ, István KUTI,
László BÖDÖR, István SZIMCSÁK (I). (Coach: Imre KOVÁCS).
FK Zeljeznicar Sarajevo: Vasilije RADOVIC, Miljan STAKA, Sulejman KULOVIC,
Vjekoslav KRAJNC, Mahmut KAPIDZIC, Rastislav MATIC, Sefik AZABAGIC, Djuro
SMAJLOVIC (II), Drago SMAJLOVIC (I), Ivica OSIM, Zvonko DUSPARA. (Coach: Vlatko
KONJEVOD).
Goal: M.T.K. Budapest: 1-0 László BÖDÖR (3').
Referee: Cesare JONNI (ITA)   Attendance; 6.000

FINAL

26-06-1963   Népstadion, Budapest: M.T.K. Budapest – Vasas SC 2-1 (1-0)
M.T.K. Budapest: Ferenc KOVALIK, György KESZEI, József DANSZKY, István JENEI,
István NAGY, Ferenc KOVÁCS (III), Mihály LACZKÓ, Mihály VASAS, László BÖDÖR,
István KUTI, István SZIMCSÁK (I). (Coach: Imre KOVÁCS).
Vasas SC: László VARGA, Sándor BAKOS, Dezsö BUNDZSÁK, László SÁROSI, Gyula
SAS, Pál BERENDI, István BOZÓ, Mihály KÉKESI, Ferenc MACHOS, László PÁL (I),
Kálmán IHÁSZ. (Coach: Rudolf ILLOVSZKY).
Goals: M.T.K. Budapest: 1-0 István NAGY (36' penalty), 2-0 István KUTI (62').
Vasas SC: 2-1 Ferenc MACHOS (84').
Referee: Branko CAHUN (YUG)   Attendance: 24.569

03-07-1963   Népstadion, Budapest: Vasas SC – M.T.K. Budapest 1-1 (0-0)
Vasas SC: László VARGA, Kálmán IHÁSZ, Kálmán MÉSZÖLY, László SÁROSI, Gyula
SAS, Pál BERENDI, István BOZÓ, Mihály KÉKESI, Ferenc MACHOS, László PÁL (I),
Tibor PÁL (II). (Coach: Rudolf ILLOVSZKY).
M.T.K. Budapest: Ferenc KOVALIK, György KESZEI, József DANSZKY, István JENEI,
István NAGY, Ferenc KOVÁCS (III), Mihály LACZKÓ, Mihály VASAS, László BÖDÖR,
István KUTI, István SZIMCSÁK (I). (Coach: Imre KOVÁCS).
Goals: Vasas SC: 1-1 Ferenc MACHOS (52').
M.T.K. Budapest: 0-1 István KUTI (49').
Referee: Concetto LO BELLO (ITA)   Attendance: 32.083

*** M.T.K. Budapest won the Cup ***

162

1964

QUARTER-FINALS

03-06-1964   Népstadion, Budapest: Vasas SC – Linzer ASK   3-1 (0-0)
Vasas SC: Antal SZENTMIHÁLYI, Kálmán IHÁSZ, Kálmán MÉSZÖLY, László SÁROSI, Sándor BAKOS, Ferenc FISTER, Tibor PÁL (II), Ferenc MACHOS, Mihály KÉKESI, Lajos PUSKÁS, János FARKAS. (Coach: Gyula NOSZKAY).
Linzer ASK: Helmut KITZMÜLLER, Heribert TRÜBRIG, Helmut LINOSSI, Heinz OBERPARLEITER, Alfred TEINITZER, Gerhard STURMBERGER, Luka LIPOSINOVIC (YUG), Adolf (Dolfi) BLUTSCH, Francisco Carlos Correia Lima "CHICO" (POR), Rudolf SABETZER, Ferdinand ZECHMEISTER. (Coach: Karl SCHLECHTA).
Goals: Vasas SC: 1-1 Ferenc MACHOS (74'), 2-1 Tibor PÁL (80'), 3-1 János FARKAS (86').
Linzer ASK: 0-1 Francisco Carlos Correia Lima "CHICO" (72').
Attendance: 20.000

10-06-1964   Praha: TJ Spartak Praha Sokolovo – M.T.K. Budapest   1-1 (1-0)
TJ Spartak Praha Sokolovo: Anton KRAMERIUS, Milan KOLLÁR, Jirí TICHÝ, Vladimír TÁBORSKÝ, Václav POTMESÍL, Jirí GURA, Bohumil VESELÝ, Ivan MRÁZ, Josef VOJTA, Václav MASEK, Pavel DYBA. (Coach: Václav JEZEK).
M.T.K. Budapest: Ferenc KOVALIK, György KESZEI, József DANSZKY, István JENEI, Mihály VASAS, Ferenc KOVÁCS (III), József TÖRÖK, István KUTI, HORVÁTH, István HALÁPI, László BÖDÖR. (Coach: Imre KOVÁCS).
Goals: TJ Spartak Praha Sokolovo: 1-0 Václav MASEK (12').
M.T.K. Budapest: 1-1 József TÖRÖK (58').
Referee: Paul SCHILLER (AUT)   Attendance: 30.000

10-06-1964   Sarajevo: FK Zeljeznicar Sarajevo – Slovan UNV Bratislava   2-1 (1-0)
FK Zeljeznicar Sarajevo: József TÖRÖK, Miljan STAKA, Vjekoslav KRAJNC, Rastislav MATIC, Dusan JOVANOVIC, Josip ZEMKO, Boris BRACULJ, Mirko GASIC, Drago SMAJLOVIC, Ivan OSIM, Ahmet DIZDAREVIC.
Slovan UNV Bratislava: Viliam SCHROJF, Jozef FILO, Ján POPLUHÁR, Ján SLOSIARIK, Peter MOLNÁR (II), Alexander HORVÁTH, Ludovit CVETLER, Jozef OBERT, Pavol MOLNÁR (I), Jozef ADAMEC, Karol JOKL. (Coach: Leopold STASTNÝ).
Goals: FK Zeljeznicar Sarajevo: 1-0 Drago SMALJOVIC (9'), 2-1 Ahmet DIZDAREVIC (65').
Slovan UNV Bratislava: 1-1 Jozef OBERT (58').
Referee: Lajos HORVÁTH (HUN)   Attendance: 16.000

10-06-1964   Linzer Stadion, Linz: Linzer ASK – Vasas SC   1-1 (1-0)
Linzer ASK: Helmut KITZMÜLLER, Heribert TRÜBRIG, Helmut LINOSSI, Gyula SZABÓ (HUN), Adolf (Dolfi) BLUTSCH, Gerhard STURMBERGER, Luka LIPOSINOVIC (YUG), Francisco Carlos Correia Lima "CHICO" (POR), Hermann FÜRST, Rudolf SABETZER, Johann (Hans) KONDERT. (Coach: Karl SCHLECHTA).
Vasas SC: László VARGA, Károly NAGY, Sándor BAKOS, Kálmán IHÁSZ, Barnabas LIEBHABER, Ferenc FISTER, Imre MATHESZ, Ferenc MACHOS, Mihály KÉKESI, Lajos PUSKÁS, János FARKAS. (Coach: Gyula NOSZKAY).
Goals: Linzer ASK: 1-0 Francisco Carlos Correia Lima "CHICO" (1').
Vasas SC: 1-1 Lajos PUSKÁS (56').
Attendance: 6.500

163

17-06-1964   Stadio Comunale, Bologna: FC Bologna – O.F.K. Beograd   1-0 (0-0)
FC Bologna: Rino RADO, Bruno CAPRA, Edmondo LORENZINI, Vanni TROMBETTA, Marcello TENTORIO, Lorenzo NONINO, Antonio RENNA, Héctor (Ettore) DE MARCO (URU), Alessandro VITALI, Mauro PANTANI, Sidio CORRADI. (Coach: Fulvio BERNARDINI).
O.F.K. Beograd: Stanoje MILORADOVIC, Miroslav MILOVANOVIC, Momcilo GAVRIC, Stojan VUKASINOVIC, Blagomir KRIVOKUCA, Zoran DAKIC, Vojislav DUKIC, SUBOTIC, Srdan CEBINAC, Dragan GUGLETA, Sretan BANOVIC. (Coach: Sava ANTIC).
Goal: FC Bologna: 1-0 Mauro PANTANI (79').
Referee: Dimitris WLACHOJANIS (AUT)

17-06-1964   Bratislava: Slovan UNV Bratislava – FK Zeljezcinar Sarajevo   3-0 (2-0)
Slovan UNV Bratislava: Viliam SCHROJF, Anton URBAN, Ján POPLUHÁR, Ján SLOSIARIK, Alexander HORVÁTH, Peter MOLNÁR (II), Vladimir PISÁRIK, Jozef ADAMEC, Pavol MOLNÁR (I), Karol JOKL, Ludovít CVETLER. (Coach: Leopold STASTNÝ).
FK Zeljeznicar Sarajevo: József TÖRÖK, Miljan STAKA, Vjekoslav KRAJNC, Rastislav MATIC, Enver KAPIDZIC, Josip ZEMKO, Boris BRACULJ, Mirko GASIC, Drago SMAJLOVIC, Ivan OSIM, Zvonko DUSPARA.
Goals: Slovan UNV Bratislava: 1-0 Vladimir PISÁRIK (1'), 2-0 Vladimir PISÁRIK (43'), 3-0 Anton URBAN (70').
Referee: Giuseppe ADAMI (ITA)

17-06-1964   Budapest: M.T.K. Budapest – TJ Spartak Praha Sokolovo   1-3 (0-2)
M.T.K. Budapest: Ferenc KOVALIK, György KESZEI, József DANSZKY, István JENEI, Mihály VASAS, Ferenc KOVÁCS (III), József TÖRÖK, László TAKÁCS, HORVÁTH, István KUTI, László BÖDÖR. (Coach: Béla VOLONTIK).
TJ Spartak Praha Sokolovo: Anton KRAMERIUS, Jirí GURA, Jirí TICHÝ, Vladimír TÁBORSKÝ, Josef VOJTA, Kvetoslav NOVÁK, Bohumil VESELY, Ivan MRÁZ, Tadeás KRAUS, Václav MASEK, Pavel DYBA. (Coach: Václav JEZEK).
Goals: M.T.K. Budapest: 1-3 HORVÁTH (68'), 2-3 Scorer not known (..').
TJ Spartak Praha Sokolovo: 0-1 Václav MASEK (17'), 0-2 Tadeás KRAUS (22'), 0-3 Václav MASEK (57').
Referee: Aleksandar SKORIC (YUG)   Attendance: 5.000

20-06-1964   Boegrad: O.F.K. Beograd – FC Bologna   2-2 (0-0)
O.F.K. Beograd: Stanoje MILORADOVIC, Miroslav MILOVANOVIC, Momcilo GAVRIC, Vojislav DUKIC, Blagomir KRIVOKUCA, Selimir MILOSEVIC, Spasoje SAMARDZIC, Dragan GUGLETA, SUBOTIC, Srdan CEBINAC, Sretan BANOVIC (expulsion 77'). (Coach: Sava ANTIC).
FC Bologna: Rino RADO, Edmondo LORENZINI, Maurizio MAGAGNI, Franco MARINI, Marcello TENTORIO, Lorenzo NONINO, Sidio CORRADI, Héctor (Ettore) DE MARCO (URU), Alessandro VITALI, Mauro PANTANI, Francisco DE MECENAS (BRA). (Coach: Fulvio BERNARDINI).
Goals: O.F.K. Beograd: 1-0 Selimir MILOSEVIC (53'), 2-1 Srdan CEBINAC (78').
FC Bologna: 1-1 Francisco DE MECENAS (72'), 2-2 Sidio CORRADI (85').
Referee: József FÉHÉRVARI (HUN)   Attendance: 8.000

164

24-06-1964   Stadión Tehelné pole, Bratislava:
Slovan UNV Bratislava – Vasas SC 1-1 (1-1)
Slovan UNV Bratislava: Viliam SCHROJF, Anton URBAN, Ján POPLUHÁR, Jozef FILO,
Alexander HORVÁTH, Peter MOLNÁR (II), Vladimír PISÁRIK, Karol JOKL, Pavol
MOLNÁR (I), Jozef ADAMEC, Jan SLOSIARIK. (Coach: Leopold STASTNÝ).
Vasas SC: Antal SZENTMIHÁLYI, Károly NAGY, Kálmán MÉSZÖLY, Kálmán IHÁSZ,
Sándor BAKOS, Ferenc FISTER, István BOZÓ, Ferenc MACHOS, Mihály KÉKESI, Lajos
PUSKÁS, János FARKAS. (Coach: Gyula NOSZKAY).
Goals: Slovan UNV Bratislava: 1-1 Karol JOKL (16').
Vasas SC: 0-1 János FARKAS (14').
Referee: Renzo RIGHETTI (ITA)   Attendance: 22.000

24-06-1964   Stadio Comunale, Bologna:
FC Bologna – TJ Spartak Praha Sokolovo 2-2 (2-1)
FC Bologna: Rino RADO, Edmondo LORENZINI, Marcello TENTORIO, MAGAGEL,
Franco MARINI, Lorenzo NONINO, SidioCORRACI, Alessandro VITALI, PANTANI,
Francisco DE MECENAS, TENNOLI.
TJ Spartak Praha Sokolovo: Anton KRAMERIUS, Jirí GURA, Jirí TICHÝ, Vladimír
TÁBORSKÝ, Josef VOJTA, Kvetoslav NOVÁK, Bohumil VESELY, Ivan MRÁZ, Tadeás
KRAUS, Václav MASEK, Pavel DYBA. (Coach: Václav JEZEK).
Goals: FC Bologna: 1-1 Marcello TENTORIO (30'), 2-1 PANTANI (40').
TJ Spartak Praha Sokolovo: 0-1 SidioCORRACI (10' own goal), 2-2 Marcello TENTORIO
(55' own goal).
Referee: Friedrich (Franz) MAYER (AUT)   Attendance: 4.000

01-07-1964   Népstadion, Budapest: Vasas SC – Slovan UNV Bratislava 1-2 (0-1)
Vasas SC: Antal SZENTMIHÁLYI, Károly NAGY, Kálmán MÉSZÖLY, Kálmán IHÁSZ,
Sándor BAKOS, Ferenc FISTER, János FARKAS, Lajos NELL, Ferenc MACHOS, Lajos
PUSKÁS, Imre MATHESZ. (Coach: Gyula NOSZKAY).
Slovan UNV Bratislava: Viliam SCHROJF, Anton URBAN, Ján POPLUHÁR, Jozef FILO,
Alexander HORVÁTH, Peter MOLNÁR (II), Vladimír PISÁRIK, Jozef TOMANEK, Karol
JOKL, Pavol MOLNÁR (I), Ludovít CVETLER. (Coach: Leopold STASTNÝ).
Goals: Vasas SC: 1-1 Lajos PUSKÁS (57').
Slovan UNV Bratislava: 0-1 Jozef TOMANEK (3'), 1-2 Kálmán MÉSZÖLY (87' *own goal*).
Referee: Gennaro MARCHESE (ITA)   Attendance: 20.000

01-07-1964   Letenský Stadion (Sparty), Praha:
TJ Spartak Praha Sokolovo – FC Bologna 3-0 (0-0)
TJ Spartak Praha Sokolovo: Anton KRAMERIUS, Jirí GURA, Jirí TICHÝ, Vladimír
TÁBORSKÝ, Kvetoslav NOVÁK, Tadeás KRAUS, Bohumil VESELY, Josef VOJTA, Ivan
MRÁZ, Václav MASEK, Pavel DYBA. (Coach: Václav JEZEK).
FC Bologna: Rino RADO, Tazio ROVERSI, Marcello TENTORIO, Edmondo LORENZINI,
Franco MARINI, Lorenzo NONINO, SidioCORRACI, Francisco DE MECENAS, Alessandro
VITALI, PANTANI, TENNOLI
Goals: TJ Spartak Praha Sokolovo: 1-0 Ivan MRAZ (68'), 2-0 Václav MASEK (76'), 3-0
Pavel DYBA (84')
Referee: Alfred HABERFELLNER (AUT)

FINAL

05-08-1964   Stadión Tehelné pole, Bratislava:
Slovan UNV Bratislava – TJ Spartak Praha Sokolovo   0-0
Slovan UNV Bratislava: Viliam SCHROJF, Anton URBAN, Alexander HORVÁTH, Jozef
FILO, Ludovít ZLOCHA, Peter MOLNÁR (II), Ludovít CVETLER, Pavol MOLNÁR (I),
Karol JOKL, Jozef ADAMEC, Viliam HRNCAR. (Coach: Leopold STASTNÝ).
TJ Spartak Praha Sokolovo: Anton KRAMERIUS, Milan KOLLÁR, Jirí TICHÝ, Vladimír
TÁBORSKÝ, Josef VOJTA, Jirí GURA, Jirí HAK, Ivan MRÁZ, Tadeás KRAUS, Václav
MASEK, Pavel DYBA. (Coach: Václav JEZEK).
Referee: Zdenek VALES (TCH)   Attendance: 30.000

02 -09-1964   Letenský Stadion (Sparty), Praha:
TJ Spartak Praha Sokolovo – Slovan UNV Bratislava   2-0 (1-0)
TJ Spartak Praha Sokolovo: Anton KRAMERIUS, Milan KOLLÁR, Jirí TICHÝ, Vladimír
TÁBORSKÝ, Josef VOJTA, Karel STEININGEL, Pavel DYBA, Ivan MRÁZ, Tadeás
KRAUS, Václav MASEK, Václav VRÁNA. (Coach: Václav JEZEK).
Slovan UNV Bratislava: Viliam SCHROJF, Anton URBAN, Ján POPLUHÁR, Jozef FILO,
Ludovít ZLOCHA, Alexander HORVÁTH, Peter MOLNÁR (II), Karol JOKL, Ivan
HRDLICKA, Viliam HRNCAR, Ludovít CVETLER. (Coach: Leopold STASTNÝ).
Goals: TJ Spartak Praha Sokolovo: 1-0 Václav MASEK (12'), 2-0 Václav MASEK (53').
Referee: Alojz OBTULOVIC (TCH)   Attendance: 30.000

*** TJ Spartak Praha Sokolovo won the Cup ***

1965

08-05-1965   Sarajevo: FK Sarajevo – Vasas SC   1-2
FK Sarajevo: Refik MUFTIC, Mirsad FAZLAGIC, Ibrahim BIOGRADLIC, Milenko BAJIC, Fahrudin PRLJACA, Aleksandar RISTIC, Svetozar VUJOVIC, Sreten SILJKUT, SEHOVIC, Dzemaludim MUSOVIC, Stjepan BLAZEVIC.
Vasas SC: László VARGA, Kálmán IHÁSZ, Kálmán MÉSZÖLY, Pál BERENDI, László SÁROSI, Mihály KÉKESI, Ferenc FISTER, Dezsö MOLNÁR, Lajos PUSKÁS, János FARKAS, Imre MATHESZ. (Coach: Rudolf ILLOVSZKY).
Goals: FK Sarajevo: Aleksandar RISTIC.
Vasas SC: Lajos PUSKÁS, János FARKAS.

26-05-1965   Népstadion, Budapest: Vasas SC – FK Sarajevo   2-0
Vasas SC: László VARGA, Sándor BAKOS, Kálmán MÉSZÖLY, Pál BERENDI, Kálmán IHÁSZ, Imre MATHESZ, Ferenc FISTER, Dezsö MOLNÁR, János FARKAS, Lajos PUSKÁS, Tibor PÁL (II). (Coach: Rudolf ILLOVSZKY).
FK Sarajevo: Ibrahim SIRCO, Milenko BAJIC, Aleksandar RISTIC, Mirsad FAZLAGIC, Ibrahim BIOGRADLIC, Svetozar VUJOVIC, Dzemaludim MUSOVIC, Sreten SILJKUT, SEHOVIC, Fahrudin PRLJACA, Stjepan BLAZEVIC.
Goals: Vasas SC: János FARKAS, Tibor PÁL.

SEMI-FINALS

23-06-1965   Praterstadion, Wien: Vasas SC – TJ Sparta CKD Praha   5-4 (3-2)
Vasas SC: László VARGA, Sándor BAKOS, Kálmán MÉSZÖLY, Kálmán IHÁSZ, Imre MATHESZ, Pál BERENDI, Dezsö MOLNÁR, Lajos PUSKÁS, János FARKAS, Ferenc FISTER, Tibor PÁL (II). (Coach: Rudolf ILLOVSZKY).
TJ Spartak CKD Praha: Anton KRAMERIUS, Milan KOLLÁR, Jirí TICHÝ, Vladimír TÁBORSKÝ, Vladimír KOS, Pavel DYBA, Tomás POSPÍCHAL, Ivan MRÁZ, Andrej KVASNÁK, Václav MASEK, Václav VRÁNA. (Coach: Václav JEZEK).
Goals: Vasas SC: 1-0 Ferenc FISTER (2'), 2-0 Lajos PUSKÁS (8'), 3-1 Lajos PUSKÁS (35'), 4-4 Dezsö MOLNÁR (84'), 5-4 Vladimír TÁBORSKÝ (109' own goal).
TJ Sparta CKD Praha: 2-1 Václav MASEK (18'), 3-2 Andrej KVASNÁK (44'), 3-3 Václav VRÁNA (67'), 3-4 Ivan MRÁZ (77').
Referee: Eduard BABAUCZEK (AUT)   Attendance: 8.000

(After extra time)

23-06-1965   Praterstadion, Wien: SK Rapid Wien – AC Fiorentina   0-3 (0-3)
SK Rapid Wien: Roman PICHLER, Paul HALLA, Wilhelm ZAGLITSCH, Josef HÖLTL,
Franz HASIL, Walter SKOCIK, Toni FRITSCH, Franz WOLNY, Rudolf NUSKE, Rudolf
FLÖGEL, Branko MILANOVIC (YUG). (Coach: Robert KÖRNER).
AC Fiorentina: Alfredo PAOLICCHI, Egidio GUARNACCI, Giuseppe BRIZI, Sergio
CASTELLETTI, Giovan Battista PIROVANO, Rino MARCHESI, Kurt Roland HAMRIN
(SWE), Mario BERTINI, Paolo NUTI, Renato BENAGLIA, Juan Carlos MORRONE (ARG).
(Coach: Giuseppe CHIAPPELLA).
Goals: AC Fiorentina: 0-1 Mario BERTINI (35'), 0-2 Kurt Roland HAMRIN (43'), 0-3 Mario
BERTINI (45').
Referee: Aleksandar SKORIC (YUG)   Attendance: 10.000

3rd PLACE MATCH

26-06-1965   Praterstadion, Wien: SK Rapid Wien – TJ Sparta CKD Praha   0-2 (0-1)
SK Rapid Wien: Andrija VERES (YUG), Paul HALLA, Wilhelm ZAGLITSCH, Josef
HÖLTL, Ewald ULLMANN, Walter SKOCIK, Franz WOLNY, Walter SEITL, Leopold
GRAUSAM, Franz HASIL Rudolf FLÖGEL. (Coach: Robert KÖRNER).
TJ Spartak CKD Praha: Anton KRAMERIUS, Jirí GURA, Jirí TICHÝ, Vladimír
TÁBORSKÝ, Josef VOJTA, Tomás POSPÍCHAL, Pavel DYBA, Ivan MRÁZ, Andrej
KVASNÁK, Václav MASEK, Václav VRÁNA. (Coach: Václav JEZEK).
Goals: TJ Sparta CKD Praha: 0-1 Václav MASEK (44'), 0-2 Václav VRÁNA (89').
Referee: Aleksandar SKORIC (YUG)   Attendance: 3.500

FINAL

26-06-1965   Praterstadion, Wien: Vasas SC – AC Fiorentina   1-0 (0-0)
Vasas SC: László VARGA, Sándor BAKOS, Kálmán MÉSZÖLY, Kálmán IHÁSZ, Imre
MATHESZ, Pál BERENDI, Dezsö MOLNÁR, Lajos PUSKÁS, János FARKAS, Ferenc
FISTER, Tibor PÁL (II). (Coach: Rudolf ILLOVSZKY).
AC Fiorentina: Alfredo PAOLICCHI, Egidio GUARNACCI, Giuseppe BRIZI, Sergio
CASTELLETTI, Giovan Battista PIROVANO, Rino MARCHESI, Kurt Roland HAMRIN
(SWE), Mario BERTINI, Paolo NUTI, Renato BENAGLIA, Juan Carlos MORRONE (ARG).
(Coach: Giuseppe CHIAPPELLA).
Goal: Vasas SC: 1-0 Kálmán MÉSZÖLY (85' penalty).
Referee: Paul SCHILLER (AUT)   Attendance: 5.000

*** Vasas SC won the Cup ***

1966

02-03-1966   Sarajevo: FK Sarajevo – Wiener Sportklub 2-1 (1-0)
FK Sarajevo: Refik MUFTIC, Mirsad FAZLAGIC, Milenko BAJIC, Svetozar VUJOVIC, Ibraham (Ibro) BIOGRADLIC, Aleksandar RISTIC, Bosko PRODANOVIC, Fahrudin PRLJACA, Dzemaludin MUSOVIC, Sreten SILJKUT, Stjepan BLAZEVIC.
Wiener Sportklub: Rudolf SZANWALD, Johann WINDISCH (expulsion 30'), Karl WEBORA, Wilhelm KAINRATH, Adolf BLUTSCH, Norbert HOF (II), Helmut METZLER, Adolf KNOLL, Wolfgang GAYER (FRG), Friedrich RAFREIDER, Johann HÖRMAYER. (Coach: Karl SCHLECHTA).
Goals: FK Sarajevo: 1-0 Dzemaludin MUSOVIC (13'), 2-1 Bosko PRODANOVIC (80').
Wiener Sportklub: 1-1 Helmut METZLER (52').
Referee: Name not known (TCH)   Attendance: 10.000

23-03-1966   Budapest: M.T.K. Budapest – SK Slavia Praha 1-0 (1-0)
M.T.K. Budapest: Sándor LANCZKOR, István JENEI, Csaba CSETÉNTYI, VARGA, A.NAGY, Lajos DUNAI, László TAKÁCS, Mihály LACZKÓ, Lajos LAKINGER, István KUTI, E.NAGY. (Coach: Ferenc KOVÁCS).
SK Slavia Praha: Josef LEDECKY, BARAN, Jirí HILDEBRANDT, Bohumil SMOLIK, Bedrich TESAR, Karel NEPOMUCKÝ, Frantisek VESELÝ, Josef KADRABA, Frantisek SINDELÁR, Josef PÍSA, Frantisek ULDRYCH. (Coach: Frantisek IPSER)
Goal: M.T.K. Budapest: 1-0 Lajos LAKINGER (28').
Referee: Francesco FRANCESCON (ITA)   Attendance: 8.000

23-03-1966   Admiraplatz, Wien: Admira-Energie Wien – TJ Jednota Trencin 2-1 (0-0)
Admira-Energie Wien: Dragomir VUKICEVIC (YUG), Michael BREIBERT, Walter STAMM, Emmerich SOMMER, Bohumil HRUSKA, Paul KOZLICEK, Anton HERZOG, Peter REITER, Felix LATZKE, Günter KALTENBRUNNER, Johann SZAUER. (Coach: Johann (Hans) PESSER).
TJ Jednota Trencin: Tibor RIHOSEK, Anton POKORNÝ, Stefan HOJSÍK, Miroslav CEMEZ, Vladimír MOJZÍS, Pavol BENCZ, Milan NAVRÁTIL, Peter ZITNANSKÝ, Rudolf SEFCIK, Vojtech MASNÝ, Ludovit KOIS. (Coach: Michal VICAN).
Goals: Admira-Energie Wien: 1-0 Bohumil HRUSKA (48'), 2-1 Günter KALTENBRUNNER (87').
TJ Jednota Trencin: 1-1 Stefan HOJSÍK (60').
Referee: Zivko BAJIC (YUG)   Attendance: 2.500

23-03-1966   Beograd: FK Crvena Zvezda Beograd – AC Napoli 2-0 (0-0)
FK Crvena Zvezda Beograd: Srboljub KRIVOKUCA, Aleksandr STOJANOVIC, Zivorad JEVTIC, Branimir VRATNJAN, Vladimir DURKOVIC, Dejan BEKIC, Dusan ANDRIC, Vojislav MELIC, Stevan OSTOJIC, Borivoje (Bora) KOSTIC, Dragan DZAJIC. (Coach: Rajko MITIC).
AC Napoli: Pacifico CUMAN, Pietro ADORNI, Mauro GATTI, Amedeo STENTI, Mario ZURLINI, Antonio GIRARDO, Giovanni BOLZONI, Vincenzo MONTEFUSCO, Guido POSTIGLIONE, Jarbas Faustinho CANÈ (BRA), Juan Carlos TACCHI (ARG). (Coach: Bruno PESAOLA (ARG)).
Goals: FK Crvena Zvezda Beograd: 1-0 Stevan OSTOJIC (61'), 2-0 Bran. VRATNJAN (82').
Referee: Josef KRNÁVEK (TCH)

30-03-1966   Praha: SK Slavia Praha – M.T.K. Budapest 2-0 (2-0)
SK Slavia Praha: Josef LEDECKY, Jan LÁLA, Jirí HILDEBRANDT, Bohumil SMOLIK,
Bedrich TESAR, Karel NEPOMUCKÝ, Frantisek VESELÝ, Josef KADRABA, Frantisek
SINDELÁR, Josef PÍSA, Frantisek ULDRYCH. (Coach: Frantisek IPSER)
M.T.K. Budapest: Sándor LANCZKOR, György KESZEI, Csaba CSETÉNTYI (expulsion
87'), VARGA, István JENEI, Lajos DUNAI, László TAKÁCS, Mihály LACZKÓ, Lajos
LAKINGER (expulsion 88'), István KUTI, József TÖRÖK. (Coach: Ferenc KOVÁCS).
Goals: SK Slavia Praha: 1-0 Josef PÍSA (35'), 2-0 Josef PÍSA (40').
Attendance: 15.000

06-04-1966   Trencin: TJ Jednota Trencin – Admira-Energie Wien 4-0 (2-0)
TJ Jednota Trencin: Tibor RIHOSEK, Vladimír MOJZÍS, Stefan HOJSÍK, Miroslav CEMEZ,
Milan HOCHEL, Rudolf SEFCIK, Milan NAVRÁTIL, Pavol BENCZ, Peter ZITNANSKÝ,
Vojtech MASNÝ, Ludovit KOIS. (Coach: Michal VICAN).
Admira-Energie Wien: Dragomir VUKICEVIC (YUG), Michael BREIBERT, Josef WAHL,
Emmerich SOMMER, Bohumil HRUSKA, Paul KOZLICEK, Anton HERZOG, Felix
LATZKE, Werner BEDERNIK, Günter KALTENBRUNNER, Karl SKERLAN. (Coach:
Johann (Hans) PESSER).
Goals: TJ Jednota Trencin: 1-0 Pavol BENCZ (31'), 2-0 Rudolf SEFCIK (43'), 3-0 Vojtech
MASNÝ (69'), 4-0 Stefan HOJSÍK (74' penalty).
Referee: György VADAS (HUN)   Attendance: 4.500

06-04-1966   Sportklubplatz, Wien: Wiener Sportklub – FK Sarajevo 3-0 (0-0)
Wiener Sportklub: Rudolf SZANWALD, Wilhelm KAINRATH, Adolf (Dolfi) BLUTSCH,
Rudolf STARK, Norbert HOF (II), Adolf KNOLL, Peter SCHMIDT, Wolfgang GAYER
(FRG), Erich HOF (I), Friedrich RAFREIDER, Helmut METZLER. (Coach: Karl
SCHLECHTA).
FK Sarajevo: Refik MUFTIC, Mirsad FAZLAGIC, Svetozar VUJOVIC, Ibraham (Ibro)
BIOGRADLIC, Milenko BAJIC, Aleksandar RISTIC, Bosko PRODANOVIC, Dzemaludin
MUSOVIC, Asim FERHATOVIC, Sreten SILJKUT, Stjepan BLAZEVIC.
Goals: Wiener Sportklub: 1-0 Friedrich RAFREIDER (53'), 2-0 Wolfgang GAYER (60'), 3-0
Friedrich RAFREIDER (83').
Referee: Gusztav BIRCSAK (HUN)   Attendance: 6.000

14-04-1966   Stadio San Paolo, Napoli: AC Napoli – FK Crvena Zvezda Beograd 2-1 (1-0)
AC Napoli: Claudio BANDONI, Pietro ADORNI, Stelio NARDIN, Amedeo STENTI, Dino
PANZANATO, Vincenzo MONTEFUSCO, Jarbas Faustinho CANÈ (BRA), Antonio
JULIANO, José João ALTAFINI, Enrique Omar SÍVORI, Juan Carlos TACCHI (ARG).
(Coach: Bruno PESAOLA (ARG)).
FK Crvena Zvezda Beograd: Srboljub KRIVOKUCA, Vladimir DURKOVIC, Zivorad
JEVTIC, Vojislav MELIC, Milan COP, Dejan BEKIC, Dragan DZAJIC, Stevan OSTOJIC,
Selimir MILOSEVIC (expulsion 34'), Dragoslav SEKULARAC, Borivoje (Bora) KOSTIC.
(Coach: Rajko MITIC).
Goals: AC Napoli: 1-0 Antonio JULIANO (44'), 2-1 José João ALTAFINI (82').
FK Crvena Zvezda Beograd: 1-1 Stevan OSTOJIC (78').
Referee: Friedrich (Franz) MAYER (AUT)   Attendance: 30.000

170

04-05-1966   Praha: TJ Slavia Praha – Wiener Sportklub 4-1 (2-1)
SK Slavia Praha: Josef LEDECKY, Jan LÁLA, Jirí HILDEBRANDT, Karel KNESL, Bohumil
SMOLIK, Frantisek SINDELÁR, Karel NEPOMUCKÝ, Frantisek VESELÝ, Josef
KADRABA, Josef PÍSA, Bedrich TESAR. (Coach: Frantisek IPSER).
Wiener Sportklub: Rudolf SZANWALD, Wilhelm KAINRATH, Karl WEBORA, Johann
WINDISCH, Rudolf STARK, Adolf (Dolfi) BLUTSCH, Adolf KNOLL, Friedrich
RAFREIDER, Peter SCHMIDT, Wolfgang GAYER (FRG), Johann HÖRMAYER. (Coach:
Karl SCHLECHTA).
Goals: TJ Slavia Praha: 1-1 Josef KADRABA (11'), 2-1 Josef KADRABA (18'), 3-1 Frantisek
VESELÝ (56'), 4-1 Frantisek VESELÝ (61').
Wiener Sportklub: 0-1 Peter SCHMIDT (6').
Referee: Bozidar BOTIC (YUG)   Attendance: 10.000

11-05-1966   Trencin: TJ Jednota Trencin – FK Crvena Zvezda Beograd 3-1 (2-0)
TJ Jednota Trencin: Tibor RIHOSEK, Anton POKORNÝ, Stefan HOJSÍK, Miroslav CEMEZ,
Vladimír MOJZÍS, Milan HOCHEL, Milan NAVRÁTIL, Pavol BENCZ, Dusan BARTOVIC,
Vojtech MASNÝ, Ludovít KOIS. (Coach: Michal VICAN).
FK Crvena Zvezda Beograd: Ratomir DUJKOVIC (89' Srboljub KRIVOKUCA), Vladimir
DURKOVIC, Milan COP, Zivorad JEVTIC, Vojislav MELIC, Dejan BEKIC, Dragan
DZAJIC, Stevan OSTOJIC, Veljko ALEKSIC, Dragoslav SEKULARAC, Borivoje (Bora)
KOSTIC. (Coach: Rajko MITIC).
Goals: TJ Jednota Trencin: 1-0 Vladimír MOJZÍS (3'), 2-0 Vojtech MASNÝ (43'), 3-1 Pavol
BENCZ (90').
FK Crvena Zvezda Beograd: 2-1 Dragan DZAJIC (55').
Referee: Gyula GERE (HUN)   Attendance: 4.000

11-05-1966   Sportklubplatz, Wien: Wiener Sportklub – TJ Slavia Praha 5-1 (2-1)
Wiener Sportklub: Rudolf SZANWALD, Wilhelm KAINRATH, Karl WEBORA, Norbert
HOF (II), Adolf KNOLL, Adolf (Dolfi) BLUTSCH, Friedrich RAFREIDER, Erich HOF (I),
Peter SCHMIDT, Wolfgang GAYER (FRG)R, Johann HÖRMAYER. (Coach: Karl
SCHLECHTA).
SK Slavia Praha: Josef LEDECKY, Jan LÁLA, Jirí HILDEBRANDT, Bohumil SMOLIK,
Karel KNESL, Karel NEPOMUCKÝ, Frantisek VESELÝ, Josef KADRABA, Frantisek
SINDELÁR, Josef PÍSA, Bedrich TESAR. (Coach: Frantisek IPSER).
Goals: Wiener Sportklub: 1-0 Adolf (Dolfi) BLUTSCH (10'), 2-0 Erich HOF (28'), 3-1
Friedrich RAFREIDER (72'), 4-1 Erich HOF (75'), 5-1 Friedrich RAFREIDER (83').
TJ Slavia Praha: 2-1 Bedrich TESAR (30').
Referee: Bruno DE MARCHI (ITA)   Attendance: 3.000

17-05-1966   Beograd: FK Crvena Zvezda Beograd – TJ Jednota Trencin 0-1 (0-0)
FK Crvena Zvezda Beograd: Srboljub KRIVOKUCA, Vladimir DURKOVIC, Zivorad
JEVTIC, Vojislav MELIC, Milan COP, Dejan BEKIC, Dragan DZAJIC, Stevan OSTOJIC,
Veljko ALEKSIC, Jovan (Kula) ACIMOVIC, Borivoje (Bora) KOSTIC. (Coach: Rajko
MITIC).
TJ Jednota Trencin: Tibor RIHOSEK, Anton POKORNÝ, Stefan HOJSÍK, Miroslav CEMEZ,
Vladimír MOJZÍS, Milan HOCHEL, Milan NAVRÁTIL, Vojtech MASNÝ, Pavol BENCZ,
Dusan BARTOVIC, Ludovit KOIS. (Coach: Michal VICAN).
Goal: TJ Jednota Trencin: 0-1 Vojtech MASNÝ (52').
Referee: Eduard BABAUCZEK (AUT)   Attendance: 30.000

SEMI-FINALS

15-06-1966   Stadio Comunale, Livorno: TJ Jednota Trencin – Vasas SC 1-0 (0-0)
TJ Jednota Trencin: Tibor RIHOSEK, Anton POKORNY, Stefan HOJSIK, Miroslav CEMEZ, Ferdinand SCHWARZ, Vladimír MOJZÍS (expulsion 89'), Milan NAVRÁTIL, Pavol BENCZ, Dusan BARTOVIC, Rudolf SEFCIK, Ludovit KOIS. (Coach: Michal VICAN).
Vasas SC: István KENDERESI, Sándor BAKOS, Gusztáv SZEPESI, Pál BERENDI, Kálmán IHÁSZ, Mihály KÉKESI, Tibor PÁL (II), Dezsö MOLNÁR, Lajos PUSKÁS, István KORSÓS, László KALMÁR.
Goal: TJ Jednota Trencin: 1-0 Milan NAVRATIL (48').
Referee: Fabio MONTI (ITA)   Attendance: 2.000

15-06-1966   Firenze: AC Fiorentina – Wiener Sportklub 4-2 (3-0)
AC Fiorentina: Alfredo PAOLICHI, Bernardo ROGORA, Ugo FERRANTE, Rino MARCHESI, Giuseppe BRIZI, Giovan Battista PIROVANO, Kurt Roland HAMRIN (SWE), Claudio MERLO, Mario BRUGNERA, Giancarlo DE SISTI, Luciano CHIARUGI. (Coach: Giuseppe CHIAPPELLA).
Wiener Sportklub: Rudolf SZANWALD, Johann WINDISCH, Karl WEBORA, Anton Hans Jörg LINHART, Adolf (Dolfi) BLUTSCH, Adolf KNOLL, Helmut METZLER, Erich HOF (I), Peter SCHMIDT, Friedrich RAFREIDER, Johann HÖRMAYER. (Coach: Karl SCHLECHTA).
Goals: AC Fiorentina: 1-0 WINDISCH (23' own goal), 2-0 BRUGNERA (27'), 3-0 Kurt Roland HAMRIN (35' penalty), 4-0 BRUGNERA (54').
Wiener Sportklub: 4-1 Erich HOF (56'), 4-2 Erich HOF (59').
Referee: Stjepan VARAZDINEC (YUG)   Attendance: 8.000

3rd PLACE MATCH

18-06-1966   Arena Garibaldi, Pisa: Vasas SC – Wiener Sportklub 4-3 (4-0)
Vasas SC: István KENDERESI, Sándor BAKOS, Kálmán IHÁSZ, Pál BERENDI, László SÁROSI, Gusztáv SZEPESI, Tibor PÁL (II), Dezsö MOLNÁR, Lajos PUSKÁS, László KALMÁR, István KORSÓS. (Coach: Lajos CSORDÁS).
Wiener Sportklub: Rudolf SZANWALD, Adolf (Dolfi) BLUTSCH, Karl WEBORA, Anton Hans Jörg LINHART, Johann WINDISCH, Adolf KNOLL, Friedrich RAFREIDER, Helmut WEISS, Erich HOF (I), Peter SCHMIDT, Johann HÖRMAYER. (Coach: Karl SCHLECHTA).
Goals: Vasas SC: 1-0 Dezsö MOLNÁR (19'), 2-0 Lajos PUSKÁS (23'), 3-0 Lajos PUSKÁS (35'), 4-0 László SÁROSI (41').
Wiener Sportklub: 4-1 Helmut WEISS (52'), 4-2 Friedrich RAFREIDER (53'), 4-3 Karl WEBORA (59').
Attendance: 3.000

FINAL

19-06-1966   Firenze: AC Fiorentina – TJ Jednota Trencin   1-0 (0-0)
AC Fiorentina: Alfredo PAOLICHI, Bernardo ROGORA, Marcello DIOMEDI, Rino
MARCHESI, Piero GONFIANTINI, Giovan Battista PIROVANO, Kurt Roland HAMRIN
(SWE), Roberto VIERI, Mario BRUGNERA, Giancarlo DE SISTI, Luciano CHIARUGI.
(Coach: Giuseppe CHIAPPELLA).
TJ Jednota Trencin: Tibor RIHOSEK, Anton POKORNÝ, Stefan HOJSÍK, Miroslav CEMEZ,
Milan HOCHEL, Ferdinand SCHWARZ, Milan NAVRÁTIL, Pavol BENCZ, Dusan
BARTOVIC, Rudolf SEFCIK, Ludovít KOIS. (Coach: Michal VICAN).
Goal: AC Fiorentina:1-0 Mario BRUGNERA (77').
Referee: Konstantin ZECEVIC (YUG)   Attendance: 15.000

*** AC Fiorentina won the Cup ***

1966-1967

FIRST ROUND

09-11-1966   Stadio Flaminio, Roma:
               SS Lazio Roma – FK Crvena Zvezda Beograd   3-0 (1-0)
SS Lazio Roma: Valerio CEI, Diego ZANETTI, Sergio CASTELLETI, Aldo ANZUINI,
Pierluigi PAGNI, Paolo CAROSI, Enrico BURLANDO, Romano BAGATTI, Can BARTU
(TUR), Juan Carlos MORRONE (ARG), Vito D'AMATO. (Coach: Maino NERI).
FK Crvena Zvezda Beograd: Dragan RACIC, Sava KARAPANDZIC, Zivorad JEVTIC,
Vojislav MELIC, Aleksandar MARKOVIC, Dejan BEKIC, Branko KLENKOVSKI, Jovan
(Kula) ACIMOVIC, Vojin LAZAREVIC, Trifun MIHAJLOVIC, Selimir MILOSEVIC.
(Coach: Miljan MILJANIC).
Goals: SS Lazio Roma: 1-0 Aleksandar MARKOVIC (39' *own goal*), 2-0 Romano BAGATTI
(70'), 3-0 Romano BAGATTI (76').
Referee: Radoslav FIALA (TCH)   Attendance: 10.000

09-11-1966   Latorca utca, Budapest:
               Budapesti Honvéd SE – TJ Spartak TAZ Trnava   1-1 (0-1)
Budapesti Honvéd SE: István ERDÖSI, József TAJTI, László MAROSI, István VÁGI, Gyula
TÓTH, Ferenc SIPOS, György NAGY, Antal NAGY, Kálmán TÓTH, Imre KOMORA,
Sándor KATONA. (Coach: József BOZSIK).
TJ Spartak TAZ Trnava: Josef GERYK, Karol DOBIÁS, Jaroslav KRAVÁRIK, Stanislav
JARÁBEK, Vladimír HAGARA, Anton HRUSECKÝ, Ladislav KUNA, Adam FARKAS,
Valerián SVEC, Jozef ADAMEC, Alojz FANDEL. (Coach: Anton MALATINSKÝ).
Goals: Budapesti Honvéd SE: 1-1 Ferenc SIPOS (54').
TJ Spartak TAZ Trnava: 0-1 Adam FARKAS (14').
Referee: TAUSIC (Nationality possibly YUG)   Attendance: 14.000

09-11-1966   Cagliari: US Cagliari – FK Sarajevo   2-1 (2-1)
US Cagliari: Adriano REGINATO, Mario MARTIRADONNA, Giuseppe LONGONI,
Pierluigi CERA, Raffaello VESCOVI, Miguel Ángel LONGO (ARG), Claudio Olinto de
Carvalho NENÉ (BRA), Bruno VISENTIN, Roberto BONINSEGNA, Ricciotti GREATTI,
Luigi RIVA. (Coach: Manlio SCOPIGNO).
FK Sarajevo: Ibrahim SIRCO, Mirsad FAZLAGIC, Milenko BAJIC, Sead JESENKOVIC,
Ibrahim (Ibro) BIOGRADLIC, Fuad MUZUROVIC, Bosko PRODANOVIC, Sreten
SILJKUT, Vahidin MUSEMIC, Fahrudin PRLJACA, Bosko ANTIC. (Coach: Miroslav
(Meho) BROZOVIC).
Goals: US Cagliari: 1-0 Luigi RIVA (..'), 2-0 Ricciotti GREATTI (..').
FK Sarajevo: 2-1 Miguel Ángel LONGO (..' *own goal*).
Referee: István ZSOLT (HUN)   Attendance:

174

16-11-1966   Slavia-stadion, Praha; SK Slavia Praha – FK Austria Wien   1-2 (1-0)
SK Slavia Praha: Josef LEDECKY, PRIKRYL, Bedrich TESAR, Jiri HILDEBRANDT,
Bohumil SMOLÍK, Frantisek MORÁVEK, Karel NEPOMUCKÝ, Frantisek VESELÝ, Josef
KADRABA, Václav BOUSKA, Miroslav ZIEGLER. (Coach: Frantisek HAVRÁNEK).
FK Austria Wien: Arkoc ÖZCAN (TUR), Heinz NOWY, Johann FRANK, Karl FRÖHLICH,
Heinz BINDER, Alfons DIRNBERGER, Horst HIRNSCHRODT, Walter HIESEL, Thomas
PARITS, Johann GEYER, Ernst FIALA. (Coach: Ernst OCWIRK).
Goals: SK Slavia Praha: 1-0 Miroslav ZIEGLER (39').
FK Austria Wien: 1-1 Thomas PARITS (72'), 1-2 Ernst FIALA (80').
Referee: Alessandro D'AGOSTINI (ITA)   Attendance: 10.000

16-11-1966   Hohe Warte, Wien: First Vienna FC – AC Fiorentina   4-3 (2-2)
First Vienna FC: Dr.Günther PAULITSCH, Hellmuth LIENER, Giuseppe Francesco Carlo
KOSCHIER, Friedrich KREMSER, Rudolf CEYKA, Otto KLARL, Heinz MARIK, Ivan
LIPOSINOVIC (YUG), Horst NEMEC, Erhard WIEGER, Franz WEIDINGER. (Coach:
Alfred KÖRNER).
AC Fiorentina: Enrico ALBERTOSI, Giovan Battista PIROVANO, Ugo FERRANTE,
Marcello DIOMEDI, Mario BERTINI, Piero LENZI, Kurt Roland HAMRIN (SWE), Claudio
MERLO, Mario BRUGNERA, Giancarlo DE SISTI, Giuseppe COSMA.
Goals: First Vienna FC: 1-0 Horst NEMEC (21'), 2-2 Horst NEMEC (37' penalty), 3-2 Franz
WEIDINGER (66'), 4-3 Ugo FERRANTE (85' own goal).
AC Fiorentina: 1-1 Mario BRUGNERA (24'), 1-2 Giuseppe COSMA (29'), 3-3 Kurt Roland
HAMRIN (78').
Referee: Gyula GERE (HUN)   Attendance: 3.000

16-11-1966   Stadión Spartak, Trnava:
               TJ Spartak TAZ Trnava – Budapesti Honvéd SE   4-0 (2-0)
TJ Spartak TAZ Trnava: Josef GERYK, Karol DOBIAS, Kamil MAJERNIK, Stanislav
JARÁBEK, Vladimír HAGARA, Anton HRUSECKÝ, Ladislav KUNA, Adam FARKAS,
Valerián SVEC, Jozef ADAMEC, Alojz FANDEL. (Coach: Anton MALATINSKÝ).
Budapesti Honvéd SE: István ERDÖSI, József TAJTI, László MAROSI, István VÁGI, Antal
TUSSINGER, Ferenc SIPOS, Antal NAGY, György NAGY, Kálmán TÓTH, Imre KOMORA,
Sándor KATONA. (Coach: József BOZSIK).
Goals: TJ Spartak TAZ Trnava: 1-0 Jozef ADAMEC (10'), 2-0 László MAROSI (40' own
goal), 3-0 Jozef ADAMEC (50' penalty), 4-0 Jozef ADAMEC (59').
Referee: Dimitris WLACHOJANIS (AUT)   Attendance: 8.000

23-11-1966   Zagreb: NK Dinamo Zagreb – AC Milan   1-0 (0-0)
NK Dinamo Zagreb: Zlatko SKORIC, Rudolf CVEK, Mirko BRAUN, Zlatko MESIC, Hrvoje
JUKIC, Filip BLASKOVIC, Marijan NOVAK, Branko GRACANIN, Slaven ZAMBATA,
Josip GUCMIRTL, Krasnodar RORA. (Coach: Branislav (Branko) ZEBEC).
AC Milan: Dario BARLUZZI, Bruno BACCHETTA, Karl Heinz SCHNELLINGER (FRG),
Bruno BAVENI, Nello SANTIN, Sergio MADDÈ, Bruno MORA, Gianni RIVERA, Ángelo
Benedicto Miguel SORMANI (BRA), AMARILDO Tavares da Silveira (BRA), Giuliano
FORTUNATO. (Coach: Arturo SILVESTRI).
Goal: NK Dinamo Zagreb: 1-0 Slaven ZAMBATA (54').
Referee: SEP (HUN)

23-11-1966   Sarajevo: FK Sarajevo – US Cagliari   3-1 (1-0)
FK Sarajevo: Ibrahim SIRCO, Mirsad FAZLAGIC, Milenko BAJIC, Sead JESENKOVIC,
Ibrahim (Ibro) BIOGRADLIC, Fuad MUZUROVIC, Bosko PRODANOVIC, Sreten
SILJKUT, Vahidin MUSEMIC, Fahrudin PRLJACA, Bosko ANTIC. (Coach: Miroslav
(Meho) BROZOVIC).
US Cagliari: Adriano REGINATO, Mario MARTIRADONNA, Giuseppe LONGONI, Sandro
TIBERI, Raffaello VESCOVI, Miguel Ángel LONGO (ARG), Claudio Olinto de Carvalho
NENÉ (BRA), Pierluigi CERA, Roberto BONINSEGNA, Ricciotti GREATTI, Bruno
VISENTIN. (Coach: Manlio SCOPIGNO).
Goals: FK Sarajevo: 1-0 Vahidin MUSEMIC (24'), 2-1 Fahrudin PRLJACA (69'), 3-1 Bosko
PRODANOVIC (82').
US Cagliari: 1-1 Ricciotti GREATTI (68').
Referee: Friedrich (Franz) MAYER (AUT)   Attendance: 7.000

23-11-1966   Wacker-Platz, Wien: FK Austria Wien – SK Slavia Praha   2-0 (2-0)
FK Austria Wien: Arkoc ÖZCAN (TUR) (46' Erich SCHREITL), Heinz NOWY, Johann
FRANK, Karl FRÖHLICH, Heinz BINDER, Alfons DIRNBERGER, Horst HIRNSCHRODT,
Josef HICKERSBERGER, Thomas PARITS, Johann GEYER, Karl KODAT. (Coach: Ernst
OCWIRK).
SK Slavia Praha: Josef LEDECKY, Jan LÁLA, Jirí HILDEBRANDT, Bohumil SMOLÍK,
Bedrich TESAR, Karel NEPOMUCKÝ, Frantisek VESELÝ, Josef KADRABA, Frantisek
MORÁVEK, Václav BOUSKA, Jaroslav SIMEK. (Coach: Mirko PARÁCEK).
Goals: FK Austria Wien: 1-0 Karl KODAT (1'), 2-0 Josef HICKERSBERGER (11').
Referee: Janos BIRÓCZKI (HUN)   Attendance: 7.000

23-11-1966   Budapest: Újpesti Dózsa SC – TJ Slovan CHZJD Bratislava   5-1 (2-1)
Újpesti Dózsa SC: Antal SZENTMIHÁLYI, Benö KÁPOSZTA, Mátyás CSORDÁS, István
NYÍRÓ, Ernö NOSKÓ, Ernö SOLYMOSI (I), László FAZEKAS, János GÖRÖCS, Ferenc
BENE, Antal DUNAI (II), Sándor ZÁMBÓ. (Coach: Lajos BARÓTI).
TJ Slovan CHZJD Bratislava: Alexander VENCEL (I), Anton URBAN, Ján POPLUHÁR,
Peter MUTKOVIC, Alexander HORVÁTH, Jozef TOMÁNEK, Ján MEDVID, Ivan
HRDLICKA, Jozef OBERT, Ludovít ZLOCHA, Ludivít CVETLER. (Coach: Ján HUCKO).
Goals: Újpesti Dózsa SC: 1-0 Antal DUNAI (II) (32'), 2-1 Ernö SOLYMOSI (I) (45' penalty),
3-1 Antal DUNAI (II) (46'), 4-1 Ferenc BENE (65'), 5-1 Ferenc BENE (85').
TJ Slovan CHZJD Bratislava: 1-1 Ludovít ZLOCHA (40').
Referee: Bruno DE MARCHI (ITA)   Attendance: 4.000

27-11-1966   Bratislava: TJ Slovan CHZJD Bratislava – Újpesti Dózsa SC   1-1 (1-1)
TJ Slovan CHZJD Bratislava: Alexander VENCEL (I), Peter MUTKOVIC, Ján POPLUHÁR,
Ernest MALASZKY, Vladimír HRIVNÁK, Jozef TOMÁNEK, Ján MEDVID, Ivan
HRDLICKA, Jozef OBERT, Ludovít ZLOCHA, Ludivít CVETLER. (Coach: Ján HUCKO).
Újpesti Dózsa SC: Antal SZENTMIHÁLYI, Benö KÁPOSZTA, Mátyás CSORDÁS, István
NYÍRÓ, Ernö SOLYMOSI (I), Ernö NOSKÓ, László FAZEKAS, János GÖRÖCS, Ferenc
BENE, Antal DUNAI (II), Sándor ZÁMBÓ. (Coach: Lajos BARÓTI).
Goals: TJ Slovan CHZJD Bratislava: 1-1 Jozef TOMÁNEK (26').
Újpesti Dózsa SC: 0-1 László FAZEKAS (9').
Referee: Paul SCHILLER (AUT)   Attendance: 4.000

30-11-1966   Bányász Stadion, Tatabánya:
             Tatabányai Bányász SC – FC Wacker Innsbruck 1-0 (1-0)
Tatabányai Bányász SC: József GELEI, Ottó LÉBER, Tibor KOVÁCS (I), László JUHOS,
Iván MENCZEL, Mihály LACZKÓ, György SZABÓ, Tibor CSERNAI, József SZEKERES,
Antal SZUROMI, Tibor SOLYMOS. (Coach: Nándor HIDEGKUTI).
FC Wacker Innsbruck: Leo TSCHENETT, Roland ESCHELMÜLLER, Josef SIKIC, Johann
EIGENSTILLER, Peter PUMM, Buffy ETTMAYER, Helmut SENEKOWITSCH, Klaus
RINNERSCHWENDTNER, Franz WOLNY, Helmut SIBER, Helmut REDL. (Coach: Leopold
STASTNY).
Goal: Tatabányai Bányász SC: 1-0 Antal SZUROMI (4').
Referee: Ratko CANAK (YUG)   Attendance: 3.000

30-11-1966   Beograd: FK Crvena Zvezda Beograd – SS Lazio Roma 2-1 (2-1)
FK Crvena Zvezda Beograd: Ratomir DUJKOVIC, Sava KARAPANDZIC, DAKIC,
Dragoljub ZIVKOVIC, Dejan BEKIC, Branko KLENKOVSKI, Vojislav MELIC, Stevan
OSTOJIC, Vojin LAZAREVIC, Jovan (Kula) ACIMOVIC, Dragan DZAJIC. (Coach: Miljan
MILJANIC).
SS Lazio Roma: Valerio CEI, Diego ZANETTI, Sergio CASTELLETI, Pietro DOTTI,
Pierluigi PAGNI, Paolo CAROSI, Vito D'AMATO, Enrico BURLANDO, Juan Carlos
MORRONE (ARG), Alberto MARI, Gianni SASSAROLI. (Coach: Maino NERI).
Goals: FK Crvena Zvezda Beograd: 1-0 Stevan OSTOJIC (24'), 2-1 Dragan DZAJIC (38').
SS Lazio Roma: 1-1 Vito D'AMATO (35').
Referee: Paul SCHILLER (AUT)   Attendance: 22.000

30-11-1966   San Siro, Milano: AC Milan – NK Dinamo Zagreb 0-0
AC Milan: Dario BARLUZZI, Angelo ANQUILLETTI, Gilberto NOLETTI, Roberto
ROSATO, Nello SANTIN, Karl Heinz SCHNELLINGER (FRG), Gianni RIVERA, Giovanni
LODETTI, Ángelo Benedicto Miguel SORMANI (BRA), Sergio MADDÈ, AMARILDO
Tavares da Silveira (BRA). (Coach: Arturo SILVESTRI).
NK Dinamo Zagreb: Zlatko SKORIC, Rudolf CVEK, Mirko BRAUN, Zlatko MESIC, Hrvoje
JUKIC, Mladen RAMLJAK, Stjepan LAMZA, Branko GRACANIN, Slaven ZAMBATA,
Josip GUCMIRTL, Krasnodar RORA. (Coach: Branislav (Branko) ZEBEC).
Referee: Ivan PLACEK (TCH)

08-12-1966   Florenze: AC Fiorentina – First Vienna FC 3-1 (2-0)
AC Fiorentina: Enrico ALBERTOSI, Bernardo ROGORA, Giovan Battista PIROVANO,
Mario BERTINI, Ugo FERRANTE, Giuseppe BRIZI, Kurt Roland HAMRIN (SWE),
Salvatore ESPOSITO, Mario BRUGNERA, Giancarlo DE SISTI, Giuseppe COSMA.
First Vienna FC: Dr.Günther PAULITSCH, Hellmuth LIENER, Giuseppe Francesco Carlo
KOSCHIER, Friedrich KREMSER, Rudolf CEYKA, Otto KLARL, Heinz MARIK, Ivan
LIPOSINOVIC (YUG), Horst NEMEC, Erhard WIEGER, Franz WEIDINGER. (Coach:
Alfred KÖRNER).
Goals: AC Fiorentina: 1-0 Kurt Roland HAMRIN (14'), 2-0 Kurt Roland HAMRIN (44'), 3-1
Kurt Roland HAMRIN (80').
First Vienna FC: 2-1 Heinz MARIK (62').
Referee: Karol GALBA (TCH)   Attendance: 21.000

177

08-12-1966   Tivoli-Stadion, Innsbruck:
                    FC Wacker Innsbruck – Tatabányai Bányász SC   1-2 (1-0)
FC Wacker Innsbruck: ... (Coach: Leopold STASTNY).
Tatabányai Bányász SC: József GELEI, Ferenc TÖRÖCSIK, Tibor KOVÁCS (I), László
JUHOS, Iván MENCZEL, Mihály LACZKÓ, György SZABÓ, Tibor CSERNAI, József
SZEKERES, Antal SZUROMI, Csaba KOVÁCS (II). (Coach: Nándor HIDEGKUTI).
Goals: FC Wacker Innsbruck: 1-0 Helmut SIBER (39').
Tatabányai Bányász SC: 1-1 György SZABÓ (68'), 1-2 Iván MENCZEL (80').
Attendance: 7.500

QUARTER-FINALS

08-03-1967   Zagreb: NK Dinamo Zagreb – FK Austria Wien   3-3 (0-1)
NK Dinamo Zagreb: Zlatko SKORIC, Rudolf CVEK, Hrvoje JUKIC, Marijan BRNCIC,
Mirko BRAUN, Filip BLASKOVIC, Branko GRACANIN, Marijan NOVAK, Ivica KIS, Josip
GUCMIRTL, Krasnodar RORA. (Coach: Branislav (Branko ZEBEC).
FK Austria Wien: Arkoc ÖZCAN (TUR), Heinz NOWY, Johann FRANK, Karl FRÖHLICH,
Robert SARA, Heinz BINDER, Horst HIRNSCHRODT, Johann BUZEK, Thomas PARITS,
Johann GEYER, Walter HIESEL. (Coach: Ernst OCWIRK).
Goals: NK Dinamo Zagreb: 1-1 Krasnodar RORA (49'), 2-2 Mirko BRAUN (60'), 3-3 Ivica
KIS (72').
FK Austria Wien: 0-1 Thomas PARITS (32'), 1-2 Thomas PARITS (51'), 2-3 Robert SARA
(71').
Referee: Fabio MONTI (ITA)   Attendance: 11.000

15-03-1967   Bányász Stadion, Tatabánya:
                    Tatabányai Bányász SC – AC Fiorentina   1-1 (1-1)
Tatabányai Bányász SC: József GELEI, Ferenc TÖRÖCSIK, Tibor KOVÁCS (I), László
JUHOS, Iván MENCZEL, Mihály LACZKÓ, György SZABÓ, Tibor CSERNAI, Gyula BÍRÓ,
Antal SZUROMI, Ferenc HOLÁNSZKY. (Coach: László HÁRI).
AC Fiorentina: Enrico ALBERTOSI, Bernardo ROGORA, Marcello DIOMEDI, Giuseppe
BRIZI, Ugo FERRANTE, Piero LENZI, Kurt Roland HAMRIN (SWE), Claudio MERLO,
Giuseppe COSMA, Mario BERTINI, Salvatore ESPOSITO. (Coach: Giuseppe
CHIAPPELLA).
Goals: Tatabányai Bányász SC: 1-0 György SZABÓ (11').
AC Fiorentina: 1-1 Kurt Roland HAMRIN (16').
Referee: Dimitris WLACHOJANIS (AUT)

15-03-1967   Sarajevo: FK Sarajevo – Újpesti Dózsa SC   1-2

15-03-1967   Praterstadion, Wien: FK Austria Wien – NK Dinamo Zagreb   1-0 (0-0)
FK Austria Wien: Arkoc ÖZCAN (TUR), Heinz NOWY, Johann FRANK, Karl FRÖHLICH,
Robert SARA, Heinz BINDER, Horst HIRNSCHRODT, Johann BUZEK, Thomas PARITS,
Johann GEYER, Walter HIESEL. (Coach: Ernst OCWIRK).
NK Dinamo Zagreb: Zlatko SKORIC, Rudolf CVEK, Hrvoje JUKIC, Marijan BRNCIC,
Mirko BRAUN, Filip BLASKOVIC, Mladen RAMLJAK, Marijan NOVAK, Josip
GUCMIRTL, Stjepan LAMZA, Krasnodar RORA. (Coach: Branislav (Branko ZEBEC).
Goal: FK Austria Wien: 1-0 Johann BUZEK (49').
Referee: Zdenek VALES (TCH)   Attendance: 8.000

22-03-1967   Roma: SS Lazio Roma – TJ Spartak TAZ Trnava 1-1 (0-0)
SS Lazio Roma: Valerio CEI, Giovanni MASIELLO, Pietro ADORNI, Paolo CAROSI, Pierluigi PAGNI, Sergio CASTELLETI, Vito D'AMATO, Enrico BURLANDO, Juan Carlos MORRONE (ARG), Arrigo DOLSO, Romano BAGATTI. (Coach: Maino NERI).
TJ Spartak TAZ Trnava: Josef GERYK, Jaroslav KRAVÁRIK, Kamil MAJERNIK, Stanislav JARÁBEK, Karol DOBIAS, Anton HRUSECKÝ, Adam FARKAS, Valerián SVEC, Ladislav KUNA, Jozef ADAMEC, Dusan KABÁT. (Coach: Anton MALATINSKY).
Goals: SS Lazio Roma: 1-0 Romano BAGATTI (57').
TJ Spartak TAZ Trnava: 1-1 Jozef ADAMEC (62').
Referee: Gusztav BIRCSAK (HUN)   Attendance: 4.630

29-03-1967   Stadio Comunale, Firenze: AC Fiorentina – Tatabányai Bányász SC 1-0 (1-0)
AC Fiorentina: Enrico ALBERTOSI, Marcello DIOMEDI, Giampiero VITALI, Giovan Battista PIROVANO, Ugo FERRANTE, Giuseppe BRIZI, Kurt Roland HAMRIN (SWE), Salvatore ESPOSITO, Mario BRUGNERA, Mario BERTINI, Luciano CHIARUGI. (Coach: Giuseppe CHIAPPELLA).
Tatabányai Bányász SC: József GELEI, Ottó LÉBER, Tibor KOVÁCS (I), Ferenc TÖRÖCSIK, Csaba KOVÁCS (II), Mihály LACZKÓ, György SZABÓ, Gyula BÍRÓ, Iván MENCZEL, József SZEKERES, Ferenc HOLÁNSZKY. (Coach: László HÁRI).
Goal: AC Fiorentina: 1-0 Kurt Roland HAMRIN (16').
Referee: Josip STRMECKI (YUG)

30-03-1967   Trnava: TJ Spartak TAZ Trnava – SS Lazio Roma 1-0 (0-0)
TJ Spartak TAZ Trnava: Josef GERYK, Jaroslav KRAVÁRIK, Kamil MAJERNÍK, Stanislav JARÁBEK, Karol DOBIAS, Anton HRUSECKÝ, Adam FARKAS, Valerián SVEC, Ladislav KUNA, Jozef ADAMEC, Dusan KABÁT. (Coach: Anton MALATINSKY).
SS Lazio Roma: Valerio CEI, Giovanni MASIELLO, Pietro ADORNI, Pietro DOTTI, Pierluigi PAGNI, Sergio CASTELLETI, Romano BAGATTI, Enrico BURLANDO, Arrigo DOLSO, Rino MARCHESI, Alberto MARI. (Coach: Maino NERI).
Goal: TJ Spartak TAZ Trnava: 1-0 Valerián SVEC (47').
Referee: Ferdinand MARSCHALL (AUT)   Attendance: 18.000

30-03-1967   Budapest: Újpesti Dózsa SC – FK Sarajevo 5-1 (3-1)

SEMI-FINALS

27-04-1967   Trnava: TJ Spartak TAZ Trnava – AC Fiorentina 2-0 (1-0)
TJ Spartak TAZ Trnava: Jaroslav MACHÁC, Karol DOBIAS, Kamil MAJERNÍK, Stanislav JARÁBEK, Emil BRUNOVSKÝ, Anton HRUSECKÝ, Ladislav KUNA, Adam FARKAS, Jaroslav KRAVÁRIK, Jozef ADAMEC, Dusan KABÁT. (Coach: Anton MALATINSKY).
AC Fiorentina: Enrico ALBERTOSI, Bernardo ROGORA, Ugo FERRANTE, Giovan Battista PIROVANO, Mario BERTINI, Giuseppe BRIZI, Kurt Roland HAMRIN (SWE), Claudio MERLO, Salvatore ESPOSITO, Giancarlo DE SISTI, Luciano CHIARUGI. (Coach: Giuseppe CHIAPPELLA).
Goals: TJ Spartak TAZ Trnava: 1-0 Jozef ADAMEC (31'), 2-0 Adam FARKAS (87').
Referee: Gyula ERMSBERGER (HUN)   Attendance: 12.000

179

10-05-1967   Firenze: AC Fiorentina – TJ Spartak TAZ Trnava   2-1 (0-0)
AC Fiorentina: Enrico ALBERTOSI, Bernardo ROGORA, Ugo FERRANTE, Giovan Battista
PIROVANO, Mario BERTINI, Giuseppe BRIZI, Kurt Roland HAMRIN (SWE), Claudio
MERLO, Mario BRUGNERA, Giancarlo DE SISTI, Giuseppe COSMA. (Coach: Giuseppe
CHIAPPELLA).
TJ Spartak TAZ Trnava: Josef GERYK, Karol DOBIAS, Kamil MAJERNÍK, Stanislav
JARÁBEK, Vladimír HAGARA, Anton HRUSECKÝ, Ladislav KUNA, Adam FARKAS,
Jaroslav KRAVÁRIK, Jozef ADAMEC, Dusan KABÁT. (Coach: Anton MALATINSKY).
Goals: AC Fiorentina: 1-1 Giuseppe COSMA (70'), 2-1 Claudio MERLO (73').
TJ Spartak TAZ Trnava: 0-1 Jozef ADAMEC (59').
Attendance: Eduard BABAUCZEK (AUT)   Attendance: 20.000

31-05-1967   Megyeri úti Stadion, Budapest:
              Újpesti Dózsa SC – FK Austria Wien   3-0 (1-0)
Újpesti Dózsa SC: Antal SZENTMIHÁLYI, József SZINI, Ernö SOLYMOSI, Kálmán
SÓVÁRI, Ernö NOSKÓ, István NYÍRÖ, László FAZEKAS, János GÖRÖCS, Ferenc BENE,
Antal DUNAI (II), Sándor ZÁMBÓ. (Coach: Lajos BARÓTI).
FK Austria Wien: Arkoc ÖZCAN (TUR), Heinz NOWY, Heinz BINDER, Karl FRÖHLICH,
Walter HIESEL, Horst HIRNSCHRODT, Kurt FOKA, Robert SARA, Thomas PARITS,
Johann GEYER, Ernst FIALA. (Coach: Ernst OCWIRK).
Goals: Újpesti Dózsa SE: 1-0 László FAZEKAS (10'), 2-0 Antal DUNAI (85'), 3-0 Ferenc
BENE (86').
Referee: Alessandro D'AGOSTINI (ITA)   Attendance: 12.000

07-06-1967   Praterstadion, Wien: FK Austria Wien – Újpesti Dózsa SC   1-2 (0-0)
FK Austria Wien: Arkoc ÖZCAN (TUR), Heinz NOWY, Alfons DIRNBERGER, Karl
FRÖHLICH, Walter HIESEL, Robert SARA, Josef HICKERSBERGER, Johann BUZEK,
Thomas PARITS, Johann GEYER, Franz HOCHLEUTNER. (Coach: Ernst OCWIRK).
Újpesti Dózsa SC: Antal SZENTMIHÁLYI, József SZINI, Ernö SOLYMOSI, Kálmán
SÓVÁRI, Ernö NOSKÓ, István NYÍRÖ, László FAZEKAS, János GÖRÖCS, Ferenc BENE,
Antal DUNAI (II), Sándor ZÁMBÓ. (Coach: Lajos BARÓTI).
Goals: FK Austria Wien: 1-0 Johann BUZEK (58' penalty).
Újpesti Dózsa SC: 1-1 Ferenc BENE (67'), 1-2 Sándor ZÁMBÓ (78').
Referee: Alojz OBTULOVIC (TCH)   Attendance: 2.000

FINAL

04-10-1967   Megyeri úti Stadion, Budapest:
Újpesti Dózsa SC – TJ Spartak TAZ Trnava   3-2 (2-2)
Újpesti Dózsa SC: Antal SZENTMIHÁLYI, Benö KÁPOSZTA, Ernö SOLYMOSI (I),
Kálmán SÓVÁRI, Ernö NOSKÓ, István NYÍRÖ, László FAZEKAS, János GÖRÖCS, Ferenc
BENE, Antal DUNAI (II), Sándor ZÁMBÓ. (Coach: Lajos BARÓTI).
TJ Spartak TAZ Trnava: Frantisek KOZINKA, Karol DOBIAS, Stanislav JARÁBEK,
Vladimír HAGARA, Emil BRUNOVSKÝ, Jaroslav KRAVÁRIK, Ladislav KUNA, Stanislav
MARTINKOVIC, Anton HRUSECKÝ, Jozef ADAMEC, Dusan KABÁT. (Coach: Anton
MALATINSKY).
Goals: Újpesti Dózsa SC: 1-0 Ferenc BENE (6'), 2-2 István NYÍRÖ (45'), 3-2 László
FAZEKAS (85').
TJ Spartak TAZ Trnava: 1-1 Ladislav KUNA (9'), 1-2 Jozef ADAMEC (17').
Referee: Aurelio ANGONESE (ITA)   Attendance: 15.000

01-11-1967   Stadión Spartak, Trnava:
TJ Spartak TAZ Trnava – Újpesti Dózsa SC   3-1 (2-1)
TJ Spartak TAZ Trnava: Frantisek KOZINKA, Jaroslav KRAVÁRIK, Stanislav JARÁBEK,
Ján ZLOCHA, Karol DOBIAS, Anton HRUSECKÝ, Ladislav KUNA, Stanislav
MARTINKOVIC, Valerián SVEC, Jozef ADAMEC, Dusan KABÁT. (Coach: Anton
MALATINSKY).
Újpesti Dózsa SC: Antal SZENTMIHÁLYI, Benö KÁPOSZTA, Ernö SOLYMOSI (I),
Kálmán SÓVÁRI, Ede DUNAI (III), Ernö NOSKÓ, László FAZEKAS, János GÖRÖCS,
Ferenc BENE, Antal DUNAI (II), Sándor ZÁMBÓ. (Coach: Lajos BARÓTI).
Goals: TJ Spartak TAZ Trnava: 1-1 Valerián SVEC (20'), 2-1 Ladislav KUNA (29'), 3-1
Jaroslav KRAVÁRIK (56').
Újpesti Dózsa SC: 0-1 Ferenc BENE (3').
Referee: Paul SCHILLER (AUT)   Attendance: 25.000

*** **TJ Spartak TAZ Trnava won the Cup** ***

181

1967-1968

QUARTER-FINALS

01-11-1967   Bányász Stadion, Tatabánya:
Tatabányai Bányász SC – TJ Internacional Slovnaft Bratislava 3-1 (2-0)
Tatabányai Bányász SC: József GELEI, István LÉVAI, Ottó LÉBER, László JUHOS, Ferenc HORVÁTH, Mihály LACZKÓ, György SZABÓ, Sándor BENCZE, János LOCKER, Tibor CSERNAI, András DELI. (Coach:László HÁRI).
TJ Internacional Slovnaft Bratislava: Peter FÜLLE, Milan HRICA, Vladimír WEISS (I), Titus BUBERNÍK, Ottmar DEUTSCH, Ivan DANO, Eduard GÁBORÍK, Jozef LEVICKÝ, Juraj SZIKORA, Michal MEDVID, Ján ONDRÁSEK. (Coach: Ladislav KACÁNI).
Goals: Tatabányai Bányász SC: 1-0 György SZABÓ (9'), 2-0 Mihály LACZKÓ (19'), 3-1 György SZABÓ (85').
TJ Internacional Slovnaft Bratislava: 2-1 Juraj SZIKORA (84').
Referee: Milivoje GUGULOVIC (YUG)   Attendance: 5.000

08-11-1967   Linzer Stadion, Linz: Linzer ASK – FK Vardar Skopje 0-0
Linzer ASK: Wilhelm HARREITHER, Heribert TRÜBRIG, Manfred LEITNER, Gerhard STURMBERGER, Siegfried HINTRINGER, Francisco Carlos Correia Lima "CHICO" (POR), Franz VIEHBÖCK, Luka LIPOSINOVIC (YUG), Helmut KÖGLBERGER, Manfred PICHLER, Alfons WURDINGER. (Coach: Frantisek BUFKA (TCH)).
FK Vardar Skopje: Dragan MUTIBARIC, RAC, PEEV, DROBAC, Atanas MECKAROV, PLACKOV, DONCIC, Sokrat MOJSOV, Petar SULINCEVSKI, Stojan VELKOVSKI, Methodije SPASOVSKI.
Referee: Zdenek VALES (TCH)   Attendance: 3.000

08-11-1967   Bratislava:
TJ Internacional Slovnaft Bratislava – Tatabányai Bányász SE 7-0 (4-0)
TJ Internacional Slovnaft Bratislava: Peter FÜLLE, Milan HRICA, Vladimír WEISS (I), Ottmar DEUTSCH, Pavol DAUCÍK, Anton OBLOZINSKÝ, Titus BUBERNÍK, Jozef LEVICKÝ, Juraj SZIKORA, Mikulás KRNÁC, Ján ONDRÁSEK. (Coach: Ladislav KACÁNI).
Tatabányai Bányász SC: József GELEI (22' Ádám ROTHERMEL), István LÉVAI, Ottó LÉBER, László JUHOS, Ferenc HORVÁTH, Mihály LACZKÓ, György SZABÓ, Sándor BENCZE, János LOCKER, Tibor CSERNAI, András DELI. (Coach:László HÁRI).
Goals: TJ Internacional Slovnaft Bratislava: 1-0 Mikulás KRNAC (16'), 2-0 Titur BUBERNIK (21'), 3-0 Juraj SZIKORA (35'), 4-0 Ján ONDRASEK (43'), 5-0 Jozef LEVICKY (75'), 6-0 MikulásKRNAC (77'), 7-0 Juraj SZIKORA (90').
Referee: Erich LINEMAYR (AUT)   Attendance: 4.000

15-11-1967   Stadion Crvena Zvezda, Beograd:
FK Crvena Zvezda Beograd – Diósgyöri VTK   3-0 (1-0)
FK Crvena Zvezda Beograd: Ratomir DUJKOVIC, Aleksandar MARKOVIC, Tomislav MILICEVIC, Miroslav PAVLOVIC, Kiril (Kiro) DOJCINOVSKI, Branko KLENKOVSKI, Zoran ANTONIJEVIC (..' Trifun MIHAJLOVIC), Stevan OSTOJIC, Vojin LAZAREVIC, Jovan ACIMOVIC, Dragan DZAJIC.
Diósgyöri VTK: Gyula TAMÁS, Pál KOVÁCS, József SALAMON, András SZUCSÁNYI, Béla GÁL, Zoltán RUTTKAI, András HORVÁTH, Imre HAJAS, Lajos SZURGENT (..' Béla VÁRKONYI), Ferenc SIKORA, László VASS. (Coach: Pál SZABÓ).
Goals: FK Crvena Zvezda Beograd: 1-0 Dragan DZAJIC (20'), 2-0 Dragan DZAJIC (65'), 3-0 Dragan DZAJIC (84').
Attendance: 8.000

15-11-1967   Praterstadion, Wien: FK Austria Wien – Atalanta Bergamo   1-2 (1-0)
FK Austria Wien: Rudolf SZANWALD, Heinz NOWY, Johann FRANK, Karl FRÖHLICH, Robert SARA, Alfons DIRNBERGER, Thomas PARITS, Vlatko MARKOVIC (YUG), Herbert POINDL, Walter HIESEL (60' Gustav PROVAZNIK), Ernst FIALA. (Coach: Ernst OCWIRK).
Atalanta Bergamo: Giuseppe VALSECCHI, Alfredo PESENTI, Giancarlo CELLA, Franco NODARI, Gian Pietro MARCHETTI, Paolo SIGNORELLI, Giancarlo DANOVA (53' Adriano NOVELLINI), Luigi MILAN, Guiseppe SAVOLDI, Lucio DELL'ANGELO, Roberto RIGOTTO.
Goals: FK Austria Wien: 1-0 Robert SARA (43').
Atalanta Bergamo: 1-1 Lucio DELL'ANGELO (55'), 1-2 Guiseppe SAVOLDI (75').
Referee: István ZSOLT (HUN)   Attendance: 51.181
(Double game played on the same day and at the same venue as the match between SK Rapid Wien and Eintracht Braunschweig in the European Champions Cup).

15-11-1967   Megyeri úti Stadion, Budapest:
Újpesti Dózsa SC – Wiener Sportklub   6-1 (4-1)
Újpesti Dózsa SC: Antal SZENTMIHÁLYI, Benö KÁPOSZTA, Ernö SOLYMOSI, Kálmán SÓVÁRI, Ede DUNAI (III), Ernö NOSKÓ, László FAZEKAS, János GÖRÖCS, Ferenc BENE, Antal DUNAI (II), Béla KUHARSZKI. (Coach: Lajos BARÓTI).
Wiener Sportklub: Wilhelm KAIPEL, Wilhelm KAINRATH, Norbert HOF (II), Rudolf NOVAK, Anton LINHART, Helmut WALLNER, Erich HOF (I), Peter SCHMIDT, Hans BUZEK, Johann HÖRMAYER, Kurt LEITNER. (Coach: GALLI).
Goals: Újpesti Dózsa SC: 1-0 Ferenc BENE (3'), 2-1 Kálmán SÓVÁRI (26'), 3-1 Ernö SOLYMOSI (41' penalty), 4-1 Norbert HOF (II) (45' *own goal*), 5-1 Antal DUNAI (II) (60'), 6-1 Ferenc BENE (70').
Wiener Sportklub: 1-1 Hans BUZEK (10').
Referee: Aurelio ANGONESE (ITA)   Attendance: 11.000

15-11-1967   Trencin: TJ Jednota Trencin – FK Zeljeznicar Sarajevo   0-0
TJ Jednota Trencin: Tibor RIHOSEK, Anton POKORNÝ, Stefan HOJSÍK, Ferdinand SCHWARZ, Miroslav CEMEZ, Vladimír MOJZIS, Dusan BARTOVIC, Milan NAVRÁTIL, Michal JANOVSKÝ, Juray JENCÍK, Milan ALBRECHT.
FK Zeljeznicar Sarajevo: Vasilije RADOVIC, Miljan STAKA, Nusret KADRIC, Blagoje BRATIC, Josip KATALINSKI, Enver HADZIABDIC, Branimir JELUSIC, D.BAJIC, Ivan OSIM, Edin SPRECO, Fikret MUJKIC. (Coach: Marcel ZIGANTE).
Referee: Friedrich (Franz) MAYER (AUT)   Attendance: 1.000

22-11-1967   Sportklub-Platz, Wien: Wiener Sportklub – Újpesti Dózsa SC   1-1 (0-1)
Wiener Sportklub: Wilhelm KAIPEL, Rudolf HACKER, Norbert HOF (II), Anton LINHART,
Emmerich PINGITZER, Peter SCHMIDT, Wilhelm KAINRATH, Hans BUZEK, Herbert
ONGER (46' Franz MATOUSEK), Kurt LEITNER, Walter ZIPS.
Újpesti Dózsa SC: Antal SZENTMIHÁLYI, Benö KÁPOSZTA, Ernö SOLYMOSI, Kálmán
SÓVÁRI, Sándor ZÁMBÓ (64' József SZINI), Ernö NOSKÓ, László FAZEKAS, János
GÖRÖCS, Ferenc BENE, Antal DUNAI (II), Béla KUHARSZKI. (Coach: Lajos BARÓTI).
Goals: Wiener Sportklub: 1-1 Kurt LEITNER (55').
Újpesti Dózsa SC: 0-1 Antal DUNAI (II) (22').
Referee: Milivoje GUGULOVIC (YUG)   Attendance: 2.500

22-11-1967   MVSC Stadion, Miskolc:
                      Diósgyöri VTK – FK Crvena Zvezda Beograd   3-1 (1-0)
Diósgyöri VTK: Gyula TAMÁS, Pál KOVÁCS, József SALAMON, András SZUCSÁNYI,
Béla GÁL, Béla VÁRKONYI, Zoltán RUTTKAI (..' István PÓCSIK), Imre HAJAS, András
HORVÁTH, Ferenc SIKORA, László VASS. (Coach: Pál SZABÓ).
FK Crvena Zvezda Beograd: Ratomir DUJKOVIC, Aleksandar MARKOVIC, Tomislav
MILICEVIC, Miroslav PAVLOVIC, Kiril (Kiro) DOJCINOVSKI, Zivan RAKIC, Zoran
ANTONIJEVIC, Stevan OSTOJIC, Vojin LAZAREVIC, Jovan ACIMOVIC (..' Branko
KLENKOVSKI), Dragan DZAJIC. (Coach: Todor ZIVANOVIC).
Goals: Diósgyöri VTK: 1-0 András SZUCSÁNYI (6'), 2-1 András HORVÁTH (80'), 3-1
András SZUCSÁNYI (84').
FK Crvena Zvezda Beograd: 1-1 Dragan DZAJIC (75').

29-11-1967   Cagliari: US Cagliari – TJ Baník Ostrava   6-0 (1-0)
US Cagliari: Adriano REGINATO, Mario MARTIRADONNA, Giuseppe LONGONI,
Pierluigi CERA, Raffaello VESCOVI, Miguel Ángel LONGO (ARG), Claudio Olinto de
Carvalho NENÉ (BRA), Francesco RIZZO, Roberto BONINSEGNA, Ricciotti GREATTI,
Luigi RIVA. (Coach: Héctor (Ettore) PURICELLI Seña (URU)).
TJ Baník Ostrava: Frantisek SCHMUCKER, Karel WEISS, SLADECEK, Jirí KOMÁNEK,
Jan KNIEZEK, Anton ONDÁK, Jozef HASPRA, Karel JÜNGER, Petr KRIZÁK, Milan
POSTULKA, Miroslav MICKA.
Goals: US Cagliari: 1-0 Luigi RIVA (37'), 2-0 Claudio Olinto de Carvalho NENÉ (56'), 3-0
Roberto BONINSEGNA (59'), 4-0 Roberto BONINSEGNA (67'), 5-0 Luigi RIVA (74'), 6-0
Mario MARTIRADONNA (84').
Referee: Paul SCHILLER (AUT)

30-11-1967   Sarajevo: FK Zeljeznicar Sarajevo – TJ Jednota Trencin   1-0 (1-0)
FK Zeljeznicar Sarajevo: Vasilije RADOVIC, Miljan STAKA, Nusret KADRIC, Blagoje
BRATIC, Josip KATALINSKI, Enver HADZIABDIC, Branimir JELUSIC, D.BAJIC, Ivan
OSIM, Edin SPRECO, Fikret MUJKIC. (Coach: Marcel ZIGANTE).
TJ Jednota Trencin:
Goal: FK Zeljeznicar Sarajevo: 1-0 Enver HADZIABDIC (16').
Attendance: 4.000

06-12-1967   Trnava: TJ Spartak TAZ Trnava – AS Roma 2-1 (1-0)
TJ Spartak TAZ Trnava: Josef GERYK, Karol DOBIAS, Ján ZLOCHA, Vladimír HAGARA,
Emil BRUNOVSKÝ, AntonHRUSECKÝ, Jaroslav KRAVÁRIK, Stanislav MARTINKOVIC,
Valerián SVEC, Ladislav KUNA,Dusan KABÁT (46' Adam FARKAS). (Coach: Anton
MALATÍNSKÝ).
AS Roma: Alberto GINULFI, Giacomo LOSI, Enzo ROBOTTI, Francesco CAPPELLI,
Ambrogio PELAGALLI (46' Giancarlo CARLONI), Luigi OSSOLA, Sergio FERRARI,
Franco CORDOVA, JAIR da Costa (BRA), Joaquin PEIRÓ Lucas (ESP), Fabio ENZO.
Goals: TJ Spartak TAZ Trnava: 1-0 Karol DOBIAS (25'), 2-0 Valerián SVEC (72').
AS Roma: 2-1 Fabio ENZO (75').
Referee: Erich LINEMAYR (AUT)   Attendance: 10.000

06-12-1967   Ostrava: TJ Baník Ostrava – US Cagliari 3-2 (3-2)
TJ Baník Ostrava: Frantisek SCHMUCKER, Karel WEISS, SLADECEK, Jirí KOMÁNEK,
Jan KNIEZEK, Karel JÜNGER, Anton ONDÁK, Josef POSTULKA, Ladislav MICHALÍK,
Milan POSTULKA, Jozef HASPRA.
US Cagliari: Adriano REGINATO, Mario MARTIRADONNA, Giuseppe LONGONI,
Comunardo NICCOLAI, Raffaello VESCOVI, Miguel Ángel LONGO (ARG), Claudio Olinto
de Carvalho NENÉ (BRA), Gerald Archibald (Gerry) HITCHENS (ENG), Francesco RIZZO,
Roberto BONINSEGNA, Luigi RIVA. (Coach: Héctor (Ettore) PURICELLI Seña (URU)).
Goals: TJ Baník Ostrava: 1-0 Milan POSTULKA (1'), 2-0 Milan POSTULKA (20'), 3-1 Jozef
HASPRA (37').
US Cagliari: 2-1 Roberto BONINSEGNA (24'), 3-2 Roberto BONINSEGNA (41').
Referee: Istvan ZSOLT (HUN)

13-12-1967   Bergamo: Atalanta Bergamo – FK Austria Wien 0-2 (0-1)
Atalanta Bergamo: Giuseppe VALSECCHI, Luciano POPPI, Giancarlo CELLA, Franco
NODARI, Gian Pietro MARCHETTI, Paolo SIGNORELLI, Adriano NOVELLINI, Elvio
SALVORI, Guiseppe SAVOLDI (46' Luigi MILAN), Lucio DELL'ANGELO, Roberto
RIGOTTO.
FK Austria Wien: Rudolf SZANWALD, Heinz NOWY, Johann FRANK, Karl FRÖHLICH,
Walter HIESEL, Robert SARA, Thomas PARITS, Adolf KNOLL, Herbert POINDL, Josef
HICKERSBERGER, Ernst FIALA. (Coach: Ernst OCWIRK).
Goals: FK Austria Wien: 0-1 Ernst FIALA (41'), 0-2 Ernst FIALA (64').
Referee: Radoslav FIALA (TCH)   Attendance: 4.000

17-12-1967   Skopje: FK Vardar Skopje – Linzer ASK 2-1 (0-1)
Goals: FK Vardar Skopje: 1-1 Stojan VELKOVSKI (60'), 2-1 SPASOVSKI (75').
Linzer ASK: 0-1 ILLE (28').
Attendance: 5.000

20-12-1967   Roma: AS Roma – TJ Spartak TAZ Trnava 1-1 (1-1)
AS Roma: Pier Luigi PIZZABALLA, Giacomo LOSI, Enzo ROBOTTI, Francesco
CAPPELLI, Francesco CARPENETTI, Ambrogio PELAGALLI, Francesco SCARATTI,
Franco CORDOVA (46' Fabio ENZO), JAIR da Costa (BRA), Joaquin PEIRÓ Lucas (ESP),
Guliano TACCOLA.
TJ Spartak TAZ Trnava: Josef GERYK, Jaroslav KRAVÁRIK, Karol DOBIAS, Ján
ZLOCHA, Vladimír HAGARA, Anton HRUSECKÝ, Stanislav MARTINKOVIC, Valerián
SVEC, Ladislav KUNA, Jozef ADAMEC, Dusan KABÁT. (Coach: Anton MALATÍNSKÝ).
Goals: AS Roma: 1-0 Guliano TACCOLA (21').
TJ Spartak TAZ Trnava: 1-1 Ladislav KUNA (42').
Referee: Ladislav (Lado) JAKSE (YUG)   Attendance: 10.000

28-02-1968   Trnava: TJ Spartak TAZ Trnava – FK Zeljeznicar Sarajevo 2-1 (1-0)
TJ Spartak TAZ Trnava: Josef GERYK, Emil BRUNOVSKÝ, Stanislav JARÁBEK, Ján
ZLOCHA, Jaroslav KRAVÁRIK, Anton HRUSECKÝ, Ladislav KUNA, Stanislav
MARTINKOVIC (..' Adam FARKAS), Valerián SVEC, Jozef ADAMEC, Dusan KABÁT.
(Coach: Karol TIBENSKÝ).
FK Zeljeznicar Sarajevo: Vasilije RADOVIC, F.HRVAT, Midhat MUJKIC, Josip
KATALINSKI, Blagoje BRATIC, Enver HADZIABDIC, Ivan OSIM, Branimir JELUSIC,
D.BAJIC (..' DERAKOVIC), Edin SPRECO, Fikret MUJKIC. (Coach: Marcel ZIGANTE).
Goals: TJ Spartak TAZ Trnava: 1-0 Stanislav MARTINKOVIC (17'), 2-0 Jozef ADAMEC
(62' penalty).
FK Zeljeznicar Sarajevo: 2-1 Branimir JELUSIC (67').
Referee: Sergio GONELLA (ITA)   Attendance: 10.000

06-03-1968   Sarajevo: FK Zeljeznicar Sarajevo – TJ Spartak TAZ Trnava 2-2 (0-1)
FK Zeljeznicar Sarajevo: Vasilije RADOVIC, F.HRVAT, Miljan STAKA, Josip
KATALINSKI, Midhat MUJKIC, Enver HADZIABDIC, Blagoje BRATIC, Branimir
JELUSIC, Ivan OSIM, Edin SPRECO, A.DERAKOVIC. (Coach: Marcel ZIGANTE).
TJ Spartak TAZ Trnava: Josef GERYK, Karol DOBIAS, Stanislav JARÁBEK, Ladislav
KUNA, Ján ZLOCHA, Jaroslav KRAVÁRIK, Anton HRUSECKÝ, Stanislav
MARTINKOVIC, Valerián SVEC, Jozef ADAMEC, Dusan KABÁT. (Coach: Karol
TIBENSKÝ).
Goals: FK Zeljeznicar Sarajevo: 1-1 Edin SPRECO (51'), 2-2 Ivica OSIM (88').
TJ Spartak TAZ Trnava: 0-1 Ján ZLOCHA (36'), 1-2 Jozef ADAMEC (72').
Referee: János BIRÓCZKI (HUN)   Attendance: 15.000

13-03-1968   Skopje: FK Vardar Skopje – US Cagliari 1-0 (0-0)
FK Vardar Skopje: Dragan MUTIBARIC, DROBAC, RAC, GEORGIJEV, Atanas
MECKAROV, PLACKOV, Mirko ILIJEVSKI, Sokrat MOJSOV (46' DONCIC), Petar
SULINCEVSKI, Stojan VELKOVSKI, Methodije SPASOVSKI.
US Cagliari: Adriano REGINATO, Mario TIDDIA, Giuseppe LONGONI, Pierluigi CERA,
Raffaello VESCOVI, Miguel Ángel LONGO (ARG), Alessio BADARI, Francesco RIZZO,
Roberto BONINSEGNA, Ricciotti GREATTI, Gerald Archibald (Gerry) HITCHENS (ENG)
(46' Luigi RIVA). (Coach: Héctor (Ettore) PURICELLI Seña (URU)).
Goal: FK Vardar Skopej: 1-0 Methodije SPASOVSKI (90').
Referee: Tibor WOTTAVA (HUN)

20-03-1968   Wacker-Platz, Wien: FK Austria Wien – Újpesti Dózsa SC 2-2 (1-1)
FK Austria Wien: Rudolf SZANWALD, Robert SARA, Gustav PROVAZNIK, Karl
FRÖHLICH, Johann FRANK, Heinz NOWY, Thomas PARITS, Walter HIESEL (56' Adolf
KNOLL), Herbert POINDL, Josef HICKERSBERGER, Ernst FIALA. (Coach: Ernst
OCWIRK).
Újpesti Dózsa SC: Antal SZENTMIHÁLYI, Benö KÁPOSZTA, Ernö SOLYMOSI (I),
Kálmán SÓVÁRI, Ede DUNAI (III), Ernö NOSKÓ, László FAZEKAS, János GÖRÖCS,
Ferenc BENE, Antal DUNAI (II), Sándor ZÁMBÓ. (Coach: Lajos BARÓTI).
Goals: FK Austria Wien: 1-1 Johann FRANK (26'), 2-1 Thomas PARITS (55').
Újpesti Dózsa SC: 0-1 Ferenc BENE (9'), 2-2 Ferenc BENE (81').
Referee: Zdenek VALES (TCH)   Attendance: 9.000

186

27-03-1968   Beograd:
FK Crvena Zvezda Beograd – TJ Internacional Slovnaft Bratislava   3-0 (1-0)
FK Crvena Zvezda Beograd: Dragan RACIC, Milovan DJORIC, Petar KRIVOKUCA,
Miroslav PAVLOVIC, Kiril (Kiro) DOJCINOVSKI, Branko KLENKOVSKI, Zoran
ANTONIJEVIC, Stevan OSTOJIC, Aleksandar MARKOVIC, Slobodan SKRBIC, Dragan
DZAJIC (..' Stevan KOVACEVIC). (Coach: Miljan MILJANIC).
TJ Internacional Slovnaft Bratislava: Peter FÜLLE, Milan HRICA, Ottmar DEUTSCH, Peter
SOLIN, Ivan DANO, Titus BUBERNÍK, Anton OBLOZINSKÝ, Jozef LEVICKÝ, Juraj
SZIKORA (..' Michal MEDVID), Mikulás KRNÁC, Ján ONDRÁSEK. (Coach: Ladislav
KACÁNI).
Goals: FK Crvena Zvezda Beograd: 1-0 Stevan OSTOJIC (24'), 2-0 Stevan OSTOJIC (..'), 3-0
Stevan KOVACEVIC (70').
Referee: Bruno DE MARCHI (ITA)   Attendance: 10.000

27-03-1968   Cagliari: US Cagliari – FK Vardar Skopje   0-1 (0-0)
US Cagliari: Pietro PIANTA, Mario TIDDIA, Giuseppe LONGONI, Ricciotti GREATTI,
Raffaello VESCOVI, Miguel Ángel LONGO (ARG), Gerald Archibald (Gerry) HITCHENS
(ENG), Francesco RIZZO, Roberto BONINSEGNA, Alessio BADARI (46' Michele MORO),
Luigi RIVA. (Coach: Héctor (Ettore) PURICELLI Seña (URU)).
FK Vardar Skopje: Dragan MUTIBARIC, DROBAC, RAC, GEORGIJEV, Atanas
MECKAROV, PLACKOV, Mirko ILIJEVSKI, Sokrat MOJSOV, KOVACEVSKI, Stojan
VELKOVSKI, Methodije SPASOVSKI.
Goal: FK Vardar Skopje: 0-1 Stojan VELKOVSKI (81').
Referee: Eduard BABAUCZEK (AUT)

27-03-1968   Megyeri úti Stadion, Budapest:
                Újpesti Dózsa SC – FK Austria Wien   4-1 (3-0)
Újpesti Dózsa SC: Antal SZENTMIHÁLYI (24' László BORBÉLY), Benö KÁPOSZTA, Ernö
SOLYMOSI (I), Kálmán SÓVÁRI, Ede DUNAI (III), Ernö NOSKÓ (46' József SZINI),
László FAZEKAS, János GÖRÖCS, Ferenc BENE, Antal DUNAI (II), András TÓTH.
(Coach: Lajos BARÓTI).
FK Austria Wien: Rudolf SZANWALD, Robert SARA, Gustav PROVAZNIK, Karl
FRÖHLICH, Heinz NOWY, Alfons DIRNBERGER, Thomas PARITS, Walter HIESEL (46'
Franz HOCHLEUTNER), Herbert POINDL, Josef HICKERSBERGER, Ernst FIALA. (Coach:
Ernst OCWIRK).
Goals: Újpesti Dózsa SC: 1-0 János GÖRÖCS (1'), 2-0 László FAZEKAS (8'), 3-0 László
FAZEKAS (30'), 4-1 Ernö SOLYMOSI (63').
FK Austria Wien: 3-1 Josef HICKERSBERGER (50').
Referee: Konstantin ZECEVIC (YUG)   Attendance: 18.000

187

03-04-1968   Bratislava:
TJ Internacional Slovnaft Bratislava – FK Crvena Zvezda Beograd   3-2 (2-1)
TJ Internacional Slovnaft Bratislava: Peter FÜLLE, Milan HRICA, Vladimír WEISS (I),
Ottmar DEUTSCH, Pavol DAUCÍK, Eduard GÁBORÍK (46' Vladimír KONDERLÍK), Titus
BUBERNÍK, Jozef LEVICKÝ, Juraj SZIKORA, Mikulás KRNÁC, Ján ONDRÁSEK. (Coach:
Ladislav KACÁNI).
FK Crvena Zvezda Beograd: Dragan RACIC, Milovan DJORIC, Petar KRIVOKUCA,
Miroslav PAVLOVIC, Kiril (Kiro) DOJCINOVSKI, Branko KLENKOVSKI, Zoran
ANTONIJEVIC, Stevan OSTOJIC, Vojin LAZAREVIC, Slobodan SKRBIC, DAKIC. (Coach:
Miljan MILJANIC).
Goals: TJ Internacional Slovnaft Bratislava: 1-0 Juraj SZIKORA (11'), 2-0 Mikulás KRNAC
(14'), 3-1 Ján ONDRASEK (50').
FK Crvena Zvezda Beograd: 2-1 Stevan OSTOJIC (35'), 3-2 Vojin LAZAREVIC (51').
Referee: Ferdinand MARSCHALL (AUT)   Attendance: 6.000

SEMI-FINALS

08-05-1968   Trnava: TJ Spartak TAZ Trnava – FK Vardar Skopje   4-1 (2-1)
TJ Spartak TAZ Trnava: Frantisek KOZINKA, Karol DOBIAS, Stanislav JARÁBEK, ..., ...,
Anton HRUSECKÝ, Ladislav KUNA, Stanislav MARTINKOVIC, Valerián SVEC (80'
Vojtech VARADÍN), Jozef ADAMEC, Dusan KABÁT. (Coach: Anton MALATINSKÝ).
FK Vardar Skopje: Dragan MUTIBARIC, RAC, MOJSOV (I), Sokrat MOJSOV (II), ..., ..., ...,
DROBAC, KOVACEVSKI, Methodije SPASOVSKI, Stojan VELKOVSKI.
Goals: TJ Spartak TAZ Trnava: 1-1 Stanislav MARTINKOVIC (23'), 2-1 Jozef ADAMEC
(26' penalty), 3-1 Jozef ADAMEC (69'), 4-1 Metodije SPASOVSKI (83' own goal).
FK Vardar Skopje: 0-1 Stojan VELKOVSKI (15').
Referee: Alessandro D'AGOSTINI (ITA)   Attendance: 11.000

29-05-1968   Megyeri úti Stadion, Budapest:
Újpesti Dózsa SC – FK Crvena Zvezda Beograd   1-0
Újpesti Dózsa SC: Antal SZENTMIHÁLYI, Benö KÁPOSZTA, Ernö SOLYMOSI (I), József
SZINI, Ede DUNAI (III), Ernö NOSKÓ, László FAZEKAS, János GÖRÖCS, Ferenc BENE,
Antal DUNAI (II), Sándor ZÁMBÓ. (Coach: Lajos BARÓTI).
FK Crvena Zvezda Beograd: Ratomir DUJKOVIC, Djoric MILOVAN, Blagoje
KRIVOKUCA (I), Petar KRIVOKUCA (II), Kiril (Kiro) DOJCINOVSKI, Sava
KARAPANDZIC, Zoran ANTONIJEVIC, Stevan OSTOJIC, Vojin LAZAREVIC, Jovan
ACIMOVIC, Trifun MIHAJLOVIC. (Coach: Miljan MILJANIC).
Goal: Újpesti Dózsa SC: 1-0 László FAZEKAS (..').

29-05-1968   Skopje: FK Vardar Skopje – TJ Spartak TAZ Trnava   2-2 (0-1)
FK Vardar Skopje: ATANASOVSKI, RAC, DONCIC, GEORGIEVSKI, Atanas
MECKAROV, PLACKOV, Mirko ILIJEVSKI, VRBICA, Stojan VELKOVSKI,
SEKULARAC (46' Vanco SPASOVKSI), Metodije SPASOVSKI.
TJ Spartak TAZ Trnava: Josef GERYK, Karol DOBIAS, Stanislav JARÁBEK, Vladimir
HAGARA, Ján ZLOCHA, Anton HRUSECKÝ, Ladislav KUNA, Stanislav MARTINKOVIC,
Valerián SVEC (88' Adam FARKAS), Alojz FANDL, Dusan KABÁT. (Coach: Anton
MALATINSKÝ).
Goals: FK Vardar Skopje: 1-1 Vancó SPASOVSKI (50'), 2-1 Mirko ILIJEVSKI (63' penalty).
TJ Spartak TAZ Trnava: 0-1 Valerián SVEC (35'), 2-2 Dusan KABAT (84').
Referee: Franz WÖHRER (AUT)   Attendance: 4.000

06-06-1968   Stadion Crvena Zvezda, Beograd:
               FK Crvena Zvezda Beograd – Újpesti Dózsa SC   4-1
FK Crvena Zvezda Beograd: Ratomir DUJKOVIC, Djoric MILOVAN, Blagoje
KRIVOKUCA (I), Petar KRIVOKUCA (II), Kiril (Kiro) DOJCINOVSKI, Rudolf BELIN,
Zoran ANTONIJEVIC, Stevan OSTOJIC, Vojin LAZAREVIC, Jovan ACIMOVIC, Trifun
MIHAJLOVIC. (Coach: Miljan MILJANIC).
Újpesti Dózsa SC: Antal SZENTMIHÁLYI, Benö KÁPOSZTA, Ernö SOLYMOSI (I), József
SZINI, Ede DUNAI (III), Ernö NOSKÓ, László FAZEKAS, János GÖRÖCS, Ferenc BENE,
Antal DUNAI (II), Sándor ZÁMBÓ. (Coach: Lajos BARÓTI).
Goals: FK Crvena Zvezda Beograd: Vojin LAZAREVIC, Ede DUNAI (*own goal*), Trifun
MIHAJLOVIC, Vojin LAZAREVIC.
Újpesti Dózsa SC: Ede DUNAI.

FINAL

16-10-1968   Spartak Stadion, Trnava:
               TJ Spartak TAZ Trnava – FK Crvena Zvezda Beograd   1-0 (0-0)
TJ Spartak TAZ Trnava: Frantisek KOZINKA, Karol DOBIAS (74' Alojz FANDEL), Kamil
MAJERNIK, Vladimir HAGARA, Vlastimil BOZIK, Anton HRUSECKÝ, Ladislav KUNA,
Adam FARKAS (46' Stanislav MARTINKOVIC), Valerián SVEC (74' Substitute not known),
Jozef ADAMEC, Dusan KABAT. (Coach: Ján HUCKO).
FK Crvena Zvezda Beograd: Dragan RACIC, Milovan DJORIC, Kiril (Kiro) DOJCINOVSKI,
Dragoslav STEPANOVIC, Blagomir KRIVOKUCA, Zoran ANTONIJEVIC, Branko
KLENKOVSKI, Stevan OSTOJIC, Vojin LAZAREVIC, Tomislav PROSEN, Josip BUKAL
(74' Substitute not known). (Coach: Miljan MILJANIC).
Goal: TJ Spartak TAZ Trnava: 1-0 Valerián SVEC (47').
Referee: Bruno DE MARCHI (ITA)   Attendance: 12.500

23-10-1968   Beograd: FK Crvena Zvezda Beograd – TJ Spartak TAZ Trnava   4-1 (1-1)
FK Crvena Zvezda Beograd: Ratomir DUJKOVIC, Milovan DJORIC, Blagomir
KRIVOKUCA, Miroslav PAVLOVIC, Kiril (Kiro) DOJCINOVSKI, Branko KLENKOVSKI,
Zoran ANTONIJEVIC, Stevan OSTOJIC, Vojin LAZAREVIC, Jovan ACIMOVIC, Dragan
DZAJIC. (Coach: Miljan MILJANIC).
TJ Spartak TAZ Trnava: Frantisek KOZINKA, Vojtech VARADIN, Kamil MAJERNIK,
Vladimir HAGARA, Vlastimil BOZIK, Anton HRUSECKY, Ladislav KUNA, Stanislav
MARTINKOVIC, Valerián SVEC, Jozef ADAMEC, Dusan KABAT. (Coach: Ján HUCKO).
Goals: FK Crvena Zvezda Beograd: 1-0 Vojin LAZAREVIC (35'), 2-1 Stevan OSTOJIC (56'),
3-1 Zoran ANTONIJEVIC (64'), 4-1 Vojin LAZAREVIC (69').
TJ Spartak TAZ Trnava: 1-1 Ladislav KUNA (39').
Referee: Erich LINEMAYR (AUT)   Attendance: 20.000

*** FK Crvena Zvezda Beograd won the Cup ***

189

1968-1969

13-11-1968   Bozsik József Stadion, Budapest:
              Budapesti Honvéd SE – FK Zeljeznicar Sarajevo 0-1
Budapesti Honvéd SE: Bertalan BICSKEI, József TAJTI, József RUZSINSZKY, Pál VÁRI,
László MAROSI, István VÁGI, Antal TUSSINGER (..' Gyula TÓTH), Lajos KOCSIS, Lajos
TICHY, Imre KOMORA, Kálmán TÓTH. (Coach: Kálmán PREINER).
FK Zeljeznicar Sarajevo:
Goal: FK Zeljeznikar Sarajevo: 0-1
Attendance: 5.000

27-11-1968   Bányász Stadion, Tatabánya:
              Tatabányai Bányász SC – TJ Sklo Union Teplice 3-3 (1-2)
Tatabányai Bányász SC: József GELEI, István LÉVAI (46' Ferenc SIMA), Tibor KOVÁCS
(I), László JUHOS, Ferenc HORVÁTH, Mihály LACZKÓ, György SZABÓ, Tibor CSERNAI,
Mihály ARANY, László HERNÁDI (60' Tivadar MONOSTORI), Attila LADINSZKY.
(Coach: György SZÜCS).
TJ Sklo Union Teplice: Jirí SEDLÁCEK, Rudolf SMETANA, Josef MYSLIVEC, Jirí
NOVÁK, Jirí SETÍNSKÝ, Karel ZENÍSEK, Frantisek JÍLEK, Premysl BICOVSKÝ, Jaroslav
VOJTA, Pavel STRATIL, Ján GOMOLA (62' Ivan STUDENT). (Coach: Antonín RÝGR).
Goals: Tatabányai Bányász SC: 1-2 Tibor CSERNAI (40'), 2-2 Ferenc HORVÁTH (65'),
Attila LADINSZKY (82').
TJ Sklo Union Teplice: 0-1 Pavel STRATIL (22'), 0-2 Pavel STRATIL (30'), 2-3 Pavel
STRATIL (75').
Referee: Josip STRMECKI (YUG)   Attendance: 4.000

04-12-1968   Sportklubplatz, Wien: Wiener Sportklub – US Cagliari 1-0 (0-0)
Wiener Sportklub: Wilhelm KAIPEL, Anton LINHART, Ernst HAIDER, Helmut WALLNER,
Horst BLANKENBURG (FRG), Norbert HOF (II), Finn LAUDRUP (DEN), Hans BUZEK,
Wolfgang GAYER (FRG), Herbert ONGER, Johann HÖRMAYER. (Coach: Johann (Hans)
PESSER).
US Cagliari: Enrico ALBERTOSI, Giulio ZIGNOLI, Giuseppe LONGONI, Pierluigi CERA,
Comunardo NICCOLAI, Giuseppe TOMASINI, Claudio Olinto de Carvalho NENÉ (BRA),
Mario BRUGNERA, Roberto BONINSEGNA, Ricciotti GREATTI, Luigi RIVA. (Coach:
Manlio SCOPIGNO).
Goal: Wiener Sportklub: 1-0 Norbert HOF (50' penalty).
Referee: SKALA (TCH)   Attendance: 5.000

190

04-12-1968   Fáy utcai Stadion, Budapest: Vasas SC – SK Sturm Graz 4-3 (2-1)
Vasas SC: László VARGA, Sándor BAKOS, Kálmán MÉSZÖLY, Kálmán IHÁSZ, Imre
MATHESZ, Iván MENCZEL, Dezsö MOLNÁR (..' János RADICS), Lajos PUSKÁS (..'
Sándor MÜLLER), János FARKAS, Ferenc FISTER, István KORSÓS. (Coach: Rudolf
ILLOVSZKY).
SK Sturm Graz: Damir GRLOCI (YUG) (..' Dr.Günther PAULITSCH), Marijan BEREK
(YUG), Heinz RUSS, Manfred REITER, Franz REITER, Walter FUCHS, Helmut WAGNER,
Walter PEINTINGER, Robert KAISER, Helmut HUBERTS (I), Anton HÖGGERL (..'
Wilhelm HUBERTS (II)). (Coach: Gerhard (Gerd) SPRINGER).
Goals: Vasas SC: 1-0 Kálmán MÉSZÖLY (17'), 2-1 Lajos PUSKÁS (45'), 3-1 Sándor
MÜLLER (50'), 4-2 István KORSÓS (63').
SK Sturm Graz: 1-1 Robert KAISER (41'), 3-2 Robert KAISER (61'), 4-3 Walter
PEINTINGER (70').
Referee: Ratko CANAK (YUG)   Attendance: 4.000

04-12-1968   Bratislava:
              TJ Internacional Slovnaft Bratislava – US Palermo 3-0 (3-0)
TJ Internacional Slovnaft Bratislava: Justin JAVOREK, Milan HRICA, Peter SOLIN, Ottmar
DEUTSCH, Vladimír WEISS (I), Anton OBLOZINSKÝ (46' Eduard GÁBORÍK), Michal
MEDVID, Jozef LEVICKÝ, Juraj SZIKORA (78' Vladimír KONDERLÍK), Mikulás KRNÁC,
Ján ONDRÁSEK. (Coach: Ladislav KACÁNI).
US Palermo: Gianvito GEOTTI, Giorgio COSTANTINI, Ido SGRAZZUTTI, Carlo LANCINI,
Mario GIUBERTONI, Franco LANDRI (46' Antonio DE BELLIS), Gilbert PERRUCCONI,
Giuseppe FURINO, Gaetano TROJA, Silvino BERCELLINO (I), Enrico NOVA. (Coach:
Carmelo DI BELLA).
Goals: TJ Internacional Slovnaft Bratislava: 1-0 Juraj SZIKORA (8' penalty), 2-0 Franco
LANDRI (24' own goal), 3-0 Michal MEDVID (45').
Referee: Ferdinand MARSCHALL (AUT)   Attendance: 1.000

04-12-1968   Sarajevo: FK Zeljeznicar Sarajevo – Budapesti Honvéd SE 1-0 (0-0)
FK Zeljeznicar Sarajevo:
Budapesti Honvéd SE: ... (Coach: Kálmán PREINER).
Attendance: 4.000

04-12-1968   Stadion Na Stínadlech, Teplice:
              TJ Sklo Union Teplice – Tatabányai Bányász SC 3-0 (2-0)
TJ Sklo Union Teplice: Jirí SEDLÁCEK, Emil STIBOR, Josef MYSLIVEC, Jirí NOVÁK, Jirí
SETÍNSKÝ, Rudolf SMETANA, Frantisek JÍLEK, Jaroslav VOJTA (..' Julius KANTOR),
Premysl BICOVSKÝ, Pavel STRATIL, Ján GOMOLA. (Coach: Antonín RÝGR).
Tatabányai Bányász SC: József GELEI, István LÉVAI (70' Ferenc TÖRÖCSIK), Tibor
KOVÁCS (I), László JUHOS, Ferenc HORVÁTH, Mihály LACZKÓ, György SZABÓ, Tibor
CSERNAI, Mihály ARANY, László HERNÁDI (80' Ferenc SIMA), Attila LADINSZKY.
(Coach: György SZÜCS).
Goals: TJ Sklo Union Teplice: 1-0 Frantisek JÍLEK (38' penalty), 2-0 Pavel STRATIL (43'),
3-0 Pavel STRATIL (51').
Referee: Franz WÖHRER (AUT)   Attendance: 3.000

191

11-12-1968   Bergamo: Atalanta Bergamo – FK Crvena Zvezda Beograd 2-4 (1-2)
Atalanta Bergamo: Claudio MANTOVANI, Enrico DORDONI, Franco NODARI (69'
MOROSINI), Ambrogio PELAGALLI, Giuseppe ZANIBONI, Ivan BERTUOLO, Corrado
NASTASIO, Paolo LAZZOTTI, Sergio CLERICI (BRA) (60' Giancarlo ROFFI), Giampaolo
INCERTI, Adriano NOVELLINI. (Coach: Stefano ANGELERI).
FK Crvena Zvezda Beograd: Dragan RACIC, Milovan DJORIC, Blagomir KRIVOKUCA,
Miroslav PAVLOVIC, Kiril (Kiro) DOJCINOVSKI, Sava KARAPANDRIC, Zoran
ANTONIJEVIC (46' Aleksandar MARKOVIC), Stevan OSTOJIC, Vojin LAZAREVIC,
Jovan ACIMOVIC, Dragan DZAJIC. (Coach: Miljan MILJANIC).,
Goals: Atalanta Bergamo: 1-2 INCERTI (20'), 2-2 Adriano NOVELLINI (47').
FK Crneva Zvezda Beograd: 0-1 Vojin LAZAREVIC (7'), 0-2 Dragan DZAJIC (16'), 2-3
Dragan DZAJIC (61'), 2-4 Stevan OSTOJIC (80').
Referee: P.SANDOR (HUN)

11-12-1968   Skopje: FK Vardar Skopje – Admira-Energie Wien 2-2 (0-1)
FK Vardar Skopje: ANATOSIOVSKI, PALEVSKI, BALEVSKI, ..., SPASOVSKI.
Admira-Energie Wien: Johann DRAXELMAYER, Karl ROSNER, Michael BREIBERT,
Walter STAMM, Heinrich STRASSER (..' Robert LENGYEL), Werner BEDERNIK, Gerhard
BÖHMER, Josef HOLATA, Wilhelm (Willy) KREUZ, Felix LATZKE, Johann (Hans)
PIRKNER. (Coach: Anton MALATINSKÝ (TCH)).
Goals: FK Vardar Skopje: 1-2 BALEVSKI (60'), 2-2 SPASOVSKI (67').
Admira-Energie Wien: 0-1 Wilhelm (Willy) KREUZ (25' penalty), 0-2 Felix LATZKE (49').
Attendance: 500

14-12-1968   Bazaly Stadion, Ostrava: TJ Baník Ostrava – NK Hajduk Split 4-1 (2-1)
TJ Baník Ostrava:Frantisek SCHMUCKER, Alfréd BARSCH, Karel HEROT, Jan KNIEZEK,
Karel WEISS, Anton ONDÁK, Karel JÜNGER, Miroslav MICKA, Milan POSTULKA,
Valerián BARTALSKÝ, Ladislav MICHALÍK (75' Josef KOLECKO). (Coach: Oldrich
UBRT).
NK Hajduk Split: Ante SIRKOVIC, Marino LEMESIC, Ivica HLEVNJAK, Vinko CUZZI,
Petar BONACIC, Miroslav FERIC, Jurica JERKOVIC, Ante IVKOVIC, Bosko BURSAC,
Miroslav VARDIC, Ivan PAVLICA. (Coach: Dusan NENKOVIC).
Goals: TJ Baník Ostrava: 1-0 Milan POSTULKA (..'), 2-0 Milan POSTULKA (8'), 3-1 Milan
POSTULKA (46'), 4-1 Ladislav MICHALÍK (49').
NK Hajduk Split: 2-1 Bosko BURSAC (..').
Referee: Aurelio ANGONESE (ITA)   Attendance: 1.000

18-12-1968   Palermo: SSC Palermo – TJ Internacional Slovnaft Bratislava 1-0 (0-0)
US Palermo: Idilio CEI, Giorgio COSTANTINI, Giuseppe FURINO, Carlo LANCINI, Mario
GIUBERTONI, Franco LANDRI, Sergio PELLIZZARO Domenicacci, Graziano LANDONI,
Gaetano TROJA (55' Enrico NOVA), Edoardo REJA, Enzo FERRARI. (Coach: Carmelo DI
BELLA).
TJ Internacional Slovnaft Bratislava: Justin JAVOREK, Milan HRICA, Peter SOLIN, Ottmar
DEUTSCH, Dr.Alexander BINOVSKY, Jozef JURCO, Anton OBLOZINSKÝ, Jozef
LEVICKÝ, Michal MEDVID (65' Mikulás KRNÁC), Juraj SZIKORA, Ján ONDRÁSEK.
(Coach: Ladislav KACÁNI).
Goal: SSC Palermo: 1-0 Sergio PELLIZZARO Domenicacci (58').
Referee: Konstantin ZECEVIC (YUG)   Attendance: 30.000

192

18-12-1968   Stadio Amsicora, Cagliari: UC Cagliari – Wiener Sportklub   2-1 (2-0)
US Cagliari: Enrico ALBERTOSI, Giulio ZIGNOLI, Giuseppe LONGONI, Pierluigi CERA,
Comunardo NICCOLAI, Giuseppe TOMASINI, Claudio Olinto de Carvalho NENÉ (BRA),
Mario BRUGNERA (46' Roberto BONINSEGNA), Gerald Archibald (Gerry) HITCHENS
(ENG) (62' Giuseppe FERRERO), Ricciotti GREATTI, Luigi RIVA. (Coach: Manlio
SCOPIGNO).
Wiener Sportklub: Wilhelm KAIPEL, Anton LINHART, Ernst HAIDER, Helmut WALLNER,
Horst BLANKENBURG (FRG), Erich HOF (I), Finn LAUDRUP (DEN) (65' Herbert
ONGER), Hans BUZEK, Wolfgang GAYER (FRG), Norbert HOF (II), Johann HÖRMAYER.
Goals: US Cagliari: 1-0 Mario BRUGNERA (14'), 2-0 Mario BRUGNERA (16').
Wiener Sportklub: 2-1 Herbert ONGER (81').
Referee: Gyula EMSBERGER (HUN)   Attendance: 15.000

22-12-1968   Split: NK Hajduk Split – TJ Baník Ostrava   2-1 (1-0)
Goals: NK Hajduk Split: BURSAC (2x).
TJ Baník Ostrava: Valerián BARTALSKÝ.

22-12-1968   Wien: Admira-Energie Wien – FK Vardar Skopje   3-0 (1-0)
Admira-Energie Wien: Johann DRAXELMAYER, Karl ROSNER, ..., Felix LATZKE, ...
(Coach: Anton MALATINSKÝ (TCH)).
FK Vardar Skopje:
Goals: Admira-Energie Wien: 1-0 Felix LATZKE (44'), 2-0 Felix LATZKE (87'), 3-0 Felix
LATZKE (90').
Attendance: 2.500

29-12-1968   Beograd: FK Crvena Zvezda Beograd – Atalanta Bergamo   5-1 (2-0)
FK Crvena Zvezda Beograd: Ratomir DUJKOVIC (64' KALGANIC), Blagomir
KRIVOKUCA, Zivorad JEVTIC, Miroslav PAVLOVIC, Kiril (Kiro) DOJCINOVSKI, Branko
KLENKOVSKI, Zoran ANTONIJEVIC (46' Slobodan JANKOVSKI), Stevan OSTOJIC,
Vojin LAZAREVIC, Jovan ACIMOVIC, Trifun MIHAJLOVIC. (Coach: Miljan MILJANIC).
Atalanta Bergamo: Giorgio DE ROSSI, Luciano POPPI, Franco NODARI (70' Giuliano
CASTOLDI), Enrico DORDONI, Piero DOTTI, Ivan BERTUOLO, Corrado NASTASIO,
Alberto SIRONI, Sergio CLERICI (BRA), Paolo LAZZOTTI, Giampaolo INCERTI (46'
Adriano NOVELLINI). (Coach: Stefano ANGELERI).
Goals: FK Crvena Zv ezda Beograd: 1-0 Zoran ANTONIJEVIC (24'), 2-0 Vojin LAZAREVIC
(42'), 3-1 Vojin LAZAREVIC (71'), 4-1 Stevan OSTOJIC (77'), 5-1 Trifun MIHAJLOVIC
(90').
Atalanta Bergamo: 2-1 Adriano NOVELLINI (63').
Referee: Egon GRUBER (AUT)

18-02-1969   Sturm-Platz, Graz: SK Sturm Graz – Vasas SC   1-2 (1-2)
SK Sturm Graz: Damir GRLOCI (YUG), Marijan BEREK (YUG), Manfred REITER,
Wilhelm HUBERTS (II), Franz REITER, Helmut WAGNER, Odilon Ribeiro TESOURINHO
(BRA), Alfred MURLASITS, Robert KAISER, Helmut HUBERTS (I), Anton HÖGGERL
(52' Ladislaus SWOBODA). (Coach: Gerhard (Gerd) SPRINGER).
Vasas SC: István KENDERESI, Sándor BAKOS, Kálmán MÉSZÖLY, Kálmán IHÁSZ,
Sándor MÜLLER, Imre MATHESZ (65' Lajos NELL), Dezsö MOLNÁR (70' Csaba
VIDÁTS), Lajos PUSKÁS, Iván MENCZEL, János FARKAS, Ferenc FISTER. (Coach:
Rudolf ILLOVSZKY).
Goals: SK Sturm Graz: 1-2 Odilon Ribeiro TESOURINHO (26').
Vasas SC: 0-1 Lajos PUSKÁS (8'), 0-2 Ferenc FISTER (18').
Referee: Dragomir Josip HORVATH (YUG)   Attendance: 3.000

QUARTER-FINALS

19-03-1969   Ostrava: TJ Baník Ostrava – FK Zeljeznicar Sarajevo   1-1 (0-0)
Goals: TJ Baník Ostrava: 1-1 Valerián BARTALSKÝ   (57').
FK Zeljeznicar Sarajevo: 0-1 A.DERAKOVIC (47').
Referee: Dimitris WLACHOJANIS (AUT)   Attendance: 3.500

26-03-1969   Stadion Crvena Zvezda, Beograd: FK Crvena Zvezda Beograd – Vasas SC   1-2
FK Crvena Zvezda Beograd: Ratomir DUJKOVIC, Milovan DJORIC, Blagomir
KRIVOKUCA, Miroslav PAVLOVIC, Kiril (Kiro) DOJCINOVSKI, Branko KLENKOVSKI,
Zoran ANTONIJEVIC (..' Slobodan JANKOVIC), Stevan OSTOJIC, Vojin LAZAREVIC,
Jovan ACIMOVIC (..' ZIVKOVIC), Dragan DZAJIC. (Coach: Miljan MILJANIC).
Vasas SC: István KENDERESI, Sándor BAKOS, Kálmán MÉSZÖLY, Csaba VIDÁTS,
Kálmán IHÁSZ, Iván MENCZEL, Sándor MÜLLER (..' Bálint TÓTH), Lajos NELL (..' Ottó
VÁRADI), Dezsö MOLNÁR, Lajos PUSKÁS, János FARKAS. (Coach: Rudolf
ILLOVSZKY).
Goals: FK Crvena Zvezda Beograd: Csaba VIDÁTS (..' own goal).
Vasas SC: Dezsö MOLNÁR, Lajos NELL.
Attendance: 30.000

02-04-1969   Wien: Wiener Sportklub – TJ Sklo Union Teplice   1-1 (1-0)
Wiener Sportklub: Wilhelm KAIPEL, Anton LINHART, Horst BLANKENBURG (FRG),
Ernst HAIDER, Helmut WALLNER, Norbert HOF (II), Herbert ONGER, Wolfgang GAYER
(FRG), Finn LAUDRUP (DEN), Anton HERZOG (65' Alfred HALA), Johann HÖRMAYER.
TJ Sklo Union Teplice: Jirí SEDLACEK, Emil STIBOR (75' Frantisek ZUREK), Josef
MYSLIVEC, Jirí NOVAK, Jirí SETINSKY, Rudolf SMETANA, Frantisek JILEK, Vladimir
ZALUD, Pavel STRATIL, Ladislav BARTIK (69' Premysl BICOVSKY), Ján GOMOLA.
(Coach: Antonin RYGR).
Goals: Wiener Sportklub: 1-0 Helmut WALLNER (15').
TJ Sklo Union Teplice: 1-1 Pavel STRATIL (88').
Referee: Francesco FRANCESCON (ITA)   Attendance: 3.500

02-04-1969   Sarajevo: FK Zeljeznicar Sarajevo – TJ Baník Ostrava   4-0 (3-0)
Goals: FK Zeljeznicar Sarajevo: 1-0 Edin SPRECO (..'), 2-0 Edin SPRECO (..'), 3-0 Fikret
MUJKIC (..'), 4-0 Josip BUKAL (..').
Referee: Gusztav BIRCSAK (HUN)

02-04-1969   Faý utcai Stadion, Budapest:
                Vasas SC – FK Crvena Zvezda Beograd   3-2 (2-0)
Vasas SC: István KENDERESI, Sándor BAKOS, Kálmán MÉSZÖLY (..' Sándor MÜLLER),
Csaba VIDÁTS, Kálmán IHÁSZ, Iván MENCZEL, Ferenc FISTER (..' Lajos NELL), Dezsö
MOLNÁR, János RADICS, Lajos PUSKÁS, János FARKAS. (Coach: Rudolf ILLOVSZKY).
FK Crvena Zvezda Beograd: Ratomir DUJKOVIC, Milovan DJORIC, Kiril (Kiro)
DOJCINOVSKI, Aleksandar MARKOVIC, Miroslav PAVLOVIC, Branko KLENKOVSKI,
Jovan ACIMOVIC, Zoran ANTONIJEVIC (..' ZIVKOVIC), Stevan OSTOJIC, Vojin
LAZAREVIC, Dragan DZAJIC. (Coach: Miljan MILJANIC).
Goals: Vasas SC: Dezsö MOLNÁR, János RADICS, János FARKAS.
FK Crvena Zvezda Beograd: Kiril (Kiro) DOJCINOVSKI, Stevan OSTOJIC.

07-04-1969   Wien: Admira-Energie Wien – TJ Internacional Slovnaft Bratislava 2-2 (0-0)
Admira-Energie Wien: Johann DRAXELMAYER, Karl ROSNER, Paul KOZLICEK, Walter
STAMM (..' Erich KREUZ), Heinrich STRASSER, Johannes DEMANTKE, Peter BÜRGER,
Wilhelm (Willy) KREUZ, Felix LATZKE, Gerhard BÖHMER, Josef HOLATA. (Coach:
Anton MALATINSKÝ (TCH)).
TJ Internacional Slovnaft Bratislava: Peter FÜLLE (65' Justin JAVOREK), Milan HRICA,
Peter SOLÍN, Ottmar DEUTSCH, Ivan DANO, Jozef JURCO, Anton OBLOZINSKÝ, Jozef
LEVICKÝ, Juraj SZIKORA (74' Mikulás KRNÁC), Michal MEDVID, Ján ONDRÁSEK.
(Coach: Ladislav KACÁNI).
Goals: Admira-Energie Wien: 1-0 Wilhelm (Willy) KREUZ (60'), 2-0 Wilhelm (Willy)
KREUZ (74').
TJ Internacional Slovnaft Bratislava: 2-1 Mikulás KRNÁC (78'), 2-2 Peter SOLÍN (82').
Referee: László VIZHANYO (HUN)   Attendance: 1.500

15-04-1969   Bratislava:
              TJ Internacional Slovnaft Bratislava – Admira-Energie Wien 1-1 (0-1)
TJ Internacional Slovnaft Bratislava: Péter FÜLLE, Milan HRICA, Peter SOLIN, Ottmar
DEUTSCH, Ivan DANO, Anton OBLOZINSKÝ, Vladimír KONDERLÍK (46' Vladimír
WEISS (I)), Jozef LEVICKÝ, Michal MEDVID, Mikulás KRNÁC, Jan ONDRASEK. (Coach:
Ladislav KACÁNI).
Admira-Energie Wien: Dragomir VUKICEVIC (YUG), Werner BEDERNIK, Karl ROSNER,
Paul KOZLICEK, Heinrich STRASSER, Karl NIKISCHER, Josef HOLATA, Anton
HERZOG, Johannes DEMANTKE (88' Peter BÜRGER), Felix LATZKE, Gerhard BÖHMER.
(Coach: Anton MALATINSKÝ (TCH)).
Goals: TJ Internacional Slovnaft Bratislava: 1-1 Ján ONDRASEK (70').
Admira-Energie Wien: 0-1 Anton HERZOG (39').
Referee: Ratko CANAK (YUG)   Attendance: 2.500

30-04-1969   Teplice: TJ Sklo Union Teplice – Wiener Sportklub 2-0 (0-0)
TJ Sklo Union Teplice: Václav KAMERNÍK, Frantisek ZUREK, Josef MYSLIVEC, Jirí
SETINSKY, Frantisek VÍTU, Rudolf SMETANA, Vladimir ZALUD, Pavel STRATIL,
Frantisek JÍLEK (80' Jirí NOVÁK), Ladislav BÁRTÍK (70' Premysl BICOVSKÝ), Ján
GOMOLA. (Coach: Antonin RYGR).
Wiener Sportklub: Wilhelm KAIPEL, Anton LINHART, Horst BLANKENBURG (FRG),
Ernst HAIDER, Helmut WALLNER (71' Werner REITBAUER), Norbert HOF (II), Josef
PRIBIL, Wolfgang GAYER (FRG), Finn LAUDRUP (DEN), Anton HERZOG, Johann
HÖRMAYER (71' Herbert ONGER).
Goals: TJ Sklo Union Teplice: 1-0 Vladimir ZALUD (68'), 2-0 Premysl BICOVSKÝ (89').
Referee: Lado JASKE (YUG)   Attendance: 8.000

07-05-1969   Bratislava: TJ Internacional Slovnaft Bratislava – Vasas SC 2-2 (1-0)
TJ Internacional Slovnaft Bratislava: Justin JAVOREK, Milan HRICA, Dr.Alexander
BINOVSKY, Ottmar DEUTSCH, Ivan DANO, Michal MEDVID, Anton OBLOZINSKÝ,
Jozef LEVICKÝ, Juraj SZIKORA, Mikulás KRNÁC, Jan ONDRASEK (70' Jozef JURCO).
(Coach: Ladislav KACANI).
Vasas SC: István KENDERESI, Sándor BAKOS, Kálmán MÉSZÖLY, Csaba VIDÁTS,
Kálmán IHÁSZ, Iván MENCZEL, Ferenc FISTER, Dezsö MOLNÁR, Lajos PUSKÁS, János
RADICS (46' Sándor MÜLLER), János FARKAS. (Coach: Rudolf ILLOVSZKY).
Goals: TJ Internacional Slovnaft Bratislava: 1-0 Juraj SZIKORA (35'), 2-0 Mikulás KRNÁC
(58').
Vasas SC: 2-1 Lajos PUSKÁS (61'), 2-2 János FARKAS (71').
Referee: Milivoje GUGULOVIC (YUG)   Attendance: 7.000

20-05-1969   Fáy utcai Stadion, Budapest:
                      Vasas SC – TJ Internacional Slovnaft Bratislava 0-1 (0-0)
Vasas SC: István KENDERESI, Sándor BAKOS, Iván MENCZEL, Csaba VIDÁTS, Kálmán
IHÁSZ, Sándor MÜLLER, Ferenc FISTER, Dezsö MOLNÁR, Lajos KOCSIS, János RADICS
(69' Lajos NELL), Lajos PUSKÁS. (Coach: Rudolf ILLOVSZKY).
TJ Internacional Slovnaft Bratislava: Péter FÜLLE, Milan HRICA, Dr.Alexander
BINOVSKY, Ottmar DEUTSCH, Ivan DANO, Jozef JURCO, Anton OBLOZINSKÝ, Jozef
LEVICKÝ, Michal MEDVID, Mikulás KRNÁC, Jan ONDRÁSEK. (Coach: Ladislav
KACÁNI).
Goal: TJ Internacional Slovnaft Bratislava: 0-1 Michal MEDVID (81').
Referee: Paul SCHILLER (AUT)   Attendance: 8.000

21-05-1969   Sarajevo: FK Zeljeznicar Sarajevo – TJ Sklo Union Teplice 1-1 (1-0)
FK Zeljeznicar Sarajevo: Vasilije RADOVIC, Midhat MUJKIC, H.SARACEVIC, Dusan
JOVANOVIC, V.BECIRSPAHIC, Blagoje BRATIC, D.BAJIC (70' Fikret MUJKIC),
Branimir JELUSIC, Ivan OSIM, Josip BUKAL, Edin SPRECO,
TJ Sklo Union Teplice: Jirí SEDLÁCEK, Emil STIBOR, Jirí NOVÁK, Josef MYSLIVEC, Jirí
SETINSKY, Rudolf SMETANA, Ladislav BÁRTÍK (46' Frantisek JÍLEK), Premysl
BICOVSKÝ, Frantisek VÍTU, Pavel STRATIL, Ján GOMOLA (87' Frantisek ZUREK).
(Coach: Antonin RYGR).
Goals: FK Zeljeznicar Sarajevo: 1-0 Josip BUKAL (29').
TJ Sklo Union Teplice: 1-1 Pavel STRATIL (..' penalty).

28-05-1969   Teplice: TJ Sklo Union Teplice – FK Zeljeznicar Sarajevo 2-1 (0-0)
TJ Sklo Union Teplice: Jirí SEDLÁCEK, Emil STIBOR (68' Frantisek ZUREK), Jirí
NOVÁK, Josef MYSLIVEC, Jirí SETINSKY, Rudolf SMETANA, Ladislav BÁRTÍK (46'
Frantisek JÍLEK), Premysl BICOVSKÝ, Frantisek VÍTU, Pavel STRATIL, Ján GOMOLA
(87' Frantisek ZUREK). (Coach: Antonin RYGR).
FK Zeljeznicar Sarajevo: Vasilije RADOVIC, Midhat MUJKIC (I), V.BECIRSPAHIC,
H.SARACEVIC, Enver HADZIABDIC, Blagoje BRATIC, Branimir JELUSIC (..'
A.DERAKOVIC), Ivan OSIM, Josip BUKAL, Edin SPRECO, D.BAJIC (70' Fikret MUJKIC
(II)).
Goals: TJ Sklo Union Teplice: 1-0 Pavel STRATIL (65'), 2-0 Frantisek JÍLEK (80').
FK Zeljeznicar Sarajevo: 2-1 Fikret MUJKIC (85').
Attendance: 6.000

196

FINAL

22-06-1969   Bratislava:
            TJ Internacional Slovnaft Bratislava – TJ Sklo Union Teplice   4-1 (2-0)
TJ Internacional Slovnaft Bratislava: Peter FÜLLE, Milan HRICA, Alexander BINOVSKY,
Ottmar DEUTSCH, Ivan DANO (9' Peter SOLÍN), Anton OBLOSINSKÝ, Michal MEDVID,
Jozef LEVICKÝ, Juraj SZIKORA, Mikulás KRNÁC (64' Jozef JURCO), Ján ONDRÁSEK.
(Coach: Ladislav KACÁNI).
TJ Sklo Union Teplice: Jirí SEDLÁCEK, Emil STIBOR, Josef MYSLIVEC, Jirí SETINSKY,
Jirí NOVÁK, Frantisek VÍTU, Premysl BICOVSKÝ, Rudolf SMETANA, Frantisek JÍLEK,
Pavel STRATIL, Ján GOMOLA. (Coach: Antonin RYGR).
Goals: TJ Internacional Slovnaft Bratislava: 1-0 Ján ONDRÁSEK (3'), 2-0 Ján ONDRÁSEK
(16'), 3-1 Anton OBLOZINSKÝ (70'), 4-1 Anton OBLOZINSKÝ (89').
TJ Sklo Union Teplice: 2-1 Ján GOMOLA (57').
Referee: Alessandro D'AGOSTINI (ITA)   Attendance: 2.000

03-07-1969   Teplice: TJ Sklo Union Teplice – TJ Internacional Slovnaft Bratislava   0-0
TJ Sklo Union Teplice: Jirí SEDLÁCEK, Emil STIBOR, Josef MYSLIVEC, Frantisek VÍTU,
Jirí SETINSKY, Rudolf SMETANA, Jirí NOVÁK (59' Ladislav BÁRTÍK), Vladimir ZALUD
(46' Premysl BICOVSKÝ), Frantisek JÍLEK, Pavel STRATIL, Ján GOMOLA. (Coach:
Antonin RYGR).
TJ Internacional Slovnaft Bratislava: Peter FÜLLE, Milan HRICA, Peter SOLÍN, Ottmar
DEUTSCH, Alexander BINOVSKY, Anton OBLOSINSKÝ, Michal MEDVID, Jozef
LEVICKÝ, Juraj SZIKORA, Mikulás KRNÁC, Ján ONDRÁSEK. (Coach: Ladislav
KACÁNI).
Referee: Antonio SBARDELLA (ITA)   Attendance: 3.000

*** TJ Internacional Slovnaft Bratislava won the Cup ***

197

1969-1970

FIRST ROUND

05-10-1969   Bratislava: TJ Internacional Slovnaft Bratislava – First Vienna FC 6-1 (2-0)
TJ Internacional Slovnaft Bratislava: Peter FÜLLE, Milan HRICA, Peter SOLÍN, Ottmar
DEUTSCH, Alexander BÍNOVSKÝ, Ján SLÁDKOVSKÝ (65' Peter LUPRICH), Anton
OBLOSINSKÝ, Jozef LEVICKÝ (80' Alexander KOVÁCS), Ladislav PETRAS, Mikulás
KRNÁC, Ján ONDRÁSEK. (Coach: Ladislav KACÁNI).
First Vienna FC: Viliam SCHROJF (TCH) (46' Paul FREYTAG), Michael BREIBERT, Josef
WAHL, Peter Dimitri PERSIDIS, Emmerich SOMMER, Alfred RIEDLBERGER (17' Peter
MÜLLER), Erich OSLANSKY, Vojtech MASNÝ (TCH), Pavol BENCZ (TCH), Josef BROZ,
Franz WEIDINGER. (Coach: Arnost (Ernst) HLOZEK (TCH)).
Goals: TJ Internacional Slovnaft Bratislava: 1-0 Ladislav PETRAS (4' penalty), 2-0 Ján
ONDRÁSEK (33'), 3-0 Ladislav PETRAS (65'), 4-1 Milan HRICA (71'), 5-1 Peter LUPRICH
(80'), 6-1 Peter SOLÍN (85').
First Vienna FC: 3-1 Vojtech MASNÝ (69').
Referee: Konstantin ZECEVIC (YUG)   Attendance: 4.000

22-10-1969   Tivoli-Stadion, Innsbruck: FC Wacker Innsbrcuk – Csepel SC 2-1 (1-1)
FC Wacker Innsbruck: Herbert RETTENSTEINER, Roland ESCHELMÜLLER, Heinz
BINDER, Peter WERNER (FRG), Werner KRIESS, Helmut SENEKOWITSCH, Johann
(Buffy) ETTMAYER, Erwin HOHENWARTER, Michael VOGEL (78' Johann
TRENKWALDER), Franz WOLNY, Kurt JARA. (Coach: Branko ELSNER).
Csepel SC: Károly FATÉR, István VELLAI, Tibor MOLNÁR, Dezsö FALUDI, Attila PETÖ,
István ROTTENBILLER (82' Sándor GULYÁS), György KANDI, Gyula MAJOR (82' István
KELEMAN), László KALMÁR, Flórián LOSONCZI, György GONDÁR. (Coach: Mihály
KESZTHELYI).
Goals: FC Wacker Innsbruck: 1-0 Franz WOLNY (23'), 2-1 Dezö FALUDI (60' own goal).
Csepel SC: 1-1 Flórián LOSONCZI (44').
Attendance: 2.000

29-10-1969   Split: NK Hajduk Split – AC Brescia 3-1 (2-1)
NK Hajduk Split: Radomir VUKCEVIC, Ivan BULJAN, Aleksandar RISTIC, Dragomir
SLICKOVIC, Dragan HOLCER, Marino LEMESIC, Ivica HLEVNJAK, Miroslav VARDIC,
Petar NADOVEZA, Jure JERKOVIC, Ivan PAVLICA. (Coach: Slavko LUSTICA).
AC Brescia: BUFFON, Mario MANERA, Giovanni BOTTI, Adolfo GORI, Giancarlo
BERCELLINO (I), Bernardo BUSI, Egidio SALVI, Luigi SIMONI, Virginio DE PAOLI, Dino
D'ALESSI (46' Giorgio FANTI), Giampaolo MENICHELLI. (Coach: Arturo SILVESTRI).
Goals: NK Hajduk Split: 1-0 Petar NADOVEZA (11'), 2-0 Ivan PAVLICA (12'), 3-1 Marino
LEMESIC (66').
AC Brescia: 2-1 Giampaolo MENICHELLI (40').
Referee: Michal JURSA (TCH)

29-10-1969   Budapest: Csepel SC – FC Wacker Innsbruck   2-1 (2-1)
Csepel SC: ... (Coach: Mihály KESZTHELYI).
FC Wacker Innsbruck: Herbert RETTENSTEINER, Werner KRIESS, Helmut
VOGGENBERGER (..' Dieter LEDERER), Heinz BINDER, Peter WERNER (FRG), Helmut
SENEKOWITSCH, Erwin HOHENWARTER, Josef OBERT (TCH), Franz WOLNY, Klaus
RINNERGSCHWENDTNER (..' Michael VOGEL), Kurt JARA. (Coach: Branko ELSNER).
Goals: Csepel SC: 1-0 Flórián LOSONCZI (10'), 2-1 László KALMÁR (33').
FC Wacker Innsbruck: 1-1 Franz WOLNY (20').
Referee: Petar KOSTOVSKI (YUG)   Attendance: 5.000

(After extra time. FC Wacker Innsbruck won on the toss of a coin).

30-10-1969   Bozsik József Stadion, Budapest:
             Budapesti Honvéd SE – SS Lazio Roma   1-1 (0-1)
Budapesti Honvéd SE: Tibor LÉVAY, József KELEMAN, József RUZSINSZKY (YC),
László MAROSI, Antal TUSSINGER, István VÁGI, Kálmán TÓTH (74' László MOLNÁR
(RC)), Lajos KOCSIS, József PÁL, Imre KOMORA, József KARAKAS. (Coach: Kálmán
PREINER).
SS Lazio Roma: Michelangelo SULFARO, Giuseppe PAPADOPULO, Mario FACCO,
Giuseppe WILSON, Carlo SOLDO (RC), Rino MARCHESI, Giuseppe MASSA (61' Giuliano
FORTUNATO), Nello GOVERNATO, Giorgio CHINAGLIA (70' Arrigo DOLSO), Gian
Piero GHIO (YC), Juan Carlos MORRONE (ARG). (Coach: Juan Carlos LORENZO (ARG)).
Goals: Budapesti Honvéd SE: 1-1 Lajos KOCSIS (46' penalty).
SS Lazio Roma: 0-1 Giorgio CHINAGLIA (45').
Referee: Dragomir Josip HORVATH (YUG)   Attendance: 10.000

12-11-1969   Faý utcai Stadion, Budapest: Vasas SC – FK Vardar Skopje   1-1 (1-0)
Vasas SC: Ferenc MÉSZÁROS, Sándor BAKOS, Kálmán MÉSZÖLY, Csaba VIDÁTS,
Kálmán IHÁSZ, Péter ANTAL (..' János RADICS), Sándor MÜLLER (..' Imre MATHESZ),
László SOMOGYVÁRI, Dezsö MOLNÁR, Lajos PUSKÁS, János FARKAS. (Coach: Rudolf
ILLOVSZKY).
FK Vardar Skopje: Dragan MUTIBARIC, DROBAC, Atanas MECKAROV, PLACKOV,
RAC, Vanco BALEVSKI, GEORGIEVSKI, Koco DIMITROVSKI (..' Josif SREBROV),
Methodije SPASOVSKI, NIKOLOVSKI (..' Ljupco ANCEVSKI), MURATOVIC. (Coach:
Caslav BOZINOVSKI).
Goals: Vasas SC: 1-0 Péter ANTAL (..').
FK Vardar Skopje: 1-1 GEORGIEVSKI (..').

19-11-1969   Kragujevac: FK Radnicki Kragujevac – TJ Lokomotiva Kosice   2-0 (1-0)
FK Radnicki Kragujevac: Branko TOPALOVIC, BOSKOVIC, Ljubisa DJORDJEVIC,
MATIC, Momcilo ZIVADINOVIC, Vladeta ZABARAC (87' MILIVOJEVIC), Vlada
RADIVOJEVIC, Slavoljub (Sava) PAUNOVIC, STEFANOVIC, Dragoljub ZIVKOVIC,
Dusan NIKOLIC. (Coach: Dusan NENKOVIC).
TJ Lokomtiva Kosice: Anton FLESAR, Andrej ISTÓK, Milan URBAN, Ján SLOSIARIK,
Ondrej KNAPP, Rudolf PSURNÝ, Ján LUZA, Jozef MÓDER (82' Pavol MYCIO), Pavol
ONDO, Vladimír HRIC, Gejza FARKAS.
Goals: FK Radnicki Kragujevac: 1-0 Dragoljub ZIVKOVIC (30'), 2-0 Dragoljub ZIVKOVIC
(82').
Referee: János ALMASI (HUN)   Attendance: 2.000

25-11-1969   Praha: SK Slavia Praha – Hellas Verona SpA   4-1 (2-1)
SK Slavia Praha: Miroslav STÁREK (2' Frantisek ZLÁMAL), Josef LINHART, Jan MARES, Jaroslav SIMEK, Emíl HAMAR, Karel KNESL, Frantisek VESELÝ, Frantisek KNEBORT, Zdenek KONECNÝ, Julius KANTOR, Dusan HERDA. (Coach: Josef FOREJT).
Hellas Verona SpA: Pierluigi PIZZABALLA, Carlo RIPARI, Paolo SIRENA, Emiliano MASCETTI, Alberto BATISTONI, Amedeo STENTI, Vito D'AMATO, Sergio MADDÈ, Sergio CLERICI (BRA) (16' Luigi MASCALAITO), Jorge Luis TORO Sánchez (CHI) (68' Roberto RANGHINO), Giovanni BUI. (Coach: Renato LUCCHI).
Goals: SK Slavia Praha: 1-1 Dusan HERDA (14'), 2-1 Frantisek KNEBORT (41' penalty), 3-1 Karel KNESL (52'), 4-1 Jaroslav SIMEK (61').
Hellas Verona SpA: 0-1 Sergio CLERICI (2').
Referee: Konstantin ZECEVIC (YUG)   Attendance: 3.000

26-11-1969   Gradski Stadion, Skopje: FK Vardar Skopje – Vasas SC   2-3 (2-2)
FK Vardar Skopje: Dragan MUTIBARIC, DROBAC, RAC, GEORGIEVSKI, Atanas MECKAROV, PLACKOV, Methodije SPASOVSKI, Josif SREBROV (..' Koco DIMITROVSKI), BAJRAKTAREVIC, Sokrat MOJSOV, MURATOVIC. (Coach: Caslav BOZINOVSKI).
Vasas SC: Ferenc MÉSZÁROS, Sándor BAKOS, Kálmán MÉSZÖLY, Csaba VIDÁTS, Kálmán IHÁSZ, Iván MENCZEL, Sándor MÜLLER, Dezsö MOLNÁR, Lajos PUSKÁS, János FARKAS, Péter TÖRÖK. (Coach: Rudolf ILLOVSZKY).
Goals: FK Vardar Skopje: BAJRAKTAREVIC, Methodije SPASOVSKI.
Vasas SC: János FARKAS, Sándor MÜLLER, Lajos PUSKÁS.

26-11-1969   Kosice: TJ Lokomotiva Kosice – FK Radnicki Kragujevac   1-0 (0-0)
TJ Lokomtiva Kosice: Anton FLESAR, Andrej ISTÓK, Ján LUZA, Ondrej KNAPP, Ján SLOSIARIK, Rudolf PSURNÝ, Vladimír HRIC, Pavol ONDO (71' Pavol MYCIO), Jozef MÓDER, Gejza FARKAS, Stefan GYUREK (88' BOGNÁR). (Coach: Milan MORAVEC).
FK Radnicki Kragujevac: Branko TOPALOVIC, Vlada RADIVOJEVIC, Ljubisa DJORDJEVIC, PILIC, MATIC, Momcilo ZIVADINOVIC, Vladeta ZABARAC (75' Slobodan KARATOSIC), STEFANOVIC (46' Slobodan PAUNOVSKY), Slavoljub (Sava) PAUNOVIC, Vladeta NIKOLIC, Dragoljub ZIVKOVIC. (Coach: Dusan NENKOVIC).
Goal: TJ Lokomotiva Kosice: 1-0 Jozef MÓDER (50').
Referee: Franz WÖHRER (AUT)   Attendance: 1.000

26-11-1969   Stadio Olimpico, Roma: SS Lazio Roma – Budapesti Honvéd SE   1-2 (1-2)
SS Lazio Roma: Michelangelo SULFARO, Giuseppe WILSON (YC), Mario FACCO, Nello GOVERNATO, Luigi POLENTES, Rino MARCHESI, Giuseppe MASSA, Ferruccio MAZZOLA (II), Giorgio CHINAGLIA, Juan Carlos MORRONE (ARG), Mario TOMY (46' Gian Piero GHIO). (Coach: Juan Carlos LORENZO (ARG)).
Budapesti Honvéd SE: Bertalan BICSKEI, József KELEMAN, József RUZSINSZKY, László MAROSI (73' József TAJTI), Imre KOMORA, István VÁGI, László PUSZTAI, Lajos KOCSIS, Lajos TICHÝ, Lajos SZURGENT, József KARAKAS. (Coach: Kálmán PREINER).
Goals: SS Lazio Roma: 1-2 Giorgio CHINAGLIA (33').
Budapesti Honvéd SE: 0-1 Lajos KOCSIS (2'), 0-2 Lajos TICHÝ (27').
Referee: KOLAS (TCH)   Attendance: 8.981

200

26-11-1969   Brescia: AC Brescia – NK Hajduk Split   0-0
AC Brescia: Lamberto BORANGA, Mario MANERA, Giovanni BOTTI, Carlo VOLPI,
Giancarlo BERCELLINO (I), Raffaello VESCOVI, Egidio SALVI, Luigi SIMONI, Virginio
DE PAOLI, Renzo RAGONESI (65' Dino D'ALESSI), Giampaolo MENICHELLI (59'
Giorgio FANTI). (Coach: Arturo SILVESTRI).
NK Hajduk Split: Radomir VUKCEVIC, Vilson DZONI, Marino LEMESIC, Dragomir
SLICKOVIC, Dragan HOLCER, Miroslav FERIC, Miroslav VARDIC, Ivica HLEVNJAK,
Petar NADOVEZA, Jure JERKOVIC, Ivan PAVLICA. (Coach: Slavko LUSTICA).
Referee: László VIZHANYO (HUN)

09-12-1969   Bundesstadion Südstadt, Maria Enzersdorf:
              Admira-Energie Wien – TJ Bohemians Praha   2-1 (1-1)
Goals: Admira-Energie Wien: 1-0 Walter STREIF (7'), 2-1 Wilhelm (Willy) KREUZ (73').
TJ Bohemians Praha: 1-1 Jan JARKOVSKÝ (8').
Attendance: 500

10-12-1969   Verona: Hellas Verona – SK Slavia Praha   0-3 (0-1)
Hellas Verona SpA: Pierluigi PIZZABALLA, Carlo RIPARI, Paolo SIRENA, Emiliano
MASCETTI, Franco NANNI, Giancarlo SAVOIA, Vito D'AMATO, Jorge Luis TORO
Sánchez (CHI), Luigi MASCALAITO, Angelo ORAZI (61' Sergio MADDÈ), Giovanni BUI.
(Coach: Renato LUCCHI).
SK Slavia Praha: Miroslav STÁREK (7' Frantisek ZLÁMAL), Josef LINHART, Jan MARES,
Bohumil SMOLÍK, Emíl HAMAR, Karel KNESL, Frantisek VESELÝ, Frantisek KNEBORT,
Zdenek KONECNÝ, Julius KANTOR, Dusan HERDA (46' Ivan KOPECKÝ). (Coach: Josef
FOREJT).
Goals: SK Slavia Praha: 0-1 Julius KANTOR (9'), 0-2 Zdenek KONECNÝ (71'), 0-3 Emíl
HAMAR (72').
Referee: Dimitris WLACHOJANIS (AUT)

07-02-1970   Praha: TJ Bohemians Praha – Admira-Energie Wien   1-2 (1-0)
TJ Bohemians Praha: Frantisek KOZINKA, Stefan SÁNDOR, Frantisek RUZICKA, Kvetoslav
NOVÁK, Miroslav VALENT, Miroslav LINHART (II), Frantisek SNÝR, Adam FARKAS,
Pavel DYBA, Jan JARKOVSKÝ (46' Antonin PANENKA), Jozef VEJVODA. (Coach:
Svatopluk PLUSKAL).
Admira-Energie Wien: Gerhard FLEISCHMANN, Helmut FÜLLENHALS, Paul KOZLICEK,
Erich KREUZ, Heinrich STRASSER, Johannes DEMANTKE, Walter STREIF, Heinz
MARIK, Wilhelm (Willy) KREUZ, Gerhard BÖHMER, Josef HOLATA. (Coach: Anton
MALATINSKÝ (TCH)).
Goals: TJ Bohemians Praha: 1-0 Frantisek SNÝR (37' penalty).
Admira-Energie Wien: 1-1 Wilhelm (Willy) KREUZ (67'), 1-2 Gerhard BÖHMER (74').
Referee: Aurelio ANGONESE (ITA)   Attendance: 3.000

25-02-1970   Wien: First Vienna FC – TJ Internacional Slovnaft Bratislava

*The match was originally scheduled for 09-12-1969, but the pitch at Hohe Warte stadium was
in too poor a condition to be used on this date. The match was then scheduled for 08-02-1970
and then later for 25-02-1970. First Vienna FC then decided to withdraw because this was too
close to the championship match against Grazer AK which was to be played on 28-02-1970).*

201

18-03-1970   Stadion Eden, Praha: SK Slavia Praha – NK Hajduk Split 1-1 (1-0)
SK Slavia Praha: Frantisek ZLÁMAL, Josef LINHART, Jan MARES, Bohumíl SMOLÍK,
Bedrich TESAR (86' Zdenek LOCHMAN), Karel KNESL, Frantisek VESELÝ, Emil
HAMÁR, Zdenek KONECKÝ (70' Jaroslav SIMEK), Jaroslav KRAVÁRIK, Julius
KANTOR. (Coach: Jaroslav FOREJT).
NK Hajduk Split: Radomir VUKCEVIC, Vilson DZONI, Marino LEMESIC, Dragomir
SLICKOVIC, Dragan HOLCER, Miroslav FERIC, Josko GLUJIC, Ivica HLEVNJAK, Ivan
BULJAN (31' Mario BOLJAT), Jure JERKOVIC, Ivan PAVLICA. (Coach: Slavko
LUSTICA).
Goals: SK Slavia Praha: 1-0 Jaroslav KRAVÁRIK (11').
NK Hajduk Split: 1-1 Miroslav FERIC (87').
Referee: Franz WÖHRER (AUT)   Attendance: 6.000

19-03-1970   Bundesstadion Südstadt, Maria Enzersdorf:
              Admira-Energie Wien – Vasas SC   0-4 (0-2)
Admira-Energie Wien: Gerhard FLEISCHMANN, Johannes DEMANTKE, Paul KOZLICEK,
Erich KREUZ, Heinrich STRASSER, Walter STREIF, Karl NIKISCHER. Heinz MARIK (55'
Karl ROSNER), Wilhelm (Willy) KREUZ, Felix LATZKE, Karl HOLATA. (Coach: Anton
MALATINSKÝ (TCH)).
Vasas SC: Gyula TAMÁS, Tibor FÁBIÁN, Kálmán MÉSZÖLY, Kálmán IHÁSZ, Péter
ANTAL, Csaba VIDÁTS, Dezsö MOLNÁR, Lajos PUSKÁS, János FARKAS, Lajos
LAKINGER, Attila LADINSZKY. (Coach: József ALBERT).
Goals: Vasas SC: 0-1 János FARKAS (20'), 0-2 Lajos PUSKÁS (35'), 0-3 Attila
LADINSZKY (50'), 0-4 János FARKAS (67').
Referee: Bruno DE MARCHI (ITA)   Attendance: 2.000

25-03-1970   Stadion Cika Daca, Kragujevac:
              FK Radnicki Kragujevac – Budapesti Honvéd SE   2-1
FK Radnicki Kragujevac:
Budapesti Honvéd SE: Bertalan BICSKEI, László MOLNÁR, József RUZSINSZKY, László
MAROSI, Pál VÁRI, István VÁGI, László PUSZTAI, Sándor PINTÉR (..' Gyula TÓTH),
Lajos SZURGENT, Imre KOMORA, József KARAKAS (..' Antal TUSSINGER). (Coach:
Kálmán PREINER).
Goals: FK Radnicki Kragujevac:
Budapesti Honvéd SE: László PUSZTAI.
Attendance: 4.000

02-04-1970   Budapest: Budapesti Honvéd SE – FK Radnicki Kragujevac 4-0
Budapesti Honvéd SE: ... (Coach: Kálmán PREINER).
FK Radnicki Kragujevac:

07-04-1970   Innsbruck:
                 FC Wacker Innsbruck – TJ Internacional Slovnaft Bratislava 0-3 (0-1)
FC Wacker Innsbruck: Leo TSCHENETT, Roland ESCHELMÜLLER, Heinz BINDER,
Johann (Hans) EIGENSTILLER, Helmut VOGGENBERGER, Peter WERNER (FRG),
Helmut SENEKOWITSCH (75' Erwin HOHENWARTER), Günther RINKER, Jozef OBERT
(TCH) (60' Werner HÖGER), Hans BUZEK, Kurt JARA. (Coach: Branko ELSNER (TCH)).
TJ Internacional Slovnaft Bratislava: Lórant MAJTHENYI, Jozef JURCO, Peter SOLÍN,
Dr.Alexander BINOVSKÝ, Ottmar DEUTSCH, Anton OBLOZINSKÝ, Peter LUPRICH,
Jozef LEVICKÝ, Juraj SZIKORA, Mikulás KRNÁC (46' Zoltán GÁL), Ján ONDRÁSEK
(Coach: Ladislav KACÁNI).
Goals: TJ Internacional Slovnaft Bratislava: 0-1 Anton OBLOZINSKÝ (11'), 0-2 Juraj
SZIKORA (87'), 0-3 Peter LUPRICH (90').
Referee: György MÜNCZ (HUN)   Attendance:2.500

10-04-1970   Split: NK Hajduk Split – SK Slavia Praha 2-2 (0-0)
NK Hajduk Split:
SK Slavia Praha: Frantisek ZLÁMAL, Josef LINHART, Jan MARES, Karel KNESL, Bedrich
TESAR, Ján LUZA, Ivan KOPECKÝ, Julius KANTOR, Frantisek KNEBORT, Jaroslav
KRAVÁRIK, Dusan HERDA. (Coach: Josef FOREJT).
Goals: NK Hajduk Split: 1-1 Ivan PAVLICA (63' penalty), 2-2 Drazen MUZINIC (78').
SK Slavia Praha: 0-1 Jaroslav KRAVÁRIK (51'), 1-2 Frantisek KNEBORT (75').
Referee: Gusztav BIRCZAK (HUN)   Attendance: 12.000

15-04-1970   Budapest: Vasas SC – Admira-Energie Wien 3-1 (0-1)
Vasas SC: Gyula TAMÁS, Tibor FÁBIÁN, Kálmán MÉSZÖLY, Ottó VÁRADI, Kálmán
IHÁSZ, Iván MENCZEL, Sándor MÜLLER, Lajos PUSKÁS, János RADICS, Lajos
LAKINGER, Dezsö MOLNÁR. (Coach: József ALBERT).
Admira-Energie Wien: Gerhard FLEISCHMANN, Johannes DEMANTKE, Karl ROSNER,
Heinrich STRASSER, Helmut FÜLLENHALS, Walter STREIF, Erich KREUZ, Wilhelm
(Willy) KREUZ, Felix LATZKE, Gerhard BÖHMER, Karl HOLATA. (Coach: Anton
MALATINSKÝ (TCH)).
Goals: Vasas SC: 1-1 Kálmán MÉSZÖLY (63'), 2-1 Iván MENCZEL (68'), 3-1 Kálmán
IHÁSZ (89').
Admira-Energie Wien: 0-1 Gerhard BÖHMER (5').
Referee: Milivoje GUGULOVIC (YUG)   Attendance: 5.000

12-05-1970   Bratislava:
                 TJ Internacional Slovnaft Bratislava – FC Wacker Innsbruck 0-1 (0-1)
TJ Internacional Slovnaft Bratislava: Lórant MAJTHENYI, Milan HRICA, Peter SOLÍN,
Dr.Alexander BÍNOVSKÝ, Pavol DAUCÍK, Anton OBLOZINSKÝ (66' Ján
SLADKOVSKÝ), Peter LUPRICH, Jozef LEVICKÝ, Juraj SZIKORA, Mikulás KRNÁC, Ján
ONDRÁSEK. (Coach: Ladislav KACÁNI).
FC Wacker Innsbruck: Herbert RETTENSTEINER, Josef PEER (46' Dieter LEDERER), Peter
WERNER (FRG), Heinz BINDER, Werner KRIESS, Johann (Hans) EIGENSTILLER, Jozef
OBERT (TCH) (68' Werner HÖGER), Helmut SENEKOWITSCH, Erwin HOHENWARTER,
Franz WOLNY, Kurt JARA. (Coach: Branko ELSNER (TCH)).
Goal: FC Wacker Innsbruck: 0-1 Kurt JARA (38').
Referee: Josip STRMECKI (YUG)   Attendance: 300

SEMI-FINALS

17-05-1970   Slavia Stadión, Praha: SK Slavia Praha – Vasas SC   1-1 (1-0)
SK Slavia Praha: Miroslav STÁREK, Jaroslav SIMEK, Jan MARES, Bohumil SMOLÍK, Bedrich TESAR (..' Zdenek KONECKÝ), Ivan KOPECKÝ, Julius KANTOR, Frantisek KNEBORT, Jaroslav KRAVÁRIK, Emil HAMÁR, Dusan HERDA. (Coach: Josef FOREJT).
Vasas SC: Gyula TAMÁS, Tibor FÁBIÁN, Kálmán MÉSZÖLY, Csaba VIDÁTS, Kálmán IHÁSZ, Iván MENCZEL, Lajos LAKINGER, Dezsö MOLNÁR, Lajos PUSKÁS, János FARKAS, Attila LADINSZKY. (Coach: József ALBERT).
Goals: SK Slavia Praha: 1-0 Iván MENCZEL (25' own goal).
Vasas SC: 1-1 Kálmán MÉSZÖLY (59').
Referee:Franz WÖHRER (AUT)   Attendance: 10.000

17-05-1970   Bozsik József Stadion, Budapest:
                 Budapesti Honvéd SE ⌐TJ Internacional Slovnaft Bratislava 0-1 (0-1)
Budapesti Honvéd SE: Bertalan BICSKEI, József TAJTI, József RUZSINSZKY, Pál VÁRI, Gyula TÓTH, István VÁGI (30' Antal TUSSINGER), László PUSZTAI, Lajos TICHY, Mihály KOZMA, Imre KOMORA, László TIBOR (54' Lajos SZURGENT). (Coach: Kálmán PREINER).
TJ Internacional Slovnaft Bratislava: Lórant MAJTHÉNYI, Milan HRICA, Peter SOLÍN, Dr.Alexander BÍNOVSKÝ, Pavol DAUCÍK, Peter LUPRICH, Anton OBLOZINSKÝ, Jozef LEVICKÝ, Juraj SZIKORA, Mikulás KRNÁC, Ján ONDRÁSEK. (Coach: Ladislav KACÁNI).
Goal: TJ Internacional Slovnaft Bratislava: 0-1 Imre KOMORA (23' own goal).
Referee: Walter FERCHER (AUT)   Attendance: 8.000

01-06-1970   Fáy utcai Stadion, Budapest: Vasas SC – SK Slavia Praha   1-0 (1-0)
Vasas SC: Gyula TAMÁS, Tibor FÁBIÁN, Kálmán MÉSZÖLY, Csaba VIDÁTS, Ottó VÁRADI, Iván MENCZEL, Lajos LAKINGER (..' Attila LADINSZKY), Péter TÖRÖK, Lajos PUSKÁS (..' Sándor MÜLLER), János FARKAS, Bálint TÓTH. (Coach: József ALBERT).
SK Slavia Praha: Miroslav STÁREK, Jan MARES, Jaroslav SIMEK, Ivan KOPECKÝ, Bohumil SMOLÍK, Bedrich TESAR (..' Ján LUZA), Jaroslav KRAVÁRIK (..' Zdenek LOCHMAN), Zdenek KONECKÝ, Emil HAMÁR, Frantisek KNEBORT, Dusan HERDA. (Coach: Josef FOREJT).
Goal: Vasas SC: 1-0 János FARKAS (12').
Referee: Ladislav (Lado) JAKSE (YUG)   Attendance: 10.000

03-06-1970   Stadion na Pasienkoch, Bratislava:
                 TJ Internacional Slovnaft Bratislava – Budapesti Honvéd SE 2-1 (0-1)
TJ Internacional Slovnaft Bratislava: Lórant MAJTHENYI, Milan HRICA, Peter SOLÍN, Dr.Alexander BÍNOVSKÝ, Ivan DANO, Anton OBLOZINSKÝ, Jozef LEVICKÝ, Peter LUPRICH, Juraj SZIKORA, Mikulás KRNÁC, Ján ONDRÁSEK. (Coach: Ladislav KACÁNI).
Budapesti Honvéd SE: Bertalan BICSKEI (46' József HAJDU), László MOLNÁR, József RUZSINSZKY, József TAJTI, Gyula TÓTH, Pál VÁRI, László PUSZTAI, Lajos KOCSIS, Lajos SZURGENT, Imre KOMORA, Mihály KOZMA. (Coach: Kálmán PREINER).
Goals: TJ Internacional Slovnaft Bratislava: 1-1 Mikulás KRNÁC (66'), 2-1 Anton OBLOZINSKÝ (81').
Budapesti Honéd SE: 0-1 Lajos KOCSIS (33').
Referee: Ratko CANAK (YUG)   Attendance: 4.000

204

FINAL

10-06-1970   Bratislava: TJ Internacional Slovnaft Bratislava – Vasas SC 2-1 (1-0)
TJ Internacional Slovnaft Bratislava: Lórant MAJTHENYI, Milan HRICA, Peter SOLÍN,
Dr.Alexander BINOVSKÝ, Pavol DAUCIK, Jozef JURCO, Peter LUPRICH (46' Ján
SLADKOVSKÝ), Jozef LEVICKÝ, Juraj SZIKORA (80' Alexander KOVACS), Mikulás
KRNÁC, Ján ONDRÁSEK (Coach: Ladislav KACÁNI).
Vasas SC: Gyula TAMAS (6' Ferenc MESZAROS), Tibor FÁBIÁN, Kálmán MÉSZÖLY,
Csaba VIDÁTS, Ottó VÁRADI, Lajos LAKINGER (70' Sándor MÜLLER), Iván
MENCZEL, Lajos PUSKÁS, Bálint TÓTH, János FARKAS (65' Péter TÖRÖK), Attila
LADINSZKY. (József ALBERT).
Goals: TJ Internacional Slovnaft Bratislava: 1-0 Mikulás KRNÁC (45'), 2-0 Mikulás KRNÁC
(50').
Vasas SC. 2-1 Péter TÖRÖK (72').
Referee: Ladislav (Lado) JAKSE (YUG)   Attendance: 3.500

20-06-1970   Fáy utcai Stadion, Budapest:
               Vasas SC – TJ Internacional Slovnaft Bratislava 4-1 (0-1)
Vasas SC: Ferenc MÉSZÁROS, Tibor FÁBIÁN, Kálmán MÉSZÖLY, Csaba VIDÁTS, Lajos
LAKINGER, Sándor MÜLLER, Iván MENCZEL (69' Ottó VÁRADI), Péter TÖRÖK (74'
Attila LADINSZKY), Lajos PUSKÁS, János FARKAS, Bálint TÓTH. (Coach: József
ALBERT).
TJ Internacional Slovnaft Bratislava: Lórant MAJTHENYI, Milan HRICA, Peter SOLÍN,
Dr.Alexander BINOVSKÝ, Ivan DANO, Juraj SZIKORA, Peter LUPRICH, Anton
OBLOZINSKÝ, Jozef LEVICKÝ, Ladislav PETRÁS, Mikulás KRNÁC. (Coach: Ladislav
KACÁNI).
Goals: Vasas SC: 1-1 Lajos PUSKÁS (48'), 2-1 János FARKAS (78'), 3-1 Sándor MÜLLER
(81'), 4-1 János FARKAS (85').
TJ Internacional Slovnaft Bratislava: 0-1 Peter SOLÍN (43').
Referee: Paul SCHILLER (AUT)   Attendance: 17.000

*** Vasas SC won the Cup ***

205

1970-1971

14-10-1970   Zenica: FK Celik Zenica – CC Catania   3-0 (2-0)
FK Celik Zenica: Momcilo VUJACIC, Slobodan DOGANDZIC, Fadil TALIC, Midhat
MUJKIC, Dragoljub GOLUBOVIC, Mehmed PINTOL, Petar MICIC, Rade RADULOVIC
(75' Meho BARJAKTAREVIC), Alojz RENIC, Branko HERCEG (63' Rifet BAJRIC), Petar
RASIC.
CC Catania: Rino RADO, Umberto STRUCCHI, Luciano LIMENA, Luciano
BUZZACCHERA, Paolo MONTANARI (75' Massimo CHERUBINI), Mauro VAIANI,
Maurizio CAVAZZONI, Giancarlo PASQUALOTTO, Pietro BAISI (43' Massimo
SILVESTRI), Angelo PERENI, Aquilino BONFANTI. (Coach: Egizio RUBINO).
Goals: FK Celik Zenica: 1-0 Midhat MUJKIC (32' penalty), 2-0 Alojz RENIC (39'), 3-0 Petar
MICIC (65').
Referee: VINCE (HUN)

14-10-1970   Graz: Grazer AK – NK Maribor   2-0 (0-0)
Goals: Grazer AK: 1-0 Walter KOLEZNIK (55'), 2-0 ARNJECIC (77').
Attendance: 2.000

22-10-1970   Maribor: NK Maribor – Grazer AK   3-1 (1-1)
NK Maribor:
Grazer AK: ..., Josef STERING (RC), ...
Goals: NK Maribor: 1-0 Mladen KRANJC (7'), 2-1 Erwin NINAUS (46' own goal), 3-1
Prosen PROSEN (60' penalty).
Grazer AK: 1-1 ARNJECIC (14').
Attendance: 3.000

28-10-1970   Fáy utcai Stadion, Budapest: Vasas SC – SV Austria Salzburg   3-1 (1-1)
Vasas SC: ... (Coach: Ferenc MACHOS).
SV Austria Salzburg: Adolf ANTRICH, Horst HIRNSCHRODT, Johann (Hans) KLOPF,
Gerhard MAIRHUBER, Artur KIBLER, Adolf (Adi) MACEK, Adolf (Dolfi) BLUTSCH, Karl
KODAT, Bernd LANGGRUBER (..' Franz WEIDINGER), Karl RITTER, Heinz LIBUDA
(FRG). (Coach: Karl SCHLECHTA).
Goals: Vasas SC: 1-0 Kálmán MÉSZÖLY (33'), 2-1 Attila LADINSZKY (60'), 3-1 Lajos
PUSKÁS (76').
SV Austria Salzburg: 1-1 Heinz LIBUDA (34').
Attendance: 6.000

28-10-1970   Hriste Slavie na Letné, Praha: SK Slavia Praha – Csepel SC   0-2 (0-2)
SK Slavia Praha: Frantisek ZLÁMAL, Josef LINHART, Jan MARES, Ivan KOPECKÝ,
Bohumil SMOLÍK, Bedrich TESAR (46' Jaroslav SIMEK), Zdenek LOCHMAN (46'Ján
LUZA), Frantisek VESELÝ, Frantisek KNEBORT, Frantisek MACHURKA, Dusan HERDA.
(Coach: Antonín RÝGR).
Csepel SC: ... (Coach: Mihály KESZTHELYI).
Goals: Csepel SC: 0-1 Jaroslav SIMEK (18' own goal), 0-2 CSORDÁS (44').
Referee: Josef BUCEK (AUT)   Attendance: 5.000

28-10-1970   Kragujevac: FK Radnicki Kragujevac – SS Lanerossi-Vicenza 1-0 (0-0)
FK Radnicki Kragujevac: Branko TOPALOVIC, Milasin MILIC, Ljubisa DJORDJEVIC,
Vlada RADIVOJEVIC, Novica MATIC, Moncilo ZIVADINOVIC, Nebojsa LICANIN,
Slobodan KARATOSIC, Slavoljub (Sava) PAUNOVIC, Vladeta NIKOLIC, Slobodan
PAUNOVSKI.
SS Lanerossi-Vicenza: Pietro PIANTA, Gianfranco VOLPATO, Andrea CISCO, Nello
SANTIN, Sergio CARANTINI, Mario CALOSI, Domenico FONTANA, Nevio SCALA,
Renato FALOPPA, Sidney Colona Cunha "CHINESINHO" (BRA) (46' Luigi MERONI),
Carlo FACCHIN. (Coach: Héctor (Ettore) PURICELLI Seña (URU)).
Goal: FK Radnicki Kragujevac: 1-0 Vlada RADIVOJEVIC (19').
Referee: RADA (HUN)

04-11-1970   Letenský Stadion, Praha: Linzer ASK – TJ Skoda Plzen 1-1 (0-0)
Linzer ASK: Helmut SAURER, Karl KIESENEBNER,Gerhard STURMBERGER, Francisco
Carlos Correia Lima "CHICO" (POR), Franz VIEHBÖCK, Peter SCHMIDT, Janos (Johann)
KONDERT, Erhard WIEGER, Heinz STREBELE, Michal MEDVID (TCH) (67' Josef
WETSCHER), Alfons WURDINGER (46' Willibald BAUER). (Coach: Wilhelm (Willy)
KMENT).
TJ Skoda Plzen: HOPP, Frantisek SUDIK, Karel KNESL, STRUNC, Josef SPINKA, Ivan
BACHNER (67' Václav KAMIR), Frantisek PLASS, Karel SÜSS, HERBST, Ivan BICAN,
Miroslav ZIEGLER. (Coach: Jirí RUBÁS).
Goals: Linzer ASK: 1-0 Alfons WURDINGER (49').
TJ Skoda Plzen: 1-1 Frantisek PLASS (86').
Referee: Josip STRMECKI (YUG)   Attendance: 400

04-11-1970   Diósgyör: Diósgyöri VTK – TJ Lokomotiva Kosice 2-0
Diósgyöri VTK: János BENCZE, Ferenc OLÁH, József SALAMON, István SÁFRÁNY, Béla
GÁL, Imre HAJAS, László VASS, Károly CSUHÁNYI, Károly FÖLDESI, András
HORVÁTH, Ferenc SIKORA. (Coach: Imre MATHESZ).
TJ Lokomotiva Kosice:
Goals: Diósgyöri VTK: 1-0 László VASS (2'), 2-0 András HORVÁTH (..').
Referee: Ratko CANAK (YUG)   Attendance: 5.000

04-11-1970   Sportstadion Itzling, Salzburg: SV Austria Salzburg – Vasas SC 3-0 (1-0)
SV Austria Salzburg: Adolf ANTRICH, Johann (Hans) KLOPF, Gerhard MAIRHUBER, Artur
KIBLER, Adolf (Adi) MACEK, Adolf (Dolfi) BLUTSCH (46' Heinz LIBUDA (FRG)), Horst
HIRNSCHRODT, Bernd LANGGRUBER (46' Gerhard FILZMOSER), Karl RITTER, Peter
GROSSER (FRG), Karl KODAT. (Coach: Karl SCHLECHTA).
Vasas SC: Gyula TAMÁS, Tibor FÁBIÁN, Kálmán MÉSZÖLY, Csaba VIDÁTS, Kálmán
IHÁSZ, Sándor MÜLLER, Lajos LAKINGER, Péter TÖRÖK (46' Ottó VÁRADI), Lajos
PUSKÁS, János FARKAS, Attila LADINSZKY. (Coach: Ferenc MACHOS).
Goals: SV Austria Salzburg: 1-0 Karl RITTER (18'), 2-0 Karl KODAT (67'), 3-0 Karl
RITTER (73').
Referee: Karol SARKA (TCH)   Attendance: 1.500

207

04-11-1970   Catania: CC Catania – FK Celik Zenica   1-0 (1-0)
CC Catania: Rino RADO, Umberto STRUCCHI, Luciano LIMENA, Luciano
BUZZACCHERA, Sergio REGGIANI, Giorgio BERNARDIS, Maurizio CAVAZZONI,
Angelo PERENI, Pietro BAISI (60' Domenico VENTURA), Romano FOGLI, Aquilino
BONFANTI. (Coach: Egizio RUBINO).
FK Celik Zenica: Momcilo VUJACIC, Slobodan DOGANDZIC, Fadil TALIC, Midhat
MUJKIC, Dragoljub GOLUBOVIC, Mehmed PINTOL, Petar MICIC, Rade RADULOVIC,
Alojz RENIC, Branko HERCEG (63' Muhamed CERIMAGIC), Petar RASIC.
Goal: CC Catania: 1-0 Maurizio CAVAZZONI (31').
Referee: Franz WÖHRER (AUT)

11-11-1970   Plzen: TJ Skoda Plzen – Linzer ASK   4-0 (3-0)
Goals: TJ Skoda Plzen: 1-0 Jozef HOFFMANN (20'), 2-0 Jozef HOFFMANN (29'), 3-0 Ivan
BICAN (34'), 4-0 Jozef HOFFMANN (84').
Referee: Ettore CARMINATI (ITA)   Attendance: 1.000

11-11-1970   Vicenza: SS Lanerossi-Vicenza – FK Radnicki Kragujevac   3-0 (0-0)
SS Lanerossi-Vicenza: Pietro PIANTA, Gianfranco VOLPATO, Nevio SCALA,
BASSANESE (46' Andrea CISCO), Nello SANTIN, Mario CALOSI, Domenico FONTANA,
Claudio TURCHETTO, Mario MARASCHI, Sidney Colona Cunha "CHINESINHO" (BRA),
Renato FALOPPA (62' Nicola CICCOLO). (Coach: Héctor (Ettore) PURICELLI Seña
(URU)).
FK Radnicki Kragujevac: Vladimir VUKOVIC, Slobodan KARATOSIC, DOROTEVIC,
Vlada RADIVOJEVIC, Novica MATIC, Vladeta NIKOLIC, Momcilo STOJANOVIC (84'
Radomir KOSTIC), Slobodan PAUNOVSKI (58' Srbislav MARINKOVIC), Slavoljub (Sava)
PAUNOVIC, Nebojsa LICANIN, Drazen MATIC.
Goals: SS Lanerossi-Vicenza: 1-0 Vlada RADIVOJEVIC (61' *own goal*), 2-0 Claudio
TURCHETTO (96'), 3-0 Nicola CICCOLO (102').
Referee: Walter FERCHER (AUT)

(After extra time)

02-12-1970   Stadio Comunale, Torino: AC Torino – M.T.K. Budapest   1-1 (0-1)
AC Torino: Luciano CASTELLINI, Marino LOMBARDO, Natalino FOSSATI, Giorgio
PUIA, Angelo CERESER, Aldo AGROPPI (46' Luciano ZECCHINI), Ferdinando ROSSI,
Giorgio FERRINI, Carlo PETRINI, Claudio SALA, Livio LUPPI (62' Stanislao BOZZI).
(Coach: Giancarlo CADÉ).
M.T.K. Budapest: József HAJDÚ, József TÖRÖK, Lajos DUNAI, Péter RAB, József OLÁH,
Csaba CSETÉNTYI, László STRASSZER, Lajos KORITÁR (75' István SÁRZÖKI), József
BECSEI, Antal SZUROMI (65' Tibor KISS), Jenö KUNSZT. (Coach: Tibor PALICSKÓ).
Goals: AC Torino: 1-1 Stanislao BOZZI (68').
M.T.K. Budapest: 0-1 Lajos KORITÁR (23').
Referee: Franz WÖHRER (AUT)   Attendance: 5.664

02-12-1970   Kosice: TJ Lokomotiva Kosice – Diósgyöri VTK   0-0
TJ Lokomotiva Kosice:
Diósgyöri VTK: János BENCZE, Pál KOVÁCS, József SALAMON, Béla KOLLÁTH, Béla
GÁL, Imre HAJAS, László VASS, Ferenc FEKETE (..' Ferenc OLÁH), András HORVÁTH,
Károly FÖLDESI, Ferenc SIKORA. (Coach: Imre MATHESZ).

06-12-1970   Hungária körúti stadion, Budapest: M.T.K. Budapest – AC Torino 2 1 (0-0)
M.T.K. Budapest: József HAJDÚ, József TÖRÖK, Lajos DUNAI, Csaba CSETÉNTYI, József
OLÁH (91' Tibor KISS), László STRASSZER, Lajos KORITÁR, István SÁRZÖKI (46'
Sándor OBORZIL), József BECSEI, Antal SZUROMI, Jenö KUNSZT. (Coach: Tibor
PALICSKÓ).
AC Torino: Luciano CASTELLINI, Marino LOMBARDO, Natalino FOSSATI, Giorgio
PUIA, Angelo CERESER, Giorgio FERRINI, Rosario RAMPANTI (91' Renato
ZACCARELLI), Sergio MADDÈ, Carlo PETRINI (60' Stanislao BOZZI), Claudio SALA,
Giovanni (Gianni) BUI. (Coach: Giancarlo CADÉ).
Goals: M.T.K. Budapest: 1-1 József BECSEI (67'), 2-1 Giorgio FERRINI (115' own goal).
AC Torino: 0-1 Giorgio PUIA (47').
Referee: Bohumil KOPCIO (TCH)   Attendance: 6.000
(After extra time)

06-12-1970   Budapest: Csepel SC – SK Slavia Praha 0-0
Csepel SC: ... (Coach: Mihály KESZTHELYI).
SK Slavia Praha: Frantisek ZLÁMAL, Josef LINHART, Jan MARES, Ivan KOPECKÝ (75'
Jaroslav SIMEK), Bohumil SMOLÍK, Ján LUZA, Bedrich TESAR, Frantisek SMOLÍK,
Frantisek VESELÝ, Frantisek MACHURKA, Dusan HERDA. (Coach: Antonín RÝGR).
Referee: Fabio MONTI (ITA)   Attendance: 8.000

QUARTER-FINALS

23-02-1971   Vicenza: SS Lanerossi-Vicenza – SV Austria Salzburg 3-2 (1-2)
SS Lanerossi-Vicenza: Pietro PIANTA, Gianfranco VOLPATO, Andrea CISCO, Nevio
SCALA, Nello SANTIN, Mario CALOSI, Oscar DAMIANI, Domenico FONTANA (63'
Renato FALOPPA), Mario MARASCHI (RC87), Sidney Colona Cunha "CHINESINHO"
(BRA), Nicola CICCOLO. (Coach: Héctor (Ettore) PURICELLI Seña (URU)).
SV Austria Salzburg: Roman PICHLER, Johann (Hans) KLOPF, Gerhard MAIRHUBER,
Horst HIRNSCHRODT (RC87), Gerhard FILZMOSER, Adolf (Dolfi) BLUTSCH, Heinz
LIBUDA (FRG), Karl KODAT, Karl RITTER, Peter GROSSER (FRG), Franz WEIDINGER.
(Coach: Karl SCHLECHTA).
Goals: SS Lanerossi-Vicenza: 1-2 Nicola CICCOLO (34'), 2-2 Mario MARASCHI (74'), 3-2
Sidney Colona Cunha "CHINESINHO" (82').
SV Austria Salzburg: 0-1 Peter GROSSER (7'), 0-2 Karl RITTER (30').
Referee: Sándor PETRI (HUN)   Attendance: 2.500
(Roman PICHLER saved a 64th minute penalty taken by Mario MARASCHI)

17-03-1971   Budapest: Csepel SC – TJ Skoda Plzen 0-0
Csepel SC: ... (Coach: Mihály KESZTHELYI).
TJ Skoda Plzen:
Referee: Sergio GONELLA (ITA)   Attendance: 4.000

24-03-1971   Bundesstadion Liebenau, Graz: Grazer AK – M.T.K. Budapest 0-0
Grazer AK: Zoran MISIC (YUG), Josef HOFBAUER, Erwin NINAUS, Giogo GRUBISIC
(YUG), Gottfried LAMPRECHT, Engelbert BREINER, Werner MAIER, Harald REBERNIG,
Walter KOLEZNIK, Johann (Charly) SCHARMANN, Karl PHILIPP. (Coach: Karl
DURSPEKT).
M.T.K. Budapest: József HAJDÚ, József TÖRÖK, József OLÁH, Péter RAB, László
STRASSZER, Csaba CSETÉNTYI, Lajos KORITÁR, István SÁRZÖKI, Lajos DUNAI,
József BECSEI, Jenö KUNSZT. (Coach: Tibor PALICSKÓ).
Referee: Michal JURSA (TCH)   Attendance: 2.000

209

31-03-1971   Miscolk: Diósgyöri VTK – FK Celik Zenica 1-0
Diósgyöri VTK: János BENCZE, Pál KOVÁCS, József SALAMON, Béla KOLLÁTH, Béla
GÁL, Imre HAJAS, László VASS, Ferenc FEKETE, András HORVÁTH (..' Károly
CSUHÁNY), István GASS, Ferenc SIKORA. (Coach: Imre MATHESZ).
FK Celik Zenica:
Goal: Diósgyöri VTK: 1-0 András HORVÁTH (..').

06-04-1971   Budapest: M.T.K. Budapest – Grazer AK 2-1 (2-1)
M.T.K. Budapest: … (Coach: Tibor PALICSKÓ).
Grazer AK: … (Coach: Karl DURSPEKT).
Goals: M.T.K. Budapest: 1-1 Lajos DUNAI (18'), 2-1 Lajos KORITÁR (23').
Grazer AK: 0-1 Walter KOLEZNIK (10').
Attendance: 6.000

07-04-1971   Zenica: FK Celik Zenica – Diósgyöri VTK 4-1
FK Celik Zenica:
Diósgyöri VTK: János BENCZE, Pál KOVÁCS, József SALAMON (..' Károly CSUHÁNY),
István SÁFRÁNY, Béla KOLLÁTH, Béla GÁL, Imre HAJAS, Ferenc SIKORA, Ferenc
FEKETE, András HORVÁTH, László VASS. (Coach: Imre MATHESZ).
Goals: FK Celik Zenica:
Diósgyöri VTK: Ferenc SIKORA.

14-04-1971   Salzburg: SV Austria Salzburg – SS Lanerossi-Vicenza 3-1 (2-1)
SV Austria Salzburg: Adolf ANTRICH, Gerhard FILZMOSER, Johann (Hans) KLOPF,
Arthur KIBLER, Gerhard MAIRHUBER, Adolf (Dolfi) BLUTSCH, Heinz LIBUDA (FRG),
Bernd LANGGRUBER (58' Karl KODAT), Karl RITTER, Peter GROSSER (FRG), Franz
WEIDINGER (66' Gustav THALER). (Coach: Karl SCHLECHTA).
SS Lanerossi-Vicenza: Pietro PIANTA, Attilio BERTI, Nevio SCALA, Domenico
FONTANA, Andrea CISCO, Mario CALOSI, Oscar DAMIANI, Sidney Colona Cunha
"CHINESINHO" (BRA), Claudio TURCHETTO, Renato FALOPPA, Nicola CICCOLO.
(Coach: Héctor (Ettore) PURICELLI Seña (URU)).
Goals: SV Austria Salzburg: 1-0 Peter GROSSER (17'), 2-0 Heinz LIBUDA (20'), 3-1 Heinz
LIBUDA (55').
SS Lanerossi-Vicenza: 2-1 Claudio TURCHETTO (32').
Referee: Ivan PLACEK (TCH)   Attendance: 4.500

14-04-1971   Plzen: TJ Skoda Plzen – Csepel SC 1-1 (1-1)
TJ Skoda Plzen:
Csepel SC: … (Coach: Mihály KESZTHELYI).
Goals: TJ Skoda Plzen: 1-1 Jozef HOFFMANN (28').
Csepel SC: 0-1 Flórián LOSONCZI (22').
Referee: Alois KESSLER (AUT)   Attendance: 2.500

SEMI-FINALS

05-05-1971   Budapest: Csepel SC – SV Austria Salzburg   2-0 (2-0)
Csepel SC: Károly FATÉR, István VELLAI, Tibor MOLNÁR, György KANDI, László
HUNYADI, Dezsö FALUDI, István ROTTENBILLER, Flórián LOSONCZI, László
KALMÁR, László TAKÁCS, György GONDÁR. (Coach: Mihály KESZTHELYI).
SV Austria Salzburg: Adolf ANTRICH, Johann (Hans) KLOPF, Horst HIRNSCHRODT,
Arthur KIBLER, Josef LARIONOWS, Heinz LIBUDA (FRG) (70' Gerhard MAIRHUBER),
Adolf (Dolfi) BLUTSCH, Gustav THALER, Karl KODAT (70' Bernd LANGGRUBER), Karl
RITTER, Franz WEIDINGER. (Coach: Karl SCHLECHTA).
Goals: Csepel SC: 1-0 László HUNYADI (25'), 2-0 Flórián LOSONCZI (26').
Referee: Alberto PICASSO (ITA)   Attendance: 6.000

05-05-1971   Zenica: FK Celik Zenica – M.T.K. Budapest   1-0
FK Celik Zenica:
M.T.K. Budapest: ... (Coach: Tibor PALICSKÓ).

19-05-1971   Sportstadion Itzling, Salzburg: SV Austria Salzburg – Csepel SC   4-1 (3-1)
SV Austria Salzburg: Adolf ANTRICH, Johann (Hans) KLOPF, Arthur KIBLER, Gerhard
MAIRHUBER, Gerhard FILZMOSER, Adolf (Dolfi) BLUTSCH, Horst HIRNSCHRODT,
Peter GROSSER (FRG), Bernd LANGGRUBER (46' Heinz LIBUDA (FRG)), Karl RITTER,
Karl KODAT. (Coach: Karl SCHLECHTA).
Csepel SC: Károly FATÉR, István VELLAI, Tibor MOLNÁR, Dezsö FALUDI, László
HUNYADI, György KANDI, Gyula MAJOR, István ROTTENBILLER (62' Attila PETÖ),
László KALMÁR, Flórián LOSONCZI, György GONDÁR. (Coach: Mihály KESZTHELYI).
Goals: SV Austria Salzburg: 1-0 Karl RITTER (24'), 2-0 Horst HIRNSCHRODT (39'), 3-0
Karl KODAT (43'), 4-1 Karl KODAT (80').
Csepel SC: 3-1 Gyula MAJOR (44').
Referee: Paolo TOSELLI (ITA)   Attendance: 2.500

26-05-1971   Budapest: M.T.K. Budapest – FK Celik Zenica   1-1
M.T.K. Budapest: ... (Coach: Tibor PALICSKÓ).
FK Celik Zenica:

FINAL

22-09-1971   Stadio Comunale, Gorizia (ITA):
              FK Celik Zenica – SV Austria Salzburg   3-1 (2-0)
FK Celik Zenica: Momcilo VUJACIC, Slobodan DOGANDZIC, Fadil TALIC, MITROVIC,
Dragoljub GOLUBOVIC, Midhat MUJKIC, Petar MICIC, Rade RADULOVIC, Svetozar
ANDREJIC, Mate GAVRAN, Mehmed BUZA.
SV Austria Salzburg: Wilhelm KAIPEL, Gerhard MAIRHUBER, Johann (Hannes)
WINKLBAUER (35' Josef LARIONOWS), Arthur KIBLER, Gerhard FILZMOSER, Horst
HIRNSCHRODT, Heinz LIBUDA (FRG), Adolf (Dolfi) BLUTSCH, Josef STADLER (46'
Klaus JANSON (FRG)), Alfred HALA, Franz WEIDINGER.
Goals: FK Celik Zenica: 1-0 Petar MICIC (28'), 2-0 Midhat MUJKIC (42' penalty), 3-1 Rade
RADULOVIC (73').
SV Austria Salzburg: 2-1 Artur KIBLER (68').
Referee: Paolo TOSELLI (ITA)   Attendance: 1.000

*** **FK Celik Zenica won the Cup** ***

211

1971-1972

GROUP A

20-10-1971   Letenský Stadion, Praha:
TJ Sparta CKD Praha – Budapesti Honvéd SE   2-3 (1-2)
TJ Sparta CKD Praha: Antonín KRAMERIUS, Pavel MELICHAR, Václav MIGAS (27' Josef PESICE), Eduard KESSEL, Oldrich URBAN, Frantisek CHOVANEC, Petr ULICNÝ, Jaroslav BARTON, Svatopluk BOUSKA, Josef JURKANIN, Václav MASEK. (Coach: Tadeás KRAUS).
Budapesti Honvéd SE: Bertalan BICSKEI, József KELEMAN, György DUDÁS, Sándor LUKÁCS, József PÁL, József TAJTI, László PUSZTAI, Lajos KOCSIS, Lajos SZÜCS, Imre KOMORA, László CSEPREGI. (Coach: József MÉSZÁROS).
Goals: TJ Sparta CKD Praha: 1-0 Frantisek CHOVANEC (3'), 2-3 Petr ULICNÝ (89').
Budapesti Honvéd SE: 1-1 Lajos SZÜCS (11'), 1-2 László CSEPREGI (13'), 1-3 Lajos KOCSIS (75').
Referee: Marijan RAUS (YUG)   Attendance: 8.000

03-11-1971   Bozsík József Stadion, Budapest:
Budapesti Honvéd SE – FK Celik Zenica   3-0
Budapesti Honvéd SE: Bertalan BICSKEI, József KELEMAN, József TAJTI, Sándor LUKÁCS, József PÁL (..' László MOLNÁR), Lajos SZÜCS, László PUSZTAI, Lajos KOCSIS, Gyula TÓTH, Imre KOMORA, László CSEPREGI (..' Zoltán BÓDI). (Coach: József MÉSZÁROS).
FK Celik Zenica:
Goals: Budapesti Honvéd SE: 1-0 Slobodan DOGANDZIC (..' own goal), 2-0 Gyula TÓTH (..'), 3-0 Lajos KOCSIS (..').
Attendance: 3.000

08-03-1972   Zenica: FK Celik Zenica – TJ Sparta CKD Praha   2-0 (1-0)
Goals: FK Celik Zenica: 1-0 Alojz RENIC (10'), 2-0 PRODANIC (66').
Referee: Walter FERCHER (AUT)   Attendance: 3.000

22-03-1972   Bozsík József Stadion, Budapest:
Budapesti Honvéd SE – TJ Sparta CKD Praha   2-1 (0-1)
Budapesti Honvéd SE: Bertalan BICSKEI, József KELEMAN, György DUDÁS, Lajos SZÜCS, Sándor LUKÁCS, József PÁL, Imre KOMORA, László PUSZTAI, Lajos KOCSIS, Imre KOZMA, László CSEPREGI. (Coach: József MÉSZÁROS).
TJ Sparta CKD Praha: Jan PAVLÍCEK, .., Vladimír KÁRA, Josef JURKANIN (25' Ivan MRÁZ0, Josef VESELÝ, Jaroslav BARTON. (Coach: Tadeás KRAUS).
Goals: Budapesti Honvéd SE: 1-1 Lajos KOCSIS (79'), 2-1 Imre KOZMA (84').
TJ Sparta CKD Praha: 0-1 Jaroslav BARTON (37').
Referee: Nikola MLADENOVIC (YUG)   Attendance: 7.000

10-05-1972   Stadion Bilino polje, Zenica: FK Celik Zenica – Budapesti Honvéd SE   3-0
FK Celik Zenica:
Budapesti Honvéd SE: ... (Coach: József MÉSZÁROS).

28-06-1972   Praha: TJ Sparta CKD Praha – FK Celik Zenica 0-2 (0-2)
TJ Sparta CKD Praha: Vladimir BRABEC (46' Jan PAVLICEK), Milan KOLLÁR, Vaclav
MIGAS, Frantisek CHOVANEC, Josef PETÁK, Oldrich URBAN, Josef PESICE, Ivan
MRÁZ, Václav MASEK, Josef JURKANIN, Karel PÉNEK. (Coach: Tadeás KRAUS).
FK Celik Zenica: BUJACIC, PRELCIC, Mirsad GALIJASEVIC, Dragoljub GOLUBOVIC,
Jasmin HAJDUK, Midhat MUJKIC, Petar MICIC, SERBO, Alojz RENIC, Mate GAVRAN,
Mehmed BUZA.
Goals: FK Celik Zenica: 0-1 Alojz RENIC (11'), 0-2 SERBO (21').
Referee: Josef BUCEK (AUT)   Attendance: 3.000

Pos	Team	Pld	W	D	L	GF	GA	GD	Pts
1	FK Celik Zenica (YUG)	4	3	0	1	7	3	+4	6
2	Budapesti Honvéd SE (HUN)	4	3	0	1	8	6	+2	6
3	TJ Sparta CKD Praha (TCH)	4	0	0	4	3	9	-6	0

*** FK Celik Zenica won the group and qualified for the Final ***

GROUP B

20-10-1971   Wien: First Vienna FC – AC Fiorentina 0-3 (0-0)
First Vienna FC: Viliam SCHROJF (TCH), Anton LINHART, Peter ACS (60' Walter FIALA),
Josef WAHL (70' Herbert PERISCHA), Hellmuth LIENER, Manfred REITER, Alfred
TRAXLER, Karl SCHLAGER, Vojtech MASNÝ (TCH), Rainer SCHLAGBAUER, Alfred
GASSNER. (Coach: Arnost (Ernst) HLOZEK (TCH)).
AC Fiorentina: Nevio FAVARO, Giancarlo GALDIOLO, Pietro GHEDIN (46' Giuseppe
LONGONI), Andrea ORLANDINI, Ugo FERRANTE, Giuseppe BRIZI, Claudio MERLO,
Dino D'ALESSI, Sergio CLERICI (BRA), Giancarlo DE SISTI, Luciano CHIARUGI. (Coach:
Nils Erik LEIDHOLM (SWE)).
Goals: AC Fiorentina: 0-1 Luciano CHIARUGI (50'), 0-2 Luciano CHIARUGI (61'), 0-3 Dino
D'ALESSI (89').
Referee: Bohumil SMEJKAL (TCH)   Attendance: 3.000

04-11-1971   Firenze: AC Fiorentina – FK Partizan Beograd 3-0 (2-0)
AC Fiorentina: Franco SUPERCHI, Giancarlo GALDIOLO, Giovanni BOTTI, Dino
D'ALESSI, Ennio PELLEGRINI, Andrea ORLANDINI, Claudio MERLO, Ferruccio
MAZZOLA (II), Sergio CLERICI (BRA) (80' Italo FLORIO), Giancarlo DE SISTI, Luciano
CHIARUGI (78' Claudio PICCINETTI). (Coach: Nils Erik LEIDHOLM (SWE)).
FK Partizan Beograd: Miodrag KNEZEVIC, Milos RADAKOVIC, Slobodan TODOROVIC
(46' MAJAKIC), Vladimir PEJOVIC, Blagoje PAUNOVIC, Radomir ANTIC, Miodrag
ZIVALJEVIC, Svemir DJORDJIC, Pavle GRUBJESIC (35' Zarko OLAREVIC), Momcilo
(Moca) VUKOTIC, Nenad BJEKOVIC.
Goals: AC Fiorentina: 1-0 Luciano CHIARUGI (24'), 2-0 Luciano CHIARUGI (37'), 3-0 Dino
D'ALESSI (65').
Referee: István ZSOLT (HUN)

01-03-1972   Beograd: FK Partizan Beograd – First Vienna FC 3-0 (2-0)
Goals: FK Partizan Beograd: 1-0 Nenad BJEKOVIC (19'), 2-0 Momcilo (Moca) VUKOTIC
(22'), 3-0 Miodrag ZIVALJEVIC (62').
Attendance: 7.000

213

22-03-1972   Firenze: AC Fiorentina – First Vienna FC   2-1 (1-0)
AC Fiorentina: Franco SUPERCHI, Giancarlo GALDIOLO, Giuseppe LONGONI, Nevio
SCALA, Ugo FERRANTE, Salvatore ESPOSITO, Claudio MERLO, Dino D'ALESSI, Sergio
CLERICI (BRA), Giancarlo DE SISTI, Luciano CHIARUGI. (Coach: Nils Erik LEIDHOLM
(SWE)).
First Vienna FC: Gernot FRAYDL, Peter ACS (57' Walter DANNHAUSER goalkeeper),
Helmut LOSCHY, Anton LINHART, Hellmuth LIENER, Herbert PERISCHA, Alfred
TRAXLER, Alfred GASSNER, Vojtech MASNÝ (TCH), Rainer SCHLAGBAUER, Rudolf
HEVERA (75' Walter FIALA). (Coach: Arnost (Ernst) HLOZEK (TCH)).
Goals: AC Fiorentina: 1-0 CHIARUGI (25'), 2-1 CLERICI (90').
First Vienna FC: 1-1 Alfred TRAXLER (82').
Referee: György MÜNCZ (HUN)   Attendance: 10.000

24-04-1972   Beograd: FK Partizan Beograd – AC Fiorentina   2-1 (1-1)
FK Partizan Beograd: Ivan CURKOVIC, Milos RADAKOVIC, Ivan GOLAC, Vladimir
PEJOVIC, Slobodan TODOROVIC, Pavle GRUBJESIC, Lija KATIC, Svemir DJORDJIC,
Miodrag ZIVALJEVIC (51' Blagoje PAUNOVIC), Radomir ANTIC, Nenad BJEKOVIC.
AC Fiorentina: Nevio FAVARO, Giancarlo GALDIOLO, Giuseppe LONGONI, Andrea
ORLANDINI, Giuseppe BRIZI, Giovanni BOTTI, Salvatore ESPOSITO, Dino D'ALESSI,
Sergio CLERICI (BRA), Giancarlo DE SISTI, Giorgio BRAGLIA (70' Ferruccio MAZZOLA
(II)). (Coach: Nils Erik LEIDHOLM (SWE)).
Goals: FK Partizan Beograd: 1-0 Nenad BJEKOVIC (11'), 2-1 Svemir DJORDJIC (52').
AC Fiorentina: 1-1 Giorgio BRAGLIA (18').
Referee: Alois KESSLER (AUT)

21-06-1972   Wien: First Vienna FC – FK Partizan Beograd   1-4 (0-1)
First Vienna FC: Walter DANNHAUSER, Peter ACS, Helmut LOSCHY, Manfred REITER,
Paul RIZZOLI (46' Peter MEISTER), Josef WAHL, Alfred TRAXLER, Rudolf HEVERA,
WOLF (74' Rainer SCHLAGBAUER), Vojtech MASNÝ (TCH), Alfred GASSNER. (Coach:
Horst FRANZ (FRG)).
FK Partizan Beograd: Mladen FURTULA (46' Miodrag KNEZEVIC), Milos RADAKOVIC,
PREMOVIC, Vladimir PEJOVIC, Ivan GOLAC, Radomir ANTIC, Nenad CVETKOVIC,
Momcilo (Moca) VUKOTIC (46' Djuro MARIC), Lija KATIC, Svemir DJORDJIC,
LICANIN.
Goals: First Vienna FC: 1-1 Vojtech MASNÝ (52' penalty).
FK Partizan Beograd: 0-1 Lija KATIC (27'), 1-2 Nenad CVETKOVIC (64'), 1-3 Nenad
CVETKOVIC (75'), 1-4 Svemir DJORDJIC (83').
Referee: Gusztav BIRCSAK (HUN)   Attendance: 3.000

Pos	Team	Pld	W	D	L	GF	GA	GD	Pts
1	AC Fiorentina (ITA)	4	3	0	1	9	3	+6	6
2	FK Partizan Beograd (YUG)	4	3	0	1	9	5	+4	6
3	First Vienna FC (AUT)	4	0	0	4	2	12	-10	0

*** AC Fiorentina won the group and qualified for the Final ***

214

FINAL

23-08-1972   Firenze: AC Fiorentina – FK Celik Zenica   0-0
AC Fiorentina: Franco SUPERCHI, Mario PEREGO, Giancarlo GALDIOLO, Nevio SCALA,
Giuseppe BRIZI, Andrea ORLANDINI, Claudio MERLO, Ángelo Benedicto Miguel
SORMANI (BRA), Sergio CLERICI (BRA), Giancarlo DE SISTI, Nello SALTUTTI. (Coach:
Nils Erik LEIDHOLM (SWE)).
FK Celik Zenica: Momcilo VUJACIC, Kemal SLJOKA, Fadil TALIC, Mirsad
GALIJASEVIC, Jasmin HAJDUK, Midhat MUJKIC, Mehmed BUZA, Goran PELES, Alojz
RENIC, Mate GAVRAN, Rifet BAJRIC.
Referee: Bohumil KOPCIO (TCH)

04-10-1972   Zenica: FK Celik Zenica – AC Fiorentina   1-0
FK Celik Zenica: Momcilo VUJACIC, Goran PELES, Fadil TALIC, Mirsad GALIJASEVIC,
Jasmin HAJDUK, Midhat MUJKIC, Mehmed BUZA, Rifet BRDAREVIC, Alojz RENIC,
Mate GAVRAN, Rifet BAJRIC.
AC Fiorentina: Franco SUPERCHI, Giancarlo GALDIOLO, Giuseppe LONGONI, Nevio
SCALA, Giuseppe BRIZI, Andrea ORLANDINI, Mario PEREGO, Claudio MERLO, Sergio
CLERICI (BRA), Giancarlo DE SISTI (2' Ennio PELLEGRINI), Ángelo Benedicto Miguel
SORMANI (BRA). (Coach: Nils Erik LEIDHOLM (SWE)).
Goal: FK Celik Zenica: 1-0 Mirsad GALIJASEVIC (89').
Referee: Ferdinand MARSCHALL (AUT)

*** FK Celik Zenica won the Cup ***

1972-1973

25-10-1972   Zenica: FK Celik Zenica – Linzer ASK   2-0 (2-0)
Goals: FK Celik Zenica: 1-0 Midhat MUJKIC (21'), 2-0 Mate GAVRAN (32').
Referee: Gyula EMSBERGER (HUN)   Attendance: 4.000

08-11-1972   Linzer Stadion, Linz: Linzer ASK – TJ Zbrojovka Brno   1-3 (0-1)
Linzer ASK: Josef SCHRÖTTNER, Stefan RATZESBERGER, Erhard WIEGER, Franz
VIEHBÖCK, Walter GEBHARDT, August STAREK, Willibald BAUER, Johann KONDERT,
Rudolf NAFZIGER, SIGMUND, Hermann ROITHNER. (Coach: Otto BARIC (YUG)).
TJ Zbrojovka Brno: BALENIK, VIDU, Josef POSPISIL, Jan KLIMES, UVIGL, Rostislav
VÁCLAVÍCEK, Ivan HRDLICKA, Vítezslav KOTÁSEK, CVETLER, MIKLOS, Jan
KOPENEC. (Coach: Frantisek HAVRÁNEK).
Goals: Linzer ASK: 1-3 NAFZINGER (90').
TJ Zbrojovka Brno: 0-1 Jan KOPENEC (6'), 0-2 CVETLER (80'), 0-3 Jan KOPENEC (89').
Referee: Ratko CANAK (YUG)   Attendance: 1.000

29-11-1972   Brno: TJ Zbrojovka Brno – FK Celik Zenica   2-1 (1-0)
Goals: TJ Zbrojovka Brno: 1-0 MIKLOS (..'), Rostislav VÁCLAVÍCEK.
FK Celik Zenica: Alojz RENIC.
Referee: Lajos SOMLAI (HUN)   Attendance: 4.000

21-03-1973   Linzer Stadion, Linz: Linzer ASK – FK Celik Zenica   1-3 (1-2)
Linzer ASK: ... (Coach: BARIC).
FK Celik Zenica:
Goals: Linzer ASK: 1-1 Gerhard STURMBERGER (36').
FK Celik Zenica: 0-1 Alojz RENIC (32'), 1-2 Alojz RENIC (41'), 1-3 Rifet BAJRIC (90').
Referee: Francesco FRANCESCON (ITA)   Attendance: 1.700

11-04-1973   Brno: TJ Zbrojovka Brno – Linzer ASK   1-1 (1-0)
TJ Zbrojovka Brno:
Linzer ASK: ..., Hubert SCHÖLL (FRG), ...
Goals: TJ Zbrojovka Brno: 1-0 Karel KROUPA (40').
Linzer ASK: 1-1 Hubert SCHÖLL (53').
Referee: Paolo TOSELLI (ITA)   Attendance: 1.200

09-05-1973   Zenica: FK Celik Zenica – TJ Zbrojovka Brno   2-1 (1-0)
Goals: FK Celik Zenica: Alojz RENIC, Goran PELES.
TJ Zbrojovka Brno: Vítezslav KOTÁSEK.
Referee: Josef SZILVASI (HUN)   Attendance: 4.000

Pos	Team	Pld	W	D	L	GF	GA	GD	Pts
1	FK Celik Zenica (YUG)	4	3	0	1	8	4	+4	6
2	TJ Zbrojovka Brno (TCH)	4	2	1	1	7	5	+2	5
3	Linzer ASK (AUT)	4	0	1	3	3	9	-6	1

*** FK Celik Zenica won the group and qualified for the Final ***

GROUP B

25-10-1972   Bologna: FC Bologna – NK Dinamo Zagreb   2-2 (0-1)
FC Bologna: Pietro BATTARA, Tazio ROVERSI, Adriano FEDELE, Francesco SCORSA, Franco CRESCI, Ivan GREGORI, Carlo LANCINI (15' MODONESE, 55' Fausto LANDINI (II)), Francesco LIGUORI, Giuseppe SAVOLDI (I), Pierino GHETTI, Roberto FILIPPI. (Coach: Bruno PESAOLA (ARG)).
NK Dinamo Zagreb: Fahrudin DAUTBEGOVIC, Celestin GASPARINI, Damir VALEC, Josip LALIC, Marijan BRNCIC, Josip KUZE, Ivica SENZEN, Josip GUCMIRTL, Nedo KOVACEVIC, Dragutin VABEC (73' Marijan CERCEK), KRANC (46' Zdenko KAFKA).
Goals: FC Bologna: 1-2 Giuseppe SAVOLDI (58'), 2-2 Adriano FEDELE (66').
NK Dinamo Zagreb: 0-1 KOVACEVIC (2'), 0-2 Adriano FEDELE (52' *own goal*).
Referee: Paul SCHILLER (AUT)

08-11-1972   Stadion Maksimir, Zagreb:
                   NK Dinamo Zagreb – Tatabányai Bányász SC   0-1 (0-1)
NK Dinamo Zagreb:
Tatabányai Bányász SC: János CSEPECZ, Mihály LACZKÓ, László HORVÁTH, Tibor KOVÁCS (I), Mihály ARANY, Lajos KOVÁCSHEGYI, István NAGY, István NYÍRÖ, György ZÖLDI, György SZABÓ, Kálmán TÓTH. (Coach:Károly LAKAT).
Goal: Tatabányai Bányász SC: 0-1 György ZÖLDI (..').
Referee: Karol SARKA (TCH)

29-11-1972   Bányász Stadion, Tatabánya: Tatabányai Bányász SC – FC Bologna   3-0 (3-0)
Tatabányai Bányász SC: János CSEPECZ, László HORVÁTH, Tibor KOVÁCS (I), István NYÍRÖ, György SZABÓ, István NAGY (70' László LÓDI), János GÖRÖCS (60' Mihály LACZKÓ), György ZÖLDI, László TAKÁCS, Mihály ARANY, Kálmán TÓTH. (Coach:Károly LAKAT).
FC Bologna: Amos ADANI, Giovanni MEI, Vittorio CAPORALE, MONTANARI, Francesco SCORSA, Aldo MALDERA (III), TREMAGLIA (77' Franco COLOMBA), Pierino GHETTI, Oriano GROP, Roberto VIERI, Eraldo PECCI. (Coach: Bruno PESAOLA (ARG)).
Goals: Tatabányai Bányász SC: 1-0 János GÖRÖCS (17'), 2-0 László TAKÁCS (28'), 3-0 László TAKÁCS (35').
Referee: Josef BUCEK (AUT)

28-03-1973   Zagreb: NK Dinamo Zagreb – FC Bologna   3-1 (2-0)
NK Dinamo Zagreb: Zelimir STINCIC, Damir VALEC, Cedomir JOVICEVIC, Icica CAR, Ivica MILJKOVIC, Filip BLASKOVIC (46' Slavko KOVACIC), Marijan CERCEK, Josip LALIC, Dragutin VABEC (71' Marijan NOVAK), Zdenko KAFKA, Krasnador RORA. (Coach: Domagoj KAPETANOVIC).
FC Bologna: Sergio BUSO, Giovanni MEI, Roberto CANESTRARI, Vittorio CAPORALE, MONTANARI, Aldo MALDERA (III), POSOCCO, Carlo LANCINI, Fausto LANDINI (II), Francesco LIGUORI, Oriano GROP. (Coach: Bruno PESAOLA (ARG)).
Goals: NK Dinamo Zagreb: 1-0 Dragutin VABEC (4'), 2-0 Josip LALIC (15'), 3-1 Dragutin VABEC (69').
FC Bologna: 2-1 Aldo MALDERA (47').
Referee: Zdenek JELÍNEK (TCH)

11-04-1973   Bányász Stadion, Tatabánya:
                     Tatabányai Bányász SC – NK Dinamo Zagreb   0-1 (0-1)
Tatabányai Bányász SC: János CSEPECZ, László HORVÁTH, Tibor KOVÁCS (I), István
KNAPIK, Lajos KOVÁCSHEGYI, István NAGY, János GÖRÖCS, György SZABÓ, László
TAKÁCS, Mihály KÖMÜVES, Ferenc TÓTH (..' György ZÖLDI). (Coach:Károly LAKAT).
NK Dinamo Zagreb: ... (Coach: Domagoj KAPETANOVIC).
Goal: NK Dinamo Zagreb: 0-1
Referee: Alois KESSLER (AUT)

09-05-1973   Stadio Comunale, Bologna: FC Bologna – Tatabányai Bányász SC   1-2 (0-1)
FC Bologna: Sergio BUSO, Giovanni MEI, Aldo MALDERA (III), Francesco SCORSA,
MONTANARI, Carlo LANCINI, Eraldo PECCI, Roberto VIERI, Fausto LANDINI (II),
Francesco LIGUORI, Oriano GROP (71' TREMAGLIA). (Coach: Bruno PESAOLA (ARG)).
Tatabányai Bányász SC: János CSEPECZ, Mihály LACZKÓ, László HORVÁTH, Tibor
KOVÁCS (I), István KNAPIK, Lajos KOVÁCSHEGYI, László TAKÁCS, Mihály ARANY,
György SZABÓ, Mihály KÖMÜVES, László HERNÁDI. (Coach:Károly LAKAT).
Goals: FC Bologna: 1-1 Fausto LANDINI (54').
Tatabányai Bányász SC: 0-1 György SZABÓ (27'), 1-2 László TAKÁCS (73').
Referee: Adolf MATHIAS (AUT)

Pos	Team	Pld	W	D	L	GF	GA	GD	Pts
1	*Tatabányai Bányász SC (HUN)*	*4*	*3*	*0*	*1*	*6*	*2*	*+4*	*6*
2	NK Dinamo Zagreb (YUG)	4	2	1	1	6	4	+2	5
3	FC Bologna (ITA)	4	0	1	3	4	10	-6	1

*** Tatabányai Bányász SC won the group and qualified for the Final ***

FINAL

27-06-1973   Stadion Bilino polje, Zenica:
                     FK Celik Zenica – Tatabányai Bányász SC   1-2 (0-0)
FK Celik Zenica:
Tatabányai Bányász SC: János CSEPECZ, Mihály LACZKÓ, László HERNÁDI, Tibor
KOVÁCS (I), László HORVÁTH, Ferenc HORVÁTH, Mihály ARANY, János GÖRÖCS,
György SZABÓ, Mihály KÖMÜVES, István NAGY (..' Ervin DÁKAI). (Coach:Károly
LAKAT).
Goals: FK Celik Zenica:
Tatabányai Bányász SC: György SZABÓ, Mihály KÖMÜVES.
Referee: Fabio MONTI (ITA)   Attendance: 7.000

01-07-1973   Bányász Stadion, Tatabánya:
                     Tatabányai Bányász SC – FK Celik Zenica   2-1 (1-1)
Tatabányai Bányász SC: János CSEPECZ, László HERNÁDI, Tibor KOVÁCS (I), Mihály
LACZKÓ, László HORVÁTH, Ferenc HORVÁTH, Mihály ARANY (..' István KNAPIK),
György SZABÓ, Mihály KÖMÜVES, Ervin DÁKAI, István NAGY. (Coach:Károly LAKAT).
FK Celik Zenica:
Goals: Tatabányai Bányász SC: Ervin DÁKAI, Ervin DÁKAI.
FK Celik Zenica:
Referee: Paul SCHILLER (AUT)   Attendance: 8.000

*** Tatabányai Bányász SC won the Cup ***

1973-1974

GROUP A

24-10-1973   Bregenz: FC Vorarlberg – SS Lanerossi-Vicenza   0-0
FC Vorarlberg: Johann SCHORN, Gerhard ROSSBACHER (46' Wolfgang GIRARDI),
Gustav THALER, Miroslav MAKSIMOVIC (YUG), Thomas SCHELLING, Dieter
ALBRICH, Otmar SOMMER (63' Bruno PEZZEY), Adolf (Dolfi) BLUTSCH, Wolfgang
SCHWARZ, Horst ROMES (FRG), Helmut METZLER. (Coach: Wolfgang SCHWARZ).
SS Lanerossi-Vicenza: Adriano BARDIN, Fabrizio GORIN, Giuseppe LONGONI, Domenico
FONTANA, Ugo FERRANTE, Fabrizio BERNI, Giuseppe (Oscar) DAMIANI, Ángelo
Benedicto Miguel SORMANI (BRA), Emiliano MACCHI (82' CINI), Renato FALOPPA (62'
Ezio VENDRAME), Gian Paolo GALUPPI. (Coach: Héctor (Ettore) PURICELLI Seña
(URU)).
Referee: Lajos SOMLAI (HUN)

07-11-1973   Bányász Stadion, Tatabánya:
                        Tatabányai Bányász SC – FC Vorarlberg   5-2 (3-0)
Tatabányai Bányász SC: Béla BRÜNYI, László HERNÁDI, István NÉDER, Mihály LACZKÓ
(..' István NAGY), László HORVÁTH, Tibor KOVÁCS (I), István KNAPIK, György SZABÓ
(..' László TAKÁCS), István SALLÓI, Mihály KÖMÜVES, Kálmán TÓTH. (Coach: Károly
LAKAT).
FC Vorarlberg: ..., Horst ROMES (FRG), ... (Coach: Wolfgang SCHWARZ).
Goals: Tatabányai Bányász SC: 1-0 István KNAPIK (..'), 2-0 György SZABÓ (..'), 3-0 Mihály
KÖMÜVES (..'), Mihály KÖMÜVES, Kálmán TÓTH.
FC Vorarlberg: Horst ROMES, Horst ROMES.

28-11-1973   Stadio Romeo Menti, Vicenza:
                        SS Lanerossi-Vicenza – Tatabányai Bányász SC   0-1 (0-0)
SS Lanerossi-Vicenza: Michelangelo SULFARO (43' Adriano BARDIN), Attilio BERTI,
Gianfranco VOLPATI, Domenico FONTANA, Mario PEREGO, Fabrizio BERNI, Giuseppe
(Oscar) DAMIANI, Ángelo Benedicto Miguel SORMANI (BRA), Emiliano MACCHI, Renato
FALOPPA, Ezio VENDRAME. (Coach: Héctor (Ettore) PURICELLI Seña (URU)).
Tatabányai Bányász SC: János CSEPECZ, László HERNÁDI, István NÉDER, Tibor
KOVÁCS (I), László HORVÁTH, István KNAPIK, Mihály LACZKÓ, György SZABÓ,
István SALLÓI (65' László TAKÁCS), Mihály KÖMÜVES, Kálmán TÓTH. (Coach: Károly
LAKAT).
Goal: Tatabányai Bányász SC: 0-1 László TAKÁCS (73').
Referee: Josip STRMECKI (YUG)

06-03-1974   Vicenza: SS Lanerossi-Vicenza – FC Vorarlberg 3-1 (1-1)
SS Lanerossi-Vicenza: Michelangelo SULFARO, Fabrizio GORIN (46' MAESTRINER),
Giuseppe LONGONI, Giorgio BERNARDIS, Ugo FERRANTE, Attilio BERTI, Giuseppe
(Oscar) DAMIANI, Domenico FONTANA, Emiliano MACCHI, Ezio VENDRAME, Luciano
SPEGGIORIN (II). (Coach: Héctor (Ettore) PURICELLI Seña (URU)).
FC Vorarlberg: Erwin FUCHSBICHLER(II), Gerhard ROSSBACHER, Reinhard KORNEXL,
Gustav THALER, Dieter ALBRICH, Otmar SOMMER, Rudolf BRUNNENMEIER (FRG),
Franz WOLNY, Franz WEIDINGER, Bruno PEZZEY, Wolfgang SCHWARZ. (Coach:
Wolfgang SCHWARZ).
Goals: SS Lanerossi-Vicenza: 1-1 Ezio VENDRAME (13'), 2-1 Emiliano MACCHI (59'), 3-1
Emiliano MACCHI (83' penalty).
FC Vorarlberg:0-1 Bruno PEZZEY (12').
Referee: Karoly PALOTAI (HUN)

20-03-1974   Bodenseestadion, Bregenz: FC Vorarlberg – Tatabányai Bányász SC 1-1 (1-0)
FC Vorarlberg: ..., Miroslav MAKSIMOVIC (YUG), Horst ROMES (FRG), ... (Coach:
Wolfgang SCHWARZ).
Tatabányai Bányász SC: Béla BRÜNYI, László HERNÁDI, Tibor KOVÁCS (I), István
NÉDER, László HORVÁTH, István NAGY, István KNAPIK (..' Mihály LACZKÓ), György
SZABÓ, István SALLÓI, László TAKÁCS, Kálmán TÓTH. (Coach: Károly LAKAT).
Goals: FC Vorarlberg: 1-0 Horst ROMES (10').
Tatabányai Bányász SC: 1-1 Miroslav MAKSIMOVIC (50' *own goal*).

10-04-1974   Bányász Stadion, Tatabánya:
                  Tatabányai Bányász SC – SS Lanerossi-Vicenza 1-1 (0-1)
Tatabányai Bányász SC: Béla BRÜNYI, László HERNÁDI, István NÉDER, Mihály
LACZKÓ, László HORVÁTH (46' István NAGY), György SZABÓ, Tibor KOVÁCS (I),
István SALLÓI, Mihály KÖMÜVES, István KNAPIK, Kálmán TÓTH. (Coach: Károly
LAKAT).
SS Lanerossi-Vicenza: Michelangelo SULFARO, Giorgio BERNARDIS, Mario PEREGO,
Ugo FERRANTE, Giuseppe LONGONI, Fabrizio GORIN, Ezio VENDRAME, Luciano
SPEGGIORIN (II), Ángelo Benedicto Miguel SORMANI (BRA) (46' Renato FALOPPA),
Domenico FONTANA, Alessandro VITALI. (Coach: Héctor (Ettore) PURICELLI Seña
(URU)).
Goals: Tatabányai Bányász SC: 1-1 Mihály KÖMÜVES (50').
SS Lanerossi-Vicenza: 0-1 Giorgio BERNARDIS (30').
Referee: Josef POUCEK (TCH)

Pos	Team	Pld	W	D	L	GF	GA	GD	Pts
1	*Tatabányai Bányász SC (HUN)*	4	2	2	0	8	4	+4	6
2	SS Lanerossi-Vicenza (ITA)	4	1	2	1	4	3	+1	4
3	FC Vorarlberg (AUT)	4	0	2	2	4	9	-5	2

*** **Tatabányai Bányász SC won the Group and qualified for the Final** ***

GROUP B

03-10-1973   Sarajevo: FK Sarajevo – Videoton SC   3-1 (0-0)
FK Sarajevo: Savo EKMECIC, Zlatko DUPOVAC, Fuad MUZUROVIC, Sulejman DEMIR,
Andjelko TESAN, Ante RAJKOVIC, Murat SARAN, Edhem SLJIVO, Dzemel CERIC,
Dragoljub SIMIC (..' Zoran LUKIC), Ranko PETKOVIC.
Videoton SC: László KOVÁCS, János NAGY (III), József KOVÁCS, SZABÓ, Gábor
HARTYÁNI, Gábor FEJES, Tibor WOLLEK, János NAGY (II), Attila BOGATI, László
KARSAI, Imre BURKA. (Coach: Ferenc KOVÁCS).
Goals: FK Sarajevo: Zoran LUKIC, Edhem SLJIVO, Ranko PETKOVIC.
Videoton SC: János NAGY (II).
Referee: Luciano GIUNTI (ITA)   Attendance: 2.000

24-10-1973   Székesfehérvar: Videoton SC – TJ ZVL Zilina   3-0 (1-0)
Videoton SC: ... (Coach: Ferenc KOVÁCS).
TJ ZVL Zilina: Frantisek SMAK, Albert RUSNAK (I), Jozef GARGULÁK, Milan
STASKOVAN, Rudolf PODOLÁK (65' Václav VOJTEK), Jozef TOMÁNEK, Stefan
TOMÁNEK, Tibor CHOBOT, Vladimír RUSNÁK, Stefan SLEZÁK, Jozef BELES. (Coach:
Teodor REIMAN).
Goals: Videoton SC: 1-0 János NAGY (II) (32'), 2-0 Attila BOGATI (67'), 3-0 József
KOVÁCS (70').
Referee: Josip STRMECKI (YUG)   Attendance: 5.000

07-11-1973   Zilina: TJ ZVL Zilina – FK Sarajevo   4-0 (3-0)
TJ ZVL Zilina: Ján CEPO, Jozef GARGULÁK, Milan STASKOVAN, Karol SULGAN,
Albert RUSNAK (I), Tibor CHOBOT, Stefan TOMÁNEK, Jozef TOMÁNEK, Vladimír
RUSNÁK, Stefan SLEZÁK (54' Zdeno KÚDELKA), Václav VOJTEK (75' Jozef ZIGO).
(Coach: Jozef MARUSIN).
FK Sarajevo: Sead GRUDA, Robert KOSAR, Fuad MUZUROVIC, Nijaz FERHATOVIC,
Ante RAJKOVIC, Sulejman DEMIR, Murat SARAN, Dragoljub SIMIC, Dzemel CERIC,
Sabit SADIKOVIC, Vahid AVDIC (46' Avdo MURGA).
Goals: TJ ZVL Zilina: 1-0 Tibor CHOBOT (11'), 2-0 Tibor CHOBOT (25' penalty), 3-0 Tibor
CHOBOT (31'), 4-0 Stefan SLEZÁK (50').
Referee: Adolf MATHIAS (AUT)   Attendance: 500

06-03-1974   Székesfehérvar: Videoton SC – FK Sarajevo   3-1 (2-0)
Videoton SC: SZABÓ, János NAGY (III), Lajos GARAMVÖLGYI, MESTER, József
KOVÁCS, Gábor FEJES, Tibor WOLLEK (..' Tamás SZALMÁSY), János NAGY (II), László
KUTI (..' László TIEBER), László KARSAI, Imre BURKA. (Coach: Ferenc KOVÁCS).
FK Sarajevo: Sead GRUDA, Nijaz FERHATOVIC (..' Hamdo RADELJAS), Fuad
MUZUROVIC, Robert KOSAR, Fahrudin PRLJACA, Sulejman DEMIR, Zoran LUKIC,
Dragoljub SIMIC, Safet SUSIC, Edhem SLJIVO, Ranko PETKOVIC (..' Hamdo
FERHATOVIC).
Goals: Videoton SC: János NAGY (II), László KARSAI, László TIEBER.
FK Sarajevo: Hamdo FERHATOVIC.
Referee: Paolo TOSELLI (ITA)   Attendance: 5.000

221

20-03-1974   Zilina: TJ ZVL Zilina – Videoton SC   5-1 (1-0)
TJ ZVL Zilina: ... (Coach: Michal BARÁNEK).
Videoton SC: ... (Coach: Ferenc KOVÁCS).
Goals: TJ ZVL Zilina: 1-0 Stefan TOMÁNEK (39'), 2-1 Miroslav KRÁL (61'), 3-1 Stefan
TOMÁNEK (72'), 4-1 Jozef TOMÁNEK (79'), 5-1 Jozef BELES (84').
Videoton SC: 1-1 László TIBER (60').
Referee: Josef BUCEK (AUT)   Attendance: 1.500

10-04-1974   Sarajevo: FK Sarajevo – TJ ZVL Zilina   3-3 (1-2)
FK Sarajevo: Savo EKMECIC, Hamdo RADELJAS, Zlatko DUPOVAC, Nijaz
FERHATOVIC, Ante RAJKOVIC, Momcilo TOSIC, Murat SARAN, Fahrudin PRLJACA,
Zoran LUKIC, Sabit SADIKOVIC, Avdo MURGA.
TJ ZVL Zilina: Frantisek PLACH, Albert RUSNÁK (I), Rudolf PODOLÁK, Jozef
TOMÁNEK, Jozef GARGULÁK, Vladimír RUSNÁK, Jozef BELES, Karol SULGAN, Stefan
TOMÁNEK, Stefan SLEZÁK, Tibor CHOBOT. (Coach: Michal BARÁNEK).
Goals: FK Sarajevo: Fahrudin PRLJACA, Avdo MURGA, Sabit SADIKOVIC.
TJ ZVL Zilina: Jozef BELES, Tibor CHOBOT, Jozef TOMÁNEK.
Referee: Gyula EMSBERGER (HUN)   Attendance: 2.000

Pos	Team	Pld	W	D	L	GF	GA	GD	Pts
1	TJ ZVL Zilina (TCH)	4	2	1	1	12	7	+6	5
2	Videoton SC (HUN)	4	2	0	2	8	9	-2	4
3	FK Sarajevo (YUG)	4	1	1	2	7	11	-4	3

*** TJ ZVL Zilina won the group and qualified for the Final ***

FINAL

08-05-1974   Stadión pod Dubnom, Zilina:
                    TJ ZVL Zilina – Tatabányai Bányász SC   2-3 (1-1)
TJ ZVL Zilina: Ján CEPO, Albert RUSNÁK (I), Jozef GARGULÁK (57' Jozef ZIGO), Karol
SULGAN, Rudolf PODOLÁK, Stefan TOMÁNEK, Jozef TOMÁNEK, Jozef BELES,
Miroslav KRÁL, Stefan SLEZÁK (63' Ladislav FRKO), Tibor CHOBOT. (Coach: Michal
BARANEK).
Tatabányai Bányász SC: Béla BRÜNYI, László HERNÁDI, István NÉDER, Mihály
LACZKÓ, László HORVÁTH, Mihály ARANY, Tibor KOVÁCS (I), István KNAPIK,
György SZABÓ, Mihály KÖMÜVES, Kálmán TÓTH. (Coach: Károly LAKAT).
Goals: TJ ZVL Zilina: 1-1 Stefan SLEZÁK (31'), 2-2 Jozef TOMÁNEK (85' penalty).
Tatabányai Bányász SC: 0-1 Mihály KÖMÜVES (2'), 1-2 Mihály KÖMÜVES (57'), 2-3
György SZABÓ (87').
Referee: Franz WÖHRER (AUT)   Attendance: 2.000

222

15-05-1974   Bányász Stadion, Tatabánya:
Tatabányai Bányász SC – TJ ZVL Zilina   2-0 (2-0)
Tatabányai Bányász SC: Béla BRÜNYI, László HERNÁDI, István NÉDER, Tibor KOVÁCS (I), László HORVÁTH, Mihály ARANY (..' Mihály LACZKÓ), István SALLOI (I), György SZABÓ, László TAKÁCS (..' János GÖRÖCS), Mihály KÖMÜVES, Kálmán TÓTH. (Coach: Károly LAKAT).
TJ ZVL Zilina: Ján CEPO, Albert RUSNÁK (I), Jozef GARGULÁK, Rudolf PODOLÁK, Stefan TOMÁNEK, Tibor CHOBOT (67' Miroslav RADOLSKÝ), Miroslav KRÁL, Jozef TOMÁNEK, Jozef ZIGO, Stefan SLEZÁK, Jozef BELES. (Coach: Michal BARÁNEK).
Goals: Tatabányai Bányász SC: 1-0 László TAKÁCS (16'), 2-0 Mihály KÖMÜVES (19').
Referee: Dusan MAKSIMOVIC (YUG)   Attendance: 12.000

*** Tatabányai Bányász SC won the Cup ***

223

1974-1975

GROUP A

02-10-1974   Bányász Stadion, Tatabánya: Tatabányai Bányász SC – NK Rijeka   3-1
Tatabányai Bányász SC: András DOMBAI, László HORVÁTH, István NÉDER, Tibor
KOVÁCS (I), István KNAPIK, György SZABÓ, Károly CSAPÓ, Imre HEGYI (..' Mihály
ARANY), Mihály KÖMÜVES (..' Mihály HERNÁDI), István HALÁSZ, Kálmán TÓTH.
(Coach: József GELEI).
NK Rijeka:
Goals: Tatabányai Bányász SC: István KNAPIK, Károly CSAPÓ, István HALÁSZ.
NK Rijeka:

23-10-1974   Rijeka: NK Rijeka – Swarovski Wacker Innsbruck   1-3 (1-1)
NK Rijeka: Borut SKULJ, Radomir STEFANOVIC, Ivan KOCIJANCIC, Dusko DEVCIC,
Mladen MUSTAC, Miroslav CUKON, Josip RAZIC, Gano CERIC, Miodrag KUSTUDIC,
Srecko JURICIC, Sergio MAKIN.
Swarovski Wacker Innsbruck: Friedrich (Friedl) KONCILIA, Engelbert KORDESCH, Rudolf
HORVATH (I), Johann (Hans) EIGENSTILLER, Bruno PEZZEY, Hans REBELE (FRG),
Franz OBERACHER, Peter KONCILIA, Ove FLINDT-Bjerg (DEN), Manfred GOMBASCH,
Günther RINKER. (Coach: Brabko ELSNER (TCH)).
Goals: NK Rijeka: 1-1 Miodrag KUSTUDIC C (36').
Swarovski Wacker Innsbruck: 0-1 Manfred GOMBASCH (14'), 1-2 Bruno PEZZEY (58'), 1-3
Manfred GOMBASCH (87').
Referee: Vlado TAUZES (YUG)   Attendance: 1.000

27-11-1974   Tivoli-Stadion, Innsbruck:
                Swarovski Wacker Innsbruck – Tatabányai Bányász SC   4-1 (2-1)
Swarovski Wacker Innsbruck: Friedrich (Friedl) KONCILIA, Engelbert KORDESCH (46'
Günther RINKER), Rudolf HORVATH (I), Bruno PEZZEY, Werner KRIESS, Manfred
GOMBASCH, Peter KONCILIA, Ove FLINDT-Bjerg (DEN), Franz OBERACHER, Kurt
WELZL, Helmut METZLER. (Coach: Branko ELSNER (TCH)).
Tatabányai Bányász SC: András DOMBAI, Mihály LACZKÓ, László HORVÁTH, István
NÉDER (..' Sándor CZAKÓ), Tibor KOVÁCS (I), István KNAPIK, Károly CSAPÓ (..' István
HALÁSZ), Mihály ARANY, György SZABÓ, Mihály KÖMÜVES, Kálmán TÓTH. (Coach:
József GELEI).
Goals: Swarovski Wacker Innsbruck: 1-1 Helmut METZLER (16'), 2-1 Peter KONCILIA
(40'), 3-1 Werner KRIESS (54'), 4-1 Franz OBERACHER (70').
Tatabányai Bányász SC: 0-1 Károly CSAPÓ (14').
Referee: Dietmar DRABEK (AUT)   Attendance: 3.500

05-03-1975   Bányász Stadion, Tatabánya:
          Tatabányai Bányász SC – Swarovski Wacker Innsbruck   0-1 (0-0)
Tatabányai Bányász SC: Béla BRÜNYI, László HORVÁTH, Tibor KOVÁCS (I),
J.HORVÁTH, István KNAPIK, Károly CSAPÓ (75' György SZABÓ), Vilmos BÁNFI, Imre
HEGYI, István HALÁSZ (46' István SALLÓI), Ervin DÁKAI, György ZÖLDI. (Coach:
József GELEI).
Swarovski Wacker Innsbruck: Friedrich (Friedl) KONCILIA, Werner KRIESS (33' Othmar
BAJLICZ), Rudolf HORVATH (I), Engelbert KORDESCH, Johann (Hans) EIGENSTILLER
(YC55), Ove FLINDT-Bjerg (DEN), Peter KONCILIA (YC44), Manfred GOMBASCH,
Werner SCHWARZ, Kurt WELZL, Günther RINKER (23' Hans REBELE (FRG)). (Coach:
Branko ELSNER (TCH)).
Goal: Swarovski Wacker Innsbruck: 0-1 Kurt WELZL (60').
Attendance: 5.000

19-03-1975   Stadion Kantrida, Rijeka: NK Rijeka – Tatabányai Bányász SC   3-1 (1-1)
NK Rijeka: Radojko AVRAMOVIC, Sergio MAKIN, Ivan KOCIJANCIC, Dusko DEVCIC,
Zvijezdan RADIN, Sava FILIPOVIC, Salih DURKALIC, Srecko JURICIC, Gano CERIC,
Josip MOHOROVIC, Miroslav ULJAN.
Tatabányai Bányász SC: János CSEPECZ, László HERNÁDI, Tibor KOVÁCS (I), László
HORVÁTH, Sándor CZAKÓ, Mihály ARANY (RC57), György ZÖLDI, Károly CSAPÓ,
Mihály KÖMÜVES, István KNAPIK, István SALLÓI. (Coach: József GELEI).
Goals: NK Rijeka: 1-0 Tibor KOVÁCS (12' *own goal*), 2-1 Gano CERIC (46'), 3-1 Salih
DURKALIC (70').
Tatabányai Bányász SC: 1-1 György ZÖLDI (35').
Referee: Josip STRMECKI (YUG)   Attendance: 1.500

13-05-1975   Innsbruck: Swarovski Wacker Innsbruck – NK Rijeka   0-0
Attendance: 2.000

Pos	Team	Pld	W	D	L	GF	GA	GD	Pts
1	*Swarovski Wacker Innsbruck (AUT)*	4	3	1	0	8	2	+6	7
2	NK Rijeka (YUG)	4	1	1	2	5	7	-1	3
3	Tatabányai Bányász SC (HUN)	4	1	0	3	5	9	-4	2

*** Swarovski Wacker Innsbruck won the group and qualified for the Final ***

GROUP B

02-10-1974   Bozsik József Stadion, Budapest:
          Budapesti Honvéd SE – AC Fiorentina   2-0 (0-0)
Budapesti Honvéd SE: Sándor GUJDÁR, József KELEMEN, Sándor LUKÁCS, Sándor
EGERVÁRI, József PÁL, Lajos SZÜCS, Gábor MORGÓS, Lajos KOCSIS, Mihály KOZMA,
Sándor PINTÉR, János FEHÉRVÁRI (79' István WEIMPER). (Coach: Károly LAKAT).
AC Fiorentina: Franco SUPERCHI, Giancarlo GALDIOLO, Moreno ROGGI, Bruno
BEATRICE, Giuseppe BRIZI, Mauro DELLA MARTIRA, Domenico CASO (74' Vincenzo
GUERINI), Claudio MERLO, Nello SALTUTTI, Giancarlo ANTOGNONI, Walter
SPEGGIORIN (I) (7' Renato CAPPELLINI). (Coach: Nereo ROCCO).
Goals: Budapesti Honvéd SE: 1-0 Sándor PINTÉR (46'), 2-0 Sándor PINTÉR (57').
Referee: Josip STRMECKI (YUG)   Attendance: 4.000

23-10-1974   Stadio Comunale, Firenze: AC Fiorentina – TJ Sklo Union Teplice   2-1 (1-1)
AC Fiorentina: Franco SUPERCHI, Giancarlo GALDIOLO, Giuseppe LELJ, Ennio
PELLEGRINI, Giuseppe BRIZI, Mauro DELLA MARTIRA, Domenico CASO, Vincenzo
GUERINI, Claudio DESOLATI, Giancarlo ANTOGNONI, Walter SPEGGIORIN (I) (61'
Gianfranco CASARSA). (Coach: Nereo ROCCO).
TJ Sklo Union Teplice: Jirí SEDLÁCEK, Jaromír MIXA, Frantisek WEIGEND (79' Jirí
SETÍNSKÝ), Zdenek KOUBEK, Miroslav JIROUSEK, Jirí NOVÁK, Vladimír ZALUD,
Jaroslav MELICHAR, Jan THOROVSKÝ, Jirí ZENÍSEK (73' Jirí FINGER), Josef
VEJVODA. (Coach: Antonín RÝGR).
Goals: AC Fiorentina: 1-0 Claudio DESOLATI (38' penalty), 2-1 Claudio DESOLATI (67').
TJ Sklo Union Teplice: 1-1 Jaroslav MELICHAR (43').
Referee: Adolf MATHIAS (AUT)

06-11-1974   Teplice: TJ Sklo Union Teplice – Budapesti Honvéd SE   2-0 (1-0)
TJ Sklo Union Teplice: Karel STUDENÝ, Jirí SETÍNSKÝ, Frantisek WEIGEND, Frantisek
VÍTU, Zdenek KOUBEK, Vladimír ZALUD (..' Jirí ZENÍSEK), Premysl BICOVSKÝ,
Jaroslav MELICHAR, Jirí SOUREK, Pavel STRATIL (..' Josef MACH), Josef VEJVODA.
(Coach: Antonín RÝGR).
Budapesti Honvéd SE: Sándor GUJDÁR, József KELEMEN, PANCSICS, Sándor LUKÁCS,
József PÁL, Lajos SZÜCS, János FEHÉRVÁRI (46' BARTOS), Lajos KOCSIS, Sándor
PINTÉR, Mihály KOZMA, István WEIMPER. (Coach: Károly LAKAT).
Goals: TJ Sklo Union Teplice: 1-0 Sándor LUKÁCS (..' own goal), 2-0 Jaroslav MELICHAR
(..').
Referee: Josef POUCEK (TCH)   Attendance: 3.000

19-03-1975   Stadio Comunale, Firenze: AC Fiorentina – Budapesti Honvéd SE   0-0
AC Fiorentina: Massimo MATTOLINI, Giancarlo GALDIOLO, Ennio PELLEGRINI, Bruno
BEATRICE, Giuseppe BRIZI, Mauro DELLA MARTIRA, Domenico CASO, Vincenzo
GUERINI, Gianfranco CASARSA (8' Claudio DESOLATI), Giancarlo ANTOGNONI, Walter
SPEGGIORIN (I) (53' Nello SALTUTTI). (Coach: Nereo ROCCO).
Budapesti Honvéd SE: Sándor GUJDÁR, József KELEMEN, Miklós PÁNCSICS, Sándor
EGERVÁRI, József PÁL, Sándor LUKÁCS, János FEHÉRVÁRI, Sándor PINTÉR, Mihály
KOZMA, Lajos SZÜCS, István WEIMPER. (Coach: Károly LAKAT).
Referee: Michal JURSA (TCH)   Attendance: 5.000

02-04-1975   Teplice: TJ Sklo Union Teplice – AC Fiorentina   2-0 (2-0)
TJ Sklo Union Teplice: Jirí SEDLÁCEK, Frantisek VÍTU, Frantisek WEIGEND, Jirí
ZENÍSEK, Jirí SOUREK, Jirí NOVÁK, Premysl BICOVSKÝ, Jaroslav MELICHAR, Jan
THOROVSKÝ (75' Zdenek BURIANEK), Pavel STRATIL, Josef VEJVODA. (Coach:
Antonín RÝGR).
AC Fiorentina: Massimo MATTOLINI, Giancarlo GALDIOLO, Ennio PELLEGRINI, Bruno
BEATRICE, Giuseppe BRIZI, Mauro DELLA MARTIRA, Paolo ROSI, Vincenzo GUERINI,
Walter SPEGGIORIN (I), Giancarlo ANTOGNONI (65' Domenico CASO), Nello SALTUTTI
(46' Claudio DESOLATI). (Coach: Nereo ROCCO).
Goals: TJ Sklo Union Teplice: 1-0 Premysl BICOVSKÝ (18'), 2-0 Jaroslav MELICHAR
(33').
Referee: Werner SPIEGL (AUT)   Attendance: 5.000

15-04-1975   Bozsik József Stadion, Budapest:
              Budapesti Honvéd SE – TJ Sklo Union Teplice 4-2 (1-1)
Budapesti Honvéd SE: Sándor GUJDÁR, Sándor EGERVÁRI, Miklós PÁNCSICS, Sándor LUKÁCS, József PÁL, Ernö VIRÁGH, Gábor MORGÓS (..' Ernö MENYHÁRT), Sándor BARTOS, István WEIMPER, Lajos SZÜCS, János FEHERVÁRI. (Coach: Károly LAKAT).
TJ Sklo Union Teplice: Jirí SEDLÁCEK (YC46), Jaromír MIXA, Frantisek VÍTU, Jirí NOVÁK (YC87), Josef VEJVODA, Miroslav JIROUSEK, Premysl BICOVSKÝ, Jan THOROVSKÝ, Pavel STRATIL, Jirí ZENÍSEK (..' Miroslav MACHÁCEK), Jaroslav MELICHAR (..' Jirí SOUREK). (Coach: Antonín RÝGR).
Goals: Budapesti Honvéd SE: 1-1 József PÁL (50'), 2-1 István WEIMPER (59'), 3-1 Sándor BARTOS (67'), 4-2 József PÁL (86').
TJ Sklo Union Teplice: 0-1 Pavel STRATIL (11'), 3-2 Jan THOROVSKÝ (79').
Referee: Lajos SOMLAI (HUN)   Attendance: 3.000

Pos	Team	Pld	W	D	L	GF	GA	GD	Pts
1	*Budapesti Honvéd SE(HUN)*	4	2	1	1	6	4	+2	5
2	TJ Sklo Union Teplice (TCH)	4	2	0	2	7	6	+1	4
3	AC Fiorentina (ITA)	4	1	1	2	2	5	-3	3

*** Budapesti Honvéd SE won the group and qualified for the Final ***

FINAL

27-05-1975   Tivoli-Stadion, Innsbruck:
              Swarovski Wacker Innsbruck – Budapesti Honvéd SE 3-1 (2-1)
Swarovski Wacker Innsbruck: Friedrich (Friedl) KONCILIA, Werner KRIESS, Engelbert KORDESCH, Bruno PEZZEY, Johann (Hans) EIGENSTILLER (..' Othmar BAJLICZ), Ove FLINDT-Bjerg (DEN), Peter KONCILIA, Werner SCHWARZ, Günther RINKER, Kurt WELZL, Helmut METZLER (..' Franz OBERACHER). (Coach: Brank ELSNER (TCH)).
Budapesti Honvéd SE: Sándor GUJDÁR, József KELEMEN, Miklós PÁNCSICS (70' Ernö VIRÁGH), Sándor LUKÁCS, József PÁL, Sándor EGERVÁRI, János FEHÉRVÁRI, Lajos SZÜCS, Sándor PINTÉR, Mihály KOZMA, István WEIMPER. (Coach: Károly LAKAT).
Goals: Swarovski Wacker Innsbruck: 1-0 Günther RINKER (26'), 2-0 Ove FLINDT-Bjerg (32'), 3-1 Kurt WELZL (86').
Budapesti Honvéd SE: 2-1 István WEIMPER (41').
Referee: Dusan MAKSIMOVIC (YUG)   Attendance: 8.000

11-06-1975   Bozsik József Stadion, Budapest:
              Budapesti Honvéd SE – Swarovski Wacker Innsbruck 1-2 (0-0)
Budapesti Honvéd SE: Sándor GUJDÁR, József KELEMEN, Sándor EGERVÁRI, Sándor LUKÁCS, József PÁL, Lajos SZÜCS, János FEHÉRVÁRI (..' Gábor MORGÓS), Lajos KOCSIS, Sándor PINTÉR, Mihály KOZMA, István WEIMPER. (Coach: Károly LAKAT).
Swarovski Wacker Innsbruck: Friedrich (Friedl) KONCILIA, Werner KRIESS, Rudolf HORVATH (I), Bruno PEZZEY, Johann (Hans) EIGENSTILLER, Ove FLINDT-Bjerg (DEN), Othmar BAJLICZ, Werner SCHWARZ, Günther RINKER, Kurt WELZL, Helmut METZLER (..' Engelbert KORDESCH). (Coach: Brank ELSNER (TCH)).
Goals: Budapesti Honvéd SE: 1-1 Lajos KOCSIS (54' penalty).
Swarovski Wacker Innsbruck: 0-1 Bruno PEZZEY (49'), 1-2 Werner SCHWARZ (81').
Referee: Sergio GONELLA (ITA)   Attendance: 11.000

*** Swarovski Wacker Innsbruck won the Cup ***

1975-1976

GROUP A

01-10-1975   Úllöi úti Stadion, Budapest: Ferencvárosi TC – TJ Zbrojovka Brno   7-1 (4-1)
Ferencvárosi TC: József HAJDÚ, Gyözö MARTOS, László BÁLINT, István MEGYESI (62'
László TAKÁCS), Tibor RAB, József MUCHA, László PUSZTAI, Tibor NYILASI, Ferenc
SZABÓ (II), Zoltán EBEDLI, István MAGYAR (70' Gusztáv KELEMEN). (Coach: Jenö
DALNOKI).
TJ Zbrojovka Brno: Josef HRON, Zdenek KLIMES, Rostislav VÁCLAVÍCEK, Josef
POSPÍSIL, Ivan LAUKO (YC6) (53' Jirí HAMRÍK), Jindrich SVOBODA, Vítezslav
KOTÁSEK, Jirí HAJSKÝ (79' Vlastimil PETRZELA), Miroslav BURES, Karel JARUSEK,
Karel KROUPA (YC68). (Coach: Frantisek HAVRÁNEK).
Goals: Ferencvárosi TC: 1-0 Ferenc SZABÓ (18'), 2-1 Ferenc SZABÓ (25'), 3-1 Tibor
NYILASI (38'), 4-1 Tibor NYILASI (43'), 5-1 László PUSZTAI (48'), 6-1 Ferenc SZABÓ
(77'), 7-1 Tibor NYILASI (88').
TJ Zbrojovka Brno: 1-1 Vítezslav KOTÁSEK (24').
Referee: György MÜNCZ (HUN)   Attendance: 25.000

21-10-1975   Brno: TJ Zbrojovka Brno – Swarovski Wacker Innsbruck   4-3 (3-2)
Goals: TJ Zbrojovka Brno: 1-0 Karel KROUPA (4'), 2-1 Jirí HAJSKÝ (28'), 3-2 Karel
KROUPA (45'), 4-3 Karel KROUPA (90').
Swarovski Wacker Innsbruck: 1-1 Jirí HAMRÍK (19' own goal), 2-2 Werner SCHWARZ
(30'), 3-3 Kurt WELZL (48').
Attendance: 1.500

05-11-1975   Tivoli-Stadion, Innsbruck:
                  Swarovski Wacker Innsbruck – Ferencvárosi TC   1-0 (0-0)
Swarovski Wacker Innsbruck: ..., Ove FLINDT-Bjerg (DEN), ...
Ferencvárosi TC: József HAJDÚ, Gyözö MARTOS, Zsolt GIRON, István MEGYESI, István
JUHÁSZ, László BRANIKOVITS, László TAKÁCS, Gusztáv KELEMEN, Ferenc SZABÓ
(II), József MUCHA, István MAGYAR. (Coach: Jenö DALNOKI). (Used subs: Zoltán
ENGELBRECHT, János STALLER, Mihály CSAJA).
Goal: Swarovski Wacker Innsbruck: 1-0 Ove FLINDT-Bjerg (57').
Attendance: 7.000

17-03-1976   Úllöi úti Stadion, Budapest:
                  Ferencvárosi TC – Swarovski Wacker Innsbruck   0-2 (0-0)
Ferencvárosi TC: József HAJDÚ, Gyözö MARTOS, László BÁLINT, Tibor RAB, István
MEGYESI, Zoltán EBEDLI, Tibor NYILASI (65' József MUCHA), László BRANIKOVITS,
Gusztáv KELEMEN, Ferenc SZABÓ (II), István MAGYAR. (Coach: Jenö DALNOKI).
Swarovski Wacker Innsbruck: Friedrich (Friedl) KONCILIA, Günther RINKER, Rudolf
HORVATH (I), Bruno PEZZEY, Johann (Hans) EIGENSTILLER, Werner SCHWARZ,
Othmar BAJLICZ, Manfred GOMBASCH, Franz OBERACHER, Kurt WELZL, Josef
STERING. (Coach: Brank ELSNER (TCH)).
Goals: Swarovski Wacker Innsbruck: 0-1 Kurt WELZL (47'), 0-2 Kurt WELZL (89').
Referee: Sándor PETRI (HUN)   Attendance: 20.000

06-04-1976   Stadion Za Luzánkami, Brno: TJ Zbrojovka Brno – Ferencvárosi TC   3-2 (3-1)
TJ Zbrojovka Brno: Eduard DOSEK, Jan KLIMES, Rostislav VÁCLAVÍCEK, Ladislav
MINARÍK, Jaroslav FARNÝ, Vítezslav KOTÁSEK, Ludovít MIKLOS (88' Jirí HAMRÍK),
Josef PESICE, Miroslav BURES, Emil HAMAR, Jirí HAJSKÝ (26' Karel JARUSEK).
(Coach: Frantisek HAVRÁNEK).
Ferencvárosi TC: József KOLLÁR, Péter VÉPI, Tamás VICZKÓ, Ferenc EIPEL, János
STALLER, István JUHÁSZ, József MÉSZÖLY, Mihály CSAJA, Gusztáv KELEMEN, István
VAD, Zoltán ENGELBRECHT (75' Pál MÉSZÖLY). (Coach: Jenö DALNOKI).
Goals: TJ Zbrojovka Brno: 1-0 Josef PESICE (9'), 2-0 Ludovít MIKLOS (16'), 3-1 Karel
JARUSEK (44').
Ferencvárosi TC: 2-1 János STALLER (21'), 3-2 Zoltán ENGELBRECHT (56').
Referee: Zdenek JELÍNEK (TCH)   Attendance: 5.000

13-04-1976   Tivoli-Stadion, Innsbruck:
              Swarovski Wacker Innsbruck – TJ Zbrojovka Brno   1-1 (1-0)
Swarovski Wacker Innsbruck: Friedrich (Friedl) KONCILIA, Günther RINKER, Rudolf
HORVATH (I), Bruno PEZZEY, Johann (Hans) EIGENSTILLER, Josef STERING (73'
Helmut METZLER), Peter KONCILIA, Manfred GOMBASCH, Franz OBERACHER, Kurt
WELZL, Karl-Heinz LERCHER. (Coach: Brank ELSNER (TCH)).
TJ Zbrojovka Brno: Eduard DOSEK, Zdenek KLIMES (63' Miroslav BURES), Rostislav
VÁCLAVÍCEK, Milos MINARÍK, Jaroslav FARNÝ, VítezslavKOTÁSEK, Josef PESICE,
Ludovít MIKLOS, Emil HAMÁR, Karel KROUPA, Jindrich SVOBODA. (Coach: Frantisek
HAVRÁNEK).
Goals: Swarovski Wacker Innsbruck: 1-0 Kurt WELZL (28').
TJ Zbrojovka Brno: 1-1 Ludovít MIKLOS (89').
Referee: Josef BUCEK (AUT)   Attendance: 3.000

Pos	Team	Pld	W	D	L	GF	GA	GD	Pts
1	Swarovski Wacker Innsbruck (AUT)	4	2	1	1	7	5	+2	5
2	TJ Zbrojovka Brno (TCH)	4	2	1	1	9	13	-4	5
3	Ferencvárosi TC (HUN)	4	1	0	3	9	7	+2	2

*** Swarovski Wacker Innsbruck won the group and qualified for the Final ***

GROUP B

30-09-1975   Franz-Horr Stadion, Wien: FK Austria/WAC Wien – Perugia AC   1-2 (0-0)
FK Austria/WAC Wien: Hubert BAUMGARTNER, Robert SARA, Erich OBERMAYER,
Josef SARA, Günther POSPISCHIL, Karl DAXBACHER, Herbert PROHASKA (46' Wilhelm
PÖLL), Johann (Hans) PIRKNER, Friedrich (Fritz) DRAZAN, Felix GASSELICH, Julio
César Araújo MORALES (URU) (56' Kurt LEITNER). (Coach: Karl STOTZ).
Perugia AC: Roberto MARCONCINI, Giancarlo RAFFAELI, Bruno BAIARDO, Pierluigi
FROSIO, Fabrizio BERNI, Mauro AMENTA, Mario SCARPA, Renato CURI, Walter Alfredo
NOVELLINO, Franco VANNINI, Sergio Domenicacci PELLIZZARO. (Coach: Ilario
CASTAGNER).
Goals: FK Austria/WAC Wien: 1-2 Kurt LEITNER (84').
Perugia AC: 0-1 Walter Alfredo NOVELLINO (51'), 0-2 Mario SCARPA (67').
Referee: László TATRAI (HUN)   Attendance: 2.000

229

22-10-1975   Perugia: Perugia AC – FK Velez Mostar   2-4 (1-1)
Perugia AC: Roberto MARCONCINI, Michele NAPPI, Giancarlo RAFFAELI, Pierluigi
FROSIO, Fabrizio BERNI, Mauro AMENTA, Roberto CICCOTELLI, Renato CURI, Walter
Alfredo NOVELLINO (46' Paolo SOLLIER), Franco VANNINI, Sergio Domenicacci
PELLIZZARO (50' Maurizio MARCHEI). (Coach: Ilario CASTAGNER).
FK Velez Mostar: Enver MARIC, Miomir METER, Dzemal HADZIABDIC, Marko COLIC,
Ahmed GLAVOCIC (70' Dubravko LEDIC), Boro PRIMORAC, Salko BILKIC (72' Mildrag
HODZIC), Marijan KVESIC, Vahid HALILHODZIC, Franjo VLADIC, Momcilo VUKOJE.
Goals: Perugia AC: 1-1 Mauro AMENTA (14' penalty), 2-1 Maurizio MARCHEI (53').
FK Velez Mostar: 0-1 Momcilo VUKOJE (7'), 2-2 Vahid HALILHODZIC (58' penalty), 2-3
Dubravko LEDIC (73'), 2-4 Franjo VLADIC (76').
Referee: Josef POUCEK (TCH)

05-11-1975   Mostar: FK Velez Mostar – FK Austria/WAC Wien   2-0 (1-0)
FK Velez Mostar:
FK Austria/WAC Wien: Hubert BAUMGARTNER, Robert SARA, Erich OBERMAYER,
Josef SARA, Günther POSPISCHIL, Karl DAXBACHER, Herbert PROHASKA, Felix
GASSELICH (..' Friedrich (Fritz) DRAZAN), Wilhelm PÖLL (..' Johann SAMER), Kurt
LEITNER, Julio César Araújo MORALES (URU). (Coach: Karl STOTZ).
Goals: FK Velez Mostar: 1-0 Vahid HALILHODZIC (29'), 2-0 Vahid HALILHODZIC (69').

07-04-1976   Perugia: Perugia AC – FK Austria/WAC Wien   1-2 (0-0)
Perugia AC: Nello MALIZIA, Giancarlo RAFFAELI, Bruno BAIARDO, Pierluigi FROSIO,
Enrico LANZI, Mauro AMENTA (46' Aldo AGROPPI), Mario SCARPA, Renato CURI,
Paolo SOLLIER (54' Maurizio MARCHEI), Franco VANNINI, Roberto CICCOTELLI.
(Coach: Ilario CASTAGNER).
FK Austria/WAC Wien: Hubert BAUMGARTNER, Günther POSPISCHIL, Erich
OBERMAYER, Josef SARA, Johann SAMER, Karl DAXBACHER, Alberto Ariel
MARTÍNEZ Piriz (URU), Felix GASSELICH (46' Friedrich (Fritz) DRAZAN), Julio César
Araújo MORALES (URU), Wilhelm PÖLL, Johann (Hans) PIRKNER. (Coach: Karl STOTZ).
Goals: Perugia AC: 1-2 Maurizio MARCHEI (89').
FK Austria/WAC Wien: 0-1 Wilhelm PÖLL (52'), 0-2 Julio César Araújo MORALES (73').
Referee: Jozef KMEC (TCH)   Attendance: 4.000

13-04-1976   Sportclub-Platz, Wien: FK Austria/WAC Wien – FK Velez Mostar   2-1 (0-0)
FK Austria/WAC Wien: Erich SCHREITL, Robert SARA, Erich OBERMAYER, Josef
SARA, Johann SAMER, Karl DAXBACHER, Herbert PROHASKA, Alberto Ariel
MARTÍNEZ Piriz (URU), Johann (Hans) PIRKNER (46' Friedrich (Fritz) DRAZAN), Felix
GASSELICH (62' Ernst BAUMEISTER), Kurt LEITNER. (Coach: Karl STOTZ).
FK Velez Mostar: Enver MARIC, Miomir METER, Boro PRIMORAC, Vladimir PECELJ,
Veselin DJURASOVID, Mario BOLFEK (68' Milidrag HODZIC), Marko COLIC (40' Mirko
DUBOVINA), Franjo VLADIC, Ramiz OMANOVIC, Vahid HALILHODZIC, Dubravko
LEDIC.
Goals: FK Austria/WAC Wien: 1-0 Alberto Ariel MARTÍNEZ Piriz (61'), 2-0 Kurt LEITNER
(72').
FK Velez Mostar: 2-1 Vahid HALILHODZIC (89').
Referee: Adolf MATHIAS (AUT)   Attendance: 4.500

28-04-1976   Mostar: FK Velez Mostar – Perugia AC   0-0
FK Velez Mostar: Slobodan MRGAN, Miomir METER, Dzemal HADZIABDIC, Mirko
DUBOVINA, Boro PRIMORAC, Vladimir PECELJ, Dragomir OKUKA, Dubravko LEDIC,
Milidrag HODZIC, Franjo VLADIC, Momcilo VUKOJE.
Perugia AC: Roberto MARCONCINI, Michele NAPPI, Giancarlo RAFFAELI, Pierluigi
FROSIO, Enrico LANZI, Franco VANNINI, Maurizio MARCHEI, Renato CURI, Walter
Alfredo NOVELLINO, Giuseppe PICELLA, Roberto CICCOTELLI. (Coach: Ilario
CASTAGNER).
Referee: György MÜNCZ (HUN)

Pos	Team	Pld	W	D	L	GF	GA	GD	Pts
1	*FK Velez Mostar (YUG)*	4	2	1	1	7	4	+3	5
2	FK Austria/WAC Wien (AUT)	4	2	0	2	5	6	-1	4
3	Perugia AC (ITA)	4	1	1	2	5	7	-2	3

*** FK Velez Mostar won the group and qualified for the Final ***

FINAL

30-06-1976   Innsbruck: Swarovski Wacker Innsbruck – FK Velez Mostar   3-1 (1-1)
Goals: Swarovski Wacker Innsburck: 1-0 Bruno PEZZEY (8'), 2-1 Kurt WELZL (60' penalty),
3-1 Franz OBERACHER (90').
FK Velez Mostar: 1-1 Vahid HALILHODZIC (9').
Attendance: 5.000

07-07-1976   Mostar: FK Velez Mostar – Swarovski Wacker Innsbruck   1-3 (0-1)
Goals: FK Velez Mostar: 1-3 Franjo VLADIC (72').
Swarovski Wacker Innsbruck: 0-1 Peter KONCILIA (31'), 0-2 Werner ZANON (61'), 0-3
Kurt WELZL (65').
Attendance: 15.000

*** Swarovski Wacker Innsbruck won the Cup ***

231

1976-1977

03-11-1976 Letenský Stadion, Praha: TJ Sparta CKD Praha – Vasas SC 2-0 (1-0)
TJ Sparta CKD Praha: Jan POSTULKA, Pavel MELICHAR, Jirí ROSICKÝ, Frantisek
CHOVANEC, Zdenek CAUDR, Jan BUSEK, Tomás STRÁNSKÝ, Václav KOTAL, Milan
CERMÁK, Pavel STRÁTIL (46' Jirí NEVRLÝ), Milan VDOVJAK. (Coach: Dusan UHRIN).
Vasas SC: Ferenc MÉSZÁROS, Péter TÖRÖK, József KANÁSZ, Béla HEGEDÜS (63' Tibor
FÁBIÁN), István SZÖKE, András KOMJÁTI, Sándor MÜLLER, Sándor ZOMBORI, István
KOVÁCS, István GASS (63' Ignác IZSÓ), Béla VÁRADY (YC). (Coach: Rudolf
ILLOVSZKY).
Goals: TJ Sparta CKD Praha: 1-0 Milan VDOVJAK (32'), 2-0 Jirí NEVRLÝ (52').
Referee: Adolf MATHIAS (AUT)   Attendance: 3.500

03-11-1976 Firenze: AC Fiorentina – FK Vojvodina Novi Sad 0-0
AC Fiorentina: Massimo MATTOLINI, Alessio TENDI, Marco ROSSINELLI, Ennio
PELLEGRINI, Mauro DELLA MARTIRA, Maurizio RESTELLI, Gianfranco CASARSA,
Domenico CASO, claudio DESOLATI, Carmelo BAGNATO (46' Sante CREPALDI),
Giuliano BERTARELLI. (Coach: Carlo MAZZONE).
FK Vojvodina Novi Sad: Ratko SVILAR, Djordje VUJKOV, Sandor MOKUS, Miroslav
VUKASINOVIC, Vasa RUTONJSKI, Zeljko JURCIC, Slobodan VUCEKOVIC, Zoran
MISIC, Petar NIKEZIC, Slobodan PAVKOVIC (68' Ivica RADOSAVLJEVIC), Dragan
BOSNJAK (66'Milorad KOSANOVIC). (Coach: Todor VESELINOVIC).
Referee: László HÁMORI (HUN)

24-11-1976 Novi Sad: FK Vojvodina Novi Sad – TJ Sparta CKD Praha 2-1 (2-0)
FK Vojvodina Novi Sad: Ratko SVILAR (..' Miladin PURAC), Djordje VUJKOV, Milorad
KOSANOVIC, Dragan BOSNJAK, Martin NOVOCELAC, Zeljko JURCIC, Petar NIKEZIC
(..' NOVAKOVIC), Zoran MISIC, Slobodan VUCEKOVIC, Slobodan PAVKOVIC, Zoran
VJESTICA. (Coach: Todor VESELINOVIC).
TJ Sparta CKD Praha: Jirí KISLINGER, Pavel MELICHAR, Jirí ROSICKÝ, Jaroslav KOTEK
(..' Tomás STRÁNSKÝ), Zdenek CAUDR, Václav KOTAL (..' Oldrich URBAN), Bohumil
VESELÝ, Jan BUSEK, Josef HOUDEK, Milan CERMÁK, Milan VDOVJAK. (Coach: Dusan
UHRIN).
Goals: FK Vojvodina Novi Sad: 1-0 Zeljko JURCIC (34'), 2-0 Zoran MISIC (38').
TJ Sparta CKD Praha: 2-1 Milan VDOVJAK (67').
Referee: Giulio CIACCI (ITA)   Attendance: 2.000

24-11-1976 Fáy utcai Stadion, Budapest: Vasas SC – AC Fiorentina 1-0 (1-0)
Vasas SC: Ferenc MÉSZÁROS, Péter TÖRÖK, József KANÁSZ, Béla HEGEDÜS, István
SZÖKE, András KOMJÁTI, István KOVÁCS, Sándor MÜLLER, István GASS (68' Ignác
IZSÓ), Sándor ZOMBORI, Béla VÁRADY. (Coach: Rudolf ILLOVSZKY).
AC Fiorentina: Massimo MATTOLINI, Giancarlo GALDIOLO (YC42), Marco ROSSINELLI,
Ennio PELLEGRINI, Mauro DELLA MARTIRA (YC40) (61' Alessio TENDI), Maurizio
RESTELLI, Domenico CASO, Steno GOLA (63' Sante CREPALDI), Gianfranco CASARSA
(YC85), Giancarlo ANTOGNONI (YC80), Claudio DESOLATI. (Coach: Carlo MAZZONE).
Goal: Vasas SC: 1-0 István KOVÁCS (17').
Referee: Miroslav KOPAL (TCH)   Attendance: 5.000

08-12-1976   Fáy utcai Stadion, Budapest: Vasas SC – FK Vojvodina Novi Sad 3-2 (2-1)
Vasas SC: Ferenc MÉSZÁROS, Péter TÖRÖK, József KANÁSZ, András KOMJÁTI, István
SZÖKE, Sándor MÜLLER (21' Béla HEGEDÜS), Sándor ZOMBORI, István KOVÁCS,
István GASS (YC87), Ignác IZSÓ, Béla VÁRADY. (Coach: Rudolf ILLOVSZKY).
FK Vojvodina Novi Sad: Ratko SVILAR (28' Miladin PURAC), Djordje VUJKOV, Zeljko
JURCIC (YC37), Vasa RUTONJSKI, Milorad KOSANOVIC (51' Dusan NENADIC),
Miroslav VUKASINOVIC (YC51), Petar NIKEZIC (YC83), Zoran MISIC, Nebojsa
VUCKOVIC, Slobodan VUCEKOVIC, Dragoljub STAKIC. (Coach: Todor VESELINOVIC).
Goals: Vasas SC: 1-0 István GASS (5'), 2-1 András KOMJÁTI (42'), 3-1 Ignác IZSÓ (61').
FK Vojvodina Novi Sad: 1-1 Petar NIKEZIC (11'), 3-2 Petar NIKEZIC (83').
Attendance: 6.000

08-12-1976   Firenze: AC Fiorentina – TJ Sparta CKD Praha 3-0 (3-0)
AC Fiorentina: Alberto GINULFI, Alessio TENDI, Sergio ZUCCHERI, Ennio PELLEGRINI,
Mauro DELLA MARTIRA, Maurizio RESTELLI, Carmelo BAGNATO, Steno GOLA (75'
Antonio DI GENNARO), Gianfranco CASARSA, Giancarlo ANTOGNONI (46' Domenico
CASO), Claudio DESOLATI. (Coach: Carlo MAZZONE).
TJ Sparta CKD Praha: Jirí KISLINGER, Pavel MELICHAR (46' Oldrich URBAN), Zdenek
CAUDR, Jirí ROSICKÝ, Jaroslav KOTEK (46' Frantisek CHOVANEC), Tomás
STRÁNSKÝ, Jan BUSEK, Bohumil VESELÝ, Václav KOTAL, Milan CERMÁK, Jirí
NEVRLÝ. (Coach: Dusan UHRIN).
Goals: AC Fiorentina: 1-0 Gianfranco CASARSA (9'), 2-0 Gianfranco CASARSA (34'
penalty), 3-0 Claudio DESOLATI (41').
Referee: Tome MANOJLOVSKI (YUG)   Attendance: 1.500

16-03-1977   Gradski Stadion, Novi Sad: FK Vojvodina Novi Sad – Vasas SC 2-2 (0-0)
FK Vojvodina Novi Sad: Ratko SVILAR, Rajko ALEKSIC, Djordje VUJKOV (46' Miroslav
VUKASINOVIC), Sándor MÓKUS, Martin NOVOSELAC, Zeljko JURCIC, László
LÖRINCZ, Dragoljub STAKIC (46' Josif ILIC), Milenko DRAGOJEVIC, Petar NIKEZIC,
Slavko LICINAR. (Coach: Todor VESELINOVIC).
Vasas SC: Ferenc MÉSZÁROS, Péter TÖRÖK, Béla HEGEDÜS, András KOMJÁTI, Mihály
KÁNTOR, István GASS, Sándor MÜLLER, Sándor ZOMBORI, István KOVÁCS (YC45),
Ignác IZSÓ, Béla VÁRADY. (Coach: Rudolf ILLOVSZKY).
Goals: FK Vojvodina Novi Sad: 1-0 Josif ILIC (47'), 2-0 Miroslav VUKASINOVIC (48').
Vasas SC: 2-1 István KOVÁCS (60'), 2-2 Béla VÁRADY (74' penalty).
Attendance: 4.000

(László LÖRINCZ was also known by the name of Laslo LERINC).

16-03-1977   Praha: TJ Sparta CKD Praha – AC Fiorentina 2-0 (1-0)
TJ Sparta CKD Praha: Jirí KISLINGER, Pavel MELICHAR, Zdenek CAUDR, Tomás
STRÁNSKÝ, Oldrich URBAN (75' Frantisek CHOVANEC), Jaroslav KOTEK, Jan BUSEK,
Bohumil VESELÝ, Pavel STRATIL, Milan CERMÁK, Milan VDOVJAK (46' BEZNOSKA).
(Coach: Arnost (Ernst) HLOZEK).
AC Fiorentina: Massimo MATTOLINI, Alessio TENDI, Sergio ZUCCHERI, Ennio
PELLEGRINI, Giancarlo GALDIOLO, Maurizio RESTELLI, Carmelo BAGNATO, Luigi
SACCHETTI, Gianfranco CASARSA, Giancarlo ANTOGNONI (30' Piero BRAGLIA), Sante
CREPALDI. (Coach: Carlo MAZZONE).
Goals: TJ Sparta CKD Praha: 1-0 Pavel STRATIL (36'), 2-0 Tomás STRÁNSKÝ (80').
Referee: Lajos SOMLAI (HUN)   Attendance: 3.000

233

06-04-1977   Novi Sad: FK Vojvodina Novi Sad – AC Fiorentina   4-2 (3-1)
FK Vojvodina Novi Sad: MiladinPURAC, Djordje VUJKOV, Sandor MOKUS, Zeljko
JURCIC, Martin NOVOSELAC, Vasa RUTONJSKI, László LÖRINCZ, Petar NIKEZIC (46'
Milenko DRAGOJEVIC), Slobodan VUCEKOVIC, Slobodan PAVKOVIC, Ivica
RADOSAVLJEVIC (46' Slavko NICINAR). (Coach: Todor VESELINOVIC).
AC Fiorentina: Alberto GINULFI, Marco MARCHI, Sergio ZUCCHERI, Alessio TENDI,
Albert FONTANI, Maurizio RESTELLI, Gianfranco CASARSA (59' Piero BRAGLIA), Steno
GOLA, Claudio DESOLATI (46' Carmelo BAGNATO), Giancarlo ANTOGNONI, Sante
CREPALDI. (Coach: Carlo MAZZONE).
Goals: FK Vojvodina Novi Sad: 1-1 Slobodan VUCEKOVIC (17'), 2-1 Slobodan
VUCEKOVIC (19'), 3-1 Slobodan VUCEKOVIC (44'), 4-1 Sandor MOKUS (49').
AC Fiorentina: 0-1 Gianfranco CASARSA (5'), 4-2 Piero BRAGLIA (71').
Referee: Dusan MAKSIMOVIC (YUG)

06-04-1977   Fáy utcai Stadion, Budapest: Vasas SC – TJ Sparta CKD Praha   2-0 (1-0)
Vasas SC: Ferenc MÉSZÁROS, Péter TÖRÖK, Béla HEGEDÜS, András KOMJÁTI, István
FÖLDHÁZI (46' István SZÖKE), István GASS, Sándor MÜLLER (YC54), Sándor
ZOMBORI, István KOVÁCS, Ignác IZSÓ, Béla VÁRADY. (Coach: Rudolf ILLOVSZKY).
TJ Sparta CKD Praha: Jirí KISLINGER, Frantisek CHOVANEC, Zdenek CAUDR, Jaroslav
KOTEK, Oldrich URBAN, Jirí ROSICKÝ (16' Pavel MELICHAR), Bohumil VESELÝ,
Tomás STRÁNSKÝ, Václav KOTAL, Milan CERMÁK (54' Jan BUSEK), Milan VDOVJAK.
(Coach: Arnost (Ernst) HLOZEK).
Goals: Vasas SC: 1-0 István KOVÁCS (27'), 2-0 István KOVÁCS (83').
Referee: Domenico SERAFINO (ITA)   Attendance: 3.500

20-04-1977   Stadio Comunale, Firenze: AC Fiorentina – Vasas SC   2-1 (1-0)
AC Fiorentina: Alberto GINULFI, Alessio TENDI, Marco ROSSINELLI (69' Marco
MARCHI), Ennio PELLEGRINI, Giancarlo GALDIOLO, Sergio ZUCCHERI (66' Luigi
SACCHETTI), Maurizio RESTELLI, Steno GOLA, Claudio DESOLATI, Antonio DI
GENNARO,Sante CREPALDI. (Coach: Carlo MAZZONE).
Vasas SC: Ferenc MÉSZÁROS, Tibor FÁBIÁN, Béla HEGEDÜS, Mihály KÁNTOR, István
GASS, András SARLÓS, László FEKETE, Sándor MÜLLER, Ignác IZSÓ, István SZÖKE
(53' Péter BECSEI), Sándor ZÁMBÓ. (Coach: Rudolf ILLOVSZKY).
Goals: AC Fiorentina: 1-0 Antonio DI GENNARO (5'), 2-1 Luigi SACCHETTI (87').
TJ Sparta Praha: 1-1 László FEKETE (55').
Referee: Radmilo RISTIC (YUG)   Attendance: 20.000

03-08-1977   Praha: TJ Sparta CKD Praha – FK Vojvodina Novi Sad   0-0
TJ Sparta CKD Praha: Ján CEPO, Václav KOTÁL, Frantisek CHOVANEC, Jaroslav KOTEK,
Zdenek CAUDR, Jan BUSEK, Antonín PRINC, Tomás STRÁNSKÝ, Vlastimil VEJNAR (87'
HFEBEJK), Milan CERMÁK, Josef RASKA. (Coach: Arnost (Ernst) HLOZEK).
FK Vojvodina Novi Sad: Slobodan JANJUS, Dragan JABLAN (87' Zoran PASIC), Djordje
VUJKOV, Vladimir TRIFUNOVIC, Miroslav JAKOVLEVIC, Dragan BOSNJAK, Zoran
MISIC, Petar NIKEZIC, Ivica RADOSAVLJEVIC, Slobodan PAVKOVIC, László LÖRINCZ
(58' Milenko DRAGOJEVIC). (Coach: Todor VESELINOVIC).
Referee: László PÁDÁR (HUN)   Attendance: 3.500

Pos	Team	Pld	W	D	L	GF	GA	GD	Pts
1	FK Vojvodina Novi Sad (YUG)	6	2	3	1	10	8	+2	7
2	Vasas SC (HUN)	6	3	1	2	9	8	+1	7
3	AC Fiorentina (ITA)	6	2	1	3	7	8	-1	5
4	TJ Sparta CKD Praha (TCH)	6	2	1	3	5	7	-2	5

*** FK Vojvodina Novi Sad won the Cup ***

1977-1978

GROUP A

28-09-1977   Stadion JNA, Beograd: FK Partizan Beograd – TJ Zbrojovka Brno   5-1 (3-1)
Goals: FK Partizan Beograd: Moncilo VUKOTIC (2x), Aleksandar TRIFUNOVIC, Pavle GRUBJESIC, Dzevad PREKAZI.
TJ Zbrojovka Brno: Karel KROUPA.
Attendance: 10.000

19-10-1977   Brno: TJ Zbrojovka Brno – AC Perugia   0-0
TJ Zbrojovka Brno: Eduard DOSEK, Josef MAZURA (46' Jan KLIMES), Rostislav VÁCLAVÍCEK, Jaroslav PETRTÝL, Karel DVORÁK, Jirí HAJSKÝ, VítezslavKOTÁSEK, Petr JANECKA (70' Miroslav BURES), Karel KROUPA, Karel JARUSEK, Jan KOPENEC. (Coach: Josef MASOPUST).
AC Perugia: Marcello GRASSI, Michele NAPPI, Antonio CECCARINI, Paolo DAL FIUME, Luciano ZECCHINI, Pierluigi FROSIO, Mario SCARPA, Mauro AMENTA, Walter Alfredo NOVELLINO (50' Mario GORETTI), Franco VANNINI, Walter SPEGGIORIN. (Coach: Ilario CASTAGNER).
Referee: Franz LATZIN (AUT)   Attendance: 4.000

14-12-1977   Perugia: AC Perugia – FK Partizan Beograd   2-1 (2-1)
AC Perugia: Marcello GRASSI, Michele NAPPI, Antonio CECCARINI, Paolo DAL FIUME, Antonio MATTEONI, Luciano ZECCHINI, Salvatore BAGNI, Mauro AMENTA (61' Guido BIONDI), Walter Alfredo NOVELLINO, Franco VANNINI, Walter SPEGGIORIN. (Coach: Ilario CASTAGNER).
FK Partizan Beograd: Petar BOROTA, Vladimir PEJOVIC, Borislav DJUROVIC, Aleksandar TRIFUNOVIC, Nenad STOJKOVIC, Jusuf HATUNIC, Ilija ZAVISIC, Nikica KLINCARSKI, Momcilo VUKOTIC, Dzevad PREKAZI, Bosko DJORDJEVIC. (Coach; Ante MLADINIC).
Goals: AC Perugia: 1-0 Walter SPEGGIORIN (3'), 2-0 Walter SPEGGIORIN (15').
FK Partizan Beograd: 2-1 Nenad STOJKOVIC (20').
Referee: Antonin WENCL (TCH)

29-03-1978   Stadion Za Luzánkami, Brno:
               TJ Zbrojovka Brno – FK Partizan Beograd   2-3 (1-1)
TJ Zbrojovka Brno: Eduard DOSEK, Josef MAZURA, Jindrich SVOBODA, Jan KLIMES, Josef POSPÍSIL, Josef PESICE, VítezslavKOTÁSEK, Petr JANECKA, Karel KROUPA (85' Libor DOSEK), Karel JARUSEK, Jan KOPENEC (16' Miroslav BURES). (Coach: Josef MASOPUST).
FK Partizan Beograd: Petar BOROTA, Ivan GOLAC (80' Dragan ARSENOVIC), Novica VULIC, Aleksandar TRIFUNOVIC, Nenad STOJKOVIC, Jusuf HATUNIC, Ilija ZAVISIC, Nikica KLINCARSKI (75' Milovan JOVIC), Slobodan SANTRAC, Momcilo VUKOTIC, Bosko DJORDJEVIC. (Coach: Ante MLADINIC).
Goals: TJ Zbrojovka Brno: 1-0 Petr JANECKA (41'), 2-3 Petr JANECKA (76').
FK Partizan Beograd: 1-1 Slobodan SANTRAC (45' penalty), 1-2 Momcilo VUKOTIC (53'), 1-3 Momcilo VUKOTIC (71').
Referee: Werner SPIEGL (AUT)   Attendance: 6.000

236

12-04-1978   Perugia: AC Perugia – TJ Zbrojovka Brno   1 0 (0-0)
AC Perugia: Marcello GRASSI, Michele NAPPI, Antonio CECCARINI, Paolo DAL FIUME, Luciano ZECCHINI, Pierluigi FROSIO, Mario GORETTI (74' Mauro AMENTA), Guido BIONDI, Walter Alfredo NOVELLINO (46' Salvatore BAGNI), Franco VANNINI, Mario SCARPA. (Coach: Ilario CASTAGNER).

TJ Zbrojovka Brno: Eduard DOSEK, Jaroslav PETRTÝL, Rostislav VÁCLAVÍCEK, Jan KLIMES, Josef POSPÍSIL, Josef PESICE, VítezslavKOTÁSEK (84' VJATER), Jirí HAJSKÝ, Miroslav BURES, Libor DOSEK, Jan KOPENEC (79' Jindrich SVOBODA). (Coach: Josef MASOPUST).
Goal: AC Perugia: 1-0 Salvatore BAGNI (53' penalty).
Referee: JUSUFBEGOVIC (YUG)

19-04-1978   Beograd: FK Partizan Beograd – AC Perugia   4-0 (0-0)
FK Partizan Beograd: Petar BOROTA, Ivan GOLAC, Borislav DJUROVIC (17' Tomislav KOVACEVIC), Aleksandar TRIFUNOVIC, Vladimir PEJOVIC, Jusuf HATUNIC, Ilija ZAVISIC, Nikica KLINCARSKI, Slobodan SANTRAC (73' Milovan JOVIC), Moncilo VUKOTIC, Bosko DJORDJEVIC. (Coach; Ante MLADINIC).
AC Perugia: Marcello GRASSI, Michele NAPPI, Antonio CECCARINI, Paolo DAL FIUME, Luciano ZECCHINI, Pierluigi FROSIO, Salvatore BAGNI, Guido BIONDI (62' Mario GORETTI), Walter Alfredo NOVELLINO, Franco VANNINI, Mario SCARPA. (Coach: Ilario CASTAGNER).
Goals: FK Partizan Beograd: 1-0 Nikica KLINCARSKI (61'), 2-0 Slobodan SANTRAC (72'), 3-0 Milovan JOVIC (87' penalty), 4-0 Ilija ZAVISIC (89').
Referee: László HÁMORI (HUN)   Attendance: 15.000

Pos	Team	Pld	W	D	L	GF	GA	GD	Pts
1	FK Partizan Beograd (YUG)	4	3	0	1	13	5	+8	6
2	AC Perugia (ITA)	4	2	1	1	3	5	-2	5
3	TJ Zbrojovka Brno (TCH)	4	0	1	3	3	9	-6	1

*** FK Partizan Beograd won the group and qualified for the Final ***

GROUP B

28-09-1977   Bozsik József Stadion, Budapest:
                Budapesti Honvéd SE – FK Vojvodina Novi Sad   6-0
Budapesti Honvéd SE: Sándor GUJDÁR, Sándor PARÓCZAI, István KOCSIS, Antal NAGY, Sándor LUKÁCS, József PÁL, Sándor PINTÉR, József PÓCZIK, László GYIMESI, Béla BODONYI, Mihály KOZMA. (Coach: Lajos TICHY).
FK Vojvodina Novi Sad:
Goals: Budapesti Honvéd SE: 1-0 József PÁL (..'), 2-0 József PÁL (..'), 3-0 Mihály KOZMA (..'), 4-0 Mihály KOZMA (..'), 5-0 József PÓCZIK (..'), 6-0 József PÓCZIK (..').
Attendance: 2.000

19-10-1977   Novi Sad: FK Vojvodina Novi Sad – Budapesti Honved SE   2-1
FK Vojvodina Novi Sad:
Budapesti Honvéd SE: ... (Coach: Lajos TICHY).

SK Rapid Wien (AUT) withdrew from the competition.

237

Pos	Team	Pld	W	D	L	GF	GA	GD	Pts
1	Budapesti Honvéd SE (HUN)	2	1	0	1	7	2	+5	2
2	FK Vojvodina Novi Sad (YUG)	2	1	0	1	2	7	-5	2

*** Budapesti Honvéd SE won the group and qualified for the Final ***

FINAL

13-12-1978   Stadion JNA, Beograd:
FK Partizan Beograd – Budapesti Honvéd SE   1-0 (0-0)
FK Partizan Beograd: Rade ZALAD, Borislav DJUROVIC, Refik KOZIC, Aleksandar TRIFUNOVIC, Vlada LAZICIC, Nenad STOJKOVIC, Ilija ZAVISIC, Zvonko ZIVKOVIC, Slobodan SANTRAC (46' Zvonko VARGA, 73' Milovan JOVIC (YC85)), Dzevad PREKAZI, Nikica KLINCARSKI. (Coach; Ante MLADINIC).
Budapesti Honvéd SE: Sándor GUJDÁR, Sándor PARÓCZAI, István KOCSIS, Antal NAGY (YC53), József VARGA (I), József PÁL, József VARGA (II), Sándor LUKÁCS, József PÓCZIK, István WEIMPER, János GEIGER (46' István SZEGÖ). (Coach: Lajos TICHY).
Goal: FK Partizan Beograd: 1-0 Aleksandar TRIFUNOVIC (64' penalty).
Attendance: 6.000

*** FK Partizan Beograd won the Cup ***

238

1978-1979

No Mitropa Cup competition was held during this season.

1979-1980

19-09-1979   Udine: Udinese AC – TJ Rudá Hvezda Cheb 3-2 (1-1)
Udinese AC: Carlo DELLA CORNA, Sauro CATELLANI, Giovanni SGARBOSSA, Angelo
CUPINI, Fulvio FELLET, Mariano RIVA (78' PANIZZA), Claudio VAGHEGGI, Claudio
BENCINA, Ciro BILARDI, Livio PIN, Nerio ULIVIERI (65' Carlo DE BERNARDI). (Coach:
Corrado ORRICO).
TJ Rudá Hvezda Cheb: Václav LAVICKA, Stanislav SMOLAGA, Jirí RUS, Zdenek
KOUBEK, Karel BUBLA, Miroslav KASPAR, Milan LINDENTHAL, Ivan BICAN, Jozef
CHOVANEC, Lubomír POKLUDA, Vladimír HRUSKA (46' Josef WUNSCH). (Coach: Jirí
LOPATA).
Goals: Udinese AC: 1-1 Nerio ULIVIERI (33'), 2-1 Angelo CUPINI (79'), 3-2 Livio PIN
(85').
TJ Rudá Hvezda Cheb: 0-1 Miroslav KASPAR (26'), 2-2 Miroslav KASPAR (82').
Referee: Josef BUCEK (AUT)

19-09-1979   Bilino, Polje, Zenica: FK Celik Zenica – Debreceni VSC 2-0 (0-0)
FK Celik Zenica: ... (Coach: Alojz RENIC).
Debreceni VSC: János LUKÁCS, János KISS, Lajos GARAMVÖLGYI, Lajos POTYÓK,
Ignác HALLA, Mihály CZIKORA, ÚJVÁRI (12' Mátyás SOMOGYI), Ernö MENYHART,
András BARTHA (52' László FELEDI), Péter BODONYI, György NÉREY. (Coach: Gyula
TELEKI).
Goals: FK Celik Zenica: 1-0 Rade RADULOVIC (85'), 2-0 Branislav KARAC (88').
Attendance: 4.000

03-10-1979   Udine: Udinese AC – FK Celik Zenica 0-0
Udinese AC: Carlo DELLA CORNA, Sauro CATELLANI, Giovanni SGARBOSSA, Angelo
CUPINI, Fulvio FELLET, Mariano RIVA (78' Pasquale FANESI), Claudio VAGHEGGI,
Livio PIN, Ciro BILARDI, Claudio BENCINA, Nerio ULIVIERI (58' Carlo DE BERNARDI).
(Coach: Corrado ORRICO).
FK Celik Zenica: Zlatko JURICEVIC, Sead PRELDZIC, Ibrahim ZUKANOVIC, Enes
DEDIC, Marin BLOUDEK, Miodrag TESIC, Rade RADULOVIC, Milojica TRIPKOVIC (46'
Goran PELES), Ranko DJORDJIC, Jasmin GRADINCIC, Branislav KARAC (46' Dragan
STOJILJKOVIC). (Coach: Alojz RENIC).
Referee: Jan VEVERKA (TCH)

03-10-1979   Stadion Lokomotiva, Cheb: TJ Rudá Hvezda Cheb – Debreceni VSC 2-1 (1-0)
TJ Rudá Hvezda Cheb: Václav LAVICKA, Stanislav SMOLAGA, Karel BUBLA, Jirí RUS,
Zdenek KOUBEK, Josef LATISLAV (56' Miroslav KASPAR), Jozef CHOVANEC (56'
Milan KONVALINKA), Milan LINDENTHAL, Lubomír POKLUDA, Vladimír HRUSKA,
Josef WUNSCH. (Coach: Jirí LOPATA).
Debreceni VSC: János LUKÁCS, János KISS (..' András SZIGETI), Lajos GARAMVÖLGYI,
Ignác HALLA, Lajos LIPÖK, Mátyás SOMOGYI, Mihály CZIKORA (..' Zoltán
SZÍJGYÁRTÓ), László FELEDI, Péter BODONYI, Ferenc TÓTH, György NÉREY. (Coach:
Gyula TELEKI).
Goals: TJ Rudá Hvezda Cheb: 1-0 Vladimír HRUSKA (21'), 2-1 Jirí RUS (88').
Debreceni VSC: 1-1 Mátyás SOMOGYI (50').
Referee: Damir MATOVINOVIC (YUG)   Attendance: 8.000

24-10-1979   Nagyerdei stadion, Debrecen: Debreceni VSC – Udinese AC   0-0
Debreceni VSC: József SZABÓ (II), János KISS (46' Lajos LIPÖK), Lajos
GARAMVÖLGYI, András SZIGETI (YC34), Ignác HALLA, János SZÜCS, Ernö
MENYHÁRT, Zoltán SZÍJGYÁRTÓ (YC48), István TÍMÁR (46' Lajos POTYÓK), László
FELEDI, Sándor JANKOVICS. (Coach: Gyula TELEKI).
Udinese AC: Ernesto GALLI, Fulvio FELLET, Giovanni SGARBOSSA (YC63), Valentino
LEONARDUZZI, Sauro CATELLANI, Pasquale FANESI (YC37) (46' Nerio ULIVIERI),
Livio PIN, Sergio VRIZ, Luigi DELNERI, Claudio VAGHEGGI (46' Carlo OSTI (YC88)),
Giuseppe BRESSANI. (Coach: Corrado ORRICO).
Referee: Franz LATZIN (AUT)   Attendance: 8.000

24-10-1979   Zenica: FK Celik Zenica – TJ Rudá Hvezda Cheb   3-1 (1-0)
Goals: FK Celik Zenica: 1-0 Jasmin GRADINCIC (32'), 2-0 Rade RADULOVIC (57'), 3-1
Rade RADULOVIC (89').
TJ Rudá Hvezda Cheb: 2-1 Milan LINDENTHAL (84').

07-11-1979   Cheb: TJ Rudá Hvezda Cheb – Udinese AC   2-0 (0-0)
TJ Rudá Hvezda Cheb: Karel CHARVÁT, Zdenek KOUBEK, Milan SVOJTKA, Miroslav
KASPAR (YC53), Stanislav SMOLAGA, Lubomír POKLUDA (46' Vladimír HRUSKA
(YC76)), Milan LINDENTHAL, Josef LATISLAV, Jirí RUS, Milan KONVALINKA, Josef
WUNSCH. (Coach: Jirí LOPATA).
Udinese AC: Carlo DELLA CORNA, Giovanni SGARBOSSA, Pasquale FANESI, Valentino
LEONARDUZZI, Fulvio FELLET (17' Carlo OSTI), Sauro CATELLANI, Giuseppe
BRESSANI, Livio PIN (68' Claudio VAGHEGGI), Silvio FRANCESCONI, Luigi DELNERI,
Nerio ULIVIERI. (Coach: Corrado ORRICO).
Goals: TJ Rudá Hvezda Cheb: 1-0 Vladimír HRUSKA (67'), 2-0 Vladimír HRUSKA (82').
Referee: Stjepan GLAVINA (YUG)

07-11-1979   Nagyerdei stadion, Debrecen: Debreceni VSC – FK Celik Zenica   0-0
Debreceni VSC: József SZABÓ (II), János KISS, Lajos GARAMVÖLGYI, András SZIGETI,
Ignác HALLA, Mátyás SOMOGYI, Lajos POTYÓK (46' Zoltán SZÍJGYÁRTÓ), Ernö
MENYHÁRT, János SZÜCS, László FELEDI, Sándor JANKOVICS. (Coach: Gyula
TELEKI).
FK Celik Zenica: Zlatko JURICEVIC, Sead PRELZDIC, Enes DEDIC, Marin BLOUDEK,
Svetislav PERDUV (YC68), Goran PELES, Jasmin GRADINCIC, Miodrag TESIC, Branislav
KARAC (YC62), Rade RADULOVIC, Ibrahim ZUKANOVIC (YC65). (Coach: Alojz
RENIC).
Attendance: 3.000

19-03-1980   Debrecen: Debreceni VSC – TJ Rudá Hvezda Cheb   2-1 (1-1)
Debreceni VSC: János GULYÁS, János SZÜCS, Lajos GARAMVÖLGYI (YC21), András
SZIGETI, Ignác HALLA, László OROSHÁZI (46' Ernö MENYHÁRT), Mátyás SOMOGYI,
Zoltán SZÍJGYÁRTÓ, András BARTHA (46' Ervin DÁKAY), László FELEDI, György
NÉREY. (Coach: Gyula TELEKI).
TJ Rudá Hvezda Cheb: Václav LAVICKA, Stanislav SMOLAGA, Vladimír CERMAK, Milan
SVOJTKA, Zdenek KOUBEK, Josef LATISLAV (65' Miroslav KASPAR), Vratislav
CHALOUPKA (YC39), Karel BUBLA, Lubomír POKLUDA, Vladimír SISMA (65' Josef
WUNSCH), Vladimír HRUSKA. (Coach: Jirí LOPATA).
Goals: Debreceni VSC: 1-0 László FELEDI (25'), 2-1 Ervin DÁKAY (49').
TJ Rudá Hvezda Cheb: 1-1 Lubomír POKLUDA (38').
Referee: Horst BRUMMEIER (AUT)   Attendance: 2.000

241

19-03-1980   Zenica: FK Celik Zenica – Udinese AC   2-3 (1-0)
FK Celik Zenica: Zlatko JURICEVIC, Svetislav PERDUV, Ibrahim ZUKANOVIC, Miodrag
TESIC, Zvonko VIDACAK, Jasmin GRADINCIC, Branislav KARAC, Rade RADULOVIC,
Sead HODZIC (30' Selver IBRAHIMOVIC), Goran PELES, Ranko DJORDJIC. (Coach:
Alojz RENIC).
Udinese AC: Carlo DELLA CORNA, Carlo OSTI, Domenico MACUGLIA, Giovanni
SGARBOSSA (46' Daniele ARRIGONI), Fulvio FELLET, Livio PIN (46' Silvio
FRANCESCONI), Claudio VAGHEGGI, Luigi DELNERI, Luigi DE AGOSTINI, Sergio
VRIZ, Nerio ULIVIERI. (Coach: Corrado ORRICO).
Goals: FK Celik Zenica: 1-0 Branislav KARAC (15'), 2-0 Ranko DJORDJIC (69').
Udinese AC: 2-1 Nerio ULIVIERI (73'), 2-2 Silvio FRANCESCONI (80'), 2-3 Claudio
VAGHEGGI (82').
Referee: Robert JACZINA (HUN)

09-04-1980   Stadio Friuli, Udine: Udinese AC – Debreceni VSC   2-0 (2-0)
Udinese AC: Ernesto GALLI, Sauro CATELLANI (46' Giovanni SGARBOSSA), Domenico
MACUGLIA, Valentino LEONARDUZZI, Fulvio FELLET, Daniele ARRIGONI, Giuseppe
BRESSANI, Silvio FRANCESCONI, Elvio PIANCA, Luigi DE AGOSTINI, Nerio
ULIVIERI.
Debreceni VSC: János LUKÁCS, János KISS, András SZIGETI, Ignác HALLA, János
SZÜCS (64' Sándor SALLAI), Mátyás SOMOGYI, András BARTHA, Ernö MENYHÁRT,
László FELEDI, Zoltán SZÍJGYÁRTÓ, Sándor JANKOVICS (..' Ervin DÁKAY). (Coach:
Gyula TELEKI).
Goals: Udinese AC: 1-0 Nerio ULIVIERI (2'), 2-0 Nerio ULIVIERI (43').
Referee: Aleksandar NIKIC (YUG)   Attendance: 3.000

09-04-1980   Cheb: TJ Rudá Hvezda Cheb – FK Celik Zenica   2-1 (1-0)
Goals: TJ Rudá Hvezda Cheb: 1-0 Milan LINDENTHAL (43'), 2-1 Jozef CHOVANEC (90').
FK Celik Zenica: 1-1 Zvonko VIDACAK (86').
Referee: László GYÖRI (HUN)   Attendance: 3.000

Pos	Team	Pld	W	D	L	GF	GA	GD	Pts
1	Udinese AC (ITA)	6	3	2	1	8	6	+2	8
2	FK Celik Zenica (YUG)	6	2	2	2	8	6	+2	6
3	TJ Rudá Hvezda Cheb (TCH)	6	3	0	3	10	10	0	6
4	Debreceni VSC (HUN)	6	1	2	3	3	7	-4	4

*** Udinese AC won the Cup ***

1980-1981

10-10-1980   Como: Como Calcio – NK Zagreb   2-0 (1-0)
Como Calcio: Giuliano GIULIANI, Gabriele RATTI, Giuseppe MAROZZI (68' Pietro
VIERCHOWOD), Giancarlo CENTI, Silvano FONTOLAN, Piero VOLPI, Doriano
POZZATO (46' Massimo MANCINI), Maurizio GIOVANNELLI, Ezio CAVAGNETTO,
Renzo GOBBO, Roberto MANDRESSI. (Coach: Giuseppe MARCHIORO).
NK Zagreb: Stjepan PANJKRET, Branko GODINIC, Damir VALEC, Jerko TIPURIC, Josip
COP, Atif LIPOVAC, Zeljko JURIN (53' Slavko KOVACIC), Stipe PERIC, Srecko
KURBASA, Mihajlo BOSNJAK, Marijan CERCEK. (Coach: Drazan JERKOVIC).
Goals: Como Calcio: 1-0 Doriano POZZATO (30'), 2-0 Pietro VIERCHOWOD (89').
Referee: László TATRAI (HUN)

05-11-1980   Stadion Kranjceviceva, Zagreb: NK Zagreb – Csepel SC   0-0
NK Zagreb: ... (Coach: Drazan JERKOVIC).
Csepel SC: Attila KOVÁCS, Lájos GODÁN, Gábor KÖHALMI, József ELEKES, György
GÁLHÍDI (YC), László LAZSÁNYI (YC), Gusztáv KELEMEN, István TÓTH (80' Béla
KINCSES), Sándor TARNÓCZI, Mihály TULIPÁN (65' Gyula HEGYI), Sándor VINCZE.
(Coach: Mihály KESZTHELYI Keszli).
Referee: Antoniín WENCL (TCH)   Attendance: 500

05-11-1980   Presov: TJ Tatran Presov – Como Calcio   4-1 (2-0)
TJ Tatran Presov: Jaroslav MATKOBIS, Stefan VARGA, Jozef OBORIL, Miroslav LABUN,
Zoltán BREUER (34' Stefan SVANA), Vladimír RUSNÁK, Bartolomej MAJERNÍK (83'
Mikulás KOMANICKÝ), Vladimír GOMBÁR, Lubomír (Lubos) ANINA, Jozef SÁLKA,
Alexander COMISSO. (Coach: Stefan HOJSÍK).
Como Calcio: William VECCHI, Pietro VIERCHOWOD, Mariano RIVA (64' Gabriele
RATTI), Giancarlo CENTI, Silvano FONTOLAN, Piero VOLPI, Massimo MANCINI,
Adriano LOMBARDI, Ezio CAVAGNETTO, Renzo GOBBO (64' Giuseppe MAROZZI),
Maurizio GIOVANNELLI. (Coach: Giuseppe MARCHIORO).
Goals: TJ Tatran Presov: 1-0 Vladimír RUSNÁK (15'), 2-0 Lubomír (Lubos) ANINA (27'),
3-0 Alexander COMISSO (46'), 4-0 Jozef SÁLKA (61').
Como Calcio: 4-1 Pietro VIERCHOWOD (87').
Referee: Josef BUCEK (AUT)   Attendance: 1.000

26-11-1980   Presov: TJ Tatran Presov – NK Zagreb   2-1 (1-1)
TJ Tatran Presov: ..., Miroslav LABUN, Vladimír RUSNÁK, Vladimír GOMBÁR, Lubomír
(Lubos) ANINA, Jozef SALKA, ... (Coach: Stefan HOJSÍK).
NK Zagreb:
Goals: TJ Tatran Presov: 1-1 Miroslav LABUN (31' penalty), 2-1 Miroslav LABUN (86').
NK Zagreb: 0-1 Josip COP (29').
Referee: László KÖRÖS (HUN)   Attendance: 1.500

26-11-1980   Béke téri Stadion, Budapest: Csepel SC – Como Calcio 0-0
Csepel SC: Attila KOVÁCS, Béla KINCSES, Gábor KÖHALMI, Gusztáv KELEMEN, József
ELEKES, György GÁLHÍDI,Károly OZSVÁTH (78' Miklós KÖKÉNY), László LAZSÁNYI
(YC80), Mihály TULIPÁN, István TÓTH, Sándor VINCZE. (Coach: Mihály KESZTHELYI
Keszli).
Como Calcio: Giuliano GIULIANI, Pietro VIERCHOWOD, Mariano RIVA (YC85),
Giancarlo CENTI, Silvano FONTOLAN, Piero VOLPI, Massimo MANCINI, Adriano
LOMBARDI (78' Renzo GOBBO), Marco NICOLETTI (YC87), Doriano POZZATO, Ezio
CAVAGNETTO. (Coach: Giuseppe MARCHIORO).
Referee: Franz LATZIN (AUT)   Attendance: 4.000

04-03-1981   Béke téri Stadion, Budapest: Csepel SC – TJ Tatran Presov 3-0 (1-0)
Csepel SC: Attila KOVÁCS, Lajos GODÁN, Gábor KÖHALMI, Antal WÉBER, György
GÁLHIDI, József VARGA, Gusztáv KELEMEN (76' Béla KINCSES), István TÓTH, Károly
OZSVÁTH, Mihály TULIPÁN (73' Gábor DÉKÁNY), Sándor VINCZE. (Coach: Mihály
KESZTHELYI Keszli).
TJ Tatran Presov: Milan VESELÝ, Stefan VARGA, Vladimír HARAJDA, Miroslav LABUN,
Anton FILARSKÝ, Andrej VALÍCEK (46' Vladimír RUSNÁK), Jozef SAJÁNEK (YC32),
Bartolomej MAJERNÍK, Alexander COMISSO, Jozef SÁLKA, Vladimír GOMBÁR. (Coach:
Stefan HOJSÍK).
Goals: Csepel SC: 1-0 Antal WÉBER (13'), 2-0 István TÓTH (54' penalty), 3-0 István TÓTH
(60' penalty).
Referee: Dr.Zoran REBAC (YUG)   Attendance: 1.000

18-03-1981   Zagreb: NK Zagreb – Como Calcio 2-1 (0-0)
NK Zagreb: LONCARIC, Nenad PODGAJSKI, Ante RUMORA (80' PETRAVIC), Branko
GODINIC (46' Drago RUKLJAC), Stipe PERIC, Atif LIPOVAC, Marijan CERCEK, Zeljko
JURIN, Srecko KURBASA, Mihajlo BOSNJAK, Miroslav ULJAN. (Coach: Drazan
JERKOVIC).
Como Calcio: Giuliano GIULIANI, Pietro VIERCHOWOD, Giuseppe MAROZZI, Maurizio
GIOVANNELLI, Gabriele RATTI, Piero VOLPI, Roberto DI NICOLA, Adriano LOMBARDI
(70' Giancarlo CENTI), Marco NICOLETTI, Renzo GOBBO, Ezio CAVAGNETTO (75'
Roberto GALIA). (Coach: Giuseppe MARCHIORO).
Goals: NK Zagreb: 1-0 Marijan CERCEK (55'), 2-0 Drago RUKLJAC (59').
Como Calcio: 2-1 Marco NICOLETTI(85' penalty).
Referee: Robert JACZINA (HUN)

18-03-1981   Stadión Tatran, Presov: TJ Tatran Presov – Csepel SC 0-0
TJ Tatran Presov: ..., Jozef OBORIL, Lubomír (Lubos) ANINA, ... (Coach: Stefan HOJSÍK).
Csepel SC: Attila KOVÁCS, Béla KINCSES, Gábor KÖHALMI, Antal WÉBER, György
GÁLHIDI, József VARGA, László LAZSÁNYI, István TÓTH, Mihály TULIPÁN (87' Gábor
DÉKÁNY), Gusztáv KELEMEN, Sándor VINCZE. (Coach: Mihály KESZTHELYI Keszli).
Referee: Horst BRUMMEIER (AUT)   Attendance: 1.500

244

08-04-1981   Béke téri Stadion, Budapest. Csepel SC – NK Zagreb 2-0 (1-0)
Csepel SC: Attila KOVÁCS, Lajos GODÁN, Gábor KÖHALMI, Antal WÉBER, György
GÁLHIDI, József VARGA (74' György DRAHOS), Gusztáv KELEMEN, István TÓTH,
Mihály TULIPÁN, László LAZSÁNYI, Sándor VINCZE. (Coach: Mihály KESZTHELYI
Keszli).
NK Zagreb: Vjeran SIMUNIC, Nenad PODGAJSKI, Stipe PERIC, Josip COP (YC89), Ante
RUMORA, Zvonko COPOR, Branimir ANTOLIC, Mihajlo BOSNJAK (75' Robert ZAGAR),
Zeljko JURIN, Srecko KURBASA (60' Slavko KOVACIC), Miroslav ULJAN. (Coach:
Drazan JERKOVIC).
Goals: Csepel SC: 1-0 László LAZSÁNYI (18'), 2-0 László LAZSÁNYI (70').
Referee: Massimo CIULLI (ITA)   Attendance: 3.500

08-04-1981   Como: Como Calcio – TJ Tatran Presov 1-0 (0-0)
Como Calcio: Giuliano GIULIANI, Giuseppe MAROZZI, Mariano RIVA, Roberto GALIA,
Silvano FONTOLAN (46' Pietro VIERCHOWOD), Gabriele RATTI, Maurizio
GIOVANNELLI, Gianni UNGARO, Ezio CAVAGNETTO (46' Roberto DI NICOLA),
Adriano LOMBARDI, Roberto MANDRESSI. (Coach: Giuseppe MARCHIORO).
TJ Tatran Presov: Ján CEPO, Stefan VARGA, Jozef OBORIL, Zoltán BREUER, Vladimír
HARAJDA, Anton FILARSKÝ (79' Alexander COMISSO), Lubomír (Lubos) ANINA, Jozef
SAJÁNEK, Vladimír RUSNÁK, Jozef SÁLKA, Andrej VALÍCEK. (Coach: Stefan HOJSÍK).
Goal: Como Calcio: 1-0 Roberto MANDRESSI (62').
Referee: Milorad VLAJIC (YUG)   Attendance: 800

21-04-1981   Zagreb: NK Zagreb – TJ Tatran Presov 1-5 (1-2)
NK Zagreb: LONCARIC, Nenad PODGAJSKI, Ante RUMORA, Robert ZAGAR (46'
PETROVIC), Stipe PERIC, Atif LIPOVAC, Zeljko JURIN, Zvonko COPOR, Slavko
KOVACIC, Mihajlo BOSNJAK, Miroslav ULJAN. (Coach: Drazan JERKOVIC).
TJ Tatran Presov: Ján CEPO, Anton FILARSKÝ, Vladimír HARAJDA, Jozef OBORIL,
Zoltán BREUER, Pavol SUSKO, Marián JOZEF, Vladimír RUSNÁK, Lubomír (Lubos)
ANINA, Ján TURÁK (46' Jozef SAJÁNEK), Andrej VALÍCEK. (Coach: Stefan HOJSÍK).
Goals: NK Zagreb: 1-1 Robert ZAGAR (34').
TJ Tatran Presov: 0-1 Andrej VALICEK (12'), 1-2 Lubomír (Lubos) ANINA (36'), 1-3 Lubos
ANINA (56'), 1-4 Vladimír RUSNÁK (57'), 1-5 Lubomír (Lubos) ANINA (85').
Referee: Claudio PIERI (ITA)   Attendance: 1.000

21-04-1981   Stadio Giuseppe Sinigaglia, Como: Como Calcio – Csepel SC 2-1 (2-1)
Como Calcio: William VECCHI, Giuseppe MAROZZI (82' Roberto MANDRESSI), Mariano
RIVA, Giancarlo CENTI (46' Renzo GOBBO), Silvano FONTOLAN, Gabriele RATTI,
Massimo MANCINI, Adriano LOMBARDI, Marco NICOLETTI, Doriano POZZATO, Ezio
CAVAGNETTO. (Coach: Giuseppe MARCHIORO).
Csepel SC: Attila KOVÁCS, Lajos GODÁN, Antal WÉBER, György GÁLHIDI, Gábor
KÖHALMI, József VARGA (68' József ELEKES), László LAZSÁNYI, Béla KINCSES,
Mihály TULIPÁN, István TÓTH, Gusztáv KELEMEN. (Coach: Mihály KESZTHELYI
Keszli).
Goals: Como Calcio: 1-1 Silvano FONTOLAN (3'), 2-1 Doriano POZZATO (35').
Csepel SC: 0-1 László LAZSÁNYI (1').
Referee: Josef POUCEK (TCH)

Pos	Team	Pld	W	D	L	GF	GA	GD	Pts
1	*TJ Tatran Presov (TCH)*	*6*	*3*	*1*	*2*	*11*	*7*	*+4*	*7*
2	Csepel SC (HUN)	6	2	3	1	6	2	+4	7
3	Como Calcio (ITA)	6	3	1	2	7	7	0	7
4	NK Zagreb (YUG)	6	1	1	4	4	12	-8	3

*** TJ Tatran Presov won the Cup ***

1981-1982

20-10-1981   Mestský Stadion, Ostrava: TJ Vítkovice – AC Milan   2-1 (1-1)
TJ Vítkovice: Miroslav HAVLÍCEK, Jindrich KUSNÍR, Ján MORAVCÍK, Rostislav
CEVELA, Milan LISANÍK, Josef MYDLO (46' Miloslav SMETANA), Jirí SOUREK, Jirí
KLICKA, Jozef MARCHEVSKÝ, Miroslav GAJDUSEK, Jan KOURIL (70' Rostislav
SIONKO). (Coach: Jirí DUNAJ).
AC Milan: Ottorino PIOTTI, Mauro TASSOTTI, Aldo MALDERA (III), Andrea ICARDI,
Fulvio COLLOVATI (46' Joseph (Joe) JORDAN (SCO)), Sergio BATTISTINI, Ruben
BURIANI, Walter Alfredo NOVELLINO (I), Roberto ANTONELLI, Francesco ROMANO,
Giuseppe INCOCCIATI (74' Massimo GADDA). (Coach: Luigi RADICE (II)).
Goals: TJ Vítkovice: 1-1 Jindrich KUSNÍR (27'), 2-1 Miroslav GAJDUSEK (90' penalty).
AC Milan: 0-1 Roberto ANTONELLI (15').
Referee: MOHÁCSI (HUN)   Attendance: 7.000

21-10-1981   Rohonci úti stadion, Szombathely:
                    Szombathelyi Haladás VSE – NK Osijek   4-2 (1-1)
Szombathelyi Haladás VSE: Péter HEGEDÜS, Imre HORVÁTH, Ferenc KIRÁLY, Csaba
VÖRÖS (80' János TAPASZTI), Tamás PRESZELLER, József NAGY, József FITOS, Ferenc
KULCSÁR, Imre HEGYI, Ferenc SZABÓ (60' Attila BOGÁTI), György GARICS. (Coach:
Péter TÖRÖK).
NK Osijek: Dusan ALEMPIC, Srecko HULJIC (YC81), Stipe PETROVIC, Ivica KALINIC,
Mile DUMANCIC, Ilija SORMAZ (52' Stjepan CORDAS), Branko ZERAVICA, Goran
POPOVIC (YC44), Petar NIKEZIC (YC,YC56), Ivan LUKACEVIC, Mirko SKRINJAR (72'
Josip ILICIC). (Coach: Josip DUVANCIC).
Goals: Szombathelyi Haladás VSE: 1-0 József NAGY (6'), 2-1 Imre HEGYI (54'), 3-1 Attila
BOGÁTI (62'), 4-1 József NAGY (66').
NK Osijek: 1-1 Petar NIKEZIC (22'), 4-2 Stjepan CORDAS (89' penalty).
Attendance: 5.000

04-11-1981   Osijek: NK Osijek – TJ Vítkovice   0-0
NK Osijek:
TJ Vítkovice: Jaroslav ZÁPALKA, Josef MYDLO, Ján MORAVCÍK, Zdenek VYHLÍDAL,
Rostislav CEVELA, Miloslav SMETANA (60' Zdenek SVATONSKÝ), Jirí KLICKA, Jirí
SOUREK, Miroslav GAJDUSEK, Petr KOKES, Jan SVOBODA (67' Jozef MARCHEVSKÝ).
(Coach: Jirí DUNAJ).
Referee: Béla SZABÓ (HUN)   Attendance: 2.000

247

04-11-1981   Stadio Giuseppe Meazza, Milano:
AC Milan – Szombathelyi Haladás VSE   2-0 (1-0)
AC Milan: Ottorino PIOTTI, Mauro TASSOTTI, Andrea ICARDI, Sergio BATTISTINI,
Fulvio COLLOVATI, Maurizio VENTURI, Alberigo EVANI (59' Ruben BURIANI),
Giuseppe INCOCCIATI, Joseph (Joe) JORDAN (SCO) (82' Roberto MANDRESSI),
Francesco ROMANO, Roberto ANTONELLI. (Coach: Luigi RADICE (II)).
Szombathelyi Haladás VSE: Péter HEGEDÜS, Tamás VICZKÓ, Csaba VÖRÖS (YC67),
Tamás PRESZELLER, József NAGY (75' Attila BOGÁTI), Ferenc KIRÁLY, Imre
HORVÁTH (84' János TAPASZTI), Ferenc KULCSÁR, György GARICS, József FITOS,
Imre HEGYI. (Coach: Péter TÖRÖK).
Goals: AC Milan: 1-0 Fulvio COLLOVATI (15'), 2-0 Giuseppe INCOCCIATI (78').
Referee: Zoran PETROVIC (YUG)   Attendance: 10.000

25-11-1981   Osijek: NK Osijek – AC Milan   1-1 (0-0)
NK Osijek: Dusan ALEMPIC, Srecko HULJIC, Mirko LULIC, Mile DUMANCIC (70' Ilija
SORMAZ), Branko ZERAVICA, Ivan SMUDLA, Milan MARICIC, Goran POPOVIC, Ivan
LUKACEVIC (67' Zlatko RASIC), Petar NIKEZIC, Ivica GRNJA. (Coach: Andrija VEKIC).
AC Milan: Ottorino PIOTTI, Mauro TASSOTTI, Andrea ICARDI, Ruben BURIANI, Fulvio
COLLOVATI, Maurizio VENTURI, Stefano CUOGHI, Walter Alfredo NOVELLINO (I),
Roberto ANTONELLI (73' Joseph (Joe) JORDAN (SCO)), Adelio MORO, Francesco
ROMANO. (Coach: Luigi RADICE (II)).
Goals: NK Osijek: 1-1 Ilija SORMAZ (89').
AC Milan: 0-1 Walter Alfredo NOVELLINO (60').
Referee: Franz LATZIN (AUT)

25-11-1981   Rohonci úti stadion, Szombathely:
Szombathelyi Haladás VSE – TJ Vítkovice   2-2 (2-2)
Szombathelyi Haladás VSE: Arnold ELLER, János TAPASZTI, Ferenc KIRÁLY, Csaba
VÖRÖS (YC5), Tamás PRESZELLER, Zoltán SZARKA (YC29) (75' Gábor NÉMETH), Imre
HORVÁTH, Ferenc KULCSÁR (YC40), Attila BOGÁTI, Ferenc SZABÓ, György GARICS.
(Coach: Péter TÖRÖK).
TJ Vítkovice: Jaroslav ZÁPALKA, Jindrich KUSNÍR (YC52), Ján MORAVCÍK, Zdenek
VYHLÍDAL (YC5), Josef MYDLO, Miloslav SMETANA (78' Zdenek SVATONSKÝ),
Rostislav SIONKO, Jirí SOUREK, Miroslav GAJDUSEK (YC39), Jan SVOBODA (68' Petr
KOKES), Jan KOURIL. (Coach: Jirí DUNAJ).
Goals: Szombathelyi Haladás VSE: 1-1 György GARICS (4'), 2-2 Ferenc SZABÓ (32').
TJ Vítkovice: 0-1 Jan KOURÍL (1'), 1-2 Jan SVOBODA (27').
Referee: Pietro D'ELIA (ITA)   Attendance: 3.000

17-03-1982   Gradski stadion, Osijek: NK Osijek – Szombathelyi Haladás VSE   3-0 (3-0)
NK Osijek: Branko DAVIDOVIC, Luka KOSTIC, Stipe PETROVIC (YC77), Miomir
METER, Ilija SORMAZ, Branka KARACIC, Ivan SMUDLA, Petar NIKEZIC, Petar GUDELJ
(46' Dragoslav PERIC), Viktor GOIC, Ivica GRNJA (62' Zlatko JURASOVIC). (Coach: Josip
DUVANCIC).
Szombathelyi Haladás VSE: Péter HEGEDÜS, Imre HORVÁTH, Ferenc KIRÁLY, József
FITOS, György KISS, Ferenc TAR, Imre HEGYI, Ferenc KULCSÁR, Tamás PRESZELLER
(62' János TAPASZTI), Attila BOGÁTI (62' Gábor NÉMETH), Ferenc SZABÓ. (Coach:
Péter TÖRÖK).
Goals: NK Osijek: 1-0 Viktor GOIC (8'), 2-0 Péter HEGEDÜS (17' *own goal*), 3-0 Ivica
GRNJA (32').
Attendance: 1.000

248

07-04-1982 Rohonci úti stadion, Szombathely:
Szombathelyi Haladás VSE – AC Milan 0-1 (0-1)
Szombathelyi Haladás VSE: Péter HEGEDÜS, Imre HORVÁTH (YC63), Csaba VÖRÖS,
Tamás PRESZELLER, Ferenc TAR, Ferenc KIRÁLY (64' Attila BOGÁTI), Ferenc SZABÓ,
Ferenc KULCSÁR, György GARICS, József FITOS (YC20), Imre HEGYI. (Coach: Péter
TÖRÖK).
AC Milan: Ottorino PIOTTI, Andrea ICARDI, Mauro TASSOTTI, Maurizio VENTURI,
Fulvio COLLOVATI, Franceschino (Franco) BARESI, Stefano CUOGHI (YC45) (54' Walter
Alfredo NOVELLINO (I)), Sergio BATTISTINI, Roberto ANTONELLI, Alberigo EVANI,
Giuseppe INCOCCIATI (81' Aldo MALDERA). (Coach: Italo GALBIATI).
Goal: AC Milan: 0-1 Sergio BATTISTINI (23').
Referee: KORHAT (TCH)   Attendance: 4.500

21-04-1982 Stadio Giuseppe Meazza, Milano: AC Milan – NK Osijek 2-1 (2-0)
AC Milan: Ottorino PIOTTI, Alberto MINOIA, Aldo MALDERA, Maurizio VENTURI (55'
Andrea ICARDI), Fulvio COLLOVATI, Franceschino (Franco) BARESI, Francesco
ROMANO, Adelio MORO (46' Sergio BATTISTINI), Roberto ANTONELLI, Alberigo
EVANI, Giuseppe INCOCCIATI. (Coach: Italo GALBIATI).
NK Osijek: Dusan ALEMPIC, Branko ZERAVICA, Miomir METER, Mile DUMANCIC,
Jasmin DZEKO, Ivica KALINIC, Luka DILBER, Goran POPOVIC, Dragan TODOROVIC
(80' Milan MARICIC), Ante RAKELA, Ivica GRNJA (46' Dragoslav PERIC). (Coach: Josip
DUVANCIC).
Goals: AC Milan: 1-0 Roberto ANTONELLI (6'), 2-0 Franceschino (Franco) BARESI (10'
penalty).
NK Osijek: 2-1 Ante RAKELA (46').
Referee: Josef POUCEK (TCH)

08-05-1982 Stadión TJ Vítkovice, Ostrava:
TJ Vítkovice – Szombathelyi Haladás VSE 6-1 (2-0)
TJ Vítkovice: Jaroslav ZÁPALKA, Jindrich KUSNÍR, Ján MORAVCÍK, Milan LISANÍK,
Karel DOSTÁL, Josef MYDLO, Jirí SOUREK, Miloslav SMETANA (46' Jirí BELES), Jozef
MARCHEVSKÝ, Jirí KLICKA, Milan ALBRECHT. (Coach: Jirí DUNAJ).
Szombathelyi Haladás VSE: Péter HEGEDÜS (28' Arnold ELLER), Gábor NÉMETH, Csaba
VÖRÖS, Ferenc KULCSÁR, György KISS, József NAGY, Imre HEGYI, István PAPP, Attila
BOGÁTI, Ferenc SZABÓ, György GARICS. (Coach: Péter TÖRÖK).
Goals: TJ Vítkovice: 1-0 Jindrich KUSNÍR (27'), 2-0 Jozef MARCHEVSKÝ (30'), 3-0 Milan
ALBRECHT (48'), 4-1 Milan LISANÍK (57'), 5-1 Jirí KLICKA (71'), 6-1 Jirí SOUREK (87').
Szombathelyi Haladás VSE: 3-1 György GARICS (51').
Referee: Maurizio MATTEI (ITA)   Attendance: 2.000

12-05-1982 Stadio Giuseppe Meazza, Milano: AC Milan – TJ Vítkovice 3-0 (1-0)
AC Milan: Ottorino PIOTTI, Andrea ICARDI, Aldo MALDERA, Maurizio VENTURI, Mauro
TASSOTTI, Franceschino (Franco) BARESI, Alberto CAMBIAGHI (69' Francesco
ROMANO), Walter Alfredo NOVELLINO (I), Joseph (Joe) JORDAN (SCO), Adelio MORO
(46' Sergio BATTISTINI), Alberigo EVANI. (Coach: Italo GALBIATI).
TJ Vítkovice: Jaroslav ZÁPALKA, Jirí BELES, Ján MORAVCÍK, Rostislav CEVELA (58'
Jindrich KUSNÍR), Milan LISANÍK, Jirí SOUREK, Jozef MARCHEVSKÝ, Zdenek
SVATONSKÝ (73' Josef MYDLO), Miloslav SMETANA, Miroslav GAJDUSEK, Milan
ALBRECHT. (Coach: Jirí DUNAJ).
Goals: AC Milan: 1-0 Franceschino (Franco) BARESI (12' penalty), 2-0 Alberto
CAMBIAGHI (50'), 3-0 Joseph (Joe) JORDAN (77' penalty).
Referee: Milorad VLAJIC (YUG)   Attendance: 20.000

16-05-1982   Ostrava: TJ Vítkovice – NK Osijek   2-1 (0-1)
TJ Vítkovice: Miroslav HAVLÍCEK, Jindrich KUSNÍR, Ján MORAVCÍK, Milan LISANÍK,
Karel DOSTÁL, Jirí SOUREK (46' Jirí BELES), Miroslav GAJDUSEK, Josef MYDLO, Jozef
MARCHEVSKÝ, Jirí KLICKA, Jan KOURIL (60' Rostislav CEVELA). (Coach: Jirí
DUNAJ).
NK Osijek:
Goals: TJ Vítkovice: 1-1 Jirí KLICKA (47'), 2-1 Jirí KLICKA (76' penalty).
NK Osijek: 0-1 Josip ILICIC (40').
Referee: Miklós NAGY (HUN)   Attendance: 1.500

Pos	Team	Pld	W	D	L	GF	GA	GD	Pts
1	AC Milan (ITA)	6	4	1	1	10	4	+6	9
2	TJ Vítkovice (TCH)	6	3	2	1	12	8	+4	8
3	NK Osijek (YUG)	6	1	2	3	8	9	-1	4
4	Szombathelyi Haladás VSE (HUN)	6	1	1	4	7	16	-9	3

*** AC Milan won the Cup ***

250

1982-1983

20-10-1982   Zemun: FK Galenika Zemun – Vasas SC   2-1
FK Galenika Zemun:
Vasas SC: ... (Coach: Rudolf ILLOVSZKY).

20-10-1982   Stadion pod Dubnom, Zilina: TJ ZVL Zilina – Hellas Verona FC   4-0 (3-0)
TJ ZVL Zilina: Ivan ZIAK, Milan ZVARÍK, Miroslav TURIANIK, Jaroslav MINTÁL, Milan
SMEHÝL, Pavol STRAPÁC, Ivan SIMCEK, Jozef NOROCKÝ, Vladimír GOFFA (77'
Vladimír MASÁR), Miroslav GERHÁT (40' Jozef BELES), Ján BERESÍK. (Coach: Kamil
MAJERNÍK).
Hellas Verona FC: Alberto TORRESIN, Emidio ODDI, Luciano MARANGON, Adriano
FEDELE, Domenico VOLPATI, Roberto TRICELLA, Luigi MANUELI, Antonio DI
GENNARO (70' Flavio FIORIO), Mauro GIBELLINI, José Guimarães DIRCEU (BRA),
Domenico PENZO (46' Pietro FANNA). (Coach: Osvaldo BAGNOLI).
Goals: TJ ZVL Zilina: 1-0 Ivan SIMCEK (2'), 2-0 Ján BERESIK (23'), 3-0 Jaroslav MINTAL
(34'), 4-0 Ivan SIMCEK (59').
Referee: Milorad VLAJIC (YUG)   Attendance: 3.000

02-11-1982   Budapest: Vasas SC – TJ ZVL Zilina   2-0
Vasas SC: ... (Coach: Rudolf ILLOVSZKY).
TJ ZVL Zilina: ... (Coach: Kamil MAJERNÍK).
Goals: Vasas SC: 1-0 Ignác IZSO (..'), 2-0 László KISS (..').
Referee: Stjepan GLAVINA (YUG)   Attendance: 3.000

03-11-1982   Stadio Marc'Antonio Bentegodi, Verona:
                Hellas Verona FC – FK Galenika Zemun   1-1 (0-1)
Hellas Verona FC: Alberto TORRESIN, Domenico VOLPATI, Adriano FEDELE, Luigi
SACCHETTI, Franco TOMMASI (46' José Guimarães DIRCEU (BRA)), Roberto
TRICELLA, Pietro FANNA (68' Roberto QUARELLA), Luigi MANUELI, Ezio SELLA,
Antonio DI GENNARO, Domenico PENZO. (Coach: Osvaldo BAGNOLI).
FK Galenika Zemun: Ratomir DUJKOVIC, MILATIC, Dragan BANKOVIC, Goran
KALUSEVIC, Milivoje ZIVKOVIC, Branko NIKOLIC, Miljan MEMISI (65' Miroslav
BAROS), Jovica KOLB, Slobodan SANTRAC (77' Zoran DIMITRIJEVIC), Dragan
LACMANOVIC, Milijan TUPAJIC.
Goals: Hellas Verona FC: 1-1 Luigi MANUELI (49').
FK Galenika Zemun: 0-1 Dragan LACMANOVIC (9').
Referee: Sándor KUTI (HUN)

24-11-1982   Fáy utcai Stadion, Budapest: Vasas SC – Hellas Verona FC   1-0 (0-0)
Vasas SC: Imre LEBONICZKY, László RÁCZ (70' Béla HEGEDÜS), Gábor SERES,
György CSIMA, Tibor BALOG, András KOMJÁTI, István BIRINYI, Géza RIXER, László
KISS, Ignác IZSÓ, Péter BIRKÁS (57' Béla VÁRADI). (Coach: Rudolf ILLOVSZKY).
Hellas Verona FC: Alberto TORRESIN, Emidio ODDI, Luciano MARANGON (49'
Domenico PENZO), Domenico VOLPATI, Luciano SPINOSI, Roberto TRICELLA, Pietro
FANNA, Luigi SACCHETTI (65' Luigi MANUELI), Antonio DI GENNARO, José
Guimarães DIRCEU (BRA), Ezio SELLA. (Coach: Osvaldo BAGNOLI).
Goal: Vasas SC: 1-0 László KISS (57').
Referee: Josip GLAZAR (YUG)

24-11-1982   Zilina: TJ ZVL Zilina – FK Galenika Zemun   2-0 (1-0)
TJ ZVL Zilina: ... (Coach: Kamil MAJERNÍK).
FK Galenika Zemun: ..., Branko NIKOLIC (YC), ...
Goals: TJ ZVL Zilina: 1-0 Jaroslav MINTAL (7'), 2-0 Vladimír GOFFA (82').
Referee: Béla SZABÓ (HUN)   Attendance: 1.000

02-03-1983   Budapest: Vasas SC – FK Galenika Zemun   3-1 (3-0)
Vasas SC: ... (Coach: Rudolf ILLOVSZKY).
FK Galenika Zemun:

02-03-1983   Stadio Marc'Antonio Bentegodi, Verona:
                Hellas Verona FC – TJ ZVL Zilina   1-1 (0-1)
Hellas Verona FC: Alberto TORRESIN, Emidio ODDI, Adriano FEDELE, Domenico
VOLPATI (46' Pietro FANNA), Franco TOMMASI, Luciano SPINOSI, Luigi MANUELI,
Luigi SACCHETTI, Ezio SELLA, José Guimarães DIRCEU (BRA), Domenico PENZO (64'
Roberto TRICELLA). (Coach: Osvaldo BAGNOLI).
TJ ZVL Zilina: Ivan ZIAK, Vladimír KINIER, Miroslav TURIANIK, Jozef NOROCKÝ,
Milan ZVARÍK, Pavol STRAPÁC, Ivan SIMCEK, Stanislav MOCÁR, Vladimír GOFFA,
Miroslav GERHÁT (82' Ján BERESÍK), Jaroslav MINTÁL. (Coach: Kamil MAJERNÍK).
Goals: Hellas Verona FC: 1-1 José Guimarães DIRCEU (73' penalty).
TJ ZVL Zilina: 0-1 Vladimír GOFFA (36').
Referee: Heinz FAHNLER (AUT)

16-03-1983   Stadion Zemun, Beograd: FK Galenika Zemun – Hellas Verona FC   4-2 (2-2)
FK Galenika Zemun: Ratomir DUJKOVIC, Vanco NIKOLOVSKI, Dragan BANKOVIC,
Slobodan MILINKOVIC, Miroslav BAROS, Miodrag VARANJES, Zoran STOJADINOVIC
(69' Zoran CIKIC), Jovica KOLB, Vladimir BULATOVIC, Milos BURSAC, Zoran PANIC.
Hellas Verona FC: Alberto TORRESIN, Emidio ODDI, Luciano SPINOSI, Adriano FEDELE,
Wladyslaw ZMUDA (POL), Franco TOMMASI (46' Roberto TRICELLA), Flavio FIORIO,
Luigi SACCHETTI, Luigi MANUELI, Domenico VOLPATI, Ezio SELLA. (Coach: Osvaldo
BAGNOLI).
Goals: FK Galenika Zemun: 1-0 Vladimir BULATOVIC (5'), 2-1 Vladimir BULATOVIC
(18'), 3-2 Vladimir BULATOVIC (50'), 4-2 Milos BURSAC (52').
Hellas Verona FC: 1-1 Luciano SPINOSI (14'), 2-2 Ezio SELLA (26').
Referee: Antonin REZNÍCEK (TCH)

16-03-1983   Zilina: TJ ZVL Zilina – Vasas SC   3-1 (1-0)
TJ ZVL Zilina: ... (Coach: Kamil MAJERNÍK).
Vasas SC: ... (Coach: Rudolf ILLOVSZKY).
Goals: TJ ZVL Zilina: 1-0 Ján BERESIK (13'), 2-0 Stanislav MOCAR (54'), 3-1 Vladimír
GOFFA (85').
Vasas SC:2-1 Sándor SEGESVARI (79').

06-04-1983   Stadio Marc'Antonio Bentegodi, Verona:
                    Hellas Verona FC – Vasas SC   1-2 (0-1)
Hellas Verona FC: Alberto TORRESIN, Emidio ODDI, Luciano MARANGON (69' Nicola
SILVESTRINI), Adriano FEDELE, Luciano SPINOSI, Luigi MANUELI, Ezio SELLA, Luigi
SACCHETTI, Antonio DI GENNARO, José Guimarães DIRCEU (BRA), Domenico PENZO
(46' Pietro FANNA). (Coach: Osvaldo BAGNOLI).
Vasas SC: László KAKAS, Tibor FARKAS, Gábor HÍRES, Sándor LUKÁCS, László RÁCZ,
András KOMJÁTI, István BIRINYI (86' Gábor SERES), Péter BIRKÁS, László KISS, Ignác
IZSÓ, Béla VÁRADI. (Coach: Rudolf ILLOVSZKY).
Goals: Hellas Verona FC: 1-1 Luciano SPINOSI (50').
Vasas SC: 0-1 Béla VÁRADI (27'), 1-2 László KISS (67').
Referee: Franz WÖHRER (AUT)

06-04-1983   Zemun: FK Galenika Zemun – TJ ZVL Zilina   2-0
Goals: FK Galenika Zemun: 1-0 Milos BURSAC (..'), 2-0 Milos BURSAC (..').

Pos	Team	Pld	W	D	L	GF	GA	GD	Pts
1	*Vasas SC (HUN)*	*6*	*4*	*0*	*2*	*10*	*7*	*+3*	*8*
2	TJ ZVL Zilina (TCH)	6	3	1	2	10	6	+4	7
3	FK Galenika Zemun (YUG)	6	3	1	2	10	9	+1	7
4	Hellas Verona FC (ITA)	6	0	2	4	5	13	-8	2

*** Vasas SC won the Cup ***

1983-1984

FINAL ROUND

18-10-1983   Teplice: TJ Sklo Union Teplice – Vasas SC 3-2 (1-0)
TJ Sklo Union Teplice: Vladimír POCTA, Miroslav BUBENÍK, Jirí SIDÁK, Frantisek FRANKE, Vlastimil HOLUB, Stanislav KOLLER, Miloslav TICHÝ, Jaroslav MELICHAR, Tomás ZAHRADNÍK (..' Milan VÍZEK), Antonín ROSA, Pavel KLOUCEK (..' Zdenek SLOWIK). (Coach: Milan KOLLÁR).
Vasas SC: László KAKAS, Béla VÁRADI, György KATONA, György CSIMA, Gyula MAGOS, László KISS, PALASZ, András SZABÓ, Dr.István BIRINYI, András KOMJÁTI, Ignác IZSÓ. (Coach: Kálmán MÉSZÖLY).
Goals: TJ Sklo Union Teplice: 1-0 Antonín ROSA (12'), 2-1 Pavel KLOUCEK (50'), 3-2 Antonín ROSA (89').
Vasas SC: 1-1 Gyula MAGOS (46'), 2-2 László KISS (76').
Referee: Arthur PERNKOPF (AUT)   Attendance: 1.500

18-10-1983   Lindenstadion, Eisenstadt: SC Eduscho Eisenstadt – FK Pristina 4-2 (2-1)
SC Eduscho Eisenstadt: Leo MARTINSCHITZ, Oswald STEIGER, Johann SCHÖLL, Franz EDER, Karl ANDRES, Michael FLEISCHHACKER (60' Johann (Hans) FÜZI), Rubén PLAZA (URU), Dr.Premysl BICOVSKÝ (TCH), Erwin SCHNEIDER, Karl RUPPRECHT (75' Hannes MARZI), Reinhold SOLLEDER. (Coach: Josef SCHNEIDER).
FK Pristina:
Goals: SC Eduscho Eisenstadt: 1-1 Karl RUPPRECHT (25'), 2-1 Sefcet SINANI (31' *own goal*), 3-1 Karl RUPPRECHT (59'), 4-1 Dr.Premysl BICOVSKÝ (68').
FK Pristina: 0-1 Agim CANA (8'), 4-2 Fadilj VOKRI (89').
Attendance: 400

02-11-1983   Budapest: Vasas SC – TJ Sklo Union Teplice 2-1 (1-0)
Vasas SC: ... (Coach: Kálmám MÉSZÖLY).
TJ Sklo Union Teplice: Vladimír POCTA, Miroslav BUBENÍK, Jirí SIDÁK, Frantisek FRANKE, Vlastimil HOLUB, Josef LATISLAV, Zdenek SLOWIK, Stanislav KOLLER, Miloslav TICHÝ, Antonín ROSA, Pavel KLOUCEK. (Coach: Milan KOLLÁR).
Goals: Vasas SC: 1-0 Ignác IZSÓ (..'), László KISS (..').
TJ Sklo Union Teplice: Antonín ROSA (..').
Referee: Sinasi BERISA (YUG)   Attendance: 1.200

02-11-1983   Pristina: FK Pristina – SC Eduscho Eisenstadt 3-3 (1-1)
FK Pristina:
SC Eduscho Eisenstadt: Leo MARTINSCHITZ, Oswald STEIGER (46' Christian FISCHER), Heinz PEISCHL, Franz EDER, Karl ANDRES, Michael FLEISCHHACKER, Rubén PLAZA (URU), Johann SCHÖLL, Erwin SCHNEIDER, Johann (Hans) FÜZI, Karl RUPPRECHT (46' Hannes MARZI). (Coach: Josef SCHNEIDER).
Goals: FK Pristina: 1-0 Scorer not known (7'), 2-1 Not known (..'), 3-1 Scorer not known (..').
SC Eduscho Eisenstadt: 1-1 Rubén PLAZA (22'), 3-2 Johann SCHÖLL (70' penalty), 3-3 Johann (Hans) FÜZI (83').
Attendance: 25.000

254

22-11-1983   Budapest: Vasas SC – FK Pristina 1-1 (0-0)
Vasas SC: ... (Coach: Kálmám MÉSZÖLY).
FK Pristina:

23-11-1983   Teplice: TJ Sklo Union Teplice – SC Eduscho Eisenstadt 4-1 (2-1)
TJ Sklo Union Teplice: Vladimír POCTA, Miroslav BUBENÍK, Frantisek FRANKE, Jirí
SIDÁK, Zdenek SLOWIK, Radislav HOUSKA, Stanislav KOLLER, Jaroslav MELICHAR,
Tomás ZAHRADNÍK (..' Petr NOVÝ), Pavel KLOUCEK, Miloslav TICHÝ. (Coach: Milan
KOLLÁR).
SC Eduscho Eisenstadt: Leo MARTINSCHITZ, Hannes MARZI, Franz EDER, Johann
SCHÖLL, Ernst BUCSICH, Heinz PEISCHL, Rubén PLAZA (URU), Dr.Premysl
BICOVSKÝ (TCH), Erwin SCHNEIDER, Karl RUPPRECHT (80' Johann (Hans) FÜZI),
Raimund RADAKOVITS (60' Reinhold SOLLEDER). (Coach: Josef SCHNEIDER).
Goals: TJ Sklo Union Teplice: 1-0 Pavel KLOUCEK (9'), 2-1 Jaroslav MELICHAR (19'), 3-1
Miloslav TICHÝ (65'), 4-1 Jaroslav MELICHAR (88').
SC Eduscho Eisenstadt: 1-1 Erwin SCHNEIDER (16').
Referee: Lajos NEMETH (HUN)   Attendance: 1.500

20-03-1984   Gradski stadion, Pristina: FK Pristina – Vasas SC 4-2 (2-2)
FK Pristina:
Vasas SC: Imre LEBOVICZKY, László PECHA, Gábor HÍRES, András KOMJÁTI, János
CSORBA, Tibor BALOG, László KISS, Ferenc CSÍK, György KATONA, Ignác IZSÓ, László
KUTI (..' Géza RIXER). Coach: Kálmán MÉSZÖLY).
Goals: FK Pristina: 1-0 Zoran BATROVIC (18'), 2-2 Haris SMAJIC (31'), 3-2 Rifat
MEHINOVIC (85'), 4-2 Jusuf TORTOSI (87').
Vasas SC: 1-1 László KUTI (24'), 1-2 György KATONA (26').
Attendance: 8.000

20-03-1984   Lindenstadion, Eisenstadt:
              SC Eduscho Eisenstadt – TJ Sklo Union Teplice 1-1 (1-1)
SC Eduscho Eisenstadt: Leo MARTINSCHITZ, Oswald STEIGER, Heinz PEISCHL, Peter
KLOIBER, Karl ANDRES, Johann SCHÖLL, Dr.Premysl BICOVSKÝ (TCH), Michael
FLEISCHHACKER, Rubén PLAZA (URU), Raimund RADAKOVITS, Erwin SCHNEIDER.
(Coach: Josef SCHNEIDER).
TJ Sklo Union Teplice: Vladimír POCTA, Miroslav BUBENÍK, Tomás ZAHRADNÍK, Jirí
SIDÁK, Zdenek SLOWIK, Radislav HOUSKA (..' Miloslav TICHÝ), Stanislav KOLLER,
Jaroslav MELICHAR, Pavel HORA, Antonín ROSA, Pavel KLOUCEK. (Coach: Milan
KOLLÁR).
Goals: SC Eduscho Eisenstadt: 1-1 Raimond RADAKOVITS (42').
TJ Sklo Union Teplice: 0-1 Jaroslav MELICHAR (38').
Attendance: 400

10-04-1984   Lindenstadion, Eisenstadt: SC Eduscho Eisenstadt – Vasas SC   2-1 (1-1)
SC Eduscho Eisenstadt: Leo MARTINSCHITZ, Oswald STEIGER (RC), Franz EDER, Peter
KLOIBER, Martin LEFOR, Johann SCHÖLL (78' Karl ANDRES), Dr.Premysl BICOVSKÝ
(TCH), Heinz PEISCHL (35' Johann (Hans) FÜZI), Rubén PLAZA (URU), Raimund
RADAKOVITS, Erwin SCHNEIDER. (Coach: Felix LATZKE).
Vasas SC: ..., András KONJÁTI (RC), ..., Gábor HÍRES, ... (Coach: Kálmán MESZÖLY).
Goals: SC Eduscho Eisenstadt: 1-1 Dr.Premysl BICOVSKÝ (21'), 2-1 Johann (Hans) FÜZI
(50').
Vasas SC: 0-1 Gábor HÍRES (16').
Attendance: 150

11-04-1984   Pristina: FK Pristina – TJ Sklo Union Teplice   2-0 (2-0)
FK Pristina:
TJ Sklo Union Teplice: Vladimír POCTA, Miroslav BUBENÍK, Jirí SIDÁK, Tomás
ZAHRADNÍK (..' Radislav HOUSKA), Jirí MALIGA, Josef LATISLAV, Stanislav KOLLER,
Miloslav TICHÝ, Pavel HORA, Antonín ROSA, Pavel KLOUCEK. (Coach: Milan
KOLLÁR).
Goals: FK Pristina: 1-0 Rifat MEHINOVIC (6'), 2-0 Jirí MALIGA (29' own goal).
Referee: Franz LATZIN (AUT)   Attendance: 1.000

24-04-1984   Városi Sporttelep, Tapolca: Vasas SC – SC Eduscho Eisenstadt   1-2 (0-0)
Vasas SC: László KAKAS, Tibor BALOG (46' László PECHA), Gábor HÍRES, Géza
MÉSZÖLY, János CSORBA, Dr.István BIRINYI, Ferenc CSÍK, László KUTI, György
KATONA (46' Géza RIXER), Péter BIRKÁS, Ignác IZSÓ. (Coach: Kálmán MESZÖLY).
SC Eduscho Eisenstadt: Leo MARTINSCHITZ, Franz EDER, Karl
RUPPRECHT, Ernst BUCSICH, Johann (Hans) FÜZI, Johann SCHÖLL, Dr.Premysl
BICOVSKÝ (TCH), Rubén PLAZA (URU) (57' Heinrich HORVATH), Raimund
RADAKOVITS, Reinhold SOLLEDER (12' Hannes MARZI). (Coach: Felix LATZKE).
Goals: Vasas SC: 1-2 László KUTI (88' penalty).
SC Eduscho Eisenstadt: 0-1 Johann SCHÖLL (60'), 0-2 Raimund RADAKOVITS (75').
Attendance: 1.000

24-04-1984   Teplice: TJ Sklo Union Teplice – FK Pristina   1-1 (1-0)
TJ Sklo Union Teplice: Vladimír POCTA, Zbynek ZÁVESKÝ, Jirí SIDÁK, Frantisek
FRANKE, Zdenek SLOWIK, Jaroslav MELICHAR (..' Radislav HOUSKA), Stanislav
KOLLER, Josef LATISLAV, Pavel HORA, Antonín ROSA, Miloslav TICHÝ (..' Ludek
JÁNSKÝ). (Coach: Milan KOLLÁR).
FK Pristina:
Goals: TJ Sklo Union Teplice: 1-0 Josef LATISLAV (29').
FP Pristina: 1-1 Fadilj MURICI (88').
Referee: Urbán ARPÁD (HUN)   Attendance: 500

Pos	Team	Pld	W	D	L	GF	GA	GD	Pts
1	SC Eduscho Eisenstadt (AUT)	6	3	2	1	13	12	+1	8
2	FK Pristina (YUG)	6	2	3	1	13	11	+2	7
3	TJ Sklo Union Teplice (TCH)	6	2	2	2	10	9	+1	6
4	Vasas SC (HUN)	6	1	1	4	9	13	-4	3

*** SC Eduscho Eisenstadt won the Cup ***

1984-1985

FINAL ROUND

17-10-1984   Kórház utcai stadion, Békéscsaba:
Békéscsabai Elöre Spartacus SC – NK Iskra Bugojno 1-1 (0-1)
Békéscsabai Elöre Spartacus SC: Imre LEBONICZKY, Tibor VÍGH, Attila KEREKES,
Sándor BARANYI (63' Miklós CSANÁLOSI), Mihály OTTLAKÁN, Zoltán
STEIGERWALD, József PÁSZTOR, János PLÁSTYIK (46' Zoltán ÚJVÁRI), József
TAKÁCS, László MOHÁCSI, István FECSKU. (Coach: István SÜLE).
NK Iskra Bugojno: Drazen LADIC, Dragan GLAMOCAK, Vatroslav PETRINOVIC, Zijad
SALKIC, Milomir CEREMIDZIC (YC72), Miralem ZJAJO (85' PAVLOVIC), Milos
RADOVIC, Goran PAVLIC, Miro STIPIC, Ante TOLIC, Dragan MIRKOVIC (89' Mladen
KAROGLAN). (Coach: Blagoje BRATIC).
Goals: Békéscsabai Elöre Spartacus SC: 1-1 László MOHÁCSI (63').
NK Iskra Bugojno: 0-1 Dragan MIRKOVIC (30').
Attendance: 3.000

24-10-1984   Bergamo: Atalanta Bergamo – TJ Baník Ostrava OKD   0-0
Atalanta Bergamo: Ottorino PIOTTI, Giampaolo ROSSI, Maurizio CODOGNO, Diego
BORTOLUZZI (67' Marino MAGRIN), Roberto SOLDA, Adelio MORO, Sauro FATTORI,
Enrico VELLA, Roberto DONADONI (72' Marco PACIONE), Glenn Peter STRÖMBERG
(SWE), Lars (Lasse) LARSSON (SWE). (Coach: Nedo SONETTI).
TJ Baník Ostrava OKD: Pavol MICHALÍK, Lubomír (Lubos) ODEHNAL, Lubomír
SRÁMEK, Dusan SRUBAR, Petr ZAJAROS, Václav PÉCHÁCEK, Jirí ZÁLESKÝ, Petr
NEMEC, Zdenek VÁLEK (81' Roman SIÁLINI), Zdenek SREINER, Werner LICKA (57'
Dusan FÁBRY). (Coach: Josef KOLECKO).
Referee: Lajos HARTMANN (HUN)

07-11-1984   Bugojno: NK Iskra Bugojno – Atalanta Bergamo   2-0 (0-0)
NK Iskra Bugojno: Josip SKARO, Dragan GLAMOCAK, Milomir CEREMIDZIC, Milos
RADOVIC, Vatroslav PETRINOVIC, Nedzad OMERHODZIC, Stojance IDIC (60' Ante
TOLIC), Jako NOVOKMET (57' Miralem ZJAJO), Zijad SALKIC, Goran PAVLIC, Dragan
MIRKOVIC. (Coach: Blagoje BRATIC).
Atalanta Bergamo: Ottorino PIOTTI, Carlo OSTI, Maurizio CODOGNO, Diego
BORTOLUZZI, Roberto SOLDA, Giampaolo ROSSI, Sauro FATTORI, Enrico VELLA (56'
Eugenio PERICO), Roberto DONADONI, Andrea AGOSTINELLI, Lars (Lasse) LARSSON
(SWE) (46' Marco PACIONE). (Coach: Nedo SONETTI).
Goals: NK Iskra Bugojno: 1-0 Nedzad OMERHODZIC (59'), 2-0 Miralem ZJAJO (80').
Referee: Jan HORA (TCH)

07-11-1984   Stadion na Bazalech, Ostrava:
                TJ Baník Ostrava OKD – Békéscsabai Elöre Spartacus SC   1-0 (1-0)
TJ Baník Ostrava OKD: Stanislav VAHALA, Lubomír (Lubos) ODEHNAL, Lubomír
SRÁMEK, Václav PÉCHÁCEK (46' Karel KULA), Petro ONDRASIK, Zdenek SREINER,
Petr NEMEC, Zdenek VÁLEK, Dusan SRUBAR, Werner LICKA, Dusan FÁBRY (46'
Roman SIÁLINI). (Coach: Josef KOLECKO).
Békéscsabai Elöre Spartacus SC: Tamás BAJI, Mihály OTTLAKÁN, Attila KEREKES,
Sándor BARANYI, György FABULYA, Zoltán STEIGERWALD, János PLÁSTYIK (YC37)
(57' István FECSKU), Ottó SULIJA, József TAKÁCS, Zoltán KANYÁRI (52' Károly
KIRÁLYVÁRI (YC89)), József SZEKERES. (Coach: István SÜLE).
Goal: TJ Baník Ostrava OKD: 1-0 Werner LICKA (44').
Referee: Pietro D'ELIA (ITA)   Attendance: 1.000

28-11-1984   Bugojno: NK Iskra Bugojno – TJ Baník Ostrava OKD   1-0 (0-0)
Goal: NK Iskra Bugojno: 1-0 Stojance IDIC (80').

28-11-1984   Kórház utcai stadion, Békéscsaba:
                Békéscsabai Elöre Spartacus SC – Atalanta Bergamo   1-2 (0-1)
Békéscsabai Elöre Spartacus SC: Imre LEBONICZKY, Tibor VÍGH, József PÁSZTOR, József
TAKÁCS (YC45), György FABULYA, Attila KEREKES, Béla MELIS, Károly
KIRÁLYVÁRI (YC73), Zoltán KANYÁRI (69' Mihály OTTLAKÁN), Ottó SULIJA (46'
János SZARVAS), József SZEKERES. (Coach: István SÜLE).
Atalanta Bergamo: Nello MALIZIA, Maurizio CODOGNO (YC60), Giampaolo ROSSI, Diego
BORTOLUZZI, Roberto SOLDA, Giorgio MAGNOCAVALLO, Sauro FATTORI (YC79),
Enrico VELLA (46' Andrea AGOSTINELLI), Marino MAGRIN, Roberto DONADONI,
Marco PACIONE. (Coach: Nedo SONETTI).
Goals: Békéscsabai Elöre Spartacus SC: 1-1 József TAKÁCS (76').
Atalanta Bergamo: 0-1 Sauro FATTORI (34'), 1-2 Marco PACIONE (89').
Referee: Heinz HOLZMANN (AUT)   Attendance: 3.000

19-03-1985   Stadion Jaklic, Bugojno:
                NK Iskra Bugojno – Békéscsabai Elöre Spartacus SC   4-0 (1-0)
NK Iskra Bugojno: Drazen LADIC, Dragan GLAMOCAK, Nedzad OMERHODZIC,
Vatroslav PETRINOVIC (YC73), Mensur STRUKAR, Miralem ZJAJO (73' Jako
NOVOKMET), Nebojsa OROZ, Goran PAVLIC (65' Miro STIPIC), Damir VRABAC, Zoran
TOSKIC, Dragan MIRKOVIC. (Coach: Blagoje BRATIC).
Békéscsabai Elöre Spartacus SC: Imre LEBONICZKY, Tibor VÍGH, János PLÁSTYIK,
Sándor BARANYI (YC75), Mihály OTTLAKÁN, Zoltán STEIGERWALD, József TAKÁCS
(61' Ottó SULIJA), Miklós CSANÁLOSI (65' Béla MELIS), Zoltán KANYÁRI, Árpád
ADORJÁN, József SZEKERES. (Coach: István SÜLE).
Goals: NK Iskra Bugojno: 1-0 Mihály OTTLAKÁN (33' own goal), 2-0 Damir VRABAC
(61'), 3-0 Damir VRABAC (68'), 4-0 Dragan MIRKOVIC (72').
Attendance: 3.000

27-03-1985   Ostrava: TJ Baník Ostrava OKD   Atalanta Bergamo   0-0
TJ Baník Ostrava OKD: Stanislav VAHALA, Jirí JURÁSEK, Lubomír SRÁMEK, Lubomír
(Lubos) ODEHNAL, Karel KULA (..' Dusan FÁBRY), Václav PÉCHÁCEK, Václav
HANYÁS (12' Werner LICKA), Petr NEMEC, Zdenek VÁLEK, Zdenek SREINER, Zdynek
OLLENDER. (Coach: Josef KOLECKO).
Atalanta Bergamo: Ottorino PIOTTI, Carlo OSTI, MILANI, Eugenio PERICO, Giampaolo
ROSSI, Giorgio MAGNOCAVALLO, Glenn Peter STRÖMBERG (SWE), Enrico VELLA,
Lars (Lasse) LARSSON (SWE) (85' Andrea AGOSTINELLI), Diego BORTOLUZZI, Sauro
FATTORI (60' Marino MAGRIN). (Coach: Nedo SONETTI).
Referee: Helmut KOHL (AUT)

03-04-1985   Bergamo: Atalanta Bergamo – NK Iskra Bugojno   1-0 (1-0)
Atalanta Bergamo: Nello MALIZIA, Carlo OSTI, Carmine GENTILE, Enrico VELLA,
Giampaolo ROSSI, Eugenio PERICO, Glenn Peter STRÖMBERG (SWE), Roberto
DONADONI, Lars (Lasse) LARSSON (SWE), Diego BORTOLUZZI (81' Giorgio
MAGNOCAVALLO), Sauro FATTORI (74' Marino MAGRIN). (Coach: Nedo SONETTI).
NK Iskra Bugojno: Drazen LADIC, Dragan GLAMOCAK, Milomir CEREMIDZIC, Milos
RADOVIC, Vatroslav PETRINOVIC, Nedzad OMERHODZIC, Nebojsa OROZ, Miralem
ZJAJO, Zoran TOSKIC, Goran PAVLIC (58' Damir VRABAC), Dragan MIRKOVIC.
(Coach: Blagoje BRATIC).
Goal: Atalanta Bergamo: 1-0 Lars (Lasse) LARSSON (42').
Referee: Robert JACZINA (HUN)

10-04-1985   Kórház utcai stadion, Békéscsaba:
            Békéscsabai Elöre Spartacus SC – TJ Baník Ostrava OKD   1-0 (0-0)
Békéscsabai Elöre Spartacus SC: Imre LEBONICZKY, Tibor VÍGH, Mihály OTTLAKÁN,
József TAKÁCS, György FABULYA, Zoltán STEIGERWALD, Árpád ADORJÁN, István
FECSKU, Zoltán KANYÁRI (YC64) (64' Zoltán ÚJVÁRI), Béla MELIS (77' Károly
KIRÁLYVÁRI), József SZEKERES. (Coach: István SÜLE).
TJ Baník Ostrava OKD: Stanislav VAHALA, Jirí JURÁSEK, Lubomír SRÁMEK, Pavel
VRBA, Alois GRUSSMANN, Jirí ZÁLESKÝ, Karel KULA, Václav HANYÁS (80' Libor
SZILAS), Zdynek OLLENDER (64' Dusan HORVÁTH), Lubomír (Lubos) ODEHNAL,
Roman SIALINI. (Coach: Josef KOLECKO).
Goal: Békéscsabai Elöre Spartacus SC: 1-0 István FECSKU (69').
Attendance: 1.000

24-04-1985   Stadio Atleti Azzuri d'Italia, Bergamo:
            Atalanta Bergamo – Békéscsabai Elöre Spartacus SC   2-2 (1-0)
Atalanta Bergamo: Nello MALIZIA, Carlo OSTI, Maurizio CODOGNO, Andrea
AGOSTINELLI, Giampaolo ROSSI, Enrico VELLA, Glenn Peter STRÖMBERG (SWE) (64'
Corrado CORTESI), Marino MAGRIN (64' Gianmario CONSONNI), Sauro FATTORI
(YC27,RC79), Roberto DONADONI, Lars (Lasse) LARSSON (SWE). (Coach: Nedo
SONETTI).
Békéscsabai Elöre Spartacus SC: Imre LEBONICZKY, Károly KIRÁLYVÁRI, József
PÁSZTOR (YC32) (75' János PLÁSTYIK), József TAKÁCS, Mihály OTTLAKÁN (RC40),
Attila KEREKES (YC82), Zoltán KANYÁRI (46' Zoltán STEIGERWALD), Árpád
ADORJÁN, Béla MELIS, István FECSKU, József SZEKERES. (Coach: István SÜLE).
Goals: Atalanta Bergamo: 1-0 Marino MAGRIN (40' penalty), 2-2 Enrico VELLA (81').
Békéscsabai Elöre Spartacus SC: 1-1 István FECSKU (54'), 1-2 Árpád ADORJÁN (61').
Referee: Damir MATOVINOVIC (YUG)   Attendance: 6.000

27-04-1985   Ostrava: TJ Baník Ostrava OKD – NK Iskra Bugojno   1-1
Goals: TJ Baník Ostrava OKD: 1-0 Petr NEMEC (..').
NK Iskra Bugojno: 1-1 Damir VRABAC (..').

Pos	Team	Pld	W	D	L	GF	GA	GD	Pts
1	*NK Iskra Bugojno (YUG)*	*6*	*3*	*2*	*1*	*9*	*3*	*+6*	*8*
2	Atalanta Bergamo (ITA)	6	2	3	1	5	5	0	7
3	TJ Baník Ostrava OKD (TCH)	6	1	3	2	2	3	-1	5
4	Békéscsabai Elöre Spartacus SC (HUN)	6	1	2	3	5	10	-5	4

*** NK Iskra Bugojno won the Cup ***

1985-1986

14-11-1985   Arena Garibaldi, Pisa: Pisa SC – TJ Sigma ZTS Olomouc   1-0 (0-0)
Pisa SC: Alessandro MANNINI, Stefano COLANTUONO, Giuseppe VOLPECINA, Roberto
CHITI (58' Klaus BERGGREEN (DEN)), Franco IPSARO PASSIONE, Domenico PROGNA,
Ciro MURO, Michele ARMENISE, Willem Cornelis Nicolaas (Wim) KIEFT (HOL), Paolo
GIOVANNELLI (86' Antonio CAVALLO), Ferruccio MARIANI. (Coach: Vincenzo
GUERINI).
TJ Sigma ZTS Olomouc: Zdenek TULIS, Jirí MALÍK, Miroslav MLEJNEK, Oto VYSKOCIL,
Ladislav KUCERNÁK (81' Pavel JERÁBEK), Leos KALVODA, Jirí FIALA, Miroslav
PRÍLOZNÝ, Jaromír FIALA, Rudolf MUCHKA, Vladimír SISMA. (Coach: Karel
BRÜCKNER).
Goal: Pisa SC: 1-0 Klaus BERGGREEN (77').
Referee: Stjepan GLAVINA (YUG)   Attendance: 14.000

14-11-1985   Stadio Porta Elisa, Lucca: Debreceni VSC – NK Rijeka   1-0
Debreceni VSC: József MEZÖ, Tamás CSEKE, Lajos NAGY, Lajos TILL, József DURÓ,
János SZÜCS, Zsolt BÜCS (..' Béla MÖRTEL), Balász MAGYAR, József SZABÓ (..' Sándor
CSABA), Zsolt MAGYAR, Sándor BENYÓ. (Coach: Lajos PUSKÁS).
NK Rijeka: Mauro RAVNIC, Igor JELAVIC, Nikica MILENKOVIC, Robert PALISKA,
Radoslav LJEPOJEVIC, Borce SREDOJEVIC, Nebojsa MALBASA, Nenad GRACAN, Darko
MATRIJAN, Predrag VALENCIC (..' Davor RADMANOVIC), Janko JANKOVIC (..' Vlado
KOTUR).
Goal: Debreceni VSC: 1-0 Béla MÖRTEL (60').
Referee: Robert MATUSÍK (TCH)   Attendance: 10.000

17-11-1985   Arena Garibaldi, Pisa: NK Rijeka – TJ Sigma ZTS Olomouc   3-2 (1-0)
NK Rijeka:
TJ Sigma ZTS Olomouc: Ivan ZIAK, Stanislav SKRÍCEK, Miroslav MLEJNEK, Petr
MRÁZEK (55' Pavel JERÁBEK), Slavomir HODUL, Jirí MALÍK, Leos KALVODA (46'
Miroslav PRÍLOZNÝ), Vladimír SISMA, Jirí FIALA, Ladislav RICHTER, Rudolf MUCHKA.
(Coach: Karel BRÜCKNER).
Goals: NK Rijeka: STANKOVIC (2x), Nebojsa MALBASA.
TJ Sigma ZTS Olomouc: Rudolf MUCHKA, Jirí FIALA.
Referee: Miklós NAGY (HUN)   Attendance: 20.000

FINAL

17-11-1985   Arena Garibaldi, Pisa: Pisa SC – Debreceni VSC   2-0 (1-0)
Pisa SC: Alessandro MANNINI, Stefano COLANTUONO (86' Roberto CHITI), Giuseppe
VOLPECINA, Ferruccio MARIANI, Franco IPSARO PASSIONE, Domenico PROGNA,
Klaus BERGGREEN (DEN), Michele ARMENISE, Willem Cornelis Nicolaas (Wim) KIEFT
(HOL), Paolo GIOVANNELLI, Ciro MURO (58' Paolo BALDIERI). (Coach: Vincenzo
GUERINI).
Debreceni VSC: József MEZÖ, Tamás CSEKE (68' István VARGA), Lajos NAGY (35' Zsolt
BÜCS), József DURÓ, Lajos TILL, János SZÜCS, Zsolt MAGYAR, Balász MAGYAR,
László SZABÓ, Béla MÖRTEL, Sándor BENYÓ. (Coach: Lajos PUSKÁS).
Goals: Pisa SC: 1-0 Stefano COLANTUONO (42'), 2-0 Wim KIEFT (77').
Referee: Robert MATUSÍK (TCH)   Attendance: 10.870

*** Pisa SC won the Cup ***

1986-1987

14-11-1986   Stadio Ferranti, Porto Sant'Elpidio:
TJ Bohemians CKD Praha – Vasas SC   3-1 (3-0)
TJ Bohemians CKD Praha: Adrian HUBEK, Zdenek SCASNÝ (68' Jaroslav JERÁBEK),
Frantisek JAKUBEC, Tomás MATEJCEK, Jirí TYMICH (66' Milan SKODA), Josef VINS,
Peter ZELENSKÝ, Milos BELÁK, Pavel CHALOUPKA, Tibor MICINEC, Zdenek VÁLEK.
(Coach: Tomás POSPÍCHAL).
Vasas SC: Attila KOVÁCS, Tibor FARKAS, József ELEKES, János CSORBA, István
SZÍJÁRTÓ, Tibor BALOG, Géza MÉSZÖLY, István BODNÁR (51' Vaszilisz TEODORU),
László GUBUCZ (37' Péter GALASCHEK), László SZBADI, Mihály BOROSTYÁN.
(Coach: István KISTELEKI).
Goals: TJ Bohemians CKD Praha: 1-0 Zdenek VÁLEK (9'), 2-0 Zdenek VÁLEK (13'), 3-0
Zdenek VÁLEK (27').
Vasas SC: 3-1 István SZÍJÁRTÓ (60').
Referee: Branko BUJIC (YUG)   Attendance: 1.000

14-11-1986   Ascoli Piceno: Ascoli Calcio – FK Spartak Subotica   2-1 (2-0)
Ascoli Calcio: Andrea PAZZAGLI, Paolo AGABITINI, Catello CIMMINO, Guiseppe
IACHINI, Aleksandar TRIFUNOVIC (YUG), Antonio DELL'OGLIO, Fulvio BONOMI,
Vittorio PUSCEDDU, Lorenzo SCRARAFONI, Guiseppe GRECO (76' Alberto
MARCHETTI), Domenico AGOSTINI (70'Giuseppe CARILLO). (Coach: Ilario
CASTAGNER).
FK Spartak Subotica: Slobodan SUJICA, JABO, Radivoje DJUROVIC, CORYAK (76' Antal
PUHALAK), Zoran ARSIC, Miodrag KOVACEVIC, Senad KARAC, Zoran DIMITRIJEVIC,
Zivko SLIJEPCEVIC, KLOB, VIKODIJEVIC (46' NJARI).
Goals: Ascoli Calcio: 1-0 GRECO (16'), 2-0 IACHINI (43').
FK Spartak Subotica: 2-1 NJARI (67').
Referee: György DRIGAN (HUN)

THIRD PLACE MATCH

16-11-1986   Stadio Ferranti, Porto Sant'Elpidio:
Vasas SC – FK Spartak Subotica   2-0 (1-0)
Vasas SC: Attila KOVÁCS, Géza MÉSZÖLY, József ELEKES, Tibor BALOG, László
GUBUCZ, István SZÍJÁRTÓ, Vaszilisz TEODORU, István BODNÁR, Péter GALASCHEK,
Mihály BOROSTYÁN, László SZBADI (65' Attila KECSKÉS). (Coach: István KISTELEKI).
FK Spartak Subotica: Slobodan SUJICA, KLOB, Rudolf RAFAI, Dragoljub LJILJAK,
Miodrag KOVACEVIC, Zoran ARSIC, Senad KARAC, Zoran DIMITRIJEVIC, Zivko
SLIJEPCEVIC (60' Antal PUHALAK), Ivica VUJICEVIC, NOVAKOVIC.
Goals: Vasas SC: 1-0 Vaszilisz TEODORU (3'), 2-0 Péter GALASCHEK (64').
Referee: Dusan KRCHNÁK (TCH)   Attendance: 1.000

FINAL

16-11-1986   Ascoli Piceno: Ascoli Calcio – TJ Bohemians CKD Praha   1-0
Ascoli Calcio: Andrea PAZZAGLI, Silvano BENEDETTI, Catello CIMMINO, Guiseppe
IACHINI, Aleksandar TRIFUNOVIC (YUG), Antonio DELL'OGLIO, Fulvio BONOMI,
Vittorio PUSCEDDU, Lorenzo SCRARAFONI (79' Alberto MARCHETTI), Guiseppe
GRECO, Massimo BARBUTI. (Coach: Ilario CASTAGNER).
TJ Bohemians CKD Praha: Milan SVENGR, Frantisek JAKUBEC, Tomás MATEJCEK, Peter
ZELENSKÝ, Jirí TYMICH, Josef VINS, Zdenek SCASNÝ, Pavel CHALOUPKA, Tibor
MICINEC, Zdenek VÁLEK, Milos BELÁK. (Coach: Tomás POSPÍCHAL).
Goal: Ascoli Calcio: 1-0 BONOMI (85' penalty).
Referee: Branko BUJIC (YUG)

*** Ascoli Calcio won the Cup ***

1987-1988

GROUP A

24-05-1988   Arena Garibaldi, Pisa: Pescara Calcio – Váci Izzó MTE   4-1 (1-1)
Pescara Calcio: … (Coach: Giovanni GALEONE).
Váci Izzó MTE: István BROCKHAUSER, Tamás KOSZTOLNIK, Tibor TALAPA, László
KÓSA, György CSIMA, Tibor NAGY, Sándor HERMANN, Attila GYIMESI (..' Csaba
CSIKÓS, Péter VÍG, József ZVARA (..' János MÓZNER), Péter DURUCSKÓ. (Coach:
Sándor HAÁSZ).
Goals: Pescara Calcio: 1-1 Rocco PAGANO (20'), 2-1 Stefano FERRETTI (59'), 3-1 Primo
BERLINGHIERI (67'), 4-1 Rocco PAGANO (82').
Váci Izzó MTE: 0-1 Péter DURUCSKÓ (5').

26-05-1988   Arena Garibaldi, Pisa:
                Pescara Calcio – TJ Slovan CHZJD Bratislava   0-1 (0-0)
Pescara Calcio:
TJ Slovan CHZJD Bratislava: …, Eugen VARGA. (Coach: Ján ZACHAR).
Goal: TJ Slovan Bratislava: 0-1 Eugen VARGA (73').

28-05-1988   Arena Garibaldi, Pisa:
                Váci Izzó MTE – TJ Slovan CHZJD Bratislava   6-0 (4-0)
Váci Izzó MTE: István BROCKHAUSER, Tamás KOSZTOLNIK, Tibor TALAPA, László
KÓSA, György CSIMA, Tibor NAGY, János PAKSI (60' Sándor HERMANN), Péter VÍG,
Tibor BALOG, János MÓZNER (77' József ZVARA), Péter DURUCSKÓ. (Coach: Sándor
HAÁSZ).
TJ Slovan CHZJD Bratislava: Karel STROMSIK, Miroslav HIRKO, Rudolf DUCKY, …
(Coach: Ján ZACHAR).
Goals: Váci Izzó MTE: 1-0 Tibor BALOG (7'), 2-0 Péter VÍG (22'), 3-0 János MÓZNER
(24'), 4-0 Tibor TALAPA (43'), 5-0 Tibor NAGY (59'), 6-0 János MÓZNER (76').
Referee: Romeo PAPARESTA (ITA)   Attendance: 2.000

Pos	Team	Pld	W	D	L	GF	GA	GD	Pts
1	*Váci Izzó MTE (HUN)*	2	*1*	*0*	*1*	*7*	*4*	*+3*	*2*
2	Pescara Calcio (ITA)	2	1	0	1	4	2	+2	2
3	TJ Slovan CHZJD Bratislava (TCH)	2	1	0	1	1	6	-5	2

*** Váci Izzó MTE won the group and qualified for the Final ***

GROUP B

24-05-1988   Arena Garibaldi, Pisa: Pisa SC – Kaposvári Rákóczi SC   2-0 (0-0)
Pisa SC: Alessandro NISTA, Antonio CAVALLO, Daniele BERNAZZANI, Mario
FACCENDA, Claudio SCLOSA (70' Aldo DOLCETTI), Stefano DIANDA, Stefano
CUOGHI, Bruno CANEO, Ricardo PACIOCCO (84' David FIORENTINI), Marinus Antonius
(Mario) BEEN (HOL), Luca CECCONI. (Coach: Giuseppe MATERAZZI).
Kaposvári Rákóczi SC: Attila KOVÁCS, János KURDI, Antal DEÁKVÁRI (..' Lajos BÓCZ),
László RÁCZ, László BARNA, László PRUKNER, Antal BÍRÓ, Zoltán KRAFT, István
ADORJÁN, Tamás CSREPKA (..' Lajos HAVASI), Gyula MEKSZ. (Coach: István
CSORDÁS).
Goals: Pisa SC: 1-0 Daniele BERNAZZANI (49'), 2-0 Luca CECCONI (65').
Attendance: 10.000

26-05-1988   Arena Garibaldi, Pisa:
               FK Vojvodina Novi Sad – Kaposvári Rákóczi SC   3-0 (2-0)
FK Vojvodina Novi Sad:
Kaposvári Rákóczi SC: Róbert SÁNDORFI, János KURDI, Zoltán KRAFT, László RÁCZ,
László BARNA, László PRUKNER (65' Antal BÍRÓ), Lájos BÓCZ, Tibor GYURICS, János
HANUSZ, Lajos HAVASI (46' István ADORJAN), Gyula MEKSZ. (Coach: István
CSORDÁS).
Goals: FK Vojvodina Novi Sad: 1-0 Marijan ZOVKO (4'), 2-0 Zoran MIJUCIC (21'), 3-0
Samid BEGANOVIC (64').
Referee: Pier-Luigi PAIRETTO (ITA)   Attendance: 1.000

27-05-1988   Arena Garibaldi, Pisa: Pisa SC – FK Vojvodina Novi Sad   1-0 (1-0)
Pisa SC: Alessandro NISTA, Antonio CAVALLO, Daniele BERNAZZANI, Mario
FACCENDA, Claudio SCLOSA, Stefano DIANDA, Stefano CUOGHI, Bruno CANEO,
Ricardo PACIOCCO (78' Aldo DOLCETTI), Marinus Antonius (Mario) BEEN (HOL) (75'
David FIORENTINI), Luca CECCONI. (Coach: Giuseppe MATERAZZI).
FK Vojvodina Novi Sad: Goran SKAVIC, Dragan GACESA, Budimir VUJACIC, Svetozar
SAPURIC, Marijan ZOVKO, Milan POPOVIC, Samid BEGANOVIC (81' Vladimir
TOKOVIC), Dragan MARKOVIC, Goran POPOVIC, Milos SESTIC (46' Ljubomir
VORKAPIC), Zoran MIJUCIC. (Coach: Ivan BRZIC).
Goal: Pisa SC: 1-0 Stefano CUOGHI (16').
Referee: László NAGY (HUN)

Pos	Team	Pld	W	D	L	GF	GA	GD	Pts
1	Pisa SC (ITA)	2	2	0	0	3	0	+3	4
2	FK Vojvodina Novi Sad (YUG)	2	1	0	1	3	1	+2	2
3	Kaposvári Rákóczi SC (HUN)	2	0	0	2	0	5	-5	0

*** Pisa SC won the group and qualified for the Final ***

30-05-1988   Arena Garibaldi, Pisa: Pisa SC – Váci Izzó MTE   3-0 (2-0)
Pisa SC: Alessandro NISTA (81' Gianpaolo GRUDINA), Antonio CAVALLO, Daniele
BERNAZZANI, Mario FACCENDA, Claudio SCLOSA, Stefano DIANDA, Stefano
CUOGHI, Bruno CANEO (82' David FIORENTINI), Aldo DOLCETTI, Marinus Antonius
(Mario) BEEN (HOL) (86' Silvio GORI), Luca CECCONI. (Coach: Giuseppe MATERAZZI).
Váci Izzó MTE: István BROCKHAUSER, Tamás KOSZTOLNIK, Tibor TALAPA, György
CSIMA, László KÓSA, Tibor NAGY, Tibor BALOG, Sándor HERMANN, János MÓZNER
(54' József ZVARA), Péter VÍG, Péter DURUCSKÓ (62' János PAKSI). (Coach: Sándor
HAÁSZ).
Goals: Pisa SC: 1-0 Luca CECCONI (33'), 2-0 Claudio SCLOSA (36'), 3-0 Daniele
BERNAZZANI (75').
Referee: Rudolf LÍSKA (TCH)   Attendance: 25.000

*** Pisa SC won the Cup ***

1988-1989

SEMI-FINALS

20-10-1988   Stadio Alberto Braglia, Modena: Bologna FC – Ferencvárosi TC 5-2 (2-0)
Bologna FC: Nello CUSIN, Gianluca LUPPI, Renato VILLA (YC68) (73' Stéphane DEMOL
(BEL)), Eraldo PECCI, Marco DE MARCHI, Ivano BONETTI, Mika A.AALTONEN (FIN),
Angelo ALESSIO, Giuseppe LORENZO (59' Massimo BONINI (SMR)), Paolo
STRINGARA, Lorenzo MARRONARO. (Coach: Luigi MAIFREDI).
Ferencvárosi TC: Miklós JÓZSA, Gyula VASZIL, Tibor SIMON, Iván BÚS, Zsolt NAGY,
Zsolt LIMPERGER (46' Antal TOPOR), László WUKOVICS, József BÁNKI (YC80) (80'
László STRAUSZ), Pál FISCHER, Sándor KINCSES, Béla DUKON. (Coach: Gyula
RÁKOSI).
Goals: Bologna FC: 1-0 Giuseppe LORENZO (43'), 2-0 Lorenzo MARRONARO (44'), 3-0
Lorenzo MARRONARO (54'), 4-2 Mika A.AALTONEN (87'), 5-2 Lorenzo MARRONARO
(90').
Ferenvárosi TC: 3-1 Sándor KINCSES (57'), 3-2 Sándor KINCSES (78').
Referee: Sinasi BERISA (YUG)   Attendance: 3.000

02-11-1988   Úllói úti Stadion, Budapest: Ferencvárosi TC – Bologna FC 3-3 (1-3)
Ferencvárosi TC: Miklós JÓZSA, Gyula VASZIL, Attila PINTÉR, József KELLER, Zsolt
NAGY, Zsolt LIMPERGER, Zsolt VAJDA (71' Zsolt PÁLING), Antal TOPOR, Pál
FISCHER, József DZURJÁK (46' László WUKOVICS), Béla DUKON. (Coach: Gyula
RÁKOSI).
Bologna FC: Roberto SORRENTINO (YC85), Gianluca LUPPI, Renato VILLA, Marco DE
MARCHI, Stéphane DEMOL (BEL), Marco MONZA (56' Paolo STRINGARA), Fabio POLI
(65' Massimo GIANNELLI), Massimo BONINI (SMR), Giuseppe LORENZO, Angelo
ALESSIO, Mika A.AALTONEN (FIN). (Coach: Luigi MAIFREDI).
Goals: Ferencvárosi TC: 1-1 Antal TOPOR (31'), 2-3 Pál FISCHER (73' penalty), 3-3 Pál
FISCHER (86' penalty).
Bologna FC: 0-1 Fabio POLI (26'), 1-2 Giuseppe LORENZO (33'), 1-3 Fabio POLI (34').
Referee: Rudolf LÍSKA (TCH)   Attendance: 7.000

*TJ Baník Ostrava OKD qualified for the final without playing a game after FK Vojvodina Novi
Sad withdrew from the competition.*

FINAL

12-11-1988   Bazaly Stadion, Ostrava: TJ Baník Ostrava OKD – Bologna FC 2-1 (1-1)
TJ Baník Ostrava OKD: Jirí RICHTER, Dusan FÁBRY, Miroslav ONUFER, Karel KULA,
Libor FRYC, Jirí ZÁLESKÝ, Radomír CHÝLEK (84' Josef ZAJÍCEK), Ivo STAS, Dusan
VRTO, Radim NECAS, Roman SIALINI. (Coach: Milan MÁCALA).
Bologna FC: Roberto SORRENTINO (40' Nello CUSIN), Gianluca LUPPI, Renato VILLA,
Paolo STRINGARA, Marco DE MARCHI, Marco MONZA, Fabio POLI, Angelo ALESSIO,
Giuseppe LORENZO (65' Massimo BONINI (SMR)), Ivano BONETTI, Mika A.AALTONEN
(FIN). (Coach: Luigi MAIFREDI).
Goals: TJ Baník Ostrava OKD: 1-1 Radomír CHÝLEK (32'), 2-1 Dusan FÁBRY (58').
Bologna FC: 0-1 Angelo ALESSIO (14').
Referee: Friedrich KAUPE (AUT)   Attendance: 1.046

268

08-12-1988   Stadio Renato Dall'Ara, Bologna:
Bologna FC – TJ Baník Ostrava OKD   1-2 (0-1)
Bologna FC: Roberto SORRENTINO, Marco DE MARCHI, Renato VILLA, Gianluca LUPPI, Stéphane DEMOL (BEL), Marco MONZA (59' Paolo STRINGARA), Fabio POLI, Ivano BONETTI, Lorenzo MARRONARO, Mika A.AALTONEN (FIN) (46' Hugo Eduardo RUBIO Montecinos (CHI)), Angelo ALESSIO. (Coach: Luigi MAIFREDI).
TJ Baník Ostrava OKD: Ludek MIKLOSKO, Petr SKARABELA, Miroslav ONUFER, Karel KULA, Viliam HÝRAVÝ (30' Dusan FÁBRY), Jirí ZÁLESKÝ, Radomír CHÝLEK, Ivo STAS (72' Václav PECHÁCEK), Václav DANEK, Radim NECAS, Roman SIALINI. (Coach: Milan MÁCALA).
Goals: Bologna FC: 1-1 Fabio POLI (79').
TJ Baník Ostrava OKD: 0-1 Václav DANEK (15' penalty), 1-2 Václav DANEK (88').
Referee: Heinz HOLZMANN (AUT)   Attendance: 5.000

*** TJ Baník Ostrava OKD won the Cup ***

1990

17-05-1990   Stadio della Vittoria, Bari: Bari AS – Pécsi Munkás SC 3-0 (1-0)
Bari AS: Alessandro MANNINI, Giampaolo CERAMICOLA, Angelo CARBONE, Angelo
TERRACENERE, Ubaldo RIGHETTI, Corrado URBANO, Carlo PERRONE, GERSON
Candido de Paulo (BRA), "JOÃO PAULO" Sérgio Luis Donizetti (BRA), Pietro
MAIELLARO, Paolo MONELLI. (Coach: Gaetano SALVEMINI).
Pécsi Munkás SC: László BODNÁR (73' KOVACESIC), Mihály KÓNYA, Gábor MÁRTON,
János PALACZKY, Károly BRAUN (21' János TOMKA), Sándor CZÉRNA, Lajos BOJÁS,
NAGY, László CZÉH, CSOBOTH, István LEHOTA (73' Bálazs BÉRCZY). (Coach: József
GARAMI).
Goals: Bari AS: 1-0 Paolo MONELLI (27'), 2-0Pietro MAIELLARO (59'), 3-0 "JOÃO
PAULO" Sérgio Luis Donizetti (66').
Referee: Robert MATUSÍK (TCH)   Attendance: 7.000

18-05-1990   Stadio Cittá Degli Ulivi, Bitonto:
              FK Radnicki Nis – Pécsi Munkás SC   1-0 (1-0)
FK Radnicki Nis: Zavisa PEJIC, Miodrag MOMCILOVIC, Zoran MILOSEVIC, Aleksandar
KUZMANOVIC, Blagoja KULEVSKI, Goran ANTIC, Nenad JAKSIC, Sasa MRKIC, Goran
STOJILJKOVIC, Josip VISNJIC, Milan TEPIC.
Pécsi Munkás SC: László BODNÁR, Mihály KÓNYA, Gábor MÁRTON, GYURKITUY,
János TOMKA, Sándor CZÉRNA, Lajos BOJÁS, NAGY, László CZÉH, CSOBOTH, István
LEHOTA. (Coach: József GARAMI).
Goal: FK Radnicki Nis: 1-0 Goran ANTIC (20').
Referee: Pier-Lugig MAGNI (ITA)   Attendance: 100

19-05-1990   Stadio Cosimo Puttilli, Barletta: Bari AS – FK Radnicki Nis 3-0 (0-0)
Bari AS: Giulio DRAGO, Giampaolo CERAMICOLA, Lorenzo AMORUSO, Angelo
TERRACENERE (70' Corrado URBANO), Ubaldo RIGHETTI, Fabio LUPO, Carlo
PERRONE (46' Angelo CARBONE), GERSON Candido de Paulo (BRA) (55' Pietro
MAIELLARO), "JOÃO PAULO" Sérgio Luis Donizetti (BRA), Fabrizio FIORETTI, Lorenzo
SCARAFONI. (Coach: Gaetano SALVEMINI).
FK Radnicki Nis: Darko ZARIC (60' Zavisa PEJIC), Zoran MILOSEVIC, Miodrag
MOMCILOVIC, Aleksandar KUZMANOVIC, Blagoja KULEVSKI, Goran ANTIC (60'
Aleksandar MOMIROVIC), Nenad JAKSIC, Sasa MRKIC, Goran STOJILJKOVIC, Josip
VISNJIC, Milan TEPIC.
Goals: Bari AS: 1-0 Fabio LUPO (63'), 2-0 Lorenzo SCARAFONI (67'), 3-0 Lorenzo
SCARAFONI (71').
Referee: Robert MATUSÍK (TCH)   Attendance: 1.000

Pos	Team	Pld	W	D	L	GF	GA	GD	Pts
1	Bari AS (ITA)	2	2	0	0	6	0	+6	4
2	FK Radnicki Nis (YUG)	2	1	0	1	1	3	-2	2
3	Pécsi Munkás SC (HUN)	2	0	0	2	0	4	-4	0

*** Bari AS won the group and qualified for the Final ***

17-05-1990   Stadio Degli Ulivi, Andria: Genoa 1893 – SK Slavia Praha IPS   0-0
Genoa 1893: Simone BRAGLIA, Vincenzo TORRENTE, Armando FERRONI (II), Gennaro
RUOTOLO, Nicola CARICOLA (II), Gianluca SIGNORINI, Stefano ERANIO, Valeriano
FIORIN, Davide FONTOLAN (II), Alberto URBAN, Franco ROTELLA. (Coach: Franco
SCOGLIO).
SK Slavia Praha IPS: Lubos PRIBYL, Roman KOMÁREK, Jaroslav SILHAVÝ, Ludek
KLUSÁCEK, Dusan SUSKO, Lubomír FAKTOR, Tomás URBAN (68' Lubos
ZÁKOSTELSKÝ), Pavel REHÁK, Robert ZÁK, Pavel VANDAS (79' Frantisek VESELÝ),
Pavel KUKA. (Coach: Ivan KOPECKÝ).
Referee: Branko BUJIC (YUG)   Attendance: 3.500

18-05-1990   Stadio Cittá Degli Ulivi, Bitonto: SK Slavia Praha IPS – NK Osijek   2-0 (1-0)
SK Slavia Praha IPS: Zdenek JÁNOS, Roman KOMÁREK, Ludek KLUSÁCEK, Dusan
SUSKO, Jaroslav SILHAVÝ (YC), Robert ZÁK (65' Lubomír FAKTOR), Frantisek VESELÝ
(85' Lubos ZÁKOSTELSKÝ), Gustáv ONDREJCÍK, Pavel KUKA, Pavel VANDAS (60'
Slavomír GALBAVÝ), Pavel REHÁK. (Coach: Ivan KOPECKÝ).
NK Osijek: Miroslav ZITNJAK, Miroslav BICANIC (65' Ivica VLADIMIR), Jasmin
SINANOVIC, Milan MARICIC, Alen PETROVIC, Miljenko MILICEVIC, Dragan
LEPINJICA (15' Midhat GLUHACEVIC), Zeljko PAKASIN, Ivica DUSPARA (72' Robert
PEVNIK (YC)), Milenko VUKCEVIC, Tomislav STAJNBRIKNER.
Goals: SK Slavia Praha IPS: 1-0 Pavel KUKA (..'), 2-0 Pavel KUKA (..').
Referee: Carlo LONGHI (ITA)   Attendance: 300

19-05-1990   Stadio della Vittoria, Bari: Genoa 1893 – NK Osijek   6-0 (3-0)
Genoa 1893: Simone BRAGLIA, Armando FERRONI (II), Nicola CARICOLA (II), Gennaro
RUOTOLO (52' Giovanni FASCE), Fulvio COLLOVATI, Gianluca SIGNORINI, Stefano
ERANIO (56' Massimiliano COVELLI), Valeriano FIORIN (YC) (65' Cristian SCAZZOLA),
Davide FONTOLAN (II), Alberto URBAN, Franco ROTELLA. (Coach: Franco SCOGLIO).
NK Osijek: Miroslav ZITNJAK, Robert PEVNIK (YC), Jasmin SINANOVIC, Milan
MARICIC, Ivica VLADIMIR, Miljenko MILICEVIC (60' Miroslav BICANIC), Midhat
GLUHACEVIC, Zeljko PAKASIN, Ivica DUSPARA, Milenko VUKCEVIC, Tomislav
STAJNBRIKNER.
Goals: Genoa 1893: 1-0 Valeriano FIORIN (8'), 2-0 Gennaro RUOTOLO (26'), 3-0 Valeriano
FIORIN (40'), 4-0 Armando FERRONI (53'), 5-0 Alberto URBAN (56'), 6-0 Nicola
CARICOLA (90').
Referee: LAZIN (HUN)   Attendance: 100

Pos	Team	Pld	W	D	L	GF	GA	GD	Pts
1	*Genoa 1893 (ITA)*	2	1	1	0	6	0	+6	3
2	SK Slavia Praha IPS (TCH)	2	1	1	0	2	0	+2	3
3	NK Osijek (YUG)	2	0	0	2	0	8	-8	0

*** Genoa 1893 won the group and qualified for the Final ***

271

21-05-1990   Stadio San Nicola, Bari: Bari AS – Genoa 1893   1-0 (1-0)
Bari AS: Alessandro MANNINI, Giampaolo CERAMICOLA (YC), Angelo CARBONE (88'
Lorenzo AMORUSO), Angelo TERRACENERE (67' Fabio LUPO), Ubaldo RIGHETTI,
Massimo BRAMBATI, Carlo PERRONE, Corrado URBANO, "JOÃO PAULO" Sérgio Luis
Donizetti (BRA), GERSON Candido de Paulo (BRA), Lorenzo SCARAFONI (61' Paolo
MONELLI). (Coach: Gaetano SALVEMINI).
Genoa 1893: Simone BRAGLIA, Armando FERRONI (II), Nicola CARICOLA (II) (YC),
Gennaro RUOTOLO, Fulvio COLLOVATI (YC), Gianluca SIGNORINI, Stefano ERANIO
(87' Massimiliano COVELLI), Valeriano FIORIN, Davide FONTOLAN (II), Alberto
URBAN, Franco ROTELLA. (Coach: Franco SCOGLIO).
Goal: Bari AS: 1-0 Carlo PERRONE (14').
Referee: Branko BUJIC (YUG)   Attendance: 3.600

*** Bari AS won the Cup ***

1991

GROUP A

01-06-1991   Stadio delle Alpi, Torino: AC Torino – SK Vorwärts Steyr   1-0 (1-0)
AC Torino: Raffaele DI FUSCO, Pasquale BRUNO, Roberto MUSSI (41' Rafael MARTÍN VÁZQUEZ (ESP)), Enrico ANNONI, Silvano BENEDETTI, Roberto CRAVERO (46' Francesco ROMANO), Luca FUSI, Giuseppe CARILLO, AMARILDO Souza do Amaral (BRA), Giorgio VENTURIN, Roberto POLICANO. (Coach: Emiliano MONDONICO).
SK Vorwärts Steyr: Manfred TROST, Peter BARAC (25' Róland Alfonso GONZÁLEZ Brenes (CRC)), Radan LUKIC (YUG), Kurt HOCHEDLINGER (67' Ljubo PETROVIC (YUG)), Frank KASTNER (FRG), Frank KIRCHHOFF (FRG) (72' Tomislav KOCIJAN), Thomas URBAN (TCH), Michael NOVAK, Franz FEIRER, Gernot KRINNER, Slobodan BRANKOVIC (YUG). (Coach: Felix LATZKE).
Goal: AC Torino: 1-0 Roberto POLICANO (42').
Referee: Mateo BEUSAN (YUG)   Attendance: 5.000
(Thomas URBAN appeared as a guest player).

02-06-1991   Stadio delle Alpi, Torino: SK Vorwärts Steyr – Veszprém FC   2-2 (0-1)
SK Vorwärts Steyr: Markus JETZINGER, Radan LUKIC (YUG) (23' Markus GRABNER), Kurt HOCHEDLINGER, Róland Alfonso GONZÁLEZ Brenes (CRC), Michael NOVAK, Frank KIRCHHOFF (FRG), Thomas URBAN (TCH), Tomislav KOCIJAN, Franz FEIRER, Gernot KRINNER, Slobodan BRANKOVIC (YUG). (Coach: Felix LATZKE).
Veszprém FC: ... (Coach: Róbert GLÁZER).
Goals: SK Vorwärts Steyr: 1-1 Slobodan BRANKOVIC (48' penalty), 2-1 Tomislav KOCIJAN (58').
Veszprém FC: 0-1 Vendel RUGOVICS (29'), 2-2 István LEHOTA (67').

03-06-1991   Stadio delle Alpi, Torino: AC Torino – Veszprém FC   1-0 (0-0)
AC Torino: Raffaele DI FUSCO, Pasquale BRUNO (RC71), Sandro COIS, Luca FUSI, Leovegildo Lins da Gama "LÉO" JÚNIOR (BRA) (70' Francesco ROMANO), Enrico ANNONI, Giuseppe CARILLO, Giorgio VENTURIN, AMARILDO Souza do Amaral (BRA), Rafael MARTÍN VÁZQUEZ (ESP) (70' Alessandro BRUNETTI), Roberto POLICANO. (Coach: Emiliano MONDONICO).
Veszprém FC: Zoltán VÉGH, László HORVÁTH, Tamás BIMBÓ, János SZÉCSI (61' László HORVÁTH (II)), Ferenc CSÍK, Miklós KELEMEN, Gyula PLOTÁR (46' Zsolt KISS), Péter BOGNÁR, János SÜLE (80' Gábor VASS), Vendel RUGOVICS (RC68), István LEHOTA. (Coach: Róbert GLÁZER or possibly DUNAI).
Goal: AC Torino: 1-0 Miklós KELEMEN (48' *own goal*).
Referee: Jozef MARKO (TCH)   Attendance: 1.271

Pos	Team	Pld	W	D	L	GF	GA	GD	Pts
1	*AC Torino (ITA)*	*2*	*2*	*0*	*0*	*2*	*0*	*+2*	*4*
2	Veszprém FC (HUN)	2	0	1	1	2	3	-1	1
3	SK Vorwärts Steyr (AUT)	2	0	1	1	2	3	-1	1

*** AC Torino won the group and qualified for the Final ***

273

01-06-1991   Pisa: Pisa SC – TJ Bohemians CKD Praha   0-0
Pisa SC: Luigi SIMONI, José Antonio CHAMOT Reguero (ARG), Davide LUCARELLI, Mauro BOCCAFRESCA, Mirko TACCOLA, Roberto BOSCO, David FIORENTINI, Paolo CRISTALLINI (70' Aldo DOLCETTI), Cristian POLIDORI, Stefano MARINI, Henrik LARSEN (DEN). (Coach: Luca GIANNINI).
TJ Bohemians CKD Praha: Radek CIMBÁL, Jirí TYMICH, Miroslav CHYTRA, Prokop VÝRAVSKÝ, Libor CIHÁK, Petr HOLOTA (86' Bedrich HAMSA), Vítezslav MOJZÍS (58' Jaroslav NOVOTNÝ), Bohus VÍGER (78' Pavel MEDYNSKÝ), Jaroslav IROVSKÝ, Frantisek MYSLIVECEK, Boris KOCÍ. (Coach: Ladislav LEDECKÝ).
Referee: László VÁGNER (HUN)

02-06-1991   Pisa: TJ Bohemians CKD Praha – FK Rad Beograd   4-2 (2-1)
TJ Bohemians CKD Praha: Radek CIMBÁL, Jirí TYMICH, Pavel MEDYNSKÝ, Prokop VÝRAVSKÝ, Libor CIHÁK, Petr HOLOTA, Jaroslav NOVOTNÝ (72' Vítezslav MOJZÍS), Bohus VÍGER, Jaroslav IROVSKÝ, Frantisek MYSLIVECEK, Boris KOCÍ (60' Vladimír SADÍLEK). (Coach: Ladislav LEDECKÝ).
FK Rad Beograd: Jovan SAVIC, Sasa NEDELJKOVIC (49' Goran ACIMOVIC), Sasa STRBAC, Milan DJUROVIC, Ivica GVOZDEN, Djordje VASIC (49' Mirko MIHIC), Milos DABIC (61' Aleksandar PAJIC), Fahredin DURAK, Nedim TUTIC, Milenko KOVACEVIC, Ljubinko DRULOVIC.
Goals: TJ Bohemians CKD Praha: 1-0 Petr HOLOTA (15'), 2-1 Boris KOCÍ (30'), 3-2 Boris KOCÍ (48'), 4-2 Libor CIHÁK (55').
FK Rad Beograd: 1-1 Milenko KOVACEVIC (17'), 2-2 Nedim TUTIC (46').
Referee: Luciano LUCI (ITA)   Attendance: 1.000

03-06-1991   Pisa: Pisa SC – FK Rad Beograd   4-1 (2-1)
Pisa SC: Luigi SIMONI, José Antonio CHAMOT Reguero (ARG), Davide LUCARELLI (46' Davide MORETTI), Mauro BOCCAFRESCA, Luciano DONDO (64' Diego Pablo SIMEONE González (ARG) (RC)), Roberto BOSCO (YC), David FIORENTINI, Paolo CRISTALLINI (73' Aldo DOLCETTI), Marco FERRANTE, Stefano MARINI, Cristian POLIDORI (YC). (Coach: Luca GIANNINI).
FK Rad Beograd: Jovan SAVIC, Zoran MIRKOVIC, Igor TASEVSKI (YC), Sasa STRBAC (46' Fahredin DURAK, Ivica GVOZDEN, Djordje VASIC, Mirko MIHIC, Goran ACIMOVIC (YC) (52' Sasa NEDELJKOVIC), Milos DABIC (62' Nedim TUTIC (YC)), Milenko KOVACEVIC, Ljubinko DRULOVIC.
Goals: Pisa SC: 1-1 Marco FERRANTE (33'), 2-1 David FIORENTINI (43'), 3-1 David FIORENTINI (60'), 4-1 Antonio CHAMOT Reguero (89').
FK Rad Beograd: 0-1 Ljubinko DRULOVIC (15').
Referee: Friedrich KAUPE (AUT)   Attendance: 500

Pos	Team	Pld	W	D	L	GF	GA	GD	Pts
1	Pisa SC (ITA)	2	1	1	0	4	1	+3	3
2	TJ Bohemians CKD Praha (TCH)	2	1	1	0	4	2	+2	3
3	FK Rad Beograd (YUG)	2	0	0	2	3	8	-5	0

*** Pisa SC won the group and qualified for the Final ***

274

04-06-1991   Stadio delle Alpi, Torino: AC Torino – Pisa SC 2-1 (0-1)
AC Torino: Raffaele DI FUSCO, Enrico ANNONI, Gianluca ATZORI (86' Alessandro
BRUNETTI, 104' Sandro COIS), Luca FUSI, Leovegildo Lins da Gama "LÉO" JÚNIOR
(BRA), Giuseppe CARILLO, Giorgio VENTURIN (59' Davide MEZZANOTTI), Francesco
ROMANO, AMARILDO Souza do Amaral (BRA) (YC), Rafael MARTÍN VÁZQUEZ (ESP),
Roberto POLICANO (RC42). (Coach: Emiliano MONDONICO).
Pisa SC: Luigi SIMONI, José Antonio CHAMOT Reguero (ARG), Mirko TACCOLA (90'
BALDINI), Mauro BOCCAFRESCA (68' Davide MORETTI (YC)), Luciano DONDO (YC),
Roberto BOSCO (YC), David FIORENTINI, Paolo CRISTALLINI, Marco FERRANTE,
Stefano MARINI, Cristian POLIDORI (89' DIANDA). (Coach: Luca GIANNINI).
Goals: AC Torino: 1-1 Rafael MARTIN VAZQUEZ (89' penalty), 2-1 Giuseppe CARILLO
(104').
Pisa SC: 0-1 Cristian POLIDORI (39').
Referee: László VÁGNER (HUN)   Attendance: 3.018

(After extra time)

*** **AC Torino won the Cup** ***

1992

27-05-1992   Stadio Pino Zaccheria, Foggia: US Foggia – FK Borac Banja Luka   2-2 (1-1)
US Foggia: Mauro ROSIN, Dan Vasile PETRESCU (ROM), Maurizio CODISPOTI, Mauro
PICASSO, Salvatore FRESI, Pasquale PADALINO, Roberto RAMBAUDI, Alessandro
PORRO (71' Gualtiero GRANDINI), Francesco BAIANO, Onofrio BARONE, Gianluca
MUSUMECI. (Coach: Zdenek ZEMAN (TCH)).
FK Borac Banja Luka: Milan SIMEUNOVIC, Stojan MALBASIC (89' Veselin
KOVACEVIC), Mario MATAJA (68' Admir SUSIC), Milorad BILBIJA, Zvonko LIPOVAC,
Goran DJUKIC, Zvonko LIPOVAC, Fuad SASIVAREVIC, Vito STAVLJANIN, Ljubisa
SUSIC (61' Samir HABIROVIC), Almir FILIPOVIC. (Coach: Zoran SMILESKI).
Goals: US Foggia: 1-0 Francesco BAIANO (13'), 2-2 Francesco BAIANO (78').
FK Borac Banja Luka: 1-1 Fuad SASIVAREVIC (21'), 1-2 Milrad BILBIJA (61').
Referee: Karel HYCL (TCH)
Penalties: 1 Francesco BAIANO   1 Fuad SASIVAREVIC
                2 Onofrio BARONE   2 Vito STAVLJANIN
                * Roberto RAMBAUDI   3 Ljubisa SUSIC
                * Dan Vasile PETRESCU   4 Milorad BILBIJA

27-05-1992   Stadio Pino Zaccheria, Foggia: BVSC Novép – TJ DAC Dunajská Streda   0-0
BVSC Novép: Károly ERDÉLYI, SZAVELSEY, Vasile ISCHAK (UKR) (87' VAHIDI),
Aleksandr NIKIFOROV (UKR), Péter KRÓNER, Zsolt HUSZÁK, Ferenc MOLNÁR (89'
Ádám VEZÉR), Attila NAHÓCZKY, István BORGULYA, Frigyes TUBOLY (72' József
FARKAS), Viktor GRATSOV (UKR) (71' József BALOGH). (Coach: István KISTELEKI).
TJ DAC Dunajská Streda: Jirí JURCÍK, Milos TOMÁS, Rostislav PROKOP, Juraj MINTÁL,
Tibor ZSÁKOVICS, Rudolf PAVLÍK, Attila PINTÉR (46' Mikulás RADVÁNYI), Július
SIMON, Tibor JANCULA, Pavol DINA, Stefan MAIXNER. (Coach: Juraj SZIKORA).
Referee: Marcello NICCHI (ITA)
Penalties: 1 József FARKAS   1 Július SIMON
                2 Zsolt HUSZÁK   2 Juraj MINTAL
                3 ERDELYI   3 Tibor JANCULA
                4 VAHIDI   4 Mikulás RADVÁNYI
                5 József BALOGH   5 Pavol DINA
                6 Péter KRÓNER   * Tibor ZSÁKOVICS

29-05-1992   Stadio Pino Zaccheria, Foggia:
FK Borac Banja Luka – BVSC Novép   1-1 (1-0)
FK Borac Banja Luka: Milan SIMEUNOVIC (YC), Stojan MALBASIC (..' Veselin KOVACEVIC), Mario MATAJA (67' Samir HABIROVIC), Milorad BILBIJA (YC), Zvonko LIPOVAC, Goran DJUKIC (YC), Zvonko LIPOVAC, Fuad SASIVAREVIC (YC), Vitomir STAVLJANIN, Ljubisa SUSIC (46' Admir SUSIC), Almir FILIPOVIC. (Coach: Zoran SMILESKI).
BVSC Novép: Károly ERDÉLYI, SZAVELSEY, Vasile ISCHAK (UKR), Aleksandr NIKIFOROV (UKR), Péter KRÓNER (YC), Zsolt HUSZÁK, Ferenc MOLNÁR (110' József BALOGH), Attila NAHÓCZKY, István BORGULYA, Frigyes TUBOLY (46' József FARKAS), Viktor GRATSOV (UKR) (116' Ádám VEZÉR). (Coach: István KISTELEKI).
Goals: FK Borac Banja Luka: 1-0 Almir FILIPOVIC (6').
BVSC Novép: 1-1 Aleksandr NIKIFOROV (68').
Referee: Roman STEINDL (AUT)   Attendance: 2.000
Penalties: 1 Milorad BILBIJA   1 Károly ERDÉLYI
               2 Fuad SASIVAREVIC   2 Attila NAHÓCZKY
               3 Vito STAVLJANIN   3 Ádám VEZÉR
               4 Almir FILIPOVIC   4 SZAVELSEY
               5 Not known   * Not known

(After extra time)

*** FK Borac Banja Luka were the last winners of the Mitropa Cup ***

SUPER MITROPA CUP

1989

FINAL

12-04-1989   Ostrava: TJ Baník Ostrava OKD – Pisa SC   3-0 (2-0)
TJ Baník Ostrava OKD: Ludek MIKLOSKO (37' Pavel SRNICEK), Roman KAIZAR, Ivo
STAS, Petr SKARABELA (30' Miroslav ONUFER), Dusan VRTO, Libor FRYC, Karel
KULA, Radim NECAS, Radek BASTA, Dusan HORVATH (60' Zbynek OLLENDER),
Radomír CHÝLEK. (Coach: Milan MÁCALA).
Pisa SC: Gianpaolo GRUDINA, Antonio CAVALLO, Davide LUCARELLI (85' Mario
BRANDINI), Mauro BOCCAFRESCA, Stefano DIANDA (YC), Daniele BERNAZZANI,
David FIORENTINI (65' Nicola MARTINI), Francesco GAZZANEO, Giuseppe
INCOCCIATI, Aldo DOLCETTI (46' Massimiliano ALLEGRI), Francis SEVEREYNS (BEL)
(55' Lamberto PIOVANELLI). (Coach: Luca GIANNINI).
Goals: TJ Baník Ostrava OKD: 1-0 Petr SKARABELA (16'), 2-0 Karel KULA (44'), 3-0
Radim NECAS (47').
Referee: László MOLNÁR (HUN)   Attendance: 1.224

25-04-1989   Pisa: Pisa SC – TJ Baník Ostrava OKD   3-1 (1-0)
Pisa SC: Gianpaolo GRUDINA, Antonio CAVALLO, Davide LUCARELLI, Mauro
BOCCAFRESCA, Stefano DIANDA, Paul Marcellus ELLIOTT (ENG), Daniele
BERNAZZANI, Aldo DOLCETTI (46' Francesco GAZZANEO), Giuseppe INCOCCIATI,
Marinus Antonius (Mario) BEEN (HOL) (110' Nicola MARTINI), Francis SEVEREYNS
(BEL) (55' Lamberto PIOVANELLI). (Coach: Lamberto GIORGIS).
TJ Baník Ostrava OKD: Pavel SRNICEK, Václav PECHÁCEK, Miroslav ONUFER, Roman
KAIZAR, Dusan VRTO, Libor FRYC, Radomír CHÝLEK, Viliam HÝRAVÝ, Radek
BASTA, Dusan HORVATH, Dusan FÁBRY (76' Zbynek OLLENDER). (Coach: Milan
MÁCALA).
Goals: Pisa SC: 1-0 Francis SEVEREYNS (4'), 2-0 Davide LUCARELLI (46'), 3-0 Giuseppe
INCOCCIATI (86').
TJ Baník Ostrava OKD: 3-1 Radek BASTA (106').
Referee: Mateo BEUSAN (YUG)

(After extra time)

*** TJ Baník Ostrava OKD won the Cup ***

278

Overall Mitropa Cup record by club

	Club name	Cntry	Part	Pd	W	D	L	GF	GA	Pts
1	Vasas SC	HUN	15	77	42	14	21	167	103	98
2	AC Sparta Praha	TCH	18	78	33	16	29	153	138	82
3	Ferencvárosi TC	HUN	15	71	31	9	31	179	140	71
4	FK Austria Wien	AUT	11	52	30	5	17	109	81	63
5	Vörös Lobogó SE/ MTK Budapest	HUN	11	50	21	17	12	108	80	59
6	Újpesti Dozsa SC	HUN	15	59	25	9	25	136	119	59
7	SK Rapid Wien	AUT	11	49	23	10	16	120	108	56
8	SK Slavia Praha	TCH	18	61	21	14	26	107	99	56
9	FC Bologna	ITA	13	55	22	9	33	101	97	53
10	Juventus FC	ITA	8	38	20	7	11	81	64	47
11	First Vienna FC	AUT	14	43	20	3	20	77	84	43
12	AC Fiorentina	ITA	9	38	18	6	14	60	52	42
13	FK Crvena Zvezda Beograd	YUG	8	39	17	7	15	72	59	41
14	SK Admira Wien	AUT	11	37	16	9	13	66	77	39
15	FK Vojvodina Novi Sad	YUG	9	36	13	11	12	57	51	37
16	FK Partizan Beograd	YUG	7	28	13	9	6	59	50	35
17	Tatabányai Bányász SC	HUN	8	28	15	8	8	45	44	35
18	Budapesti Honvéd SE	HUN	9	39	14	6	19	75	71	34
19	FC Celik Zenica	YUG	4	25	13	4	8	38	22	30
20	Spartak TAZ Trnava	TCH	4	24	10	7	7	39	38	27
21	TJ Slovan CHZJD Bratislava	TCH	8	27	10	7	10	33	43	27
22	AS Ambrosiana Inter	ITA	7	28	11	5	12	64	69	27
23	FC Swarovski Wacker Innsbruck	AUT	4	18	11	2	5	31	20	24
24	TJ Internacional Slovnaft Bratislava	TCH	3	19	10	4	5	39	23	24
25	NK Dynamo Zagreb	YUG	5	24	9	5	10	33	37	23
26	TJ Baník Ostrava	TCH	8	26	7	9	10	33	51	23
27	TJ Sklo Union Teplice	TCH	3	18	7	6	5	30	25	20
28	AC Torino	ITA	5	16	9	1	6	35	31	19
29	Atalanta Bergamo	ITA	4	18	5	8	5	26	28	18
30	Hungária FC Budapest	HUN	11	28	6	6	16	50	66	18
31	Genoa 1893	ITA	5	16	6	5	5	30	27	17
32	FK Zeljeznicar Sarajevo	YUG	4	16	6	5	5	20	17	17
33	Udinese AC	ITA	3	13	6	4	3	25	20	16
34	Csepel SC	HUN	3	14	5	6	3	15	10	16
35	TJ Jednota Trencin	TCH	3	14	6	2	6	24	17	14
36	NK Hajduk Split	YUG	5	12	5	3	4	17	27	13
37	Pisa SC	ITA	3	8	6	1	1	14	3	13
38	U.D.A. Praha/Dukla Praha	TCH	4	14	4	5	5	19	23	13
39	BSK Beograd/OFC Beograd	YUG	7	18	6	1	11	26	46	13
40	AC Milan	ITA	3	10	5	2	3	13	9	12

Overall Mitropa Cup record by club

	Club name	Cntry	Part	Pd	W	D	L	GF	GA	Pts
41	TJ Tatran Presov	TCH	2	12	5	2	5	21	19	12
42	SK Kladno/ TJ SONP Kladno	TCH	3	13	5	2	6	25	25	12
43	CS Rapid Bucuresti	ROM	2	9	4	3	2	13	10	11
44	TJ Zbrojovka Brno	TCH	3	12	4	3	5	19	27	11
45	AS Roma	ITA	6	16	4	3	9	24	39	11
46	FK Vardar Skopje	YUG	3	10	3	4	3	12	16	10
47	Wiener Sportklub	AUT	5	16	4	2	10	29	40	10
48	TJ Slovan Nitra	TCH	1	7	3	3	1	20	16	9
49	FK Velez Mostar	YUG	2	8	4	1	3	15	12	9
50	Diosgyöri VTK	HUN	3	8	4	1	3	9	11	9
51	HSK Gradjanski Zagreb	YUG	3	9	3	3	3	11	15	9
52	SK Zidenice	TCH	3	10	4	1	5	22	29	9
53	Wiener AC	AUT	3	11	4	1	6	21	30	9
54	SS Lazio Roma	ITA	4	14	3	3	8	25	30	9
55	NK Iskra Bugojno	YUG	1	6	3	2	1	9	3	8
56	FK Radnicki Beograd	YUG	1	6	3	2	1	13	9	8
57	TJ Vítkvice	TCH	1	6	3	2	1	12	8	8
58	Spartak Hradec Kralové	TCH	1	6	4	0	2	11	8	8
59	SC Eduscho Eisenstadt	AUT	1	6	3	2	1	13	12	8
60	SS Lanerossi-Vicenza	ITA	2	8	3	2	3	11	9	8
61	Perugia AC	ITA	2	8	3	2	3	8	12	8
62	Debreceni (Bocskai) VSC	HUN	4	12	3	2	7	6	19	8
63	TJ ZVL Zilina	TCH	1	6	3	1	2	10	6	7
64	FK Pristina	YUG	1	6	2	3	1	13	11	7
65	FK Galenica Zemun	YUG	1	6	3	1	2	10	9	7
66	Como Calcio	ITA	1	6	3	1	2	7	7	7
67	Rudá Hvezda Brno	TCH	1	8	2	3	3	10	10	7
68	FK Sarajevo	YUG	5	14	3	1	10	18	33	7
69	Bari AS	ITA	1	3	3	0	0	7	0	6
70	Phöbus FC Budapest	HUN	1	4	3	0	1	15	9	6
71	TJ Rudá Hvezda Cheb	TCH	1	6	3	0	3	10	10	6
72	FC Radnicki Kragujevic	YUG	2	6	3	0	3	5	9	6
73	Grasshopper-Club	SUI	2	6	2	2	2	12	17	6
74	SV Austria Salzburg	AUT	1	7	3	0	4	14	13	6
75	US Cagliari	ITA	3	8	3	0	5	13	11	6
76	SC Wacker Wien	AUT	3	8	1	4	3	14	20	6
77	TJ Skoda Plzen	TCH	1	4	1	3	0	6	2	5
78	Cervená Hviezda Bratislava	TCH	2	5	2	1	2	18	13	5
79	TJ Bohemians Praha	TCH	3	6	2	1	3	9	8	5
80	NK Rijeka	YUG	2	6	2	1	3	8	10	5

Overall Mitropa Cup record by club

	Club name	Cntry	Part	Pd	W	D	L	GF	GA	Pts
81	Linzer ASK	AUT	5	13	0	5	8	11	29	5
82	Ascoli Calcio	ITA	1	2	2	0	0	3	1	4
83	Videoton SC	HUN	1	4	2	0	2	8	9	4
84	US Palermo	ITA	2	4	2	0	2	4	5	4
85	Dynamo Praha	TCH	2	4	2	0	2	9	13	4
86	SK Viktoria Zizkov	TCH	1	5	2	0	3	15	13	4
87	SSC Napoli	ITA	2	5	1	2	2	4	10	4
88	Békéscsabai Elöre Spartacus SC	HUN	1	6	1	2	3	5	10	4
89	NK Osijek	YUG	2	8	1	2	5	8	17	4
90	FK Lokomotiv Sofia	BUL	1	4	1	1	2	8	7	3
91	Grazer AK	AUT	1	4	1	1	2	4	5	3
92	TJ Lokomotiva Kosice	TCH	2	4	1	1	2	1	4	3
93	SK Prostéjov	TCH	2	6	1	1	4	11	12	3
94	Szombathelyi Haladás VSE	HUN	1	6	1	1	4	7	16	3
95	Pescara Calcio	ITA	1	2	1	0	1	4	2	2
96	FK Borac Banja Luka	YUG	1	2	0	2	0	3	3	2
97	NK Maribor	YUG	1	2	1	0	1	3	3	2
98	BVSC Novép	HUN	1	2	0	2	0	1	1	2
99	Salgótarjáni BTC	HUN	1	2	1	0	1	3	4	2
100	Széged FC	HUN	1	2	1	0	1	2	4	2
101	CC Catania	ITA	1	2	1	0	1	1	3	2
	FK Radnicki Nis	YUG	1	2	1	0	1	1	3	2
103	1.Simmeringer SC	AUT	1	2	1	0	1	3	6	2
104	Lausanne-Sports	SUI	1	2	1	0	1	2	6	2
105	Levski Sofia	BUL	1	2	1	0	1	1	5	2
106	SK Slavija Sarajevo	YUG	1	2	1	0	1	3	11	2
107	Váci Izzó MTE	HUN	1	3	1	0	2	7	7	2
108	US Sampdoria	ITA	1	3	0	2	1	4	7	2
109	1.Wiener Neustädter SC	AUT	1	3	1	0	2	5	10	2
110	FC Ripensa Timisoara	ROM	1	4	1	0	3	9	12	2
	Stiinta Timisoara	ROM	1	4	1	0	3	9	12	2
112	FC Vorarlberg	AUT	1	4	0	2	2	4	9	2
113	Young Fellows Zürich	SUI	2	5	1	0	4	4	13	2
114	SV Stickstoff Linz	AUT	2	5	0	2	3	11	21	2
115	ACS Venus Bucuresti	ROM	3	6	1	0	5	6	19	2
116	Hellas Verona	ITA	2	8	0	2	6	6	20	2
117	US Foggia	ITA	1	1	0	1	0	2	2	1
118	TJ DAC Dunajska Streda	TCH	1	1	0	1	0	0	0	1
119	Veszprém FC	HUN	1	2	0	1	1	2	3	1
	SK Vorwärts Steyr	AUT	1	2	0	1	1	2	3	1

Mitropa Cup record by club

	Club name	Cntry	Part	Pd	W	D	L	GF	GA	Pts
121	Kispesti AC	HUN	1	2	0	1	1	3	5	1
122	AC Brescia	ITA	1	2	0	1	1	1	3	1
123	Dukla Pardubice	TCH	1	2	0	1	1	0	2	1
124	SK Viktoria Plzen	TCH	1	2	0	1	1	4	8	1
125	SK Sturm Graz	AUT	1	2	0	0	2	4	6	0
126	TJ Sigma Olomouc	TCH	1	2	0	0	2	2	4	0
127	HASK Zagreb	YUG	1	2	0	0	2	2	5	0
	Teplitzer FK	TCH	1	2	0	0	2	2	5	0
129	FK Spartak Subotica	YUG	1	2	0	0	2	1	4	0
130	US Alessandria	ITA	1	2	0	0	2	2	6	0
131	Pécsi Munkás SC	HUN	1	2	0	0	2	0	4	0
132	CCA Bucuresti	ROM	1	2	0	0	2	4	9	0
133	FK Rad Beograd	YUG	1	2	0	0	2	3	8	0
134	Kaposvári Rákóczi SC	HUN	1	2	0	0	2	0	5	0
135	FC Bern	SUI	1	2	0	0	2	2	11	0
136	Floridsdorf AC	AUT	1	2	0	0	2	1	10	0

Overall Mitropa Cup record by country

	Country name	Cntry	Part	Pd	W	D	L	GF	GA	Pts
1	Hungaria	HUN	106	423	176	82	165	843	740	434
2	Czechoslovakia	TCH	104	410	155	97	158	714	699	407
3	Italy	ITA	92	334	137	67	139	575	567	341
4	Yugoslavia	YUG	79	297	115	67	115	460	490	297
5	Austria	AUT	78	284	118	49	116	539	584	281
6	Romania	ROM	8	25	7	3	15	41	62	17
7	Switzerland	SUI	6	15	4	2	9	20	47	10
8	Bulgaria	BUL	2	6	2	1	3	9	12	5